New Syllabus
Mathematics 1

Consultants:
Prof Lee Peng Yee
Dr Fan Liang Huo

Teh Keng Seng BSc, Dip Ed
Looi Chin Keong BSc, Dip Ed

$\pi r^2 h$

$\sin A = \sin (180^\circ - A)$

$a^2 - b^2$

$\triangle XYZ \equiv \triangle PQR$

shinglee publishers pte ltd

SHINGLEE PUBLISHERS PTE LTD

120 Hillview Avenue #05-06/07
Kewalram Hillview Singapore 669594
Tel: 7601388 Fax: 7625684
e-mail: sales@shinglee com.sg

First Published 1982
Reprinted 1983, 1984, 1985, 1986
Second Edition 1987
Reprinted 1987, 1988, 1989, 1990, 1991
Third Edition 1992
Reprinted 1992, 1993, 1994, 1995
Fourth Edition 1997
Reprinted 1997, 1999
Fifth Edition 2001
Reprinted 2002

ISBN 9971 61 971 7

Cover design by Dave Cheong Wan Kong

Acknowledgement

The authors and publishers are grateful to Suntec City Development Pte Ltd
for the photograph on page 178.

In some cases, we are unable to trace the copyright holder and would welcome
information which enable us to contact the company or person responsible.

Printed in Singapore by KHL Printing Co Pte Ltd

PREFACE

New Syllabus Mathematics is a series of four books. These books follow the Mathematics Syllabus for Secondary Schools, implemented from 2001 by the Ministry of Education, Singapore. The whole series covers the complete syllabus for the Singapore-Cambridge GCE 'O' Level Mathematics.

The fifth edition of New Syllabus Mathematics 1 retains the goals and objectives of the previous edition, but has been revised to meet the requests of users of the fourth edition and to keep materials up-to-date as well as to give students a better understanding of the contents.

All topics are comprehensively dealt with to give students a firm grounding in the subject. Explanations of concepts and principles are concise and written in clear language with supportive illustrations and examples. Examples and exercises have been carefully graded to aid students in progressing within, as well as up, each level. Those exercises marked with a ✳ are either tricky or involve more calculations. "Problem Solving" and "Exploration", placed at the end of the chapter, contain more difficult and challenging questions requiring students to apply their knowledge and experience in solving them.

Numerous revision exercises are provided at appropriate intervals to enable students to recapitulate what they have learnt. In addition, there are mid-year and end-of-year examination specimen papers.

Important features which have been retained in this edition to facilitate learning are:

- an interesting introduction at the beginning of each chapter complete with photographs or graphics
- brief specific instructional objectives for each chapter
- in-class activities (investigation / discussion / problem solving)
- activities and interesting information in the marginal text (clip-notes, "Down Memory Lane", "Back In Time", "Investigate", "Check This Out!", "It's A Fact", "Just For Fun", "Are You Game Enough?", "For Your Information", "Library Corner", "Problems" and "IT")

Problem-solving heuristics are subsequently introduced at appropriate sections of the book to reinforce problem-solving skills. In addition, questions which call for problem-solving skills are also set in the margin for students to do at their own pace and time.

Ample opportunities are also provided for mathematical investigative and communicative activities.

It is hoped that these features will help students learn mathematics with more zest and excel in the subject.

CONTENTS

CHAPTER 1

Whole Numbers

In this chapter, you will learn how to

- ▲ represent numbers on the number line and order them;
- ▲ use the symbols =, ≠, >, <, ≥, ≤;
- ▲ perform mental calculations with whole numbers;
- ▲ perform calculations with whole numbers using a calculator;
- ▲ check the accuracy of a calculation by estimation.

Preliminary Problem

When you log onto an internet website, have you ever noticed that the site will show that you are their number xxxxx visitor? The idea of counting is used to monitor the number of times a website has been visited.

The popularity of a website corresponds closely to the number of "hits" or the number of visitors it receives. Commercial websites boost their earnings through advertisements which depend on the number of visitors to the sites.

The Concept of Whole Numbers

Numeral System

We use numbers everyday. The number system that we use is called the **Hindu-Arabic** system. It is based on ten symbols called **digits**. They are

$$0, 1, 2, 3, 4, 5, 6, 7, 8 \text{ and } 9.$$

They also form the ten smallest **whole numbers**. Any other whole number can be written using the ten digits and the idea of **place values**.

Using two or three digits, we can write the next nine hundred and ninety whole numbers

$$10, 11, \dots 20, 21, \dots, 98, 99, 100, 101, \dots 200, 201, \dots, 998, 999.$$

Very large whole numbers can be written with more digits. In July 1996, the estimated population of Singapore was 3 396 924 people or three million three hundred ninety-six thousand nine hundred and twenty-four people, in words.

Here are the place values for the seven digits of the number that represents the Singapore population.

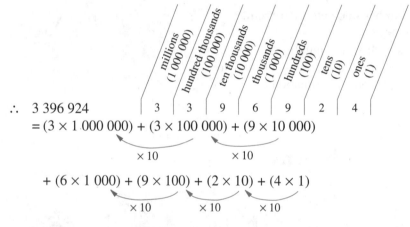

$$\therefore \quad 3\ 396\ 924$$
$$= (3 \times 1\ 000\ 000) + (3 \times 100\ 000) + (9 \times 10\ 000)$$
$$\overset{\times 10}{} \qquad \overset{\times 10}{}$$
$$+ (6 \times 1\ 000) + (9 \times 100) + (2 \times 10) + (4 \times 1)$$
$$\overset{\times 10}{} \qquad \overset{\times 10}{} \qquad \overset{\times 10}{}$$

Did you notice that the Hindu-Arabic numeration system is built on groups of 1, $10 = 10 \times 1$, $100 = 10 \times 10$, $1\ 000 = 10 \times 100$ and so on?

Thus, the system is known as the **base ten** system or the **decimal** system.

Ordering of Whole Numbers

All the whole numbers can be arranged in the following **order**.

In 3 396 924, from the right to the left
4 represents 4 ones or
4 × 1,
2 represents 2 tens or
2 × 10,
9 represents _____ or _____
6 represents 6 thousands or 6 × 1 000.
9 represents _____ or _____
3 represents _____ or _____
3 represents 3 millions or 3 × 1 000 000

Can you complete the above?

Use of Zero as a Place-holder
Can you imagine what will happen when zeros are omitted from the numerals 403 and 4 030?

$$0, 1, 2, 3, 4, 5, \dots$$

The Babylonians (around 2000 BC) used the symbols ◢ *and* ▾ *to represent ten and one respectively.*

◢◢◢ ▾▾▾
◢　▾▾

represents 45.

The Romans (around 100 BC) used letters as symbols for numbers. The basic Roman numerals are I (one) V (five) X (ten) L (fifty) C (one hundred) D (five hundred) M (one thousand). The numerals are written in a definite order and the principles of subtraction and addition are employed. 1999 is represented by MCMXCIX. Since M represents 1 000, CM represents 1 000 – 100 or 900, XC represents 100 – 10 or 90, IX represents 10 – 1 or 9. Can you figure out how DCCCLXXXVIII represents 888? Now, can you see how efficient the Hindu-Arabic system is?

They follow one another.

If we know a number, we know the next one that follows it. Can you think how we can obtain the next number?

The whole numbers get larger and larger in the above order. There is a first whole number. Is there a last whole number?

There is no largest whole number.

In Mathematics, we use the symbol '>' to denote 'is greater than' and the symbol '<' to denote 'is less than'. For example, we write '7 > 4' to express '7 is greater than 4' and we write '3 < 6' to express '3 is less than 6'.

We use the symbol '≠' to denote 'is not equal to', for example, we write '$a \neq 8$' for 'a is not equal to 8'.

We use the symbol '≥' to denote 'is greater than or equal to'. For example, we write '$a \geq 9$' for 'a is greater than or equal to 9'.

We use the symbol '≤' to denote 'is less than or equal to'. For example, we write '$b \leq 10$' for 'b is less than or equal to 10'.

Natural, Even and Odd Numbers

The whole numbers 1, 2, 3, 4, 5, 6 … are **natural numbers**.
In other words all whole numbers except 0 are natural numbers.

The whole numbers 0, 2, 4, 6, 8, … are **even numbers**.
These numbers can be divided by 2 exactly.

We use natural numbers in counting.

The whole numbers 1, 3, 5, 7, 9 … are **odd numbers**.
These numbers cannot be divided by 2 exactly.

A whole number is either an even number or an odd number.
Do you know why this is so?

Example 1

List　(a)　*all the natural numbers less than 5;*
　　　(b)　*all the even numbers between 20 and 43;*
　　　(c)　*all the odd numbers between 15 and 25.*

▼ S o l u t i o n

(a)　The natural numbers less than 5 are 1, 2, 3 and 4.
(b)　The even numbers between 20 and 43 are 22, 24, 26, 28, 30, 32, 34, 36, 38, 40 and 42.
(c)　The odd numbers between 15 and 25 are 17, 19, 21 and 23.

Even numbers can be exactly divided by 2, eg

$$\frac{4}{2\sqrt{8}}$$
$$\frac{8}{0}$$

The Number Line

In Mathematics, it is often useful to represent whole numbers by points on a line called the **number line**.

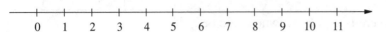

Draw a line. Choose any point on the line and label it 0. Starting with 0, mark off equal intervals of any suitable length. Label the points marked 1, 2, 3, 4, … as shown in the figure above. The arrow on the extreme right indicates that the list of numbers continues in the same way indefinitely.

A number on the number line is always greater than any number to its left and smaller than any number to its right, i.e. $4 > 3$ and $4 < 5$.

The number line below shows that $a > b > c$.

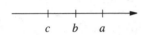

Example 2

Draw a number line to represent the whole numbers
(a) 2, 4, 6 and 8;   *(b) greater than 4.*

▼**Solution**

(a) We use dots to indicate the whole numbers, 2, 4, 6 and 8.

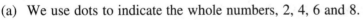

(b) We use dots to indicate the first few whole numbers that are greater than 4.

This arrow indicates that there are some more whole numbers greater than 4.

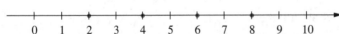

Example 3

Use a number line to find 3 + 4.

▼**Solution**

We start by drawing a number line.

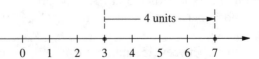

 Chapter 1   Whole Numbers

Ancient civilizations used different systems of numerals.

The early Egyptians (around 3000 BC) used the following symbols for different numerals.

| (one)

∩ (ten)

ℓ (one hundred)

⚱ (one thousand)

ⱴ (ten thousand)

♀ (one hundred thousand)

ⱶ (one million)

2 362 is represented by

Begin at 3 and then move 4 units to the right as shown in the above diagram.

We end at 7 and thus,

$$3 + 4 = 7.$$

═ Exercise 1a ═

1. In 1997, the Ministry of Education selected more than 80 000 students from schools and other educational institutions to obtain base-line indices on students' feelings and perceptions about the nation.

   The survey findings indicated that more than 90% of students from Primary Six level onwards took pride in being Singaporeans and more than 80% of them accepted friends of different religious beliefs. 83% to 95% of Primary Three students answered three out of five general knowledge questions about the country correctly.

   (a) Given that exactly a students were selected for the survey, write an inequality statement for a. $a > 8000$

   (b) If the actual percentages of students who take pride in being Singaporeans and accept friends of different religious beliefs were $b\%$ and $c\%$ respectively, write an inequality statement for each of b and c. $b > 90\%$ $c > 80\%$

   (c) Given that $d\%$ of Primary Three students answered three out of five general knowledge questions about the country correctly, write an inequality statement for d. $83 \leq d \leq 95$

2. List the following numbers:

   (a) Natural numbers less than 8. $1,2,3,4,5,6,7$
   (b) Even numbers between 25 and 35. $26,28,30,32,34$
   (c) Odd numbers between 40 and 53. $41,43,45,47,49,51$
   (d) Whole numbers > 63 but < 70. $64,65,66,67,68,69$
   (e) Whole numbers which are multiples of 3 and between 22 and 40. $24,27,30,33,36,39$
   (f) Even numbers > 84 but < 99. $86,88,90,92,94,96,98$
   (g) Odd numbers ⩾ 55 but < 65. $55,57,59,61,63.$
   (h) Even numbers > 72 but ⩽ 90. $74,76,78,80,82,84,86,88,90$

3. Draw the number line to represent the following numbers:

   (a) 1, 3, 5 and 7.
   (b) 5, 7, 10 and 14.
   (c) Whole numbers < 6.
   (d) Natural numbers ⩾ 7.
   (e) Whole numbers ⩾ 3 but ⩽ 9.
   (f) Whole numbers < 19 but ⩾ 8.
   (g) Natural numbers > 2 but ⩽ 7.
   (h) Natural numbers > 3 but < 13.

4. Display each addition using the number line.

   (a) $2 + 6 = 8$
   (b) $7 + 4 = 11$
   (c) $3 + 5 + 8 = 16$

Addition and Subtraction of Whole Numbers

There are different ways to carry out addition and subtraction of whole numbers. Here is a general paper-and-pencil method. When adding and subtracting whole numbers, we write the numbers in vertical columns, aligning digits according to their place value. The following examples illustrate how to use the general method to do addition and subtraction of whole numbers.

Example 4

Evaluate (a) 68 + 27; (b) 523 + 268 + 95.

▼ Solution

(a)

tens	units	
6	8	8 + 7 = 15
+ 2	7	60 + 20 = 80
1	5	(from the units column)
8	0	(from the tens column)
9	5	

∴ 68 + 27 = 95

or

tens	units
¹6	8
+ 2	7
9	5

Notes:

3 + 8 + 5 = 10 + 6

Bring 10 to the tens column.

20 + 60 + 90 + 10 = 180
= 100 + 80

Bring 100 to the hundreds column.

500 + 200 + 100 = 800
800 + 80 + 6 = 886

Can you explain how the subtraction is carried out?

(b)

hundreds	tens	units
¹5	¹2	3
2	6	8
+	9	5
8	8	6

∴ 523 + 268 + 95 = 886

Example 5

Calculate (a) 658 – 436; (b) 835 – 479.   3 9 6

▼ Solution

(a)

hundreds	tens	units
6	5	8
– 4	3	6
2	2	2

Check:
436
+ 222
658

(b)

hundreds	tens	units
⁷8	¹²3	¹⁵5
– 4	7	9
3	5	6

Check:
¹4 ¹7 9
+ 3 5 6
8 3 5

══ Exercise 1b ══

1. Do the following additions:

(a)
```
  ¹ ¹
  934
  715
+  86
 1735
```

(b)
```
  ⁴ ⁵
 4 801
 2 191
+ 8 463
 15455
```

2. Do the following subtractions:

(a)
```
 ⁵ ⁹ ⁰ ⁴
 60 152
– 1 895
 58257
```

(b)
```
 ⁸ ¹⁰ ² ³
 91 346
– 88 978
  2388
```

3. Copy and complete the following:

(a)
$$\begin{array}{r} 2\ 4\ 9 \\ +\ \boxed{5}\ 8\ \boxed{6} \\ \hline 8\ \boxed{3}\ 5 \end{array}$$

(b)
$$\begin{array}{r} 2\ \boxed{8}\ 4 \\ -\ \boxed{1}\ 9\ \boxed{6} \\ \hline 8\ 8 \end{array}$$

(c)
$$\begin{array}{r} \boxed{6}\ 6\ 3 \\ 7\ \boxed{9}\ 2 \\ +\ 5\ 8\ \boxed{7} \\ \hline \boxed{2}\ 0\ 4\ 2 \end{array}$$

4. In each of the following, find the digits represented by the letters x, y and z.

(a)
$$\begin{array}{r} 7\ x\ 2 \\ -\ y\ 3\ 9 \\ \hline 4\ 8\ z \end{array}$$
$x = 2$
$y = 2$
$z = 3$

(b)
$$\begin{array}{r} 3\ x\ y\ z\ 9 \\ +\ \ \ x\ y\ 9\ z \\ \hline 4\ 3\ z\ z\ x \end{array}$$
$x = 6$
$y = 8$
$z = 7$

(c)
$$\begin{array}{r} x\ 5\ 4\ 8\ y\ z\ x \\ -\ \ \ y\ x\ 4\ 9\ 8\ 0 \\ \hline 8\ z\ z\ y\ 5\ x \end{array}$$
$x = 1$
$y = 7$
$z = 3$

(d)
$$\begin{array}{r} 2\ x\ y\ z \\ 2\ x\ y\ z \\ +\ \ \ 4\ x\ 8 \\ \hline 4\ z\ y\ y \end{array}$$
$x = 2$
$y = 6$
$z = 9$

5. Using some of the single digit whole numbers, form:

(a) the smallest and the largest 5-digit numbers and find their difference;

(b) two 5-digit numbers such that their sum is

    (i) the largest;

    (ii) the smallest;

(c) two 5-digit numbers such that their difference is the smallest.

Commutative and Associative Law of Addition

Commutative Law of Addition

We know that $3 + 5 = 8$ and $5 + 3 = 8$,

$\therefore \quad 5 + 3 = 3 + 5$

Using the number line, we obtain the same result for $3 + 5$ and $5 + 3$ as shown below:

Begin at 3 and then move 5 units to the right.

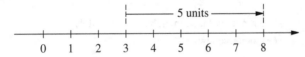

Begin at 5 and then move 3 units to the right.

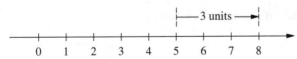

We can see that the order of adding any two numbers does not affect the result. This is the **Commutative Law of Addition**.

> **If x and y represent two whole numbers, then**
>
> $$x + y = y + x$$

It is obvious that $8 - 5$ and $5 - 8$ will not give the same results.

Thus, subtraction is not commutative. In general, if x and y represent two whole numbers, then $x - y \neq y - x$, where $x \neq 0$, $y \neq 0$.

If a cashier first scans in an item costing \$3 and then an item costing \$5, the total amount obtained must be the same as that which would be obtained if the item costing \$5 were scanned in first.

In our everyday life, there are things that we must do in a certain order. For example, we have to put on our socks before we put on our shoes.

Can you give examples of things that we can do in any order and things that we must do in a definite order?

Associative Law of Addition

We know that $2 + 3 + 5 = (2 + 3) + 5$

$$= 5 + 5$$
$$= 10$$

Also, $\quad\quad 2 + 3 + 5 = 2 + (3 + 5)$

$$= 2 + 8$$
$$= 10$$

$$\therefore \quad (2 + 3) + 5 = 2 + (3 + 5)$$

This shows that the order of grouping numbers together in addition does not affect the answer. We say that addition is associative. This property is called the **Associative Law of Addition**.

> **If x, y and z represent three whole numbers, then**
> $$(x + y) + z = x + (y + z)$$

Do you think subtraction is associative? Why? *No because when you subtract the numbers aren't always going*

Applying the commutative law and associative law of addition can often help us add whole numbers more easily.

Example 6

Calculate   (a) $9 + 17 + 3$;   (b) $10 + 8 + 4$;   (c) $18 + 5 + 2 + 6$.

▼ **Solution**

(a) $9 + 17 + 3 = 9 + (17 + 3)$ $\quad$ (Associative law)

$$= 9 + 20$$
$$= 29$$

(b) $16 + 8 + 4 = 16 + 4 + 8$ $\quad$ (Commutative law, interchanging 8 and 4)

$$= (16 + 4) + 8 \quad \text{(Associative law)}$$
$$= 20 + 8$$
$$= 28$$

(c) $18 + 5 + 2 + 6 = (18 + 2) + (5 + 6)$ $\quad$ (Commutative law, interchanging 5 and 2)

$$= 20 + 11$$
$$= 31$$

═══ Exercise 1c ═══

1. State each number represented by a.
   (a) $15 + 39 = 39 + a$ $\quad a = 15$
   (b) $a + 269 = 269 + 854$ $\quad a = 854$
   (c) $32 + 75 + a = 18 + 32 + 75$ $\quad a = 18$
   (d) $15 + a + 69 = 69 + 15 + 23$ $\quad a = 23$

2. Apply either the commutative law or associative law or both in the following mental calculations:
   (a) $14 + 6 + 9$
   (b) $14 + 21 + 9$
   (c) $31 + 16 + 9$
   (d) $25 + 28 + 15$
   (e) $67 + 52 + 33$
   (f) $123 + 66 + 77$
   (g) $28 + 22 + 41 + 59$
   (h) $49 + 51 + 101 + 99$
   (i) $7 + 25 + 13 + 75$
   (j) $11 + 26 + 4 + 89$

3. Calculate

(a) $25 + 43 + 75$ (b) $14 + 28 + 36 + 50$ (c) $145 + 80 + 55$ (d) $74 + 39 + 61 + 26$

(e) $9 + 25 + 41 + 125$ (f) $650 + 128 + 350 + 22$

Multiplication and Division of Whole Numbers

From the diagram given on the right we can see

$$4 \times 5 = 5 + 5 + 5 + 5 = 20$$
$$6 \times 3 = 3 + 3 + 3 + 3 + 3 + 3 = 18$$

Multiplication is the same as **repeated addition** of the same number. From the above we can also get

$$20 \div 4 = 5 \quad \text{or} \quad 20 \div 5 = 4$$
$$18 \div 6 = 3 \quad \text{or} \quad 18 \div 3 = 6$$

As in the case of addition and subtraction of whole numbers, there is a general paper-and-pencil method to carry out multiplication and division of whole numbers, taking into consideration the place values of the digits. The following examples illustrate how to use this general method to carry out multiplication and division of whole numbers.

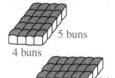

5 buns
4 buns
3 buns
6 buns

To find the total number of buns, all we need to know are the number of rows of buns and the number of buns in each row. Thus, in the diagram there are

    $4 \times 5 = 20$ *buns*
and $6 \times 3 = 18$ *buns*
respectively.

Example 7

Calculate   (a) 46×15;   (b) 318×509.

▼ **Solution**

(a)
```
     46
  ×  15   ←  (15 = 10 + 5)
    230   ←  (5 × 46)
  + 460   ←  (10 × 46)
    690
```

(b)
```
        318
  ×     509   ←  (509 = 500 + 0 + 9)
       2862   ←  (9 × 318)
       0000   ←  (0 × 318)
  + 159000   ←  (500 × 318)
     161862
```

Example 8

Divide 64 by 4.

▼ **Solution**

In short division, working is done mentally.

Using long division:

```
       1 6
  4 ) 6 4
      − 4      Bring 4 down.
      ② 4
      − 2 4    The remainder 2 tens
        0      is added to 4.
```

Using short division:

```
        2     ←  This 2 is the same as
  4 ) 6 4        the circled 2 shown on
     1 6         the left.
```

Example 9

Divide 6 239 by 27.

▼ **Solution**

Long division

```
        231   quotient
27 )  6 239
     - 5 4
       83
     - 81
       29
     - 27
        2   remainder
```

Short division

```
             8 2
27 ) 6 2 3 9
       2 3 1   remainder 2
```

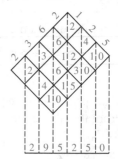

The following shows an increasing method of multiplication developed by the Arabs.

2 362 × 125 = 295 250

229 × 785 = 179 765

Can you figure out how the method works?

⬤ ⬤ ⬤ ⬤ ⬤ ⬤ ⬤ ⬤ ⬤ ⬤

═══ **Exercise 1d** ═══

1. Do the following:

   (a) 326 × 19   (b) 537 × 160   (c) 671 × 407

2. Do the following using short division:

   (a) 992 ÷ 8   (b) 6 444 ÷ 9   (c) 34 566 ÷ 7

3. Evaluate the following divisions:

   (a) 704 ÷ 22   (b) 4 446 ÷ 13   (c) 6 919 ÷ 11

Laws of Multiplication of Whole Numbers

Commutative Law

Using the number line, the products of 3 × 4 and 4 × 3 are obtained as shown in the figure below.

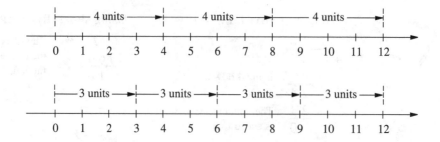

The diagram above illustrates the **Commutative Law of Multiplication** by showing that

$$3 \times 4 = 4 \times 3$$

> **If x and y represent two whole numbers, then**
> $$x \times y = y \times x$$

Compute $27 \div 3$ and $3 \div 27$. $3\overline{)27}\ \ \ \ \ \ 27\overline{)3.0}$

Is $27 \div 3$ equal to $3 \div 27$? Is the division commutative?

No, the division is not commutative

Associative Law

The product $2 \times 3 \times 4$ may be found in two different ways, i.e.,

$(2 \times 3) \times 4 = 6 \times 4 = 24$
$2 \times (3 \times 4) = 2 \times 12 = 24$
$\therefore \quad (2 \times 3) \times 4 = 2 \times (3 \times 4)$

In general, the property is called the **Associative Law of Multiplication**:

> **If x, y and z represent three whole numbers, then**
> $$(x \times y) \times z = x \times (y \times z)$$

Calculate $(9 \div 3) \div 3$ and $9 \div (3 \div 3)$.

Is $(9 \div 3) \div 3$ equal to $9 \div (3 \div 3)$? Is the division associative?

$999999999999999 = 1990$
Insert $+$, $-$, $\times$ or $\div$ in suitable places on the left-hand side of $=$ so as to make the above equation true.

Distributive Laws

(1) John did $5 + 9$ or 14 hours of community work. Hence, he received $4 \times 14 = 56$ points

(2) For the first half of the year, he received 4×5, or 20, points. For the second half of the year, he received 4×9, or 36, points. Hence, for the whole year he received $20 + 36$, or 56, points.

John did 5 hours and 9 hours of community work in the first and second half of the year respectively. He was awarded 4 points for each hour of community work. Let us find the total points John received for the whole year.

The points he received can be calculated in two ways as shown below:

(1) $4 \times (5 + 9) = 4 \times 14 = 56$

(2) $(4 \times 5) + (4 \times 9) = 20 + 36 = 56$

Clearly, $4 \times (5 + 9) = (4 \times 5) + (4 \times 9)$

In general, for any three whole numbers x, y and z we have $x \times (y + z) = x \times y + x \times z$. This is called the **Distributive Law of Multiplication over Addition**.

We also have the **Distributive Law of Multiplication over Subtraction**, that is for any three whole numbers, x, y and z, we have

$$x \times (y - z) = x \times y - x \times z.$$

Let us look at an example.

Ezar, John's classmate, performed 8 hours of community service for the first half of the year and a total of 15 hours for the whole year. The points Ezar was awarded for the second half of the year can be obtained as shown below:

(1) $4 \times (15 - 8) = 4 \times 7 = 28$

(2) $(4 \times 15) - (4 \times 8) = 60 - 32 = 28$

$\therefore \quad 4 \times (15 - 8) = (4 \times 15) - (4 \times 8)$

In summary,

> **If x, y and z represent three whole numbers, then**
> $$x \times (y + z) = x \times y + x \times z$$
> $$x \times (y - z) = x \times y - x \times z$$

(I) Ezar did $(15 - 8)$ or 7 hours of community work for the second half of the year. Hence, he received $4 \times 7 = 28$ points.

(II) For the whole year, he received 4×15 or 60 points. The first half of the year, he received 4×8 or 32 points. Hence, he received $60 - 32$, or 28, points for the second half of the year.

═══ Exercise 1e ═══

1. Fill in the boxes with +, – or ×:

 (a) $6 \boxed{\times} 4 = 4 \boxed{\times} 6 = 24$

 (b) $23 \boxed{+} 11 = 11 \boxed{+} 23 = 34$

 (c) $107 \boxed{+} 33 = 33 \boxed{+} 107 = 140$

 (d) $6 \boxed{\times} 15 = 15 \boxed{\times} 6 = 90$

 (e) $35 \boxed{\times} 7 = 7 \boxed{\times} 35 = 245$

 (f) $263 \boxed{+} 103 = 103 \boxed{+} 263 = 366$

2. Put a numeral in each box to make the equation true:

 (a) $6 \times (5 + \boxed{7}) = 6 \times 5 + 6 \times 7$

 (b) $10 \times (4 + 5) = 10 \times \boxed{4} + 10 \times \boxed{5}$

 (c) $11 \times 12 + 6 \times 12 = (11 + 6) \times \boxed{12}$

 (d) $2 \times (\boxed{6} - 5) = (2 \times 6) - (2 \times 5)$

 (e) $(10 \times 13) - (9 \times 13) = (10 - 9) \times \boxed{13}$

 (f) $(6 - 5) \times 9 = (\boxed{6} \times 9) - (5 \times \boxed{9})$

Applying the above laws of multiplication can often help us do the calculations more easily.

$9 = 3 \times 3 = 3 + 3 + 3$
$\quad = 2 + 3 + 4$

$\therefore$ 9 can be written as a sum of three consecutive numbers, 2, 3 and 4.

$40 = 5 \times 8 = 8 + 8 + 8 +$
$\qquad 8 + 8$
$\quad = 6 + 7 + 8 +$
$\qquad 9 + 10$

$63 = 3 \times 21 = 21 + 21 +$
$\qquad 21$
$\quad = 20 + 21 +$
$\qquad 22$

Example 10

Do the following sums mentally:

(a) $25 \times 29 \times 4$;   (b) $45 \times 3 + 45 \times 7$;

(c) $33 \times 17 - 33 \times 7$;   (d) 4×98;

(e) 25×16;   (f) $5 \times 72 - 5 \times 12$.

▼ **Solution**

(a) $25 \times 29 \times 4 = 25 \times 4 \times 29$ (Commutative law)
$\qquad\qquad = 100 \times 29 = 2\,900$ (Associative law)

(b) $45 \times 3 + 45 \times 7 = 45 \times (3 + 7)$ (Distributive law)
$\qquad\qquad = 45 \times 10 = 450$

(c) $33 \times 17 - 33 \times 7 = 33 \times (17 - 7)$ (Distributive law)
$\qquad\qquad = 33 \times 10 = 330$

$63 = 7 \times 9 = 9 + 9 + 9 +$
$\qquad 9 + 9 + 9 +$
$\qquad 9$
$\qquad = 6 + 7 + 8 +$
$\qquad 9 + 10 + 11$
$\qquad + 12$

Can you write 30, 33, 42 and 22 each as a sum of consecutive numbers?

Can any one of them be written as a sum of consecutive numbers in more than one way?

⦾ ⦾ ⦾ ⦾ ⦾ ⦾ ⦾ ⦾ ⦾ ⦾

(d) $4 \times 98 = 4 \times (100 - 2)$ (Write 98 as $100 - 2$)
$\qquad = 4 \times 100 - 4 \times 2$ (Distributive law)
$\qquad = 400 - 8 = 392$

(e) $25 \times 16 = 25 \times 4 \times 4$ (Write 16 as 4×4)
$\qquad = 100 \times 4$ (Associative law)
$\qquad = 400$

(f) $5 \times 72 - 5 \times 12 = 5 \times 2 \times 36 - 5 \times 2 \times 6$ (Write 72 as 2×36
$\qquad = 10 \times (36 - 6)$ and 12 as 2×6)
$\qquad = 10 \times 30 = 300$ (Distributive law)

1, 10, 100 … are friendly numbers.

═ Exercise 1f ═

1. **(a)** Find the product of 273 and 111 and then multiply the result by 8.
   (b) Find the product of 273 and 888 directly.
   (c) Will **(a)** or **(b)** give you the product 273×888 more easily?

2. Find the product of the three numbers 33, 444 and 99.

3. Calculate the following mentally.
   (a) $45 \times 7 + 45 \times 3 = 450$
   (b) $62 \times 4 + 62 \times 6 = 620$
   (c) $59 \times 19 - 59 \times 9 = 590$
   (d) $48 \times 77 - 38 \times 77 = 770$

   (e) $89 \times 15 + 11 \times 15 = 1500$
   (f) $61 \times 123 - 23 \times 61 = 610$
   (g) $1\ 291 \times 1\ 291 - 1\ 291 \times 1\ 281$
   (h) $5 \times 816 \times 20 = 81600$
   (i) $25 \times 1\ 999 \times 4 = 199900$
   (j) $2 \times 6\ 505 \times 50 = 650500$
   (k) $888 \times 50 = 44400$
   (l) $8\ 888 \times 25 = 222200$
   (m) $8\ 888 \times 125$
   (n) $4 \times 9 \times 9 \times 25 =$
   (o) $4 \times 8 \times 9 \times 5 \times 5 =$
   (p) $25 \times 7 \times 4 \times 11 =$
   (q) $8 \times 999 =$
   (r) $1\ 999 \times 5 =$

In-Class Activity

Mental calculations involving special 2-digit numbers

Work in pairs.

1. Calculate the following products:
   (i) $76 \times 74 = 5624$ **(ii)** $32 \times 38 = 1216$ **(iii)** $65 \times 65 = 4225$
   (a) When you compare the tens digits and the units digits, what do you notice about each pair of numbers?
   (b) Did you obtain $76 \times 74 = 5\ 624$? = Yes

2. Investigate how the digits of 76, 74 and 5 624 are related by studying the diagram below.

$76 \times 74 = 5624$

$$
\begin{array}{ccccc}
 & \times & & & 6 \times 4 \\
7\ 6 & \times & 7\ 4 & = & 56\ \ 24 \\
\downarrow & & \downarrow & & \\
7 & & 8 & & 7 \times 8 \\
 & \times & & &
\end{array}
$$
(+ 1)

3. Investigate whether the same relationships exist for 1(ii) and 1(iii).

4. With a little practice, do you think you can use the relationships to calculate the product of such a pair of numbers mentally?

5. Find the product of each of the following mentally:
   (a) $67 \times 63 = $ 4221 (b) $96 \times 94 = $ 9024 (c) $58 \times 52 = $ 3016 (d) $85 \times 85 = $ 7225
   (e) 75×75 5625 (f) $109 \times 101 = $ 20 (g) 268×262

6. Practice with your partner by giving each other products of such pairs of numbers to work out mentally.

Order of Operations

Confusion arises when we try to evaluate 19 – 3 + 7.

Which operation should we perform first?

If we perform the addition first, we obtain

$$19 - (3 + 7) = 19 - 10$$
$$= 9$$

If we perform the subtraction first, we obtain

$$(19 - 3) + 7 = 16 + 7$$
$$= 23$$

Obviously, $9 \neq 23$ and hence $19 - (3 + 7) \neq (19 - 3) + 7$

Similarly, $(10 \times 6) + 4 \neq 10 \times (6 + 4)$ $(10 \times 6) + 4 = 64$
$10 \times (6 + 4) = 100$

and $(20 \div 5) - 3 \neq 20 \div (5 - 3)$ $(20 \div 5) - 3 = 1$
$20 \div (5 - 3) = 10$

From the discussion above, we know that some rules are needed for performing operations.

Some Simple Rules for Performing Arithmetical Operations

The following rules are applicable to arithmetical operations:

1. If an expression contains brackets, simplify the expression within the brackets first. For example:
$$3 + (5 - 3) = 3 + 2 = 5$$

2. If an expression contains more than one pair of brackets, that is, there are brackets within brackets, simplify the expression within the innermost pair of brackets first. For example:
$$3 + [15 - (3 + 4)] = 3 + [15 - 7]$$
$$= 3 + 8 = 11$$

3. If an expression contains only additions and subtractions, work from left to right. For example:
$$28 + 12 - 9 = 40 - 9 = 31$$

4. If an expression contains only multiplications and divisions, work from left to right. For example:

$$125 \div 5 \times 15 = 25 \times 15 = 375$$

5. If an expression contains all the four operations (i.e.) addition, subtraction, multiplication and division), do multiplications or divisions before additions or subtractions. For example:

$$12 + 3 \times 4 - 35 \div 7 = 12 + 12 - 5$$
$$= 24 - 5 = 19$$

═ Exercise 1g ═

1. In each case, fill in the box with >, < or =:

(a) $9 \times 3 - 11 \boxed{=} 16$

(b) $5 \times 11 + 6 \times 3 \boxed{>} 60$

(c) $56 \div 8 \times 4 - 15 + 9 \boxed{<} 25$

(d) $72 \div (18 - 60 \div 5) \boxed{>} 10$

(e) $2 \times [2 + 3 \times (2 + 5)] \boxed{>} 45$

(f) $24 \times 7 \times 8 \div 12 \boxed{<} 112$

(g) $2 \times 35 \div 5 + 96 \div 3 \boxed{} 50$

(h) $2\,464 \div (1 + 3 + 3 \times 4) \boxed{} 54$

(i) $105 + 27 \times 8 - 144 \div 9 \boxed{} 337$

(j) $(8 \times 9 - 108 \div 12) \times 2 - 57 \boxed{} 70$

2. Insert parentheses in each of the following expressions to make the resulting statement true. For example, the statement $11 - 5 - 4 = 10$ will be true if brackets are inserted around $5 - 4$ because $11 - (5 - 4) = 11 - 1 = 10$.

(a) $12 - 7 - 2 = 7$

(b) $3 \times 5 + 7 = 36$

(c) $3 \times 5 + 2 \times 4 = 39$

(d) $3 \times 5 + 2 \times 4 = 84$

(e) $3 \times 5 + 2 \times 4 = 68$

(f) $4 \times 6 - 3 \times 5 = 60$

3. Calculate:

(a) $98 - 32 - 15 + 21$

(b) $24 \times 7 \times 8 \div 12$

(c) $25 \div 5 \times 5 \div 25$

(d) $(47 - 25) + (52 - 47) \times 8$

(e) $(32 - 16) + (85 - 37) \div 2$

(f) $[(12 + 18) \times 3 - 5] \div 17$

(g) $(50 + 60) \times [40 \div (60 - 50)]$

(h) $[50 \times 3 + (50 - 10) \times 3] \div 6$

(i) $9\,000 \div [1\,500 \div 30 \div 10 \times (90 + 30)]$

(j) $[5 \times 52 - (5 \times 52 + 5 \times 36) \div 2] \div 5$

(k) $[567 - (175 - 132) \times 9] + (35 - 18) \times 6$

(l) $[(325 + 45) \div 5 \times 7] - (78 - 65) \times 2$

(m) $75 - 38 \div 2 + 75 \div 5 \times 7 + 81 \div 3$
$\div 9 \times 7 - 15 + 6 \times 7$

4. A shopkeeper buys 18 T-shirts and 12 skirts for \$144. If the T-shirts cost \$4 each, find the cost of each skirt by completing and calculating the following:

$$(144 - 18 \times \boxed{}) \div \boxed{}$$

5. A fruit seller buys 8 crates of oranges at \$18 per crate and 10 crates of apples at \$20 per crate. There are 72 oranges in each crate of oranges and 100 apples in each crate of apples. If he sells the oranges at 3 for a dollar and apples at 4 for a dollar, find his profit by completing and simplifying the following expression:

$$\boxed{} \times (\boxed{} \div 3 - 18) + 10 \times (100 \div \boxed{} - \boxed{})$$

6. In a pet shop, two goldfish cost as much as five tropical fish. If Wei Meng pays \$20 for 10 tropical fish, how many goldfish can he buy with \$40? Obtain your answer by simplifying an expression like those in Question 3.

7. A shop charges the customers \$2 for binding a book. There will be no charge if customers are not satisfied with the service. In the last two days, the shop bound 38 and 45 books respectively and received \$156. How many books were not bound to the satisfaction of the customers? Obtain your answer by simplifying an expression like those in Question 3.

Rounding off Whole Numbers

As of 1998, there are 702 100 foreigners in Singapore of which 5 000 are Australians.

Can you complete the following? 702 100 could have been obtained from a number which has been rounded off to the nearest 100. While 5 000 could also have been obtained when a number has been rounded off to the nearest 1 000.

(a) 702 100 could have been rounded off to the nearest ____.

(b) 5 000 could have been rounded off to the nearest ____.

Can you give other daily life examples in which you need to work with estimates rather than exact values?

It was mentioned at the beginning of this chapter that the estimated population of Singapore in July 1996 was 3 396 924 people.

It is usually not useful to give such an accurate estimate of the population of Singapore. We will get a better idea of how large or how small the population was if the estimate was to be given as 3.4 million or 3 400 000 people.

On 20th March 1999, *The Straits Times* published the population figure under the heading "Singapore with 4 million people" and gave our population as 3.87 million or 3 870 000.

3 400 000 (three million and four **hundred thousand**) has been obtained by **rounding 3 396 924** off to the nearest **hundred thousand** (100 000) and **3 870 000** (three million and eight hundred and **seventy thousand**) could have been rounded off to the nearest ten thousand (**10 000**).

By comparing the two rounded off figures, we grasp very quickly that the population has increased by about 470 000 people in less than three years.

There are other occasions where it is better to work with estimates. For example, we may budget $1 000 for a trip that would cost at least $850.

A certain type of printing paper is sold in reams of 500 sheets. If you need 2 345 sheets of printing paper, how many reams of paper must you buy?

In-Class Activity

Work with a partner.

1. (a) Is 20 or 30 a better estimate of 24?
   (b) Is 20 nearer to 24 than 30?
   The diagram below shows the section of the number line from 20 to 30.

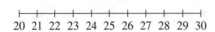

   (i) Is 25 half way between 20 and 30?
   (ii) Can you locate the point representing 24?
   (iii) Can we say that 24 is nearer to 20 than 30 because the units digit of 24 is less than the units digit of 25, i.e. 4 < 5?
   (iv) 30 is nearer to 27 than 20. Why?
   (v) Can we say that when 24 is rounded to 20 and 27 to 30, 24 and 27 have been rounded to the nearest 10?

25 is exactly between 20 and 30. By convention, we round 25 to 30, correct to the nearest ten.

2. Now, consider 824 and 827.

    (a) In each case, fill in the box with > or <:

        (i) 824 is nearer to 820 than 830 because 4 ☐ 5.

        (ii) 827 is nearer to 830 than 820 because 7 ☐ 5.

    (b) In each case, fill in the box with the correct number:

        (i) 824 = 8 ☐ 0   (correct to the nearest 10)

        (ii) 827 = 8 ☐ 0   (correct to the nearest 10)

3. Consider 845 and 855.

    (a) In each case, fill in the box with >, <, = or ≠:

        (i) 845 is nearer to 800 than 900 because the tens digit, 4 ☐ 5.

        (ii) 855 is nearer to 900 than 800 because the tens digit, 5 ☐ 5 and the units digit, 5 ☐ 0.

    (b) In each case, find a digit for each ☆:

        (i) 845 = 8 ☆☆   (correct to the nearest 100)

        (ii) 855 = ☆☆☆   (correct to the nearest 100)

4. We say that 24 and 27 are approximately equal to 20 and 30 respectively and we write $24 \approx 20$ and $27 \approx 30$. In other words, 20 and 30 are estimates of 24 and 27 respectively.

In each case, fill in the blank with the correct number:

    (a) $824 \approx$ _____ and $827 \approx$ _____.

    (b) $845 \approx$ _____ and $855 \approx$ _____.

From the above activity, we can conclude the following:

(i) To round off a whole number to the nearest ten, consider the units digit. If it is less than 5, simply replace it by 0. If it is 5 or more, add 1 to the tens digit and replace the units digit by 0.

(ii) To round off a whole number to the nearest hundred, consider the tens digit. If it is less than 5, simply replace the tens and the units digits by zeros. If it is 5 or more, add 1 to the hundreds digit and replace the tens and units digits by zeros.

(iii) The same procedure can be extended to round off a whole number to a specified place as shown below:

    Step 1   Find the digit in the specified place.

    Step 2   Consider the next digit to the right.

        (a) If the digit is less than 5, replace it and all the digits to its right by zeros.

        (b) If the digit is 5 or more, replace it and all digits to its right by zeros after adding 1 to the digit in the specified place.

Example 11

Write   *(a) 4 178 correct to the nearest 10;*   *(b) 98 142 correct to the nearest 100;*

        (c) 48 653 correct to the nearest 1 000.

Solution

        + 1

(a) 4 1 7 8 = 4 1 8 0   (correct to the nearest 10)

        This digit is more than 5.

(b) 9 8 1 4 2 = 9 8 1 0 0 (correct to the nearest 100)

+ 0

This digit is less than 5.

+ 1

(c) 4 8 6 5 3 = 4 9 0 0 0 (correct to the nearest 1 000)

This digit is more than 5.

≡ Exercise 1h ≡

1. With a population of 4 million and a land area of 585 sq km, Singapore has a population density of 6 838 people per sq km.

   (a) Round 585 off to the nearest
       (i) 10   (ii) 100

   (b) Round 6 838 off to the nearest
       (i) 10   (ii) 100   (iii) 1 000

2. It will take 10 076 Boeing 747s to ship out 4 million Singaporeans who would in turn fit into 2 222 MRT trains.

   (a) Round 2 222 off to the nearest
       (i) 100   (ii) 1 000

   (b) Round 10 076 off to the nearest
       (i) 10   (ii) 100   (iii) 1 000
       (iv) 10 000

3. A pop group sold 82 649 copies of their latest album. What is the number of copies sold to the nearest

   (a) ten   (b) hundred
   (c) thousand   (d) ten thousand?

4. Round the following figures correct to the

   (i) nearest ten

   (ii) nearest hundred
   (iii) nearest thousand

   (a) 55 726   (b) 380 014
   (c) 9 969 972   (d) 76 636 792

5. If a whole number n, rounded to the nearest 10, is 50, then the possible values of n are $45 \leqslant n \leqslant 54$ or $45 \leqslant n < 55$. Similarly if a whole number m, rounded off to the nearest 100, is 2 500, then the possible values of m are $2\,450 \leqslant m < 2\,550$.

   (a) In Singapore, about 15 000 National Service recruits are enlisted annually. If the actual number of recruits enlisted in a particular year is a and 15 000 is the value of a rounded off to the nearest 1 000, write down the possible values of a.

   (b) In Singapore, there are about 250 000 operationally ready servicemen in the SAF. If the actual number of operationally ready servicemen at a particular moment is b and 250 000 is the value of b rounded off to the nearest 10 000, write down the possible values of b.

Use of Calculators

There are different types of calculators we can use in Mathematics. Therefore, it is important that you follow the instructions given in the handbook that comes with your calculator.

Below are some important keys of the calculator.

0 to 9   Numeral keys

+, −, ×, ÷   Operation keys

=   Equal key

ON/C   All clear key

( )   Bracket keys

Before you use a calculator make sure that it is functioning properly. You can check this by performing some simple calculations to which you already know the answers.

For example,

3 × 2 ÷ 3 must give 2 or 6 666 666 ÷ 2 must give 3 333 333, etc.

Example 12

Use the calculator to find the values of the following:

(a) *34 + 785;*   (b) *357 × 174;*   (c) *966 ÷ 23.*

▼ **Solution**

The steps	Final display
(a) 34 + 785 =	819
(b) 357 × 174 =	62 118
(c) 966 ÷ 23 =	42

NB: Many calculators available in the market observe rules for order of operations. Check your calculator for this by entering, say 7 + 3 × 6. If you obtain 25, then your calculator does observe the rules for order of calculations. If you obtain 60, then it does not. It pays to obtain a calculator which observes such rules so that you can work from left to right without having to worry about the order of calculations.

Example 13

Evaluate using the calculator,

(a) *569 + 24 × 77;*   (b) *3 255 ÷ 15 × 64;*   (c) *(27 × 15 − 88) × 79.*

▼ **Solution**

The steps	Final Display
(a) 569 + 24 × 77 = or EXE	2 417
(b) 3 255 ÷ 15 × 64 =	13 888
(c) (27 × 15 − 88) × 79 =	25 043

"What is your favourite number?" John asked his little sister.

"Three", she said.

"I will use my calculator to work out a product to give you a string of your favourite number," John said.

John pressed 12345679 on his pocket calculator which has a 10-digit display. He multiplied this number by 27 and the product was 333333333. His sister was thrilled and told John, "I also like the number 9. Can you give me a string of 9's?"

"No problem," replied John. John pressed 12345679 again and this time he multiplied this number by 81 and the result was 999999999.

Can you multiply two numbers so as to give a string of 5's, 7's, 8's, and so on?

When Sumei opens a book, two pages face her. If the product of the two page numbers is 3 192, what are the two page numbers?

Many calculators provide a **memory storage space**. It is useful for computing complex expressions.

| STO | or | Min | Memory Entry Key

This key will transfer the number displayed to memory and it cancels the previous contents in the memory. To clear the memory, press zero | STO |.

| RCL | or | MR | Memory Recall Key

It will display the contents of the memory without clearing it.

For example, $\dfrac{323 + 7\,594}{285 - 198}$ *can be obtained by pressing*

285 – 198 | = | | STO | 323 + 7 594 | = | | ÷ | | RCL | | = | to get 91.

Can you work out the above with the use of bracket keys?

NB: Human and machine errors may affect the **accuracy** of a calculation. Hence, it is important to estimate mentally results of calculations for checking purposes. For example, $89 \times 68 \approx 90 \times 70 = 6\,300$. Since $90 > 89$ and $70 > 68$, the exact value of 89×68 should be around but less than 6 300. If you obtain an answer that is a lot less than 6 300 or one that is more than 6 300, then you know that you have obtained a wrong answer.

Example 14

Estimate mentally the results of the following calculations. State in each case whether the estimated answer is greater or less than the exact answer.

(a) $7\,800 \times 19$ *(b)* $425 \times 1\,015$ *(c)* $16\,800 \div 99$

▼ **Solution**

(a) $7\,800 \times 19 \approx 7\,800 \times 20 = 156\,000$
     $156\,000 > 7\,800 \times 19$

(b) $425 \times 1\,015 \approx 425 \times 1\,000 = 425\,000$
     $425\,000 < 425 \times 1\,015$

(c) $16\,800 \div 99 \approx 16\,800 \div 100 = 168$
     $168 < 16\,800 \div 99$

═ Exercise 1i ═

1. Make an estimate of each of the following and then use a calculator to get the exact answer.

	Estimate	Exact answer
(a) 84×103	_____	_____
(b) $2\,496 \div 48$	_____	_____
(c) 782×105	_____	_____
(d) $12\,883 \div 991$	_____	_____
(e) $3\,420 \times 998$	_____	_____

2. For each of the following, two answers are given. Only one answer is correct. Use estimation to identify the correct answer.

                                 Correct answer

(a) 298×11
    (i) 4 268   **(ii)** 3 278 _____

(b) $7\ 238 \div 77$
    (i) 94   **(ii)** 84   _____

(c) $806\ 577 \div 87$
    (i) 8 421   **(ii)** 9 271 _____

(d) 589×95
    (i) 55 955   **(ii)** 62 945_____

(e) 673×108
    (i) 72 684   **(ii)** 83 664_____

3. Use a calculator to compute the following:

    (a) $43\ 749\ 888 + 9\ 046\ 302$

(b) $26\ 070\ 000 - 58\ 999$
(c) $87\ 415 \times 738$
(d) $745\ 153 \div 683$
(e) $7\ 769 \times 324 \times 189$
(f) $415\ 125 \div 45 \div 369$
(g) $55\ 069 - 9\ 968 \div 178$
(h) $49\ 138 - 89 \times 397$
(i) $3\ 007 \times 518 + 475 \times 70\ 562$
(j) $8\ 318 \times 978 - 1\ 547 \times 739$
(k) $5\ 097 \times 1\ 574 - 47\ 827 \div 283$
(l) $3\ 278 + 184 \times 237 - 136 \times 118$
(m) $14\ 234 - 3\ 477 + 16\ 762 \div 29 - 5\ 436$
(n) $7\ 532 \times 7\ 156 - 31\ 188 \div 113 + 37\ 254$
(o) $107\ 163 \div 189 \times 6\ 051 - 31\ 779 \div 321$
(p) $(1\ 213 + 673) \times (76\ 541 - 3\ 116)$
(q) $131 \times (3738 + 556 - 1\ 365) \div 29 \times (543 + 6\ 351)$

Summary

1. The numbers 1, 2, 3, 4, 5, … are **natural** numbers.

   The numbers 0, 1, 2, 3, 4, … are **whole** numbers.

   The numbers 0, 2, 4, 6, 8, … are **even** numbers.

   The numbers 1, 3, 5, 7, 9, … are **odd** numbers.

2. A **number line** is a straight line on which each point represents a number.
   A number on the number line is always greater than any number to its left and smaller than any number to its right.

3. **Commutative Laws**
   Addition and multiplication of whole numbers are commutative. For any two whole numbers x and y, we have

   $$x + y = y + x \quad \text{and} \quad x \times y = y \times x.$$

   Subtraction and division are not commutative as $x - y \neq y - x$ (if $x \neq 0$; $y \neq 0$) and $x \div y \neq y \div x$ (if $x \neq 0$; $y \neq 0$) in general.

4. **Associative Laws**
   Addition and multiplication of whole numbers are associative. For any three whole numbers x, y and z, we have

   $$(x + y) + z = x + (y + z) \quad \text{and} \quad (x \times y) \times z = x \times (y \times z).$$

5. Distributive Laws

Multiplication is distributive over addition and subtraction. For any three whole numbers x, y and z, we have:

$$x \times (y + z) = x \times y + x \times z; \quad (x + y) \times z = x \times z + y \times z;$$
$$x \times (y - z) = x \times y - x \times z; \quad (x - y) \times z = x \times z - y \times z.$$

6. Rule for Order of Operations

When an expression of arithmetic operations contains brackets, work with the expressions within the brackets first. (If there are brackets within brackets, work with the innermost pair of brackets first.)

When an expression contains addition, subtraction, multiplication and division, do multipliation and division before addition and subtraction.

When an expression contains only addition and subtraction or only multiplication and division, work from left to right.

═ Review Questions 1 ═

1. Without using a calculator, find the value of each of the following. (a) and (b) have been done for you.

   (a) $96 + 8 + 28 + 2 + 72 + 4 + 15$

   $= (96 + 4) + (8 + 72) + (28 + 2) + 15$
   $= 100 + 80 + 30 + 15$
   $= 225$

   (b) $3\ 648 + 999$
   $= 3\ 648 + (1\ 000 - 1)$
   $= (3\ 648 + 1\ 000) - 1$
   $= 4\ 648 - 1$
   $= 4\ 647$

   (c) $102 + 7 + 45 + 198 + 3$
   (d) $1\ 720 + 863 + 280 + 137$
   (e) $135 + 798 + 465 + 202$
   (f) $4\ 685 + 3\ 999$
   (g) $999 + 99 + 9$
   (h) $998 + 1\ 246 + 9\ 998$

2. Evaluate the following mentally:

   (a) 302×5 (b) $2 \times 135 \times 5$
   (c) $2 \times 8 \times 9 \times 5$ ✱(d) $25 \times 7 \times 4 \times 11$
   ✱(e) $700 \div 25$ ✱(f) $1\ 600 \times 25$
   ✱(g) $99\ 800 \div 20 \div 5$
   ✱(h) 44×46 ✱(i) 197×193

3. Without using a calculator, evaluate the following:

   (a) $40 \times 5 + 50 \times 6 - 7 \times 60$
   (b) $(57 + 43 - 7 \times 5) \times 20 + 4 \times 90$
   (c) $(325 - 127) \div 9 + 136 - 11 \times 11$
   (d) $16 \div [18 - (32 - 100 \div 5) \div 6]$
   (e) $1 \div 1 + 0 \div 26 + 26 \div 1$
   (f) $7 \times 3 - 77 \div 11 + 16$
   (g) $56 \div 8 + (47 - 17) \div 5 - 13$
   (h) $(32 \times 5 - 60) \times 25 - 90 \times 15$
   (i) $[4 \times 15 + 72 \div 8 - (47 - 23) \div 6] \times 2$
   (j) $105 \div 5 + 15 \times 3 - (6 \times 12 - 54 \div 9)$
   (k) $79 - 6 \times 81 \div 9 + 65 \div 13 - 11$
   (l) $(640 \div 80 + 54 \div 6) \times 20 - 840 \div 7$

4. Estimate the results of the following calculations:

   (a) $97 \times 1\ 003$
   (b) $3\ 648 \times 999$
   (c) $199 \times 21 \times 998$
   (d) $19 \times 499 \div 51$
   (e) $4\ 201 \div 58$
   (f) $160\ 015 \div 801$
   ✱(g) $39 \div 5 + 51 \times 4 - 7 \times 19$
   ✱(h) $389 \div 13 + 2\ 604 \div 13$
   ✱(i) $1\ 999 \div 501 \times 49$
   ✱(j) $(599 + 402 - 298 \times 2) \times 49$

Problem Solving

1. Complete the following:

(a)
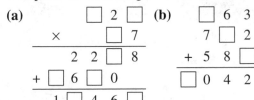
$$
\begin{array}{r}
\square\ 2\ \square \\
\times\qquad \square\ 7 \\
\hline
2\ 2\ \square\ 8 \\
+\ \square\ 6\ \square\ 0 \\
\hline
1\ \square\ 4\ 6\ \square
\end{array}
$$

(b)
$$
\begin{array}{r}
\square\ 6\ 3 \\
7\ \square\ 2 \\
+\ 5\ 8\ \square \\
\hline
\square\ 0\ 4\ 2
\end{array}
$$

(c)
$$
\begin{array}{r}
\square\ 0\ \square\ \square\ 3 \\
-\quad \square\ 7\ 2\ \square \\
\hline
7\ 7\ 7
\end{array}
$$

(d)
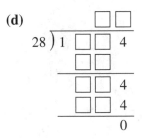

2. Fill each of the ▢ with a digit so as to make the long division correct.

(a)
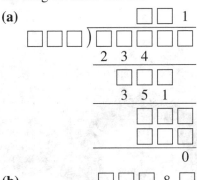

(b)
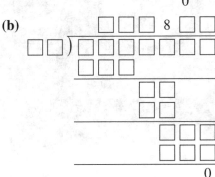

3. Given that a 6-digit number 199 6 ▢▢ is exactly divisible by 95, find the last two digits of the number.

4. Fill in the numbers 1, 2, 3, 4, 5, 6, 7, 8 and 9 so that the sum of the numbers on each side of the triangle will be equal to 17.

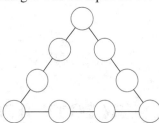

5. Insert +, −, ×, ÷ and brackets to make the following sentences true. The first one has been done.

(a) $(3 + 3) \div 3 - 3 \div 3 = 1$
(b) 3 3 3 3 3 = 2   **(c)** 3 3 3 3 3 = 3
(d) 3 3 3 3 3 = 4   **(e)** 3 3 3 3 3 = 5
(f) 3 3 3 3 3 = 6   **(g)** 3 3 3 3 3 = 7
(h) 3 3 3 3 3 = 8   **(i)** 3 3 3 3 3 = 9
(j) 3 3 3 3 3 = 10

6. Insert +, −, ×, ÷ and brackets to make the following sentences true. The first one has been done.

(a) $(5 + 5) \div 5 - 5 \div 5 = 1$
(b) 5 5 5 5 5 = 2   **(c)** 5 5 5 5 5 = 3
(d) 5 5 5 5 5 = 4   **(e)** 5 5 5 5 5 = 5
(f) 5 5 5 5 5 = 6   **(g)** 5 5 5 5 5 = 7
(h) 5 5 5 5 5 = 8   **(i)** 5 5 5 5 5 = 10

7. Given that $\triangle + \square + \Diamond = 9$ $\triangle + \square + \bigcirc = 8$
$\triangle + \Diamond + \bigcirc = 7$ $\square + \Diamond + \bigcirc = 6$
Find the value of $\triangle$, $\square$, $\Diamond$ and $\bigcirc$.

8. Fill in the numbers 1, 2, 3, 4, 5, 6, 7, 8 and 9 so that the sum of the numbers on each side of the triangle will be equal to 23.

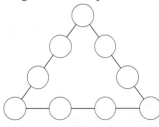

9. Use eight 8's to make a total of 1 000. (Use +, −, ×, ÷ or brackets as you see fit.)

CHAPTER 2

Factors and Multiples

In this chapter, you will learn

▲ about prime numbers;

▲ how to find the highest common factor (HCF) and the lowest
common multiple (LCM) of two or more numbers;

▲ how to find squares, square roots, cubes and cube roots
of numbers.

Preliminary Problem

In the picture, the alarm clock and the
two watches display the same time.
Suppose the alarm clock shows the
correct time, while the two watches do not.
If, for every minute, the watch on the left is
slower by 5 seconds, while that on the right
is faster by 5 seconds, how many minutes
later do you think all three will display the
same time again?

In-Class Activity

Work with a partner. You will need a box of toothpicks for the activity.

1. Start with 10 toothpicks. Can you arrange them into groups (more than 1) of equal numbers of toothpicks (more than 1) with no leftovers?

2. Repeat the above with 1, 2, 3, …, 9 toothpicks and also with 11, 12, 13, …, 20 toothpicks.

3. Classify the numbers 1, 2, 3, …, 20 according to how each number can be arranged by copying and completing the following table:

List I	List II	List III
The number 1: 1 group of 1 toothpick or $1 = 1 \times 1$	The number 2: 1 group of 2 toothpicks; 2 groups of 1 toothpick or $2 = 1 \times 2 = 2 \times 1$ The number 3: 1 group of 3 toothpicks; 3 groups of 1 toothpick or $3 = 1 \times 3 = 3 \times 1$	The number 4: 1 group of 4 toothpicks; 4 groups of 1 toothpick; 2 groups of 2 toothpicks or $4 = 1 \times 4 = 4 \times 1 = 2 \times 2$ The number 6: 1 group of 6 toothpicks; 6 groups of 1 toothpick; 2 groups of 3 toothpicks; 3 groups of 2 toothpicks or $6 = 1 \times 6 = 6 \times 1 = 2 \times 3 = 3 \times 2$

Factors and Multiples

From the above activity, we have

$$18 = \mathbf{1} \times 18 = \mathbf{2} \times 9 = \mathbf{3} \times 6 = \mathbf{6} \times 3 = \mathbf{9} \times 2 = \mathbf{18} \times 1.$$

We call each of the numbers 1, 2, 3, 6, 9 and 18 a **factor** of 18. Conversely, we call 18 a **multiple** of each of the numbers 1, 2, 3, 6, 9 and 18. Clearly, when 18 is divided by any one of its factors, the remainder is zero. We say that 18 is **divisible** by 1, 2, 3, 6, 9 and 18.

Example 1

(a) *List the factors of 60.* (b) *List the multiples of 5.*

▼ Solution

(a) We have $60 = 1 \times 60 = 2 \times 30 = 3 \times 20 = 4 \times 15 = 5 \times 12 = 6 \times 10$.
Thus, the factors of 60 are 1, 2, 3, 4, 5, 6, 10, 12, 15, 20, 30, 60.

(b) By multiplying 5 with 1, 2, 3, 4 and so on, we obtain the multiples of 5, i.e. the multiples of 5 are 5, 10, 15, 20, ….

Prime Numbers and Composite Numbers

In Chapter 1, we classified natural numbers into even and odd numbers. In the activity above, we see another way of classifying natural numbers. We classify the numbers according to the number of factors they have.

Did you notice that each of your List II numbers on Page 25 has exactly **two** different factors, 1 and itself? Such natural numbers are called **prime numbers**.

> **A natural number which has only two different factors, 1 and the number itself, is a prime number.**

For example: 2, 3, 5, 7, 11, …

Each of the List III numbers has more than two different factors. Such natural numbers are known as **composite numbers**.

> **A natural number which has more than two different factors is a composite number.**

For example: 4, 6, 8, 9, 10, …

The number 1 is neither a prime number nor a composite number. Why?

In-Class Activity

You may work on this activity with a partner.

1. Copy on a piece of paper the numbers from 1 to 100 inclusive and arrange them in 10 rows as shown below.

1	2	3	4	5	6	7	8	9	10
11	12	13	14	15	16	17	18	19	20
21	22	23	24	25	26	27	28	29	30
31	32	33	34	35	36	37	38	39	40
41	42	43	44	45	46	47	48	49	50
51	52	53	54	55	56	57	58	59	60
61	62	63	64	65	66	67	68	69	70
71	72	73	74	75	76	77	78	79	80
81	82	83	84	85	86	87	88	89	90
91	92	93	94	95	96	97	98	99	100

   (a) Cross out the number 1.
   (b) Circle the number 2 and cross out all the other multiples of 2.
   (c) Circle the number 3 and cross out all the other multiples of 3.
   (d) Circle the number 5 and cross out all the other multiples of 5.
   (e) Circle the number 7 and cross out all the other multiples of 7.
   (f) Continue the process until all numbers are either circled or crossed out.

2. Answer the following questions:
   (a) What is the reason for crossing out the number 1?
   (b) What are the circled numbers?
   (c) What are the numbers crossed out?
   (d) List the number of prime numbers that are less than 100.

(e) What is the largest prime number less than 100?

(f) What are the first 20 composite numbers?

(g) Is every odd number a prime number?

(h) Is every even number a composite number?

The above process of finding all the prime numbers less than a given number is called the **Sieve of Eratosthenes** in honour of a Greek mathematician, Eratosthenes.

3. There is a statement which says that "every even number greater than 2 can be expressed as the sum of two prime numbers". For example, $4 = 2 + 2$, $8 = 3 + 5$ and $12 = 7 + 5$. This statement is called **Goldbach's Conjecture**. It is a conjecture because it has not yet been proven.

For each of the following numbers, verify Goldbach's Conjecture by expressing the number as a sum of two prime numbers:

(a) 16 **(b)** 36 **(c)** 64 **(d)** 98

4. Prime numbers such as 5 and 7 that differ by 2 are called **twin primes**. Mathematicians believe that there is an infinite number of pairs of twin primes. 1 000 000 061 and 1 000 000 063 are twin primes. List five other pairs of twin primes.

═══ Exercise 2a ═══

1. Write down all the factors of each of the following.

   (a) 16 **(b)** 28 **(c)** 96
   (d) 100 **(e)** 120 **(f)** 210

2. Write down the first six multiples of the following numbers.

   (a) 4 **(b)** 7 **(c)** 9
   (d) 12 **(e)** 17 **(f)** 21

3. Circle the numbers that have 18 as a factor.

   54, 126, 198, 240, 320

4. Underline the numbers which are factors of 144.

   1, 2, 3, 4, 8, 9, 12, 14, 16, 32, 48, 144

5. Identify the multiples of 8 from the following numbers.

   14, 24, 32, 54, 56, 36, 72, 30, 64, 18, 40, 78, 96, 108, 120

6. State the numbers that have 224 as a multiple in the following.

   3, 4, 12, 14, 24, 28, 32, 36, 56

7. Use a calculator to find all the factors of the following numbers.

   (a) 480 **(b)** 600 **(c)** 960
   (d) 936 **(e)** 1 080 **(f)** 1 200

8. John has 48 orange-flavoured sweets and Susan has 45 lime-flavoured sweets.

   (a) John wishes to divide his sweets equally into bags. List all the possible ways he can do this. (For example, he can have 6 bags of 8 sweets.)

   (b) Susan also wishes to divide her sweets equally into bags. List all the possible ways she can do this.

   (c) Peter, their good friend, suggests that they combine the sweets and divide them equally into bags in such a way that each bag has equal number of orange-flavoured and lime-flavoured sweets. Explain how this can be done.

9. Determine whether each of the following is a prime number or a composite number:

   (a) 2 **(b)** 15 **(c)** 17
   (d) 21 **(e)** 27 **(f)** 29

10. Name the the next five prime numbers after 30.

11. To test whether a given number is a prime number.

    (a) Is 221 a prime number? Use a calculator to divide 221 successively by the prime numbers 2, 3, 5, 7, ... You can stop the process when

(i) a prime number divides 221 exactly. If this happens, then 221 will not be a prime number (e.g. 25 is not a prime number because 5 divides 25 exactly).

(ii) a prime number does not divide 221 exactly and the number in the display is less than the prime number. If this occurs, then 221 will be a prime number (e.g. 13 is a prime number since $13 \div 2 = 6.5 > 2$; $13 \div 3 = 4.3 > 3$; $13 \div 5 = 2.6 < 5$).

(b) Repeat the above procedure to determine whether each of the following is a prime number.

(i) 101   **(ii)** 227   **(iii)** 323
(iv) 997   **(v)** 1 007   **(vi)** 2 761

12. Find two prime numbers whose sum is an odd number. Must one of the numbers be 2?

13. Can the product of two prime numbers be
   (a) an odd number;
   (b) an even number;
   (c) a prime number?

14. 37 and 73 are prime numbers with reversed digits. Name another pair of two-digit prime numbers with reversed digits?

Tests of Divisibility

Is 50 346 divisible by 2?   Is 1 776 divisible by 3?   Is 123 436 divisible by 4?
Is 17 325 divisible by 5?   Is 738 divisible by 9?   Are 6 721 and 8 162 divisible by 11?

We can find out whether a number is divisible by another by actually working out the division. However, this can be quite tedious. There are some short-cuts for determining whether one number is divisible by another number. These methods, called **tests of divisibility**, are shown below.

111, 333, 555, 777, 999 are divisible by 3 while 222, 444, 666, 888 are divisible by 6. Why?

A palindromic number is one which reads the same forwards or backwards. Some examples are: 121, 2 332, 1 234 321, etc. Can you show that all palindromic numbers with an even number of digits are divisible by 11?

1. A number is divisible by 2 if it is even. 50 346 is even. Hence, it is divisible by 2.

2. A number is divisible by 3 if the sum of the digits is divisible by 3.
   1 776 is divisible by 3 as $1 + 7 + 7 + 6 = 21$ is divisible by 3.

3. A number is divisible by 4 if the number formed by the last two digits is divisible by 4.
     123 436 is divisible by 4 as 36 is divisible by 4.

4. A number is divisible by 5 if the last digit is 0 or 5.
     17 325 is divisible by 5.

5. A number is divisible by 9 if the sum of its digits is divisible by 9.
     738 is divisible by 9 as $7 + 3 + 8 = 18$ is divisible by 9.

6. A number is divisible by 10 if the last digit is 0.
     124 830 is divisible by 10.

7. A number is divisible by 11 if the difference between the sum of the digits in the odd places and the sum of the digits in the even places is equal to 0 or is a multiple of 11.
     6 721 is divisible by 11 as $6 + 2 = 7 + 1$ or $6 - 7 + 2 - 1 = 0$.
     8 162 is divisible by 11 as $(8 + 6) - (1 + 2) = 11$
     or $8 - 1 + 6 - 2 = 11$.

Example 2

Test each of the following numbers for divisibility by 2, 3, 4, 5, 10 and 11:

(a) 660   (b) 510   (c) 639   (d) 49 610

▼ **Solution**

(a) 660 is divisible by 2 since it is even.
     660 is divisible by 3 since 6 + 6 + 0 = 12 is divisible by 3.
     660 is divisible by 4 since 60 is divisible by 4.
     660 is divisible by 5 and 10 as its last digit is 0.
     660 is divisible by 11 as (6 + 0) − 6 = 0.
     ∴   660 is divisible by 2, 3, 4, 5, 10 and 11.

(b) 510 is divisible by 2, 3, 5 and 10.

(c) 639 is divisible by 3 as 6 + 3 + 9 = 18 is divisible by 3.

(d) Since 4 − 9 + 6 − 1 + 0 = 0 or (4 + 6 + 0) − (9 + 1) = 0, 49 610 is divisible by 2, 5, 10 and 11.

Can you give the reasons for the answers to (b), (c) and (d)?

Exercise 2b

1. Which of the following numbers are divisible by 2, 4 or 5?

    (a) 10   (b) 24   (c) 60
    (d) 108   (e) 135   (f) 189
    (g) 240   (h) 315   (i) 648
    (j) 756   (k) 1 024   (l) 2 410

2. Which of the following numbers are divisible by 3, 9 or 11?

    (a) 18   (b) 72   (c) 126
    (d) 441   (e) 649   (f) 825
    (g) 1 419   (h) 9 372   (i) 666 633

3. Which of the following numbers are divisible by 6, 10, 12 or 15?

    (a) 552   (b) 650   (c) 264
    (d) 255   (e) 420   (f) 7 830

4. How would you test a number for divisibility by 30? Are 660, 540, 645 and 610 divisible by 30?

5. Test 4 237, 6 496, 7 770 and 8 514 for divisibility by 14.

6. If a number is divisible by 8, must it also be divisible by 2? By 4? Explain your answer.

7. If a number is divisible by 3, must it also be divisible by 9? Explain your answer.

Prime Factorisation

Every natural number (except 1) is either a prime number or a composite number. A composite number can be expressed as the product of two or more prime numbers, which are called **prime factors**. The process of **decomposition** of a composite number into prime factors is known as **prime factorisation**.

For example, $30 = 2 \times 3 \times 5$
and $60 = 2 \times 2 \times 3 \times 5.$

2, 3 and 5 are called the prime factors of 30. They are also the prime factors of 60. A **factor tree** can be used to express a composite number as a product of its prime factors.

The factor tree illustrates the prime factorisation of 60.

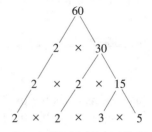

Index Notation

To be brief, we write 5×5 as 5^2 and read it as *5 squared* or *square of 5*.

$5 \times 5 \times 5$ is written as 5^3 and is read as *5 cubed* or *the cube of 5*.

$5 \times 5 \times 5 \times 5$ is written as 5^4 and is read as *5 to the power of 4*.

Similarly, $2 \times 2 \times 2 \times 2 \times 2 \times 2$ is written as 2^6 and is read as *2 is raised to the power of 6*.

In general, $\underbrace{a \times a \times \ldots \times a}_{n \text{ factors}}$ is written as a^n and is read as *a to the power of n*.

This index notation a^n gives us a more precise method of expressing the factors of a number.

For example, $12 = 2 \times 2 \times 3$ can be written as $12 = 2^2 \times 3$
$40 = 2 \times 2 \times 2 \times 5$ can be written as $40 = 2^3 \times 5$
$60 = 2 \times 2 \times 3 \times 5$ can be written as $60 = 2^2 \times 3 \times 5$
$72 = 2 \times 2 \times 2 \times 3 \times 3$ can be written as $72 = 2^3 \times 3^2$

Example 3

Express 252 in prime factors.

Solution

Method 1

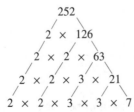

From the above factor tree, we have $252 = 2 \times 2 \times 3 \times 3 \times 7$
$= 2^2 \times 3^2 \times 7$ (using index notation)

Method 2

2	2 5 2
2	1 2 6
3	6 3
3	2 1
7	7
	1

(Start by dividing the number by the smallest prime factor and continue dividing until you get 1 as shown.)

$\therefore$ $252 = 2 \times 2 \times 3 \times 3 \times 7$
$= 2^2 \times 3^2 \times 7$

Exercise 2c

1. Express the following using index notation:
   (a) 7×7 (b) $2 \times 2 \times 5 \times 5$ (c) $3 \times 7 \times 7 \times 7$
   (d) $5 \times 5 \times 11 \times 11 \times 11$ (e) $2 \times 2 \times 13 \times 13 \times 31 \times 2$
   (f) $5 \times 5 \times 5 \times 19 \times 29 \times 19 \times 23 \times 29$

2. Express each of the following as a product of prime factors using index notation:
   (a) 28   (b) 48   (c) 54   (d) 88
   (e) 108   (f) 144   (g) 192   (h) 256

3. Complete the following factor trees:

   (a)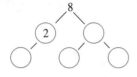

   $8 = \underline{} \times \underline{} \times \underline{}$

   (b)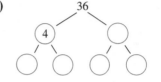

   $36 = \underline{} \times \underline{} \times \underline{} \times \underline{}$

   (c)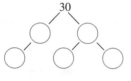

   $30 = \underline{} \times \underline{} \times \underline{}$

   (d)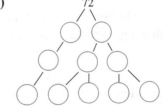

   $72 = \underline{} \times \underline{} \times \underline{} \times \underline{} \times \underline{}$

4. Factorise each of the following into prime factors using the 'factor tree' method:
   (a) 16   (b) 40   (c) 45   (d) 56
   (e) 60   (f) 84   (g) 114   (h) 120

5. Factorise each of the following numbers into prime factors:
   (a) 100   (b) 125   (c) 147   (d) 216
   (e) 225   (f) 360   (g) 567   (h) 648

Highest Common Factor (HCF)

Suppose Mary, an art elective program student, is working on an assignment. She plans to cover a 30 cm by 36 cm sheet of paper completely with identical square patterns. Can you help her to find the side of the largest possible square?

First, consider dividing each side into groups of equal lengths. This is equivalent to finding the factors of 30 and 36. Making a complete list from the smallest to the largest, we have:

The factors of 30 are   (1)   (2)   (3)   5   (6)   10   15   30
The factors of 36 are   (1)   (2)   (3)   4   (6)   9   12   18   36

1, 2, 3 and 6 are **common factors** to 30 and 36, the largest being 6. 6 is called the **Highest Common Factor (HCF)** of 30 and 36. Returning to the above problem, we now know that the side of the largest possible square is 6 cm.

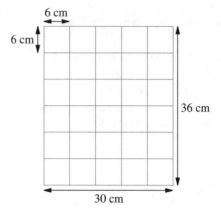

The diagram illustrates that Mary's sheet of paper can be covered completely with 30 squares each of side 6 cm.

Listing all the possible factors of numbers to find the HCF of the numbers as shown above can be tedious. The following provides two alternative methods:

Method 1

The prime factorisation of 30 and 36 is shown below:

$$30 = \boxed{2} \times \boxed{3} \times \boxed{5}$$
$$36 = \boxed{2^2} \times \boxed{3^2} \times \boxed{1}$$

(Use index notation.)
Choose the smaller number from each set.

$$2 \quad \times \quad 3 \quad \times \quad 1$$

∴ the HCF of 30 and 36 is $2 \times 3 \times 1 = 6$.

The HCF of a set of numbers will be less than the numbers or equal to one of the numbers.

Method 2

| Step 1 | 2 | 30 36 |
| Step 2 | 3 | 15 18 |
| Step 3 | | 5 6 | ← 1 is their only common factor. Stop here.

$$\text{HCF} = \boxed{2 \times 3} = 6$$

In step 1, we know that 30 and 36 are divisible by 2 because they are both even numbers.

In step 2, we divide 30 and 36 by 2 and write the quotients (15 and 18). We know that 15 and 18 are divisible by 3.

In step 3, we divide 15 and 18 by 3 and write the quotients (5 and 6).

Since 5 and 6 have no common factors except 1, we stop our computation.

We multiply the numbers listed on the left side of the above problem: $2 \times 3 = 6$.

∴ the HCF of 30 and 36 is 6.

Example 4

Find the HCF of 60, 180 and 210.

$$
\begin{aligned}
60 &= 2 \times 2 \times 3 \times 5 &= \boxed{2^2} \times \boxed{3} \times \boxed{5} \times \boxed{1} \\
180 &= 2 \times 2 \times 3 \times 3 \times 5 &= \boxed{2^2} \times \boxed{3^2} \times \boxed{5} \times \boxed{1} \\
210 &= 2 \times 3 \times 5 \times 7 &= \boxed{2} \times \boxed{3} \times \boxed{5} \times \boxed{7} \\
& & \quad\ \ 2 \quad\ \ 3 \quad\ \ 5 \quad\ \ 1
\end{aligned}
$$

Choose the smallest number from each set.

∴ the HCF of 60, 180 and 210 is $2 \times 3 \times 5 \times 1 = 30$.

Alternatively,

$$
\begin{array}{c|ccc}
2 & 60 & 180 & 210 \\
3 & 30 & 90 & 105 \\
5 & 10 & 30 & 35 \\
\hline
 & 2 & 6 & 7
\end{array}
$$

← 2, 6 and 7 have no common factor except 1. Stop here.

$$\text{HCF} = \boxed{2 \times 3 \times 5} = 30$$

∴ the HCF of 60, 180 and 210 is 30.

═ Exercise 2d ═

1. Find all the common factors of:

   (a) 6 and 9   (b) 12 and 16
   (c) 15 and 18   (d) 21 and 28
   (e) 27 and 36   (f) 30 and 45
   (g) 36 and 60   (h) 45 and 75

2. Find the HCF of the following:

   (a) 12 and 30   (b) 12 and 42
   (c) 14 and 28   (d) 15 and 75
   (e) 16 and 40   (f) 16 and 48
   (g) 20 and 45   (h) 21 and 56
   (i) 24 and 64   (j) 24 and 108
   (k) 28 and 56   (l) 36 and 243
   (m) 45 and 42   (n) 90 and 108
   (o) 99 and 165   (p) 324 and 128

3. Find the HCF of:

   (a) 27, 63 and 208   (b) 84, 63 and 126
   (c) 192, 160 and 96 (d) 48, 72 and 132
   (e) 112, 64 and 96
   (f) 30, 75, 90 and 135

   (g) 36, 168, 144 and 252
   (h) $2^3 \times 3^2 \times 5$ and $2^2 \times 3^4 \times 5^3$
   (i) $2 \times 5^2 \times 7$ and $2^3 \times 3^4 \times 5^3 \times 7^2$

4. James wants to cover a floor measuring 90 cm by 120 cm with square tiles of the same size. Given that he uses only whole tiles, find

   (a) the largest possible length of the side of each tile;
   (b) the number of tiles that are needed to cover the floor.

5. Paul has three pieces of rope with lengths of 140 cm, 168 cm and 210 cm. He wishes to cut the three pieces of rope into smaller pieces of equal length with no remainders.

   (a) What is the greatest possible length of each of the smaller pieces of rope?
   (b) How many of the smaller pieces of rope of equal length can he get?

Least Common Multiple (LCM)

Mary, the art elective program student, is working on a second assignment. She first designs a rectangular pattern measuring 9 cm by 12 cm. She then makes copies of the rectangular pattern. Next she uses the rectangular patterns to form a square. How many rectangular patterns does she need to form the smallest square? What is the length of a side of this square?

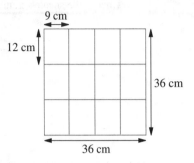

The diagram shows that Mary needs 12 rectangular patterns to form the smallest square of side 36 cm.

The length, in cm, of the side of a square that can be formed is a multiple of both 9 and 12.

Can you think why?

Consider the possible multiples of 9 and 12.

The multiples of 9 are   9   18   27   (36)   45   54   63   (72)   81   90   99   (108) .. .. ..
The multiples of 12 are   12   24   (36)   48   60   (72)   84   96   (108) .. .. ..

The first three multiples common to 9 and 12 are 36, 72 and 108.

The smallest of all the common multiples of 9 and 12 is 36 and we call 36 the **Least Common Multiple (LCM)** of 9 and 12.

Returning to our problem, we now know that the side of the smallest square is 36 cm. The number of rectangular patterns needed to create such a square is $4 \times 3 = 12$.

Example 5

Find the LCM of 30 and 36.

▼ **Solution**

Multiples of 30 = {30, 60, 90, 120, 150, 180, 210, …}

Multiples of 36 = {36, 72, 108, 144, 180, 216, …}

∴ the LCM of 30 and 36 is 180.

The above method of finding the LCM of two numbers is tedious. The following are two simpler methods:

Method 1

Using prime factorisation, we have

$$30 = \boxed{2} \times \boxed{3} \times \boxed{5}$$
$$36 = \boxed{2^2} \times \boxed{3^2} \times \boxed{1}$$

$$2^2 \times 3^2 \times 5$$

⎱ Choose the bigger number from each set.

∴ the LCM of 30 and 36 is $2^2 \times 3^2 \times 5 = 180$.

Method 2

$$\begin{array}{c|cc} 2 & 30 & 36 \\ 3 & 15 & 18 \\ \hline & 5 & 6 \end{array}$$

(Carry out the division as in the case of finding the HCF.)

→ Multiply the numbers on the left with the numbers at the bottom to obtain the LCM.

∴ the LCM of 30 and 36 is $2 \times 3 \times 5 \times 6 = 180$.

Example 6

Find the LCM of 18, 24 and 36.

▼ **Solution**

Using prime factorisation, we have

$$18 = 2 \times 3 \times 3 \quad = \boxed{2} \times \boxed{3^2}$$
$$24 = 2 \times 2 \times 2 \times 3 = \boxed{2^3} \times \boxed{3}$$
$$36 = 2 \times 2 \times 3 \times 3 = \boxed{2^2} \times \boxed{3^2}$$

$$2^3 \qquad 3^2$$

⎱ Choose the largest number from each set.

∴ the LCM of 18, 24 and 36 is $2^3 \times 3^2 = 72$.

Alternatively, we have

$$\begin{array}{c|ccc} 2 & 18 & 24 & 36 \\ 3 & 9 & 12 & 18 \\ 2 & 3 & 4 & 6 \\ 3 & 3 & 2 & 3 \\ \hline & 1 & 2 & 1 \end{array}$$

(4 and 6 have a common factor 2. Divide 4 and 6 by 2.)
(Carry 3 to the next line.)
(Divide the two 3's by 3 and carry 2 to the next line.)
(Stop dividing when any two of the numbers have no common factors except 1.)

∴ the LCM of 18, 24 and 36 is $2 \times 3 \times 2 \times 3 \times 1 \times 2 \times 1 = 72$.

What do you notice about the LCM of a set of numbers? Can the LCM be smaller than one of the numbers?

1. Find the LCM of each of the following pairs of numbers:

   (a) 3 and 7   (b) 5 and 13   (c) 6 and 9   (d) 6 and 15

   (e) 7 and 21   (f) 8 and 12   (g) 12 and 9   (h) 15 and 25

   (i) 24 and 18   (j) 30 and 25   (k) 65 and 135   (l) 81 and 54

   (m) 100 and 75   (n) 120 and 135   (o) 144 and 36   (p) 225 and 105

   (q) 250 and 125   (r) 400 and 160   (s) 63 and 490

2. Find the LCM of:

   (a) 6, 9 and 15   (b) 3, 12 and 16   (c) 8, 9 and 12   (d) 14, 18 and 21

   (e) 28, 44 and 68   (f) 65, 175 and 135   (g) 18, 12, 6 and 8   (h) 6, 12, 9 and 24

3. Find the LCM of each of the following pairs of numbers:

   (a) $2^2 \times 3^3 \times 5^4$ and $2 \times 3^4 \times 5^3 \times 7$ (b) $2^3 \times 3^4 \times 5$ and $2^2 \times 3^3 \times 5^2$

   (c) $2^2 \times 5 \times 7$ and $2^3 \times 3^2 \times 5^2 \times 11$

4. Find the HCF and LCM of each of the following:

   (a) 18 and 42   (b) 21 and 28   (c) 26 and 39

   (d) 140 and 210   (e) 150 and 45   (f) 336 and 224

5. Two lighthouses flash their lights every 20 seconds and 30 seconds respectively. Given that they flash together at 8 p.m., when will they next flash together?

6. Three bells toll at intervals of 8 minutes, 15 minutes and 24 minutes respectively. If they toll together at 3 p.m., at what time will they next toll together again?

Squares and Square Roots

The area of a square of side 6 cm is given by

$$6 \times 6 = 36 \text{ cm}^2.$$

Therefore 36 is said to be the **square** of 6. For short, we write $6^2 = 36$ and we read 'the square of 6 is 36' or simply '**6 squared is 36**'.

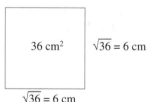

$\sqrt{36} = 6$ cm

Clearly, to find the side of a square whose area is 36 cm² we find a positive number x such that $36 = x \times x$ or x^2.

Now, $x = 6$ and we say that 6 is the positive **square root** of 36 and we write $\sqrt{36} = 6$.

Similarly, $2 \times 2 = 2^2 = 4$ and $\sqrt{4} = 2$

           $3 \times 3 = 3^2 = 9$ and $\sqrt{9} = 3$

           $4 \times 4 = 4^2 = 16$ and $\sqrt{16} = 4$

           $5 \times 5 = 5^2 = 25$ and $\sqrt{25} = 5$

           $7 \times 7 = 7^2 = 49$ and $\sqrt{49} = \sqrt{7^2} = 7$

Notice that 4, 9, 16, 25 and 49 are squares of whole numbers. These numbers are called **perfect squares**.

4, 9, 16 and 25 are perfect squares.

We use the symbol $\sqrt{}$ to denote a square root.

Find the two-digit number which has the square of the sum of its digits equal to the number obtained by reversing its digits.

In general, if a number y can be expressed as $y = x^2$, we say that y is the square of x and x is a square root of y.

Example 7

Find the positive square root of (a) 784; (b) 2 025.

▼ Solution

Working: Use prime factorisation

(a) $784 = (2 \times 2) \times (2 \times 2) \times (7 \times 7)$

$\quad\quad = (2 \times 2 \times 7)^2$

$\quad \sqrt{784} = \sqrt{(2 \times 2 \times 7)^2}$

$\quad\quad\quad = \sqrt{28^2}$

$\quad\quad\quad = 28$

2	7 8 4
2	3 9 2
2	1 9 6
2	9 8
7	4 9
	7

(b) $2\,025 = 5 \times 5 \times 3 \times 3 \times 3 \times 3$

$\quad\quad\quad = (5 \times 3 \times 3)^2$

$\quad \sqrt{2\,025} = \sqrt{(5 \times 3 \times 3)^2}$

$\quad\quad\quad\quad = \sqrt{45^2}$

$\quad\quad\quad\quad = 45$

5	2 0 2 5
5	4 0 5
3	8 1
3	2 7
3	9
	3

Example 8

Find the square of (a) 15; (b) 35.

▼ Solution

(a) $15^2 = 15 \times 15$
$\quad\quad = 225$

(b) $35^2 = 35 \times 35$
$\quad\quad = 1\,225$

Can you find 55^2 and 95^2 mentally?

Cubes and Cube Roots

The volume of a cube of side 6 cm is given by

$\quad 6 \times 6 \times 6 = 216 \text{ cm}^3$.

Therefore 216 is said to be the **cube** of 6. In short, we write $6^3 = 216$ and we read 'the cube of 6 is 216' or simply '**6 cubed is 216**'.

Clearly, to find the side of a cube whose volume is 216 cm³, we find a number x such that $216 = x \times x \times x$ or x^3. Now, $x = 6$ and we say that 6 is the **cube root** of 216 and we write $\sqrt[3]{216} = 6$.

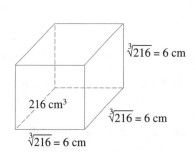

Similarly,
$$2 \times 2 \times 2 = 2^3 = 8 \quad \text{and} \quad \sqrt[3]{8} = 2$$
$$3 \times 3 \times 3 = 3^3 = 27 \quad \text{and} \quad \sqrt[3]{27} = 3$$
$$4 \times 4 \times 4 = 4^3 = 64 \quad \text{and} \quad \sqrt[3]{64} = 4$$
$$5 \times 5 \times 5 = 5^3 = 125 \quad \text{and} \quad \sqrt[3]{125} = 5$$

We use the symbol $\sqrt[3]{}$ to denote a cube root.

Notice that 8, 27, 64 and 125 are cubes of whole numbers. These numbers are called **perfect cubes**.

In general, if a number y can be expressed as $y = x^3$, we say that y is the cube of x and x is the cube root of y.

Find the two-digit number which has the sum of the cubes of its digits equal to three times itself.

Example 9

Find the cube root of (a) 512; (b) 5 832.

▼ **Solution**

(a) $512 = (2 \times 2 \times 2) \times (2 \times 2 \times 2) \times (2 \times 2 \times 2)$
$\qquad = 8 \times 8 \times 8$
$\qquad = 8^3$

$\therefore \quad \sqrt[3]{512} = \sqrt[3]{8^3} = 8$

Working

2	512
2	256
2	128
2	64
2	32
2	16
2	8
2	4
	2

(b) $5\,832 = (2 \times 3 \times 3) \times (2 \times 3 \times 3) \times (2 \times 3 \times 3)$
$\qquad = 18 \times 18 \times 18$
$\qquad = 18^3$

$\therefore \quad \sqrt[3]{5\,832} = \sqrt[3]{18^3} = 18$

2	5 832
2	2 916
2	1 458
3	729
3	243
3	81
3	27
3	9
	3

═ Exercise 2f ═

1. Find all the perfect squares that are less than 150.

2. Copy the following numbers and circle those that are perfect squares:
   8, 16, 18, 25, 33, 49, 50, 72, 81, 100, 1, 125, 144, 200, 169, 111, 225, 400

3. Fill in the following table.

x	11	12	13	14	15	16	17	18	19	20
x^2										

4. Replace each box with the correct answer:
   (a) Given that $8 \times 8 = 64$, then $\sqrt{64} = \square$.
   (b) Given that $12 \times 12 = 144$, then $\sqrt{144} = \square$.
   (c) Given that $17 \times 17 = 289$, then $\sqrt{289} = \square$.
   (d) Given that $(3 \times 4 \times 5) \times (3 \times 4 \times 5) = 3\,600$, then $\sqrt{3\,600} = \square$.

5. Find the square root of each of the following numbers:
   (a) 36   (b) 81   (c) 144   (d) 196
   (e) 256   (f) 324   (g) 441   (h) 484

6. Use a calculator to factorise the following (into prime numbers) and hence find the square root of each of the following numbers:
   (a) 1 156   (b) 1 296   (c) 1 764
   (d) 9 801   (e) 11 025   (f) 34 596

7. Calculate the cubes of 3, 4, 7, 8, 9 and 10.

8. Replace each box with the correct answer:
   (a) Given that $11 \times 11 \times 11 = 1\,331$, then $\sqrt[3]{1\,331} = \square$.
   (b) Given that $19 \times 19 \times 19 = 6\,859$, then $\sqrt[3]{6\,859} = \square$.
   (c) Given that $13^3 = 2\,197$, then $\sqrt[3]{2\,197} = \square$.
   (d) Given that $(3 \times 4) \times (3 \times 4) \times (3 \times 4) = 1\,728$, then $\sqrt[3]{1\,728} = \square$.
   (e) Given that $(4 \times 5 \times 9)^3 = 5\,832\,000$, then $\sqrt[3]{5\,832\,000} = \square$.

9. Using a calculator, completely factorise each of the following numbers and hence find its cube root:
   (a) 3 375   (b) 4 096   (c) 13 824   (d) 21 952
   (e) 46 656   (f) 91 125   (g) 262 144   (h) 373 248

10. Find the area of a square of side 56 cm.

11. What is the length of a side of a square whose area is 2 304 cm²?

12. What is the volume of a cube of side 11 cm?

13. Given that the volume of a cube is 2 744 cm³, find the length of its edge.

Mental Estimation

What is the square root of 48? What is the cube root of 65?

48 can be written as $48 = 4 \times 4 \times 3$.

65 can be written as $65 = 5 \times 13$.

Clearly, 48 and 65 cannot be expressed respectively as a^2 and b^3, where a and b are whole numbers. Thus, 48 is not a perfect square and 65 is not a perfect cube. $\sqrt{48}$ and $\sqrt[3]{65}$ are not whole numbers but decimals.

In this section, we are concerned with finding estimates of numbers such as $\sqrt{48}$ and $\sqrt[3]{65}$.

We observe that 48 is close to 49 which is a perfect square.

∴ $\sqrt{48} \approx \sqrt{49} = 7$ (Is the exact value of $\sqrt{48}$ greater or less than 7?)

The above process can also be done mentally.

Similarly, 65 is close to 64 which is a perfect cube.

∴ $\sqrt[3]{65} \approx \sqrt[3]{64} = 4$ (Is the exact value of $\sqrt[3]{65}$ greater or less than 4?)

Example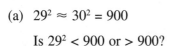

Estimate each of the following:

(a) 29^2 (b) 19^3 (c) 401^2

(d) 104^3 (e) $\sqrt{99}$ (f) $\sqrt[3]{999}$

 **Solution**

(a) $29^2 \approx 30^2 = 900$

Is $29^2 < 900$ or > 900?

(b) $19^3 \approx 20^3 = 8\,000$

Is $19^3 < 8\,000$ or $> 8\,000$?

Similarly, (c) and (d) can be worked out in the same way.

(c) $401^2 \approx 400^2 = 160\,000$

Is $401^2 < 160\,000$ or $> 160\,000$?

(d) $104^3 \approx 100^3 = 1\,000\,000$

Is $104^3 < 1\,000\,000$ or $> 1\,000\,000$?

(e) $\sqrt{99} \approx \sqrt{100} = \sqrt{10 \times 10} = 10$

Is $\sqrt{99} < 10$ or > 10?

(f) $\sqrt[3]{999} \approx \sqrt[3]{1\,000} = \sqrt[3]{10 \times 10 \times 10} = 10$

Is $\sqrt[3]{999} < 10$ or > 10?

Notes:

$30^2 = (3 \times 10) \times (3 \times 10)$
$\quad = 3 \times 3 \times 10 \times 10$
$\quad = 9 \times 100$
$\quad = 900$

$20^3 = (2 \times 10) \times (2 \times 10)$
$\quad \times (2 \times 10)$
$\quad = 2 \times 2 \times 2 \times 10 \times 10$
$\quad \times 10$
$\quad = 8 \times 1\,000$
$\quad = 8\,000$

The Use of Calculators

We can use scientific calculators to find the square, square root, cube and cube root of a number very easily. Below are some function keys for the purpose.

$\boxed{\sqrt{}}$	square root key
$\boxed{x^2}$	square key
$\boxed{y^x}$	power key
$\boxed{\sqrt[x]{}}$	x^{th} root key

To find $\sqrt{25}$, press 25 $\boxed{\sqrt{}}$ and the display gives 5, the square root of 25.

For calculators with Direct Algebraic Logic (DAL), the sequence of pressing the keys is $\boxed{\sqrt{}}$ 25 $\boxed{=}$.

We shall show the sequence following the DAL in all our examples.

Example 11

Use your calculator to evaluate the following:

(a) $14^2 + \sqrt[3]{2\,744} - \sqrt{529}$ 　　(b) $\dfrac{\sqrt[3]{729} \times 39^2}{\sqrt{169}}$ 　　　(c) $\dfrac{\sqrt{65\,536} + 8^3}{11^2 - \sqrt[3]{15\,625}}$

▼ **Solution**

Sequence of pressing keys:　　　　　　　　　　Final display

(a)　14 $\boxed{x^2}$ $\boxed{+}$ 3 $\boxed{\sqrt[x]{}}$ 2 744 $-$ $\boxed{\sqrt{}}$ 529 $\boxed{=}$ 　　　　187

(b)　3 $\boxed{\sqrt[x]{}}$ 729 $\boxed{\times}$ 39 $\boxed{x^2}$ $\boxed{\div}$ $\boxed{\sqrt{}}$ 169 $\boxed{=}$ 　　　1 053

(c)　$\boxed{(}$ $\boxed{\sqrt{}}$ 65 536 $\boxed{+}$ 8 $\boxed{x^y}$ 3 $\boxed{)}$ $\boxed{\div}$

　　$\boxed{(}$ 11 $\boxed{x^2}$ $\boxed{-}$ 3 $\boxed{\sqrt[x]{}}$ 15 625 $\boxed{)}$ $\boxed{=}$ 　　　　8

or

　　11 $\boxed{x^2}$ $-$ 3 $\boxed{\sqrt[x]{}}$ 15 625 $\boxed{=}$ $\boxed{\text{STO}}$

　　$\boxed{\sqrt{}}$ 65 536 $\boxed{+}$ 8 $\boxed{y^x}$ 3 $\boxed{=}$ $\boxed{\div}$ $\boxed{\text{RCL}}$ $\boxed{=}$ 　　　8

Note: Some calculators also have the $\boxed{\sqrt[3]{}}$ key for finding the cube root of a number. Try to use this key to work out the above calculations.

1. Estimate mentally the following:

   (a) 41^2 (b) 58^2 (c) 112^2 (d) 32^3

   (e) 39^3 (f) 98^3 (g) 198^2 (h) 301^3

2. Give an estimate of each of the following mentally:

   (a) $\sqrt{37}$ (b) $\sqrt[3]{26}$ (c) $\sqrt{63}$

   (d) $\sqrt[3]{124}$ (e) $\sqrt{84}$ (f) $\sqrt{142}$

   (g) $\sqrt[3]{1\,004}$ (h) $\sqrt{897}$

3. Evaluate the following using a calculator:

   (a) 26^2 (b) 37^2 (c) 78^2 (d) 99^2

   (e) 123^2 (f) 13^3 (g) 29^3 (h) 34^3

   (i) 67^3 (j) 109^3 (k) $\sqrt{961}$

   (l) $\sqrt{2\,209}$ (m) $\sqrt{3\,481}$

   (n) $\sqrt{11\,236}$ (o) $\sqrt{69\,169}$

   (p) $\sqrt[3]{4\,096}$ (q) $\sqrt[3]{68\,921}$

   (r) $\sqrt[3]{314\,432}$ (s) $\sqrt[3]{753\,571}$

   (t) $\sqrt[3]{1\,906\,624}$

   (u) $18^2 + 11^3 - \sqrt{484} + \sqrt[3]{4\,913}$

   (v) $\sqrt{676} \times 9^3 - 17^2 + \sqrt{2\,704}$

   (w) $24^3 \div \sqrt{4\,096} + \sqrt[3]{512} \times 44^2$

   (x) $\sqrt[3]{1\,331} \times \sqrt{2\,916} - 42^3 \div 21^2$

   (y) $\dfrac{7^3 \times \sqrt{576} + \sqrt[3]{512}}{\sqrt{7\,744} - 2^3}$

Summary

1. A **prime number** is a natural number which has only two different factors, 1 and the number itself. Prime numbers are 2, 3, 5, 7, 11, 13, 17, etc.

2. A **composite number** is a natural number which has more than two different factors. Composite numbers are 4, 6, 12, 15, 24, 32, etc.

3. A composite number can be expressed as the product of two or more prime numbers.

4. The process of expressing a composite number as the product of prime factors is called **prime factorisation**.

5. Divisibility:
   (a) A number is divisible by 2 if it is even.
   (b) A number is divisible by 3 if the sum of the digits is divisible by 3.
   (c) A number is divisible by 4 if the number formed by the last two digits is divisible by 4.
   (d) A number is divisible by 5 if the last digit is 0 or 5.
   (e) A number is divisible by 9 if the sum of its digits is divisible by 9.
   (f) A number is divisible by 11 if the difference between the sum of the digits in the odd places and the sum of the digits in the even places is equal to 0 or is a multiple of 11.

6. Index notation:
   In general, $\underbrace{a \times a \times \ldots \times a}_{n \text{ factors}}$ is written as a^n and is read as a to power of n.

7. The largest of the factors common to two or more numbers is called the **Highest Common Factor** (HCF) of the numbers.

8. The smallest of the common multiples of two or more numbers is called the **Least Common Multiple** (LCM) of the numbers.

9. If a number y can be expressed as $y = x^2$, we say that y is the **square** of x and x is a **square root** of y.

If x is a whole number, then y is a **perfect square**.

10. If a number y can be expressed as $y = x^3$, we say that y is the **cube** of x and x is the **cube root** of y.

Review Questions 2

1. State whether each of the following is true or false:
   (a) The prime numbers between 1 and 20 are 2, 3, 5, 7, 9, 11, 13, 17 and 19.
   (b) The HCF of 16, 20, 24 and 32 is 8.
   (c) The smallest number that is divisible by 10, 15 and 20 is 60.
   (d) 1 725 when expressed as a product of prime factors is $23 \times 15 \times 5$.
   (e) 9 996 is divisible by 11 because $9 + 9 + 9 + 6 = 33$ which is divisible by 11.
   (f) The HCF of 4×3^2, 3×4^2 and $2 \times 3 \times 5$ is $4^2 \times 3^2 \times 5$.
   (g) $\sqrt{802\,500}$ lies between 800 and 900.
   (h) An approximation of 89^2 is 8 100 which is less than the exact value of 89^2.

2. Find the HCF of each of the following:
   (a) 144, 162   (b) 12, 18, 30   (c) 65, 78, 104   (d) 10, 15, 20, 30

3. Find the LCM of each of the following:
   (a) 12, 30   (b) 16, 18, 48   (c) 42, 63, 105   (d) 88, 220, 528

4. How many whole numbers are between each of the following pairs of numbers?
   (a) $\sqrt{7}$ and $\sqrt{80}$ (b) $\sqrt[3]{7}$ and $\sqrt[3]{215}$ (c) $\sqrt[3]{18}$ and $\sqrt{120}$

5. Evaluate each of the following using a calculator:
   (a) $\sqrt{27^2 + 36^2}$ (b) $\sqrt{136^2 - 64^2}$ (c) $29^2 + 19^3 + \sqrt{676} - \sqrt[3]{50\,653}$
   (d) $58^2 \div \sqrt[3]{24\,389} \times \sqrt{3\,721} + 33^2$ (e) $\dfrac{26^3 \div \sqrt{2\,704} \times \sqrt[3]{42\,875}}{25 \times \sqrt{1\,849} - 14^3 + 40^2 + 79}$.

6. Use your calculator to verify each of the following:
   (a) $718^2 + 1\,199^2 = 145^2 + 1\,390^2 = 625^2 + 1\,250^2 = 1\,953\,125$
   (b) $3^2 + 16^2 + 24^2 = 29^2$
   (c) $3^3 + 4^3 + 5^3 = 6^3$
   (d) $55^2 + 56^2 + 57^2 + 58^2 + 59^2 + 60^2 = 61^2 + 62^2 + 63^2 + 64^2 + 65^2$

*7. John, Peter and Paul were each given a piece of string of equal length. John cut his into equal lengths of 2 m; Peter cut his into equal lengths of 3 m; and Paul cut his into equal lengths of 5 m. If there was no remainder in each case, find the shortest length of string given to each of them.

*8. What is the shortest length which can be divided into 4 cm, 8 cm or 2 cm portions without remainders?

*9. Find two numbers if their LCM is 120 and their HCF is 4. (Give three possible answers.)

*10. Find all the possible values of the digits X and Y if the six-digit number $123X4Y$ is divisible by 4 and 9.

*11. A three-digit number is the product of four prime numbers. Given that the three digits of the number are all prime and different and that the sum of its prime factors is 30, find the number.

1. Given the mathematical expression

   $$\bigcirc\bigcirc \times \bigcirc\bigcirc = \bigcirc\bigcirc \times \bigcirc\bigcirc\bigcirc = 5\ 568,$$

   fill the nine circles with the numbers 1, 2, 3, 4, 5, 6, 7, 8 and 9 to make it true.

2. Given a six-digit number 568*XYZ*, find the values of *X*, *Y* and *Z* such that the number is divisible by 3, 4 and 5 and is also the smallest six-digit number starting with 568.

3. 1 and 49 are both perfect squares. Can you find a number
   (a) *n* such that $13^2 + n$ and $13^2 - n$ are both perfect squares;
   (b) *m* such that $41^2 + m$ and $41^2 - m$ are both perfect squares?
   Note: $1 = 5^2 - 24$
           $49 = 5^2 + 24$

4. There is a two-digit number *x*. 58 divided by *x* leaves a remainder of 2, 73 divided by *x* leaves a remainder of 3 and 85 divided by *x* leaves a remainder of 1. Find *x*.

5. Four wires with lengths of 126 cm, 140 cm, 154 cm and 238 cm are to be cut into pieces all of the same length. What is the greatest possible length for the pieces if there should be no wire left?

6. Four racing cars go round a track in 48 seconds, 1 minute, 1 minute 5 seconds and 1 minute 18 seconds respectively. If they start from the same point, how many minutes would have passed before they are side by side again?

7. Can you explain why the sum of three consecutive whole numbers is always divisible by 3?

Number Sequences and Problem Solving

In this chapter, you will learn

▲ how to recognise simple patterns from various number sequences;
▲ to continue a given number sequence using different strategies;
▲ about problem-solving heuristics.

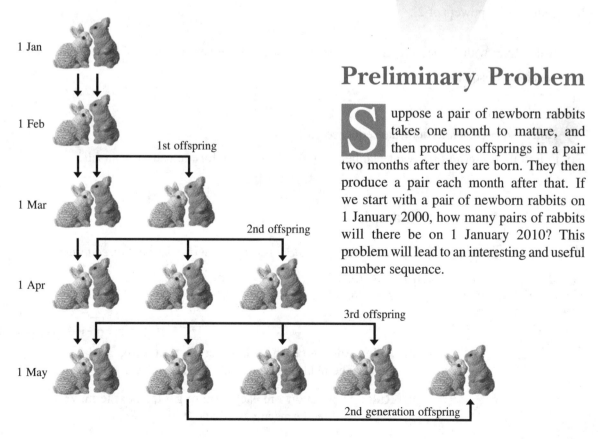

1 Jan

1 Feb

1st offspring

1 Mar

2nd offspring

1 Apr

3rd offspring

1 May

2nd generation offspring

Preliminary Problem

Suppose a pair of newborn rabbits takes one month to mature, and then produces offsprings in a pair two months after they are born. They then produce a pair each month after that. If we start with a pair of newborn rabbits on 1 January 2000, how many pairs of rabbits will there be on 1 January 2010? This problem will lead to an interesting and useful number sequence.

Number Sequences

Consider the following natural numbers:

1, 2, 3, 4, 5, 6, 7, 8, 9, 10, ...

We know that the numbers which come after 10 are 11, 12, 13, 14 and so on. We are able to continue writing down the numbers because each successive number follows the preceding one according to a specific rule. We say that the natural numbers form a **number sequence**. The numbers in a sequence are the **terms** of the sequence.

For the sequence of natural numbers, the rule is: start with 1, then add 1 to each term to get the next term.

Here are other examples of number sequences:

(a) Sequence of even numbers

2, 4, 6, 8, 10, 12, ...

Rule: Start with 2, then add 2 to each term to get the next term or multiply each term of the sequence 1, 2, 3, 4, 5, 6, ... by 2.

(b) Sequence of odd numbers

1, 3, 5, 7, 9, 11, ...

Rule: Start with 1, then add 2 to each term to get the next term or subtract 1 from each term of the sequence 2, 4, 6, 8, 10, 12, ...

(c) Sequence of powers of 2

1, 2, 4, 8, 16, 32

Rule: Start with 1, then multiply each term by 2 to get the next term.

(d) Sequence of squares

1, 4, 9, 16, 25, 36, ...

or

$1^2, 2^2, 3^2, 4^2, 5^2, 6^2, ...$

Rule: Square each term of the sequence 1, 2, 3, 4, 5, 6, ...

Try to find the pattern of the sequence below and state the rule for the pattern yourself.

1, 8, 27, 64, 125, 216, ...

Can you continue this sequence?

$1 \times 8 + 1 = 9$
$12 \times 8 + 2 = 98$
$123 \times 8 + 3 = 987$
$\vdots \qquad\qquad \vdots$

How about this one?

$0 \times 9 + 8 = 8$
$9 \times 9 + 7 = 88$
$98 \times 9 + 6 = 888$
$\vdots \qquad\qquad \vdots$

Fill in the two missing numbers in the sequence below:

1, 4, 9, 61, 52, ____, 94, ____, 18, 1, 121, ...

State a rule for this sequence.

Example 1

For each sequence, state a rule and write the next three terms:

(a) 3, 8, 13, 18 ...   *(b) 38, 32, 26, 20 ...*
(c) 2, 6, 18, 54 ...   *(d) 128, 64, 32, 16 ...*

Solution

(a) **Rule:** Add 5 to each term to get the next term.
   The next three terms are 23, 28 and 33.

(b) **Rule:** Subtract 6 from each term to get the next term.
   The next three terms are 14, 8 and 2.

(c) **Rule:** Multiply each term by 3 to get the next term.
The next three terms are 162, 486 and 1 458.

(d) **Rule:** Divide each term by 2 to get the next term.
The next three terms are 8, 4 and 2.

══ Exercise 3a ══

1. Identify a rule and complete the following number sequences:

   (a) 2, 5, 8, 11, ___, ___, ___
   (b) 0, 10, 20, 30, ___, ___, ___
   (c) 52, 59, 66, 73, ___, ___, ___
   (d) 80, 72, 64, 56, ___, ___, ___
   (e) 37, ___, 55, 64, ___, ___
   (f) 59, ___, 51, 47, ___, ___

2. State a rule and write the next three terms of each sequence.

   (a) 1, 3, 9, 27, …
   (b) 6, 12, 24, 48, …
   (c) 1 600, 800, 400, 200, …
   (d) 4, 12, 36, 108, …

3. For each of the following sequences, state a rule and write down the next two terms:

   (a) 14, 19, 24, 29, …
   (b) 28, 39, 50, 61, …
   (c) 73, 67, 61, 55, …
   (d) 99, 90, 81, 72, …
   (e) 15, 30, 60, 120, …
   (f) 2 187, 729, 243, 81, …

4. Identify a rule and complete the following:

   (a) 1, 3, 6, 10, ___, ___, ___
   (b) 17, 22, 27, 32, ___, ___, ___
   (c) 50, 45, 44, 39, 38, ___, ___, ___
   (d) 12, 10, 11, 9, ___, ___, ___
   (e) 2, 5, 10, 13, 26, ___, ___, ___
   (f) 1, 1, 2, 3, 5, 8, 13, ___, ___, ___

In-Class Activity

Carry out the activity with a partner.

1. Triangular Numbers

(a) Draw a triangular array of dots on a piece of paper with 1 dot in the first row, 2 dots in the second row, 3 dots in the third row, and so on as shown on the right.

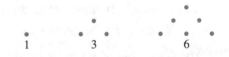

(b) The sequence of triangular array of dots corresponds to the number sequence 1, 3, 6, …. Add the next two triangles and then write down the two subsequent terms of the corresponding number sequence.

(c) Copy and complete the pattern below.

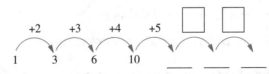

(d) These numbers are called **triangular numbers**. State the rule for writing down the numbers.

2. Fibonacci Sequence

(a) The number sequence resulting from the problem described at the beginning of the chapter: 1, 1, 2, 3, 5, … is known as a **Fibonacci sequence**. Write down the next two terms and figure out the rule for generating the next number in the sequence.

(b) Using the rule for generating a Fibonacci sequence, write down the next four terms of the Fibonacci sequence starting with

(i) 0, 1   **(ii)** 4, 2   **(iii)** 3, 3.

(c) The second and the third terms of a Fibonacci sequence are 3 and 10 respectively. Write down the first 8 terms of the sequence.

(d) Consider any three consecutive terms of the Fibonacci sequence 1, 1, 2, 3, 5, … . Multiply the end terms and square the middle term. Does the product differ from the square by 1? Check whether this is true for any other three consecutive terms.

(e) Consider the pattern:

$$1^2 + 1^2 = 1 \times 2$$
$$1^2 + 1^2 + 2^2 = 2 \times 3$$
$$1^2 + 1^2 + 2^2 + 3^2 = 3 \times 5$$
$$1^2 + 1^2 + 2^2 + 3^2 + 5^2 = 5 \times 8$$

Write down the next three lines.

3. Pascal's Triangle

(a) The following triangle of numbers is called **Pascal's triangle**.

```
              1
          1       1
        1     2     1
      1     3    3     1
    1    4    6    4     1
              ⋮
```

Each term is obtained by adding the two terms immediately above. For example, the number 2 in the third row is obtained by adding 1 and 1 which are above. The first 4 in the fifth row is obtained by adding 1 and 3 which are immediately above. (See diagram on the right)

Write down the next two rows of the triangle.

(b) The table of numbers on the right is formed in the same way as the Pascal's triangle.

(i) Write down the next six rows.

(ii) Find the sum of the terms of the upward diagonals.

(iii) Name the sequence of numbers formed by these diagonal sums.

(iv) Write down the next five diagonal sums.

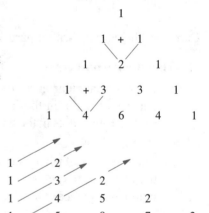

(c) In the diagram on the right, diagonals are drawn starting at each 1.

(i) Find the sum of the terms along the diagonals.

(ii) Do you find the Fibonacci sequence in the Pascal's triangle?

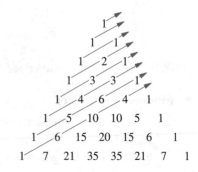

General Term in a Number Sequence

The sequence of even numbers 2, 4, 6, 8, 10, 12, ... can be rewritten as

$$2 \times 1, 2 \times 2, 2 \times 3, 2 \times 4, 2 \times 5, 2 \times 6, ..., 2 \times n, ...$$

The expression $2 \times n$ or $2n$ is the **formula** for the **nth term** or the **general term** of the number sequence. By varying the values of the letter n in the formula, we obtain corresponding values of the formula $2n$ and thus generating terms of the number sequence. The letter n is called a **variable**.

Similarly, the sequence of odd numbers 1, 3, 5, 7, 9, 11, ... can be rewritten as

$$2 \times 1 - 1, 2 \times 2 - 1, 2 \times 3 - 1, 2 \times 4 - 1, 2 \times 5 - 1, ..., 2n - 1, ...$$

The formula for the nth term of the sequence of odd numbers is $2n - 1$.

Clearly, the formula for the nth term of the number sequence, $1 = 1^2, 4 = 2^2, 9 = 3^2, 25 = 5^2, 36 = 6^2$, ... is n^2.

Example 2

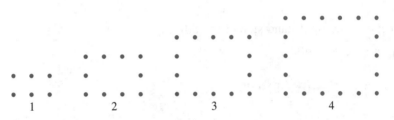

1	2	3	4

The diagram shows the first four of a sequence of figures. Figures 1 and 2 contain 6 dots and 10 dots respectively. The sequence continues as shown in Figures 3, 4 and so on. Let n denote the figure number and d the corresponding number of dots.

(a) *Count the number of dots in each of the Figures 3 and 4 and write down the next 2 terms of the number sequence 6, 10, ...*

(b) *Find a formula that connects n and d, i.e., a formula for the nth term of the sequence in (a).*

(c) *Using the formula in (b), find*
   (i) *the number of dots there will be in Figure 30;*
   (ii) *the numbering of the figure that has 42 dots.*

Solution

(a) The next two terms are 14 and 18 respectively.

(b) Notice that $6 = 4 \times 1 + 2,$ (Figure **1**)
                   $10 = 4 \times 2 + 2,$ (Figure **2**)
                   $14 = 4 \times 3 + 2,$ (Figure **3**)
                   $18 = 4 \times 4 + 2,$ (Figure **4**)

   ∴   for Figure n, the number of dots, $d = 4 \times n + 2 = 4n + 2.$

(c) (i)   To find the number of dots there will be in Figure 30, we find the value of d when n has a value 30, i.e. when $n = 30$.

      Replacing n by 30 in the formula $d = 4n + 2$, we have

      $$d = 4 \times 30 + 2 = 122.$$

   ∴   there are 122 dots in Figure 30.

(ii) By writing $42 = 4 \times 10 + 2$ and comparing with the formula $d = 4 \times n + 2$, we have $n = 10$ when $d = 42$.

∴ the numbering of the figure that has 42 dots is 10.

Example 3

Consider the pattern:
$$2 = 1 \times 2$$
$$6 = 2 \times 3$$
$$12 = 3 \times 4$$
$$20 = 4 \times 5$$
$$\vdots$$
$$110 = k \times (k + 1)$$
$$\vdots$$

Write down (a) the 8th line in the pattern;   (b) the value of k.

Solution

(a) From the pattern, the right-hand side of the 8th line is 8×9.

∴ the 8th line is $72 = 8 \times 9$.

(b) Since $110 = 10 \times 11 = 10 \times (10 + 1)$,

∴ $k = 10$.

═ Exercise 3b ═

1. Consider the pattern:
$$1 + 3 = 4 = 2^2 = (1 + 1)^2$$
$$1 + 3 + 5 = 9 = 3^2 = (2 + 1)^2$$
$$1 + 3 + 5 + 7 = 16 = 4^2 = (3 + 1)^2$$
$$1 + 3 + 5 + 7 + 9 = 25 = 5^2 = (4 + 1)^2$$
$$\vdots$$
$$1 + 3 + 5 + \ldots + a = b = c^2 = (d + 1)^2$$
$$\vdots$$

(a) Write down the fifth and sixth lines in the pattern.
(b) Write down the 11th line in the pattern.
(c) Given that $b = 169$, find the values of a, c and d.

2. Consider the pattern:
$$2 + 1^2 = 3$$
$$2 + 2^2 = 6$$
$$2 + 3^2 = 11$$
$$2 + 4^2 = 18$$
$$\vdots$$
$$2 + x^2 = 66$$
$$\vdots$$

(a) Write down the 6th line in the pattern.
(b) Find the value of x.

3. Consider the pattern:

$$1^2 - 0^2 = 1 = 1 + 0$$
$$2^2 - 1^2 = 3 = 2 + 1$$
$$3^2 - 2^2 = 5 = 3 + 2$$
$$4^2 - 3^2 = 7 = 4 + 3$$
$$\vdots$$
$$m^2 - n^2 = 81 = m + n$$
$$\vdots$$

(a) Write down the 10th line in the pattern. (b) Find the value of $598^2 - 597^2$.

(c) Find the values of m and n.

4. Consider the pattern:

$$\frac{1 \times 2}{2} + (1 - 1)^2 = 1$$
$$\frac{2 \times 3}{2} + (2 - 1)^2 = 4$$
$$\frac{3 \times 4}{2} + (3 - 1)^2 = 10$$
$$\frac{4 \times 5}{2} + (4 - 1)^2 = 19$$
$$\vdots$$
$$\frac{110}{2} + (p - 1)^2 = q$$
$$\vdots$$

(a) Write down the 11th line in the pattern. (b) Find the values of p and q.

5.

Diagram 1   Diagram 2   Diagram 3   Diagram 4

A sequence of diagrams consisting of shaded and unshaded small triangles is shown above. Diagrams 1 and 2 contain 3 and 6 shaded triangles respectively. The sequence continues as shown in Diagrams 3 and 4 and so on. Let n denote the diagram number and t the corresponding number of shaded triangles.

(a) By counting the number of shaded triangles in each of the Diagrams 3 and 4, write down the next 2 terms of the number sequence 3, 6, ...

(b) Find a formula that connects n and t.

(c) Using the formula in (b), find

    (i) the number of shaded triangles there will be in Diagram 50;

    (ii) the numbering of the diagram that has 87 shaded triangles.

6.

Figure 1   Figure 2   Figure 3   Figure 4

The above shows the first four of a sequence of figures. Figures 1 and 2 contain 4 and 9 small triangles respectively. The sequence continues as shown in Figures 3 and 4 and so on. Let N denote the figure number and T the corresponding number of small triangles.

(a) By counting the number of small triangles in Figures 3 and 4, write down the next 2 terms of the number sequence 4, 9, ...

(b) Find a formula that connects N and T.

(c) Using the formula in (b), find
   (i) the number of small triangles there will be in Figure 9;
   (ii) the numbering of the figure that has 121 small triangles.

Problem Solving

In-Class Activity

So far, in this chapter, you have learnt how to

(i) recognise simple patterns from various number sequences;
(ii) generalise the terms in the number sequences following the pattern;
(iii) associate patterns of figures with sequences of numbers.

The above are useful for problem solving.

In the following activities, you shall explore various **heuristics** or strategies of solving problems.

You may do the first problem with a partner and the second problem with four others in a group.

Problem 1

How many logs are there in the stack shown below?

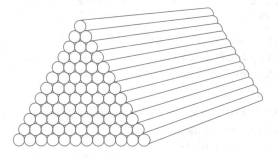

Step 1: **Simplify the problem and use a model**

Use coins to model a different number of layers of logs from the top starting with 1, 2, 3 and 4 layers as shown below.

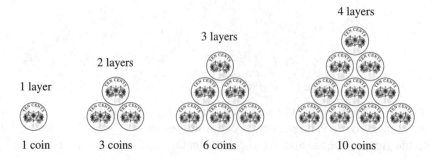

Step 2: **Look for a pattern**

(a) Use the piles of coins in the figure above to complete the following:

1 layer $= 1$ $= 1$

2 layers $= 1 + \square$ $= 3$

3 layers $= 1 + 2 + \square$ $= 6$

4 layers $= 1 + \square + 3 + \square = 10$

(b) Does the following rule completely describe the sequence?

Rule: The rth term of the sequence is obtained by adding the first r natural numbers so that

the 5th term $= 1 + 2 + 3 + 4 + 5 = 15$,

the 6th term $= 1 + 2 + 3 + 4 + 5 + 6 = 21$,

the 7th term $= 1 + 2 + 3 + 4 + 5 + 6 + 7 = 28$, and so on.

(c) Write down the 8th, 9th and 10th terms of the sequence.

(d) How many layers of logs are there in the stack?

(e) Which term of the sequence corresponds to the number of logs in the stack?

(f) Find the number of logs in the stack.

Alternatively:

The sequence of numbers 1, 3, 6, 10 can be written as follows:

1 layer : $1 = \dfrac{1 \times 2}{2} = \dfrac{1 \times (1 + 1)}{2}$

2 layers : $3 = \dfrac{2 \times 3}{2} = \dfrac{2 \times (2 + 1)}{2}$

3 layers : $6 = \dfrac{3 \times 4}{2} = \dfrac{3 \times (3 + 1)}{2}$

4 layers : $10 = \dfrac{4 \times 5}{2} = \dfrac{4 \times (4 + 1)}{2}$

(a) Do you notice an emerging pattern showing how the number of logs is connected to the number of layers in the stack?

(b) Can you state the rule for the pattern?

(c) Using the rule, find the number of logs when the number of layers in the stack is

(i) 8;   (ii) 9;   (iii) 10.

(d) Use the rule to find the number of logs in the stack shown. Does your answer agree with that obtained earlier?

(e) As a challenge, find the number of layers in such a stack of 820 logs.

Problem 2

John invites his Chinese, Malay and Indian friends for a Chinese New Year party. They shake hands to greet one another. Each person shakes hands with every other person exactly once. How many total handshakes are there if there are 20 people including John attending the party?

Step 1: **Simplify the problem and act it out**

Have two of you shake hands. Next, three of you shake hands exactly once with one another. Each time, count the number of handshakes. Repeat this with four of you and five of you respectively.

Step 2: Use tabulation and look for a pattern

(a) Tabulate your results by copying and completing the table below.

Number of people (n)	2	3	4	5
Number of handshakes (N)	$1 = \dfrac{(2-1) \times 2}{2}$	$3 = \dfrac{(3-1) \times 3}{2}$		

(b) Write down the formula connecting n, the number of people and N, the number of handshakes.

(c) Use the formula to find how many handshakes there are when 20 people shake hands with one another exactly once.

Alternatively, in **Step 1** above, you can use **diagrams**.
The first two diagrams, involving two people, A and B, and three people, A, B and C, respectively, are shown below.

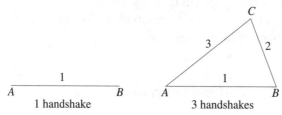

1 handshake   3 handshakes

Add the next two diagrams, involving four people, A, B, C and D, and five people, A, B, C, D and E, respectively.

State a rule and write down the next twenty terms of the following sequence:

1, 3, 6, 10, 15, ...

(a) Multiply each number in the sequence by 8 and add 1. What do you notice?

(b) Choose any two consecutive numbers in the sequence and add them. What do you notice?

(c) Select any two consecutive numbers in the sequence. Square each of them and add. Do you get another number in the same sequence?

More Problem Solving

From the above activities, we see that a problem may be solved in more than one way and in solving the above problems, we have used different strategies or heuristics like:

- simplifying the problem
- using a model
- using tabulation
- acting it out
- looking for a pattern

Some other strategies you will find useful are:

- drawing a diagram
- making an organised list
- writing an equation
- using trial-and-error
- thinking of a related problem
- eliminating the unlikely possibilities
- solving a simpler problem
- changing your point of view
- working backwards
- making a supposition
- solving part of the problem

In the next few examples, we shall consider two of the above problem-solving strategies, i.e., drawing a diagram and changing your point of view. We shall introduce some of the other strategies in later chapters.

Some problems are best approached by drawing diagrams. They help us to have a clearer picture of the problems.

Example 4

A boy scout in a jungle is heading south. He takes a right turn and walks for 40 m. Then he takes a left turn and walks again for a further 50 m. He then takes a left turn and walks for another 45 m. Finally, he takes a right turn. In which direction is he heading now?

▼Solution

The following diagram illustrates the movement of the boy scout. Notice that the distance which the boy scout walks is not important in arriving at the answer.

The diagram tells us that the boy scout is heading south.

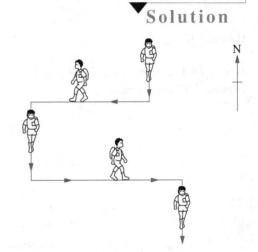

Example 5

Suppose in the Tiger Cup soccer tournament, 8 teams qualify for the final round. If the organisers adopt a single-elimination method for the final round, i.e., winners play against winners until only 1 team is left, what is the total number of games played? How many games would the eventual champion team have played?

▼Solution

Draw a diagram showing the progress of the tournament as shown below.

From the diagram, the number of games played = 4 + 2 + 1 = 7.

The champion is the only team that is left and therefore must survive each elimination round. From the diagram, there are 3 elimination rounds. Thus the champion team would have to play 3 games.

We can also use **logical reasoning** to find the total number of games played. Since 1 team is eliminated in each game played, we need 7 games to eliminate 7 teams to leave 1 champion team.

STRATEGY: **Change your point of view**

You probably have the experience of failing to solve a problem because of the way you think of the problem or because the method you use does not work. Therefore, if necessary, you must change your point of view so that you can think of more innovative ideas and suggestions.

Example 6

Use only 4 lines to join the 9 points without lifting your pencil.

▼ **S o l u t i o n**

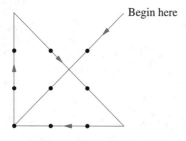

Begin here

Many of us may fail when solving this problem because we restrict ourselves to drawing lines within the confines of the 9 points. If we extend our viewpoint, we would realise that we can draw lines beyond the confines of the 9 points as shown. We can then easily solve the problem.

Example 7

The diagram shows 12 matchsticks arranged to form 6 equilateral triangles. Can you rearrange these 12 matchsticks to form 8 equilateral triangles of the same size?

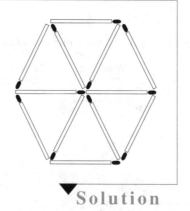

▼ **S o l u t i o n**

Most of us would probably first attempt to arrange these matchsticks on a flat surface such as the table-top or what mathematicians call a 2-dimensional plane. No matter how hard we try we will not succeed in the task.

There are seven colours in a rainbow: red, orange, yellow, green, blue, indigo and violet. These colours can be remembered as ROYGBIV.

A design consists of a circle divided in half. The top and bottom halves are to be painted with different colours from the seven colours of a rainbow such that the colours must be in the same order as those given above. For example, RO, RB, OI and so on are acceptable, while OR, GR, BY and so on are unacceptable. In how many ways can the circle be painted?

In another design there are three triangles in a row and each triangle is to be painted with a different colour in the same way. In how many ways can the triangles be coloured?

Have you ever thought of arranging these matchsticks in 3-dimension as shown in the diagram below (the matchsticks form a pyramid, with the triangle *ABC* as its base)? Each 3-dimensional figure consists of 6 matchsticks forming 4 equilateral triangles of the same size. Thus, we have succeeded in forming 8 equilateral triangles of the same size using 12 matchsticks.

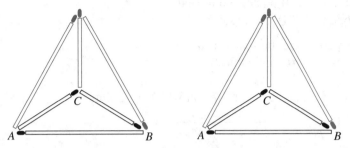

From the above examples, we see that when solving problems, be it mathematical, scientific or social, or even everyday life problems, the solutions may not be too difficult to obtain if we can be open-minded and think of all possible options or strategies, such as drawing diagrams or looking at the problems from a totally different point of view.

═══ Exercise 3c ═══

1. How many segments will there be when 49 points divide a given line segment?

   (a) Study the diagram below and complete the table that follows.

No. of points	1	2	3	4	5	6
No. of segments	1 + 1 = 2	2 + 1 = 3				

   (b) Hence, write down the number of segments there will be when 49 points divide the given line segment.

   (c) How many points are needed to divide a given line segment into 101 segments?

2. 20 people go to a restaurant for a buffet dinner. They request to be seated at the same table. The restaurant has only small square tables that can be joined end to end to form a large long table. If each small square table can seat only one person on each side, how many of such small tables are needed to seat this group of people?

   (a) Study the diagram below and complete the tables (i) and (ii) that follow.

   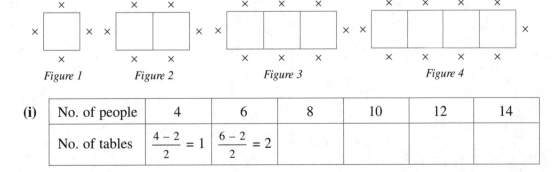

   Figure 1   Figure 2   Figure 3   Figure 4

(i)	No. of people	4	6	8	10	12	14
	No. of tables	$\frac{4-2}{2} = 1$	$\frac{6-2}{2} = 2$				

No. of tables	1	2	3	4	5	6
No. of people	2(1)+2=4	2(2)+2=6				

(b) How many tables will be needed to seat
  (i) 20 people;   **(ii)** 30 people?

(c) How many people can be seated if there are
  (i) 22 tables;   **(ii)** 36 tables?

3. The diagram shows a line segment, AB, on which 18 points (P_1, P_2, ..., P_{18}) are marked.

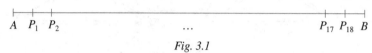

Fig. 3.1

(a) Study the diagram below and complete the table that follows.

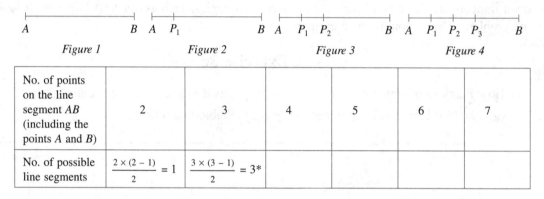

No. of points on the line segment AB (including the points A and B)	2	3	4	5	6	7
No. of possible line segments	$\frac{2 \times (2-1)}{2} = 1$	$\frac{3 \times (3-1)}{2} = 3*$				

* The three line segments are AP_1, P_1B and AB.

(b) What is the total number of possible line segments in Fig. 3.1?

4. Sixteen players participate in a table-tennis tournament. If the organisers adopt a round robin method, i.e., each player will meet each of the other players once, what will be the total possible number of tournament matches played?

[*Hint:* Model 16 players with 16 points on a line segment so that a line segment joining any two points represents a match played. How many possible triangles are there in Fig. 3.2? Since the triangles have a common vertex, V, the number of possible triangles is the same as the number of possible bases.]

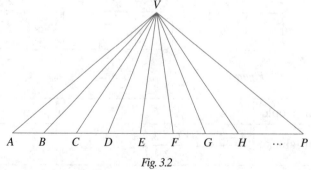

Fig. 3.2

5. A man was trying to swim to a buoy placed at a distance of 200 m out in the sea. It took him 1 min to swim 20 m. Then a wave pushed him back 10 m and he rested for another 1 min before swimming again. He continued in this way for the rest of the journey. How long would it take the man to swim to the buoy?

6. Twenty-seven people entered a chess competition which runs in a single-elimination format. How many tournament games will the champion have to play? What is the total number of tournament games played?

7. Making cuts across the diameter, a saw-mill worker can cut a log into 3 pieces in 3 minutes. How long will it take the worker to cut a log of the same size into 11 pieces?

8. How can you place 15 cows into 4 pens so that there is an odd number of cows in each pen?

9. Remove 8 toothpicks from the following arrangement so that only 2 squares are left.

<hr>

S u m m a r y

1. A **number sequence** is a set of numbers arranged in such a way that each successive number follows the preceding one according to a specific rule. The numbers in a sequence are known as the **terms** of the sequence.

2. Some heuristics for problem solving are:

   - change your point of view
   - make an organised list
   - work backwards
   - make a supposition
   - use trial-and-error
   - think of a related problem
   - simplify the problem
   - eliminate the unlikely possibilities

   - draw a diagram
   - look for a pattern
   - write an equation
   - solve a simpler problem
   - solve part of the problem
   - use tabulation
   - use a model
   - act it out

1. State the rule and write down the next three terms in the following sequences:
   (a) 1, 7, 13, 19, ...
   (b) 12, 15, 21, 30, ...
   (c) 0, 2, 2, 4, 6, 10, ...
   (d) 101, 97, 93, 89, ...
   (e) 5, 9, 13, 17, ...
   (f) 3, 6, 11, 18, ...

2. Fill in each box with an appropriate number. State the rule you used to obtain your answer.
   (a) 1, 3, ☐, 27, 81
   (b) ☐, 12, 24, 48, 96
   (c) 2, 4, 7, 11, ☐
   (d) 60, 55, 54, 49, 48, 43, ☐
   (e) 1, 5, 6, 11, 17, ☐
   (f) 41, 40, 38, 35, 31, ☐
   (g) 2, 5, 11, 23, 47, ☐

3. Consider the pattern:

$$11 - 2 = 3^2$$
$$1\,111 - 22 = 33^2$$
$$111\,111 - 222 = 333^2$$
$$\vdots$$
$$x - y = 33\,333\,333^2$$

   (a) Write down the 5th line in the pattern.
   (b) Find the values of x and y.

4. (a) Consider the pattern:

$$1 = \frac{1 \times (1 + 1)}{2}$$
$$1 + 2 = 3 = \frac{2 \times (2 + 1)}{2}$$
$$1 + 2 + 3 = 6 = \frac{3 \times (3 + 1)}{2}$$
$$1 + 2 + 3 + 4 = 10 = \frac{4 \times (4 + 1)}{2}$$
$$\vdots$$
$$1 + 2 + 3 + 4 + \ldots + k = 45 = \frac{k \times (k + 1)}{2}$$
$$\vdots$$

   (i) Write down the 7th line in the pattern.
   (ii) Find the value of k.

   (b) Consider the pattern:

$$1^3 = 1 = 1^2$$
$$1^3 + 2^3 = 1 + 8 = 9 = 3^2$$
$$1^3 + 2^3 + 3^3 = 1 + 8 + 27 = 36 = 6^2$$
$$1^3 + 2^3 + 3^3 + 4^3 = 1 + 8 + 27 + 64 = 100 = 10^2$$
$$\vdots$$
$$1^3 + 2^3 + 3^3 + \ldots + x^3 = 1 + 8 + 27 + \ldots + y = z = 36^2$$
$$\vdots$$

   (i) Write down the 6th line in the pattern.
   (ii) Making use of the pattern in (a), find the values of x, y and z.

*5. Using toothpicks, we can form patterns consisting of different layers of triangles as shown in the diagram below.

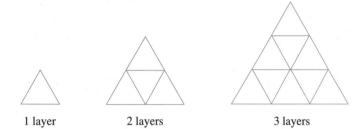

| 1 layer | 2 layers | 3 layers |

The number of toothpicks used form the following pattern:

Number of layers	Number of toothpicks
1	$1 \times 3 + 3 \times 0$
2	$2 \times 3 + 3 \times 1$
3	$3 \times 3 + 3 \times 3$
4	$4 \times 3 + 3 \times 6$
5	$5 \times 3 + 3 \times 10$
...	...
k	$k \times 3 + 3 \times \dfrac{k \times (k-1)}{2}$
...	...

How many toothpicks are needed to form

(a) an 8-layer triangular pattern;

(b) a 20-layer triangular pattern and a 40-layer triangular pattern?

Exploration

1. Each small triangle in the diagram on the right has three adjacent dots as vertices. Are there more dots than small triangles? Explain your reason.

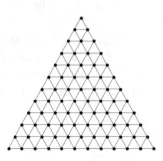

2. In the diagram below, Figure 1 shows an equilateral triangle. Figure 2 is obtained from Figure 1 by adding new equilateral triangles all round the outside of the equilateral triangle. Figure 3 is obtained from Figure 2, and Figure 4 is obtained from Figure 3 in a similar manner.

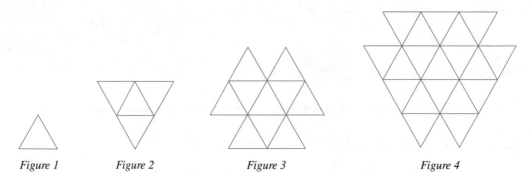

| Figure 1 | Figure 2 | Figure 3 | Figure 4 |

Show how many small triangles are in Figure 30. How many small triangles will there be in Figure 100?

3. Fill in the next line in the following sequence and explain your answer:

$$3$$
$$1\ 3$$
$$1\ 1\ 1\ 3$$
$$3\ 1\ 1\ 3$$
$$1\ 3\ 2\ 1\ 1\ 3$$
$$1\ 1\ 1\ 3\ 1\ 2\ 2\ 1\ 1\ 3$$
$$\vdots$$

4. The following array of 800 natural numbers contain many squares of nine numbers. Three of them are shown below.

1	2	3	4	5	6	7	8
9	10	11	12	13	14	15	16
17	18	19	20	21	22	23	24
25	26	27	28	29	30	31	32
⋮	⋮	⋮	⋮	⋮	⋮	⋮	⋮
793	794	795	796	797	798	799	800

(a) The sum of the numbers in one of these squares is 99. What are the sums of the numbers of the other two squares?

(b) Find the largest possible sum of a square of nine numbers in the above array.

(c) If a square is moved one place to the right, calculate the increase in value of the sum.

(d) If a square is moved one place upwards, calculate the decrease in value of the sum.

(e) Is it possible to find a square of nine numbers in the above array in which the sum is

    (i) 1 060;

    (ii) 2 871?

Explain your answer.

CHAPTER 4

Fractions and Decimals

In this chapter, you will learn how to

▲ interpret the meanings of fractions and decimals and use them;
▲ convert fractions to decimals and decimals to fractions;
▲ compare and arrange fractions and decimals;
▲ calculate with fractions and decimals, with or without the calculator;
▲ round off decimals to a specific degree of accuracy.

Preliminary Problem

A good picture requires sufficient light to enter the camera and fall on the film. The amount of light is controlled by the size of the aperture (an opening in front of the camera) and the duration it remains open. The aperture-size varies and is indicated by a sequence of numbers: 1.4, 2, 2.8, 4, 5.6, 8, 11, 16 and 22, while the duration follows a sequence of fractions of a second:

$$\frac{1}{2}, \frac{1}{4}, \frac{1}{8}, \frac{1}{15}, \frac{1}{30}, \frac{1}{60}, \frac{1}{125}, \frac{1}{250}, \frac{1}{500}, \frac{1}{1\,000}, \frac{1}{2\,000} \text{ and } \frac{1}{4\,000}.$$

The picture was taken with an aperture of size 5.6, left opened for $\frac{1}{250}$ of a second. The result is a sharp, frozen image of the moving basketballer. A longer duration of, say, $\frac{1}{60}$ may lead to a blurred picture which may be a deliberate attempt to show action.

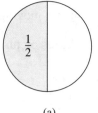

When an object is divided into equal parts, each part is called a **fraction** of the object.

Fractions

If 5 boys were to share a cake equally, we need to cut the cake into 5 equal parts and each boy will receive one part (see Fig. 4.1).

$\frac{1}{5}$ of the cake

Fig. 4.1

What number expresses the part each boy receives? A whole number? Each part of the cake is called one-fifth of the cake, written as $\frac{1}{5}$. If 3 boys take $\frac{1}{5}$ of the cake each, then we have given away three-fifths of the cake, written as $\frac{3}{5}$. $\frac{1}{5}$ and $\frac{3}{5}$ are called fractions.

A fraction is a number written as a quotient, i.e., one number divided by another.

In the fraction $\frac{3}{5}$, 3 is the **numerator** and 5 is the **denominator**.

In the fraction $\frac{5}{8}$, which is the numerator and which is the denominator?

Exercise 4a

For all the exercises in this chapter, a calculator is not allowed unless otherwise stated.

1. Write the following fractions in numerals:
   (a) one-sixth   (b) two-ninths
   (c) five-eighths   (d) six-thirteenths
   (e) five-twelfths (f) eleven-hundredths

2. Write the following fractions in words:
   (a) $\frac{1}{9}$ (b) $\frac{2}{7}$ (c) $\frac{5}{20}$ (d) $\frac{35}{100}$

3. What fraction describes how much of each figure is shaded?
   (a)

   (b)
   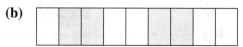

Equivalent Fractions

Equivalent fractions have the same value. For example, $\frac{1}{2}$ and $\frac{2}{4}$ are equivalent fractions.

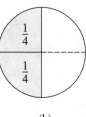

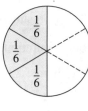

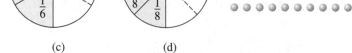

(a)   (b)   (c)   (d)

Fig. 4.2

Fig. 4.2 shows that $\frac{1}{2}$, $\frac{2}{4}$, $\frac{3}{6}$ and $\frac{4}{8}$ represent the same portion of a whole. $\frac{1}{2}$, $\frac{2}{4}$, $\frac{3}{6}$ and $\frac{4}{8}$ are called **equivalent fractions** and we have

$$\frac{1}{2} = \frac{2}{4} = \frac{3}{6} = \frac{4}{8}.$$

*Can you think of a few more fractions equivalent to $\frac{1}{2}$?*

Notice that $\quad \frac{1}{2} = \frac{1 \times 2}{2 \times 2} = \frac{2}{4} \qquad \frac{4}{8} = \frac{4 \div 4}{8 \div 4} = \frac{1}{2}$

$\frac{1}{2} = \frac{1 \times 3}{2 \times 3} = \frac{3}{6} \qquad \frac{3}{6} = \frac{3 \div 3}{6 \div 3} = \frac{1}{2}$

Hence, the value of a fraction remains unchanged if both the numerator and the denominator are multiplied or divided by the same number,

i.e.

$$\frac{a}{b} = \frac{a \times c}{b \times c} \quad \text{and} \quad \frac{a}{b} = \frac{a \div c}{b \div c} \quad \text{where } c \neq 0$$

The above rules are useful for the conversion of equivalent fractions.

 ## Simplifying Fractions

We often simplify a fraction by **reducing** it to its **lowest terms**. A fraction in its **lowest terms** has a numerator and a denominator that have no common factor except 1. Thus, reducing a fraction to lowest terms is done by converting it to the simplest fraction equivalent to it.

The ancient Egyptians were the first to use fractions. However, they only used fractions with a numerator of one.

Thus, they write $\frac{3}{8}$ as $\frac{1}{4} + \frac{1}{8}$, etc.

For example,

$$\frac{120}{375} = \frac{120 \div 5}{375 \div 5} = \frac{24}{75}, \quad \frac{24}{75} = \frac{24 \div 3}{75 \div 3} = \frac{8}{25}.$$

In practice, this is done by **"cancelling"**. Thus,

What do you think the Egyptians would write for the fractions $\frac{3}{5}$, $\frac{9}{20}$, $\frac{2}{3}$ and $\frac{7}{12}$?

$$\frac{\overset{8}{\cancel{24}}\cancel{120}}{\underset{25}{\cancel{375}}\,\cancel{75}} = \frac{8}{25} \quad \text{(In ``cancelling'', we are doing the divisions in our minds.)}$$

When the answer to a mathematical problem is in the form of a fraction, the result is usually expressed in its lowest terms.

Example 1

Reduce $\dfrac{70}{245}$ to its lowest terms.

$$\frac{70}{245} = \frac{70 \div 5}{245 \div 5} = \frac{14 \div 7}{49 \div 7} = \frac{2}{7}$$

Working:

$$\frac{\overset{\overset{2}{\cancel{14}}}{\cancel{70}}}{\underset{\underset{7}{\cancel{49}}}{\cancel{245}}} = \frac{2}{7} \quad \text{(Divide first by 5, then by 7.)}$$

Alternatively, using prime factorisation, $\dfrac{70}{245} = \dfrac{2 \times \cancel{5} \times \cancel{7}}{\cancel{5} \times \cancel{7} \times 7} = \dfrac{2}{7}$.

= Exercise 4b =

1. Copy and complete the following:

(a) $\dfrac{3}{5} = \dfrac{\square}{20}$
(b) $\dfrac{30}{100} = \dfrac{3}{\square}$
(c) $\dfrac{4}{13} = \dfrac{\square}{169}$

(d) $\dfrac{250}{750} = \dfrac{1}{\square}$
(e) $\dfrac{7}{9} = \dfrac{105}{\square}$
(f) $\dfrac{17}{9} = \dfrac{\square}{99}$

2. What set of equivalent fractions is shown by the coloured regions below?

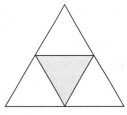 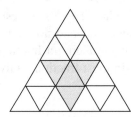 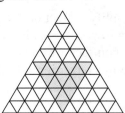

3. Draw a diagram to show that (a) $\dfrac{1}{3} = \dfrac{3}{9}$ and (b) $\dfrac{2}{5} = \dfrac{6}{15}$.

4. Copy and complete the following:

(a) $\dfrac{2}{3} = \dfrac{8}{\square} = \dfrac{\square}{27} = \dfrac{20}{\square}$
(b) $\dfrac{3}{4} = \dfrac{\square}{8} = \dfrac{24}{\square} = \dfrac{21}{\square}$

5. Reduce the following fractions to their lowest terms:

(a) $\dfrac{29}{58}$
(b) $\dfrac{64}{88}$
(c) $\dfrac{66}{143}$
(d) $\dfrac{75}{90}$
(e) $\dfrac{625}{1\,000}$
(f) $\dfrac{3\,528}{6\,552}$

6. Indicate which of the following pairs of fractions are equivalent:

(a) $\dfrac{4}{6}$ and $\dfrac{10}{15}$
(b) $\dfrac{21}{28}$ and $\dfrac{12}{16}$
(c) $\dfrac{20}{48}$ and $\dfrac{35}{84}$
(d) $\dfrac{5}{16}$ and $\dfrac{34}{111}$

7. Reduce the following fractions to their lowest terms:

(a) $\dfrac{35}{50}$ (b) $\dfrac{26}{39}$ (c) $\dfrac{66}{143}$ (d) $\dfrac{29}{58}$

(e) $\dfrac{28}{42}$ (f) $\dfrac{84}{300}$ (g) $\dfrac{198}{462}$ (h) $\dfrac{525}{1\,155}$

Proper Fractions, Improper Fractions and Mixed Numbers

In each of the fractions $\dfrac{3}{4}$, $\dfrac{7}{9}$ and $\dfrac{123}{125}$, did you notice that the numerator is less than the denominator? They are examples of **proper fractions**. The fractions we have looked at so far are all proper fractions.

(a)
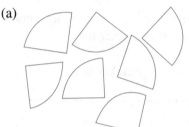

(b)
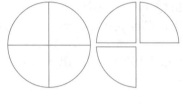

Fig. 4.3

Fig. 4.3 illustrates that 7 quarters or $\dfrac{7}{4}$ can be written as

$$\frac{7}{4} = \left(1 \text{ and } \frac{3}{4}\right) = 1 + \frac{3}{4}.$$

We write $\left(1 \text{ and } \dfrac{3}{4}\right)$ or $\left(1 + \dfrac{3}{4}\right)$ as $1\dfrac{3}{4}$.

$\dfrac{7}{4}$ is an example of an **improper fraction** which has the numerator *greater than* the denominator.

$\dfrac{7}{7}$ is also an improper fraction because its numerator is the *same as* the denominator.

$1\dfrac{3}{4}$ is an example of a **mixed number** which contains an **integral part** and a **fractional part**.

A mixed number can be expressed in fraction form as an improper fraction. The process of converting a mixed number into an improper fraction is illustrated by the following examples:

(a) $2\dfrac{3}{4} = \dfrac{2 \times 4}{4} + \dfrac{3}{4} = \dfrac{2 \times 4 + 3}{4} = \dfrac{11}{4}$

(b) $7\dfrac{5}{9} = \dfrac{7 \times 9}{9} + \dfrac{5}{9} = \dfrac{7 \times 9 + 5}{9} = \dfrac{68}{9}$

To express an improper fraction as a mixed number, we divide the numerator by the denominator. The quotient obtained is the integral part and the remainder is the numerator of the fractional part.

*You know that $5\dfrac{1}{2}$ is read as 'five and a half': it means $5 + \dfrac{1}{2}$, but we leave out the addition sign and write what we call a **mixed number**. A mixed number is the sum of a whole number and a fraction.*

fractional part

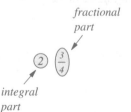

integral part

For example,

(a)

$$\frac{37}{14} = 2\frac{9}{14}$$

$$\begin{array}{r} 2 \text{ (quotient)} \\ 14\overline{)\ 37} \\ -28 \\ \hline 9 \text{ (remainder)} \end{array}$$

(b)

$$\frac{123}{7} = 17\frac{4}{7}$$

$$\begin{array}{r} 17 \text{ (quotient)} \\ 7\overline{)\ 123} \\ -7 \\ \hline 53 \\ -49 \\ \hline 4 \text{ (remainder)} \end{array}$$

Can you explain why the above procedure works?

Divide the distance between 0 and 1 into 4 equal parts.

Order of Fractions

In Chapter 1, we learnt how to represent a whole number on the number line. Can you also represent fractions on the number line?

Fig. 4.4 shows the fractions $\frac{1}{2}$ and $\frac{3}{4}$ on the number line.

$$\begin{array}{ccccc} & & & & \\ 0 & & \frac{1}{2} & \frac{3}{4} & 1 \end{array}$$

Fig. 4.4

From the number line, we know that $\frac{3}{4}$ is greater than $\frac{1}{2}$.

Where would you mark $\frac{1}{4}$, $\frac{7}{10}$ and $\frac{9}{10}$ on the above number line?

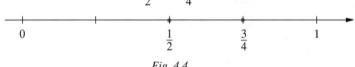

Comparing Fractions

The positions of $\frac{1}{4}$, $\frac{7}{10}$ and $\frac{9}{10}$ on the number line indicate that $\frac{9}{10} > \frac{7}{10} > \frac{1}{4}$. Clearly, $\frac{9}{10} > \frac{7}{10}$ because $9 > 7$. Comparing $\frac{1}{4}$ and $\frac{7}{10}$, two fractions with different denominators, can be done as follows:

$$\frac{7}{\textcircled{10}} = \frac{7 \times 2}{10 \times 2} = \frac{14}{\textcircled{20}}; \quad \frac{1}{\textcircled{4}} = \frac{1 \times 5}{4 \times 5} = \frac{5}{\textcircled{20}} \qquad \text{(20 is the LCM of 4 and 10)}$$

$$\frac{7}{10} > \frac{1}{4} \text{ since } \frac{14}{20} > \frac{5}{20}.$$

In general, if two fractions have the same denominator, then the larger the numerator, the larger the fraction. In contrast, if two fractions have the same numerator, then the larger the denominator, the smaller the fraction.

For two fractions with different denominators or (numerators), we can convert the fraction to an equivalent fraction with the same denominator (or numerator) and then use the above rule to compare them.

Example 2

Arrange the fractions $\frac{5}{13}$, $\frac{3}{13}$, $\frac{7}{13}$ and $\frac{10}{13}$ in descending order.

▼
Solution

Descending order means from the largest to the smallest.

$\frac{10}{13} > \frac{7}{13} > \frac{5}{13} > \frac{3}{13}$ because $10 > 7 > 5 > 3$.

Hence the arrangement of the fractions in descending order is $\frac{10}{13}$, $\frac{7}{13}$, $\frac{5}{13}$, $\frac{3}{13}$.

Example 3

Arrange the fractions $\frac{3}{4}$, $\frac{5}{9}$ and $\frac{7}{12}$ in ascending order.

▼
Solution

The fractions $\frac{3}{4}$, $\frac{5}{9}$ and $\frac{7}{12}$ have different denominators. To compare the fractions, we convert them to equivalent fractions with the same denominator.

The LCM of 4, 9 and 12 is 36.

$$\frac{3}{4} = \frac{3 \times 9}{4 \times 9} = \frac{27}{36}; \quad \frac{5}{9} = \frac{5 \times 4}{9 \times 4} = \frac{20}{36}; \quad \frac{7}{12} = \frac{7 \times 3}{12 \times 3} = \frac{21}{36}.$$

$$\frac{20}{36} < \frac{21}{36} < \frac{27}{36} \quad \text{or} \quad \frac{5}{9} < \frac{7}{12} < \frac{3}{4}.$$

Hence, the arrangement of the fractions in ascending order is $\frac{5}{9}$, $\frac{7}{12}$, $\frac{3}{4}$.

═ Exercise 4c ═

1. Which of the following are
   (i) proper fractions, (ii) improper fractions,
   (iii) mixed numbers?

   (a) $\frac{4}{5}$ **(b)** $\frac{23}{7}$ **(c)** $\frac{11}{13}$ **(d)** $3\frac{1}{7}$

   (e) $\frac{3}{14}$ **(f)** $2\frac{3}{4}$ **(g)** $\frac{9}{8}$ **(h)** $6\frac{4}{5}$

2. Express each of these mixed numbers as improper fractions.

   (a) $2\frac{1}{3}$ **(b)** $1\frac{3}{11}$ **(c)** $7\frac{5}{9}$ **(d)** $4\frac{3}{5}$

   (e) $5\frac{3}{4}$ **(f)** $3\frac{5}{6}$ **(g)** $2\frac{5}{13}$ **(h)** $14\frac{2}{11}$

3. Express each of these improper fractions as whole or mixed numbers.

   (a) $\frac{22}{7}$ **(b)** $\frac{12}{4}$ **(c)** $\frac{35}{6}$ **(d)** $\frac{42}{9}$

   (e) $\frac{84}{5}$ **(f)** $\frac{124}{8}$ **(g)** $\frac{111}{11}$ **(h)** $\frac{145}{13}$

4. Which of the two fractions is smaller?

   (a) $\frac{4}{10}$, $\frac{9}{10}$ **(b)** $\frac{1}{16}$, $\frac{1}{4}$

   (c) $\frac{5}{12}$, $\frac{1}{3}$ **(d)** $\frac{4}{7}$, $\frac{5}{9}$

5. Which of the three fractions is the largest?

   (a) $\frac{1}{7}$, $\frac{6}{7}$, $\frac{4}{7}$ **(b)** $\frac{1}{2}$, $\frac{1}{4}$, $\frac{1}{3}$

   (c) $\frac{3}{4}$, $\frac{7}{8}$, $\frac{3}{16}$ **(d)** $\frac{4}{15}$, $\frac{2}{3}$, $\frac{5}{9}$

6. Peter, the center on the basketball team, is $1\frac{7}{10}$ m tall. His rival for the position is $1\frac{5}{8}$ m tall. Who will more likely be selected for the position if they are equal in all aspects except in height?

7. Mary, Susan and Joan went fishing. Mary caught a sea bass that weighed $2\frac{2}{3}$ kg; Susan caught one that weighed $2\frac{7}{8}$ kg and Joan caught one that weighed $2\frac{3}{4}$ kg. Who caught the heaviest sea bass?

8. Arrange the following fractions in ascending order:

(a) $\dfrac{11}{12}, \dfrac{5}{8}, \dfrac{3}{4}$ (b) $\dfrac{2}{3}, \dfrac{4}{9}, \dfrac{5}{6}$

(c) $\dfrac{1}{3}, \dfrac{4}{7}, \dfrac{1}{2}$ (d) $\dfrac{7}{11}, \dfrac{5}{6}, \dfrac{2}{3}$

9. Arrange the following fractions in descending order:

(a) $\dfrac{3}{4}, \dfrac{5}{6}, \dfrac{5}{9}, \dfrac{7}{12}$ (b) $\dfrac{3}{4}, \dfrac{4}{5}, \dfrac{7}{10}, \dfrac{11}{12}$

(c) $\dfrac{2}{3}, \dfrac{5}{12}, \dfrac{1}{2}, \dfrac{5}{8}$ (d) $\dfrac{7}{9}, \dfrac{5}{6}, \dfrac{13}{18}, \dfrac{2}{3}$

Addition and Subtraction of Fractions with Same Denominators

We can only add the numerators together if they have the same denominator.

For example,

$$\frac{3}{7} + \frac{2}{7} = \frac{5}{7}.$$

Fig. 4.5 shows that $\dfrac{2}{7} + \dfrac{3}{7} = \dfrac{2+3}{7} = \dfrac{5}{7}$

$$\boxed{\frac{1}{7}}\boxed{\frac{1}{7}}\boxed{\frac{1}{7}}\boxed{\frac{1}{7}}\boxed{\frac{1}{7}}\boxed{\frac{1}{7}}\boxed{\frac{1}{7}}$$

Fig. 4.5

Fig. 4.6 shows that $\dfrac{6}{7} - \dfrac{2}{7} = \dfrac{6-2}{7} = \dfrac{4}{7}$

Fig. 4.6

The general rules for the addition and subtraction of fractions with the same denominator are

$$\frac{a}{c} + \frac{b}{c} = \frac{a+b}{c} \qquad \text{and}$$

$$\frac{a}{c} - \frac{b}{c} = \frac{a-b}{c}, \text{ where } a, b, c \text{ are whole numbers and } c \neq 0.$$

Addition and Subtraction of Fractions with Different Denominators

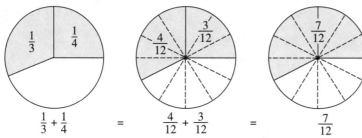

$$\frac{1}{3} + \frac{1}{4} \qquad = \qquad \frac{4}{12} + \frac{3}{12} \qquad = \qquad \frac{7}{12}$$

Fig. 4.7

If two fractions have different denominators, we must first change them to equivalent fractions which have a common denominator.

Fig. 4.7 shows $\frac{1}{3} + \frac{1}{4} = \frac{4}{12} + \frac{3}{12} = \frac{7}{12}$.

Notice that $\frac{1}{3}$ and $\frac{1}{4}$ are converted into $\frac{4}{12}$ and $\frac{3}{12}$, i.e., fractions with the same denominator.

Similarly,

The sum of $\frac{1}{2}$, $\frac{1}{3}$ and $\frac{1}{4}$ of the enrolment of ABC school is exactly the enrolment of XYZ school. The sum of $\frac{1}{5}$, $\frac{1}{6}$, $\frac{1}{7}$ and $\frac{1}{8}$ of the enrolment of ABC school is exactly the enrolment of PQR school. What are the enrolments of these schools, assuming that no school has more than 1 000 pupils?

$$\frac{4}{9} + \frac{5}{6} = \frac{4 \times 2}{9 \times 2} + \frac{5 \times 3}{6 \times 3}$$

$$= \frac{8}{18} + \frac{15}{18}$$

$$= \frac{8 + 15}{18}$$

$$= \frac{23}{18} = 1\frac{5}{18}$$

$$\frac{7}{8} - \frac{2}{5} = \frac{7 \times 5}{8 \times 5} - \frac{2 \times 8}{5 \times 8}$$

$$= \frac{35}{40} - \frac{16}{40}$$

$$= \frac{35 - 16}{40}$$

$$= \frac{19}{40}$$

Note: The LCM of 9 and 6 is 18. The LCM of 8 and 5 is 40.

In adding or subtracting fractions with different denominators, we must first express the fractions in the same denominator. We always use the LCM of the denominators as the common denominator.

Example 4

Evaluate (a) $\dfrac{7}{10} + \dfrac{3}{8}$ and (b) $\dfrac{5}{8} + \dfrac{3}{4} + \dfrac{5}{6}$.

▼ **Solution**

(a)
$$\dfrac{7}{10} + \dfrac{3}{8} = \dfrac{28}{40} + \dfrac{15}{40}$$

(The LCM of 10 and 8 is 40.)

$$= \dfrac{43}{40}$$

$$= 1\dfrac{3}{40}$$

(b)
$$\dfrac{5}{8} + \dfrac{3}{4} + \dfrac{5}{6} = \dfrac{15}{24} + \dfrac{18}{24} + \dfrac{20}{24}$$

(The LCM of 8, 4 and 6 is 24.)

$$= \dfrac{15 + 18 + 20}{24}$$

$$= \dfrac{53}{24}$$

$$= 2\dfrac{5}{24}$$

Addition and Subtraction of Mixed Numbers

Example 5

Evaluate (a) $3\dfrac{8}{15} + 1\dfrac{5}{8}$; (b) $6\dfrac{1}{6} - 1\dfrac{3}{4}$.

▼ **Solution**

(a)
$$3\dfrac{8}{15} + 1\dfrac{5}{8} = (3 + 1) + \left(\dfrac{8}{15} + \dfrac{5}{8}\right)$$

(Add the whole numbers and fractions separately.)

$$= 4 + \dfrac{64 + 75}{120}$$

(The LCM of 15 and 8 is 120.)

$$= 4 + \dfrac{139}{120}$$

$$= 4 + 1\dfrac{19}{120}$$

$$= 5\dfrac{19}{120}$$

(b)
$$6\dfrac{1}{6} - 1\dfrac{3}{4} = (5 - 1) + \left(1\dfrac{1}{6} - \dfrac{3}{4}\right)$$

$$= 4 + \left(\dfrac{7}{6} - \dfrac{3}{4}\right)$$

$$= 4 + \dfrac{14 - 9}{12}$$

$$= 4\dfrac{5}{12}$$

Do you know why $6\dfrac{1}{6}$ is written as $5 + 1\dfrac{1}{6}$ instead of $6 + \dfrac{1}{6}$?

(c) $4\dfrac{7}{10} + \dfrac{7}{15} - 2\dfrac{5}{6} = (4 - 2) + \left(\dfrac{7}{10} + \dfrac{7}{15} - \dfrac{5}{6}\right)$

$= 2 + \dfrac{21 + 14 - 25}{30}$ (The LCM of 10, 15 and 6 is 30.)

$= 2 + \dfrac{10}{30}$

$= 2\dfrac{1}{3}$

Exercise 4d

1. Find the values of the following, giving your answers in the simplest form:

   (a) $\dfrac{1}{4} + \dfrac{2}{4}$

   (b) $\dfrac{14}{20} + \dfrac{7}{20}$

   (c) $\dfrac{39}{50} + \dfrac{21}{50} + \dfrac{15}{50}$

   (d) $\dfrac{3}{14} + \dfrac{9}{14} + \dfrac{11}{14}$

2. Evaluate the following, expressing your answers in the simplest form:

   (a) $\dfrac{5}{6} - \dfrac{4}{6}$

   (b) $\dfrac{5}{8} - \dfrac{3}{8}$

   (c) $\dfrac{23}{30} - \dfrac{11}{30} - \dfrac{7}{30}$

   (d) $\dfrac{37}{49} - \dfrac{17}{49} - \dfrac{6}{49}$

3. Calculate the following:

   (a) $\dfrac{2}{7} + \dfrac{3}{6}$

   (b) $\dfrac{7}{10} + \dfrac{12}{35}$

   (c) $\dfrac{14}{35} - \dfrac{3}{10}$

   (d) $\dfrac{19}{30} - \dfrac{9}{20}$

4. Evaluate the following:

   (a) $3\dfrac{3}{5} + \dfrac{1}{5}$

   (b) $3\dfrac{1}{6} + 2\dfrac{5}{9}$

   (c) $2\dfrac{1}{7} + 3\dfrac{5}{8}$

   (d) $6\dfrac{1}{100} + 3\dfrac{1}{8}$

   (e) $2\dfrac{7}{100} + 1\dfrac{3}{40}$

   (f) $6\dfrac{7}{8} - 3\dfrac{4}{8}$

   (g) $7\dfrac{1}{5} - 3\dfrac{3}{10}$

   (h) $6\dfrac{2}{3} - 4\dfrac{1}{4}$

   (i) $9\dfrac{2}{5} - 5\dfrac{1}{3}$

   (j) $6\dfrac{7}{12} - 3\dfrac{3}{8}$

5. Evaluate the following:

   (a) $\dfrac{4}{7} + \dfrac{5}{21} + \dfrac{11}{42}$

   (b) $\dfrac{5}{8} + \dfrac{21}{10} - \dfrac{17}{20}$

   (c) $5\dfrac{27}{28} - 2\dfrac{3}{7} + \dfrac{13}{14}$

   (d) $4\dfrac{2}{3} + 1\dfrac{3}{5} - 1\dfrac{1}{4}$

   (e) $5\dfrac{3}{4} - 2\dfrac{5}{6} - 1\dfrac{8}{15} + 4\dfrac{7}{20}$

   (f) $2\dfrac{1}{7} + 4\dfrac{5}{8} - 3\dfrac{9}{14} + 1\dfrac{1}{4}$

   (g) $4\dfrac{3}{5} - 1\dfrac{2}{15} - 2\dfrac{7}{9} - \dfrac{2}{45}$

   (h) $2\dfrac{19}{24} - \dfrac{1}{18} + \dfrac{61}{72} - \dfrac{1}{36}$

6. On Thursday, Jean ran $1\frac{2}{3}$ km. On Friday, she ran $2\frac{3}{5}$ km. Find the total distance she ran in two days.

7. John has $9\frac{1}{4}$ litres of paint. After using $4\frac{1}{2}$ litres for painting a room, how much paint has he left?

8. During the school's spring cleaning day, Robin and his classmates spent $1\frac{1}{4}$ hours and $1\frac{1}{12}$ hours cleaning two classrooms assigned to them respectively.
   (a) Find the total time they spent.
   (b) Which classroom took them longer to clean?
   (c) How much longer did they spend in cleaning one classroom than the other?

9. Mary has $6\frac{3}{4}$ cups of flour. She used $2\frac{1}{2}$ cups of flour in one recipe and $2\frac{1}{4}$ cups of flour in another.
   (a) How much flour did she use altogether?
   (b) How much flour has she left?

10. The police conduct regular anti-secret society operations among youths. On a Friday night, the officers spent $\frac{3}{4}$ hour, $1\frac{1}{2}$ hours and $2\frac{1}{4}$ hours checking on youths at three youth hangouts respectively. Find the total time the officers spent on their operation.

Multiplication of a Fraction by a Whole Number

We know that 3×4 can be written as $3 + 3 + 3 + 3 = 12$.

Similarly, $\frac{3}{5} \times 4$ can be written as $\frac{3}{5} + \frac{3}{5} + \frac{3}{5} + \frac{3}{5} = \frac{3 + 3 + 3 + 3}{5} = \frac{3 \times 4}{5}$

$$= \frac{12}{5} = 2\frac{2}{5} \qquad \text{(see Fig. 4.8)}$$

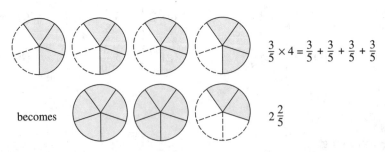

$\frac{3}{5} \times 4 = \frac{3}{5} + \frac{3}{5} + \frac{3}{5} + \frac{3}{5}$

becomes

$2\frac{2}{5}$

Fig. 4.8

This leads us to a rule for the multiplication of a fraction by a whole number.

$$\frac{a}{b} \times c = \frac{a \times c}{b}, \text{ where } a, b, c \text{ are whole numbers and } b \neq 0.$$

Fractions of Quantities

Example 6

John ordered 100 rewritable compact discs and 300 recordable compact discs for his computer store. His supplier delivered only $\frac{3}{4}$ of the rewritable compact discs and $\frac{3}{5}$ of the recordable compact discs he ordered. How many compact discs did he receive altogether?

Solution

$\frac{3}{4}$ of $100 = \frac{3}{4} \times 100 = 75$; $\frac{3}{5}$ of $300 = \frac{3}{5} \times 300 = 180$.

Therefore, he received altogether $75 + 180 = 255$ compact discs.

Multiplication of Fractions

Mr. Lee has two bookstores. In October, his book distributor sent him only $\frac{5}{6}$ of an order for a school textbook, which he had expected to distribute equally between his two stores. What fraction of his original order will each store receive?

Each store will get $\frac{1}{2}$ of the books received, but the books received make up of only $\frac{5}{6}$ of the original order.

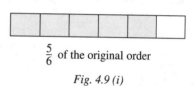

$\frac{5}{6}$ of the original order

Fig. 4.9 (i)

Each store will receive $\frac{1}{2}$ of $\frac{5}{6}$ of the original order. Fig. 4.9 illustrates that

$$\frac{1}{2} \text{ of } \frac{5}{6} = \frac{1}{2} \times \frac{5}{6} = \frac{1 \times 5}{2 \times 6} = \frac{5}{12}.$$

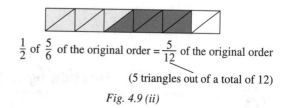

$\frac{1}{2}$ of $\frac{5}{6}$ of the original order $= \frac{5}{12}$ of the original order

(5 triangles out of a total of 12)

Fig. 4.9 (ii)

This leads us to a rule for the multiplication of fractions.

$$\frac{a}{b} \times \frac{c}{d} = \frac{a \times c}{b \times d}, \text{ where } a, b, c, d \text{ are whole numbers and } b \neq 0, d \neq 0.$$

Where $d = 1$, we have $\frac{a}{b} \times c = \frac{a \times c}{b}$, which is the rule for the multiplication of a fraction and a whole number discussed earlier.

Example 7

Evaluate (a) $\dfrac{3}{8} \times \dfrac{5}{7}$ *and (b)* $2\dfrac{2}{3} \times \dfrac{5}{14}$.

Solution

(a) $\dfrac{3}{8} \times \dfrac{5}{7} = \dfrac{3 \times 5}{8 \times 7}$

$\qquad = \dfrac{15}{56}$

(b) $2\dfrac{2}{3} \times \dfrac{5}{14} = \dfrac{8}{3} \times \dfrac{5}{14}$

$\qquad\qquad = \dfrac{8 \times 5}{3 \times 14}$

$\qquad\qquad = \dfrac{40}{42} = \dfrac{20}{21}$

Note: Mixed numbers must be changed to improper fractions before multiplication. Sometimes, "cancellations" can be done before multiplication. This alternative method for (b) is shown below:

$$2\dfrac{2}{3} \times \dfrac{5}{14} = \dfrac{\overset{4}{\cancel{8}}}{3} \times \dfrac{5}{\underset{7}{\cancel{14}}}$$

$$= \dfrac{4 \times 5}{3 \times 7} = \dfrac{20}{21}$$

Example 8

Calculate (a) $\dfrac{5}{7} \times \dfrac{8}{15} \times \dfrac{14}{3}$ *and (b)* $2\dfrac{1}{3} \times 3\dfrac{3}{7} \times \dfrac{3}{4}$.

Solution

(a) $\dfrac{\overset{1}{\cancel{5}}}{\underset{1}{\cancel{7}}} \times \dfrac{8}{\underset{3}{\cancel{15}}} \times \dfrac{\overset{2}{\cancel{14}}}{3} = \dfrac{1 \times 8 \times 2}{1 \times 3 \times 3}$

$\qquad\qquad\qquad = \dfrac{16}{9} = 1\dfrac{7}{9}$

(b) $2\dfrac{1}{3} \times 3\dfrac{3}{7} \times \dfrac{3}{4} = \dfrac{\overset{1}{\cancel{7}}}{\underset{1}{\cancel{3}}} \times \dfrac{\overset{6}{\cancel{24}}}{\underset{1}{\cancel{7}}} \times \dfrac{\overset{1}{\cancel{3}}}{\underset{1}{\cancel{4}}}$

$\qquad\qquad\qquad = 6$

Division of a Fraction by a Whole Number

Let us consider, from another point of view, the fraction of Mr Lee's original order each of his two stores will receive.

Dividing $\dfrac{5}{6}$ of his original order by two, we have $\dfrac{5}{6} \div 2$.

From Page 75, we have found that each store will receive $\dfrac{1}{2} \times \dfrac{5}{6} = \dfrac{5}{12}$.

Thus, $\dfrac{5}{6} \div 2 = \dfrac{5}{6} \times \dfrac{1}{2} = \dfrac{5 \times 1}{6 \times 2} = \dfrac{5}{12}$. $\left(\text{By commutative law, } \dfrac{1}{2} \times \dfrac{5}{6} = \dfrac{5}{6} \times \dfrac{1}{2} \right)$

This leads us to a rule for the division of a fraction by a whole number.

$$\frac{a}{b} \div c = \frac{a}{b} \times \frac{1}{c} = \frac{a}{b \times c}, \text{ where } a, b, c \text{ are whole numbers and } b \neq 0, c \neq 0.$$

 ## Division of a Fraction by Another Fraction

On another occasion, Mr. Lee's distributor delivered only $\frac{3}{4}$ of his original order. He satisfies one of his two stores first by giving the store the expected quantities, which make up of half of what he ordered. What fraction of the books delivered will this store receive?

(a) Method 1

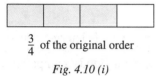

$\frac{3}{4}$ of the original order

Fig. 4.10 (i)

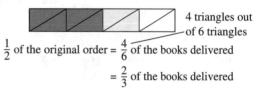

4 triangles out of 6 triangles

$\frac{1}{2}$ of the original order $= \frac{4}{6}$ of the books delivered

$= \frac{2}{3}$ of the books delivered

Hence, the store will receive $\frac{2}{3}$ of the books delivered.

Fig. 4.10 (ii)

(b) Method 2

Now, consider

$$⑦ \times \frac{3}{4} = \frac{1}{2}.$$

Thus, $⑦ = \frac{1}{2} \div \frac{3}{4} = \frac{2}{3}$.

However, we also have $\frac{1}{2} \times \frac{4}{3} = \frac{1 \times 4}{2 \times 3} = \frac{4}{6} = \frac{2}{3}$.

Therefore, $\frac{1}{2} \div \frac{3}{4} = \frac{1}{2} \times \frac{4}{3}$.

This leads to a rule for dividing a fraction by another fraction.

$$\frac{a}{b} \div \frac{c}{d} = \frac{a}{b} \times \frac{d}{c} = \frac{a \times d}{b \times c}, \text{ where } a, b, c, d \text{ are whole numbers and}$$

$$b \neq 0, c \neq 0, d \neq 0.$$

Example 9

Evaluate (a) $3\frac{1}{2} \div \frac{3}{4}$; *(b)* $\frac{24}{55} \div \frac{8}{11}$; *(c)* $1\frac{4}{13} \times 7\frac{4}{5} \div 11\frac{1}{3}$.

Solution

(a) $3\frac{1}{2} \div \frac{3}{4} = \frac{7}{2} \div \frac{3}{4}$

$= \frac{7}{2} \times \frac{4}{3} = \frac{14}{3} = 4\frac{2}{3}$

(b) $\frac{24}{55} \div \frac{8}{11} = \frac{24}{55} \times \frac{11}{8}$

$= \frac{3}{5}$

(c) $1\frac{4}{13} \times 7\frac{4}{5} \div 11\frac{1}{3} = \frac{17}{13} \times \frac{39}{5} \div \frac{34}{3}$

$$= \frac{17}{13} \times \frac{39}{5} \times \frac{3}{34}$$

$$= \frac{9}{10}$$

Note: In the above procedure to express each mixed number as an improper fraction, we changed '÷' to '×' and inverted the divisor.

$\frac{1}{3}$ *of a number of animals are cows,* $\frac{1}{4}$ *are sheep,* $\frac{1}{5}$ *are horses,* $\frac{1}{6}$ *are deer and 4 are dogs. How many animals are there altogether?*

Exercise 4e

1. Calculate the following:

   (a) $20 \times \frac{4}{5}$

   (b) $\frac{5}{6} \times 8$

   (c) $\frac{2}{3} \times \frac{5}{7}$

   (d) $\frac{4}{13} \times 3\frac{1}{4}$

   (e) $10 \div \frac{2}{3}$

   (f) $\frac{9}{28} \div \frac{6}{7}$

   (g) $1\frac{5}{7} \div \frac{4}{21}$

   (h) $8\frac{2}{7} \div 3\frac{9}{10}$

2. Evaluate the following, expressing your answers in the simplest form:

   (a) $3\frac{1}{2} \times 4\frac{4}{5} \times \frac{5}{14}$

   (b) $2\frac{1}{7} \times 1\frac{3}{46} \times 1\frac{5}{18} \times \frac{5}{7}$

   (c) $5\frac{1}{4} \div 2\frac{4}{5} \div 1\frac{7}{9}$

   (d) $3\frac{1}{9} \times 3\frac{3}{5} \div 2\frac{1}{10}$

   (e) $\frac{8}{18} \times \frac{15}{20} \div \frac{24}{15} \times \frac{42}{35}$

3. Find the following:

   (a) $\frac{1}{5}$ of 20 pupils

   (b) $\frac{3}{5}$ of 15 oranges

   (c) $\frac{4}{7}$ of 56 km

   (d) $\frac{5}{8}$ of 24 hours

   (e) $\frac{2}{9}$ of 36 kg

4. A school has $6\frac{3}{4}$ kg of detergent in stock. During the 'Use Your Hands' campaign, each class will be given $\frac{3}{8}$ kg of detergent. There are 28 classes in the school.

   (a) What fraction of the school will be supplied with the detergent in stock?
   (b) How much detergent will be required altogether for the whole school?
   (c) How much more detergent does the school need to order?
   (d) If the school gives out the detergent in stock to the 15 lower secondary classes first,
       (i) how much detergent will be given out;
       (ii) how much detergent in stock will be left?

5. (a) Last year Peter spent a total of $8\frac{1}{6}$ hours on community service. Visits to old folks' homes made up $\frac{4}{7}$ of the total time. How much time did he spend in visiting old folks' homes?

   (b) This year Peter plans to spend $1\frac{1}{5}$ of his time spent last year on community service.
       (i) Find the time he will spend on community service.
       (ii) How much more time will he spend this year than last year?

Arithmetical Operations on Fractions

Can you spot the errors in each of the following?

(a) $2 = \dfrac{8}{4} = \dfrac{8}{2+2}$

$= \dfrac{8}{2} + \dfrac{8}{2} = 4 + 4 = 8$

(b) $\dfrac{3+4}{3} = \dfrac{3}{3} + 4$

$= 1 + 4 = 5$

(c) $\dfrac{2}{3} + \dfrac{4}{5} = \dfrac{10}{15} + \dfrac{12}{15}$

$= \dfrac{10+12}{15+15} = \dfrac{22}{30} = \dfrac{11}{15}$

Keep in mind the following rules when doing arithmetic operations on fractions.

1. When an expression contains brackets, simplify the expression within the brackets first.

2. When an expression contains brackets within brackets, simplify the expression within the innermost pair of brackets first.

3. When an expression contains only additions and subtractions, work from left to right.

4. When an expression contains only multiplications and divisions, work from left to right.

5. When an expression contains addition, subtraction, multiplication and division, do multiplication and division before addition and subtraction.

Note: The above rules are the same as rules for whole numbers.

Example 10

Evaluate the following:

(a) $\left(\dfrac{1}{2} + \dfrac{1}{3} \right) \times \dfrac{1}{4}$

(b) $\dfrac{1}{3} \times \left(\dfrac{1}{2} + \dfrac{1}{4} \right) \div \dfrac{1}{6}$

(c) $\left(\dfrac{3}{4} \times \dfrac{1}{3} - \dfrac{1}{12} \right) \div \dfrac{1}{2}$

(d) $5\dfrac{1}{3} \times 4\dfrac{1}{2} - 3\dfrac{1}{4} \times \dfrac{8}{13}$

▼ Solution

(a) $\left(\dfrac{1}{2} + \dfrac{1}{3} \right) \times \dfrac{1}{4}$ (Calculate the expression within the brackets first.)

$= \left(\dfrac{3+2}{6} \right) \times \dfrac{1}{4}$

$= \dfrac{5}{6} \times \dfrac{1}{4}$

$= \dfrac{5}{24}$

(b) $\dfrac{1}{3} \times \left(\dfrac{1}{2} + \dfrac{1}{4} \right) \div \dfrac{1}{6}$ (Calculate the expression within the brackets first. Work from left to right.)

$= \dfrac{1}{3} \times \left(\dfrac{2+1}{4} \right) \div \dfrac{1}{6}$

$= \dfrac{1}{3} \times \dfrac{3}{4} \times \dfrac{6}{1}$

$= \dfrac{3}{2}$

$= 1\dfrac{1}{2}$

(c) $\left(\dfrac{3}{4} \times \dfrac{1}{3} - \dfrac{1}{12} \right) \div \dfrac{1}{2}$ (Within brackets, do multiplication before subtraction.)

$= \left(\dfrac{1}{4} - \dfrac{1}{12} \right) \div \dfrac{1}{2}$

$= \left(\dfrac{3-1}{12} \right) \times \dfrac{2}{1}$

$= \dfrac{2}{12} \times 2$

$= \dfrac{1}{3}$

(d) $5\dfrac{1}{3} \times 4\dfrac{1}{2} - 3\dfrac{1}{4} \times \dfrac{8}{13}$ (Do multiplication before subtraction.)

$= \dfrac{16}{3} \times \dfrac{9}{2} - \dfrac{13}{4} \times \dfrac{8}{13}$

$= 24 - 2$

$= 22$

1. Evaluate the following:

(a) $\dfrac{1}{3} \times \left(\dfrac{1}{3} + \dfrac{1}{4} \right)$

(b) $\left(\dfrac{3}{4} - \dfrac{1}{2} \right) \times \dfrac{2}{3}$

(c) $\left(1\dfrac{3}{4} - \dfrac{1}{2} \right) \div \dfrac{1}{3}$

(d) $\left(\dfrac{4}{5} + \dfrac{1}{3} \right) \div \dfrac{2}{3}$

(e) $3\dfrac{3}{4} \times \left(4\dfrac{1}{5} - 2\dfrac{5}{9} \right)$

(f) $3\dfrac{3}{4} \div \left(2\dfrac{1}{3} - \dfrac{1}{4} \right)$

2. Find the values of the following, expressing your answers in the simplest form:

(a) $\dfrac{1}{3} \times \left(\dfrac{1}{3} + \dfrac{3}{4} \right) \div \dfrac{5}{2}$

(b) $\dfrac{1}{3} \times \left(\dfrac{1}{4} - \dfrac{1}{12} + \dfrac{1}{2} \right)$

(c) $\left(\dfrac{1}{2} + \dfrac{1}{3} \right) \div \left(\dfrac{2}{3} \times \dfrac{1}{8} \right)$

(d) $1\dfrac{3}{4} \times \left(\dfrac{4}{9} + \dfrac{2}{3} \right) \times \left(1\dfrac{1}{5} - \dfrac{1}{2} \right)$

(e) $\dfrac{2}{3} \times \dfrac{1}{4} - \dfrac{1}{12} \div \dfrac{1}{2}$

(f) $5\dfrac{1}{3} \times 4\dfrac{1}{2} - 3\dfrac{1}{4} \times 1\dfrac{5}{6}$

 ## Problem Solving Involving Fractions

Example 11

Four boys shared a certain sum of money. The first received $\dfrac{1}{6}$ of it, the second $\dfrac{1}{4}$ and the third $\dfrac{1}{2}$. If the fourth boy received $5, how much was the sum of money shared?

▼ **Solution**

Use a model

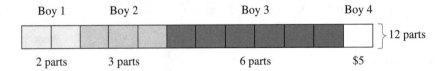

From the model, the fourth boy shared 1 part of a total of 12 parts.

∴ 1 part = $5 and thus, 12 parts = 12 × $5 = $60.

The sum of money shared is $60.

Alternatively, the first three boys together received $\dfrac{1}{6} + \dfrac{1}{4} + \dfrac{1}{2} = \dfrac{2+3+6}{12} = \dfrac{11}{12}$ of the money. The fourth boy thus received $\left(1 - \dfrac{11}{12} \right) = \dfrac{1}{12}$ of the money.

$\dfrac{1}{12}$ of the money = $5 or $\dfrac{1}{12}$ × the money = $5.

∴ the money = $5 ÷ $\dfrac{1}{12}$ = $5 × 12 = $60.

Example 12

Peter has 45 English and Chinese books. $\frac{4}{5}$ of the English books and $\frac{3}{4}$ of the Chinese books are fiction. The total number of fiction books he has is 35.

How many of his fiction books are in English?

▼**Solution**

Method 1: Make a list

Fraction of English fiction books $\dfrac{4}{5}, \dfrac{8}{10}, \dfrac{12}{15}, \dfrac{16}{20}, \mathbf{\dfrac{20}{25}}, \dfrac{24}{30}, \ldots$

Fraction of Chinese fiction books $\dfrac{3}{4}, \dfrac{6}{8}, \dfrac{9}{12}, \dfrac{12}{16}, \mathbf{\dfrac{15}{20}}, \dfrac{16}{24}, \ldots$

Study the fractions in bold from the lists.

The sum of the numerators = 20 (number of English fiction) + 15 (number of Chinese fiction)
                               = 35 (number of fiction Peter has)

The sum of the denominators = 25 + 20 = 45 (Total number of books Peter has)

∴   20 of his fiction books are in English.

Method 2: Use a model

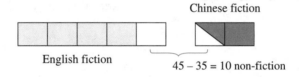

Rearrange the squares and triangles as shown below.

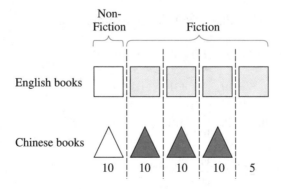

Each pair of square and triangle represents 10 books.

A single square represents 45 − 4 × 10 = 5 books.

∴   The number of English fiction books = 4 × 5 = 20.

1. James uses $\frac{1}{3}$ of his land for growing durians, $\frac{1}{4}$ for bananas, $\frac{3}{8}$ for guavas and the remaining 9 hectares for mangoes. What is the total area of his land?

2. A sum of money is shared among three brothers. The eldest receives $\frac{7}{13}$ of it and the next receives $\frac{2}{3}$ of the remainder. If the youngest brother receives $6, find the sum of money shared.

3. There are 42 pupils in a class. $\frac{3}{4}$ of the boys and $\frac{2}{3}$ of the girls travel to school by bus. The total number of boys and girls who travel to school by bus is 30.

   (a) How many boys are there in the class?
   (b) How many girls travel to school by bus?

4. The Mathematics Club in a school has 53 members. $\frac{5}{7}$ of the girl members and $\frac{3}{5}$ of the boy members are from lower secondary. The total number of lower secondary members is 35. How many members of the club are boys?

5. Mary has two tanks of fish. If she transfers 15 fish from the larger tank to the smaller tank, then the number of fish in the smaller tank will be $\frac{5}{7}$ of the number of fish in the larger tank. Given that there are 35 fish in the smaller tank originally, find the number of fish in the larger tank before the transfer of fish.

6. As part of the 'Learning Journeys' program, 73 pupils travelled on two buses, one air-conditioned and one non-air-conditioned, to the Singapore Discovery Centre. Three-fifths of the pupils on the air-conditioned bus were girls. There were 17 boys in the non-air-conditioned bus. The number of girls on the two buses were equal. How many pupils were there on the air-conditioned bus?

Decimals

*A **decimal number** is a different way of writing fractions.*

In the decimal system, a number like 4 269 can be expressed as

$$4\ 269 = 4 \times 1\ 000 + 2 \times 100 + 6 \times 10 + 9 \times 1$$

$\div 10 \qquad \div 10 \qquad \div 10$

Can we express a fraction like $4\ 269\frac{39}{100}$ in the same manner?

We know that $4\ 269\frac{39}{100} = 4\ 269 + \frac{39}{100}$

$$= 4\ 269 + \frac{30}{100} + \frac{9}{100}$$

$$= 4 \times 1\ 000 + 2 \times 100 + 6 \times 10 + 9 \times 1 + 3 \times \frac{1}{10} + 9 \times \frac{1}{100}$$

$\div 10 \qquad \div 10 \qquad \div 10 \qquad \div 10 \qquad \div 10$

$4\ 269\frac{39}{100}$ means 4 thousands, 2 hundreds, 6 tens, 9 ones, 3 tenths and 9 hundredths.

Similarly,

$$123\frac{456}{1\ 000} = 1 \times 100 + 2 \times 10 + 3 \times 1 + 4 \times \frac{1}{10} + 5 \times \frac{1}{100} + 6 \times \frac{1}{1\ 000}$$

and $\quad \dfrac{7\ 891}{10\ 000} = 7 \times \dfrac{1}{10} + 8 \times \dfrac{1}{100} + 9 \times \dfrac{1}{1\ 000} + 1 \times \dfrac{1}{10\ 000}$

$4\ 269\frac{39}{100}$ can be written as $4\ 269.39$.

Insert a dot here to separate the fractional part which consists of the tenths, hundredths, etc. from the integral part which consists of the ones, tens, etc.

*A dot called the **decimal point** is placed after the units column to separate the whole number part from the fractional part.*

Similarly,

$$123\frac{456}{1\ 000} = 123.456 \quad \text{and} \quad \frac{7\ 891}{10\ 000} = 0.789\ 1$$

Insert a dot here.

Add a zero before the dot when the integral part is zero.

Also, $\dfrac{4}{100} = 0 \times \dfrac{1}{10} + 4 \times \dfrac{1}{100} = 0.04$

This zero indicates 0 tenths.

and $\quad 3\dfrac{4}{1\ 000} = 3 \times 1 + 0 \times \dfrac{1}{10} + 0 \times \dfrac{1}{100} + 4 \times \dfrac{1}{1\ 000}$

$\qquad\qquad = 3.004$

The dot which we use to separate the fractional part from the integral part in a number is called the **decimal point**.

A number written with a decimal point is known as a **decimal**.

Examples of decimals are 4 269.39, 123.456, 0.789 1, 0.04 and 3.004.

In a decimal, the places occupied by the digits after the decimal point are called **decimal places**. 4 269.39, 123.456 and 0.789 1 have 2, 3 and 4 decimal places respectively.

A decimal 123.456 would have been written as 123\456 by Francis Vieta in 1600, 123 (456 by Johannes Kepler in 1616, 123 : 456 by John Napier in 1617, 123⁴⁵⁶ by Henry Briggs in 1624 and 123|456 by William Aughtred in 1631.

Note that

$$4\ 269.39 = 4\ 269\frac{39}{100} = \frac{426\ 939}{100}, \quad 123.456 = 123\frac{456}{1\ 000} = \frac{123\ 456}{1\ 000},$$

$$0.789\ 1 = \frac{7\ 891}{10\ 000}, \quad 0.04 = \frac{4}{100} \quad \text{and} \quad 3.004 = 3\frac{4}{1\ 000} = \frac{3\ 004}{1\ 000}.$$

Did you notice that the number of decimal places corresponds to the number of zeros in the denominators?

A decimal is a fraction whose denominator is 10 or a power of 10.

Conversion of Fractions into Decimals

Example 13

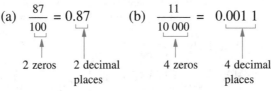

Express each of the following as a decimal:

(a) $\dfrac{87}{100}$ (b) $\dfrac{11}{10\,000}$ (c) $34\dfrac{97}{1\,000}$

▼ Solution

To change a fraction into a decimal, divide the numerator by the denominator.

(a) $\dfrac{87}{100} = 0.87$ (b) $\dfrac{11}{10\,000} = 0.001\,1$

2 zeros   2 decimal places   4 zeros   4 decimal places

(c) $34\dfrac{97}{1\,000} = 34.097$

3 zeros   3 decimal places

Fractions whose denominators can be changed to 10 or powers of 10 can be converted to decimals mentally using the method shown in Example 13.

Example 14

Express each of the following as a decimal:

(a) $\dfrac{3}{5}$ (b) $\dfrac{3}{4}$ (c) $\dfrac{27}{25}$ (d) $\dfrac{21}{4}$

▼ Solution

(a) $\dfrac{3}{5} = \dfrac{6}{10}$ (Multiply both the numerator and the denominator by 2 mentally. Write the decimal using the method in Example 13.)
$= 0.6$

(b) $\dfrac{3}{4} = \dfrac{75}{100}$ (Multiply both the numerator and the denominator by 25.)
$= 0.75$

(c) $\dfrac{27}{25} = \dfrac{108}{100}$
$= 1.08$

(d) $\dfrac{21}{4} = 5\dfrac{1}{4} = 5 + \dfrac{1}{4}$ $\left(\text{Note: } \dfrac{1}{4} = 0.25\right)$
$= 5 + 0.25$
$= 5.25$

For a fraction whose denominator cannot be changed to 10 or a power of 10 easily, the decimal form is obtained by dividing the numerator of the fraction by its denominator.

For example, $\dfrac{5}{8} = 5 \div 8$
$= 0.625$

$$
\begin{array}{r}
0.625 \\
8\,\overline{)\,5.000} \\
4\,8 \\
\hline
20 \\
16 \\
\hline
40 \\
40 \\
\hline
\end{array}
$$

Conversion of Decimals into Fractions

Example 15

Express (a) 0.95 and (b) 0.015 as fractions in their lowest terms.

Solution

(a) $0.95 = \dfrac{95}{100} = \dfrac{19}{20}$

2 decimal places   2 zeros in the denominator

(b) $0.015 = \dfrac{15}{1\,000} = \dfrac{3}{200}$

3 decimal places   3 zeros in the denominator

Example 16

Express (a) 11.25 and (b) 31.75 as fractions in their lowest terms.

Solution

(a) $11.25 = 11 + 0.25$

$\qquad = 11 + \dfrac{25}{100}$

$\qquad = 11 + \dfrac{1}{4}$

$\qquad = 11\dfrac{1}{4} \quad \left(\text{Use } 0.25 = \dfrac{1}{4}\right)$

(b) $31.75 = 31 + 0.75$

$\qquad = 31 + \dfrac{75}{100}$

$\qquad = 31 + \dfrac{3}{4}$

$\qquad = 31\dfrac{3}{4} \quad \left(\text{Use } 0.75 = \dfrac{3}{4}\right)$

Exercise 4h

1. Express the following fractions as decimals:

(a) $\dfrac{43}{100}$ (b) $\dfrac{57}{1\,000}$ (c) $\dfrac{8}{10\,000}$ (d) $\dfrac{27}{20}$ (e) $\dfrac{33}{4}$

(f) $2\dfrac{3}{10}$ (g) $15\dfrac{96}{1\,000}$ (h) $7\dfrac{5}{10\,000}$ (i) $85\dfrac{3}{25}$ (j) $2\dfrac{31}{50}$

(k) $19\dfrac{3}{125}$ (l) $101\dfrac{11}{100\,000}$

2. Express the following as fractions in their lowest terms:

(a) 0.75   (b) 0.36   (c) 0.025   (d) 0.006   (e) 0.105
(f) 3.75   (g) 0.012 5   (h) 15.25   (i) 84.625

3. Change the following into decimals:

(a) $\dfrac{13}{8}$ (b) $\dfrac{67}{80}$ (c) $\dfrac{215}{80}$ (d) $\dfrac{245}{280}$ (e) $\dfrac{19}{32}$ (f) $\dfrac{94}{64}$

Recurring Decimals

In-Class Activity

1. Divide 1 by 8. Does the division process come to an end?
2. Divide 1 by 3. Does the division process come to an end? If it does not, do you observe anything interesting? Can you suggest a way of writing the answer?
3. Divide 7 by 12. Does any digit keep repeating itself? Suggest a way to write the answer.
4. Divide 13 by 99. How many digits keep repeating? Suggest a way to write the answer.
5. Divide 41 by 333. How many digits keep repeating? Suggest a way to write the answer.
6. Divide 1 by 7. Suggest a way to write the answer.

There is an end to the division process when we divide 1 by 8, i.e., $1 \div 8 = 0.125$. Therefore, 0.125 is called a **non-recurring** decimal.

When dividing 1 by 3, the digit 3 repeats itself and we get

$$1 \div 3 = \frac{1}{3} = 0.333 \ldots = 0.\dot{3}.$$

$0.\dot{3}$ is called a **recurring decimal**. The dot above '3' indicates that '3' is the repeating digit. Similarly, we write

$$\frac{7}{12} = 0.583\,333 \ldots = 0.58\dot{3} \qquad \frac{13}{99} = 0.131\,313 \ldots = 0.\dot{1}\dot{3}$$

$$\frac{41}{333} = 0.123\,123\,123 \ldots \qquad \frac{1}{7} = 0.142\,857\,142\,857 \ldots$$

$$= 0.\dot{1}2\dot{3} \qquad\qquad\qquad = 0.\dot{1}4285\dot{7}$$

It is more convenient to write $0.\dot{1}2\dot{3}$ as $0.\dot{1}2\dot{3}$ and $0.\dot{1}42\,85\dot{7}$ as $0.\dot{1}42\,85\dot{7}$. Hence, the first dot and the last dot mark the beginning and end of a repeating block of digits.

Some numbers such as $\frac{5}{27}$ $(= 0.185\,185\,185 \ldots)$ cannot be written as decimal with a finite number of decimal places, but result in a number of digits that repeat infinitely. These are called **recurring decimals**.

═══ Exercise 4i ═══

1. Express the following fractions as recurring decimals:

   (a) $\frac{2}{3}$ (b) $\frac{5}{11}$ (c) $\frac{29}{33}$ (d) $\frac{5}{22}$ (e) $\frac{4}{7}$ (f) $\frac{35}{72}$

2. Express each of the following as a decimal and indicate whether it is recurring or non-recurring:

   (a) $\frac{4}{9}$ (b) $\frac{7}{3}$ (c) $\frac{61}{90}$ (d) $\frac{59}{99}$ (e) $\frac{97}{125}$ (f) $\frac{13}{44}$

Order of Decimals

We can represent decimals on the number line. Fig. 4.13 shows the number line with an interval of 1 unit divided into 10 equal parts. The values 0.2, 0.4 and 0.8 are marked as shown below:

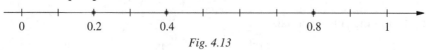

Fig. 4.13

Since 0.2 is to the left of 0.4 and 0.4 is to the left of 0.8, we have $0.2 < 0.4 < 0.8$.

In-Class Activity

1. **(a)** Without using the number line, how can you tell that 0.2 < 0.4 < 0.8?

   (b) Do you agree that 0.2 < 0.4 < 0.8 because 2 < 4 < 8?

2. Is it reasonable to say that 0.7 < 1.4 because 0 < 1 and 1.4 < 1.8 because 4 < 8?

3. Do you agree that 2.02 < 2.04 < 2.08 because 2 < 4 < 8? What about 2.08 < 2.12? Do you agree that 2.08 < 2.12 because 0 < 1? Similarly, can you see that 2.16 > 2.12 because 6 > 2?

The rule for comparing decimals is as follows:

> **Compare the digits which have the same place value from left to right, skipping the equal digits. Examine the first pair of unequal digits, the greater decimal being the decimal with the greater digit.**

Consider the following recurring decimals:

$\frac{1}{7} = 0.\dot{1}42\,85\dot{7}$

$\frac{1}{11} = 0.\dot{0}\dot{9}$

$\frac{1}{13} = 0.\dot{0}76\,92\dot{3}$

$\frac{1}{17}$
$= 0.\dot{0}58\,823\,529\,411\,764\,\dot{1}$

(a) Are the denominators of the fractions prime numbers?
(b) Are there even numbers of digits in the repeating blocks?
(c) Divide each repeating block in half and add the two parts. For example,
142 857 gives
$\begin{array}{r} 142 \\ + 857 \\ \hline 999 \end{array}$
(d) Do you notice an interesting general pattern?

Example 17

Arrange the following sets of decimals in descending order:

(a) 1.209, 1.234   *(b) 7.3, 6.5, 6.9*

▼ **Solution**

(a) 1 . 2 [3] 4 > 1 . 2 [0] 9   since 3 > 0

   ∴   the correct descending order is 1.234, 1.209.

(b) [7] . 3 > [6] . 5 and [6] . 9   since 7 > 6

   6 . [9] > 6 . [5]   since 9 > 5

   ∴   the correct descending order is 7.3, 6.9, 6.5.

Example 18

Arrange $\frac{9}{4}$, 2.23 and 2.232 in ascending order.

▼ **Solution**

$\frac{9}{4} = 2\frac{1}{4} = 2.25$ $\left(\text{Express } \frac{9}{4} \text{ as a decimal using } \frac{1}{4} = 0.25. \right)$

2 . 2 [5] 0 > 2 . 2 [3] 2 and 2 . 2 [3] 0   since 5 > 3

2 . 23 [2] > 2 . 23 [0] since 2 > 0   ⎿── Add 0 to get the same number of decimal places.

∴   the correct ascending order is 2.23, 2.232, $\frac{9}{4}$.

1. Copy the number line given below and indicate 0.3, 0.6, 1.1, 0.15 and 1.45 on it.

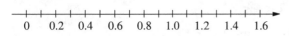

0   0.2   0.4   0.6   0.8   1.0   1.2   1.4   1.6

2. Fill in the boxes with the correct decimals.

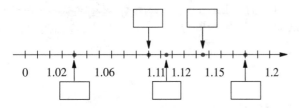

0   1.02   1.06   1.11 1.12   1.15   1.2

3. Represent the following decimals on the number line and arrange them in ascending order:

(a) 2.7, 2.4, 2.1
(b) 3.03, 3.16, 3.12
(c) 0.02, 0.08, 0.035, 0.065
(d) 1.22, 1.28, 1.31, 1.25, 1.38, 1.345

4. Fill in each box with '<' or '>':

(a) 4.13 ☐ 4.17   (b) $\frac{16}{5}$ ☐ 3.19

(c) $5\frac{1}{4}$ ☐ 6.04

(d) 0.005 4 ☐ 0.005 19

(e) $\frac{9}{100}$ ☐ 0.075 ☐ 0.044

(f) 27.11 ☐ 28.01 ☐ 29.001

5. Arrange the following in descending order:

(a) 0.3, 0.8, 0.4   (b) $\frac{5}{4}$, 1.54, $1\frac{3}{4}$

(c) 1.88, 1.13, 1.9

(d) $\frac{13}{20}$, 0.6̇5̇, 0.6̇05̇, 0.6̇5

(e) 3.14, $\frac{22}{7}$, 3.1̇4̇, 3.1̇4

(f) 2.102, 2.012, 2.201, 2.0̇2̇

Addition and Subtraction of Decimals

When two decimals are added together or subtracted from each other, the decimal points must be placed directly one below the other.

Example 19

Evaluate   *(a) 137.45 + 145.25 + 12.106;   (b) 733.75 − 123.98;*
(c) 123.14 + 52.76 − 152.75.

▼ **Solution**

Decimal points aligned.

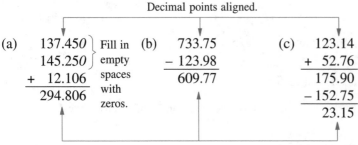

(a)   137.450 ⎱ Fill in   (b)   733.75   (c)   123.14
      145.250 ⎰ empty   − 123.98   + 52.76
    + 12.106   spaces   609.77   175.90
      294.806   with   − 152.75
                zeros.   23.15

Decimal point in the answer.

Decimals are added and subtracted in the same way as whole numbers. It is simplest to work in columns when adding decimals. Keep the decimal points under each other and write the digits in the correct place value columns.

Exercise 4k

1. Do the following additions:

(a)
$$\begin{array}{r} 0.825 \\ 0.073 \\ + \ 0.46 \\ \hline \end{array}$$

(b)
$$\begin{array}{r} 63.008 \\ 18.7 \\ 9.82 \\ + \ 245.2 \\ \hline \end{array}$$

(c)
$$\begin{array}{r} 828 \\ 17.9 \\ 61.38 \\ + \ \ \ 9.182 \\ \hline \end{array}$$

(d)
$$\begin{array}{r} 83.4 \\ 6.78 \\ 135.009 \\ + \ \ 42.014 \\ \hline \end{array}$$

2. Do the following subtractions:

(a)
$$\begin{array}{r} 649.08 \\ - \ 51.63 \\ \hline \end{array}$$

(b)
$$\begin{array}{r} 300 \\ - \ 28.09 \\ \hline \end{array}$$

(c)
$$\begin{array}{r} 9.06 \\ - \ 8.999 \\ \hline \end{array}$$

3. Do the following additions:

(a) 3.45 + 15.52
(b) 0.872 + 56.43 + 239.8
(c) 83.72 + 16.43 + 1.4 + 25.63
(d) 11.42 + 9.865 + 3.1 + 7.98

4. Do the following subtractions:

(a) 7.02 – 4.55   (b) 20 – 6.72
(c) 9.6 – 4.751   (d) 10 – 0.366
(e) 610.57 – 602.57   (f) 325.5 – 18.674

5. (a) Find the sum of 79.8, 7.98 and 0.798.
(b) Subtract 29.7 from 244.93.
(c) What is the difference between the sum of 93.71 and 8.51 and the sum of 79.93 and 33.509?

General Multiplication of Decimals

To find the product of decimals, multiply the numbers in the same way as for whole numbers first. Then put in the decimal point. The number of decimal places in the answer must correspond to the total number of decimal places in the decimals being multiplied.

Consider the product of 23.45 and 2.3.

$$23.45 \times 2.3 = \frac{2\ 345}{100} \times \frac{23}{10}$$
$$= \frac{2\ 345 \times 23}{1\ 000}$$

The product of 2 345 and 23 is obtained as shown below:

$$\begin{array}{r} 2\ 345 \\ \times \ \ \ \ 23 \\ \hline 7\ 035 \\ 46\ 90 \\ \hline 53\ 935 \\ \hline \end{array}$$

$$\therefore \quad 23.45 \times 2.3 = \frac{53\ 935}{1\ 000} = 53.935$$

2 decimal places   1 decimal place   3 decimal places

Example 20

Evaluate (a) 46.75 × 2.12, (b) 256.7 × 0.005 6 and (c) 7.06 × 72.675.

Solution

(a)
$$\begin{array}{r} 4\ 675 \\ \times \ \ \ \ 212 \\ \hline 9\ 350 \\ 46\ 75 \\ 935\ 0 \\ \hline 991\ 100 \\ \hline \end{array}$$

46.75 × 2.12 = 99.110 0.

2 decimal places   2 decimal places   4 decimal places

We may omit the two zeros at the end as they have no value. Hence, the answer is 99.11.

(b)
```
      2 567
    ×    56
     15 402
     128 35
    143 752
```

$$256.7 \times 0.005\ 6 = 1.437\ 52$$

1 decimal place   4 decimal places   5 decimal places

The answer in this case is 1.437 52.

(c)
```
        706    or        72 675    or simply as
    ×   72 675      ×        706                      72 675
        3 530            436 050                   ×      706
        49 42            000 00                       436 050
        423 6           50 872 5                     50 872 5
        1 412          51 308 550                   51 308 550
        49 42
     51 308 550
```

∴ $7.06 \times 72.675 = 513.085\ 5$

Multiplication of a Decimal by Powers of 10

Example 21

Evaluate (a) 2.75 × 10, (b) 2.75 × 100 and (c) 2.75 × 1 000.

▼ **Solution**

(a) $275 \times 10 = 2\ 750$
   ∴ $2.75 \times 10 = 27.50 = 27.5$

(b) $275 \times 100 = 27\ 500$
   ∴ $2.75 \times 100 = 275.00 = 275$

(c) $275 \times 1\ 000 = 275\ 000$
   ∴ $2.75 \times 1\ 000 = 2\ 750.00 = 2\ 750$

As a useful rule,

> **When we multiply a decimal by 10, 100, 1 000, etc., we move the decimal point 1, 2, 3, etc. places respectively to the right.**

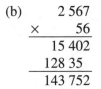

It's a Fact

The Dewey decimal system of classifying library books was invented by the American librarian Melvil Dewey. In this system, books are divided into 10 main categories. Each category is then further divided into 10 smaller categories and so on. Thus, a mathematics book may be numbered 510.7.

Investigate

Compare 2.75 and 27.5. Notice that if we move the decimal point in 2.75 one place to the right, we will get 27.5.

If we move the decimal point in 2.75 two places to the right, we will get 275.

What will we get if we move the decimal point in 2.75 three places to the right?

Division of a Decimal by Powers of 10

How will the position of the decimal point in a decimal change when the decimal is divided by 10, 100, 1 000, etc.?

The rule for division of a decimal by powers of 10 is as follows:

> **When we divide a decimal by 10, 100, 1 000 etc., we move the decimal point 1, 2, 3, etc. places respectively to the left.**

Example 22

Evaluate (a) 48.6 ÷ 10, (b) 45.62 ÷ 100 and (c) 34.81 ÷ 1 000.

Solution

(a) $48.6 \div 10 = 4.86$ (Move the decimal point 1 place to the left.)

(b) $45.62 \div 100 = 045.62 \div 100$ (Move the decimal point 2 places to the left.)
$$= 0.456\ 2$$

(c) $34.81 \div 1\ 000 = 0\ 034.81 \div 1\ 000$ (Move the decimal point 3 places to the left.)
$$= 0.034\ 81$$

Division of a Decimal by a Decimal

Can you form 100 by writing an equation using four 8's?

Dividing a decimal by a whole number is relatively easy.

For example, consider $24.5 \div 5$.

Remember, 24.5 is the **dividend** and 5 is the **divisor**.

```
                ┌──── Line up the decimal points.
                ▼
          4.9
    5 ) 24.5
       − 20
         45
         45
```

$\therefore \quad 24.5 \div 5 = 4.9$

When dividing a decimal by a decimal, it is easier to use the idea of equivalent fractions to convert the divisor to a whole number.

For example, $\dfrac{2.345}{0.05} = \dfrac{2.345}{0.05} \times \dfrac{100}{100}$

$= \dfrac{234.5}{5}$

$= 46.9$ (see working)

Line up the decimal points.

$$\begin{array}{r} 46.9 \\ 5\,\overline{)\,234.5} \\ 20 \\ \hline 34 \\ 30 \\ \hline 4\,5 \\ 4\,5 \\ \hline \end{array}$$

The rule for dividing one decimal by another decimal is as follows:

Multiply the divisor and the dividend by the same power of 10 so that the divisor becomes a whole number, then perform a long division, remembering to line up the decimal points.

Note: It is easier to shift the decimal points the same number of places in the dividend and divisor to make the divisor a whole number.

For example, consider $3.439\,8 \div 0.49$.

$3.439\,8 \div 0.49 = 343.98 \div 49 = 7.02$ (see working)

(Move the decimal points in the dividend and divisor two places to the right.)

$$\begin{array}{r} 7.02 \\ 49\,\overline{)\,343.98} \\ 343 \\ \hline 98 \\ 98 \\ \hline \end{array}$$

Exercise 4l

1. Evaluate the following:
   (a) 0.5×0.6
   (b) 8.41×0.3
   (c) 0.82×0.03
   (d) 7.3×0.9
   (e) 0.08×0.09
   (f) 2.33×0.32

2. Find the exact value of the following:
   (a) $6 \times 0.004\,75$
   (b) 13.75×43
   (c) 7.89×3.2
   (d) 15.68×102
   (e) $120 \times 0.2 \times 3.2$
   (f) 3.418×0.45
   (g) 3.94×0.023
   (h) $0.5 \times 0.4 \times 0.07$

3. Evaluate the following:
   (a) 0.736×10
   (b) 18.517×100
   (c) 15.029×100
   (d) $17.9 \times 1\,000$
   (e) $0.006\,6 \times 1\,000$
   (f) $10\,000 \times 0.012\,4$

4. Evaluate the following:
   (a) $753.8 \div 10$
   (b) $0.029 \div 10$
   (c) $624 \div 100$
   (d) $0.006\,6 \div 100$
   (e) $4\,000 \div 1\,000$
   (f) $86.5 \div 1\,000$

5. Evaluate the following:
   (a) $63.6 \div 6$
   (b) $1.71 \div 0.3$
   (c) $0.165 \div 1.5$
   (d) $720 \div 0.09$
   (e) $0.444 \div 0.04$
   (f) $7.647 \div 0.25$

6. Evaluate:
   (a) $(0.01 \div 0.005)^2$
   (b) $(0.3)^2 \div (0.1)^2$
   (c) $0.8^3 \div 0.2^2$
   (d) $\dfrac{0.055 \times 8.1}{4.5}$
   (e) $\dfrac{0.44 \times 12^2}{0.055}$
   (f) $\dfrac{0.04 \times 0.25^3}{0.008}$

Money

We know that,

> 100 cents = $1
> 75¢ can be written as $0.75.
> $3 and 75¢ can be written as $3.75.
> $3 and 5¢ can be written as $3.05.
> $3 and 50¢ can be written as $3.50.

Common denominations of coins and notes used in Singapore are:

Coins: 1¢, 5¢, 10¢, 20¢, 50¢, $1
Notes: $1, $2, $5, $10, $20, $50, $100, $500

Example 23

I spent $19.90, $26.95 and $46.50 on three different sports items. How much change would I get back if two $50 notes were used to pay for the goods?

▼ **Solution**

Amount of money spent = $19.90 + $26.95 + $46.50
= $93.35

$$
\begin{array}{r}
\$19.90 \\
\$26.95 \\
+ \ \$46.50 \\
\hline
\$93.35
\end{array}
$$

Amount of change = (2 × $50) − $93.35
= $100 − $93.35 = $6.65

Example 24

Bars of soap of a particular brand are sold at $5.40 for 8 in store A and $3.60 for 5 in store B. Which store offers a cheaper price?

▼ **Solution**

Store *A*:   8 for $5.40   or   1 for $5.40 ÷ 8 = 67.5 cents
Store *B*:   5 for $3.60   or   1 for $3.60 ÷ 5 = 72 cents
∴   store *A* offers a cheaper price.

Alternatively,
Store *A*:   8 for $5.40   or   8 × 5 = 40 for $5.40 × 5 = $27
Store *B*:   5 for $3.60   or   5 × 8 = 40 for $3.60 × 8 = $28.80
∴   store *A* offers a cheaper price.

══ Exercise 4m ══

1. How many 5-cent coins will give $3?

2. If 4 pears cost as much as 5 oranges and an orange costs 32¢, how much does a pear cost?

3. Find the total cost of 3 mangoes at $1.40 each, 2 nectarines at $1.95 each and 15 apples at $0.79 for 3.

4. Find the total bill for the following:

$1\frac{1}{2}$ kg of T-bone steak at $9.98 per kg,

$\frac{3}{4}$ kg of beef cubes at $6.96 per kg,

$\frac{1}{2}$ kg of tiger prawns at $14.14 per kg.

$\frac{1}{4}$ kg of boneless chicken breast at $8.28 per kg.

What will be the change if a $50 note is used to pay the bill?

5. Facial tissues are sold in packs of 3 for $1.95 or packs of 5 for $2.80. Which is the better buy?

Rounding Off Decimals

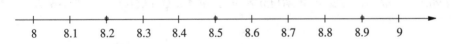

Sometimes it is impractical or meaningless to have too many decimal places in a decimal. For example, it is absurd to give the speed of a car as 48.234 56 km/h. Here, we will learn how to round off a decimal to a desired number of decimal places.

Example *25*

Round off (a) 8.2, (b) 8.9 and (c) 8.5 to the nearest whole number.

▼ **Solution**

```
+---+----+----+----+----+----+----+----+----+----+--->
8   8.1  8.2  8.3  8.4  8.5  8.6  8.7  8.8  8.9  9
```

(a) The number line above shows that 8.2 lies between 8 and 9 but is closer to 8.

∴ 8.2 ≈ 8 (correct to the nearest whole number)

(b) The number line shows that 8.9 lies closer to 9 than to 8.

∴ 8.9 ≈ 9 (correct to the nearest whole number)

(c) Similarly, it shows that 8.5 is exactly halfway between 8 and 9. For such cases, it is common to round up.

∴ 8.5 ≈ 9 (correct to the nearest whole number)

The symbol ≈ represents approximation. For example, when we say that 8.1 is approximately equal to 8, we can write 8.1 ≈ 8.

The following are steps to follow when rounding off a decimal:

1. Include one extra digit for consideration.

2. Simply drop the extra digit if it is less than 5. If it is 5 or more, add 1 to the previous digit before dropping the extra digit.

Example 26

Write the following numbers correct to (i) the nearest whole number, (ii) 2 decimal places and (iii) 3 decimal places:

(a) 9.716 8   (b) 19.214 7   (c) 0.825 14

Solution

(a) (i) 9.716 8 ≈ 10

↑

This digit is more than 5.

(ii) 9.716 8 ≈ 9.72

↑

This digit is more than 5.

(iii) 9.716 8 ≈ 9.717

↑

This digit is more than 5.

(b) (i) 19.214 7 ≈ 19

↑

This digit is less than 5.

(ii) 19.214 7 ≈ 19.21

↑

This digit is less than 5.

(iii) 19.214 7 ≈ 19.215

↑

This digit is more than 5.

(c) (i) 0.825 14 ≈ 1

↑

This digit is more than 5.

(ii) 0.825 14 ≈ 0.83

↑

This digit is 5.

(iii) 0.825 14 ≈ 0.825

↑

This digit is less than 5.

Example 27

Express   (a) $\dfrac{5}{14}$ as a decimal correct to 3 decimal places, and

        (b) $\dfrac{14}{37}$ as a decimal correct to 4 decimal places.

Solution

(a)
```
        0.357 1
   14 ) 5.000 0        This division is carried
        4 2            out up to 4 decimal places,
        ────           1 decimal place more than
         80            required.
         70
        ────
        100
         98
        ────
         2 0
         1 4
        ────
           6
```

(b)
```
        0.378 37
   37 ) 14.000 00       This extra digit is greater
        11 1            than 5.
        ────
         2 90
         2 59
        ─────
          310
          296
        ─────
          14 0
          11 1
        ─────
           2 90
           2 59
          ─────
             31
```

∴ $\dfrac{5}{14}$ ≈ 0.357

(correct to 3 decimal places)

∴ $\dfrac{14}{37}$ ≈ 0.378 4

(correct to 4 decimal places)

Exercise 4n

1. Write the following correct to **(i)** the nearest whole number and **(ii)** 2 decimal places:

   (a) 5.424 67   **(b)** 15.824   **(c)** 7.862   **(d)** 130.829

2. Write the following correct to 3 decimal places:

   (a) 712.892 6   **(b)** 0.002 72   **(c)** 0.827 4   **(d)** 7.024 489

3. Express $\dfrac{2}{7}$ as a decimal and give your answer correct to 3 decimal places.

4. Express the following fractions as decimals correct to 2 decimal places:

   (a) $\dfrac{4}{9}$ **(b)** $\dfrac{7}{11}$ **(c)** $\dfrac{9}{14}$ **(d)** $\dfrac{11}{15}$

 Use of Calculator

To do operations involving fractions and decimals, we need the Decimal Point Key $\boxed{.}$ and the Fraction Key $\boxed{a^b/c}$.

For example,

(a) To find 14.7×8.74, press $14\ \boxed{.}\ 7\ \boxed{\times}\ 8\ \boxed{.}\ 74\ \boxed{=}$ to get 128.478.

(b) To find $3\dfrac{2}{5} \div \dfrac{3}{4}$, press $3\ \boxed{a^b/c}\ 2\ \boxed{a^b/c}\ 5\ \boxed{\div}\ 3\ \boxed{a^b/c}\ 4\ \boxed{=}$ and the display screen shows

   $4 \rfloor 8 \rfloor 15$, i.e., $3\dfrac{2}{5} \div \dfrac{3}{4} = 4\dfrac{8}{15}$.

(c) To find $1\dfrac{1}{5} + 3\dfrac{2}{3} \times 1\dfrac{3}{4}$, press $1\ \boxed{a^b/c}\ 1\ \boxed{a^b/c}\ 5\ \boxed{+}\ 3\ \boxed{a^b/c}\ 2\ \boxed{a^b/c}\ 3\ \boxed{\times}\ 1\ \boxed{a^b/c}\ 3\ \boxed{a^b/c}\ 4$

   $\boxed{=}$ to get $7 \rfloor 37 \rfloor 60$, i.e. $7\dfrac{37}{60}$.

Some calculators might have different keys for displaying decimals and fractions. Check the manual of your calculator before using it.

Example 28

Evaluate each of the following using a calculator:

(a) $2.6 \times 2.7 \times (3.5 + 6.1)$ (b) $\dfrac{3.2^3 + 4.3^2}{\sqrt{47.5} - 2.74}$ (c) $\dfrac{\dfrac{2}{5} + \dfrac{3}{4}}{1\dfrac{2}{3} + \dfrac{3}{4} - \dfrac{5}{6}}$

Solution

The steps: Final display:

(a) $2\ \boxed{.}\ 6\ \boxed{\times}\ 2\ \boxed{.}\ 7\ \boxed{\times}\ \boxed{(}\ 3\ \boxed{.}\ 5\ \boxed{+}\ 6\ \boxed{.}\ 1\ \boxed{)}\ \boxed{=}$ 67.392

(b) $3.2\ \boxed{y^x}\ 3\ \boxed{+}\ 4.3\ \boxed{x^2}\ \boxed{=}\ \boxed{\div}\ \boxed{(}\ \boxed{\sqrt{}}\ 47.5 - 2.74\ \boxed{)}\ \boxed{=}$ 12.34530324

(c) 1 $\boxed{a^b/c}$ 2 $\boxed{a^b/c}$ 3 $\boxed{+}$ 3 $\boxed{a^b/c}$ 4 $\boxed{-}$ 5 $\boxed{a^b/c}$ 6 $\boxed{=}$ $\boxed{\text{STO}}$

2 $\boxed{a^b/c}$ 5 $\boxed{+}$ 3 $\boxed{a^b/c}$ 4 $\boxed{=}$ $\boxed{÷}$ $\boxed{\text{RCL}}$ $\boxed{=}$

Making words with your calculator.

Most calculators have a liquid crystal display panel. Some of the numbers displayed look like letters when viewed upside down. The letters available are shown below.

0 = O	5 = S
1 = l	6 = g
3 = E	7 = L
4 = h	8 = B

Enter 0.773 4 and turn your calculator upside down. What do you see?

Can you try to form some words with your calculator? Take note that you have to reverse the order of the digits to be entered.

Example 29

John uses his calculator to compute (a) 43.958 12 – 28.340 75 + 41.823 58 and (b) $\dfrac{502 \times \sqrt{24.98}}{9.96}$. *He obtains the following answers: (a) 57 and (b) 346, both correct to the nearest whole number. Estimate the results of John's calculations and state whether John has obtained the correct answer.*

▼ **Solution**

(a) $43.958\,12 - 28.340\,75 + 41.823\,58 \approx 44 - 28 + 42$
$$= 58$$

Since John's answer is close to the estimated value, it is likely that he has obtained the correct answer.

(b) $\dfrac{502 \times \sqrt{24.98}}{9.96} \approx \dfrac{500 \times \sqrt{25}}{10}$
$$= 250$$

Since John's answer is not very close to the estimated value, it is likely that he has not obtained the correct answer.

Note: The correct answer to $\dfrac{502 \times \sqrt{24.98}}{9.96}$ is 252 (correct to the nearest whole number).

═══ Exercise 4o ═══

1. Use your calculator to evaluate each of the following, giving your answer correct to 3 decimal places if it is not exact:

(a) 37.56×12.45

(b) $44.75 \div 1.25$

(c) $121.35 - 12.75 + 46.32$

(d) $52.35 \times 6.78 \div 13.57$

(e) $5.69 + 3.64 \times 2.79$

(f) $55.69 - 6.94 \div 1.78$

2. Use your calculator to evaluate each of the following, giving your answer as (i) a fraction and (ii) a decimal correct to 2 decimal places:

(a) $\dfrac{1}{5} + \dfrac{3}{4}$

(b) $3\dfrac{2}{3} - 1\dfrac{5}{6}$

(c) $3\dfrac{1}{5} \times 1\dfrac{2}{3} - 1\dfrac{1}{6}$

(d) $\left(3\dfrac{1}{3}\right)^2 \times 4\dfrac{5}{6}$

(e) $7\dfrac{1}{8} \div 4\dfrac{3}{4} + 1\dfrac{5}{6}$

(f) $\left(5\dfrac{3}{4}\right)^3 \div \left(4\dfrac{3}{5}\right)^2$

3. Make an estimate of the following and then use your calculator to work out the answers correct to 2 decimal places.

	Estimate	Answer (correct to 2 decimal places)
(a) 97.45 + 20.15 − 49.89	_____	_____
(b) 80.17 ÷ 7.91 × 99.93	_____	_____
(c) 0.996 3 + 101.11 × 30.96	_____	_____
(d) 300.972 − 99.983 2 ÷ 10.106 7	_____	_____
(e) $\dfrac{9.879 \times 46.071}{22.998\,2}$	_____	_____

Summary

1. A fraction is a number of the form $\dfrac{a}{b}$ where $b \neq 0$ and a, b are whole numbers. a is called the **numerator** and b is called the **denominator**.

2. $\dfrac{2}{4}$, $\dfrac{3}{6}$, $\dfrac{4}{8}$ and $\dfrac{5}{10}$ have the same value as $\dfrac{1}{2}$. They are equivalent fractions of $\dfrac{1}{2}$.

3. A **proper fraction** is one whose numerator is less than the denominator, e.g. $\dfrac{2}{5}$, $\dfrac{3}{7}$.

4. An **improper fraction** is one whose numerator is the same as or is greater than the denominator. e.g. $\dfrac{8}{8}$, $\dfrac{7}{4}$.

5. A **mixed number** is one that contains an integral part and a fractional part, e.g. $1\dfrac{3}{4}$, $2\dfrac{1}{2}$.

6. In general, if two fractions have the same denominator, then the larger the numerator, the larger the fraction. In contrast, if two fractions have the same numerator, the larger the denominator, the smaller the fraction.

7. The value of a fraction remains unchanged if both the numerator and denominator are multiplied or divided by the same number, e.g. $\dfrac{3}{5} = \dfrac{3 \times 4}{5 \times 4} = \dfrac{12}{20}$ and $\dfrac{16}{40} = \dfrac{16 \div 4}{40 \div 4} = \dfrac{4}{10}$.

8. To **simplify** a fraction is to reduce it to its **lowest terms** or simplest form, e.g. $\dfrac{16}{40} = \dfrac{4}{10} = \dfrac{2}{5}$.

9. A decimal is a fraction whose denominator is 10 or a power of 10.

10. When we **multiply** a decimal by 10, 100, 1 000, etc., we move the decimal point 1, 2, 3, etc. places respectively to the **right**.

11. When we **divide** a decimal by 10, 100, 1 000, etc., we move the decimal point 1, 2, 3, etc. places respectively to the **left**.

12. Steps for rounding off a decimal:
    (a) Include one extra digit for consideration.
    (b) Drop the extra digit if it is less than **5**. Otherwise, add 1 to the previous digit before dropping the extra digit.

Review Questions 4

1. Arrange the following fractions in ascending order:
   (a) $\dfrac{3}{4}, \dfrac{7}{10}, \dfrac{4}{5}$
   (b) $\dfrac{2}{3}, \dfrac{7}{12}, \dfrac{5}{8}$
   (c) $\dfrac{7}{12}, \dfrac{4}{7}, \dfrac{9}{14}, \dfrac{25}{42}$

2. Arrange the following fractions in descending order:
   (a) $\dfrac{5}{8}, \dfrac{7}{12}, \dfrac{5}{9}, \dfrac{13}{24}$
   (b) $\dfrac{6}{35}, \dfrac{5}{21}, \dfrac{2}{7}, \dfrac{4}{15}$
   (c) $\dfrac{2}{5}, \dfrac{6}{11}, \dfrac{7}{15}, \dfrac{9}{20}, \dfrac{13}{25}$

3. Yuanwei weighs $45\dfrac{13}{24}$ kg. Xinyu weighs $45\dfrac{5}{9}$ kg. Who is heavier?

4. Evaluate the following, expressing your answers in the simplest form:
   (a) $2\dfrac{1}{3} + 1\dfrac{5}{12}$
   (b) $4\dfrac{5}{7} - 2\dfrac{5}{21}$
   (c) $\dfrac{41}{12} - \dfrac{23}{8}$
   (d) $\dfrac{2}{3} - \dfrac{1}{6} + \dfrac{4}{5}$
   (e) $8\dfrac{1}{3} - 1\dfrac{1}{9} - \dfrac{5}{18} - 2\dfrac{5}{6}$
   (f) $2\dfrac{17}{27} - \dfrac{1}{18} + \dfrac{61}{72} - \dfrac{1}{54}$

5. Calculate the following:
   (a) $2\dfrac{3}{11} \times 1\dfrac{8}{25}$
   (b) $3\dfrac{3}{4} \div 2\dfrac{1}{2}$
   (c) $1\dfrac{6}{15} \times 3\dfrac{8}{9} \div \dfrac{7}{8}$
   (d) $\dfrac{2\dfrac{3}{5} - 1\dfrac{1}{2}}{3\dfrac{2}{3}}$
   (e) $1\dfrac{1}{4} - \left(\dfrac{2}{3} \times \dfrac{1}{3} + \dfrac{1}{9}\right) \div \dfrac{4}{9}$
   (f) $\dfrac{3}{49} \div \dfrac{1}{7} + \left(\dfrac{1}{5} + \dfrac{7}{10}\right) \times \dfrac{4}{21}$
   (g) $8\dfrac{1}{2} - 2\dfrac{1}{3} - 1\dfrac{6}{7} \times \dfrac{3}{13}$
   (h) $2 \times 2\dfrac{2}{5} \times \left(3\dfrac{1}{4} + 1\dfrac{7}{16}\right)$

6. Evaluate the following without using a calculator:
   (a) $17.2 + 13.8$
   (b) $16.83 - 7.57$
   (c) 1.72×0.091
   (d) $0.042 \div 0.35$
   (e) $80 \times 0.6 \times 2.5$
   (f) $16.52 \div 0.04$

7. Use a calculator to evaluate each of the following, giving your answer correct to 2 decimal places if it is not exact:
   (a) $\left(1\dfrac{1}{4}\right)^3 \times \dfrac{6}{25} \div \dfrac{5}{6}$
   (b) $\dfrac{9.35^2 + 96.1^3}{65.9^3 - 38.4^2}$
   ★(c) $\dfrac{\dfrac{4}{7} + \dfrac{2}{9}}{2\dfrac{3}{5} - 1\dfrac{5}{8} + 5\dfrac{3}{4}}$
   (d) $522.76 \times 647.15 \div 322.11 + 631.7 \div 524.38$
   (e) $\dfrac{4}{9} \times \left(\dfrac{5}{8} + \dfrac{5}{6} - \dfrac{2}{3}\right) \div \dfrac{2}{5} \times \left(\dfrac{3}{4} + \dfrac{1}{5}\right)$

8. John paid $9.25 for a number of packets of instant noodles costing $1.85 for 5. How many packets of noodles did John buy? If he were to buy 40 packets of the same noodles, would $15 be enough to pay for them?

Problem Solving

1. Which of the two fractions $\dfrac{1993}{1994}$ and $\dfrac{1995}{1996}$ is larger? Explain the reason without making the denominators of the two fractions the same or converting the fractions into decimals.

2. We can write $\dfrac{1}{6}$ as the sum of two fractions with numerators equal to 1. For example,
$$\frac{1}{6} = \frac{1}{12} + \frac{1}{12} \text{ and } \frac{1}{6} = \frac{1}{7} + \frac{1}{42}.$$
There are three other ways of writing $\dfrac{1}{6}$ in the same form. Can you find them?

3. Calculate $\left(5\dfrac{1}{3} + \dfrac{2\frac{1}{4} - 1\frac{1}{5}}{1\frac{1}{3} + 1\frac{1}{2}} \right) \times \dfrac{1\frac{1}{3} + 1\frac{1}{2}}{5\frac{1}{3} \times \left(1\frac{1}{3} + 1\frac{1}{2} \right) + 2\frac{1}{4} - 1\frac{1}{5}}$.

4. Evaluate $\dfrac{1}{1 \times 2} + \dfrac{1}{2 \times 3} + \dfrac{1}{3 \times 4} + \dfrac{1}{4 \times 5} + \ldots + \dfrac{1}{1995 \times 1996}$.

5. Evaluate $0.0\dot{1} + 0.1\dot{2} + 0.2\dot{3} + 0.3\dot{4} + 0.4\dot{5} + 0.5\dot{6}$.

6. $\dfrac{4}{7}$, $0.\dot{5}\dot{1}$, $\dfrac{23}{47}$, $0.5\dot{1}$, $\dfrac{13}{25}$ and $\dfrac{5}{9}$ are 6 of 8 numbers. When these numbers are arranged in ascending order the fourth number is $0.5\dot{1}$. If these numbers are arranged in descending order, which is the fourth number?

7. Identify a rule and then write the next three terms for the sequence $1, \dfrac{3}{2}, \dfrac{7}{4}, \dfrac{15}{8}, \dfrac{31}{16}, \dfrac{63}{32} \ldots$. What can you say about the value of the term as it continues?

8. In a boys' school, $\dfrac{5}{8}$ of the boys play football and $\dfrac{4}{7}$ play rugby. If every boy plays at least one of the two games, find the fraction of the boys who play both.

Revision Exercise I No. 1

1. Evaluate the following mentally:
   (a) $12 + 4 + 18$
   (b) $2 \times 16 \times 5$
   (c) 32×25
   (d) 66×64

2. Estimate the following mentally, giving your answer correct to 1 significant figure:
   (a) $101 \times \sqrt{81}$
   (b) $\sqrt[3]{26} \times 502 \div 49$
   (c) $\sqrt{65} \times \sqrt[3]{63} \div 17$

3. Find the HCF and LCM of 12, 15 and 18.

4. Evaluate the following:
   (a) $18 - 18 \times \dfrac{5}{6}$
   (b) $\left(7\dfrac{1}{6} - 2\dfrac{7}{15}\right) \div 9\dfrac{2}{5}$
   (c) $\dfrac{2}{2 + \dfrac{1}{1 + \frac{1}{2}}}$

5. Write down the next two terms in the following number sequences:
   (a) $5, 9, 13, 17, \ldots$
   (b) $\dfrac{1}{2}, \dfrac{2}{3}, \dfrac{3}{4}, \dfrac{4}{5}, \ldots$
   (c) $1 \times 3, 2 \times 4, 3 \times 5, 4 \times 6, \ldots$

6. Use a calculator to evaluate each of the following, giving your answer correct to 2 decimal places:
   (a) $\sqrt{89} + \sqrt[3]{116} - \sqrt{41}$
   (b) $12.79^3 \div (5.83)^2$
   (c) $\sqrt{9.69^3 - 5.67^2}$
   (d) $\dfrac{172.68 \times (12.93)^2}{13.84^3}$

7. Find the value of the following:
   (a) $\dfrac{\sqrt{9} + \sqrt{144}}{\sqrt{25}}$
   (b) $\dfrac{2 \times \sqrt{64} + 3 \times \sqrt[3]{8}}{\sqrt{121}}$
   (c) $\dfrac{1}{8} + \dfrac{1}{\sqrt[3]{125}} - \dfrac{1}{4}$
   (d) $\sqrt{\dfrac{7}{8} + \dfrac{4}{5} + \dfrac{9}{8} + \dfrac{6}{5}}$

8. (a) Round off 2 876 to the nearest hundred.
   (b) Express $\dfrac{2}{3}$ as a decimal correct to 2 decimal places.
   (c) Change 0.425 into a fraction in its simplest form.
   (d) Which of the decimals, 2.9, 2.84 and 2.847, is the smallest?

9. A family of 2 adults and 4 children visited Sentosa during the June school holidays. An adult ticket costs $18.90 and a child-ticket cost $12.80 during the promotional period. If the family enjoyed the promotion price,
   (a) what is the total cost of the tickets for the family?
   (b) what would be the change if a $100-note was used to purchase the tickets?

10. A teacher distributes 255 pencils, 425 sheets of graph paper and 595 sheets of writing paper equally to a group of students.
   (a) Calculate the smallest and largest possible number of students in the group.
   (b) Calculate the smallest and largest number of pencils, graph paper and writing paper each student can receive.

Revision Exercise I No. 2

1. Write down the next three terms in the following number sequences:
   (a) $91, 87, 82, 76, \ldots$
   (b) $1, 4, 3, 6, 5, \ldots$
   (c) $-48, -36, -24, -12, \ldots$

2. Evaluate each of the following:
   (a) $3 \times 0.74 - \dfrac{3}{4} + 4.006$
   (b) $\dfrac{2}{5} \times 2.5 + 4.5 \div 1.5$

3. $\dfrac{4}{9}$ of the passengers in an MRT train are men, $\dfrac{2}{5}$ of them are women and the rest are children. If there are 72 women, find
   (a) the total number of passengers in the train;
   (b) how many more men than children there are in the train.

4. (a) Find the LCM of the following:
   (i) 56, 63
   (ii) 8, 56, 140
   (iii) 35, 45, 55

(b) Find the HCF of the following:
  (i) 32, 48, 72   **(ii)** 54, 90, 240

5. Evaluate

(a) $45 \times (6 + 2) \div 18$;

(b) $[66 - 6 \times 6 \div (6 + 6)] - 6$;

(c) $180 \div \{23 - [30 \div (3 \times 7 - 15)]\}$.

6. (a) Express $\dfrac{5}{16}$ as a decimal.

(b) Change 0.225 into a fraction in its lowest form.

(c) Express 9.906 correct to
  (i) 2 decimal places;
  (ii) 2 significant figures.

7. Cane sugar is sold at $2.88 for a 900 g pack or at $1.65 for a 500 g pack. Which is more expensive and by how much per kilogram?

8. Find the exact value of

(a) 0.28×3.5 **(b)** $17.9 - 5.67$

(c) $0.816 \div 0.4$ **(d)** $\sqrt{25} - \sqrt[3]{27}$

9. Consider the number pattern:

$$1^2 - 2 \times 1 = -1,$$
$$2^2 - 2 \times 2 = 0,$$
$$3^2 - 2 \times 3 = 3,$$
$$4^2 - 2 \times 4 = 8,$$
$$5^2 - 2 \times 5 = 15,$$
$$\vdots$$
$$x^2 - 2x \quad = 63,$$
$$\vdots$$

(a) Write down the 6th line in the number pattern.

(b) Find the value of x.

10. Evaluate each of the following, giving your answer as a fraction in its lowest term:

(a) $2\dfrac{1}{5} + 3\dfrac{4}{5} \times \dfrac{1}{2}$ **(b)** $4\dfrac{1}{2} \times \dfrac{3}{4} + \dfrac{1}{4}$

(c) $5\dfrac{1}{3} - 2\dfrac{1}{2} \div \dfrac{1}{2}$

Revision Exercise I No. 3

1. Find the difference between $5^2 - \left(3\dfrac{1}{2}\right)^2$ and $\left(5 - 3\dfrac{1}{2}\right)^2$.

2. Find the exact value of

(a) $33.559 \div 0.037$

(b) $2 \times 2.41 \times (3.27 + 1.44)$

(c) $0.2 \times 0.3 \div 0.001\ 2$

3. (a) Express 0.56 as a fraction in its lowest terms.

(b) Express $\dfrac{2}{7}$ as a decimal, giving your answer correct to 2 decimal places.

4. Evaluate the following giving each answer as a fraction in its lowest terms:

(a) $3\dfrac{1}{4} - 2\dfrac{3}{5}$ **(b)** $\dfrac{1}{4} \div \left(\dfrac{1}{3} + \dfrac{3}{4}\right)$

(c) $\sqrt{\dfrac{7}{8} \times \dfrac{3}{4} \div 1\dfrac{1}{6}}$ **(d)** $\dfrac{2\dfrac{3}{4} - \dfrac{3}{8}}{\dfrac{8}{9} \times \dfrac{3}{4} \div \dfrac{4}{17}}$

5. If $3\ 920 = 2^x \times 5^y \times 7^z$, find the possible values of x, y and z.

6. (a) Express **(i)** 48 and **(ii)** 324 as a product of prime factors.

(b) Find the HCF of
  (i) 49, 63;   **(ii)** 36, 54, 75.

(c) Find the LCM of
  (i) 56, 72;   **(ii)** 21, 35, 42.

7. Write down the next two terms in each of the following number sequences:

(a) $-9, -6, -3, 0, \ldots$

(b) 33, 44, 55, 66, $\ldots$

(c) 13, 26, 39, 52, $\ldots$

8. List all the prime numbers between 15 and 45.

9. Mrs Lee was given $1\ 200 every month for the household expenses. She used $\dfrac{17}{24}$ of it to buy food for the family, $\dfrac{5}{7}$ of the remainder for clothes and other expenses. She puts the remaining money into the bank as savings for the family. Find the amount she put into the bank.

10. (a) Arrange the fractions $\dfrac{3}{4}, \dfrac{5}{6}, \dfrac{11}{12}, \dfrac{8}{9}$ in ascending order.

(b) Arrange the fractions $\dfrac{2}{5}, \dfrac{1}{4}, \dfrac{3}{8}, \dfrac{1}{3}$ in descending order.

Revision Exercise I No. 4

1. Evaluate
   (a) $3.09 \div 1.03$ (b) $52.6 - 3.5 \times 1.4$
   (c) $12.3 - 2 \times (3 - 5.4)$
   (d) $3.5 \div 4 - 2.6$

2. Simplify
   (a) $\dfrac{11}{32} + \dfrac{9}{16} - \dfrac{5}{48}$
   (b) $\dfrac{7}{16} + \dfrac{1}{4} \times \dfrac{2}{3} - \dfrac{3}{8}$

3. Is 212 345 divisible by
   (a) 2;   (b) 3;   (c) 4;
   (d) 5;   (e) 9;   (f) 11?

4. (a) Express the following fractions as decimals:
   (i) $\dfrac{7}{40}$ (ii) $\dfrac{33}{80}$ (iii) $\dfrac{9}{25}$ (iv) $\dfrac{21}{16}$
   (b) Express each of the following decimals as a fraction in its lowest terms:
   (i) 0.066   (ii) 0.575
   (iii) 0.875   (iv) 0.437 5

5. A water pump can fill a tank at the rate of 750 litres per hour. A tank has a capacity of 9 000 litres. Find the time needed to fill $\dfrac{7}{15}$ of the tank.

6. The entrance fee to an amusement park during a promotional period was \$4.75 for an adult and \$2.85 per child. Mr Ong took all his little nephews to the park and paid a total of \$30.40 as entrance fee. How many children did Mr Ong bring?

7. Mrs Goh bought 4 bags of rice at \$5.28 per bag, 5 packets of biscuits at \$1.25 per packet and 2.8 kg of meat at \$7.40 per kg. Assuming that GST was absorbed by the retailer, calculate the total amount she spent. What will be the change if she paid for all these with a \$50-note?

8. Find the LCM and HCF of
   (a) 12, 16, 32 .   (b) 20, 24, 140.

9. Write down the next two terms in the following number sequences:

   (a) 1, 8, 27, 64, ...
   (b) 4, 16, 64, 256, ...
   (c) 1, 2, 4, 7, 11, ...

10. (a) Which of the fractions, $\dfrac{1}{2}, \dfrac{3}{7}, \dfrac{2}{5}$ and $\dfrac{4}{9}$, is the largest?
    (b) Which of the fractions, $\dfrac{5}{6}, \dfrac{3}{5}, \dfrac{2}{9}$ and $\dfrac{3}{10}$, is the smallest?

Revision Exercise I No. 5

1. Simplify the following:
   (a) $\left(3\dfrac{1}{4} + 2\dfrac{1}{6} - 4\dfrac{3}{8}\right) \div 1\dfrac{2}{3}$
   (b) $\left(2\dfrac{1}{2} + \dfrac{1}{7}\right) \div \left(3\dfrac{1}{2} - 2\dfrac{1}{13}\right)$
   (c) $2\dfrac{2}{3} \times 1\dfrac{3}{4} + 1\dfrac{7}{8} \times \dfrac{1}{2}$
   (d) $1\dfrac{3}{4} + 1\dfrac{5}{16} \times \dfrac{4}{9} - 1\dfrac{5}{8}$

2. 3 cars leave Town A for Town B on a straight road. Car A stops every 60 m, Car B stops every 80 m and Car C stops every 180 m. After how many metres will the 3 cars stop at the same place?

3. Evaluate each of the following showing each step clearly:
   (a) $(15 - 6)^2 + (18 - 15)^3 - \sqrt[3]{64}$
   (b) $26 - 46 \times 0.5 + 2^3$

4. Evaluate
   (a) $\sqrt{6\,400}$ (b) $\sqrt{1\dfrac{9}{16}}$
   (c) $\sqrt[3]{2\dfrac{10}{27}}$ (d) $\sqrt[3]{2\dfrac{93}{125}}$

5. Use a calculator to evaluate
   (a) $\sqrt{88} + \sqrt[3]{117} - \sqrt{39}$;
   (b) $\dfrac{6\sqrt[3]{10} + 5\sqrt{17}}{9\sqrt{5}}$;
   (c) $\sqrt[3]{36.05^3 - (4.85 + 0.28)^2}$;
   giving each answer correct to 2 decimal places.

6. Write down
   (a) all the positive even integers less than 15;
   (b) all the positive odd integers less than or equal to 11;
   (c) all the prime numbers less than 25;
   (d) all the factors of 32.

7. Find the HCF and LCM of the following:
   (a) 48, 64   (b) 54, 63, 84
   (c) 60, 72, 120   (d) 64, 84, 112

8. Tickets to an Arts festival concert are priced at $35 each for seats at the front rows and at $15 each for seats at the back rows. There are 12 front rows with 26 seats in each row and 18 back rows with 28 seats in each row. If $\frac{5}{6}$ of all the front row seats and $\frac{6}{7}$ of the back row seats are sold, how much is the total in ticket sales?

9. (a) Express, as a fraction, the difference between the largest and the smallest fraction of the following:
   $$\frac{4}{7}, \frac{5}{8} \text{ and } \frac{7}{12}.$$
   (b) Which of the fractions, $\frac{2}{5}, \frac{6}{11}, \frac{7}{15}, \frac{9}{20}$ and $\frac{13}{25}$, is the smallest?
   (c) Arrange the following numbers in ascending order:
   $$0.571\dot{4}, 0.57\dot{1}\dot{4}, \frac{4}{7}, 0.5\dot{7}1\dot{4}$$

10. Write down the next three terms in the following number sequences:
    (a) 2, 5, 10, 17, ...
    (b) 10, 2, 0.3, 0.04, ...
    (c) 10, 8, 6, 4, ...
    (d) 1, 4, 5, 9, 14, ...
    (e) 1, $\frac{1}{2}, \frac{1}{4}, \frac{1}{8}$, ...

CHAPTER 5

Real Numbers

In this chapter, you will learn how to

- ▲ use negative numbers in practical situations;
- ▲ perform calculations with integers;
- ▲ recognise rational and irrational numbers;
- ▲ perform calculations with rational numbers;
- ▲ use a calculator to find an approximate value of an irrational number.

Preliminary Problem

The main peak of the Jade Dragon Snow Mountain in China is at an altitude of 5 596 metres above sea level. Riding in a cable car, the two young ladies reached the altitude of 4 500 metres, from which they climbed another 150 metres to arrive at the Dragon Spruce Meadow. At a temperature of 10°C below freezing point, the ladies enjoyed having a photo taken with their fruit of labour.

In this chapter you will learn about negative numbers, which were first used by the Indians for accounting purposes in the 6th and 7th centuries. If we take the altitude of the Dragon Spruce Meadow to be 0 metre altitude, then we use +946 m to indicate that the peak is 946 m above the Dragon Spruce Meadow and –150 m to indicate that the cable car terminal is 150 m below the Dragon Spruce Meadow. Similarly, we use –10°C to represent a temperature that is 10°C below 0°C.

Negative Numbers

The concept of **negative numbers** is derived from many of our real life situations. Here are some examples.

We normally record the temperature 10°C above zero as 10°C, and correspondingly, we record the temperature 10°C below zero as –10°C.

Sea level is usually taken as zero altitude. If a bird flies 50 m above zero altitude, we use 50 m to represent how high the bird is flying above sea level.

Correspondingly, if a submarine dives in 50 m, we will use –50 m to represent its depth below sea level.

In business, if a store sells an item $3 above the cost price and another item $3 below the cost price, then we can use +$3 and –$3 to record how much profit and loss the store makes on the two transactions respectively.

Tom and Johnson walk away from the same place but in opposite directions. If Tom walked 15 m heading towards the East, and Johnson walked 12 m heading towards the West, then we can use 15 m and –12 m to record how far and in which directions they walked respectively.

Fig. 5.1

In the above examples, 10, 50, 3 and 15 are called positive numbers, and –10, –50, –3 and –12 are called negative numbers. Can you give some other examples where both positive and negative numbers are used?

In Mathematics, numbers with the sign "–" are called negative numbers. "–" is read as "negative".

Integers

Each positive number (natural numbers) corresponds to a negative number. For example, +1 (for emphasis, we attach '+' sign to a positive number) corresponds to –1, +2 to –2, +3 to –3, and so on.

The whole numbers (zero and the natural numbers) together with the negative numbers, are called **integers**.

The integers can be displayed on the number line as shown in Fig. 5.2.

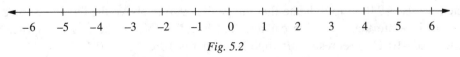

Fig. 5.2

The natural numbers 1, 2, 3, 4, … are also called **positive integers**. The corresponding negative numbers –1, –2, –3, –4, … are called **negative integers**. Zero is an integer but is neither positive nor negative.

From the number line, 3 < 4 but –3 > –4. Why?

Numerical Value or Absolute Value of an Integer

Positions of –2 and 2 on the number line indicate that –2 < 2 but they are of the same **distance** from zero. –2 and 2 are said to have the same **numerical value**, or absolute value.

The numerical or absolute value of a number is its distance from zero on the number line.

The numerical or absolute value of a number is **always positive**.

We write the numerical or absolute value of a number x as $|x|$. Thus, $|-2| = |2| = 2$.

Example 1

Given the numbers –8, 9 and –20,

(a) arrange the numbers in ascending order;   *(b) find the numerical values of the numbers;*
(c) arrange the numerical values of the numbers in descending order.

▼ Solution

(a) The required arrangement of the numbers is –20, –8, 9 since –20 < –8 < 9.

(b) Distances between –8, 9, –20 and zero on the number line are 8 units, 9 units, 20 units respectively.

∴ $|-8| = 8$, $|9| = 9$, $|-20| = 20$.

(c) The required arrangement of the numerical values is 20, 9, 8.

═══ Exercise 5a ═══

1. **(a)** Dennis withdrew $50 from his savings account. Is this transaction considered positive or negative?

   (b) Copy and complete the following:
   (i)   An ascent of –20 m means a descent of _____ m.
   (ii)   A clockwise rotation of –90° means an anticlockwise rotation of _____°.
   (iii) Walking 9 km from East to West means walking _____ km from West to East.

2. Copy and complete the following:

   (a) If –6 represents 6 m below sea-level, then +30 represents _____.
   (b) If +40 represents depositing $40 in the bank, then a withdrawal of $35 is _____.
   (c) If +60° represents rotating 60° clockwise, then –30° represents _____.
   (d) If +45 represents a speed of 45 km/h of a car moving to the East, then –45 represents

   _____.

3. Suppose time is measured in years and zero stands for the year 2000.

  (a) What number stands for the year 1999?   **(b)** What number stands for the year 2002?
  (c) What number stands for the year 1996?

4. Put the correct sign, < or >, between each pair of temperatures below.

  (a) $-4°, 4°$ **(b)** $8°, -2°$ **(c)** $-13°, -5°$ **(d)** $-1°, 5°$ **(e)** $-3°, -4°$ **(f)** $-20°, -19°$

5. Translate each of the following into a mathematical statement using either a < or a > sign:

  (a) A temperature of $-5°$ is colder than a temperature of $12°$.
  (b) A gain of \$200 is better than a loss of \$120.
  (c) A depth of 40 m below sea level is lower than a depth of 25 m below sea level.

6. Arrange the numbers in each group in ascending order.

  (a) $-2, -6, 0, -60, -90$ **(b)** $1, -1\ 500, 2, -1$

7. Use a number line to illustrate each of the following:

  (a) $-5, -2, 0, 5, -3$ **(b)** $\ldots, -10, -8, -6, -4, \ldots$
  (c) The set of integers greater than -4 and less than 2.
  (d) The set of integers between -2 and $+6$.

8. Fill in the boxes with > or <:

  (a) $8\ \square\ -8$ **(b)** $-11\ \square\ -6$ **(c)** $0\ \square\ -2$ **(d)** $(-12)^2\ \square\ -200$

  (e) $-\sqrt{64}\ \square\ \sqrt[3]{125}$ **(f)** $\sqrt[3]{-27}\ \square\ -\sqrt{16}$

Addition of Integers

You have learnt how to add positive integers. You have also learnt how to add them using the number line. Below is an example.

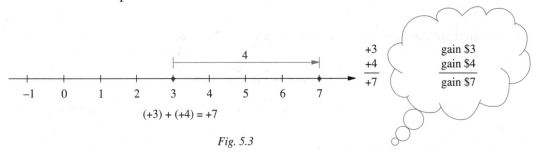

$$(+3) + (+4) = +7$$

$+3$	gain \$3
$+4$	gain \$4
$+7$	gain \$7

Fig. 5.3

Now, let us use the number line to add two negative integers e.g. -2 and -7. (See Fig. 5.4)

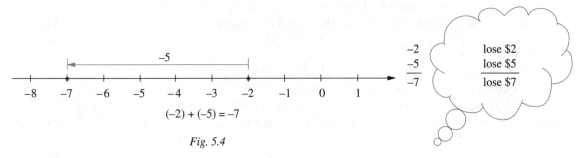

$$(-2) + (-5) = -7$$

-2	lose \$2
-5	lose \$5
-7	lose \$7

Fig. 5.4

The above discussion suggests the following rules for adding two numbers with the **same signs**.

1. To add two positive numbers, add their numerical values. The result is positive.

$$(+x) + (+y) = +(x + y)$$

To make the rule easy for remembering, you may simply remember

$$(+) \ + \ (+) \ = \ (+)$$
$$(\text{gain}) + (\text{gain}) = (\text{gain})$$

2. To add two negative numbers, add their numerical values and place a negative sign before the result.

$$(-x) + (-y) = -(x + y)$$

To make the rule easy for remembering, you may simply remember

$$(-) \ + \ (-) \ = \ (-)$$
$$(\text{loss}) + (\text{loss}) = (\text{loss})$$

Example 2

Find the sum of the following:

(a) $(-3) + (-8)$

(b) $(-71) + (-43)$

▼ Solution

(a) $(-3) + (-8) = -(3 + 8) = -11$ ($|-3| = 3$ and $|-8| = 8$)

(b) $(-71) + (-43) = -(71 + 43) = -114$ ($|-71| = 71$ and $|-43| = 43$)

Exercise 5b

1. Use the number line to find the values of the following:

(a) $(-1) + (-4)$

(b) $(-2) + (-3)$

(c) $(-6) + (-1)$

(d) $(-4) + (-2)$

(e) $(+3) + (+5)$

(f) $(-2) + (-7)$

2. Evaluate the following:

(a) $(-5) + (-6)$

(b) $(-9) + (-7)$

(c) $(-3) + (-11)$

(d) $(+12) + (+8)$

(e) $(-10) + (-11)$

(f) $(-4) + (-7) + (-9)$

(g) $(-8) + (-17) + (-5)$

Next, let us add a positive integer and a negative integer.

Fig. 5.5 shows the addition of +6 and −2.

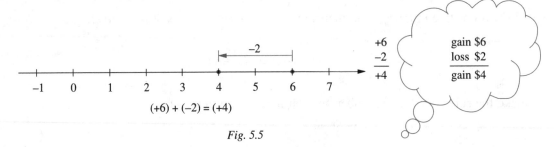

$$(+6) + (−2) = (+4)$$

Fig. 5.5

Fig. 5.6 shows the addition of −7 and +2.

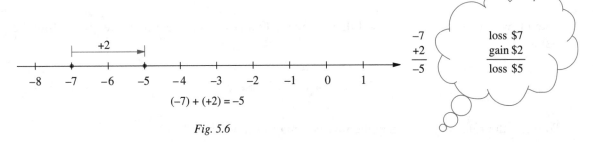

$$(−7) + (+2) = −5$$

Fig. 5.6

The above discussion suggests the following rules for adding two numbers with the **different signs**.

To add a positive and a negative number, find the difference of their numerical values by subtracting the smaller numerical value from the larger numerical value. Place the sign of the number having the larger numerical value before the result.

$$
\begin{aligned}
\text{For any } x > 0, y > 0, \quad & (+x) + (−y) = +(x − y) && \text{if } x > y \\
& (+x) + (−y) = −(y − x) && \text{if } y > x \\
& (−x) + (+y) = −(x − y) && \text{if } x > y \\
& (−x) + (+y) = +(y − x) && \text{if } y > x
\end{aligned}
$$

You may simply remember

$$
\left(\begin{array}{c} + \\ \text{gain} \end{array} \right) + \left(\begin{array}{c} − \\ \text{loss} \end{array} \right) = \left(\begin{array}{c} + \\ \text{gain} \end{array} \right) \quad \text{if} \quad \left(\begin{array}{c} + \\ \text{gain} \end{array} \right) > \left(\begin{array}{c} − \\ \text{loss} \end{array} \right)
$$

$$
\left(\begin{array}{c} + \\ \text{gain} \end{array} \right) + \left(\begin{array}{c} − \\ \text{loss} \end{array} \right) = \left(\begin{array}{c} − \\ \text{loss} \end{array} \right) \quad \text{if} \quad \left(\begin{array}{c} − \\ \text{loss} \end{array} \right) > \left(\begin{array}{c} + \\ \text{gain} \end{array} \right)
$$

Example 3

Find the following sums: *(a)*   *−6 + 18*   *(b)*   *23 + (−68)*

▼**Solution**

(a) $−6 + 18 = (−6) + (+18) = +(18 − 6) = +12 = 12.$ (+18 has a larger absolute value of 18)

(b) $23 + (−68) = (+23) + (−68) = −(68 − 23) = −45.$ (−68 has a larger numerical value of 68)

Example 4

Find the following sums:

(a) $[-5 + (-9)] + [16 + (-21)]$

(b) $-13 + 14 + (-7)$

▼ Solution

(a) $[-5 + (-9)] + [16 + (-21)]$
$= [(-5) + (-9)] + [(+16) + (-21)]$
$= [-(5 + 9)] + [-(21 - 16)]$
$= (-14) + (-5) = -(14 + 5) = -19$

(b) $-13 + 14 + (-7)$
$= [(-13) + (+14)] + (-7)$
$= [+(14 - 13)] + (-7)$
$= (+1) + (-7) = -(7 - 1) = -6.$

═══ Exercise 5c ═══

1. Use the number line to evaluate the following:
   - **(a)** $-1 + 4$
   - **(b)** $-3 + 2$
   - **(c)** $3 + (-4)$
   - **(d)** $2 + (-6)$
   - **(e)** $5 + (-1)$
   - **(f)** $-5 + 4$

2. Calculate the following.
   - **(a)** $-5 + 13$
   - **(b)** $-11 + 19$
   - **(c)** $14 + (-7)$
   - **(d)** $23 + (-12)$
   - **(e)** $-37 + 22$
   - **(f)** $-45 + 19$
   - **(g)** $25 + (-66)$
   - **(h)** $74 + (-89)$
   - **(i)** $101 + (-200)$

3. Evaluate the following.
   - **(a)** $-7 + (-11) + 9$
   - **(b)** $-10 + 17 + (-21)$
   - **(c)** $34 + (-18) + 9$
   - **(d)** $81 + (-6) + (-62)$
   - **(e)** $51 + 14 + (-100)$
   - **(f)** $-27 + 71 + 12$
   - **(g)** $[-7 + (-14)] + [-45 + 92]$
   - **(h)** $[31 + (-48)] + [-16 + (-120)]$

4. The temperature of a piece of meat was $-8°C$ when it was taken out of a freezer. After several minutes of warming, its temperature rose by $17°C$. What is the new temperature of the piece of meat?

5. A company's profits and losses for the first quarter of a certain year are as shown below.

   January: $6 000 (profit)
   February: $2 000 (loss)
   March: $5 500 (loss)

   (a) Translate the company's performance for the first quarter into a mathematical statement.

   (b) How much profit or loss did the company make in the first quarter?

Subtraction of Integers

We think of subtraction (–) as the **reverse** or **opposite** of addition (+).

On the number line, to **add** 5, we move 5 units to the **right**. Thus, to **subtract** 5, we move 5 units to the **left**. Recall also that to add –5, we move 5 units to the left. Thus, to **add** –5, we move 5 units to the **left** and to **subtract** –5, we move 5 units to the **right**.

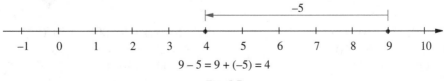

$$9 - 5 = 9 + (-5) = 4$$

Fig. 5.7

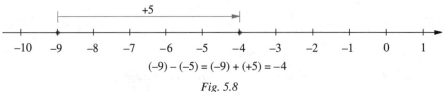

$$(-9) - (-5) = (-9) + (+5) = -4$$

Fig. 5.8

Fig. 5.7 represents both $9 - 5$ and $9 + (-5)$.

Fig. 5.8 represents both $(-9) - (-5)$ and $(-9) + (+5)$.

Hence, $9 - 5 = 9 + (-5) = 4$
$$(-9) - (-5) = (-9) + (+5) = -4$$

Similarly, $(-9) - 5 = (-9) + (-5) = -14$
$$9 - (-5) = 9 + 5 = 14.$$

The above discussion suggests the following rule for subtracting integers.

> **To subtract integers, change the sign of the integer being subtracted and add according to the rules for addition of integers.**
>
> $$x - y = x + (-y)$$

Example 5

Evaluate the following:

(a) $9 - 14$ *(b)* $-12 - 6$ *(c)* $-10 - (-7)$ *(d)* $4 - (-11)$

▼ Solution

(a) $9 - 14$ is the same as $9 - (+14)$. Change $+14$ to -14. Add 9 and -14.
   $\therefore$ $9 - 14 = 9 + (-14) = -(14 - 9) = -5$.

(b) $-12 - 6$ is the same as $-12 - (+6)$. Change $+6$ to -6. Add -12 and -6.
   $\therefore$ $-12 - 6 = -12 + (-6) = -(12 + 6) = -18$.

(c) Change -7 in $-10 - (-7)$ to $+7$. Add -10 and $+7$.
   $\therefore$ $-10 - (-7) = -10 + (+7) = -(10 - 7) = -3$.

(d) Change -11 in $4 - (-11)$ to $+11$ or simply 11. Add 4 and 11.
   $\therefore 4 - (-11) = 4 + 11 = 15$.

Example 6

Do the following:

(a) $280 + (-120) - (-320) + 50$ *(b)* $-(-700) + (-500) - 130 + 70$

▼ Solution

(a) $280 + (-120) - (-320) + 50$
  $= (280 - 120) + 320 + 50$
  $= 160 + 320 + 50 = 530$

(b) $-(-700) + (-500) - 130 + 70$
  $= 700 - 500 - 130 + 70$
  $= 200 - 130 + 70$
  $= 70 + 70 = 140$

Exercise 5d

1. Use the number line to do the following.

   (a) $-2 - 3$ **(b)** $1 - 5$

   (c) $0 - 4$ **(d)** $-3 - 3$

   (e) $1 - (-3)$ **(f)** $-2 - (-2)$

   (g) $5 - (-1)$ **(h)** $-7 - (-3)$

   (c) $-6 - (-3) - 1$ **(d)** $4 - (-9) - 5$

   (e) $-2 - (-6) - 3$ **(f)** $5 - 7 - (-10)$

   (g) $4 - (-8) - 6 - (-11)$

   (h) $-12 - 7 - (-9) - 3$

   (i) $15 - 20 - 13 - 32$

2. Evaluate the following.

   (a) $8 - 3$ **(b)** $2 - 9$

   (c) $-4 - 7$ **(d)** $-6 - 11$

   (e) $10 - (-5)$ **(f)** $7 - (-7)$

   (g) $-6 - (-7)$ **(h)** $-23 - (-34)$

   (i) $-42 - 23$ **(j)** $16 - (-54)$

   (k) $-127 - 143$ **(l)** $106 - 144$

3. Evaluate the following.

   (a) $-3 - (6 - 9)$ **(b)** $-4 - (2 - 5)$

4. Find the values of the following expressions.

   (a) $-12 - (-24) + (-36)$

   (b) $-40 + 15 - 27 + 11$

   (c) $(-5 - 6) - (15 - 5)$

   (d) $-324 + 12 - 56$

   (e) $[-2 + (-10)] - [15 + (-20)]$

   (f) $146 - (-200) + (-100) - 150$

   (g) $-176 + (-123) - (-167) + 103$

   (h) $-14 + 26 - 37 - 45 + 56 - 67 - 71$

   (i) $19 - 27 + 34 + 43 - 58 - 66 - 76 + 81$

Multiplication of Integers

We already know the rule for multiplying positive integers using a number line. For example, $3 \times 2 = 6$.

$3 \times 2 = 2 + 2 + 2 = 6.$

Similarly, for multiplying a positive integer by a negative number, for example $3 \times (-2)$, we have

$3 \times (-2) = (-2) + (-2) + (-2) = -6 = -(3 \times 2).$

We know $2 \times 3 = 3 \times 2 = 6$. Similarly we have $(-2) \times 3 = 3 \times (-2) = -(3 \times 2) = -(2 \times 3)$.

Scientists have found that the lowest possible temperature is $-273°C$. The temperature is referred to as the absolute zero. The boiling points of some gases are given below:

   Hydrogen $-253°C$
   Nitrogen $-196°C$
   Oxygen $-183°C$

If mixtures of the above three gases are cooled to $-260°C$ and then allowed to warm, which of the gases will escape first?

Simply remember the rule for signs as:

$(+)(-) = (-)$
$(-)(+) = (-)$

In general, if both x and y represent positive integers, then

$$x \times (-y) = -(x \times y) \text{ or } (-x) \times y = -(x \times y).$$

In other words, the product of a positive integer and a negative integer is a negative integer.

Example 7

Evaluate the following:

(a) $9 \times (-4)$

(b) $(-8) \times 6$

(a) $9 \times (-4) = -(9 \times 4) = -36$

(b) $(-8) \times 6 = -(8 \times 6) = -48$

We know that the product of two positive integers is a positive integer. Will the product of two negative integers be a negative integer or a positive integer?

Let us consider $(-1) \times (-1)$ first, we know $1 \times (-1) = -1$. It is reasonable to have $(-1) \times (-1) = -(1 \times (-1)) = +1$. Similarly for $(-2) \times (-3)$, we have $(-2) \times (-3) = (-1) \times 2 \times (-1) \times 3 = -(-1) \times 2 \times 3 = +2 \times 3$.

> **In general, if x and y are any two positive integers, then**
>
> $$x \times y = + (x \times y) \text{ or } (-x) \times (-y) = + (x \times y).$$
>
> **In other words, the product of two negative integers is a positive integer.**

Simply remember the rule for signs as:

$(+)(+) = (+)$
$(-)(-) = (+)$
$(+)(-) = (-)$
$(-)(+) = (-)$

Example 8

Evaluate the following:

(a) $(-8) \times (-3)$

(b) $(-7) \times (-13)$

(a) $(-8) \times (-3) = + (8 \times 3) = 24$

(b) $(-7) \times (-13) = + (7 \times 13) = 91$

Example 9

Evaluate the following:

(a) $(-8) \times (4) - (-5) \times 3$

(b) $(-7 + 6) \times (-11)$

(c) $9 \times (-2) \times (-2) \times 10$

$-(-15)$ means $(-1)(-15)$

(a) $(-8) \times 4 - (-5) \times (3) = -32 - (-15)$
$= -32 + 15$
$= -17$

(b) $(-7 + 6) \times (-11) = (-1) \times (-11)$
$= 11$

(c) $9 \times (-2) \times (-2) \times 10 = (-18) \times (-2) \times 10 = 36 \times 10 = 360$

Division of Integers

We know division is the inverse operation of multiplication. For example, $3 \times 2 = 6$, $6 \div 3 = 2$ and $6 \div 2 = 3$ and similarly as $3 \times (-2) = -6$ we naturally have $(-6) \div 3 = -2 = -(6 \div 3)$ and $-(6) \div (-2) = 3$.

In general, if x and y are any two positive integers, then

(1) $(-x) \div y = -(x \div y) = x \div (-y)$.
(2) $(-x) \div (-y) = +(x \div y)$.

We know that if x is a positive integer $0 \times x = 0$.

Therefore, $0 \div x = 0$. Similarly, as $0 \times (-x) = 0$, we say $0 \div (-x) = 0$.

Think what should be $-(x) \div 0$?

Can we divide an integer by 0? Consider $5 \div 0$ and assume that $5 \div 0 = x$. If it is true, by the relationship of division and multiplication then $5 = 0 \times x = 0$ but this is impossible. Therefore we say an integer divided by 0 is undefined.

Simply remember the rule for signs as:

$$\frac{(-)}{(+)} = (-)$$

$$\frac{(+)}{(+)} = (+)$$

Simply remember the rule for signs as:

$$\frac{(+)}{(-)} = (-)$$

$$\frac{(-)}{(-)} = (+)$$

"$\neq$" denotes "is not equal to"

There is no answer for the division of any number by 0.

Example 10

Evaluate the following:

(a) $-100 \div (-20)$ (b) $625 \div (-25)$
(c) $0 \div (-14)$ (d) $16 \div 0$

Solution

(a) $-100 \div (-20) = 100 \div 20 = 5$

(b) $625 \div (-25) = -(625 \div 25) = -25$

(c) $0 \div (-14) = 0$

(d) $16 \div 0$ is undefined.

=== Exercise 5e ===

Evaluate the following:

(a) $3 \times (-7)$ (b) $(-3) \times (-2)$ (c) $(-4) \times 8$ (d) $0 \times (-5)$ (e) $(-20) \times (-14)$
(f) $-4 \times (0)$ (g) $(-4) \div 2$ (h) $(-122) \div (-2)$ (i) $(-144) \div 24$ (j) $275 \div (-5)$
(k) $0 \div 25$ (l) $(-16) \div (-2)$ (m) $0 \div (-13)$ (n) $480 \div (-30)$
(o) $(-3) \times (-4) \times (-8) \times (-2)$
(q) $(-3) \times 0 \times (-8) \times (-5) \times 4$
(p) $(-2) \times 0 \times (-7) \times (-4) \times 5$
(r) $(-2) \times (-7) \times (-2) \times (-1)$

Rules for Operating on Integers

Addition and multiplication of integers obey the commutative law.

e.g. $2 + (-5) = -3 = (-5) + 2$ $2 \times (-5) = -10 = (-5) \times 2$

   $(-3) + (-4) = -7 = (-4) + (-3)$ $(-3) \times (-4) = 12 = (-4) \times (-3)$

Addition and multiplication of integers obey the associative law.

e.g. $[2 + (-5)] + 7 = -3 + 7 = 4$ $[2 \times (-5)] \times 7 = -10 \times 7 = -70$

   $2 + (-5 + 7) = 2 + 2 = 4$ $2 \times (-5 \times 7) = 2 \times (-35) = -70$

For integers, multiplication is distributive over addition and subtraction.

e.g. $-2 \times (-3 + 4) = -2$

   $-2 \times (-3) + (-2) \times 4 = -2$

   $\therefore \quad -2 \times (-3 + 4) = -2 \times (-3) + (-2) \times 4$

   $(-3 - 4) \times (-2) = 14$

   $-3 \times (-2) - 4 \times (-2) = 14$

   $\therefore \quad (-3 - 4) \times (-2) = -3 \times (-2) - 4 \times (-2)$

The rules for order of operations on integers are the same as those for whole numbers.

For example,

(a) $-3 \times (5 - 3) = -3 \times 2$ (Simplify the expression within the brackets first.)

   $= -6$

(b) $-3 \times [-15 + (7 - 2)] = -3 \times (-15 + 5)$ (Simplify the expression within the innermost pair of brackets first.)

   $= -3 \times (-10)$

   $= 30$

(c) $-28 + 12 - 9 = (-28 + 12) - 9$ (Work from left to right.)

   $= -16 - 9 = -25$

(d) $-125 \div 5 \times (-10) = (-125 \div 5) \times (-10)$ (Work from left to right.)

   $= (-25) \times (-10) = 250$

(e) $-12 + (-3) \times 4 - 35 \div (-7) = -12 + [(-3) \times 4] - [35 \div (-7)]$

   $= -12 + (-12) - (-5)$ (Do multiplication and division first.)

   $= -24 + 5 = -19$

(f) $2 - (-3)^2 = 2 - (9) = -(9 - 2)$ $[(-3)^2 = (-3) \times (-3) = 9]$

   $= -7$

1. Are subtraction and division of integers commutative?

2. Are subtraction and division of integers associative?

═ Exercise 5f ═

1. Copy and complete the following by filling in an appropriate operation symbol in each box:

   (a) $(-5) \;\square\; 3 = 3 \;\square\; (-5) = -15$ (b) $23 \;\square\; (-11) = -11 \;\square\; 23 = 12$

   (c) $-64 \;\square\; (-36) = -36 \;\square\; (-64) = -100$ (d) $-6 \;\square\; (-15) = -15 \;\square\; (-6) = 90$

2. Replace each $\square$ with an integer.

   (a) $(-3) \times (\square + 8) = (-3) \times (-28) + (-3) \times 8 = \square$

   (b) $(-16) \times 12 + 6 \times 12 = (-16 + 6) \times \square = \square$

    (c) $(-5) \times (-4 - \square) = [(-5) \times (-4)] - [(-5) \times (-14)] = \square$

    (d) $(-11) \times (8 - 9) = [(-11) \times \square] - [(-11) \times \square] = \square$

    (e) $(-11 \times 10) - (-9 \times 10) = [-11 - (-9)] \times \square = \square$

    (f) $[-15 - (-5)] \times (-9) = [\square \times (-9)] - [(-5) \times \square] = \square$

*3. Evaluate the following:

    (a) $5 \times 2 - (-3)$ **(b)** $5 \times [3 \times (-2) - 10]$

    (c) $\sqrt{10 - 3 \times (-2)}$ **(d)** $[3 - (-2)]^3$

    (e) $24 \times (-2) \times 5 \div (-6)$ **(f)** $(16 - 24) - (57 - 77) \div (-2)$

    (g) $[(12 - 18) \div 3 - 5] \times (-4)$ **(h)** $160 \div (-40) - 20 \div (-5)$

    (i) $2 \times (-2) + (-2) \times (-3) + 2 \times (-3)$ **(j)** $\{[(-15 + 5) \times 2 + 8] - 32 \div 8\} - (-7)$

    (k) $[3 \times (-3) - 4 \times (-2) + 5 \times 2] + [-2 \times (-3) + 8 \times (-2) - 8 \times 2]$

 ## *Rational Numbers*

When we add two whole numbers, the result is always a whole number. However, if we subtract one whole number from another, do we always obtain a whole number? We know that $5 - 3 = 2$ and $3 - 5 = -2$.

not a whole number

Thus subtraction of whole numbers does not always produce a whole number. This explains the need to include negative numbers to form the set of integers.

When we multiply two integers, we always obtain an integer. However, if we divide one integer by another, do we always obtain an integer?

We know that $6 \div 2 = 3$ and $2 \div 6 = \dfrac{1}{3}$.

not an integer

Thus, the division of two integers does not necessarily result in an integer. Hence, there is a need to include fractions to form a bigger set of numbers known as the set of **rational numbers**

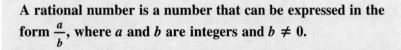

A rational number is a number that can be expressed in the form $\dfrac{a}{b}$, where a and b are integers and $b \neq 0$.

From the definition of a rational number, we see that fractions such as $-\dfrac{3}{4}, \dfrac{1}{2}$ and $\dfrac{5}{3}$ are rational numbers. If we replace b in $\dfrac{a}{b}$ by the integer 1, we have $\dfrac{a}{b} = \dfrac{a}{1} = a$. Hence, the integers $6 = \dfrac{6}{1}, -5 = \dfrac{-5}{1}, -10 = \dfrac{-10}{1}$, $0 = \dfrac{0}{1}$ and so on are rational numbers.

Example 11

Evaluate the following:

(a) $2 - \dfrac{10}{3}$

(b) $3 - 5\dfrac{3}{4}$

(c) $-\dfrac{4}{5} \times \left(-\dfrac{15}{28}\right)$

(d) $\left(-2\dfrac{1}{2}\right)^2 - \left(-\dfrac{1}{2}\right)^3$

▼ Solution

(a) $2 - \dfrac{10}{3} = \dfrac{6 - 10}{3} = -\dfrac{4}{3} = -1\dfrac{1}{3}$

(b) $3 - 5\dfrac{3}{4} = 3 - \dfrac{23}{4}$ $\qquad \left(\text{Write } 5\dfrac{3}{4} \text{ as } \dfrac{23}{4}.\right)$

$\qquad = \dfrac{12 - 23}{4} = -\dfrac{11}{4} = -2\dfrac{3}{4}$

Alternatively, $3 - 5\dfrac{3}{4} = (3 - 5) - \dfrac{3}{4}$ $\qquad \left(-5\dfrac{3}{4} = -5 - \dfrac{3}{4}\right)$

$\qquad\qquad\qquad = -2 - \dfrac{3}{4} = -2\dfrac{3}{4}$

(c) $-\dfrac{4}{5} \times \left(-\dfrac{15}{28}\right) = \dfrac{4}{5} \times \dfrac{15}{28} = \dfrac{3}{7}$

(d) $\left(-2\dfrac{1}{2}\right)^2 - \left(-\dfrac{1}{2}\right)^3 = \left(-\dfrac{5}{2}\right)^2 - \left(-\dfrac{1}{8}\right)$ $\qquad \left[\left(-\dfrac{1}{2}\right)^3 = \left(-\dfrac{1}{2}\right) \times \left(-\dfrac{1}{2}\right) \times \left(-\dfrac{1}{2}\right) = -\dfrac{1}{8}\right]$

$\qquad\qquad\qquad = \dfrac{25}{4} + \dfrac{1}{8}$ $\qquad \left[\left(-\dfrac{5}{2}\right)^2 = \left(-\dfrac{5}{2}\right) \times \left(-\dfrac{5}{2}\right) = \dfrac{25}{4}\right]$

$\qquad\qquad\qquad = \dfrac{50 + 1}{8}$

$\qquad\qquad\qquad = \dfrac{51}{8} = 6\dfrac{3}{8}$

Example 12

Evaluate

(a) $\left(\dfrac{1}{5} - \dfrac{1}{2}\right) \div \left(-\dfrac{2}{3} \times \dfrac{1}{8}\right)$ *and* (b) $-\dfrac{1}{2} \div \dfrac{3}{18} - \left(\dfrac{1}{5} - \dfrac{7}{10}\right) \times \left(-\dfrac{4}{21}\right)$.

▼ Solution

(a) $\left(\dfrac{1}{5} - \dfrac{1}{2}\right) \div \left(-\dfrac{2}{3} \times \dfrac{1}{8}\right) = \left(\dfrac{2 - 5}{10}\right) \div \left(-\dfrac{1}{12}\right)$

$\qquad\qquad\qquad = \dfrac{-3}{10} \div \left(-\dfrac{1}{12}\right) = \dfrac{3}{10} \times \dfrac{12}{1} = \dfrac{18}{5} = 3\dfrac{3}{5}$

(b) $-\dfrac{1}{2} \div \dfrac{3}{18} - \left(\dfrac{1}{5} - \dfrac{7}{10}\right) \times \left(-\dfrac{4}{21}\right) = -\dfrac{1}{2} \div \dfrac{3}{18} - \left(\dfrac{2 - 7}{10}\right) \times \left(-\dfrac{4}{21}\right)$

$\qquad\qquad\qquad = -\dfrac{1}{2} \times \dfrac{18}{3} - \left(-\dfrac{5}{10}\right) \times \left(-\dfrac{4}{21}\right)$

$\qquad\qquad\qquad = -3 - \dfrac{2}{21} = -\left(3 + \dfrac{2}{21}\right) = -3\dfrac{2}{21}$

Exercise 5g

1. Evaluate the following. Express each answer in its lowest terms.

   (a) $\dfrac{5}{8} - \left(-\dfrac{1}{8}\right)$ **(b)** $-\dfrac{13}{15} + \left(-\dfrac{2}{15}\right)$ **(c)** $2\dfrac{1}{5} - 3\dfrac{3}{10}$ **(d)** $-7\dfrac{1}{5} - \left(-3\dfrac{3}{10}\right)$

   (e) $-\dfrac{1}{2} + \dfrac{1}{4} - \dfrac{2}{3}$ **(f)** $-\dfrac{1}{10} + \left(-\dfrac{4}{5}\right) - \left(-\dfrac{1}{4}\right)$ **(g)** $-\dfrac{1}{2} - \dfrac{1}{4} - \left(-\dfrac{9}{10}\right)$

   (h) $-2\dfrac{3}{7} + \dfrac{13}{14} - 5\dfrac{27}{28}$ **(i)** $\dfrac{1}{3} + \left(\dfrac{-1}{2}\right)^2$ **(j)** $2\dfrac{1}{2} + \left(-\dfrac{1}{2}\right)^3 + \left(-\dfrac{1}{2}\right)^4$

2. Evaluate the following. Express each answer in its lowest terms.

   (a) $-5 \times \left(-\dfrac{9}{10}\right)$ **(b)** $\dfrac{4}{9} \times \left(-\dfrac{3}{10}\right)$ **(c)** $\dfrac{3}{4} \div \left(\dfrac{-2}{3}\right)^2$ **(d)** $\dfrac{11}{12} \times \left(-\dfrac{23}{33} + \dfrac{7}{11}\right)$

   (e) $-3\dfrac{1}{4} \times 1\dfrac{3}{5} \times \left(-1\dfrac{2}{13}\right)$ **✶(f)** $\dfrac{3}{5} \times \left(-\dfrac{1}{4} - \dfrac{1}{6}\right) \div \left(-2\dfrac{1}{3} + 1\dfrac{1}{4}\right)$

   ✶(g) $\left(-1\dfrac{1}{6} \times 2\dfrac{1}{2} \times 1\dfrac{3}{5}\right) \div \left[1\dfrac{1}{4}\left(-2\dfrac{3}{10}\right) \times 1\dfrac{2}{3}\right]$

 ## *Irrational Numbers*

Fig. 5.9 shows some rational numbers represented on the number line.

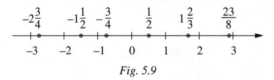

Fig. 5.9

Are there any points on the number line which do not represent rational numbers? The answer is "yes". There are points on the number line which represent numbers like $\sqrt{2}$, $\sqrt{7}$, π, $\sqrt{11}$ and so on. These numbers cannot be expressed as ratios of two integers, so they are not rational. Such numbers are called **irrational numbers**.

> **An irrational number cannot be expressed as a ratio of two integers.**

 ## *Real Numbers*

The rational numbers and the irrational numbers **completely** fill the number line and form the set of **real numbers**.

The relationship between the various sets of numbers we have discussed is shown in Fig. 5.10.

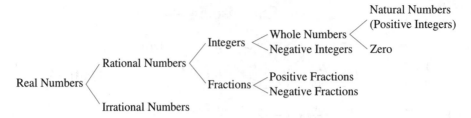

$$\text{Real Numbers} \begin{cases} \text{Rational Numbers} \begin{cases} \text{Integers} \begin{cases} \text{Whole Numbers} \begin{cases} \text{Natural Numbers (Positive Integers)} \\ \text{Zero} \end{cases} \\ \text{Negative Integers} \end{cases} \\ \text{Fractions} \begin{cases} \text{Positive Fractions} \\ \text{Negative Fractions} \end{cases} \end{cases} \\ \text{Irrational Numbers} \end{cases}$$

Fig. 5.10

Use of Calculators

The following are approximations of π:

Archimedas (287–212 BC): $3\frac{10}{71} < \pi < 3\frac{1}{7}$

Zu Chongzhi (5th century): $3.1415926 < \pi < 3.1415927$

Vieta (1593): 3.14159265 358979323

Ludoff von Ceulen (1615): 35 decimal places

Abraham Sharp (1717): 72 places

W. Shanks (1873): 707 places

Computer (1958): 10 000 places

Ludoff and Shanks both devoted their entire life trying to calculate π more accurately. In contrast, a modern computer (1958) took only 1 hour and 40 minutes to find the value of π correct to 10 000 decimal places. The Chuduovky brothers set the one billion mark in 1989 by computing 1 011 196 691 digits of π.

How many digits of π has the latest computer calculated?

The following keys are available on a calculator for calculations involving negative numbers and irrational numbers:

$+/-$	Sign Change Key
π	Pi Key, which is 3.141 592 654 correct to 9 decimal places.
$\sqrt{}$	Square Root Key
$\sqrt[x]{}$	Root Key

For example,

(a) to find $-65 + 47 \times (-79)$, press $\boxed{+/-}$ 65 $\boxed{+}$ 47 $\boxed{\times}$ $\boxed{+/-}$ 79 $\boxed{=}$ to get $-3\,778$,

(b) to find $-3\frac{2}{3} \div \left(-1\frac{5}{6}\right)$, press $\boxed{+/-}$ 3 $\boxed{a^{b}/c}$ 2 $\boxed{a^{b}/c}$ 3 $\boxed{\div}$ $\boxed{+/-}$ 1 $\boxed{a^{b}/c}$ 5 $\boxed{a^{b}/c}$ 6 $\boxed{=}$ to get 2,

(c) to find $-23.4 \div \pi$, press $\boxed{+/-}$ 23.4 $\boxed{\div}$ $\boxed{\pi}$ $\boxed{=}$ to get $-7.448\,451\,33$.

Like π, irrational numbers such as $\sqrt{2}$, $\sqrt{3}$, $\sqrt{5}$, $\sqrt[3]{2}$, $\sqrt[3]{3}$, $\sqrt[3]{4}$ and so on cannot be determined exactly. We can only find approximate values of these irrational numbers using a calculator.

For example, to find $\sqrt{2}$, press $\boxed{\sqrt{}}$ 2 $\boxed{=}$ to get 1.414 213 562,

to find $\sqrt{3}$, press $\boxed{\sqrt{}}$ 3 $\boxed{=}$ to get 1.732 050 808,

to find $\sqrt[3]{4}$, press 3 $\boxed{\sqrt[x]{}}$ 4 $\boxed{=}$ to get 1.587 401 052,

to find $\sqrt[3]{5}$, press 3 $\boxed{\sqrt[x]{}}$ 5 $\boxed{=}$ to get 1.709 975 947.

As your calculator might be different, please check your calculator manual before using it.

Example 13

Use a calculator to evaluate (a) $\dfrac{\sqrt{3}}{2}$, (b) $\dfrac{1}{\sqrt{7}-1}$ and (c) $\dfrac{\sqrt{5}+\sqrt{2}}{\sqrt{2}-\sqrt{5}}$ correct to 2 decimal places.

▼ **Solution**

Sequence of pressing keys: Final display

(a) $\boxed{\sqrt{}}$ 3 $\boxed{\div}$ 2 $\boxed{=}$ 0.866 025 403

(b) 1 $\boxed{\div}$ $\boxed{(}$ $\boxed{\sqrt{}}$ 7 $\boxed{-}$ 1 $\boxed{)}$ $\boxed{=}$ 0.607 625 218

(c) $\boxed{\sqrt{}}$ 5 $+$ $\boxed{\sqrt{}}$ 2 $\boxed{=}$ $\boxed{\div}$ $\boxed{(}$ $\boxed{\sqrt{}}$ 2 $-$ $\boxed{\sqrt{}}$ 5 $\boxed{)}$ $\boxed{=}$ -4.44 151 844

The answers are thus (a) 0.87, (b) 0.61 and (c) -4.44.

═══ **Exercise 5h** ═══

1. State whether each of the following is a rational or irrational number:

(a) $\dfrac{1}{5}$ (b) -4 (c) 0.6

(d) $\sqrt{5}$ (e) $\sqrt{6}$ (f) $\sqrt{9}$

(g) 0 (h) 2π (i) $\sqrt[3]{8}$

(j) 3.142 (k) $\dfrac{22}{7}$ (l) $\sqrt{100}$

(m) $\sqrt{1\,000}$ (n) $\sqrt[3]{1\,000}$ (o) $\dfrac{\pi}{2}$

2. State whether each of the following statements is true or false:

(a) An integer is a rational number.
(b) A rational number is an integer.
(c) A real number is either a rational or an irrational number.
(d) The set of real numbers consists of positive numbers, negative numbers and zero.
(e) Every irrational number is a real number.
(f) A fraction is an irrational number.

3. Use a calculator to compute each of the following:

(a) $-5\,165 + 2\,844 + 8\,416$
(b) $-4\,715 \times (-78)$ (c) $-29\,187 \div 69$
(d) $597 \times (-57) - 4\,648 \div (-83)$

(e) $-\dfrac{2}{21} + \dfrac{1}{43}$ (f) $-\dfrac{47}{98} \times \dfrac{518}{77}$

(g) $-\dfrac{51}{23} \div \left(-\dfrac{48}{62}\right)$

(h) $\dfrac{-\dfrac{7}{19} + \dfrac{5}{18}}{-\dfrac{6}{13} - \left(-\dfrac{11}{7}\right)}$ *(i) $\dfrac{\left(-\dfrac{4}{7}\right)^2 - \left(-\dfrac{2}{5}\right)^3}{-\sqrt{\dfrac{64}{625}} \div \sqrt[3]{\dfrac{8}{125}}}$

4. Use a calculator to evaluate the following. Give your answer correct to 2 decimal places.

(a) $\sqrt{129}$ (b) $\sqrt[3]{81}$

(c) $-\dfrac{\pi^2}{4}$ (d) $\sqrt{\dfrac{45}{8}}$

(e) $\sqrt{5} - \sqrt{3}$ (f) $\sqrt{14^2 + 19^2}$

(g) $\pi \times (79.67)^2$

(h) $\dfrac{1}{3} \times \pi \times (43.6)^2 \times 56.9$

*(i) $\dfrac{\sqrt[3]{12} - \sqrt{6}}{\sqrt{50} - \sqrt[3]{111}}$ *(j) $\sqrt{\dfrac{46^2 + 83^2 - 65^2}{2 \times 46 \times 83}}$

═══ **S u m m a r y** ═══

1. The set of **integers** is $Z = \{\dots, -4, -3, -2, -1, 0, 1, 2, 3, 4, \dots\}$.

2. Addition of Integers

(a) For any two negative integers $-x$ and $-y$,

$$-x + (-y) = -(x + y).$$

(b) For a positive integer x and a negative integer $-y$,

$$x + (-y) = x - y \text{ if } x > y \text{ and } x + (-y) = -(y - x) \text{ if } y > x.$$

3. Subtraction of Integers

For any two integers a and b, $a - b = a + (-b)$.

4. Multiplication of Integers

For any two positive integers x and y,

(a) $x \times (-y) = -(x \times y)$ and $(-x) \times y = -(x \times y)$,

(b) $x \times y = +(x \times y)$ and $(-x) \times (-y) = +(x \times y)$.

5. Division of Integers

For any two positive integers x and y,

(a) $0 \div x = 0$ and $0 \div (-x) = 0$,

(b) $(-x) \div y = -(x \div y)$ and $x \div (-y) = -(x \div y)$,

(c) $x \div y = +(x \div y)$ and $-x \div (-y) = +(x \div y)$.

6. Rational Numbers

A rational number is a number which can be expressed in the form $\dfrac{a}{b}$, where a and b are integers and $b \neq 0$.

7. Irrational Numbers

An irrational number cannot be expressed as a ratio of two integers.

8. Real Numbers

The rational numbers and the irrational numbers together form the set of real numbers. The diagram below shows the relationship between the various sets of numbers we have discussed.

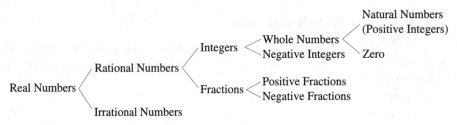

Review Questions 5

1. Evaluate each of the following:

(a) $13 - (-54)$ **(b)** $(-74) - (-46)$ **(c)** $11 + (-33)$ **(d)** $-12 - 88$

(e) $[-13 + (-15)] + (-8)$ **(f)** $500 - (-200) - 210 - 100$

(g) $777 - (-111) - (-222) + 20$ **(h)** $-(-129) + (-119) - 301 + 12$

2. Evaluate each of the following:

(a) $(-4) \times (-5) \times (-6)$ **(b)** $(-3 + 6) \times (-4)$ **(c)** $(-3 - 5) \times (-3 - 4)$

(d) $(-3 - 15) \div (-6)$ **(e)** $4 \times (-5) \div (-2)$ **(f)** $-5 \times 6 - 18 \div (-3)$

(g) $2 \times (-3)^2 - 3 \times 4$ **(h)** $[-3 \times (-2)] \times (2 - 5)^2$ **(i)** $3 \times 5^2 - 2 \times (-3) \times 2$

3. Evaluate the following:

(a) $(-2)^2 - (-2 \times 3) + (2 \times 3^2)$ **(b)** $5 \times (-2)^3 + (-4)^2 \times (-3)$

(c) $(-4)^2 \div (-8) + 3 \times (-2)^3$

(d) $(-2)^3 - \left(-2 \times \dfrac{1}{2}\right) + 3(-1)^2$

(e) $4 \times 3^2 \div (-6) - (-1)^3 \times (-3)^2$

(f) $-2 \times (-2)^3 \times (-2) \times 3 + (-2) \times 3 \times (-1)^2$

*4. Evaluate each of the following and express the result in its lowest terms:

(a) $\dfrac{1}{5} - \left(\dfrac{1}{3} + \dfrac{1}{2}\right)$

(b) $-2\dfrac{3}{4} + \left(-\dfrac{1}{2} \times 1\dfrac{1}{3}\right)$

(c) $\left(-2\dfrac{1}{2} \div 2\dfrac{1}{4}\right) - \left(-\dfrac{2}{3}\right)$

(d) $\dfrac{1}{\sqrt{64}} - \sqrt{16} + \sqrt{\dfrac{4}{9}}$

(e) $\dfrac{\dfrac{2}{3} - 4\dfrac{1}{2}}{4\dfrac{1}{2} \times \left(-\dfrac{2}{3}\right)}$

(f) $(-5)^2 + \left(3\dfrac{1}{2}\right)^2 - \left(-5 + 3\dfrac{1}{2}\right)^2$

5. Which of the fractions $-\dfrac{5}{6}, -\dfrac{9}{11}, -\dfrac{11}{13}$ is the smallest?

*6. Arrange the following numbers in ascending order:

(a) $1.428,\ 1.42\dot{8},\ 1.\dot{4}2\dot{8},\ 1\dfrac{3}{7}$

(b) $-3\dfrac{7}{11},\ -3.6\dot{3},\ -3.63,\ -3.\dot{6}$

(c) $-1.43\dot{5},\ -1.4\dot{3}\dot{5},\ -1\dfrac{4}{9},\ -1.\dot{4}3\dot{5}$

Problem Solving

1. Write down any three real numbers and the integer −1. Find the sum s_1 of these four numbers. Multiply any two of the four numbers at a time. Add the six possible products to obtain the sum s_2. Now, multiply any three of the four numbers at a time. Add the four possible products to obtain the sum s_3. Multiply all the four numbers to obtain the product s_4. Calculate the sum $s_1 + s_2 + s_3 + s_4$. What do you obtain?

   Repeat the above process with another three real numbers and the integer −1. What do you notice? Have a few of your friends work at the same time with other real numbers and the integer −1. Compare the results you and your friends obtain. Are you all surprised with the outcome? Discuss with your friends to obtain an explanation for the outcome.

2. If n is an integer and the numbers $n + 1$, $2n + 1$ and $8n + 1$ are divisible by 3, 5 and 7 respectively, what is the largest negative value of n?

3. Identify a rule and then write the next three terms of each of the following sequence:

   (a) $-\dfrac{1}{1}, \dfrac{2}{1}, -\dfrac{3}{2}, -\dfrac{5}{3}, \dfrac{8}{5}, -\dfrac{13}{8}, \ldots$

   (b) $\dfrac{9}{2}, \dfrac{11}{9}, -\dfrac{20}{11}, \dfrac{31}{20}, \dfrac{51}{31}, -\dfrac{82}{51}, \ldots$

4. The boiling point of alcohol is 82°C and the boiling point of water is 100°C. A mixture of alcohol and water is heated to a temperature of 95°C and by then there is only water left. The boiling point of liquid nitrogen is −196°C, that of xenon is −108°C and of oxygen −183°C. A mixture of liquid nitrogen, xenon and oxygen is at a temperature of −215°C. The mixture is then warmed to a temperature of −185°C. Which of the liquidified gas has evaporated?

CHAPTER 6

Estimation and Approximation

In this chapter, you will learn how to

▲ round off numbers and measures to a specified degree of accuracy;
▲ make estimates of numbers and measures.

Preliminary Problem

Can you estimate the number of oranges in the picture shown? Many a time we have to make estimates and approximation. A methodical way of making estimates is a far better method than making wild guesses.

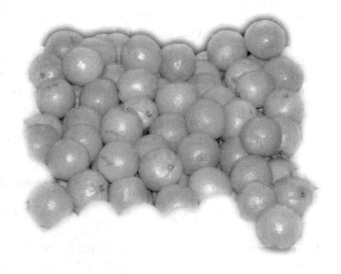

Estimation and Rounding

In our daily life, we often need to use estimation when getting a precise answer is impossible, unnecessary, or inconvenient.

Estimation often involves rounding. In rounding, we may **round up**, **round down** or round off to the nearest. For example, we round up 850 to 1 000 when we budget for a trip that will cost at least $850. At the car park, the car park charges are often rounded up. For example, you pay $1.80 for 1 hour and 50 minutes of parking at 45 cents every half hour. At NTUC supermarkets, the bill is round down to the nearest 5 cents. For example, if your bill is $12.03, you pay $12.00 and if your bill is $12.09, you pay $12.05. In Mathematics we round off a number to the nearest. For example, to round 3.824 and 2.815 each to 2 decimal places, we round down 3.824 to 3.82 and round up 2.815 to 2.82.

Example 1

Estimate the cost of 8 copies of a textbook at $10.49 each.

Solution

To estimate the cost of 8 copies of the textbook, we may choose to round $10.49 to the nearest 10 cents and obtain the result as shown below. The actual cost is also provided for comparison.

Estimate cost: $10.50   Actual cost: $10.49
                  ×   8   ×   8
                 ───────   ───────
                   $84.00 $83.92

For a quick estimate, which can be done mentally, round $10.49 to the nearest dollar and the estimate is $10 × 8 = $80.

In-Class Activity

You may carry out this activity individually.

It is useful to estimate the total sum of a bill to avoid overpayment.

For example you can estimate the total amount of a supermarket receipt. This is done by rounding the cost of each item to the nearest 50 cents and keeping a running total mentally from the first item to the last item.

The table below is drawn up from a supermarket receipt. Observe how the estimation is done.

SALE	Actual Cost ($)	Estimated Cost ($)	Running total ($)
P BUTTER	4.50	4.50	4.50
B/SARDINE	3.50	3.50	8.00
COD FISH	1.30	1.50	9.50
M+M PLAIN	0.60	0.50	10.00
ALMOND CHO	2.85	3.00	13.00
HI LO MILK	2.85	3.00	16.00
F/P KAYA	1.60	1.50	17.50
F/SPREAD	2.85	3.00	20.50
TAPIOCA CRISP	2.40	2.50	23.00
SUBTOTAL	22.45		
TOTAL	22.45		

$\therefore$ The estimated total amount = $23.00

You notice that the estimated total is very close to the actual total.

1. Collect supermarket receipts with at least 5 items. Without seeing the actual total, estimate the total amount by rounding the cost of each item and adding them mentally. Compare your estimate with the actual total.

2. Exchange the receipts with other students and repeat the process.

3. Choose a receipt with more than 10 items. Use it to start a friendly competition among your classmates. Give a round of applause to the winner, the student who takes the shortest time to estimate the total mentally.

Example 2

Make an estimate and pick the nearest answer in each of the following cases:

(a) $\dfrac{3\,902}{23\,839}$ (i) 0.02   (ii) 0.2   (iii) 2   (iv) 20   (v) 200

(b) $\dfrac{4.19 \times 0.030\,9}{0.022\,2}$ (i) 0.006   (ii) 0.06   (iii) 0.6   (iv) 6   (v) 60

(c) $\dfrac{52.41 \times 0.044}{0.001\,18}$ (i) 20   (ii) 200   (iii) 2 000   (iv) 20 000   (v) 200 000

(d) $\sqrt{990}$ (i) 10   (ii) 30   (iii) 100   (iv) 300   (v) 1 000

(e) $\sqrt{\dfrac{8.05 \times 24.78}{1.984}}$ (i) 0.1   (ii) 1   (iii) 10   (iv) 100   (v) 1 000

▼ Solution

(a) $\dfrac{3\,902}{23\,839}$ is roughly $\dfrac{4\,000}{20\,000}$, i.e., 0.2. Therefore the answer is (ii).

(b) $\dfrac{4.19 \times 0.030\,9}{0.022\,2}$ is roughly $\dfrac{4 \times 0.03}{0.02}$, i.e., 6. Therefore the answer is (iv).

(c) $\dfrac{52.41 \times 0.044}{0.001\,18}$ is roughly $\dfrac{50 \times 0.04}{0.001}$, i.e., 2 000. Therefore the answer is (iii).

(d) $\sqrt{990}$ is roughly $\sqrt{900}$, i.e., 30. Therefore, the answer is (ii).

(e) $\sqrt{\dfrac{8.05 \times 24.78}{1.984}}$ is roughly $\sqrt{\dfrac{8 \times 25}{2}}$, i.e., $\sqrt{100}$ which is equal to 10. Therefore the answer is (iii).

Exercise 6a

1. During a sale, one kilogram of fish was sold for \$4.95. Estimate how many kilograms of fish you could buy with \$20.

2. Without doing an exact calculation, determine whether you can afford all the items below if you have only \$30.

   – 1 two-kilogram bottle of corn oil for \$6.95.
   – 5 cans of peach at \$1.95 per can.
   – 300 g of beef at \$1.02 per 100 g.
   – 24 packets of recombined milk at \$2.85 for 6.

3. Given below are the prices of three brands of soap. Determine which brand is the cheapest.

Brand	No. of bars	Net weight of each bar	Price
A	3	100 g	\$1.30
B	6	100 g	\$2.35
C	4	125 g	\$2.85

4. Estimate each of the following mentally and choose the correct answer in each case:

   (a) $3.14 \times 80.5 =$
   (i) 2.527 7   (ii) 25.277
   (iii) 252.77   (iv) 2 527.7

   (b) $91.44 \div 0.36 =$
   (i) 2.54   (ii) 25.4
   (iii) 254   (iv) 2 540

   (c) $\sqrt{917} =$
   (i) 3.028 2   (ii) 30.282
   (iii) 302.82   (iv) 3 028.2

   (d) $\sqrt[3]{998} =$
   (i) 9.993   (ii) 31.591
   (iii) 3.159   (iv) 99.93

   (e) $\dfrac{4\,927}{9\,835} =$
   (i) 0.5   (ii) 5
   (iii) 50   (iv) 500

5. Estimate each of the following and pick the closest answer in each case:

   (a) $4\,831.9 \times 229.78 =$
   (i) 10 000   (ii) 100 000
   (iii) 1 000 000   (iv) 10 000 000

   (b) $17\,913 \times 0.963 =$
   (i) 180   (ii) 1 800
   (iii) 18 000   (iv) 180 000

   (c) $\dfrac{52.47 \times 0.083}{0.001\,98} =$
   (i) 200   (ii) 2 000
   (iii) 20 000   (iv) 200 000

   (d) $\dfrac{2\,857 \times (0.5)^2}{0.004\,9} =$
   (i) 1 500   (ii) 15 000
   (iii) 150 000   (iv) 1 500 000

   (e) $\sqrt{0.081\,5} =$
   (i) 0.09   (ii) 0.03
   (iii) 0.9   (iv) 0.3

 Approximations in Measurements and Accuracy

In most of our daily situations we do not need to use highly sensitive measuring devices. How accurate our measurements are depends on what we need the information for. For example, if we use a compass to guide us from one end of the school to the other, it would not be a serious error if we are 1° off course. However, 1° off course on a journey from the earth to the moon will mean an error of 644 000 km!

Besides the errors arising from the use of different instruments, human error is another source of error. In an athletics meet, the time for the first placing of a 100-m race given by two timekeepers may be slightly different. That is why in a school athletics meet there are usually two or more timekeepers for the first few placings.

In fact, all physical measurements such as mass, length, time, area and volume can never be absolutely accurate. They are only approximations. The accuracy of a measurement depends on the measuring instruments and the person taking the measurement. Both of them can never be absolutely accurate.

In-Class Activity

You can do this activity with a partner.

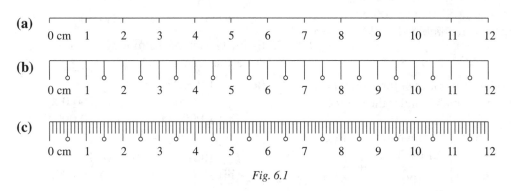

Fig. 6.1

1. Make a photocopy of Fig. 6.1 and paste it on a piece of vanguard sheet. Cut out the three strips and use them as rulers for this activity.

2.

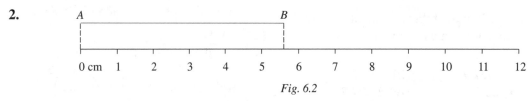

Fig. 6.2

In Fig. 6.2, we say that the length of AB is **6 cm to the nearest cm** as the end point is nearer to 6 cm.

(a) Draw three lines of lengths between 5 cm and 10 cm each.

(b) Use the first ruler (Fig. 6.1(a)) to measure the lengths of the line drawn by the other.

(c) What are the lengths of the lines to the nearest cm?

3. Fig. 6.3 shows the same line AB measured using the second ruler (Fig. 6.1(b)).

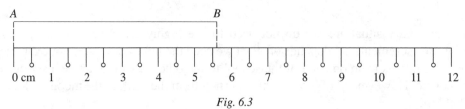

Fig. 6.3

Notice that the end point B is nearer to 5.5 cm. We say that the length of AB is **5.5 cm to the nearest 0.5 cm**. Do you agree that we achieve a greater accuracy by using the second ruler to measure the length of AB.

(a) Use your second ruler to measure the lengths of your lines.

(b) What are their lengths to the nearest 0.5 cm?

4. If we divide each centimetre (cm) into 10 equal parts like the third ruler (Fig. 6.1(c)), we can measure AB even more accurately.

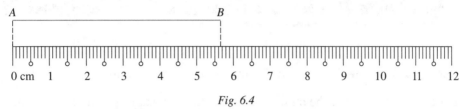

Fig. 6.4

Fig. 6.4 shows that the end point B lies between the sixth-tenth and seventh-tenth of a centimetre mark. However, it is nearer to 5.6 cm. We say that the length of AB is **5.6 cm to the nearest $\frac{1}{10}$ or 0.1 cm**.

(a) Use your third ruler to measure the lengths of the lines you have drawn.

(b) What are their lengths to the nearest 0.1 cm?

Rounding of Decimals (Revision)

The rules for rounding a decimal to a required number of decimal places have been dealt with in Chapter 4. The following examples serve as a revision.

For example, **(a)** 3.128 cm $\approx$ 3.1 cm, rounded off to the nearest 0.1 cm.

(b) 2.765 cm $\approx$ 2.8 cm, rounded off to the nearest 0.1 cm.
(c) 45.7 kg $\approx$ 46 kg, rounded off to the nearest kg.
(d) 12.45 kg $\approx$ 12 kg, rounded off to the nearest kg.
(e) 42.449 kg $\approx$ 42.4 kg, rounded off to the nearest 0.1 kg.
(f) 528 g $\approx$ 530 g, rounded off to the nearest 10 g.
(g) 21.85 cm $\approx$ 22 cm, rounded off to the nearest cm.
(h) 15.22 s $\approx$ 15.2 s, rounded off to one decimal place.

Note: If we round 5.01 to the nearest tenth, the answer should be 5.0 and not 5, because 5 can be interpreted as an approximation of 5.01 to the nearest whole number but not to the nearest 0.1. Although 5.0 and 5 are equal as numbers they indicate different degrees of accuracy.

Accuracy and Significant Figures

The accuracy of a measurement is indicated by the number of figures or digits, called **significant figures** or **digits**, that it contains. Suppose that a line PQ, with an actual length of 5.01 cm, is measured using ruler 1 (Fig. 6.1(a)) and ruler 3 (Fig. 6.1(c)) respectively. The measurements of PQ would be 5 cm (to the nearest cm) and 5.0 (to the nearest 0.1 cm) respectively.

We say that

5 cm is the length of PQ (measured) correct to **one** significant figure

and   5.0 cm is the length of PQ correct to **two** significant figures.

Significant Figures and Estimation

Estimation can be done by rounding a number to a specified decimal place. It can also be done by rounding to a specified number of significant figures. Consider a HDB flat priced at $485 500. To get a quick idea of the affordability of the flat, we may estimate the price by rounding it to $500 000, an approximation of $485 500 to one significant figure.

 ## Rounding a Number to a Given Number of Significant Figures

We have the following **rules** for rounding a number to a given number of significant figures:

1. Consider the place values of the number from left to right, starting with the first non-zero figure. Include one extra figure for consideration.

2. If the extra figure is less than 5, drop the extra figure and all other following figures to the right. Use zeros to keep the place values if necessary. (e.g. correct to 4 significant figures, 2.040 45 = 2.040 and not 2.04; correct to 3 significant figures, 0.400 127 = 0.400 and not 0.4.)

3. If the extra figure is 5 or more, add 1 to the previous figure before dropping the extra figure and all other following figures. Use zeros to keep the place values if necessary.

To find how many number of significant figures there are in a number we have the following rules:

1. The following figures in a number are significant:
   (a) All non-zero figures (e.g. 7.12 has three significant figures).
   (b) All zeros between significant figures (e.g. 2003 has four significant figures).
   (c) All zeros at the end of a decimal (e.g. 22.300 has five significant figures).

2. The following figures in a number are not significant:
   (a) All zeros at the beginning of a decimal less than 1 (e.g. 0.000 325 has three significant figures).
   (b) All zeros at the end of a number may or may not be significant. It depends on how the estimation is made (e.g. in 0.020 25 correct to 1 significant number, 0.02, the zeros are not significant).

For example,
1. 0.060 52 = 0.06 correct to 1 significant figure.
2. 0.065 2 = 0.065 correct to 2 significant figures.
3. 0.003 824 = 0.004 correct to 1 significant figure.
4. 0.003 824 = 0.003 8 correct to 2 significant figures.
5. 0.003 824 = 0.003 82 correct to 3 significant figures.

The zeros in 1–5 are not significant.

6. 2.005 7 = 2.0 correct to 2 significant figures.
7. 2.005 7 = 2.01 correct to 3 significant figures.
8. 2.005 7 = 2.006 correct to 4 significant figures.

The zeros in 6–8 are significant.

9. 0.834 = 0.83 correct to 2 significant figures.
10. 0.600 27 = 0.600 correct to 3 significant figures.

11. $0.059\ 002 = 0.059\ 00$ correct to 4 significant figures.
12. $4\ 276 = 4\ 000$ correct to 1 significant figure.
13. $4\ 276 = 4\ 300$ correct to 2 significant figures.
14. $4\ 276 = 4\ 280$ correct to 3 significant figures.
15. $40\ 004 = 40\ 000$ correct to 1 significant figure.
        (if the estimation is made, correct to the nearest 10 000)
16. $40\ 004 = 40\ 000$ correct to 2 significant figures.
        (if the estimation is made, correct to the nearest 1 000)
17. $40\ 004 = 40\ 000$ correct to 3 significant figures.
        (if the estimation is made, correct to the nearest 100)
18. $40\ 004 = 40\ 000$ correct to 4 significant figures.
        (if the estimation is made, correct to the nearest 10)

Example 3

Estimate the following, giving your answers correct to 1 significant figure:

(a) $\dfrac{74.97}{2.52}$

(b) $\sqrt{\dfrac{12.02 \times 24.99}{3.001}}$

When we are asked to estimate to 1 significant figure, we normally estimate to 2 significant figures in the working and then round off to 1 significant figure for the final answer. Similarly, for 2 significant figures, work with 3 significant figures before rounding off and so on.

▼**Solution**

(a) $\dfrac{74.97}{2.52} \approx \dfrac{75}{2.5} = \dfrac{750}{25} = 30$

$\therefore \dfrac{74.97}{2.52} \approx 30$ (correct to 1 significant figure)

(b) $\sqrt{\dfrac{12.02 \times 24.99}{3.001}} \approx \sqrt{\dfrac{12 \times 25}{3}} = \sqrt{100} = 10$

$\therefore \sqrt{\dfrac{12.02 \times 24.99}{3.001}} \approx 10$ (correct to 1 significant figure)

Example 4

(a) *Express 0.061 54 correct to*
   (i) *three decimal places and state the number of significant figures in the result;*
   (ii) *three significant figures and state the number of decimal places in the result.*

(b) *Express 12.205 7 correct to*
   (i) *two decimal places and state the number of significant figures in the result;*
   (ii) *five significant figures and state the number of decimal places in the result.*

▼**Solution**

(a) (i) $0.061\ 54 = 0.062$ (correct to three decimal places)
      0.062 has two significant figures.
   (ii) $0.061\ 54 = 0.061\ 5$ (correct to three significant figures)
      0.061 5 has four decimal places.

(b) (i) $12.205\ 7 = 12.21$ (correct to two decimal places)
      12.21 has four significant figures.

(ii) $12.205\ 7 = 12.206$ (correct to five significant figures)

12.206 has three decimal places.

Exercise 6b

1. Round off the following:
   - (a) 456 g to the nearest 10 g
   - (b) 722 g to the nearest 100 g
   - (c) 3.27 cm to the nearest cm
   - (d) 123.452 cm to 1 decimal place
   - (e) 18.2 to the nearest whole number
   - (f) 31.256 m to the nearest 10 m
   - (g) 12.35 cm to the nearest 0.1 cm
   - (h) 4 325 pupils to the nearest 100 pupils
   - (i) 845 km to the nearest 10 km
   - (j) 22.58 mm to the nearest $\dfrac{1}{10}$ mm

2. State the number of significant figures in each of the following:
   - (a) 15.0
   - (b) 27.3
   - (c) 30 756
   - (d) 4.02
   - (e) 63
   - (f) 9.5
   - (g) 30.08
   - (h) 48.20
   - (i) 6 000 000
   - (j) 0.028 3
   - (k) 0.74
   - (l) 0.000 65

3. Express the following numbers correct to the number of significant figures indicated within the brackets:
   - (a) 3.084   (2)
   - (b) 1.483 56   (4)
   - (c) 0.003 46   (1)
   - (d) 16.047   (1)
   - (e) 3.141 59   (2)
   - (f) 0.574 38   (2)
   - (g) 0.056 78   (3)
   - (h) 217.006   (5)
   - (i) 3.598   (3)
   - (j) 15.703 7   (4)
   - (k) 0.003 56   (2)
   - (l) 5.98   (2)
   - (m) 0.035 1   (2)
   - (n) 17.97   (3)
   - (o) 8.353   (2)
   - (p) 120.408   (5)
   - (q) 4.826   (3)
   - (r) 12.096   (2)
   - (s) 0.049 72   (2)
   - (t) 0.080 46   (2)
   - (u) 0.010 10   (3)
   - (v) 0.103 49   (3)

4. (a) Estimate the value of $\dfrac{7.94}{2.01}$ correct to 1 significant figure.
   (b) Use your result to estimate the value of $\dfrac{79\ 400}{0.000\ 201}$.

5. Estimate the value of $\dfrac{21.83 \times 0.498}{220.1}$, giving your answer correct to 1 significant figure.

6. Use a calculator to evaluate the following, giving your answer correct to 3 significant figures.
   - (a) $(0.218\ 7)^3$
   - (b) $\sqrt[3]{0.086\ 42}$
   - (c) $\sqrt{25.6^2 + 17.89^2}$
   - (d) $\sqrt{\dfrac{1\ 976 \times (14.98)^2}{(59.87)^2}}$

7. Express 28.136 275 correct to two significant figures. How many decimal places are there in the result?

8. Express 0.211 087 94 correct to three significant figures. Write down the number of decimal places in the result.

9. Express 0.008 345 7 correct to four decimal places. State the number of significant figures in the answer.

10. Express 117.964 8 correct to two decimal places. How many significant figures are there in the answer?

Summary

Rules for rounding a number to a given number of significant figures:

(a) Count the given number of significant figures from left to right, starting with the first non-zero figure. Include one extra figure for consideration.

(b) If the extra figure is less than 5, drop the extra figure and all other following figures. Use zeros to keep the place value if necessary.

(c) If the extra figure is 5 or more, add 1 to the previous figure before dropping the extra figure and all other following figures. Use zeros to keep the place value if necessary.

Rules for determining the number of significant figures:

(a) The following figures in a number are significant:
  (i) All non-zero figures.
  (ii) All zeros between significant figures.
  (iii) All zeros at the end of a decimal.

(b) The following figures in a number are not significant:
  (i) All zeros at the beginning of a decimal less than 1.
  (ii) All zeros at the end of a whole number may or may not be significant. It depends on how the estimation is made.

Review Questions 6

1. Estimate each of the following mentally and pick the correct answer in each case:

   (a) $4.07 \times 6.998 =$
(i) 0.284 8	**(ii)** 2.848
(iii) 28.48	**(iv)** 284.8

   (b) $29.7 \div 5.03 =$
(i) 0.590 5	**(ii)** 5.905
(iii) 59.05	**(iv)** 590.5

   (c) $\sqrt{899} + \sqrt[3]{1\,029} =$
(i) 4.008	**(ii)** 40.08
(iii) 400.8	**(iv)** 4 008

   (d) $\dfrac{6.003 - 5.12 \times 0.992}{5.97 \div 3.103} =$
(i) 0.048	**(ii)** 0.48
(iii) 4.8	**(iv)** 48

2. Estimate each of the following and pick the closest answer in each case:

   (a) $4\,962.8 \times 312.93 =$
(i) 1 500 000	**(ii)** 150 000
(iii) 15 000	**(iv)** 1 500

   (b) $\dfrac{9.103\,4 - 7.990\,2}{(10.012\,3)^2} =$
(i) 0.001	**(ii)** 0.01
(iii) 0.1	**(iv)** 1.0

   (c) $\dfrac{45.117 \div 8.97}{4.983 \times 0.002\,104} =$
(i) 50	**(ii)** 500
(iii) 5 000	**(iv)** 50 000

   (d) $\dfrac{3.989\,7 \times 2.100\,5}{(0.019\,9)^3} =$
(i) 1 000 000	**(ii)** 100 000
(iii) 10 000	**(iv)** 1 000

3. Express the following correct to the number of decimal places or significant figures indicated within the brackets:
(a)	0.085 67	(3 decimal places)
(b)	0.085 67	(3 significant figures)
(c)	5.096	(3 significant figures)
(d)	726 990	(2 significant figures)
(e)	0.058 76	(2 decimal places)
(f)	0.058 76	(1 significant figure)
(g)	0.006 138	(3 significant figures)
(h)	0.003 549	(3 decimal places)

4. Estimate, correct to 1 significant figure, the value of $52.976\,03 - 31.321\,86$.

5. Estimate, correct to 1 significant figure, the value of

   (a) $\dfrac{79.81}{1.62}$; **(b)** $\dfrac{66.4}{0.031\,9}$.

Problem Solving

1. Find the approximate value of $\dfrac{31.98 \div 8.03}{48.109 - 29.989 \times 0.995}$, giving your answer correct to 1 significant figure.

2. Estimate the value of $20.02 \times 9.99 - 6.112 \times \dfrac{16.027}{(1.977)^3}$ correct to 2 significant figures.

3. Estimate, correct to 1 significant figure, the value of $\sqrt{136.05 - (2.985 + 7.001)^2}$.

4. A Singaporean has assets of $5 billion ($5 000 000 000). If he spends $10 every second, how long will it take for him to spend all his money?

Basic Algebra

In this chapter, you will learn how to

▲ use letters to represent numbers;
▲ express basic arithmetical processes algebraically;
▲ substitute numbers for letters in formulae and expressions;
▲ manipulate simple algebraic expressions.

Preliminary Problem

P etrol costs $1.21 per litre.

How much will it cost to fill up a full tank of petrol if the tank can hold up to 45 litres of petrol?

How much will it cost to fill up 12 full tanks if each tank can hold up to 50 litres of petrol?

How much will it cost to fill up x full tanks if each tank can hold up to y litres of petrol?

Algebraic Expressions

Consider the following statements:

(a) I think of a number and when I add 5 to it the result is 9.

(b) I would like to buy 5 mangoes and 4 durians. If the price of a durian is twice that of a mango, I would have to pay $18.

(c) Twice my age plus three times the age of my mother will add to 120 years.

Translate the above statements using mathematical statements:

(a) We shall use $\square$ to represent the number I think of. The statement can be written simply as $\square + 5 = 9$.

 We can make the above mathematical statement correct by filling in the correct number in $\square$.

(b) We can use $\triangle$ to represent the price of a mango, then the price of a durian will be $(2\,\triangle)$. We write $5 \times \triangle + 4 \times (2\,\triangle) = \$18$.

(c) We let $\square$ to represent my age and $\triangle$ to represent the age of my mother. We write $2 \times \square + 3 \times \triangle = 120$.

Example 1

Use mathematical symbols, $\square$ and/or $\triangle$, to rewrite the following statements:

(a) I think of a number, and if I subtract 3 from it the result is 15.
(b) I think of two numbers; twice the first number when added to the second number is less than 50.
(c) I think of two numbers. Adding 5 to the first number and dividing the result by the second number gives 5.

▼Solution

(a) $\square - 3 = 15$ (b) $2 \times \square + \triangle < 50$ (c) $(\square + 5) \div \triangle = 5$

Example 2

Use mathematical symbols $\square$ and/or $\triangle$ to rewrite the following statements:

(a) I bought 5 exercise books and the total cost is $2.75.
(b) Aunty Tan gave each of the 5 boys some sweets and each of the 6 girls 2 more sweets than the boys. Altogether she gave away 100 sweets.
(c) Mrs Kunna bought 3 blouses and 4 skirts for her daughter. She paid a total of $245.

▼Solution

(a) $5 \times \square = \$2.75$
(b) $5 \times \square + 6 \times (\square + 2) = 100$
(c) $3 \times \square + 4 \times \triangle = \$245$

Exercise 7a

1. Use □ and/or △ and mathematical symbols to rewrite the following statements:

   (a) I think of a number, multiply it by 7 and the result is 91.
   (b) I think of a number, subtract 5 from it and multiply the result by 4. The final answer is 28.
   (c) I think of a number, multiply it by 5 and add 4 to the result. The final answer is 19.
   (d) I think of a number, subtract 2 from it and multiply the result by 3 to give a final result of 12.
   (e) I think of a number and add 15 to it. The result multiplied by another number gives a final answer of 84.
   (f) I buy 2 toy cars and the total cost is $32.
   (g) Amy bought a meal and two soft toys from a fast-food outlet for a total cost of $8.40.
   (h) Twice Jeffrey's age and five times Anita's age will add up to 47 years.
   (i) The Tan family bought 5 music CDs and 3 VCDs for a total cost of $98.
   (j) The total labour cost to transport a total of 320 chairs and 450 tables is $128.
   (k) An apprentice painter can work at only $\frac{3}{4}$ the rate of a master painter. Two apprentice painters and 4 master painters together can paint a block of flats in 6 days.
   (l) A company allocates a budget of not more than $3 000 per month to maintain a car and two lorries.
   (m) It takes 2 hours and 40 minutes for Jason to complete 3 exercises for Maths and 2 exercises for Geography.

Fundamental Algebra

We used different shapes to represent numbers in our earlier discussion. As the number of unknowns increases we may find it inconvenient to use many different shapes. It will be easier if we use letters to represent these unknowns.

In algebra, we use numbers as well as letters such as A, B, C, a, b and c to stand for any numerical values we choose. Algebra is an extension of arithmetic.

Notations in Algebra

The signs $+$, $-$, $\times$, $\div$, $=$, etc, are used in algebra as in arithmetic.

1. In arithmetic, $5 + 4 = 9$ means that the sum of 5 and 4 is equal to 9. In algebra, $x + y = z$ means that the sum of two numbers represented by x and y is equal to the number represented by z.

   If $x = 4$, $y = 3$, then z stands for 7.
   If $x = 4$, $z = 8$, then y stands for 4.

   Similarly, $x - y = z$ means that the difference between two numbers represented by the letters x and y is equal to the number represented by the letter z.

   Note: if $x + y = z$ stands for 9, then x and y may stand for any pair of numbers whose sum is 9, for example, 4 and 5, 7 and 2, and 1.7 and 7.3.

2. In arithmetic, $5 \times 4 = 20$ means that the product of 5 and 4 is 20. In algebra $a \times b = c$ means that the product of two numbers a and b is equal to the number represented by the letter c. Normally we write $a \times b = c$ simply as $ab = c$, omitting the multiplication sign. Similarly $x = a \times b \times c$ is simply written as $x = abc$.

Note: (1) When we multiply y by 3, we normally write it as $3y$ and **not** $y3$.
(2) When we multiply x by 1, we write it simply as x and **not** $1x$ or $x1$.

Can we write 5×4 simply as 54?

3. In arithmetic, $36 \div 4 = 9$ means that 36 divided by 4 gives 9. In algebra $a \div b = c$ means that the number represented by a is divided by the number represented by the letter b to give the result represented by the letter c. Also $a \div b$ is normally written as $\dfrac{a}{b}$.

4. In arithmetic, $3 \times 3 \times 3 \times 3$ may be written as 3^4, and 7^5 means $7 \times 7 \times 7 \times 7 \times 7$. In algebra $a \times a \times a \times a$ is written as a^4 and y^5 means $y \times y \times y \times y \times y$.

Example 3

Write an algebraic expression for each of the following:

(a) Subtract 2x from y and multiply the difference by z.
(b) Divide the sum of x and y by the difference when x is subtracted from y.

**Solution**

(a) When $2x$ is subtracted from y, we have $y - 2x$. Multiplying the difference by z gives the result $(y - 2x)z$.

(b) The sum of x and y is $(x + y)$. When x is subtracted from y, the difference is $(y - x)$. The final result is $\dfrac{x + y}{y - x}$.

Example 4

Is $3a^2 = (3a)^2$? Explain your answer.

Solution

$3a^2$ means the product of 3 and a^2 i.e., $3 \times a \times a$.
$(3a)^2$ means the product of $3a$ and $3a$ i.e., $3a \times 3a$.

$$3a \times 3a = 3 \times a \times 3 \times a$$
$$= 9a^2$$

Hence, $\qquad\qquad 3a^2 \neq (3a)^2$

 ## Polynomials, Variables, Coefficients and Constant Terms

An algebraic expression involves numbers, and operational signs such as $+$, $-$, $\times$ and $\div$. The $+$ and $-$ signs in an algebraic expression separate it into terms.

For example, $8y + 7z$ consists of 2 terms,
$7x^2 - 2xy + 7y^2$ consists of 3 terms,
while ab consists of only 1 term.

A **polynomial** is an algebraic expression consisting of one or more terms. For example, the expressions $x + 5$, $x + 3y$, $5x + 7y$ and $x^2 + 4x - 3$ are polynomials.

Consider the algebraic expressions: (a) $4x$ (b) $5x + 7$

The polynomial in (a) will take on different values for different values of x given.

For example,   when $x = 2, 4x = 4 \times 2 = 8$
$x = 3, 4x = 4 \times 3 = 12$
$x = 5, 4x = 4 \times 5 = 20$ and so on.

Since the value of $4x$ varies according to the value given to x, x is called a **variable**.

In the term $4x$, the constant factor 4 is called the **coefficient** of the term. Thus, the coefficient of x in $5\boldsymbol{x}$ is 5, the coefficient of xy in $7\boldsymbol{xy}$ is 7, the coefficient of abc in $23\boldsymbol{abc}$ is 23, and so on.

What is the coefficient of x^2 in $25x^2$?

The polynomial in (b) will take on different values for different values of x given.

For example,   when $x = 2, 5x + 7 = 5 \times 2 + 7 = 17$
$x = 3, 5x + 7 = 5 \times 3 + 7 = 22$
$x = 5, 5x + 7 = 5 \times 5 + 7 = 32$ and so on.

Notice that the value of the polynomial depends on x; the numeral 7 always remains unchanged. We call this numeral a **constant term** or simply a **constant**.

Each polynomial has a **degree** which is given by the **highest power** of the variable.

For example, in $8x^3 - 7x^2 + 5x + 3$, the highest power of the variable x is 3. Therefore, the degree of the polynomial $8x^3 - 7x^2 + 5x + 3$ is 3.

What is the degree of the polynomial of $5x^2 - 3x^3 + 5x^4 - 7x + 2$?

Usually, a polynomial is expressed such that the degrees of the terms appear in **descending order**, for example, $3x^3 + 2x^2 - 4x + 7$. Sometimes it is expressed with the degrees of the terms appearing in **ascending order**, for example, $3 + 5x - 7x^2 + 8x^3$.

1. A **variable** is a changing quantity, usually denoted by a letter in algebraic equations and expressions, that might have any one of a range of possible values.

2. A **coefficient** is a multiplying factor. In $2x^2 + 3x = 0$, x is a variable, and the coefficient of x^2 is 2 and that of x is 3.

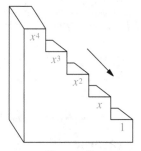

Descending

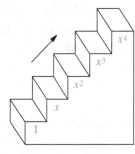

Ascending

Example 5

Write an algebraic expression for each of the following:

(a) Add 2x to 3y.   (b) Subtract 5x from 12.   (c) Multiply u by 3v.
(d) Divide 3k by 7x.   (e) Subtract the product of x and 3y from the sum of p and q.

Solution

(a) $2x + 3y$

(b) $12 - 5x$

(c) $u \times 3v = 3uv$

(d) $3k \div 7x = \dfrac{3k}{7x}$

(e) $p + q - x \times 3y = p + q - 3xy$

Example 6

Ali is three times as old as Beng and Beng is five years older than Chandra. If Beng is x years old, write algebraic expressions for each of the following:

(a) Ali's age today.   (b) Chandra's age today.
(c) Ali's age in 5 years' time.
(d) The sum of Ali's and Beng's ages in 2 years' time.
(e) The sum of Beng's and Chandra's ages 4 years ago.

Solution

(a) Ali's age is $3x$ years old.
(b) Chandra's age is $(x - 5)$ years old.
(c) Ali will be $(3x + 5)$ years old.
(d) In 2 years' time, Ali will be $(3x + 2)$ years old and Beng will be $(x + 2)$ years old. The sum of their ages is $(3x + 2) + (x + 2) = (4x + 4)$.
(e) Four years ago, Beng was $(x - 4)$ years old and Chandra was $(x - 5 - 4)$, i.e., $(x - 9)$ years old. The sum of their ages then was $(x - 4) + (x - 9) = (2x - 13)$ years old.

Example 7

Write an algebraic expression for each of the following:

(a) The sum of three consecutive integers, of which x is the middle integer.
(b) The product of two consecutive odd integers, of which x is the smaller integer.
(c) The total cost of x 10¢ stamps and 25 y¢ stamps.

Solution

(a) The integer after x is $(x + 1)$ and the one before x is $(x - 1)$. The sum of the three consecutive integers is $(x - 1) + x + (x + 1) = 3x$.
(b) The greater of the two consecutive odd integers is $(x + 2)$. The product of the two integers is $x \times (x + 2)$ or $x(x + 2)$.
(c) The cost of x 10¢ stamps $= (x \times 10)¢ = 10x¢$.
    The cost of 25 y¢ stamps $= (25 \times y)¢ = 25y¢$.
    The total cost $= (10x + 25y)¢$.

Example 8

Evaluate 2x + 5y when

(a) *x = 3 and y = 5;*   (b) *x = 2 and y = –1;*   (c) *x = –2 and y = 3.*

Solution

(a) When $x = 3$ and $y = 5$, $2x + 5y = 2(3) + 5(5) = 6 + 25 = 31$.
(b) When $x = 2$ and $y = -1$, $2x + 5y = 2(2) + 5(-1) = 4 - 5 = -1$.
(c) When $x = -2$ and $y = 3$, $2x + 5y = 2(-2) + 5(3) = -4 + 15 = 11$.

It has been said that the language of science is mathematics and the grammar of mathematics is algebra.

Example 9

Evaluate the following when a = 3, b = 4 and c = 6:

(a) *a(2c – b)*   (b) *ab[(3b – c) – a]*

(c) *(a + b)(c – b) + ab*   (d) $\dfrac{a + b}{c} + \dfrac{a + c}{c - b}$

Solution

(a) $a(2c - b) = 3(2 \times 6 - 4) = 3(12 - 4) = 3(8) = 24$

(b) $ab[(3b - c) - a] = 3 \times 4[(3 \times 4 - 6) - 3]$
$$= 12[(12 - 6) - 3]$$
$$= 12[6 - 3] = 12(3) = 36$$

(c) $(a + b)(c - b) + ab = (3 + 4)(6 - 4) + 3 \times 4$
$$= 7 \times 2 + 12 = 14 + 12 = 26$$

(d) $\dfrac{a + b}{c} + \dfrac{a + c}{c - b} = \dfrac{3 + 4}{6} + \dfrac{3 + 6}{6 - 4} = \dfrac{7}{6} + \dfrac{9}{2}$
$$= \dfrac{7 + 9 \times 3}{6} = \dfrac{7 + 27}{6} = \dfrac{34}{6} = 5\dfrac{2}{3}$$

═ Exercise 7b ═

1. Express the following polynomials so that the degrees of the terms are in descending order:

    (a) $3x + 7x^2 + 4 - 5x^3$
    (b) $7x^4 - 4x + 7x^3 - 5x^2$
    (c) $4x^2 + 5x^3 - 7x + 4$
    (d) $7x^2 + 5x^5 - 6x^3 + 7$

2. Express the following polynomials so that the degrees of the terms are in ascending order:

    (a) $7x + 4x^3 + 4 - 3x^2$
    (b) $8x^3 - 9x^2 + 4x^5 - 4x$
    (c) $2a^2 - 4a + 3a^5 - 4a^6$
    (d) $4b^3 - 3b + 7b^5 - 4b^2$

3. Write an algebraic expression for each of the following:

    (a) Add $2x$ to 14.
    (b) Subtract 14 from $5a$.
    (c) Multiply 4 by $2k$.
    (d) Divide $8x$ by $24y$.
    (e) Add $2x$ to twice $3y$.
    (f) Subtract $5x$ from half of y.

4. Translate each of the following word expressions into algebraic expressions:

    (a) The sum of a number $2x$ and a number y.
    (b) The product of 7 and a number k.
    (c) Fifteen subtracted from twice the number t.

(d) Three times the number u decreased by four.

(e) Eight more than half of a number v.

(f) The total value of h 50¢ coins and k $2 notes in dollars.

(g) The total cost of buying x sets of stamps to commemorate the 50th Anniversary of the Inter-Religious Organisation (IRO) at $1.82 per set, and y sets of the Rabbit Zodiac series at $2.22 per set.

5. If $a = 2$, $b = -3$, $c = 4$, $d = 5$ and $e = -6$, find the value of each of the following:

(a) $3a - 3(2c - e)$ **(b)** $4(a - 3b) - 5c$

(c) $4c - (a - 2b - e)$ **(d)** $9c - 3(2d + c)$

(e) $7e - 5b^2 + 4ac$ **(f)** $5abe - 4(e + c)^2$

6. Write an algebraic expression for each of the following:

(a) The cost of x litres of petrol at $1.10 per litre.

(b) Three times the variable x divided by the sum of 3 and k.

(c) Five times the number which is 3 more than h.

(d) One quarter of the number which is 4 less than m.

(e) The total number of eggs in k cartons where each carton contains n eggs.

(f) The total distance travelled by a car for x hours at a constant speed of z km/h.

7. Mary is x years old. Write an algebraic expression for each of the following:

(a) Three times Mary's age next year.

(b) Five times Mary's age six years ago.

$*$**(c)** The present age of Mary's aunt if her aunt is four times as old as Mary will be 2 years from now.

$*$**(d)** The present age of Mary's niece if her niece is 3 years less than one-third Mary's age 5 years ago.

8. If $a = 2$, $b = -3$ and $c = 4$, evaluate each of the following:

(a) $\dfrac{5ac - 2b^2}{2ab}$ **(b)** $\dfrac{3a^3 + 2b^2 - 4c}{2a + 4b}$

(c) $\dfrac{5a + 3bc - c^2}{2ac - 4b}$ **(d)** $\dfrac{7a + 8b + 2c}{3c - 2b - 4a}$

(e) $\dfrac{2c - 4b + 5ab}{(c + a)(c - a)}$ **(f)** $\dfrac{\left(\dfrac{a}{b}\right)\left(\dfrac{c}{b}\right)}{\dfrac{a}{b} - \dfrac{a}{c}}$

(g) $\dfrac{\dfrac{2}{b} + \dfrac{c}{a}}{\dfrac{c}{a} - \dfrac{a}{c}}$ **(h)** $\dfrac{\dfrac{1}{a} - \dfrac{2}{b}}{\dfrac{a}{b} \div \dfrac{1}{c}}$

Three boxes of fruit, the first containing oranges, the second containing apples and the third containing half of oranges and half of apples are labelled O, A and OA to indicate their contents. However, you are told that the labels have been switched so that every box is now incorrectly labelled.

You are to re-label the boxes so that the labels are correct. You are allowed to draw only one fruit from any of the 3 boxes.

Some Rules in Algebra

1. In algebra, terms of the same kind, called **like terms**, can be combined into a single term; added to or subtracted from one another. For example,

(a) $3a + 5a = 8a$ (b) $7b - 3b = 4b$

(c) $2a + 5b + 4a + 8b = (2a + 4a) + (5b + 8b) = 6a + 13b$

(d) $9c + 7d - 4c - 5d = (9c - 4c) + (7d - 5d) = 5c + 2d$

(e) $7a + 9b - 5a - 4b + 2a - b = (7a - 5a + 2a) + (9b - 4b - b)$
$= 4a + 4b$

Can you simplify $5x^2 + 3x$ or $2x^3 - 3x^2$?

2. In multiplication and division, the coefficients and the variables are multiplied or divided. For example,

(a) $3 \times 6a = 3 \times 6 \times a = 18a$

(b) $2a \times 5a = 2 \times a \times 5 \times a = 10a^2$

(c) $12m \times 3n = 12 \times m \times 3 \times n = 36mn$

(d) $3(a - b) = 3 \times a - 3 \times b = 3a - 3b$

(e) $-a \times (-2ab) = (-1) \times a \times (-2) \times a \times b$
$= (-1) \times (-2) \times a \times a \times b = 2a^2b$

(f) $14m \div 7 = \dfrac{14m}{7} = 2m$

(g) $18a \div 10b = \dfrac{18a}{10b} = \dfrac{9a}{5b}, \ b \neq 0$

(h) $\sqrt{9a^4} = \sqrt{3 \times 3 \times a \times a \times a \times a} = 3a^2$

3. The terms $3a^2$ and $2a$ are unlike terms. Therefore they cannot be combined into a single term by adding or subtracting.

Exercise 7c

1. Simplify the following expressions:
   (a) $4x + 7x + 3x$
   (b) $5c - 7c + 2c$
   (c) $4a - 6b - 3a$
   (d) $2c + 4d - 5d$
   (e) $13x + 6y - 6x$
   (f) $11pq - 7pq$
   (g) $ef - 3ef + 4ef$
   (h) $5de + 8de - bc$
   (i) $p^2 + 4p^2 - 3p^2$
   (j) $9a^2 - 7a^2 + 2a^2$
   (k) $q^3 - q^3 - q^3$
   (l) $3t^3 + t - 2t^3$

2. Simplify the following expressions:
   (a) $5n \times 12$
   (b) $-2 \times 6a$
   (c) $-4 \times (-2k)$
   (d) $\dfrac{1}{3} \times 15a$
   (e) $2 \times \dfrac{3m}{4}$
   (f) $-16b \times \dfrac{1}{4}$
   (g) $-\dfrac{2}{5} \times 20n$
   (h) $-\dfrac{3}{7}a \times \left(-4\dfrac{2}{3}\right)$
   (i) $51u \div 17$
   (j) $(-11c) \div 121$
   (k) $(-27v) \div (-3)$
   (l) $18 \div (6a) \quad (a \neq 0)$

(m) $45 \div (-15d) \quad (d \neq 0)$
(n) $(-32) \div 8 \times (-5m)$

3. Simplify the following expressions:
   (a) $2k \times (-7k)$
   (b) $-4b \times (-8b)$
   (c) $-1\dfrac{1}{2}x \times 6x$
   (d) $-\dfrac{3}{4}y \times \left(-\dfrac{8}{9}y\right)$
   (e) $3a \times 5b$
   (f) $2m \times (-7n)$
   (g) $-\dfrac{3}{5}u \times (-20v)$
   (h) $54b \div 9a \quad (a \neq 0)$
   (i) $(-24m) \div (-18n) \quad (n \neq 0)$
   (j) $2a \times 7a \times (-5b)$
   (k) $\sqrt{d^4e^2}$
   (l) $2xy \div 3y^2 \times 5x^2 \quad (y \neq 0)$
   (m) $\dfrac{c^2}{5} \div \dfrac{cd}{25} \quad (c, d \neq 0)$
   (n) $3d \times 2de \times def$
   (o) $\sqrt{25c^6d^4}$

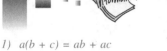

Use of Brackets in Simplification

1) $a(b + c) = ab + ac$
2) $a(b - c) = ab - ac$
3) $-a(b + c) = -ab - ac$
4) $-a(b - c) = -ab + ac$
5) $a(-b + c) = -ab + ac$
6) $a(-b - c) = -ab - ac$
7) $-a(-b + c) = ab - ac$
8) $-a(-b - c) = ab + ac$

When brackets occur in an algebraic expression, the rules by which operations are performed apply exactly as in arithmetic:

(a) Simplify the expression within the brackets first.

(b) When an expression contains more than one pair of brackets, simplify the expression within the innermost pair of brackets first, for example, $[2c - 4(c - 1)] = [2c - 4c + 4] = 4 - 2c$

(c) If an expression in brackets is multiplied by a number, **each term** within the brackets must be multiplied by that number when the brackets are removed, for example, $4(a - 2b + 3c) = 4a - 8b + 12c$

(d) The expression $\dfrac{x}{y}$ ($y \neq 0$) is called an algebraic fraction.

In the fractions $\dfrac{2x - 3}{4}$ and $\dfrac{5x - 7}{6}$, the numerators can be placed within brackets.

Thus, $\dfrac{2x - 3}{4}$ can be written as $\dfrac{(2x - 3)}{4}$ or $\dfrac{1}{4}(2x - 3)$ and $\dfrac{5x - 7}{6}$ can be written as $\dfrac{(5x - 7)}{6}$ or $\dfrac{1}{6}(5x - 7)$.

The procedure for simplifying algebraic fractions is similar to that of simplifying ordinary fractions.

Example 10

Simplify (a) $3a + 5b - 3c - 2b + 7c - a + 4c - 6b + 8a$;
(b) $3x + 2(x + 4) - (2x - 3) + 5x - 7$;
(c) $2[4p - 3(m + p)]$.

▼ **Solution**

(a) $3a + 5b - 3c - 2b + 7c - a + 4c - 6b + 8a$
$= (3 - 1 + 8)a + (5 - 2 - 6)b + (-3 + 7 + 4)c = 10a - 3b + 8c$

(b) $3x + 2(x + 4) - (2x - 3) + 5x - 7 = 3x + 2x + 8 - 2x + 3 + 5x - 7$
$= (3 + 2 - 2 + 5)x + (8 + 3 - 7)$
$= 8x + 4$

(c) $2[4p - 3(m + p)] = 2(4p - 3m - 3p)$
$= 2(p - 3m)$
$= 2p - 6m$

Example 11

Simplify the following expressions:

(a) $\dfrac{2x - 3}{5} + \dfrac{x - 3}{3}$

(b) $\dfrac{2x - 7}{3} - \dfrac{2x - 6}{9}$

(c) $\dfrac{x + y}{2} + \dfrac{3x - y}{5} - \dfrac{7(2x - 4)}{6}$

▼ **Solution**

(a) The LCM of 5 and 3 is 15.

$\dfrac{2x - 3}{5} + \dfrac{x - 3}{3}$

$= \dfrac{3(2x - 3)}{15} + \dfrac{5(x - 3)}{15}$

$= \dfrac{3(2x - 3) + 5(x - 3)}{15}$

$= \dfrac{6x - 9 + 5x - 15}{15}$

$= \dfrac{11x - 24}{15}$

(b) The LCM of 3 and 9 is 9.

$\dfrac{2x - 7}{3} - \dfrac{2x - 6}{9}$

$= \dfrac{3(2x - 7)}{9} - \dfrac{(2x - 6)}{9}$

$= \dfrac{3(2x - 7) - (2x - 6)}{9}$

$= \dfrac{6x - 21 - 2x + 6}{9}$

$= \dfrac{4x - 15}{9}$

(c) $\dfrac{x+y}{2} + \dfrac{3x-y}{5} - \dfrac{7(2x-4)}{6} = \dfrac{15(x+y) + 6(3x-y) - 35(2x-4)}{30}$

$$= \dfrac{15x + 15y + 18x - 6y - 70x + 140}{30}$$

$$= \dfrac{-37x + 9y + 140}{30}$$

═ Exercise 7d ═

1. Simplify the following expressions:

   (a) $5(a + 2b) - 3b$

   (b) $4u - 3(2u - 5v)$

   (c) $-2a - 3(a - b)$

   (d) $6x - 2(4y + x)$

   (e) $7m - 2n - 2(3n - 2m)$

   (f) $-3(2h - k) + 4(k - 3h)$

   (g) $5x(a - 6b + 5c) - 2x(b - c)$

   (h) $3(5x - 4y) - 2(x - 4y)$

   (i) $-4(a - 3b) - 5(a - 3b)$

   (j) $5(3p - 2q) - 2(3p + 2q)$

   (k) $a + 3(2a - 3b + c) + 7c$

   (l) $5k - 3(b + 3k) - 3b$

   (m) $(x + y) - 2(3x - 4y + 3)$

   (n) $3(p - 2q) - 4(2p - 3q - 5)$

2. Write down the simplest forms for the following:

   (a) $\dfrac{1}{2}\left[2x + \dfrac{1}{2}(4x - 12)\right]$

   (b) $\dfrac{2}{5}[12p - (5 + 2p)]$

   (c) $a - \{b - (c + d)\}$

   (d) $4\{2x + 5 - (3x - 2)\}$

   (e) $a - \{6a + 2(1 - 3a)\}$

   (f) $2\{(3p - 2q) - (p - q)\}$

   (g) $-2[3a - 4\{a - (2 + a)\}]$

   (h) $5[3c - \{d - 2(c + d)\}]$

   (i) $11x - \{5y - 3(2x + y)\}$

   (j) $-a - [b - \{a - (b - a)\}]$

   (k) $(w + r) - 4(3t - 2w) + 6(t - 2r)$

   (l) $\dfrac{1}{2}(4x - 2y) - \dfrac{2}{3}(9x - 3y) - 2(x - y)$

   (m) $-4[5(2x + 3y) - 4(x + 2y)]$

   (n) $8[3(4x + 5y) - 2(6x - 5y)]$

   (o) $3a - 4[3(1 - 2a) - 2(3 - 5a)]$

   (p) $7a - 2[3(5a - b) - 2(4a + b)]$

   (q) $5a - [3a - 2(a - 2b)]$

   (r) $2[y - 3(2y + x)] - 3x$

3. Simplify the following algebraic fractions:

   (a) $\dfrac{x}{5} + \dfrac{2x - 4}{7}$

   (b) $\dfrac{2x + 7}{3} + \dfrac{6x - 3}{5}$

   (c) $\dfrac{4x + 1}{5} + \dfrac{3x - 1}{2}$

   (d) $\dfrac{2x - 7}{4} - \dfrac{x - 6}{7}$

   (e) $\dfrac{3(x - 2)}{4} - \dfrac{4(2x - 3)}{5}$

   (f) $\dfrac{2(x + 3)}{5} - \dfrac{1}{2} + \dfrac{3x - 4}{4}$

Addition and Subtraction of Polynomials

Example 12

Find the sum of $4x^2 - 9x + 3$ and $x^2 - 2x - 8$.

▼ Solution

The expressions are arranged so that the like terms are grouped in the same columns. Then, each column is added.

$$4x^2 - 9x + 3$$
$$+\quad x^2 - 2x - 8$$
$$\overline{5x^2 - 11x - 5}$$

∴   the sum is $5x^2 - 11x - 5$.

Alternatively, if we use brackets, we write

$$(4x^2 - 9x + 3) + (x^2 - 2x - 8) = 4x^2 - 9x + 3 + x^2 - 2x - 8$$
$$= 5x^2 - 11x - 5$$

Example 13

Find the sum of $2a + 3b - 4c$, $3a - 2b$, $-4a + 5c$ and $a - 2b + c$.

 **Solution**

The expressions are arranged so that the like terms are grouped in the same columns. Then, each column is added.

$$2a + 3b - 4c$$
$$3a - 2b$$
$$-4a \qquad + 5c$$
$$+\quad a - 2b + \ c$$
$$\overline{2a - \ b + 2c}$$

∴   the sum is $2a - b + 2c$.

Alternatively, $(2a + 3b - 4c) + (3a - 2b) + (-4a + 5c) + (a - 2b + c)$
$$= 2a + 3b - 4c + 3a - 2b - 4a + 5c + a - 2b + c$$
$$= 2a - b + 2c$$

Example 14

Subtract $x^3 - 5x^2 + 6x - 7$ from $2x^3 - 7x^2 + 11x + 6$.

 **Solution**

Again, the expressions are arranged in order. The expression to be subtracted is placed below the other expression and like terms are grouped in the same columns.

$$2x^3 - 7x^2 + 11x + 6$$
$$-\ (x^3 - 5x^2 + \ 6x - 7)$$
$$\overline{x^3 - 2x^2 + \ 5x + 13}$$

∴   the result is $x^3 - 2x^2 + 5x + 13$.

This shows that if the expressions are written down as in arithmetic, the result is obtained by changing the sign of each term in the lower line and then adding. Alternatively, if we use brackets, we write

$(2x^3 - 7x^2 + 11x + 6) - (x^3 - 5x^2 + 6x - 7)$
$= 2x^3 - 7x^2 + 11x + 6 - x^3 + 5x^2 - 6x + 7$
$= x^3 - 2x^2 + 5x + 13$

$$2x^3 - 7x^2 + 11x + 6$$
$$+\ -x^3 + 5x^2 - \ 6x + 7$$
$$\overline{x^3 - 2x^2 + \ 5x + 13}$$

Example 15

Subtract 3a + 4b – 2c – 5d from 2a + 5b – d.

$$
\begin{array}{l}
\quad 2a + 5b \quad\quad - d \\
- (3a + 4b - 2c - 5d) \\
\hline
\quad - a + \ b + 2c + 4d
\end{array}
$$

∴ the result is $-a + b + 2c + 4d$.

Note: Since there is no term involving c in the first line, there is a gap.

═══ Exercise 7e ═══

1. Find the sum of the following expressions:

(a) $x^2 - 3x - 1$, $3x^2 + 2x + 9$

(b) $x^3 + 5x^2 + 2$, $4x^2 - 3x - 10$

(c) $-2a^3 - 3a^2 + 4a + 6$, $2a^3 + 5a^2 + 7$

(d) $4a + 6b + 5c$, $-3a - 9b$, $a + 3b - 4c$

(e) $p + 2q - 4r$, $2p - 3q + 5r$, $3p - q + 2r$

(f) $5x - 4y$, $6y - 7z$, $3z - 4x$

(g) $2x^3 + 3x^2 + 1$, $2x^3 - 2x^2 + 6x$, $4x^2 - 2x + 9$, $-3x^3 + 5$

(h) $9p + 12q - 3r - 4s$, $-8q + 4s$, $-7p + q + 2r$, $p + 4r - 5s$

(i) $5xy - 6yz + 7zx$, $xy + 5yz - 6zx$, $-6xy + yz + zx$

(j) $x^3 - 5x^2 + 4x - 7$, $x^4 + 2x^3 + x^2 - 7x + 4$, $x^4 - 7x + 8$

(k) $x^5 - 3x^4 + 5x^2 - 2x + 3$, $2x^5 + 7x^2 - 8$, $-3x^5 + 7x^4 - 4x^2 + 5x - 9$

(l) $3x^2y + xy - xy^2$, $5x^2y + 2xy - 7xy^2$, $2x^2y + 7xy + 9xy^2$

2. Subtract

(a) $3x^2 - x - 1$ from $4x^2 + 3x - 3$;

(b) $3x^2 - 5x$ from $2x^2 - 4x - 5$;

(c) $a - 2b + 6c$ from $3a + 3b - 4c$;

(d) $2q - 3r - s$ from $p - 4q - 6r$;

(e) $3x^2 + 2x - 4$ from $x^3 - 3x^2 - 5x + 6$;

(f) $2a^3 + 3a^2 - 6a + 7$ from $a^3 - 4a + 5$;

(g) $8a - 3b + 5c - 2d$ from $10a - b - 4c - 6d$;

(h) $2a^5 - 3a^4 + 7a^3 - 6$ from $7a^5 + 4a^4 - 2a^3 + 3a + 2$;

(i) $a^4 + 4a^2 + 7$ from $5a^5 + 2a^4 - 3a^3 + 2a^2 - 9$;

(j) $2a^5 + 3a^4 - 7a^3 + 4a^2 + 8$ from $2a^6 - 3a^5 - 7a^4 + 4a^3 - 8a^2 + 3a$.

3. Simplify the following expressions:

(a) $(3a^2 + 7a) + (2a^2 - 9a)$

(b) $(-2a + 7b) - (a + 4b)$

(c) $6(2a + 3b - 7ab) - 4(5a - 2b + 5ab)$

(d) $(3a + 4b - 5c) + (2a - 7b - 6c) + (8a - 5b + 9c)$

(e) $2(a + b - 3c) - 4(a - b + c) + 5a$

(f) $5(b + a - 6c) - 7(c - b + 6a)$

(g) $3(a - 5c) - 4(b - a) + 3(c - b)$

(h) $6(a - 3b + 5c) - 4(5b - c + 2a) - 5(2a - 4c + 3b)$

(i) $8(3a - 4b + c) + 5(2a - 3b + c) - 3(2c - 9a + 7b)$

(j) $9(2a - 7c + 4b) - 4(b - c) - 7(-c - 4b)$

Summary

1. In algebra, we use symbols, e.g. a, x^2 and xy, to represent numbers and variables. We add or subtract the like terms by adding or subtracting the coefficients, e.g. $2a + 5a = 7a$ and $7b - 3b = 4b$. We do not add the coefficients of unlike terms, so adding $3x$ and $4y$ gives $3x + 4y$.

2. When an expression of arithmetic operations contains brackets, work with the expressions within the brackets first. (If there are brackets within brackets, work with the innermost pair of brackets first.)

3. If an expression in brackets is multiplied by a number, each term within the brackets must be multiplied by that number when the brackets are removed.

Review Questions 7

1. Given that $a = -2$ and $b = 7$, evaluate the following expressions:

   (a) $4a + 5b$ (b) $2a^2$ (c) $3a - 4b$

   (d) $a(b - a)$ (e) $b - a^2$ (f) $(b - a)^2$

2. Given that $a = \dfrac{1 + b}{1 - b}$, calculate the value of a when $b = -3$, giving your answer as a fraction in its lowest terms.

3. Given that $\dfrac{1}{v} + \dfrac{1}{u} = \dfrac{1}{f}$, find the value of f when $v = 10$ and $u = 15$.

4. Simplify each of the following expressions:

   (a) $4[e - 3\{f - 6(f - e)\}]$

   (b) $-3 + m - \{2 - (m - 4)\}$

   (c) $10 + \dfrac{1}{3}[4k - (18 + 7k)]$

   (d) $1 - 3(1 + x) + \{2 - (4x - 7)\}$

   (e) $18 - [10 - x - (9 - x)]$

   (f) $-2[3x - (4 - 5) - (6 - 8)x]$

   (g) $\dfrac{1}{2}\left[16x - \dfrac{2}{3}(6x - 12)\right]$

   (h) $a - [b - \{c - (d + e)\}]$

   (i) $9[5a - 2\{3a - (7 - 2a)\}]$

   (j) $5x - [2x - \{3x - 3(x - 2y) + y\}]$

   (k) $5a - 2[3a - 7(a - 2) - 5]$

   (l) $3[4x - \{2x + 5(x - 2y) + 3x\}]$

   (m) $\dfrac{a + b}{3} - \dfrac{b + c}{2} + \dfrac{4a - c}{5}$

   (n) $\dfrac{2(3a + b)}{a} + \dfrac{4(2a - b)}{3a}$

   (o) $\dfrac{6x - y}{5} + \dfrac{3x - 4}{10} - \dfrac{5(x - 2)}{6}$

   (p) $\dfrac{4(x - 5)}{7} - \dfrac{5(x - y)}{6} + \dfrac{7x - z}{21}$

5. Work out the polynomial we must use to subtract $(3p^2 + 2pq + 7q^2)$ from, to get $(7p^2 + 5pq - 3q^2)$.

6. Subtract the sum of $(3x^2 - 4x + 3)$ and $(2x^2 + 7x - 5)$ from $(4x^2 + 2x - 17)$.

7. Subtract the sum of $(a^2 + 5ab + b^2)$ and $(2a^2 - 4ab + 5b^2)$ from the sum of $(5a^2 - 7ab + 4b^2)$ and $(7a^2 - 2ab + 3b^2)$.

Problem Solving

1. If $a = 3$, $b = -4$ and $c = -2$, evaluate each of the following:

   (a) $\dfrac{3a - b}{2c} + \dfrac{3a - c}{c - b}$

   (b) $\dfrac{2c - a}{3c + b} - \dfrac{5a + 4c}{c - a}$

   (c) $\dfrac{a + b + 2c}{3c - a - b} - \dfrac{5c}{4b}$

   (d) $\dfrac{b - c}{3c + 4b} \div \left(\dfrac{bc}{a} + \dfrac{ac}{b} \right)$

2. The average salary of m male employees and f female employees of a company is $\$A$. If the average salary of the male employees is $\$B$, find an expression for the average salary of the female employees.

3. At a famous "roti prata" shop, for every two people who order egg prata, there are five people who order plain prata.

   (a) If a people ordered egg prata, how many people ordered plain prata?
   (b) If b people ordered plain prata, how many people ordered egg prata?
   (c) If there are a total of c people in the shop, how many of them ordered egg prata?

4. A collection of coins contain only 10-cent and 5-cent coins. There are x 5-cent coins in the collection. Write an algebraic expression for each of the following:

   (a) The total value of the 5-cent coins.
   (b) The total value of the 10-cent coins if there are three times as many 10-cent as 5-cent coins.
   (c) The total value of the coins if for every three 10-cent coins there are five 5-cent coins.

8

Algebraic Equations

In this chapter, you will learn how to

▲ solve simple algebraic equations;
▲ construct simple linear equations from given situations and solve these equations.

Preliminary Problem

Albert Einstein derived the simple yet elegant formula, $E = mc^2$, to measure the amount of energy released when a quantity of matter is destroyed. This idea has been used by other scientists to develop the atomic bomb. An atomic explosion produces a 'mushroom-shaped' cloud which may look majestic but is actually very destructive and harmful.

Open Sentences

Consider the following sentences and state whether each of them is true or false:

(a) 5 is greater than 4.
(b) 4 is a factor of 32.
(c) $4 + 5 = 7$
(d) London is an island.

Clearly, we can conclude that sentences (a) and (b) are true while sentences (c) and (d) are false.

Now, consider the following sentences:

(e) $7 + \square = 13$.
(f) 3 is a factor of $\triangle$.
(g) $\bigcirc$ is the capital of Malaysia.

We cannot say whether sentences (e), (f) and (g) are true or false because it is not given in the sentence what the symbols $\square$, $\triangle$ and $\bigcirc$ stand for. We call such sentences **open sentences** and the symbols $\square$, $\triangle$ and $\bigcirc$ **unknowns** or **variables**. An open sentence is a sentence which contains one or more unknowns. An open sentence can be true or false depending on what we replace the unknown(s) in the sentence with.

Normally, we use letters such as a, b, c, x, y and z to represent unknowns. Open sentences that include numbers, variables and operation symbols in mathematics are called **mathematical sentences**. In particular, (e) and (f) are called open mathematical sentences.

Simple Equations

An open mathematical sentence which contains an equal sign "=" is called an equation. The following are some simple equations:

(a) $x - 5 = 7$ (b) $2x + 7 = 26$ (c) $\dfrac{x + 5}{2} = 3x - 2$ (d) $x^2 + x = 6$

Equations like $3x - 5 = x + 7$ which contain only one unknown or variable are called equations in one unknown.

To solve an equation means to find the value of the unknown so that the equation becomes a true or correct sentence. The value found is called the **solution** of the equation.

Example 1

What does x stand for if   (a) x + 5 = 11;   (b) x – 6 = 14?

Solution

By observation, we deduce that

(a) x stands for 6 because $6 + 5 = 11$.

(b) x stands for 20 because $20 - 6 = 14$.

Example 2

Find two different integers x and y such that $x^y = y^x$.

What does x stand for if   (a) $3x = 18$;   (b) $\dfrac{x}{5} = 7$?

▼ **Solution**

By observation, we deduce that

(a) x stands for 6 because $3 \times 6 = 18$.

(b) x stands for 35 because $\dfrac{35}{5} = 7$.

═ Exercise 8a ═

1. Find the solution of each of the following equations by observation:

   (a) $3a - 4 = a$

   (b) $3 \times 47 = 3a$

   (c) $2a + 8 = 16$

   (d) $50 - 5a = 10$

   (e) $\dfrac{24}{a} = 3$

   (f) $\dfrac{a}{3} = \dfrac{25}{5}$

   (g) $\dfrac{1}{2}a - \dfrac{1}{3}a = 2$

   (h) $\dfrac{3}{4}a - 3 = \dfrac{1}{2}a$

   (i) $\dfrac{1}{3}a - 3 = 0$

   (j) $1.5a + 2 = 5$

   (k) $0.5a - 1 = 4$

   (l) $0.1a + 1.5 = 2$

2. If a is an integer, find the possible solutions, if any, for each of the following by observation:

   (a) $a^2 = 4$

   (b) $9 - a^2 = 0$

   (c) $a^2 + 16 = 0$

   (d) $\sqrt{a} = 5$

   (e) $\sqrt[3]{a} = 3$

   (f) $\sqrt[3]{a} = -2$

   (g) $\sqrt[3]{a + 4} = 4$

   (h) $\sqrt{2a + 1} = 7$

Solving Simple Equations

We can use the idea of a balance to help us solve equations. Consider the case where the contents of the two scale pans balance each other. They will remain balanced if equal weights are added to both sides or if equal weights are taken away from both sides.

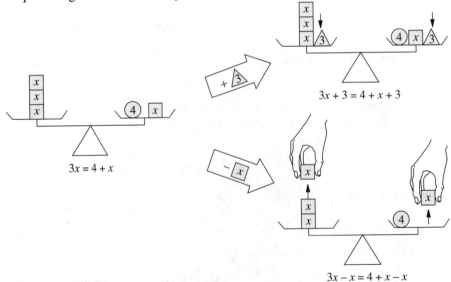

What will happen to the scales below if the weights of the contents of both sides are trebled or halved?

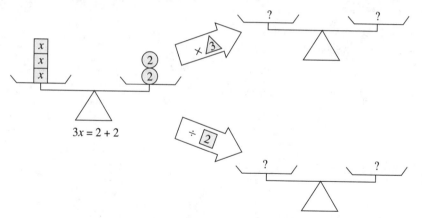

$3x = 2 + 2$

The above discussion leads to the following rules:

> To balance an equation,
> 1. equal numbers may be added to each side;
> 2. equal numbers may be subtracted from each side;
> 3. each side may be multiplied by equal numbers;
> 4. each side may be divided by equal numbers except zero.

We shall use the above rules to solve simple equations.

Example 3

Solve   (a) $n - 4 = 6$,   (b) $3x + 2 = 8$.

▼ Solution

(a) $n - 4 = 6$
      $n - 4 + 4 = 6 + 4$ (Add 4 to both sides.)
          $\therefore \quad n = 10$

Check: $10 - 4 = 6$

(b) $3x + 2 = 8$
      $3x + 2 - 2 = 8 - 2$ (Subtract 2 from both sides.)
              $3x = 6$

Check:
$3(2) + 2 = 6 + 2 = 8$

              $\dfrac{3x}{3} = \dfrac{6}{3}$ (Divide both sides by 3.)
          $\therefore \quad x = 2$

Example 4

Solve   (a) $3a - 1 = 5$;   (b) $5(x + 3) + 2(x + 1) = 5 - 4x$.

▼ Solution

(a) $3a - 1 + 1 = 5 + 1$ (Add 1 to both sides.)
              $3a = 6$
          $\therefore \quad a = 2$

(b) $5(x + 3) + 2(x + 1) = 5 - 4x$

$\qquad 5x + 15 + 2x + 2 = 5 - 4x$

$\qquad\qquad\quad 7x + 17 = 5 - 4x$

$\qquad 7x + 17 + 4x = 5 - 4x + 4x$ (Add $4x$ to both sides.)

$\qquad 11x + 17 - 17 = 5 - 17$ (Subtract 17 from both sides.)

$\qquad\qquad\quad 11x = -12$

$\qquad\qquad\quad \dfrac{11x}{11} = -\dfrac{12}{11}$ (Divide both sides by 11.)

$\qquad \therefore \quad x = -1\dfrac{1}{11}$

Can you check to see if the solution obtained is correct?

Example 5

Solve $2x - (x + 5) = 2 - (7 - x)$.

▼ **Solution**

$2 - (7 - x) \neq 2 - 7 - x$

$2x - (x + 5) = 2 - (7 - x)$

$\quad 2x - x - 5 = 2 - 7 + x$

$\qquad x - 5 = x - 5$

$\quad x - 5 + 5 = x - 5 + 5$ (Add 5 to both sides.)

$\qquad\quad x = x$

Notice that the above equation is true for all values of x. An equation such as this is called an **identity**

═ Exercise 8b ═

1. Find the value of the unknown in each equation:
   - (a) $2a = 10$
   - (b) $11x = 66$
   - (c) $2y = 0$
   - (d) $4a = -20$
   - (e) $-12e = 36$
   - (f) $-9p = 0$
   - (g) $x - 7 = 0$
   - (h) $a + 11 = 0$
   - (i) $3d - 1 = 0$

2. Solve the following equations:
   - (a) $2x + 15 = 27 - 4x$
   - (b) $15 - 5x = 24 - 8x$
   - (c) $2(c - 4) = 3(c - 2)$
   - (d) $3(2a + 3) = 4a + 3$
   - (e) $5x = x + 4$
   - (f) $-d + 3d = 14$
   - (g) $a + 4 = 7 - a$
   - (h) $3d - 12 = d + 2$

3. Solve the following equations and indicate whether they are identities.
   - (a) $5x - 7 = 2x + 3x - 7$
   - (b) $6(a - 1) - 2(a + 3) = 4(a - 3)$
   - (c) $5x + 7 = 4(x + 3) + 2x - 4$
   - (d) $5m - 52 = 7(m + 2) + 2m$
   - (e) $3(4x + 13) - 5(2x + 3) = 2x + 24$
   - (f) $2(5x - 7) - 4(x + 2) = 18(x - 4)$
   - (g) $(5m - 2) - 2(m + 1) = (3m - 4)$

Example 6 (optional)

Solve the equation $\dfrac{x-1}{3} = \dfrac{2x+5}{7}$.

Solution

$$\frac{x-1}{3} = \frac{2x+5}{7}$$

$7(x-1) = 3(2x+5)$ (Multiply both sides by the LCM of 3 and 7 ie. 21)

$7x - 7 = 6x + 15$

$7x - 7 + 7 = 6x + 15 + 7$ (Add 7 to both sides)

$7x - 6x = 6x + 22 - 6x$ (Subtract $6x$ from both sides)

$\therefore \quad x = 22$

Example 7

Solve the equation $1\frac{4}{5}x - \frac{3}{5} = 1\frac{1}{5}x + 10\frac{1}{5}$.

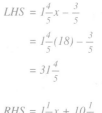

Solution

$$1\frac{4}{5}x - \frac{3}{5} = 1\frac{1}{5}x + 10\frac{1}{5}$$

$$1\frac{4}{5}x - \frac{3}{5} + \frac{3}{5} = 1\frac{1}{5}x + 10\frac{1}{5} + \frac{3}{5} \quad \left(\text{Add } \frac{3}{5} \text{ to both sides}\right)$$

$$1\frac{4}{5}x - 1\frac{1}{5}x = 1\frac{1}{5}x + 10\frac{4}{5} - 1\frac{1}{5}x \quad \left(\text{Subtract } 1\frac{1}{5}x \text{ from both sides}\right)$$

$$\frac{3}{5}x = 10\frac{4}{5}$$

$$x = 10\frac{4}{5} \times \frac{5}{3} \quad \left(\text{Multiply both sides by } \frac{5}{3}\right)$$

$$\therefore \quad x = 18$$

Example 8

Solve the equation $2.4x - 3.2 = 1.6x + 1.12$

Solution

$$2.4x - 3.2 = 1.6x + 1.12$$

$2.4x - 3.2 + 3.2 = 1.6x + 1.12 + 3.2$ (Add 3.2 to both sides)

$2.4x - 1.6x = 1.6x + 4.32 - 1.6x$ (Subtract $1.6x$ from both sides)

$$0.8x = 4.32$$

$$x = \frac{4.32}{0.8} \quad \text{(Divide both sides by 0.8)}$$

$$x = 5.4$$

Note: It is not necessary to write down the statements in the brackets when you are solving the equations.

Example 9

Solve the equation $2.3(2x - 7) = 3.3x - 4.6$ giving your answer correct to 3 significant figures.

▼ **Solution**

$$2.3(2x - 7) = 3.3x - 4.6$$
$$4.6x - 16.1 = 3.3x - 4.6$$
$$4.6x - 16.1 + 16.1 = 3.3x - 4.6 + 16.1 \quad \text{(Add 16.1 to both sides)}$$
$$4.6x = 3.3x + 11.5$$
$$4.6x - 3.3x = 3.3x + 11.5 - 3.3x \quad \text{(Subtract 3.3x from both sides)}$$
$$1.3x = 11.5$$
$$x = \frac{11.5}{1.3} \quad \text{(Divide both sides by 1.3)}$$
$$x = 8.85 \quad \text{(Correct to 3 significant figures)}$$

Can you check to see if the solution obtained is correct?

═ Exercise 8c ═

1. Solve the following equations: (* indicate that these are optional questions.)

(a) $x + \dfrac{x}{5} = 12$

(b) $\dfrac{2}{5} = \dfrac{3}{x}$

(c) $\dfrac{2}{3}x + 14 = 0$

(d) $\dfrac{3}{5}x - \dfrac{3}{7} = \dfrac{5}{7}$

(e) $2\dfrac{1}{2}y = 10 - 1\dfrac{2}{3}y$

(f) $\dfrac{d}{3} - \dfrac{d}{4} = 1$

(g) $\dfrac{n}{2} + \dfrac{n}{3} = 30$

(h) $\dfrac{1}{2}a - 2 = \dfrac{3}{5}a + 4$

*(i) $m + 2 = \dfrac{2 - m}{3} - 2$

(j) $\dfrac{k}{2} - \dfrac{k}{5} - \dfrac{k}{6} = 2$

(k) $\dfrac{x}{5} - \dfrac{x}{4} + \dfrac{x}{6} = 3$

(l) $\dfrac{2}{3}x + 4 = x - \dfrac{1}{3}$

(m) $\dfrac{5x}{2} = \dfrac{4}{3} + 2x$

*(n) $\dfrac{2x - 1}{5} + \dfrac{x + 3}{8} = 0$

(o) $\dfrac{2x + 3}{4} - \dfrac{x - 5}{6} = 0$

*(p) $\dfrac{1}{2} = \dfrac{1}{y + 2} - 1$

*(q) $\dfrac{2}{x} + 1 = \dfrac{5}{x} + 2\dfrac{1}{2}$

*(r) $\dfrac{5}{a - 2} = \dfrac{7}{a + 6}$

2. Solve the following equations, giving your answers correct to 3 significant figures where necessary:

(a) $0.2x = 0.5x + 3$

(b) $3 + 0.4x = 1.9x$

(c) $2.3 - 0.3x = 1.7x + 2$

(d) $3.5x - 7.8 = 1.6x - 0.2$

(e) $5x + 1.6 = 7.5x + 3.2$

(f) $4(0.7x + 1.3) = 8.6$

(g) $5(0.6x + 3.4) = 3.5x$

(h) $1.2(2x - 3) = 1.45$

(i) $2.4(x + 1) = 3.7x - 1.4$

(j) $3.4(3x - 2) = 4.8x - 1.9$

Formulae

A **formula** expresses a rule in algebraic terms. It uses variables to write instructions in short form for performing a calculation. For example, to find the area of a rectangle, we use the formula: $A = l \times b$ or lb. We have used the letter A to stand for the area, l for the length and b for the breadth.

This is a short form of a rule. In words, this rule can be written as: "The area of a rectangle is equal to the product of its length and breadth".

If P represents the perimeter of the rectangle, then we have $P = 2(l + b)$. If the values of l and b are known, we can find the values of A and P.

For example, if $l = 4$ and $b = 3$, then
$$A = 4 \times 3 = 12$$
$$P = 2(4 + 3) = 14$$

The above example shows that if we know the values of l and b, then we can find the corresponding values of A and P. We can also find the value of l if A and b are given. This is an example of the process of replacing letters by numbers and this process is called **substitution**

Example 10

The formula for the volume V of a cuboid is V = lbh where l is the length, b is the breadth and h is the height. Find the volume of the cuboid where

(a) l = 5 cm, b = 4 cm and h = 3 cm;　　　*(b) l = 8 cm, b = 6 cm and h = 5 cm.*

▼ **Solution**

(a)　$V = lbh$
　　　$= 5 \times 4 \times 3 = 60$
　　$\therefore$　volume of the cuboid $= 60$ cm³

(b)　$V = lbh$
　　　　$= 8 \times 6 \times 5 = 240$
　　　$\therefore$　volume of the cuboid $= 240$ cm³

Example 11

If $a = \dfrac{b}{c - b}$, find (a) a when b = 5 and c = 7; (b) b when a = 3 and c = 10.

▼ **Solution**

(a)　$a = \dfrac{5}{7 - 5}$

　　　$= \dfrac{5}{2}$

　　　$= 2\dfrac{1}{2}$

(b)　　　　　$3 = \dfrac{b}{10 - b}$

　　　$3(10 - b) = b$

　　　　$30 - 3b = b$

　　　　　　$30 = 4b$

　　　$\therefore$　$b = 7\dfrac{1}{2}$

═ Exercise 8d ═

Take the value of π as $3\dfrac{1}{7}$, where necessary.

1. If $V = \dfrac{1}{3} Ah$, find V when $A = 43$ and $h = 6$.

2. If $F = \dfrac{9c}{5} + 32$, find F when $c = 30$.

3. If $S = 4\pi r^2$, find S when $r = 10\dfrac{1}{2}$.

4. If $T = \pi(R^2 - r^2)$, find T when $R = 4$ and $r = 3$.

5. If $a = \dfrac{y^2 - xz}{5}$, find a when $x = 4$, $y = 7$ and $z = 6$.

6. If $k = \dfrac{x + y}{3}$, find x when $k = 12$ and $y = 4$.

7. If $t = \dfrac{v - u}{a}$, find a when $t = 1$, $u = 1\dfrac{2}{3}$ and $v = 3\dfrac{1}{2}$.

8. If $U = \pi(r + h)$, find r when $U = 16\frac{1}{2}$ and $h = 2\frac{3}{4}$.

9. If $v^2 = u^2 + 2gs$, find s when $v = 20$, $u = 10$ and $g = 10$.

10. If $\dfrac{m}{x + q} = N$, find q when $m = 9$, $x = 2$ and $N = 1\frac{4}{5}$.

11. If $n - y = \dfrac{4y - n}{m}$, find n when $y = 3$ and $m = 7$.

12. If $\dfrac{a}{b} + e = \dfrac{c}{b}$, find c when $a = 4$, $b = 12$ and $e = -\dfrac{1}{6}$.

✴13. If $y + b = \dfrac{ay + c}{b}$, find c when $y = 12$, $a = 14$ and $b = 3$.

✴14. If $\dfrac{1}{a} = \dfrac{1}{b} + \dfrac{1}{c} + \dfrac{1}{d}$, find c when $a = 2$, $b = 3$ and $d = 5$.

✴15. If $\dfrac{m(ny - x^2)}{z} + n = 5n$, find y when $n = 4$, $x = 2$, $m = 6$ and $z = 8$.

✴16. If $c = \dfrac{a}{b} - \dfrac{d - e}{f - d}$, find f when $a = 2$, $b = 3$, $c = 4$, $d = 5$ and $e = 6$.

Construction of Formulae

To construct a formula, choose letters to represent the quantities. Usually, the first letter of the word is used. Then express the rule in algebraic terms. For example, the sum, S kg, of the weights of two boys, one weighing m kg and the other n kg, is expressed as $S = m + n$.

Example 12

Find a formula for the sum (S) of any three consecutive even numbers.

▼ Solution

Let the smallest number be n.

The next number is $(n + 2)$ and the biggest number is $(n + 4)$.

$\quad S = n + (n + 2) + (n + 4)$
$\quad S = n + n + 2 + n + 4$
$\therefore \quad S = 3n + 6$ or $3(n + 2)$

═ Exercise 8e ═

1. Using the letters suggested, construct a simple formula in each case:

(a) The sum (S) of three numbers a, b and c.

(b) The product (P) of two numbers x and y.

(c) The difference (D) between the ages of two boys; one being a years old and the other e years old.

(d) The area (A) of a semicircle whose radius is r.

(e) The cost $(\$C)$ of m eggs at 12 cents each.

(f) The average age (A) of 4 boys whose ages are m, n, p and q years.

(g) The vertical angle $(x°)$ of an isosceles triangle whose base angle is $y°$.

(h) The time (T) in minutes for a train journey of a hours b minutes.

(i) The total cost ($\$T$) of d chairs at $\$p$ each and c tables at $\$q$ each.

✳**(j)** A car travels x km/h for p km and makes another journey at y km/h for q km.

Find

(i) the total distance (r km) the car travels;

(ii) the formula for the average speed.

Writing Algebraic Expressions

Example 13

How many days are there in (a) 5 weeks; (b) n weeks?

▼ **Solution**

There are 7 days in a week.

(a) There are (7×5) = 35 days in 5 weeks.

(b) There are ($7 \times n$) = $7n$ days in n weeks.

Example 14

A girl is now 10 years old. How old will she be (a) 5 years later; (b) t years later?

How old was she (c) 3 years ago; (d) x years ago?

What are the possible values of x? Can x be 15?

▼ **Solution**

The girl becomes 1 year older every year.

One year later, she will be ($10 + 1$) = 11 years old.

(a) 5 years later, she will be ($10 + 5$) = 15 years old.

(b) t years later, she will be ($10 + t$) years old.

(c) 3 years ago, she was ($10 - 3$) = 7 years old.

(d) x years ago, she was ($10 - x$) years old.

The possible values of x are 10, 9, 8, 7, 6, 5, 4, 3, 2, 1 and 0.
x cannot be 15 since the girl is now only 10 years old.

Example 15

A car travels at a speed of 55 km/h. How far will it travel in (a) 2 hours; (b) t hours?

▼ **Solution**

In 1 hour, the car travels 55 km.

(a) In 2 hours, the car will travel (55×2) km, i.e., 110 km.

(b) In t hours, the car will travel ($55 \times t$) km, i.e., $55t$ km.

1. How many grams are there in 5 kg? How many grams are there in x kg?

2. What is the cost of 6 magazines at $4 each? What is the cost of p magazines at $4 each? Find also the cost of p magazines at $q each.

3. Four tennis balls have a total mass of m kg. Find the mass of each ball.

4. If a horse runs at b km/h, how far can it go in 2 hours if it keeps the same speed?

5. How many minutes are there in m hours?

6. How many weeks are there in y days?

7. If Dan has x dollars, how many marbles can he buy if each marble costs five cents?

8. Write the number which is half as big as b.

9. Find the time taken by a cyclist to travel 21 km if he is travelling at v km/h.

10. A shopkeeper buys an armchair for $a and then sells it at a profit of $b. What is the selling price of the armchair?

11. A boy is b years old and his father is 6 times as old as him. Find the father's age. Find also the sum of their ages in y years' time.

12. Mrs Jones's age is equal to the sum of the ages of her two daughters. If the younger daughter is x years old and the elder is 4 years older, how old is Mrs Jones?

13. Find the three consecutive numbers in which n is the middle number.

14. A motorist drives for 5 hours at u km/h and for 3 hours at v km/h. Find the total distance travelled.

Problem Solving with Algebra

One of the most powerful mathematical tools to solve problems is by **using an equation and solving it**. We shall look at this problem-solving method more closely. (Alternative methods will be shown too if they are shorter and easier than the method of using an equation).

Setting Up Equations

In order to solve word problems in mathematics we often need to translate them into mathematical equations first. First consider these problems:

1. "When I subtract 3 from a number, the result is the same as if I had halved the number. Find the number."

2. The sum of two consecutive odd numbers is 64. Find the two numbers.

For the first question if we let x represent the number, we can write the given question mathematically as:

$$x - 3 = \frac{1}{2}x$$

For the second question, let x be the smaller of the two consecutive odd numbers, then the larger one will be $x + 2$. We can then write the mathematical equation as:

$$x + (x + 2) = 64$$

Exercise 8g

1. In each of the following, let x denote the unknown. Derive an equation involving x:
   (a) When a certain number is increased by 7, the result is 18.
   (b) When a number is decreased by 2 and the result multiplied by 3, the final result is 24.
   (c) When 5 is subtracted from a certain number and the result multiplied by 7, the final result is 63.
   (d) When a certain number is subtracted from 24 and the result divided by 5, the final result is 4.
   (e) The sum of three consecutive numbers is 63.
   (f) One number is bigger than the other number by 3 and the sum of these two numbers is 43.
   (g) Six times of a certain number is 16 more than twice the number.
   (h) The length of a rectangle is 5 m more than its width and the perimeter of the rectangle is 32 m.
   (i) The length of a rectangle is twice its width and the perimeter is 54 m.

2. Peter has five times as much money as David. If Peter gives $28 to David, both of them will have equal amounts of money. How much money did Peter have at the beginning?

3. There are a total of 225 pupils in Secondary one. If the number of pupils who pay their school fees through GIRO scheme is 14 times the number of pupils who do not, find the number of pupils who did not join the scheme.

4. $4 800 is divided among three brothers A, B and C. A receives three times as much as B and C receives twice as much as B. If B receives $$x$, form an equation in x.

5. Three wallets and two handbags cost $450 and a handbag costs twice as much as a wallet. If a wallet costs $$x$, form an equation in x.

Example 16

A man is now 3 times as old as his son. In 10 years' time, the sum of their ages will be 76. How old was the man when his son was born?

Problems

If 10 cats can catch 10 mice in 10 minutes, how many cats are required to catch 100 mice in 100 minutes?

▼ **Solution**

Strategy: Use an equation

Let the present age of the son be x years old.
The man is now $3x$ years old.
In 10 years' time, the son will be $(x + 10)$ years old.
In 10 years' time, the man will be $(3x + 10)$ years old.

$$(x + 10) + (3x + 10) = 76$$
$$4x + 20 = 76$$
$$4x = 56$$
$$x = 14$$

Hence, the man is now $(3 \times 14) = 42$ years old.

∴ the man was $(42 - 14) = 28$ years old when his son was born.

Alternatively, we can **use models** to solve the above problem.

Age now son: [ ] man: [ ][ ][ ]

Age when the son was born son: 0 years old man: [ ][ ]

Age in 10 years' time from now son: [ ] 10 years + man: [ ][ ][ ] 10 years = 76 years

∴ 4 shaded parts = 76 − 20 = 56 years
 1 shaded part = 56 ÷ 4 = 14 years
 2 shaded parts = 2 × 14 = 28 years
∴ the man was 28 years old when the son was born.

Example 17

Find three consecutive odd numbers whose sum is 57.

▼ **S o l u t i o n**

Strategy: Use an equation

Let the smallest of the three consecutive odd numbers be x.
The other odd numbers are $x + 2$ and $x + 4$.

$$x + (x + 2) + (x + 4) = 57$$
$$3x + 6 = 57$$
$$3x = 51$$
$$x = 17$$

∴ the three consecutive odd numbers are 17, 19 and 21.

Alternatively, we can find the solution by **making a systematic list**. We shall start with 11, 13, 15, … etc. Do you think it is necessary to start the list with 1, 3, 5, …?

11, 13, 15, ⑰, ⑲, ㉑, 23, 25, 27, …

Check: 17 + 19 + 21 = 57

The three circled odd numbers add up to 57.

∴ the three consecutive odd numbers are 17, 19 and 21.

Example 18

A woman buys 50 eggs for $6.60. Some cost 12 cents each and the rest 14 cents each. How many of each kind of eggs has she bought?

▼ **S o l u t i o n**

Strategy: Use an equation

Let x be the number of eggs she buys at 12 cents each.
No. of eggs bought at 14 cents each = $(50 − x)$.
Cost of x eggs at 12 cents each = $12x$ cents.
Cost of $(50 − x)$ eggs at 14 cents each = $(50 − x) × 14$ cents

$$12x + 14(50 - x) = 660$$
$$12x + 700 - 14x = 660$$
$$40 = 2x$$
$$x = 20$$

∴   no. of eggs bought a 12 cents each = 20.
∴   no. of eggs bought at 14 cents each = 50 − 20 = 30.

Check:
$20(12¢) + 30(14¢)$
$= \$2.40 + \$4.20$
$= \$6.60$

Example 19

John walked for 45 minutes at the rate of 3 km/h and then ran for half an hour at a certain speed. At the end of that time he was 6 km away from the starting point. How fast did he run?

Solution

Strategy: Use an equation

Let the speed at which he ran be x km/h.

Distance = Speed × Time

∴   the distance he walked = $\left(\dfrac{45}{60} \times 3\right)$ km = $\dfrac{9}{4}$ km

The distance he ran = $\left(\dfrac{1}{2} \times x\right)$ km = $\dfrac{x}{2}$ km

$$\frac{9}{4} + \frac{x}{2} = 6$$

$$\frac{9 + 2x}{4} = 6 \qquad \text{(Remember that when an equation is divided or multiplied by a number, every term}$$
$$\text{must be divided or multiplied by that number.)}$$

$$9 + 2x = 24$$
$$2x = 15$$
$$x = \frac{15}{2} = 7\frac{1}{2}$$

∴   John ran at a speed of $7\dfrac{1}{2}$ km/h.

═ Exercise 8h ═

1. What are the four consecutive numbers whose sum is 50?

2. If a number is trebled, it gives the same result as when 28 is added to it. What is the number?

3. When a number is added to another number 5 times as large, the result is 24. What is the first number?

4. Joe and Ahmad have 80 marbles altogether. Ahmad has 4 times as many marbles as Joe. How many marbles does each boy have?

5. Arasoo is 4 years older than Peter. Ali is 2 years younger than Peter. If the sum of their ages is 47, what are their respective ages?

6. Lilian and Susan share $30 between themselves. If Susan gets twice as much as Lilian, find each girl's share.

7. When loaded with bricks, a lorry weighs 11 600 kg. If the bricks weigh three times as heavy as the empty lorry, find the weight of the bricks.

8. When a number is added to two-thirds of itself, the result is 45. Find the number.

9. The numerator of a fraction is 5 less than the denominator. If 1 is added to both the numerator and the denominator the fraction would become $\frac{2}{3}$. Find the fraction.

10. The cost of mooncakes with double egg yolks cost 50 cents more than those with only a single egg yolk. Mrs Tan bought 6 mooncakes with double egg yolks and 5 with only a single egg yolk. If she paid $36 for the 11 mooncakes, how much does a mooncake with double egg yolks cost?

11. Tom, Dick and Harry share $256. Dick's share is four times as much as Tom's and Tom's share is one-third of Harry's. How much is each of their share?

∗12. Meng Kuang had saved a small sum of money from his weekly pocket money. After receiving a total of $108 as hong bao money from his relatives during the Chinese New Year, he decided to donate one-fifth of his money to the Community Chest of Singapore. His other siblings also donated a total of $148 to the Community Chest. If their total contribution to the Community Chest was $200, how much did Meng Kuang save originally?

∗13. A group of boys had to choose between playing soccer and badminton. The number of boys choosing soccer was three times that of those choosing badminton. Asking 12 boys who chose soccer to play badminton would make the number of players for each game equal. Find the number who chose badminton originally.

Summary

To solve an equation, we can

1. add equal numbers to each side;

    e.g. if $x - 5 = 7$,

    then $(x - 5) + 5 = 7 + 5$

2. subtract equal numbers from each side;

    e.g. if $x + 4 = 15$

    then $(x + 4) - 4 = 15 - 4$

3. multiply each side by the same number;

    e.g. if $\frac{1}{3}x = 8$

    then $3\left(\frac{1}{3}x\right) = 3(8)$

4. divide each side by the same number, except 0.

    e.g. if $3x = 21$

    then $\frac{3x}{3} = \frac{21}{3}$

Review Questions 8

1. Solve the following equations:

    (a) $\dfrac{8 - x}{3} = \dfrac{2x + 3}{5}$

    (b) $\dfrac{x + 2}{6} = \dfrac{2x + 7}{4}$

    (c) $\dfrac{x}{2} = 5 + \dfrac{x}{3}$

    (d) $\dfrac{9}{4x} - 5 = 4$

    (e) $\dfrac{2x + 1}{6} - \dfrac{x - 3}{4} = \dfrac{5}{12}$

    (f) $\dfrac{x + 3}{7} - \dfrac{2(x - 4)}{3} = 1$

    (g) $\dfrac{3x - 4}{5} - \dfrac{x + 1}{4} = \dfrac{2x - 4}{3}$

    (h) $\dfrac{x}{3} + \dfrac{x - 3}{4} - \dfrac{2x - 7}{2} = 0$

2. State whether the following equations are identities. Give solutions to those that are equations.

   (a) $3x - 5 = (x + 2) - (7 - 2x)$ (b) $7(x + 2) - 5(x - 6) = 12(x + 5)$

   (c) $3(t - 4) + 5(t + 4) = 7(t - 3)$ (d) $6(a - 4) = 2(a - 10) - 4(1 - a)$

   (e) $\frac{1}{2}(x - 3) - \frac{1}{3}(x + 6) = \frac{1}{6}(x - 21)$ (f) $\frac{1}{3}(x - 4) + \frac{1}{4}(x - 5) = \frac{1}{7}(x - 9)$

3. A man has a number of ducks costing $10 each and three times as many chickens costing $6 each. If the total cost of ducks and chickens is $420, find the number of chickens the man has.

4. Three families, A, B, and C, share 480 kg of rice. B gets twice as much as A, and C gets half as much as B. How much does each family get?

5. A shopkeeper buys some eggs at 15 cents each. Six of them are broken while the rest are sold at 20 cents each. If he makes a profit of $4.80, find how many eggs he bought.

6. Tiong Beng worked part time at a fast food restaurant during the school holidays. He was paid the normal hourly rate of $2.80 per hour. Overtime rate is one and a half times the normal rate. He received $173.60 for 54 hours of work. How many hours did he work overtime?

7. Peter has 25 sweets and Lilian has 55. How many sweets must Peter give Lilian so that Lilian will have 4 times as many sweets as Peter?

8. With a fixed amount of money $M, Mr Phua can use it to pay the wages of a local worker for 40 days or to pay the wages of an unskilled foreign worker for 60 days. If he employs one local worker and one unskilled foreign worker for a renovation project, how many days can the $M be enough to pay for these two workers?

9. Drawing pencils cost 8 cents each and coloured pencils cost 11 cents each. Two dozen assorted pencils cost $2.16. How many coloured pencils are there?

10. A man travels from A to B at 4 km/h and from B to A at 6 km/h. The total journey takes 45 minutes. Find the distance travelled.

11. A number is 5 times another number. By adding 8 to each number, the first number becomes only 3 times the second. What are the two numbers?

12. How can the number 45 be divided into two parts so that 4 times one part is 9 less than 5 times the other?

*13. A man normally takes 5 hours to travel at a certain speed from city A to city B. One day, he increases his speed by 4 km/h and finds that the journey from A to B takes half an hour less than the normal time. Find his normal speed.

*14. The sum of the ages of Fandi and Ahmad is 38. Seven years ago, Fandi was three times as old as Ahmad. Find their present ages.

*15. Aramugum has enough money to buy 24 apples. If the price of each apple is reduced by 5 cents, he will be able to buy an extra 6 apples with the same sum of money. Find the original cost of each apple.

Problem Solving

1. A tank can be fully filled with water using a pipe that fills 20 litres in a minute. A bigger pipe that can fill 25 litres in a minute will take one minute less to fill the same tank. How many minutes does the smaller pipe take to fill the tank?

2. Mary is twice as old as John and half as old as Bob. In 22 years' time, Bob will be twice as old as John. How old is Mary?

3. Alice and Belinda start off simultaneously from two towns to meet one another. If Alice travels 2 km/h faster than Belinda, they would meet in 3 hours. If Belinda travels 1 km/h slower and Alice' speed is two-thirds of her previous speed, they would meet in 4 hours. How far apart are the two towns?

4. At a fast-food restaurant, for every three people who ordered a cheeseburger, there are five people who ordered an apple pie. The number of people who ordered the cheeseburger is 5 more than the people who ordered the apple pie. If the total number of people who ordered food is 1 678, how many people ordered apple pie?

5. Given that A, B, C and D are whole numbers such that $A + B = 8$, $B + C = 11$, $B + D = 13$ and $C + D = 14$, find the values of A, B, C and D.

6. Given that A, B, C and D are whole numbers such that $A \times B = 8$, $B \times C = 28$, $C \times D = 63$ and $B \times D = 36$, find the values of A, B, C and D.

Revision Exercise II No. 1

1. What is the sum of $4x$ dollars and $4x$ cents? Express your answer in cents.

2. Simplify $2x - \{[2x - 3(2y - 3x) - (5y - 2x) - 9y] - 3x\}$.

3. Simplify
   - (a) $15a \div 5$;
   - (b) $4c \times 7c$;
   - (c) $a \times 5 \times b$;
   - (d) $a \times 5 \times 2 + c$;
   - (e) $\frac{2}{3} \times 21a^2$;
   - (f) $5xy \times 0$;
   - (g) $2xy + 0$;
   - (h) $15x - 3 \times 5x$;
   - (i) $8a + 2 \times 6a$;
   - (j) $4x + 8x \div 2$.

4. Solve the following equations:
   - (a) $3x - (2x - 1) = 7$
   - (b) $8(7 - x) = (3x - 1)$
   - (c) $8 - \frac{3}{4}(x - 4) = \frac{1}{8}(x + 1)$
   - (d) $\frac{x - 1}{2} - \frac{x - 2}{3} = \frac{x - 3}{4}$

5. (a) Find the value of $3x^2 + 14x - 7$ when $x = 5$.
   (b) If $x = 2$ is a solution of the equation $x^2 - 7x + k = 0$, find the value of k.

6. A father is 36 years old and his son is 6 years old. In how many years' time will the father be twice as old as his son?

7. Evaluate each of the following showing each step clearly
   - (a) $(-3)^3 + (-2)^2 \times (4 - 7)$
   - (b) $2 \times (3 - 7)^3 - 4 \times 7$
   - (c) $5 \times (-4)^2 - 6 \times (18 - 23)^3$

8. Simplify each of the following and give your answer as a fraction in its simplest form.
   - (a) $3\frac{4}{5} \times \left(-1\frac{1}{2}\right) + 2\frac{1}{3} \div \left(-1\frac{1}{3}\right)$
   - (b) $2\frac{4}{9} - \frac{3}{2} \times \left(\frac{2}{3} - \frac{3}{2}\right)^2$

9. Copy and complete the following using one of the symbols >, = or <:
   - (a) $5 \square 2$
   - (b) $-5 \square -2$
   - (c) $\frac{1}{3} \square 0.33$
   - (d) $-7 \square 14 \div (-2)$

10. Evaluate the following:
    - (a) $(-100) - (350)$
    - (b) $(-13) \times (-2)$
    - (c) $(-64) \div (-4)$
    - (d) $(-5) + 7 + (-6) + 16$

Revision Exercise II No. 2

1. Simplify $2a - \{4[b - 3(a - 2 \times b - 2a)] - 10(3b - 5a)\}$.

2. Given that $a = 1$, $b = 2$, $c = 0$ and $d = -3$, evaluate
   - (a) $\frac{a^2 bd}{3a - d}$;
   - (b) $\frac{d^2 + bc}{b + a}$;
   - (c) $a^2 + b^2 + d^2$;
   - (d) $a^3 + b^3 + d^3$.

3. Solve
   - (a) $\frac{x}{4} + \frac{1}{6} = \frac{x}{2} + \frac{1}{8}$;
   - (b) $\frac{3x + 2}{4} + \frac{x - 2}{3} = 2 + \frac{x - 5}{2}$.

4. I think of a number, halve it and then subtract 1 from it. The result is double the amount obtained by dividing the number by 3 and subtracting 4 from it. Find the number.

5. Ali earns \$480 a month and Ahmad earns \$720 a month. How many months must Ali work to earn as much as Ahmad does in 6 months?

6. Evaluate the following:
   - (a) $18 \times \{[11 + 3) \div 7] - 2\}$
   - (b) $[5 \times (-9)] - [(-9) \times (-3)]$
   - (c) $(-25) \div (-5) + 24 \div (-6)$
   - (d) $\frac{(-10)^2 \times 12}{8 \times (-2)}$

7. Evaluate
   - (a) $\left(1\frac{5}{11} + \frac{7}{22}\right) \div \left(\frac{7}{15} + \frac{2}{5}\right)$;
   - (b) $\dfrac{5\frac{3}{4} + 2\frac{2}{3} \times 1\frac{5}{16}}{\frac{2}{5} \div \frac{4}{15}}$;
   - (c) $\left(-5\frac{1}{2}\right) + \left[4\frac{1}{2} \times \left(-\frac{1}{12}\right)\right]$.

8. Estimate the value of

(a) $\dfrac{64.11}{1.62}$;

(b) $56.967\,13 - 34.230\,67$;

(c) $\dfrac{7.14 \times 0.206}{0.050\,7 \times \sqrt{48.902}}$;

correct to 1 significant figure.

9. A car travels x km in t hours. Assuming the speed is constant, how many metres does it travel in one second?

10. Use your calculator to evaluate

(a) $4(25 - 4\pi)$;

(b) $\dfrac{\dfrac{2}{7} + \sqrt{15} \times \sqrt[3]{3}}{\sqrt{5} \div \dfrac{11}{2}}$;

(c) $\dfrac{10.92^3 \times \sqrt{7.42}}{5.68^2} + \sqrt[3]{\dfrac{5.16 \times 6.42}{1.56 \times 4.72}}$;

giving each answer correct to 3 decimal places.

Revision Exercise II No. 3

1. Remove the brackets and simpify
$2(p + r + s) + (2p - 3q - 4r - s) - (4p - q - 5r + 2s)$.

2. Given that $a = 5$, $b = 6$ and $c = -1$, evaluate

(a) $3a + b + c$;　　(b) $\dfrac{ab}{2c}$;

(c) $2a + 3b - 4c$;　　(d) $ab - bc$.

3. Solve the following equations:

(a) $\dfrac{1}{3}x + 15 = 2x$

(b) $3(1.5x - 0.2) = 0.5x$

(c) $\dfrac{x + 1}{5} + \dfrac{x - 1}{5} = 6$

(d) $\dfrac{3x - 5}{6} + 2 = \dfrac{5x - 4}{5}$

4. A bookshelf can hold 45 books, each 6.3 cm thick. How many books can it hold if each book is 2.1 cm thick?

5. A mother is now three times as old as her daughter. If the sum of their ages five years ago was fifty, how old is the mother now?

6. Evaluate the following:

(a) $63 \div (-9)$

(b) $[7 \times (-2)] + [6 \times (-5)]$

(c) $(-8) \times (-15) - 22$

7. Use a calculator to evaluate the following giving your answers correct to 2 decimal places:

(a) $\sqrt{62.5^3 - 58.5^2}$　　(b) $\dfrac{(36.27)^2 \div 21.68}{15.86 \div (2.66)^2}$

(c) $\dfrac{(4.62^2 + 2.68^2) \div 3.42}{\sqrt[3]{168.4^2 + 26.8^2}}$

8. Replace each $\square$ with '>' or '<'.

(a) $\dfrac{4}{7} \square \dfrac{3}{7}$　　　　(b) $1\dfrac{2}{5} \square 2\dfrac{1}{5}$

(c) $-5 \square -4$　　　　(d) $\dfrac{7}{12} \square \dfrac{7}{13}$

(e) $0.54 \square 0.539\,9$

(f) $-0.001 \square 0.000\,1$

9. Given that $23.78 \times 583.5 = 13\,875.6$, find the value

(a) $0.237\,8 \times 58.35$

(b) $13.875\,6 \div 0.023\,78$

10. Evaluate each of the following, giving your answer as a fraction in its lowest term.

(a) $\dfrac{\dfrac{3}{4} - 3\dfrac{1}{2}}{2\dfrac{1}{3} \times \left(-\dfrac{3}{2}\right) + \dfrac{1}{4}}$

(b) $\left(\dfrac{-3}{5}\right) \times \left(2\dfrac{1}{2}\right) - 2 \times \left(-1\dfrac{1}{3}\right)^2$

Revision Exercise II No. 4

1. Round off

(a) the number 5.335 2 to 2 decimal places;

(b) the number 0.090 38 to 2 significant figures;

(c) the number 4 972 to the nearest hundred;

(d) the number 12 097 to the nearest ten.

2. Simplify

(a) $2x^2 - 5x - 2(1 - 2x + 3y^2)$;

(b) $(x - 3y + 4z) - (x - y - 2z)$.

3. Simplify

$$\frac{1}{2}(x - y) + \frac{1}{3}(2x - 5y) - \frac{1}{5}(6x - 5y).$$

4. A student paid $5.40 for 30 pencils. Some pencils cost 10 cents each and others cost 20 cents each. How many pencils of the 10-cents type did he buy?

5. Find x when

(a) $9x = 15$; (b) $\frac{3}{4}x = 6$;

(c) $18 = 32 - x$; (d) $\frac{1}{2}x + 6 = 8$;

(e) $6x - 3x = 31 - 25$; (f) $1.2x = x + 1$.

6. A boy cycles $12x$ km in 5 hours. How far can he cycle in $3y$ hours at the same speed?

7. Estimate each of the following correct to 1 significant figure:

(a) $4\,980 \times 409$ (b) $2\,986 \times 304$
(c) $100\,523 \div 19$ (d) $199\,607 \div 51$

8. Find the approximate value of each of the following, giving your answer correct to 1 significant figure:

(a) $\dfrac{11.01 \times 0.661}{2\,199}$ (b) $\dfrac{83.9}{0.040\,7}$

(c) $\sqrt{\dfrac{16.01 \times 36.0}{3.999}}$ (d) $\sqrt[3]{\dfrac{9.06 \times 20.94}{7.025}}$

9. Given that $x = 2$, $y = -3$, $z = 4$ and $k = -1$, evaluate each of the following:

(a) $xy - 3zk + 2x$ (b) $y(2z - 3kx - xz)$

(c) $\dfrac{3x - 4z}{4y - 5k}$ (d) $\dfrac{4k}{3x - y + z}$

10. Peter is 24 years younger than his father. In 5 years' time, his father will be 3 times as old as Peter.

(a) How old is Peter now?
(b) How old will Peter's father be in 25 years' time?

Revision Exercise II No. 5

1. Given that $a = 3$, $b = 2$, $x = 0$ and $y = 1$, evaluate

(a) $a^2 - b^2$; (b) $ab + xy$;
(c) $ax - (b - y)^2$; (d) $ab^2 - xy^3$.

2. Simplify $\dfrac{7x - 1}{2} + \dfrac{2x + 3}{6} - \dfrac{5x - 4}{2}$.

3. Solve $\dfrac{6x}{5} - \dfrac{x - 1}{4} = x$.

4. Find x when

(a) $7x = 42$; (b) $6x = 16$;
(c) $2x + 19 = 41$; (d) $3x = 7 + 8$;
(e) $6x - 32 = 2x$; (f) $3.4x = x - 3$.

5. Simplify

(a) $2m \times 6n$; (b) $18xy \times \dfrac{1}{6}$;

(c) $7 \times 4a$; (d) $8a + 2a \div 4$.

6. (a) Round off 6.236 to 2 significant figures.
(b) Round off 2.594 74 to 3 decimal places.
(c) Write down, correct to the nearest whole number, the value of $\sqrt[3]{998}$.

7. Find the value of each of the following:

(a) $\dfrac{(-16) + (-20)}{(-9)}$ (b) $\dfrac{(-5) \times (11 - 15)}{8 \times [-19 - (-9)]}$

(c) $(-6) \times (-8) - 3 \times (-5) - (-6)^2$

(d) $\dfrac{3 - 5 - (-8)}{4 \times (-5)}$

8. Given that $x = 5$, $y = -4$, $z = -2$, $h = 0$ and $k = -1$, evaluate each of the following:

(a) $5x - 3yk + 4hz$ (b) $xy(2x - 4k + xhz)$

(c) $\dfrac{5x - 3z}{xhk - 5yk}$ (d) $\dfrac{2k}{xh - yz}$

9. (a) Ali is six times as old as his daughter Rohana. How old was Ali when Rohana was born if the sum of their ages will be 49 in 7 years' time?
(b) Peter is 8 years younger than Joanne. In 5 years' time, Joanne will be twice as old as Peter. How old will Peter be in 15 years' time?

10. Use your calculator to evaluate each of the following, giving your answer correct to 4 significant figures.

(a) $\dfrac{28.75^2 - \sqrt[3]{45.67}}{84.4 + \sqrt{75.6}}$ (b) $\dfrac{56.34^4}{384.7^2 - 46.5^3}$

(c) $46.9^2 - 15.3 \times \sqrt{47.4}$

(d) $\sqrt{5\,487} \div (48.3 - \sqrt[3]{784})$

Note: Take $\pi = \dfrac{22}{7}$ unless otherwise stated for all the Specimen Papers.

Mid-year Examination Specimen Paper 1

Part 1 (50 marks)   Time: 1 h

*Answer **all** the questions. Calculators are **not** to be used in this section.*

1. State whether each of the following statements is true or false:
   (a) The first four prime numbers are 1, 2, 3 and 5. [1]
   (b) Every prime number is a rational number. [1]
   (c) 3.141 59 is an irrational number. [1]
   (d) $\left(2\dfrac{3}{4} + 1.25\right)$ is an integer. [1]

2. (a) Find the HCF of 36, 48 and 60. [1]
   (b) Find the LCM of 130, 195 and 325. [2]

3. Simplify the following and give each answer as a single fraction:
   (a) $3\dfrac{1}{6} + 1\dfrac{2}{3} \div 1\dfrac{1}{2}$ [2]
   (b) $\dfrac{14}{15} \times 1\dfrac{1}{54} \div 4\dfrac{5}{18}$ [2]

4. Evaluate each of the following:
   (a) $14 + (-20) - (-30)$ [1]
   (b) $(-2)^2 \times (-1)^5$ [1]
   (c) $210 \div (-7) + 10$ [1]
   (d) $327 \times 129 \times 0$ [1]

5. (a) Express 0.875 as a fraction in its lowest terms. [2]
   (b) Express $1\dfrac{31}{80}$ as a decimal. [2]

6. (a) Express 32.748 7 correct to
      (i) 2 decimal places; [1]
      (ii) 3 significant figures. [1]
   (b) Simplify $\dfrac{18.9 \times 6.3}{12.6 \times 0.108}$, giving your answer as a decimal. [2]

7. Express 4 624 in prime factors and hence, or otherwise, find the value of $\sqrt{4\,624}$. [3]

8. (a) Subtract $(10x^4 - 7x^3 - 2x^2 - 3x - 5)$ from $(3x^4 - 7x^3 - 10x^2 + 7x - 2)$. [2]
   (b) Add $(-5x^2 + 12x + 17)$ to $(2x^3 + 7x^2 - 4x - 7)$. [2]

9. One-fifth of a plank is sawn off and three-eighths of the remaining piece is then thrown away. What fraction of the original plank remains? [3]

10. Lamp posts along one side of a street are 6 m apart. If they extend for one and a half kilometres, find the number of lamp posts along the street. [3]

11. Solve $\dfrac{3}{4}x + \dfrac{1}{2} = \dfrac{2}{3}x$. [4]

12. An apple costs x cents. An orange costs y cents more than an apple. Express the cost of 8 apples and 12 oranges in terms of x and y. [4]

13. Given that $a = \dfrac{1}{2}, b = \dfrac{1}{3}, c = -\dfrac{1}{4}$ and $d = 0$, find the value of $\dfrac{1}{a+b} - \dfrac{1}{bc - ad}$. [3]

14. Identify a rule for each of the following number sequences, and then complete it:
   (a) 0.4, 0.5, 0.7, 1.0, 1.4, ____, ____ [1]
   (b) 3, 4, 8, 17, 33, 58, ____, ____ [2]

Part II (50 marks)   Time: 1 h 15 min

*Answer **all** the questions. Calculators may be used in this section.*

Section A (22 marks)

1. (a) Simplify $5x - \{8x - [7 - (4x - 8 - 2x)]\} - 5$. [3]
   (b) If $u = \dfrac{1}{2}h(a + b)$, find a when $u = 84$, $h = 7$ and $b = 16$. [3]

2. John is $1\dfrac{1}{3}$ times as heavy as Mary. If their total mass is 112 kg, find the mass of John. [4]

3. Consider the following pattern:

$$\frac{1}{1 \times 2} = 1 - \frac{1}{2}$$

$$\frac{1}{2 \times 3} = \frac{1}{2} - \frac{1}{3}$$

$$\frac{1}{3 \times 4} = \frac{1}{3} - \frac{1}{4}$$

$$\vdots \qquad \vdots$$

$$\frac{1}{342} = \frac{1}{a} - \frac{1}{b}$$

(a) Write down the 8th line in the pattern. [1]

(b) Using the above, find the value of $\frac{1}{50} - \frac{1}{51}$. [1]

(c) Find the value of a and of b. [2]

4. (a) The product of two numbers is $1\frac{1}{5}$. If one of the numbers is $\frac{1}{5}$, find the sum of the two numbers. [4]

(b) Solve the equation
$$\frac{4x + 1}{2} = \frac{2x - 1}{4} + \frac{x + 3}{8}.$$ [4]

Section B (28 marks)

5. Evaluate each of the following, giving your answer correct to 4 significant figures where necessary. (Take $\pi = 3.142$)

(a) $\left(\frac{2}{5}\right)^2 + 4\frac{3}{4} \div 1\frac{1}{4}$ **(b)** $\frac{15.76 + 3.58^3}{\sqrt{14.75 \div 0.03}}$

(c) $\frac{25\pi}{7.58 + 6.76^2}$ **(d)** $\frac{4}{26.7} - \frac{6}{\sqrt[3]{0.73}}$ [8]

6. (a) Estimate the value of $\frac{\sqrt{2\,505} \times 8.705}{4.98 \times 2.907}$ giving your answer as a whole number. [2]

(b) Given that $6.5 \times 232 = 1\,508$, find the value of
(i) 0.065×2.32 [2]
(ii) $1.508 \div 650$ [2]
showing your working clearly.

7. Simplify each of the following expressions
(a) $5h - 3[4k - 6m + 2\{3h - (2h + 3k)\}]$ [3]

(b) $2x + \frac{3y - 4x}{3} - \frac{2x - 4y}{5}$ [3]

8. (a) Solve the equation $\frac{3x + 5}{4} = 2x - 7$. [3]

(b) If $\frac{h}{k} = \frac{h - 2m}{g}$, find the value of g when $h = 5$, $k = 4$ and $m = -2$. [2]

(c) Subtract the sum of $3x^3 + 4x^2 - 7x + 5$ and $2x^3 - 4x - 4$ from $7x^3 - 4x^2 - 13$, giving your answer in ascending powers of x. [3]

Mid-year Examination Specimen Paper 2

Part I (50 marks)   Time: 1 h

*Answer **all** the questions. Calculators are **not** to be used in this section.*

1. (a) Find the LCM of 77, 132 and 198. [2]

(b) Find the smallest number which, when divided by 16, 20 or 24, leaves a remainder of 3. [2]

2. Evaluate **(a)** $2 \times 2\frac{2}{5} \times \left(3\frac{1}{4} + 1\frac{7}{16}\right)$, [2]
(b) $2 \times 2.41 \times (3.27 + 1.44)$. [2]

3. Simplify **(a)** $12a - 2(3a + 5) + 10$, [2]
(b) $3(2x - y) - 2(3x - y)$. [2]

4. Solve
(a) $4(y + 2) - (3y - 1) = 5 - (2y + 3)$; [2]
(b) $4(2x - 1) - 12 = 16 - 2x$. [2]

5. A father is 45 years old and his son is 9 years old. In how many years' time will the father be three times as old as the son? [4]

6. John has $3.75 and David has twice as much money as John. How much money do they have altogether? [3]

7. Simplify **(a)** $4 - \left(1\frac{3}{4}\right)^2$; [2]

(b) $\frac{2}{7} + \frac{1}{2} \div \frac{3}{14}$. [2]

8. Express $\frac{7}{33}$ as

   (a) a recurring decimal; [2]
   (b) a decimal correct to 4 decimal places. [1]

9. (a) Estimate the value of $\frac{7.984 \times 9.017}{3.967 \times 0.304}$, correct to the nearest whole number. [2]

   (b) Use your result in (a) to find the value of $\frac{7\,984 \times 90.17}{0.396\,7 \times 304}$. [1]

10. Write down the difference between $3y$ minutes and $25y$ seconds, giving your answer in seconds. [3]

11. Identify a rule for each of the following number pattern, and then complete it:

   (a) 7, 9, 13, 21, 37, _____, _____ [2]

   (b) $\frac{3}{5}$, $\frac{5}{8}$, $\frac{9}{13}$, $\frac{3}{4}$, _____, _____ [2]

12. On a certain morning, the temperature in London was $-14°C$, the temperature in Hong Kong was $8°C$ while the temperature in Singapore was $24°C$.

   (a) Find the difference in temperature between London and Singapore. [1]
   (b) The temperature in Shanghai was mid-way between the temperature of London and Hong Kong. Find the temperature of Shanghai on that morning. [2]

13. Simplify $\frac{2x - 5}{3} - \frac{2(3x + 1)}{5} - 2x$. [3]

14. If $a = 2$, $b = 0$, $c = 1$ and $d = -3$, evaluate

   (a) $ac - 2d^2 + 3bd$; [2]
   (b) $(2ad)^2 - 2cd^2 + 2bc^3$. [2]

Part II (50 marks)   Time: 1 h 15 min

*Answer **all** the questions. Calculators may be used in this section.*

Section A (22 marks)

1. Evaluate each of the following:

   (a) $16 - 3 \times (-2)$ [1]
   (b) $45 + 16 \div (-2)^3$ [1]

   (c) $\{[(215 + 25) \div 5 \times 6] - 132 \div 8\} \times 4$ [2]

2. Evaluate each of the following, giving your answer correct to 4 significant figures: (Take $\pi = 3.142$)

   (a) $3.26^3 - \sqrt{0.45}$ [2]
   (b) $\frac{35\pi}{\sqrt[3]{4.87^5 + 9.76^4}}$ [2]

3. Solve (a) $\frac{5 - x}{3} = 1 + \frac{1 - x}{4}$, [4]

     (b) $\frac{3}{x} + \frac{1}{3x} = \frac{1}{3}$. [4]

4. (a) The sum of two numbers is 35; half of the smaller number is equal to $\frac{1}{3}$ of the greater number. Find the numbers. [4]

   (b) Simplify $\frac{a - 1}{5} + \frac{2a - 3}{4}$. [2]

Section B (28 marks)

5. John and Derek had $24 and $50 respectively. They spent the same amount of money on some books. How much money did each boy spend if Derek had 3 times as much money as John after buying the books? [4]

6. (a) If $h^2 = \frac{k}{2x} - \frac{g}{5y^2}$, find the value of x when $y = 3$, $h = -2$, $k = -1$ and $g = 4$. [3]

   (b) A ribbon is 14 m long. Fourteen pieces, each of length 25 cm, are cut from it. The remaining piece is cut into equal lengths of 40 cm. How many pieces of length 40 cm are there? What is the length of the piece that is left over? [4]

7. The numerals $-2, -1, 1, 2, 3, 4, 5$ and 6 are written on eight separate cards, with one number on each card.

   (a) List the pairs of cards that have a sum of 4. [2]
   (b) List the pairs of cards that have a product of 2. [2]
   (c) List the groups of three cards that have a sum of 10. [3]

8. (a) Simplify
$2x^2 - 5x - 2x(3 - 4x) + 2(3x - 1)$. [2]

(b) Subtract $2x^3 - 5 + 4x$ from the sum of $2x - 5x^2 + 3x^3$ and $7x^2 + 5x^3 - 4$. [3]

9. Consider the pattern

$$1 = 1 = 1^2$$
$$1 + 3 = 4 = 2^2$$
$$1 + 3 + 5 = 9 = 3^2$$
$$1 + 3 + 5 + 7 = 16 = 4^2$$
$$\vdots \quad \vdots$$

(a) Write down the tenth line in the pattern. [1]

(b) Find the value of $1 + 3 + 5 + \ldots + 29$. [2]

(c) Given that $1 + 3 + 5 + \ldots + (2x - 1) = 13^2$, find the value of x. [2]

Mid-year Examination Specimen Paper 3

Part I (50 marks)   Time: 1 h

*Answer **all** the questions. Calculators are **not** to be used in this section.*

1. Evaluate
$-20 + 2[-38 - 20 \times (-8) + 5 - (-10 - 20)]$. [3]

2. Find the HCF and LCM of $3^2 \times 5$, 3×5^2 and $2^3 \times 3 \times 5$. [4]

3. Express 3 136 as a product of prime factors and hence, find the value of $\sqrt{3\,136}$. [3]

4. Solve the equation $\dfrac{5x}{6} - \dfrac{2}{3} = \dfrac{x}{2} + \dfrac{1}{6}$. [3]

5. Copy and complete the following statements with '<' or '>':

(a) 2 _____ 21   **(b)** -1 _____ 2

(c) -1 _____ -2 **(d)** $x + 1$ _____ $x + 2$ [4]

6. Find the value of a from the formula
$A = \dfrac{1}{2}h(a + b)$ if $A = 117$, $h = 13$ and $b = 11$. [3]

7. Find the exact value of $\dfrac{0.03 \times 0.49}{42}$, giving your answer as a decimal. [2]

8. Which of the following numbers is/are divisible by both 2 and 4?

102, 336, 3 306, 11 048 [4]

9. Simplify each of the following, giving your answer as a fraction in its lowest terms:

(a) $2\dfrac{2}{3} \times 1\dfrac{4}{5} - 1\dfrac{3}{10}$ [2]

(b) $3\dfrac{3}{4} - 1\dfrac{1}{2} \div 2\dfrac{2}{3}$ [2]

10. Identify a rule for each of the following number sequences, and then complete it.

(a) 3, 5, 8, 12, 17, 23, _____, _____ [2]

(b) $\dfrac{2}{3}$, 1, $1\dfrac{2}{3}$, $2\dfrac{2}{3}$, 4, $5\dfrac{2}{3}$, _____, _____ [2]

11. (a) Express $\dfrac{5}{8}$ as a decimal. [1]

(b) Change 0.86 into a fraction in its lowest terms. [1]

(c) Express 0.002 56 correct to 2 significant figures. [1]

(d) Express 2.445 7 correct to one decimal place. [1]

12. Simplify each of the following expressions:

(a) $x + 2(3x - y) - 5(y - x)$ [2]

(b) $-5(2x - z) + 2z - x$ [2]

13. Given that $a = 2$, $b = -1$ and $c = 5$, evaluate

(a) $3(c - b) + 2bc$; [2]

(b) $3a^2 - 2bc + b^3$. [2]

14. Ah Beng has $38 and Ah Lian has $20. If Ah Beng gives some money to Ah Lian, Ah Beng will then have one-third of what Ah Lian has. How much does Ah Beng give to Ah Lian? [4]

Part II (50 marks)   Time: 1 h 15 min

*Answer **all** the questions. Calculators may be used in this section.*

Section A (22 marks)

1. Evaluate each of the following and give your answer correct to 4 significant figures:

(a) $2 \times 5.12 \div \sqrt{7.96}$ [2]

(b) $\sqrt[3]{42.6} + 8.75 \div 0.14$ [2]

2. **(a)** Given that $H = \dfrac{V(P - R)}{500}$, find the value of P when $V = 80$, $H = 3.2$ and $R = 65$. [3]

   (b) Solve $\dfrac{x}{3} - \dfrac{3x - 5}{2} = 6$. [4]

3. Mr Li's age is four times his son's. Six years ago, Mr Li was ten times as old as his son. How old are they now? [4]

4. **(a)** An apple costs a cents while a pear costs b cents more than an apple. Find, in terms of a and b, the cost of 5 apples and 7 pears. [4]

   (b) Write the following using mathematical symbols:

   (i) 7 is greater than 5 but less than 10. [1]

   (ii) a lies between b and c where a, b and c are numbers. [2]

Section B (28 marks)

5. Copy and complete the following number patterns:

   (a) 1, 2, 4, 7, 11, 16, 22, _____, _____ [2]

   (b) 1, 2, 5, 10, 17, 26, 37, _____, _____ [2]

6. **(a)** Four girls, A, B, C and D, share a box of chocolates among themselves. A takes $\dfrac{1}{4}$ of the chocolates, B takes $\dfrac{3}{8}$ of the remainder and C takes $\dfrac{5}{9}$ of the left-overs. What fraction of the chocolates does D have? [4]

   (b) What polynomial must be subtracted from $2x^5 + 3x^2 + 5x - 7$ to give $6x^5 - 4x^4 + 2x^2 - 8x$? [3]

7. If $37.56 \div 2.31 = 16.26$, find the value of

   (a) $0.375\,6 \div 23.1$ [2]

   (b) $1.626 \times 23\,100$ [2]

   showing your working clearly.

8. **(a)** There are seven consecutive even numbers. If the largest number is x, write an algebraic expression for the middle term. If the middle term is 48, find the value of the smallest term. [4]

(b) Use the distributive property to evaluate 876×999. [2]

9. **(a)** Simplify $\dfrac{3x}{7y} \div \sqrt{\dfrac{81x^4}{49y^2}} + \dfrac{15}{x}$. [3]

   (b) Solve the equation $\dfrac{3x - 4}{7} = \dfrac{2}{3}(x + 5)$. [4]

Mid-year Examination Specimen Paper 4

Part I (50 marks)   **Time: 1 h**

*Answer **all** the questions. Calculators are **not** to be used in this section.*

1. Arrange the following numbers in ascending order:

   $0.1\dot{7}$, $0.1\dot{7}$, 0.177, 0.178 [3]

2. Find the LCM and HCF of 135, 180 and 270. [4]

3. Express 5 832 as a product of prime factors and hence, find the cube root of 5 832. [3]

4. Simplify
   $25 - (-3) + [12 \times (-3) + 15 - (-35)] \div 7$. [3]

5. Simplify **(a)** $1\dfrac{3}{4} - \dfrac{3}{8} \times \dfrac{2}{9}$, [2]

   (b) $1\dfrac{1}{2} \div 2 - \dfrac{1}{2}$. [2]

6. If $x = 3$, $y = 2$ and $z = -1$, find the value of $\dfrac{2z^2 - 5x}{xz - y}$. [3]

7. Simplify $\dfrac{2x - 1}{3} - \dfrac{2(x - 2)}{5}$. [3]

8. Solve the following equations:

   (a) $10x - 9 = 19 + 9x$ [2]

   (b) $2\dfrac{1}{4}x = 18$ [2]

9. What polynomial must be added to $2x^3 - 5x^2 + 7x - 4$ to give $9 + 3x - 5x^2 + 6x^3$? [3]

10. Solve $2 - \dfrac{1}{2}(x - 2) = \dfrac{3}{4}(x + 3) - \dfrac{1}{4}(x - 5)$. [4]

11. A man is 3 times as old as his son. Five years ago, he was 4 times as old as his son. Find their present ages. [4]

12. Write an algebraic expression for each of the following:

   (a) The distance a car travels in x hours if its speed is 70 km/h.

   (b) The number of 22-cent stamps you can buy with $\$x$.

   (c) The number of grammes in k kilogrammes. [3]

13. Simplify $25xy - 3x(5x - y) + 2[5(x - 4y) - 7(x - y)]$. [3]

14. Simplify $\dfrac{3\frac{2}{3} - 1\frac{4}{5}}{\left(1\frac{1}{2}\right)^2 + 2\frac{1}{4}}$. [3]

15. David cycles x km in 3 hours. If he maintains the same speed, how far can he cycle in $12y$ minutes? [3]

Part II (50 marks)   Time: 1 h 15 min

*Answer **all** the questions. Calculators may be used in this section.*

Section A (22 marks)

1. Find the value of $\dfrac{(2.06 + 1.24)^2}{3.4^2 - 1.5^2}$, giving your answer correct to 2 decimal places. [3]

2. If $x = -1$, find the value of $3x^3 + 2x^2 + 5x + 9$. [3]

3. Solve the equation $\dfrac{3x - 1}{3} - \dfrac{x + 3}{5} = 8$. [4]

4. Arrange the following fractions in ascending order: $\dfrac{34}{51}$, $\dfrac{76}{95}$, $\dfrac{88}{121}$, $\dfrac{169}{273}$. [2]

5. The product of two numbers is $2\frac{2}{3}$. If one number is $\frac{3}{5}$, find their sum. [4]

6. A man's salary is $\$1\,200$ a month. He spends $\frac{5}{8}$ of it on food and lodging, $\frac{1}{5}$ of the remainder on transport and saves the rest. Calculate the amount of money he saves. [6]

Section B (28 marks)

7. (a) Evaluate each of the following, giving your answer correct to 4 significant figures:

   (i) $\dfrac{\sqrt{54.6} \times 74.5^3}{46.7 - 0.8^4}$ [2]

   (ii) $\dfrac{84.5 + 7.5 \div 1.6}{\sqrt[3]{46.8} - \sqrt[4]{89.4}}$ [2]

   (b) Simplify $\dfrac{x - y}{2} - \dfrac{2x - 3y}{7}$. [3]

8. (a) Consider the number pattern

$$1^2 - 0^2 = 1$$
$$2^2 - 1^2 = 3$$
$$3^2 - 2^2 = 5$$
$$4^2 - 3^2 = 7$$
$$\vdots$$
$$x^2 - y^2 = 157$$

   (i) Write down the tenth line of the pattern.

   (ii) Find the value of $99^2 - 98^2$.

   (iii) Find the value of x and y in $x^2 - y^2 = 157$. [4]

   (b) Simplify $\sqrt[3]{64x^6 y^9} - \dfrac{1}{2}[7 - (5 - 6x)]$. [3]

9. (a) If the value of $3x^3 + 2x^2 + xy + 7$ is equal to 40 when $x = -2$, find the value of y. [3]

   (b) $\frac{4}{7}$ of the passengers in an MRT train are men, $\frac{1}{3}$ of them are women and the rest are children. If there are 42 children, find

   (i) the total number of people in the train; [2]

   (ii) how many more men than women there are in the MRT train. [3]

10. (a) Copy and complete the following number sequence:

   5, 6, 10, 19, 35, 60, _____, _____ [2]

   (b) The sum of three consecutive odd numbers is 237. Find the largest of the three numbers. [4]

Mid-year Examination Specimen Paper 5

Part I (50 marks)   **Time: 1 h**

*Answer **all** the questions. Calculators are **not** to be used in this section.*

1. Evaluate
   (a) $365 - 23 \times 10 - 32 \div (-4)$;   [2]
   (b) $34 \times 6 + 5 - 4 \div 16$.   [2]

2. If $a = \dfrac{1}{4}$, $b = \dfrac{-1}{3}$ and $c = \dfrac{3}{5}$, evaluate each of the following, giving your answer as a fraction in its lowest terms:
   (a) $3a - 2b + c$;
   (b) $2a - 3b \div 5c$.   [4]

3. Find the HCF and LCM of $(2 \times 5 \times 7)$, $(3^3 \times 5)$ and $(2^2 \times 3^3 \times 5)$.   [4]

4. Find the value of $x^2 - 4x + 2$ when x is
   (a) 0;   (b) 1;   (c) $\dfrac{1}{2}$;   (d) −1.   [4]

5. Simplify   (a) $5a - b - (4a + 3b)$;   [2]
              (b) $2(m - 2n) - 7m$.   [2]

6. Evaluate $42 \div 6 \times 3 - 8 \times 5 - 70 \div (-5) \times 8 \div (-2)$.   [3]

7. Simplify   (a) $\dfrac{3}{5} + \dfrac{4}{7} - \dfrac{3}{35}$,   [2]

              (b) $\dfrac{2}{5} + \dfrac{1}{3} \times \dfrac{2}{5}$.   [2]

8. Solve the equation $2(x - 1) = 5 - (x + 2)$.   [3]

9. Express 2 304 as a product of prime factors and hence, find the value of $\sqrt{2\,304}$.   [3]

10. Arrange the fractions $\dfrac{2}{3}, \dfrac{4}{9}, \dfrac{5}{7}$ and $\dfrac{8}{11}$ in descending order.   [3]

11. Subtract $5x^2 - 3x - 2$ from $2x^3 - 3x^2 + 5x - 7$.   [3]

12. Use the distributive law to simplify each of the following:
    (a) 567×99;   [2]
    (b) $63 \times 7\dfrac{2}{5} - 17 \times 7.4 + \dfrac{37}{5} \times 24$.   [2]

13. The cost of printing name cards is given by the equation $y = k + \dfrac{3\,000}{x}$ where y cents is the cost per card, x is the number of cards printed and k is a constant.
    (a) Given that $y = 10$ when $x = 600$, find the value of k.
    (b) Calculate the cost per card if 750 cards are printed.
    (c) How many cards will be printed if the cost per card is to be 7.5 cents?   [4]

14. (a) List the whole numbers between $\sqrt[3]{65}$ and $\sqrt{65}$.   [2]
    (b) What is the value of the number that is mid-way between −24 and 6?   [1]

Part II (50 marks)   **Time: 1 h 15 min**

*Answer **all** the questions. Calculators may be used in this section.*

Section A (22 marks)

1. Evaluate each of the following:
   (a) $\dfrac{2}{14.5} - \dfrac{7.2}{4.5^3}$ [2]

   (b) $\sqrt{54.89} \div \dfrac{5}{1.27^2} - 6.89$ [2]

2. Solve the equation:
   $3(m^2 - 2m) = 7 - m^2 + m(4m - 8)$.   [3]

3. The table below shows a man's deposits and withdrawals in dollars. If he had $520 in his savings account initially, calculate his balance after his withdrawals and last deposit of $75.   [4]

Deposits (in $)	Withdrawals (in $)
65	44
30	134
20	25
40	55
60	50
75	

4. If $x = \dfrac{5y}{z - 4y}$, find the value of y when $x = 3$ and $z = 2$. [4]

5. (a) Subtract $2\dfrac{1}{2}$ from the sum of $3\dfrac{1}{6}$ and $4\dfrac{5}{8}$. [3]

   (b) Subtract the sum of $(2x^2 + 5x - 3)$ and $(4x^3 + 3x - 9)$ from the product of $2x$ and $(3x^2 - 5x - 4)$. [4]

Section B (28 marks)

6. (a) The sum of three consecutive odd numbers is 141, find the largest of the three numbers. [4]

   (b) Five teachers took a group of students for a movie. Each adult ticket cost $7.20 and students' tickets were sold at half price. If the total cost for the group was $212.40, calculate the number of children in the group. [3]

7. (a) Solve the equation $x - 2 = \dfrac{x - 4}{3}$. [4]

(b) Copy and complete the following number sequence:

   7, 4, 8, 6, 11, 10, 16, 16, 23, 24, _____, _____ [2]

8. (a) Similar bars of soap are sold in packs of 3 for $2 or packs of 8 for $5.20. Find the difference in the price for 48 bars of soap. [3]

   (b) Mr Tan gave $240 to his wife, $\dfrac{2}{5}$ of the remainder of his money to his son and kept the rest. If he had $195 left, how much money did he have originally? [3]

   (c) The temperature in Arrowtown for six days are $-4°C$, $-12°C$, $-18°C$, $2°C$, $4°C$ and $-8°C$. Find the average temperature for these six days. [2]

9. (a) The result of adding 90 to a number is the same as multiplying that number by 6. Find the number. [3]

   (b) John is 4 years older than David and Joe is 2 years younger than David. If the sum of their ages is 41, how old will John be in 8 years' time? [4]

CHAPTER 9

Perimeter and Area of Simple Geometrical Figures

In this chapter, you will learn how to

▲ find the perimeter and area of simple geometrical figures;
▲ solve problems involving these figures and figures related to them.

Preliminary Problem

The picture shows the famous "Fountain of Wealth', the world's largest fountain. Located at Suntec City in Singapore, it has attracted many visitors from all over the world. The bronze fountain has a circular ring of perimeter 66 m and a base area of 1 683 m².

Perimeter

The perimeter of a closed plane figure is the distance to go along one round of the plane.

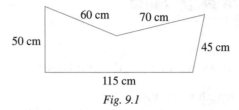

60 cm   70 cm

50 cm

45 cm

115 cm

Fig. 9.1

In Fig. 9.1, the perimeter of the closed figure = (50 + 60 + 70 + 45 + 115) cm
= 340 cm

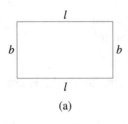

l

b b

l

(a)

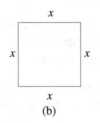

x

x x

x

(b)

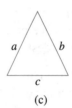

a b

c

(c)

Fig. 9.2

The perimeter of the rectangle in Fig. 9.2(a) is

$P = (2l + 2b)$ units
$= 2(l + b)$ units

The perimeter of the square in Fig. 9.2(b) is

$P = 2(x + x)$ units
$= 4x$ units

The perimeter of the triangle in Fig. 9.2(c) is

$P = (a + b + c)$ units

In-Class Activity

Adam intends to build a house of floor area 144 m².

Area = 144 m² y m

x m

Complete the following table to get some possible different perimeters, but the same area, of the floor:

x (m)	1	2	4	6	8	12	16	18	24	36	72	144
y (m)	144	72	36	24								
Perimeter (m)	290	148										

(a) Which design do you think is the cheapest to build? What is its perimeter?

(b) Which is the most expensive design to build?

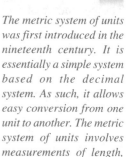

Units of Length or Distance

We often use the following units to measure lengths or distances.

Metre (m): The basic unit of length is the metre.
This is normally used to measure distance between two places within a small compound. For example, the distance between your school gate and the school hall is measured in metres.

Centimetre (cm): This is a unit used to measure the length of small objects or the distance between two neighbouring points. For example, the length of your desk is measured in centimetres.

Millimetre (mm): This is normally used for measuring small lengths or thickness. For example, the thickness of a page of this book is given in millimetres.

Kilometre (km): This is used to measure the distance between two places far away from each other. For example, the distance between Hongkong and Singapore is measured in kilometres.

The above units are related as shown below:

> 1 centimetre (cm) = 10 millimetres (mm)
> 1 metre (m)   = 100 centimetres (cm)
> 1 kilometre (km) = 1 000 metres (m)

The metric system of units was first introduced in the nineteenth century. It is essentially a simple system based on the decimal system. As such, it allows easy conversion from one unit to another. The metric system of units involves measurements of length, area, mass, capacity and volume; all these units being related through the decimal notation.

In-Class Activity

Work with a partner.

Use a measuring tape to measure and then record the perimeter of your

(a) classroom blackboard;   (b) classroom floor.

Example 1

Find the perimeter of the given figure.

Solution

Perimeter of the figure
= [2 + 2(5) + 6 + 3 + 2(8) + (2 + 6 + 3)] cm
= (2 + 10 + 6 + 3 + 16 + 11) cm
= 48 cm

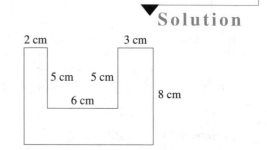

1. Find the perimeter of each of the following geometrical figures:
   (a) A triangle of sides 8 cm, 9 cm and 10 cm.
   (b) A rectangle with length 9 cm and breadth 7 cm.
   (c) A square of side 7 cm.

2. Find the perimeter of each of the following figures. All measurements are in cm:

   (a)   (b) 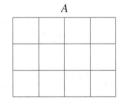   (c)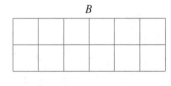

3. A piece of wire is bent to form a square of side 8 cm. It is then reshaped to form a rectangle of length 10 cm and breadth x cm. Find x.

4. A boy is asked to run 15 times round the edge of a rectangular field measuring 30 m by 25 m. Find the total distance the boy ran.

5. The length of a rectangular plot of land is twice its breadth. If its perimeter is 102 m, calculate its breadth.

6. Find, in cm, the perimeter of a rectangle measuring a m by b cm.

Area of Simple Figures

Which is bigger — a football field or a basketball court? The football field is bigger because it covers a larger surface than the basketball court. In other words, the football field has a larger area.

Fig. A and Fig. B consist of squares of the same size. Count the number of squares in each. What do you notice? Can we say that A and B cover the same amount of space, i.e., they have the same area?

> **Area is the measure of the amount of surface covered.**

Units of Area

We often use the following units to measure area.

Square centimetre (cm²): We usually use unit squares to compare areas. A square of side 1 cm is used as a standard unit. We call this unit area 1 square centimeter (1 cm²). See Fig. 9.3.

1 cm

1 cm

Fig. 9.3

Square millimetre (mm²): In Fig. 9.4, each small square has an area of 1 square millimetre (1 mm²).

$$1 \text{ cm} = 10 \text{ mm}$$
$$\therefore \quad 1 \text{ cm}^2 = 10 \text{ mm} \times 10 \text{ mm} = 100 \text{ mm}^2$$

10 mm

10 mm

Fig. 9.4

Square millimetres are used to measure the areas of very small shapes.

Square metre (m²): The square metre is used to measure the area of large surfaces such as the floor area of a flat.

$$1 \text{ m} = 100 \text{ cm}$$
$$\therefore \quad 1 \text{ m}^2 = 100 \text{ cm} \times 100 \text{ cm} = 10\,000 \text{ cm}^2$$

Hectare (ha): The hectare is used to measure large land areas such as farms.

$$1 \text{ ha} = 10\,000 \text{ m}^2$$

Square km (km²): The square kilometre is used to measure the area of a very large surface such as the area of a country.

$$1 \text{ km} = 1\,000 \text{ m}$$
$$\therefore \quad 1 \text{ km}^2 = 1\,000 \text{ m} \times 1\,000 \text{ m}$$
$$= 1\,000\,000 \text{ m}^2 = 100 \text{ ha}$$

The British used feet, inches, yards, furlongs, miles, etc. to measure length, and acre to measure area.

Find out what these units are and compare them with the SI units.

The largest freshwater lake in the world is Lake Superior, one of the Great Lakes of North America. It covers an area of 82 350 km², roughly 130 times the size of Singapore.

Example 2

Express   *(a)*   *975 cm² in m²;*   *(b)*   *2.65 km² in m²;*
           (c)   *48 000 m² in ha;*   *(d)*   *5 mm² in cm².*

▼ **Solution**

(a) $975 \text{ cm}^2 = \underline{\hspace{1cm}} \text{ m}^2$

$$1 \text{ cm} = \frac{1}{100} \text{ m}$$
$$1 \text{ cm}^2 = \frac{1}{100} \text{ m} \times \frac{1}{100} \text{ m}$$
$$= \frac{1}{10\,000} \text{ m}^2$$
$$\therefore \quad 975 \text{ cm}^2 = 975 \times \frac{1}{10\,000} \text{ m}^2$$
$$= 0.097\,5 \text{ m}^2$$

(b) $2.65 \text{ km}^2 = \underline{\hspace{1cm}} \text{ m}^2$

$$1 \text{ km} = 1\,000 \text{ m}$$
$$1 \text{ km}^2 = 1\,000 \times 1\,000 \text{ m}$$
$$= 1\,000\,000 \text{ m}^2$$
$$\therefore \quad 2.65 \text{ km}^2 = 2.65 \times 1\,000\,000 \text{ m}^2$$
$$= 2\,650\,000 \text{ m}^2$$

(c) $48\,000 \text{ m}^2 = \underline{\hspace{1cm}} \text{ ha}$
$$10\,000 \text{ m}^2 = 1 \text{ ha}$$
$$1 \text{ m}^2 = \frac{1}{10\,000} \text{ ha}$$
$$\therefore \quad 48\,000 \text{ m}^2 = 48\,000 \times \frac{1}{10\,000} \text{ ha}$$
$$= 4.8 \text{ ha}$$

(d) $5 \text{ mm}^2 = \underline{\hspace{1cm}} \text{ cm}^2$

$$1 \text{ mm} = \frac{1}{10} \text{ cm}$$
$$1 \text{ mm}^2 = \frac{1}{10} \text{ cm} \times \frac{1}{10} \text{ cm}$$
$$= \frac{1}{100} \text{ cm}^2$$
$$\therefore \quad 5 \text{ mm}^2 = 5 \times \frac{1}{100} \text{ cm}^2 = 0.05 \text{ cm}^2$$

Area of a Rectangle

Consider a rectangle of length l units and breadth b units (see Fig. 9.5). The rectangle is made up of b rows, each with l unit squares.

No. of unit squares in the rectangle = $l \times b$

$\therefore$　area of rectangle = $(l \times b)$ unit^2

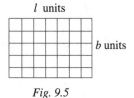

l units

b units

Fig. 9.5

In general,

> **area of a rectangle = length × breadth**

Hence,　　length = $\dfrac{\text{area}}{\text{breadth}}$, breadth = $\dfrac{\text{area}}{\text{length}}$

Problem Solving — Draw a diagram

Many problems can be made easier by **drawing a diagram**.

Example 3

The area of a rectangle is 40 cm^2 and one of its sides is 8 cm long. Find the breadth and the perimeter of the rectangle.

▼ **Solution**

Draw a simple diagram like this

8 cm

Area = 40 cm^2

Breadth of the rectangle = $\dfrac{40 \text{ cm}^2}{8 \text{ cm}}$ = 5 cm

Perimeter of the rectangle = 2(8 + 5) cm = 26 cm

Example 4

The perimeter of a rectangle is 22 cm and its breadth is 4 cm. Find its area.

▼ **Solution**

We can **draw a diagram** and then **form an equation** to solve the problem.

Let the length of the rectangle be x cm.

Then $2(x + 4) = 22$
$$2x + 8 = 22$$
$$2x = 14$$
$$x = 7$$

∴   the area of the rectangle = (7×4) cm^2 = 28 cm^2

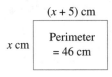

Example 5

The width of a rectangle is 5 cm less than its length, and its perimeter is 46 cm. Find its width and its area.

▼ Solution

Let the width of the rectangle be x cm.

Then the length is $(x + 5)$ cm.

Perimeter = $2[x + (x + 5)]$ cm = 46 cm
$$4x + 10 = 46$$
$$\therefore \quad 4x = 36$$
$$x = 9$$

∴   Its width is 9 cm and its length is 14 cm.
∴   Its area = (9×14) cm^2
          = 126 cm^2

Example 6

A rectangular field is 13 m long and 10 m wide. It has a cement path $3\frac{1}{2}$ m wide around it. What is the area of the cement path?

▼ Solution

Area of the field and cement path = (20×17) m^2 = 340 m^2

Area of the field = (13×10) m^2 = 130 m^2

∴   area of cement path = $(340 - 130)$ m^2 = 210 m^2

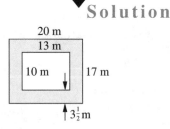

═══ **Exercise 9b** ═══

1. Copy and fill in the missing numbers:

   (a) 8.5 cm^2 = _____ m^2
   (b) 2.5 mm^2 = _____ cm^2
   (c) 6.3 m^2 = _____ cm^2
   (d) 40.6 cm^2 = _____ mm^2
   (e) 44.4 km^2 = _____ ha
   (f) 3.1 ha   = _____ m^2
   (g) 53.7 m^2 = _____ km^2

   (h) 0.28 km^2 = _____ m^2
   (i) 53 200 mm^2 = _____ m^2
   (j) 69 450 cm^2 = _____ m^2
   (k) 3.4 ha   = _____ km^2
   (l) 462 m^2 = _____ ha

2. Copy and complete the table below for each given rectangle:

	Length	Breadth	Perimeter	Area
(a)	6 m	4 m		
(b)	8 m			48 m²
(c)		2.2 m		8.8 m²
(d)	4.5 m		23 m	
(e)		26 mm	98 mm	

3. Find the number of 15-centimetre square tiles required to cover a rectangular floor 5.4 m long and 4.05 m wide.

4. Find the area, in square centimetres, of a rectangular strip of board 3.28 m long and 75 mm wide.

5. A square cardboard of side 20 m has a 4 m wide border round three of its sides. Find the area of the border.

6. A paper box without a lid is 25 cm long. 16 cm wide and 5 cm deep. How many square centimetres of paper have been used to make the box?

7. Find the cost required to carpet a hall 8 m by 5.5 m if a rectangular section 2 m by $1\frac{1}{2}$ m is taken out to provide for the fire-place and the carpet costs $52.50 per m².

8. A swimming pool 25 m by 10 m has a concrete border all round. Find the area of the concrete border if it is 2.5 m wide at the sides and 5 m at the ends.

9. The perimeter of a square is 36 cm. Find its area.

∗10. Find the total area of cardboard used in making a match box, complete with the sliding portion, 4 cm long, 2.5 cm wide and 1.2 cm deep (ignore the thickness of the cardboard).

11. Find, in hectares, the area of the figure shown below. Give your answer correct to 2 decimal places.

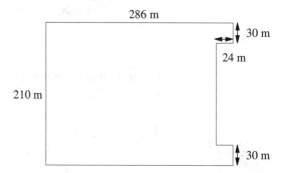

12. The length of a rectangle is 8 cm more than its width. If its perimeter is 56 cm, find its length and its area.

Area of a Parallelogram

A **parallelogram** is a quadrilateral in which the opposite pairs of sides are parallel.

We can obtain a rectangle from a parallelogram. To do so, draw on a piece of paper a parallelogram *ABCD* as shown in Fig. 9.6.

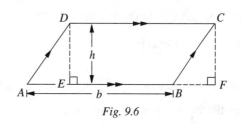

Fig. 9.6

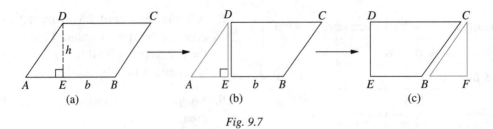

Fig. 9.7

Cut off $\triangle AED$ and place it in the position BFC (Fig. 9.7(c)). A rectangle $EFCD$ is obtained. Do you agree that the parallelogram $ABCD$ and the rectangle $EFCD$ have the same area?

Area of the parallelogram $ABCD$ = Area of the rectangle $EFCD$
$$= DC \times DE$$

But $DC = AB$ (opposite sides of a parallelogram)

$\therefore$ area of parallelogram $ABCD = AB \times DE$
$$= b \times h$$
$$= \text{base} \times \text{height}$$

In general,

area of a parallelogram = base × height = $b \times h$

 ## Area of a Triangle

Look at the square $ABCD$, the rectangle $PQRS$ and the parallelogram $HIJK$ in Fig. 9.8.

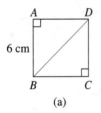 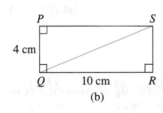 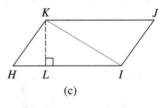

Fig. 9.8

The square $ABCD$ in Fig. 9.8(a) is cut into two halves by the diagonal BD. Similarly, the diagonal QS cuts the rectangle $PQRS$ in Fig. 9.8(b) into two equal right-angled triangles PQS and SQR.

Area of square $ABCD = BC \times CD$

$\therefore$ area of $\triangle BCD = \dfrac{1}{2} \times BC \times CD$

Since BC is the base and CD is the height of $\triangle BCD$,

$\therefore$ area of $\triangle BCD = \dfrac{1}{2} \times \text{base} \times \text{height}$.

How would you deduce that in Fig. 9.8(b), area of $\triangle QRS = \dfrac{1}{2} \times QR \times RS = \dfrac{1}{2} \times \text{base} \times \text{height}$?
If QS is taken as the base, where should the height of $\triangle QRS$ be?

The diagonal *KI* cuts the parallelogram *HIJK* in Fig. 9.8(c) into two identical triangles which are not right-angled.

Area of $HIJK = HI \times KL$

$\therefore$ area of $\triangle HIK = \dfrac{1}{2} \times HI \times KL$

HI is the base and *KL* is the height of $\triangle HIK$.

$\therefore$ area of $\triangle HIK = \dfrac{1}{2} \times$ base $\times$ height

In general

$$\text{area of a triangle} = \frac{1}{2} \times \text{base} \times \text{height}$$

$$= \frac{1}{2}\, bh$$

 ## *Area of a Trapezium*

A **trapezium** is a quadrilateral with one pair of parallel sides. Fig. 9.9 shows a trapezium *ABCD* in which *AD* is parallel to *BC* with a height of *AH*. The trapezium is divided into $\triangle ABC$ and $\triangle ACD$.

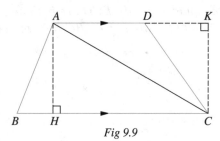

Fig 9.9

Four rectangular cards of identical size are arranged as shown below. You are to move only one card so as to form a square.

Area of trapezium $ABCD$ = area of $\triangle ABC$ + area of $\triangle ACD$

$$= \left(\frac{1}{2} \times BC \times AH \right) + \left(\frac{1}{2} \times AD \times CK \right)$$

Note: $AH = CK$

Area of trapezium $ABCD = \dfrac{1}{2}\, AH\,(BC + AD)$

$$= \frac{1}{2} \times \text{height} \times \text{sum of parallel sides}$$

In general,

$$\text{area of a trapezium} = \frac{1}{2} \times \text{height} \times \text{sum of parallel sides}$$

Example 7

Find the areas of the following figures:

(a)

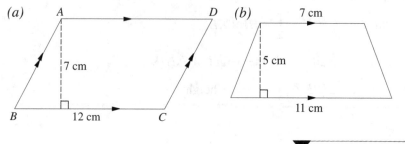

▼ **Solution**

(a) Area of parallelogram $ABCD$ = base × height
$$= (12 \times 7) \text{ cm}^2 = 84 \text{ cm}^2$$

(b) Area of trapezium = $\frac{1}{2}$ × height × sum of parallel sides

$$= \left[\frac{1}{2} \times 5 \times (7 + 11) \right] \text{cm}^2 = 45 \text{ cm}^2$$

Example 8

In the figure below, the sides AB and DC of the quadrilateral ABCD are both perpendicular to the diagonal AC. Given AB = 2 cm, DC = 8 cm and the area of △ABC = 6 cm², calculate

(a) the length of AC;
(b) the area of the quadrilateral ABCD.

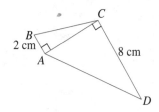

▼ **Solution**

(a)   Area of $\triangle ABC = \frac{1}{2} \times AB \times AC$

∴ $\frac{1}{2} \times AB \times AC = 6$

$\frac{1}{2} \times 2 \times AC = 6$

∴ $AC = 6$ cm

(b) Area of $\triangle ACD = \frac{1}{2} \times AC \times CD$

$$= \left(\frac{1}{2} \times 6 \times 8 \right) \text{cm}^2 = 24 \text{ cm}^2$$

∴   the area of the quadrilateral $ABCD = (6 + 24) \text{ cm}^2 = 30 \text{ cm}^2$

Example 9

Find the value of *x* in the following figures:

(a)

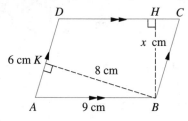

(b)

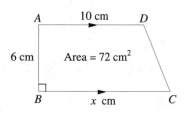

Solution

(a) Area of parallelogram *ABCD*
$$= AB \times BH = AD \times BK$$
$$9 \times x = 6 \times 8$$
$$\therefore \quad x = \frac{6 \times 8}{9} = 5\frac{1}{3}$$

(b) Area of trapezium $ABCD = \frac{1}{2} \times AB \times (AD + BC)$
$$72 = \left[\frac{1}{2} \times 6 \times (10 + x)\right]$$
$$24 = 10 + x$$
$$\therefore \quad x = 14$$

Example 10

Find the total area of the shaded parts in the diagram.

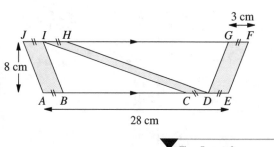

Solution

The total area of the shaded parts is made up of 3 parallelograms of the same base length (3 cm) and of the same height (8 cm).
∴   area of shaded region = [3(3 × 8)] cm² = 72 cm²

Example 11

In the figure on the right, *AB* = 17 cm, *BC* = 25 cm, *AP* = 8 cm, *BQ* = 5 cm, *CR* = 14 cm and *CS* = 3 cm. Find the area of the shaded region.

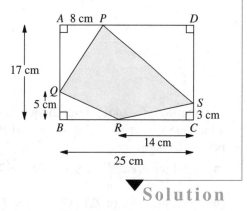

Solution

Area of shaded region *PQRS* = area of *ABCD* − area of triangles (*APQ* + *PDS* + *CSR* + *BQR*)

Area of $ABCD = (17 \times 25)$ cm^2 = 425 cm^2

Area of $\triangle APQ = \dfrac{1}{2} \times AP \times AQ = \left[\dfrac{1}{2} \times 8 \times (17 - 5)\right]$ cm^2 = 48 cm^2

Area of $\triangle PDS = \dfrac{1}{2} \times PD \times DS = \left[\dfrac{1}{2} \times (25 - 8) \times (17 - 3)\right]$ cm^2 = 119 cm^2

Area of $\triangle SRC = \dfrac{1}{2} \times RC \times SC = \left(\dfrac{1}{2} \times 14 \times 3\right)$ cm^2 = 21 cm^2

Area of $\triangle BRQ = \dfrac{1}{2} \times BR \times BQ = \left[\dfrac{1}{2} \times (25 - 14) \times 5\right]$ cm^2 = 27.5 cm^2

$\therefore$ Area of $PQRS$ = (425 − 48 − 119 − 21 − 27.5) cm^2 = 209.5 cm^2

Exercise 9c

1. Find the area of the triangle PQR in the following cases:

(a)

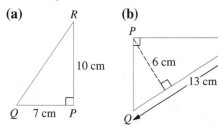

(b)

(c)

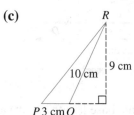

2. In the diagram below, the area of $\triangle PQR$ is 255 cm^2 and the length of QR is 30 cm. Find the length of PS.

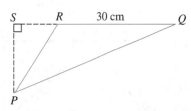

3. For questions (a) to (c), refer to the figure in which QS is perpendicular to PR and PK is perpendicular to QR.
    (a) Find the area of $\triangle PQR$ if $PR = 17$ cm and $QS = 12$ cm.
    (b) Find the area of $\triangle PQS$ if $QS = 7$ cm, $PR = 14$ cm and $SR = 9$ cm.

(c) Find QS if $PR = 14$ cm and the area of $\triangle PQR = 147$ cm^2.

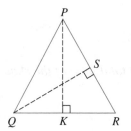

4. Copy and complete the following table for each parallelogram:

	(a)	(b)	(c)
Base (cm)	12		7.8
Height (cm)	7	6	
Area (cm^2)		42	42.9

5. In the diagram, $AB = 20$ cm, $BC = 21$ cm, $AD = 10$ cm and $DE = 10.5$ cm. Angles ABC and ADE are right angles. If $\triangle ADE$ is removed from $\triangle ABC$, what is the area of the shaded region that remains?

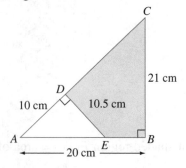

6. Copy and complete the following table for each trapezium:

	(a)	**(b)**	**(c)**
Height (cm)	6	14	8
Parallel side 1 (cm)	7	8	
Parallel side 2 (cm)	11		5
Area (cm²)		126	72

✱**7.** What is the cost of spraying insecticide on a field measuring 2 000 m by 3 200 m if the cost is $22 per hectare? (1 ha = 10 000 m²)

✱**8.** Find the unknowns, marked *x*, in the following figures:

(a)

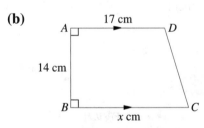

Area of *ABCD* = 124 cm²

(b)

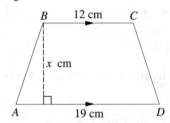

Area of *ABCD* = 280 cm²

(c)

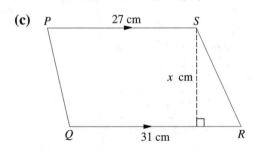

Area of *PQRS* = 348 cm²

(d)

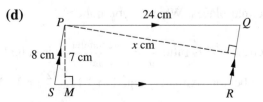

9. Find the areas of the following shaded parts:

(a)

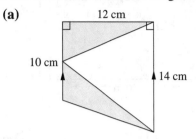

(b)

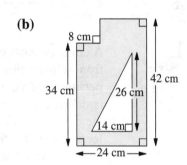

(c)   **(d)**

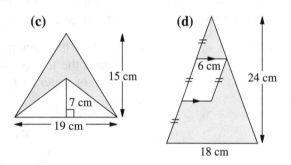

✱**(e)**

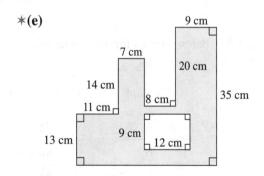

(f)

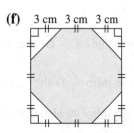

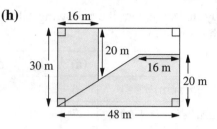

(g)

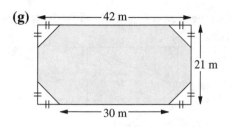

Perimeter of a Circle

The circumference of the Earth's equator is approximately 40 000 km. An imaginary belt of 40 000 km will fit the equator nicely. If we increase the length of the belt by 1 m, will it be possible for a cat to squeeze through? How far above the surface of the equator will the belt be?

A circle consists of points that are all equidistant from a particular point called the **centre**. The **perimeter** of a circle, or the length of its boundary, is called the **circumference**. The distance from the centre of a circle to any point on its circumference is called the **radius**. The **diameter** of the circle is twice the length of its radius.

The diameter of a tin can be found by placing it between two books as shown in Fig. 9.10.

To find the circumference of the tin can, simply wrap a strip of paper round the top as shown in Fig. 9.11. Then measure the length of the strip of paper to get the circumference.

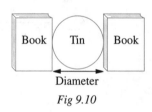

Fig 9.10

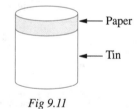

Fig 9.11

The table below shows the circumferences and diameters of several tin cans found by the above methods.

Tin Can	Circumference (c)	Diameter (d)	$\frac{c}{d}$
A	48.5 cm	15.5 cm	
B	40.0 cm	12.7 cm	
C	31.3 cm	9.9 cm	
D	26.1 cm	8.3 cm	

In each case, find the value of $\frac{c}{d}$ correct to two decimal places. What do you notice?

As a matter of fact, the ratio $\frac{c}{d}$ is the same for all circles. This ratio $\frac{c}{d} = \frac{\text{circumference}}{\text{diameter}}$ is called **pi** and is denoted by the symbol π. Usually π is taken to be approximately equal to 3.14, $\frac{22}{7}$ or 3.142.

To find the circumference of a circle, we use $\dfrac{\text{circumference}}{\text{diameter}} = \dfrac{c}{d} = \pi$.

Therefore $c = \pi d$.

Since $d = 2r$ where r denotes the radius of the circle, $c = 2\pi r$.

Hence,

> **circumference of a circle, $c = \pi d$ or $2\pi r$, where d = diameter and r = radius.**

Area of a Circle

Is the circle perfectly round?

Look at the following figures:

(a)

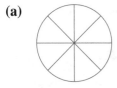
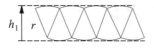

(b)

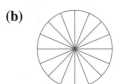
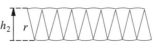

(*h* gets closer and closer to *r*)

(c)

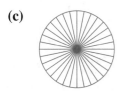
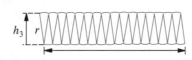

The length of the base gets closer and closer to πr.

Fig. 9.12

In Fig. 9.12(a), a circle is divided into 8 equal parts and rearranged as shown. In Fig. 9.12(b) and (c), the circles are divided into 16 and 32 equal parts respectively. In each case, the parts are rearranged in a straight line as shown. Notice that the figures resulting from the rearrangements of the parts tend to look like parallelograms. As the number of equal parts increases, the area of the resulting figure, which is the same as the area of the **original circle**, will be closer and closer to the area of a parallelogram. Notice also that the height h of the parallelogram gets closer and closer to r, the radius of the circle, and the length of the base gets closer and closer to πr, which is half of the circumference of the circle.

$\therefore$ area of the parallelogram = base × height
$$= \pi r \times r = \pi r^2$$

> **Area of a circle = πr^2, where r = radius.**

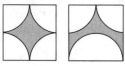

Example 12

A circle has a radius of 7 m. Find its area and circumference. $\left(Take\ \pi = \dfrac{22}{7}\right)$

Solution

Area of circle $= \pi r^2 = \left(\dfrac{22}{7} \times 7 \times 7\right) m^2$

$\qquad\qquad = 154\ m^2$

Circumference of circle $= 2\pi r = \left(2 \times \dfrac{22}{7} \times 7\right) m$

$\qquad\qquad\qquad\qquad = 44\ m$

Example 13

The area of a circle is 78.5 cm². Calculate the circumference of the circle. (Take $\pi = 3.14$)

Solution

Area of circle $= \pi r^2$

$\qquad 78.5 = 3.14 r^2$

$\qquad\quad r^2 = \dfrac{78.5}{3.14} = 25$

$\qquad\quad r = \sqrt{25} = 5$

$\therefore$ circumference of circle $= 2\pi r$

$\qquad\qquad\qquad\qquad = 2(3.14)(5)\ cm$

$\qquad\qquad\qquad\qquad = 31.4\ cm$

Example 14

The diameter of the wheel of a car is 0.35 m. Find the number of revolutions made by the wheel per minute when the car is travelling at 33 km/h. $\left(Take\ \pi = \dfrac{22}{7}\right)$

Solution

In 60 minutes, the car travels $(33 \times 1\ 000)$ m.

In 1 minute, the car travels $\dfrac{33 \times 1\ 000}{60}$ m.

Number of revolutions made per minute $= \dfrac{\text{distance travelled}}{\text{circumference of wheel}}$

$\qquad\qquad\qquad\qquad = \dfrac{33 \times 1\ 000}{60} \times \dfrac{1}{\pi d}$

$\qquad\qquad\qquad\qquad = \dfrac{33 \times 1\ 000}{60} \times \dfrac{7}{22} \times \dfrac{100}{35}$

$\qquad\qquad\qquad\qquad = 500$

Example 15

In the figure, ABCD is a rectangle of length 24 cm and breadth 16 cm. Given that $CQ = PB = \frac{1}{2}PQ$, calculate the area of the trapezium PQRS.

▼**Solution**

Strategy 1: Use an equation

$PQ = 8$ cm, $RQ = \frac{1}{4} AB = 6$ cm and $PS = \frac{3}{4} AB = 18$ cm

Using the formula $\frac{1}{2} \times$ height $\times$ sum of parallel sides

= area of trapezium,

area of $PQRS$ = $\frac{1}{2} \times 8 \times (6 + 18)$

= 96 cm²

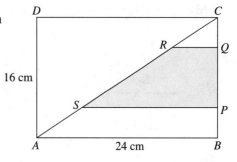

Strategy 2: Draw a diagram

Divide the rectangle into 8 equal parts as shown. If we move the shaded triangle X onto Y, the total shaded area is equal to $\frac{1}{4}$ of the big rectangle.

∴ area of $PQRS$ = $\frac{1}{4} \times 16 \times 24$

= 96 cm²

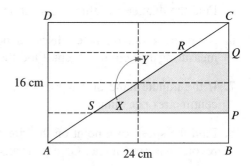

Exercise 9d

Take π to be $\frac{22}{7}$ for this exercise unless otherwise stated.

1. Copy and complete the following table below for each circle:

	(a)	(b)	(c)	(d)
Radius	10 m			
Diameter				3.6 m
Circumference		176 mm		
Area			616 cm²	

2. Calculate the circumference and area of each circle, given its diameter:

   (a) 70 mm   (b) 28 cm   (c) 35 cm   (d) $\frac{14}{3}$ cm

3. Calculate the circumference and area of each circle, given its radius (take $\pi = 3.14$), giving your answer correct to 2 decimal places:

   (a) 3.5 cm   (b) 13.8 m   (c) 0.37 m   (d) 5.25 cm

✱**4.** Find the perimeter and area of each of the following figures. All dimensions are given in cm and the circular portions are semicircles.

(a)

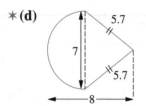

28

(b)

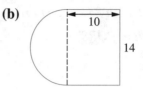

10

14

(c)

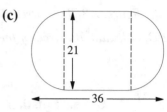

21

36

✱**(d)**

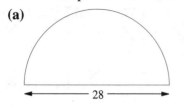

5.7

7

5.7

8

(e)

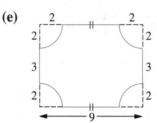

2   2

2   2

3   3

2   2

9

(f)

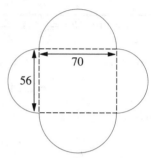

70

56

5. Two wire circles of diameters 12 cm and 8 cm are cut and then joined to make one large circle. Find the diameter of this larger circle.

6. As many 8-cm diameter discs as possible are cut from a sheet of rectangular cardboard measuring 170 cm by 90 cm. Find the area of the sheet that is left.

7. If the minute hand of a big clock is 1.12 m long, find the rate at which its tip is moving in centimetres per minute.

8. Find the speed of a point on the rim of a 24-cm diameter fly-wheel which is turning at 2 800 revolutions per minute. Give your answer in metres per second.

✱**9.** A lorry travels at 50 km/h. Given that the diameter of its wheel is 88 cm, find how many revolutions per minute the wheel is turning. Give your answer to the nearest whole number.

10. Find the difference between the perimeter of a square of area 1 m² and the circumference of a circle of the same area.

Summary

1. For a rectangle with length l units and breadth b units, the perimeter = $2(l + b)$ units and the area = $(l \times b)$ units².

2. Area of a parallelogram = base × height

3. Area of a triangle = $\dfrac{1}{2}$ × base × height

4. Area of a trapezium = $\dfrac{1}{2}$ × height × sum of parallel sides

5. For a circle with radius r units, the circumference = $2\pi r$ units and the area = πr^2 unit².

Take π to be $\frac{22}{7}$ for this exercise.

1. $\triangle APQ$ is enclosed within the rectangle $ABCD$ as shown in the figure below. Calculate the area of $\triangle APQ$.

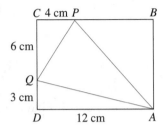

2. In the figure, $ABCD$ is a rectangle of length 8 cm and breadth 6 cm. If $BP = CP$, calculate the area of trapezium $ABPQ$, where AQC is a diagonal of the rectangle.

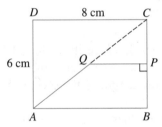

3. A piece of wire 48 cm long is bent to form a rectangle whose length is twice its width. Calculate its area.

4. The length of a rectangle is 4 cm longer than its width and its perimeter is 44 cm. Find the length and area of the rectangle.

5. A rectangular driveway 12 m long and $4\frac{1}{2}$ m wide is to be covered by similar square tiles of side 25 cm each. Find the number of tiles needed to cover the driveway.

6. The area of a trapezium is 36 cm² and the perpendicular distance between its parallel sides is 6 cm. If the lengths of these parallel sides are x cm and y cm, find the value of $(x + y)$. Given further that x is twice as big as y, find the values of x and y.

7. A bucket of water is brought up from a well 9.68 m deep by a rope which winds round a drum 22 cm in diameter. How many turns of the handle are required to bring up a bucket from the bottom of the well?

8. A racing track is a circular ring with inner diameter 140 m and track 7 m wide. How much further does a motorist on the outside rim travel, when he goes round the circuit once, than another who goes round the circuit on the inside rim?

∗9. The diagram shows three semicircles. Calculate the perimeter and area of the shaded region.

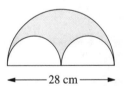

Problem Solving

$\left(\text{Take } \pi = \frac{22}{7}\right)$

1. A single turn of wire wound onto a 5-cm diameter transformer has a mass of 5.5 g. What is its length if the mass of the complete coil of the wire is $1\frac{3}{4}$ kg?

2. A goat, tethered by a rope 1.5 m long, eats a square metre of grass in 14 minutes. Find the time taken if it is to eat all the grass within its reach.

3. A metal disc of radius 6 cm costs 66 cents. Find the cost of 3 square metres of the metal.

4. In the figure below, AB is the diameter of the big semicircle. AK and BK are the diameters of the two smaller semicircles. Given $AK = x$ cm and $BK = y$ cm, find, in terms of x and y, the area of the shaded region enclosed by the three semicircles.

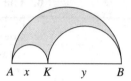

5. The figure shows a rectangular cardboard with 4 semicircles being cut off. Find the area of the remaining cardboard in terms of r.

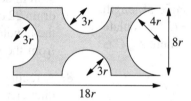

6. Kumar walks round a rectangular field the length of which is twice its width. He then walks round another rectangular field half as wide but having the same perimeter as the first field. If the difference in area between the two fields is 432 m², find the length of the second field.

7. The diagram shows 4 circles of equal radius touching each other. If the radius of each circle is 12 cm, calculate the area of the shaded region.

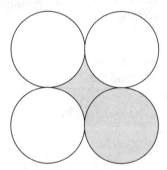

CHAPTER 10

Volume and Surface Area

In this chapter, you will learn how to

▲ find the volume and surface area of cubes, cuboids, prisms and cylinders;

▲ solve problems involving volumes made up of the above solids;

▲ solve problems involving density.

Preliminary Problem

The picture shows the land being cleared for the construction of infrastructure for a new township. The contractor has deliberately left some heaps of soil behind. Do you know that the purpose of this is to estimate the volume of soil taken from the site?

Volume

Fig. 10.1 shows a piece of wood, a brick and a matchbox.

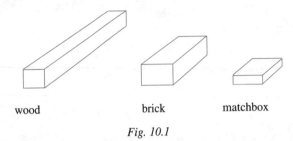

wood   brick   matchbox

Fig. 10.1

Which one of them occupies the least amount of space? Obviously, the matchbox occupies the least space. But which of the other two, the piece of wood or the brick, occupies more space? To answer this question, we first have to make some measurements and then obtain the volume of each object.

Units of Volume

The British System of measure uses pints, gallons, quarts and barrels as units for volume. Find out what these units are and compare them with the SI units.

As with the case of the area of a plane figure, we compare the volume of an object with a standard unit. A standard unit for volume is a cube with side 1 cm (see Fig. 10.2). We call this 1 cubic centimetre, written as 1 cm^3.

Fig. 10.2

Similarly, a cube with side 1 mm will have a volume of 1 mm^3 and that with side 1 m will have a volume of 1 m^3.

Volume of a Cuboid

Fig. 10.3 shows a rectangular block with dimensions 5 cm by 1 cm by 1 cm. The block contains 5 unit cubes, each of volume 1 cm^3. So the volume of the block is $(5 \times 1 \times 1)$ cm^3 = 5 cm^3.

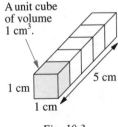

A unit cube of volume 1 cm^3.

Fig. 10.3

Fig. 10.4 shows a rectangular block with dimensions 5 cm by 2 cm by 1 cm. It contains 10 unit cubes. Hence, the volume of the block is $(5 \times 2 \times 1)$ cm³ = 10 cm³.

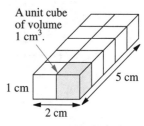

A unit cube of volume 1 cm³.

1 cm
2 cm
5 cm

Fig. 10.4

The rectangular block in Fig. 10.5 has dimensions 5 cm by 2 cm by 4 cm. It contains 4 layers of the block shown by Fig. 10.4. Hence, it is made of (4×10) unit cubes = 40 unit cubes and its volume is $(5 \times 2 \times 4)$ cm³ = 40 cm³.

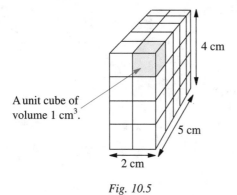

A unit cube of volume 1 cm³.

4 cm
5 cm
2 cm

Fig. 10.5

A prism is a solid figure with a flat base and parallel upright edges. A glass prism breaks up white light into different colours.

NB: Each of the rectangular blocks in Figs. 10.3, 10.4 and 10.5 is called a **rectangular prism** or a **cuboid**

From the above discussion, we see that we can find the volume of a cuboid by multiplying together the length, width and height, which must all be measured in the same units. That is, the volume, V, of a cuboid L units long, W units wide and H units high is given by

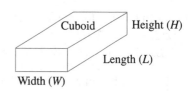

Cuboid   Height (H)
Length (L)
Width (W)

Fig. 10.6

$$V = (L \times W \times H) \text{ unit}^3$$

↑

Area of the base

A cube can be considered as a special cuboid whose length, width and height are equal, i.e., $L = W = H$. The volume of a cube whose side is L units long is given by

$$V = (L \times L \times L) \text{ unit}^3$$
$$= L^3 \text{ unit}^3$$

Surface Area of a Cuboid

If we unfold a cardboard cuboid, we get a *net* of the cuboid as shown in Fig. 10.7. This net will help us find the total surface area of the cuboid.

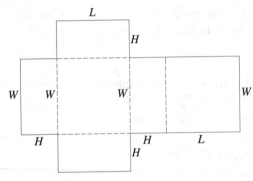

Fig. 10.7

There are several different ways of unfolding the
same cardboard cuboid to obtain different nets
of the same solid. Fig. 10.8 shows another net of
the same cuboid. Can you draw another net for
the same cuboid?

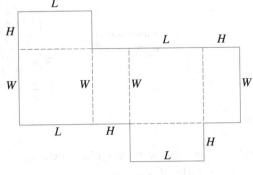

Fig. 10.8

From Fig. 10.7, the surface area of a cuboid of length L units, width W units and height H units
= $[2(L \times W) + 2(L \times H) + 2(W \times H)]$ units^2
= $2(L \times W + L \times H + W \times H)$ units^2.

In the case of a cube where the length, width and height are all equal, i.e. $L = W = H$, the total surface
area
= $2(L \times L + L \times L + L \times L)$
= $2(L^2 + L^2 + L^2)$ units^2
= $6L^2$ units^2.

Example 1

Express (a) 1 cm^3 in mm^3 and (b) 1 m^3 in cm^3.

Solution

(a) Since 1 cm = 10 mm, a cube with side 10 mm has a volume 1 cm^3.
   i.e., 1 cm^3 = $(10 \times 10 \times 10)$ mm^3
                = 1 000 mm^3

(b) Similarly, since 1 m = 100 cm.
                1 m^3 = $(100 \times 100 \times 100)$ cm^3
                     = 1 000 000 cm^3

Example 2

The figure below shows a rectangular prism 9 cm long and 7 cm wide. Given that the volume of the prism is 315 cm³, find

(a) the height of the prism;
(b) its surface area.

▼Solution

(a) $L = 9$, $W = 7$, $H = ?$

   Volume of the prism $= L \times W \times H$
$$315 = 9 \times 7 \times H$$
$$H = \frac{315}{9 \times 7} = 5$$

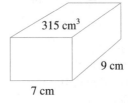

∴   the height of the prism is 5 cm.

(b) The surface area of the prism $= 2(9 \times 7 + 9 \times 5 + 7 \times 5)$ cm²
$$= 286 \text{ cm}^2$$

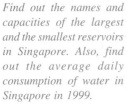

 Volume of Fluids

Find out the names and capacities of the largest and the smallest reservoirs in Singapore. Also, find out the average daily consumption of water in Singapore in 1999.

The volume of fluids, or liquids, is measured using special units. These units are the millilitre (m*l*), the litre (*l*) and the kilolitre (k*l*). Normally, we buy milk and petrol by the litre and we take medicine by the millilitre.

$$1 \text{ m}l = 1 \text{ cm}^3$$
$$1 \text{ litre} = 1\ 000 \text{ m}l = 1\ 000 \text{ cm}^3$$
$$1 \text{ kilolitre} = 1\ 000 \text{ litres} = 1 \text{ m}^3$$

Example 3

A container is in the form of a cuboid 20 cm long, 3 cm wide and 14 cm high. Find the volume of the liquid, in litres, that the container can hold (i.e., the capacity of the container).

▼Solution

The volume of the container $= (20 \times 3 \times 14)$ cm³ $= 840$ cm³
$$1\ 000 \text{ cm}^3 = 1 \text{ litre}$$

∴   the volume of the liquid $= \frac{840}{1\ 000}$ litre $= 0.84$ litre

Example 4

Express (a) 3 600 000 mm³ in (i) cm³ and (ii) ml;
(b) 0.7 m³ in (i) cm³ and (ii) litres.

▼Solution

(a) (i)
$$10 \text{ mm} = 1 \text{ cm}$$
$$1\ 000 \text{ mm}^3 = 1 \text{ cm}^3$$
$$3\ 600\ 000 \text{ mm}^3 = \frac{3\ 600\ 000}{1\ 000} \text{ cm}^3$$
$$= 3\ 600 \text{ cm}^3$$

(ii)
$$1 \text{ cm}^3 = 1 \text{ m}l$$
$$3\ 600 \text{ cm}^3 = 3\ 600 \text{ m}l$$

(b) (i)
$$1 \text{ m} = 100 \text{ cm}$$
$$1 \text{ m}^3 = 1\ 000\ 000 \text{ cm}^3$$
$$0.7 \text{ m}^3 = (0.7 \times 1\ 000\ 000) \text{ cm}^3$$
$$= 700\ 000 \text{ cm}^3$$

(ii)
$$1\ 000 \text{ cm}^3 = 1 \text{ litre}$$
$$700\ 000 \text{ cm}^3 = \frac{700\ 000}{1\ 000} \text{ litres}$$
$$= 700 \text{ litres}$$

═ Exercise 10a ═

1. Find the volume and surface area of the following cuboids, and draw its net:

(a)

10 cm
8 cm
6 cm

(b)

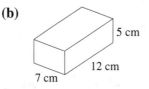
5 cm
12 cm
7 cm

(c)

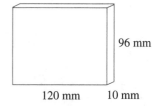
96 mm
120 mm   10 mm

(d)

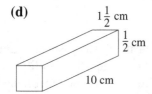
$1\frac{1}{2}$ cm
$\frac{1}{2}$ cm
10 cm

(e)

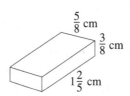
$\frac{5}{8}$ cm
$\frac{3}{8}$ cm
$1\frac{2}{5}$ cm

(f)

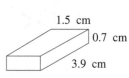
1.5 cm
0.7 cm
3.9 cm

2. Copy and complete the following table for each cuboid:

	Length	Width	Height	Volume	Surface Area
(a)	24 mm	18 mm	5 mm		
(b)	5 cm	3 cm		120 cm³	
(c)		6 cm	$3\frac{1}{2}$ cm	52.5 cm³	
(d)	12 m		6 m	576 m³	
(e)	$2\frac{1}{4}$ cm	8 cm		$58\frac{1}{2}$ cm³	
(f)	9 cm	12 cm			426 cm²

3. Find the capacity of each of the following rectangular tanks, giving your answer in litres:
   (a) Height = 3.6 m, length = 5.5 m, width = 3.5 m.
   (b) Height = 2.7 m, length = 4.75 m, width = 2.6 m.

(c) Height = 0.15 m, length = 0.24 m, width = 0.19 m.

(d) Height = 38 cm, length = 52 cm, width = 18 cm.

4. Find the total surface area of a solid cube of volume 64 cm³.

5. A man sells sugarcane juice in 200 m*l* cups. How many cups of sugarcane juice can he dispense from his big rectangular tank of length 65 cm, width 40 cm and height 54 cm?

∗6. An open water tank with length 20 cm and width 15 cm holds 4.8 litres of water. Calculate the height of the water level in the tank and the total surface area of the cuboid in contact with the water.

7. A rectangular tank measures 4 m long, 2 m wide and 4.8 m high. Initially it is half filled with water. Find the depth of water in the tank after 4 000 litres more of water are added to it.

8. A rectangular water tank of length 60 cm and width 40 cm contains water up to a depth of 30 cm. A piece of ice measuring 20 cm by 15 cm by 12 cm is dropped into the tank of water. Calculate the new depth of water when the ice melts completely, assuming its volume decreases by $\frac{1}{10}$.

9. It took two and a half years and 2.85 million m³ of earth to fill the disused Sin Seng quarry at Rifle Range Road.

(a) If each truck can carry a maximum load of 6.25 m³ of earth per trip, how many trips are needed to fill the entire quarry?

(b) If the cost of transport, material and administration for each truck load is $55, how much would it cost to fill the quarry?
The quarry site now provides an area of approximately 3 hectares for future development. Calculate the cost of one m² of the land. (1 hectare = 10 000 m²)

10. In November 1998, the government announced in Parliament a $10.5 billion package to help the country overcome the Asian economic crisis. If the $10.5 billion is to be issued in $2 notes, what will be the volume of all the $2 notes, assuming that a $2-note has a length of 13.3 cm, a width of 6.4 cm and a thickness of 0.15 mm. Give your answer in m³.

Density

Which is heavier, 1 kg of iron or 1 kg of feathers?

The density of a substance is defined as the mass of one unit volume of the substance.

$$\text{Density} = \frac{\text{mass}}{\text{volume}}$$

We usually express density in g/cm³ or kg/m³.

If 1 cm³ of a certain substance weighs 3.5 g, we say that the density of the substance is 3.5 g per cm³ or 3.5 g/cm³. Similarly, if the mass of 1 m³ of a substance is 500 kg, then the density of the substance is 500 kg/m³.

Example 5

If 15 cm³ of a solid weighs 42 g, find the density of the solid.

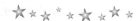**Solution**

15 cm³ of the solid weighs 42 g.

1 cm³ of the solid weighs $\dfrac{42}{15}$ g = 2.8 g.

∴ the density of the solid is 2.8 g/cm³.

Example 6

The density of a substance is 2.5 g/cm³. If the substance has a volume of 32 cm³, find its mass.

**Solution**

Mass = density × volume
    = (2.5 × 32) g = 80 g

∴ the mass of the substance is 80 g.

If the population of the world is 5×10^9, what is the length of the edge of a cubical box that could hold this many people assuming that the volume of an average person is 5.4×10^{-2} m³?

Example 7

The diagram shows a rectangular solid weighing 360 g. Find (a) its volume, and (b) its density in (i) g/cm³ and (ii) kg/m³.

**Solution**

(a) Volume of cuboid = $L \times W \times H$
        = (12 × 3 × 2) cm³ = 72 cm³

∴ the volume of the solid is 72 cm³.

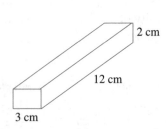

2 cm

12 cm

3 cm

(b) (i) Density = $\dfrac{\text{mass}}{\text{volume}} = \dfrac{360}{72}$ g/cm³ = 5 g/cm³

(ii) 5 g = $\dfrac{5}{1\,000}$ kg

1 cm³ = $\left(\dfrac{1}{100} \times \dfrac{1}{100} \times \dfrac{1}{100}\right)$ m³ = $\dfrac{1}{1\,000\,000}$ m³

Density = $\left(\dfrac{5}{1\,000} \div \dfrac{1}{1\,000\,000}\right)$ kg/m³ = 5 000 kg/m³

∴ the density of the solid is 5 g/cm³ or 5 000 kg/m³.

Exercise 10b

1. Find the density of a metal if 25 g of it has a volume of 8 cm³.

2. Calculate the density of a solid if 40 cm³ of it weighs 96.4 g.

3. If 12 cm³ of a liquid weighs 15.6 g, find the density of the liquid.

4. Calculate the mass of a piece of solid of volume 26 cm³ and density 2.8 g/cm³.

5. Calculate the volume of a piece of cork of mass 105 g and density 0.84 g/cm³.

6. Calculate the volume of a liquid of mass 3.4 kg and density 13.6 g/cm³.

7. A rectangular block, 12 cm by 8 cm by 7 cm, has a density of 2.8 g/cm³. Find
   (a) its volume;   (b) its mass.

8. A rectangular block, 14 cm by 22 cm by 4 cm, has a mass of 9.4 kg. Find
   (a) its volume;   (b) its density.

Right Prisms

In general, a right prism is a solid which has two parallel planes of the same shape and size. Also, its lateral surface are perpendicular to its parallel ends.

Cut out a large number of identical triangles from a piece of cardboard and pile them up as shown in Fig. 10.8. A solid is formed. This solid is called a triangular prism. The two parallel planes, *PQR* and *P'Q'R'*, are triangular in shape and the *triangular prism* takes its name from these planes.

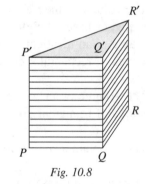

Fig. 10.8

A cuboid is a prism with rectangular planes (see Fig. 10.9). Hence, it is called a rectangular prism. Notice that, in Fig. 10.8, the other three surfaces, which are called the lateral surfaces of the triangular prism, are all rectangular, and that *PP'*, *QQ'* and *RR'* are all perpendicular to the planes *PQR* and *P'Q'R'*. Similarly, in Fig. 10.9, the four lateral surfaces of the cuboid are rectangular and *AA'*, *BB'*, *CC'* and *DD'* are perpendicular to the planes *ABCD* and *A'B'C'D'*. These prisms are called **right prisms**.

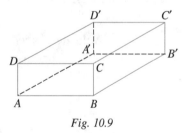

Fig. 10.9

Fig. 10.10 and Fig. 10.11 show a right pentagonal and a hexagonal prism respectively.

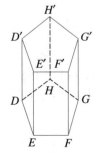

Fig. 10.10

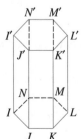

Fig. 10.11

A right prism has a **uniform cross-section**, i.e., the cross-section of the prism is identical to the two parallel ends (see Fig. 10.12).

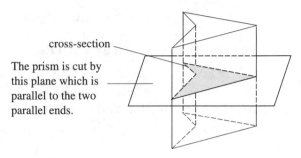

cross-section

The prism is cut by this plane which is parallel to the two parallel ends.

Fig. 10.12

Volume of a Prism

The three prisms shown in Fig. 10.13 are obtained by stacking up a large number of respective identical shapes cut out from cardboards.

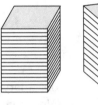  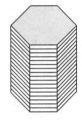

The volume of the right rectangular prism or cuboid
= area of base × height
= area of an identical cardboard × height of rectangular stack
= area of rectangular cross-section × distance between parallel rectangular ends

Fig. 10.13

The volume of a right triangular prism
= area of triangular cross-section × distance between parallel triangular ends

Try to obtain a similar formula as the ones above for the volume of a hexagonal prism.

In general, for a right prism, the volume is given by

> **volume = area of cross-section × distance between parallel ends**
> **= base area × height**

Surface Area of a Prism

Fig. 10.14 shows a right prism whose base is a polygon.

Let A denote the surface area of the prism. Suppose the height of the prism is H and the lengths of the sides of the base are L_1, L_2, L_3, L_4, L_5 and L_6.

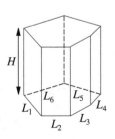

H

L_6 L_5 L_4

L_1

L_2 L_3

Fig. 10.14

A net of the prism is shown on the right.

The dotted lines indicate the folds.

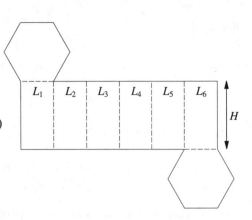

The area, A, is given by

$A = L_1H + L_2H + L_3H + L_4H + L_5H + L_6H + 2(\text{base area})$
  $= (L_1 + L_2 + L_3 + L_4 + L_5 + L_6)H + 2(\text{base area})$
  $= \text{perimeter of base} \times \text{height} + 2(\text{base area})$

In general,

> **surface area of a right prism = perimeter of the base × height + 2(base area)**

Example 8

Draw a net of the right prism shown on the right and then find its volume and surface area.

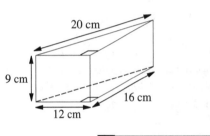

Solution

Here is a net of the right prism.

Area of the base $= \left(\dfrac{1}{2} \times 12 \times 16\right)$ cm^2 = 96 cm^2

Volume of the solid = area of the base × height
  = (96×9) cm^3 = 864 cm^3

Perimeter of the base = $(12 + 16 + 20)$ cm = 48 cm

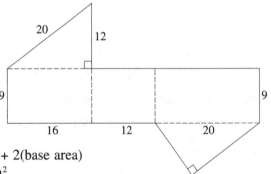

Total surface area = perimeter of the base × height + 2(base area)
  = $[48 \times 9 + 2(96)]$ cm^2 = 624 cm^2

Example 9

Find the volume and surface area of the right prism shown.

Solution

Volume of the right prism = $(12 \times 8 \times 14)$ cm^3
  = 1 344 cm^3

Surface area of the right prism
= $2(12 \times 8 + 8 \times 14 + 14 \times 12)$ cm^2
= $2(96 + 112 + 168)$ cm^2 = 752 cm^2

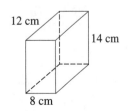

Example 10

Find the volume and surface area of the right pentagonal prism shown.

Solution

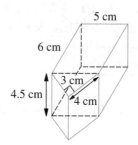

Area of the base $= \left[(6 \times 5) + \left(\dfrac{1}{2} \times 3 \times 4 \right) \right]$ cm² = 36 cm²

∴ volume of the prism $= (36 \times 4.5)$ cm³
$$= 162 \text{ cm}^3$$

Area of the lateral surfaces = perimeter of the base × height
$$= [(6 + 5 + 6 + 4 + 3) \times 4.5] \text{ cm}^2$$
$$= 108 \text{ cm}^2$$

∴ total surface area of the prism $= [108 + 2(36)]$ cm²
$$= 180 \text{ cm}^2$$

Example 11

Find the volume of wood used in making an open rectangular box 2 cm thick, given that its internal dimensions are 54 cm long, 46 cm wide and 18 cm deep.

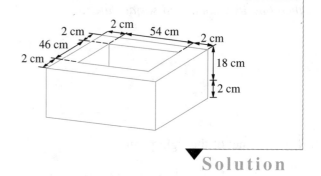

Solution

External length $= (54 + 2 + 2)$ cm = 58 cm

External breadth $= (46 + 2 + 2)$ cm = 50 cm

External height $= (18 + 2)$ cm = 20 cm

External volume $= (58 \times 50 \times 20)$ cm³ = 58 000 cm³

Internal volume $= (54 \times 46 \times 18)$ cm³ = 44 712 cm³

∴ volume of wood used $= (58\ 000 - 44\ 712)$ cm³
$$= 13\ 288 \text{ cm}^3$$

═══ **Exercise 10c** ═══

1. Draw a net of each of the following right prisms and find its volume.

(a)

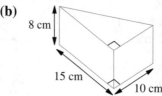

25 cm, 36 cm, 20.5 cm

(b)

8 cm, 15 cm, 10 cm

(c)

9 cm, 26 cm, 12 cm

(d)

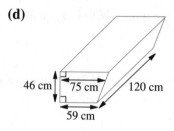

46 cm, 75 cm, 120 cm, 59 cm

(e)

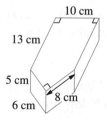

7 cm, 28 cm, 16 cm, 38 cm, 18 cm

(f)

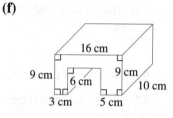

16 cm, 9 cm, 9 cm, 6 cm, 10 cm, 3 cm, 5 cm

(g)

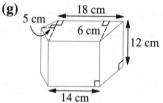

5 cm, 18 cm, 6 cm, 12 cm, 14 cm

(h)

10 cm, 13 cm, 5 cm, 6 cm, 8 cm

(i)

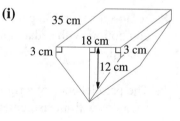

35 cm, 18 cm, 3 cm, 3 cm, 12 cm

2. The figure shows a right prism standing on a horizontal, rectangular base *BCDE*. The triangle *ABC* is a vertical cross-section of the solid prism.

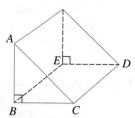

Copy and complete the table below:

	AB	BC	CD	Area of △ABC	Volume of prism
(a)	3 cm	4 cm	7 cm		
(b)	9 cm		11 cm	63 cm²	
(c)		15 cm	300 cm		72 000 cm³
(d)	24.6 cm	7.8 cm			38 376 cm³

∗3. Not taking into consideration the thickness of the walls and roof, find the air space in the hall with the dimensions given in the figure:

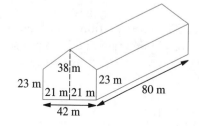

38 m, 23 m, 21 m, 21 m, 23 m, 80 m, 42 m

∗4. Find the volume and the surface area of the solid, which is in the shape of a right prism, as shown:

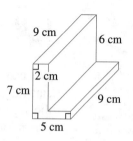

9 cm, 6 cm, 2 cm, 7 cm, 9 cm, 5 cm

∗5. A swimming pool is 50 m long and 25 m wide. It is 1 m deep at the shallow end and 8 m deep at the other end. Find the volume of water in the pool when it is full as well as the total area of the pool which is in contact with the water (refer to figure).

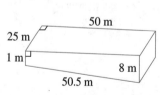

50 m, 25 m, 1 m, 8 m, 50.5 m

6. Find the volume and surface area of a right prism of height 20 cm whose base is a square of side 15 cm.

7. $4\frac{1}{2}$ litres of oil are poured into a rectangular container whose cross-section is a square of side 12 cm. What is the depth of the oil in the container?

8. A closed box is 135 cm long, 80 cm wide and 60 cm deep internally. It is to be lined on its sides and bottom with cedar veneer of negligible thickness. Find, in square metres, the area of veneer needed.

9. The parallel ends of a right prism, 15 cm long, are isosceles triangles with measurements shown below. Find
   (a) the volume;
   (b) the surface area of the prism.

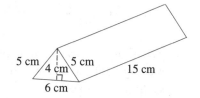

10. The internal dimensions of an open concrete tank are 1.8 m long, 0.8 m wide and 1.2 m high. Find the capacity of the tank in litres. If the concrete is 0.1 m thick, find also, in cubic metres, the volume of concrete used.

11. A trough, in the form of an open rectangular box, is 1.85 m long, 45 cm wide and 28 cm deep externally. If the trough is made of wood 2.5 cm thick, find, in cubic centimetres, the volume of wood required.

12. A tin which is 12 cm long, 9 cm wide and 4 cm deep holds 120 g of tea. If 1 kg of the same tea is packed into a tin which has a 12-cm square base, how tall will the tin have to be?

*13. The cross-section of a drain is a rectangle 30 cm wide. If water 3.5 cm deep flows along the drain at a rate of 22 cm per second, how many litres of water will flow through each minute?

Cylinders

Formally, the cylinder shown here is called a right circular cylinder. In this book, we use 'cylinder' to represent a 'right circular cylinder'.

We can form a cylindrical solid by vertically stacking up a pile of 50-cent coins as shown in the figure. This solid is called a right circular prism or simply a right cylinder. Its cross-sectional area is a circle. Steel pipes, oil drums and many tin containers for liquids and preserved food are all common examples of cylinders. Can you name other objects which are cylindrical in shape?

a stack of 50-cent coins

Volume of a Cylinder

Since a cylinder is a right prism with uniform cross-section, we can find its volume by applying the same method used in finding the volume of a right prism,

i.e.,

volume of a cylinder = base area × height

Thus, the volume of a cylinder of base radius r and height h is given by

volume = $\pi r^2 h$

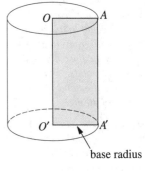

base radius

Surface Area of a Cylinder

Fig. 10.15(a) shows two equal circles of radius r and a rectangle of height h. It is a net of a cylinder. To form the cylinder shown in Fig. 10.15(b), we roll up the rectangle and bring the two edges AB and CD together. The two equal circles formed will become the top and base circles of the cylinder. Obviously, the length of the rectangle is equal to $2\pi r$, the circumference of each circle.

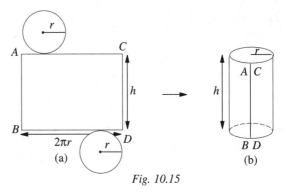

Fig. 10.15

∴ the area of the curved surface of the cylinder
= area of rectangle $ABCD$ = $2\pi rh$

Surface area of a solid cylinder = the area of curved surface + 2 × the area of the base circle
$$= 2\pi rh + 2\pi r^2 = 2\pi r(h + r)$$

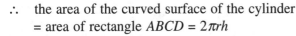
Example 12

The diameter of the base of a right circular cylinder is 14 cm and its height is 10 cm. Find the volume and surface area of the solid cylinder. $\left(Take\ \pi = \dfrac{22}{7} \right)$

▼**Solution**

$r = \dfrac{14}{2} = 7$, $h = 10$

Volume = $\pi r^2 h$

$\quad = \left(\dfrac{22}{7} \times 7^2 \times 10 \right)$ cm^3

$\quad = 1\ 540$ cm^3

∴ the volume is $1\ 540$ cm^3.

Surface area = $2\pi r(h + r)$

$$= \left[2 \times \frac{22}{7} \times 7 \times (10 + 7)\right] \text{cm}^2$$

$$= 748 \text{ cm}^2$$

∴   the surface area is 748 cm².

Example 13

Find the mass, in kg, of a cylindrical metal bar 1.2 m long and 1.4 cm in radius. (The density of the metal is 7.5 g/cm³.)

▼ **Solution**

$r = 1.4$ cm, $h = 1.2$ m = 120 cm

Volume = $\pi r^2 h$

$$= \left(\frac{22}{7} \times 1.4 \times 1.4 \times 120\right) \text{cm}^3$$

$$= 739.2 \text{ cm}^3$$

Mass = density × volume
    = (7.5 × 739.2) g
    = 5 544 g
    = 5.544 kg

∴   the mass of the bar is 5.544 kg.

Example 14

If water flows through a 56-mm diameter pipe at the rate of 3 m/s, what volume of water, in litres, is discharged per minute? $\left(\text{Take } \pi = \frac{22}{7}\right)$

▼ **Solution**

$r = 28$ mm = 2.8 cm, $h = 3$ m = 300 cm

Volume of water discharged per second = $\pi r^2 h$

$$= \left(\frac{22}{7} \times 2.8 \times 2.8 \times 300\right) \text{cm}^3$$

$$= 7 \, 392 \text{ cm}^3$$

Volume of water discharged per minute = (7 392 × 60) cm³
                    = 443 520 cm³
                    = 443.5 litres   (correct to 1 decimal place)

∴   443.5 litres of water are discharged per minute.

Example 15

A circular metal sheet 30 cm in diameter and 0.25 cm thick is melted and then recast into a cylindrical bar of diameter 5 cm. Find the length of the bar.

▼ **Solution**

Volume of circular sheet = $\left(\pi \times 15 \times 15 \times \dfrac{1}{4} \right)$ cm³

Let the length of the bar be x cm.

Volume of bar = $\left(\pi \times \dfrac{5}{2} \times \dfrac{5}{2} \times x \right)$ cm³

Volume of bar = Volume of circular sheet

$$\pi \times \dfrac{5}{2} \times \dfrac{5}{2} \times x = \pi \times 15 \times 15 \times \dfrac{1}{4}$$

$$x = \dfrac{\pi \times 15 \times 15 \times \dfrac{1}{4}}{\pi \times \dfrac{5}{2} \times \dfrac{5}{2}} = 9$$

∴ the bar is 9 cm long.

In this example, no numerical value is used for π.

Hollow Cylinders

Imagine a solid cylinder of radius R and height h. Suppose another cylinder of smaller radius r (i.e. $r < R$) but of the same height h is scooped out from it. This results in a tube, or a hollow cylinder, as shown in Fig. 10.16. The volume of the hollow cylinder is the difference between the volumes of the two solids.

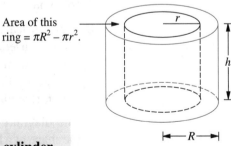

Area of this ring = $\pi R^2 - \pi r^2$.

Fig. 10.16

∴ **Volume of a hollow cylinder**
$$= \pi R^2 h - \pi r^2 h = \pi h (R^2 - r^2)$$

NB: An open cylinder refers to one with a base but without a lid. A closed cylinder refers to one with a base and a lid.

Problems

A cube of side 3 cm is painted green on all its 6 faces. It is to be cut into 27 1-cm cubes. How many cuts do you need to make?

3 cm
3 cm
3 cm

How many small cubes have
(1) no painted faces at all;
(2) 1 face painted green;
(3) 2 faces painted green;
(4) 3 faces painted green;
(5) 4 faces painted green?

You are now given a 4-cm cube which is also painted green on all its faces. How many cuts do you need to make to reduce it to 64 1-cm cubes?

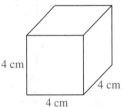

4 cm
4 cm
4 cm

How many small cubes have
(1) 4 faces painted green;
(2) 3 faces painted green;
(3) 2 faces painted green;
(4) 1 face painted green;
(5) no painted faces at all?

Example 16

The figure on the right shows a section of a steel pipe. Given the internal radius of the pipe is 2.1 cm, the external radius is 2.5 cm and the length of the pipe is 12 cm, find

(a) the volume of steel used;

(b) its total surface area. (Take $\pi = 3.14$)

▼ Solution

(a) $R = 2.5$, $r = 2.1$, $h = 12$
The cross-section of the pipe is a ring.
Area of ring $= [\pi(2.5)^2 - \pi(2.1)^2]$ cm^2
$= 1.84\pi$ cm^2

Volume of pipe $= (18.4\pi \times 12)$ cm^3
$= (1.84 \times 3.14 \times 12)$ cm^3
$= 69.3$ cm^3 (correct to 1 decimal place)
∴ the volume of steel used $= 69.3$ cm^3.

(b) Total surface area of pipe
$=$ areas of internal and external curved surfaces $+$ area of 2 rings
$= [(2\pi \times 2.1 \times 12) + (2\pi \times 2.5 \times 12) + (2 \times 1.84\pi)]$ cm^2
$= (50.4\pi + 60\pi + 3.68\pi)$ cm^2
$= 358.2$ cm^2 (correct to 1 decimal place)

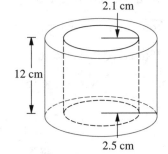

═══ Exercise 10d ═══

In this exercise, take π to be $\frac{22}{7}$ unless otherwise stated.

1. Find the volume and total surface area of each of the following cylindrical solids:

(a)
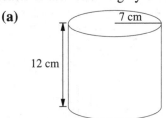

(b)
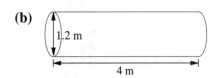

(c)
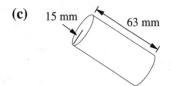

2. Find the diameters of the cylinders given the following:
   (a) volume 704 cm^3, height 14 cm;
   (b) volume 12 320 cm^3, height 20 cm.

3. Find the heights of the cylinders given the following:
   (a) volume 528 cm^3, diameter 4 cm;
   (b) volume 1 056 m^3, radius 4 m.

4. A cylindrical can of radius 5 cm and height 8 cm is used to pour water into a larger cylinder of radius 20 cm and height 2 m. How many times must this be done to fill the larger cylinder?

5. The diagram shows a drinking trough in the shape of a half-cylinder with dimensions as shown. Find its capacity in litres.

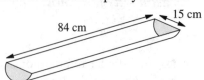

6. The diagram shows a metal pipe with an outer diameter of 28 mm and an inner diameter of 20 mm. Its length is 3.5 m. Find the volume, in cm³, of the metal used in making the pipe.

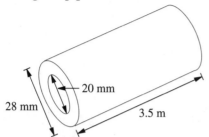

7. In a toy factory, 200 wooden solid cylinders 7 cm long and 35 mm in diameter have to be painted. What is the total surface area, in cm², that needs to be painted?

8. 500 cylindrical cans, without top lids and each 14 cm high with diameter 8 cm, are to be made from a sheet of metal. Find, in m², the total area that needs to be painted externally. (Take $\pi = 3.14$)
Correct your answer to one decimal place.

9. A railway tunnel 147 m long is to be bored with a circular cross section of radius 5 m. What volume of soil has to be excavated? If the soil is to be taken away in wagons of capacity 75 m³ each, how many wagons are needed?

10. A beer cask has a height of 63 cm and a diameter of 50 cm. Find its capacity in litres. How many glasses full of beer can it serve if the capacity of each glass is 0.6 litre?

11. A cylindrical solid, whose base radius and height are 10 cm and 14 cm respectively, has a density of 8.6 g/cm³. Find
    (a) its volume;   (b) its mass.

12. A cylindrical solid with a base radius of 7 cm and a height of 20 cm has a mass of 2.6 kg. Find
    (a) its volume;   (b) its density.

13. Assuming that a $1 coin is cylindrical with a diameter of 2.24 cm and a thickness of 2.5 mm, find the volume of the coin, giving your answer in cm³. If the density of the coin is 5.4 g/cm³, find its weight, correct to 2 decimal places.

The Singapore government announced a $10.5 billion recovery package in Parliament in 1998 to help the country overcome the Asian economic crisis. If the $10.5 billion is to be given out in $1 coins, what is the volume of all the coins? (Give your answer in m³, correct to 1 decimal place.) Also find the weight of all the $10.5 billion coins, giving your answer in tonnes, correct to the nearest tonnes.

Summary

1. The volume of an object is the amount of space it occupies. A standard unit for volume is 1 cm³, which is the volume of a cube of side 1 cm.

2. (a) Volume of a cuboid L units long, W units wide and H units high $= (L \times W \times H)$ unit³.
   (b) Volume of a cube with side L units long $= L^3$ unit³.
   (c) Volume of a right prism = base area × height.

3. (a) Surface area of a cuboid, L units long, W units wide and H units high
       $= 2(L \times W + L \times H + W \times H)$ unit².
   (b) Surface area of a cube with side L units long $= 6L^2$ unit².

4. For a cylinder of base radius r and height h, curved surface area $= 2\pi rh$, total surface area $= 2\pi rh + 2\pi r^2$ or $2\pi r(h + r)$ and volume $= \pi r^2 h$.

5. The volume of a hollow cylinder with external radius R, internal radius r and height h is given by $V = h(\pi R^2 - \pi r^2)$.

Take π to be $\dfrac{22}{7}$, where necessary, for the following questions:

∗1. (a) Find the volume and surface area of each of the following right prisms:

(i)

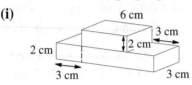

(ii)

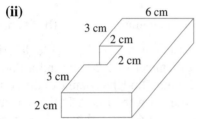

(b) Find the volume and surface area of the following solid, which is made up of two cylinders:

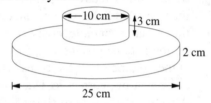

2. The following shows the nets of certain solids. State the name of each of the solids formed and draw a sketch of the solid.

(a)

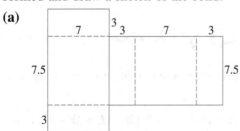

(b)

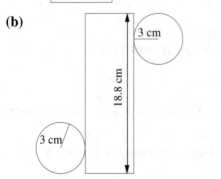

(c)

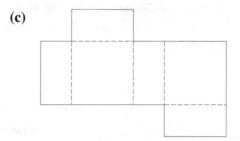

(d)

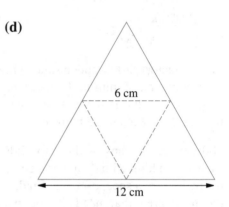

(e)

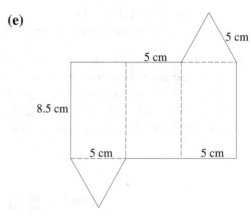

(f)

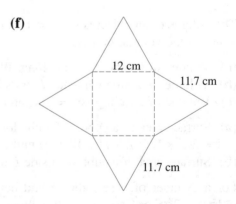

3. A room 8 m long and 5.5 m wide contains 123.2 m³ of air. Find the height of the room.

4. A brick measures 18 cm by 9 cm by 6 cm. Find the number of bricks that will be needed to build a wall 4.5 m wide, 18 cm thick and 3.6 m high.

5. A water tank, 0.8 m long, 0.8 m wide and 2.4 m deep is half-full of water. How many times can a watering-can be filled if its capacity is approximately 12 litres?

6. How many matchboxes, each 80 mm by 75 mm by 18 mm, can be packed into a box 72 cm by 60 cm by 45 cm internally?

7. The following figure shows a trough 15 m long. Its cross-section is a trapezium. Find the amount of water that the trough can hold in litres.

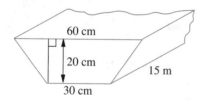

8. A slab of marble is 2.4 m long, 28 cm wide and 5 cm thick. If the density of the marble is 3.1 g/cm³, what is its mass?

9. A rectangular wooden beam is 24 cm by 16 cm in cross-section and 6 m long. Find the mass of the beam if the wood has a density of 750 kg/m³.

10. Find the mass of the water that has fallen onto a flat roof 10.4 m long and 6.5 m wide, when 25 mm of rain is recorded. (The mass of 1 cm³ of water is 1 g.)

11. How many cubic metres of concrete are needed to surround a rectangular pond $4\frac{1}{4}$ m by 4 m with a border $\frac{1}{4}$ m wide and 18 cm thick?

12. 132 litres of oil is poured into a cylindrical drum, 40 cm in diameter. What is the depth of the oil in the drum?

13. Ten open cylindrical containers are to be painted on the outside, including the base. Each container has a radius of 30 cm and a height of 28 cm. Given that 150 g of paint is needed to paint an area of 1 m², find the amount of paint required to paint the ten cylinders. Give your answer in kg.

14. A cylindrical barrel 70 cm in diameter and 80 cm in height is filled with water. A leak at the bottom drains away 0.2 litres of water every minute. How long will it take for the water level to drop by 6 cm?

15. The Singapore Expo has an exhibition area of 60 000 m², making it the largest exhibition centre in the region. If the average height of the exhibition centre is 4.85 m, find the volume of air in the centre. If the density of air is approximately 1.26 kg/m³, find the mass of air contained in the centre.

16. It took two and half years and 2.85 million m³ of earth to fill the disused Sin Seng quarry in Rifle Range Road.
    (a) If each truck can carry 5.75 m³ of earth per trip, how many trips are needed to fill the quarry?
    (b) Taking one year to be 365 days, find the number of truck loads ferried per day for the above project, giving your answer correct to the nearest whole number.

Take π to be $\dfrac{22}{7}$, where necessary, for the following questions.

1. (a) Calculate the volume and surface area of each of the following right prisms:

(i)

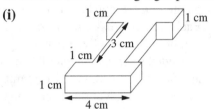

(ii)

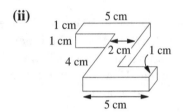

(b) Calculate the volume and surface area of the following solid, which is made up of a cylinder and a right prism:

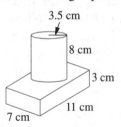

2. The figure shows the dimensions of the cross-section of a girder which is 2.5 m long. Find

(a) the volume of the girder;
(b) the surface area;
(c) its weight if the material weighs 7.8 g per cm³.

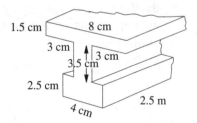

3. The figure shows a closed container of uniform cross-section. The cross-section consists of rectangle *ADCB* and a quadrant *DEC* of a circle, centre *D*. Given *AB* = 14 cm, *AD* = 9 cm and *BH* = *CG* = *EF* = *AI* = 20 cm, calculate

(a) the area of the cross-section *ADECB*;
(b) the volume of the container;
(c) the area of the surface *BCEFGH*.

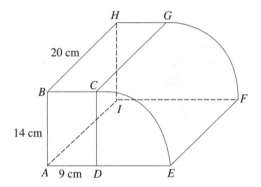

4. A section of a metal pipe has internal diameter 4.2 cm and external diameter 5.0 cm. If the length of the metal used for the pipe is 8.9 cm, calculate the volume of the metal used for making the pipe. If the metal costs $8 per kg and 1 m³ of the metal has a mass of 2 700 kg, find the cost of the pipe.

5. A cuboid of dimension 70 cm by 50 cm by 30 cm has "square holes" measuring 10 cm by 10 cm in the centre of three faces of the cuboid, as shown. Calculate the volume and the surface area of the remaining solid.

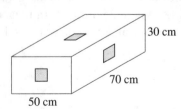

CHAPTER 11

Ratio, Rate and Proportion

In this chapter, you will learn how to

▲ find the ratio of two or more quantities;
▲ recognize and use common measures of rate;
▲ solve problems involving rate;
▲ use direct and inverse proportions;
▲ solve problems involving ratios and proportions.

Preliminary Problem

The picture shows an ancient sundial used in China for measuring the time of the day.

The measurement of time is essential to calculate the speed of a moving object. It is also needed in many other situations such as measuring the rate of one's heart beat, the rate of change of force in the measure of power and the rate at which your body digests food.

Ratio

In a secondary one class of 45 pupils, 15 of the pupils are girls. We can compare the number of boys and the number of girls in the class using two different ways:

(1) There are 15 more boys than girls in the class. Here, we are comparing the number of boys and the number of girls in the class by finding their difference.

(2) The number of boys in the class is twice that of girls. Here, we are comparing the number of boys and the number of girls by finding a fraction consisting of the number of boys over the number of girls. The fraction is thus $\frac{30}{15}$.

The fraction obtained in (2) is an example of a **ratio** which is used to compare two quantities of the same kind.

A ratio may be written with two dots in between the numbers. In our example, the boy-girl ratio in the class is expressed as 30 : 15, or $\frac{30}{15}$.

30 : 15 means 'the ratio of 30 to 15'.

In general, the ratio of a to b, where a and b represent two quantities and b is not zero, is written as $a : b$, or $\frac{a}{b}$.

In-Class Activity

If the ratio of the length of Fatimah's hair to that of Fandi's hair is 3 : 1, can we make the following conclusions?

1. Fatimah's hair is 3 times as long as Fandi's hair;
2. Fatimah's hair is very long;
3. Fatimah is 3 times as old as Fandi;
4. Fatimah is 3 times taller than Fandi.

Equivalent Ratios

Expressing a ratio in its simplest form is the same as reducing it to its lowest term. Thus 25 : 15 in its simplest terms is 5 : 3.

We usually express a ratio in its simplest form.

We know that $\frac{30}{15} = \frac{2}{1}$, thus 30 : 15 = 2 : 1. We say that 30 : 15 and 2 : 1 are **equivalent ratios**.

NB: The **order** in which the ratio is expressed is important. Using the previous example of the class of 45 pupils, the boy-girl ratio is 30 : 15 = 2 : 1, or $\frac{2}{1}$, while the girl-boy ratio is 15 : 30 = 1 : 2, or $\frac{1}{2}$.

A ratio has **no units**. It is merely a number which indicates how many times one quantity is as great as the other or what fraction one quantity is of another. For example, the boy-girl ratio of 2 : 1 indicates that the number of boys is twice that of girls, and the girl-boy ratio of 1 : 2, or $\frac{1}{2}$, indicates that there are half as many girls as there are boys.

Example 1

Find the ratio of (a) 50 g to 200 g and (b) 700 g to 1 kg.

▼ **Solution**

Divide both terms of the ratio by the HCF of the terms, i.e., 50.

(a) The ratio of 50 g to 200 g can be found using two different methods.

Method 1 $50 : 200 = \frac{50}{200} = \frac{1}{4} = 1 : 4$

Method 2 $50 : 200 = \frac{50}{50} : \frac{200}{50} = 1 : 4$

∴   the ratio of 50 g to 200 g is 1 : 4.

(b) 700 g and 1 kg are of different units and thus we have to express them in the same units first.

It is easier to express 1 kg as 1 000 g.

∴   the ratio of 700 g to 1 kg is 700 : 1 000 or 7 : 10.

Ratios can be used to compare more than two quantities. For example, three men, *A*, *B* and *C*, share the profit of a business. They receive $4 000, $3 000 and $1 000 respectively. The ratio of their share of the profit is then 4 000 : 3 000 : 1 000 or 4 : 3 : 1.

═══ Exercise 11a ═══

1. Copy and complete the following equivalent ratios:

   (a) $2 : 3 = \square : 9$ **(b)** $\square : 8 = 12 : 32$
   (c) $6 : 24 = 3 : \square$ **(d)** $12 : \square = 36 : 21$

2. Express each of the following ratios in its simplest form:

   (a) 6 : 10   **(b)** 44 : 8
   (c) 3.6 : 4.5   **(d)** 0.4 : 20
   (e) $1\frac{1}{2} : 2$ **(f)** 32 : 40 : 24
   (g) $1\frac{1}{3} : \frac{2}{3} : \frac{1}{6}$ **(h)** 1.2 : 2 : 2.8
   (i) $1.4 : \frac{2}{5} : \frac{1}{3}$ **(j)** $6\frac{2}{5} : 9.6 : 16$

3. Express each of the following as a ratio of the first quantity to the second, in its lowest term, **(i)** in the form a : b, **(ii)** as a fraction:

   (a) 25 cents, 80 cents
   (b) 210°, 360°
   (c) 250 cm, 1 m
   (d) 80 cents, $1.20
   (e) 1 kg 250 g, 3 kg
   (f) 3 min 30 s, 1 h

4. In a carpark, the ratio of red cars to green is 5 : 6, while that of green cars to blue is 3 : 10. Find the ratio of red cars to blue cars.

5. A school has an enrolment of 630 local students and 120 foreign students. Find the ratio of foreign students to local students.

6. A man earns $1 200 and spends $450 per month. Find the ratio of **(a)** his income to his expenditure and **(b)** his savings to his income.

7. Three people, *A*, *B* and *C*, share $416 among themselves. *A* receives $169 and *B* receives $156. Find the ratio in which the sum of money is shared.

8. The interior angles of a quadrilateral are 40°, 60°, 120° and 140°. Find the ratio of these angles according to the order given.

9. The sides of two squares are 4 cm and 6 cm. Find the ratio of **(a)** their areas and **(b)** their perimeters.

10. The table below shows how 117 people travel to work.

Taxi	MRT Train	Bus	Car
9	21	72	15

Find the ratio of people using the four different modes of transport.

Increase and Decrease in Ratio

$\frac{11}{9}$ *is an improper fraction.*

If the number of teachers in a school is increased from 45 to 55, then the ratio no. of present staff : no. of previous staff = 55 : 45 = 11 : 9.

$$\frac{\text{no. of present staff}}{\text{no. of previous staff}} = \frac{55}{45} = \frac{11}{9}$$

We say that the number of teachers has been **increased in the ratio** 11 : 9, or $\frac{11}{9}$. In other words, the number of present staff is $\frac{11}{9}$ times that of previous staff. Hence, we have no. of present staff = $\frac{11}{9}$ × no. of previous staff.

Notice that when a number *x* is multiplied by an improper fraction, its value is increased.

Example 2

Increase $20 in the ratio 6 : 5; what is the result?

▼**Solution**

The new value is $20 × $\frac{6}{5}$ = $24.

A newspaper agent orders 84 copies of newspapers everyday. During the holidays, he decreases his order to 63 copies. The ratio no. of copies ordered during the holidays : usual no. of copies ordered = 63 : 84 = 3 : 4, or $\frac{3}{4}$.

We say that the number of copies ordered per day has been **decreased in the ratio** 3 : 4, or $\frac{3}{4}$, during the holidays. In other words, the number of copies ordered per day during the holidays is $\frac{3}{4}$ of the usual number of copies ordered.

$\frac{3}{4}$ *is a proper fraction.*

i.e., new no. of copies ordered during the holidays = $\frac{3}{4}$ × usual no. of copies ordered

To decrease a number x, we multiply it by a proper fraction.

Example 3

Find the result of decreasing 56 m in the ratio 7 : 8.

▼Solution

The new length is $\left(56 \times \frac{7}{8}\right)$ m = 49 m.

Example 4

In what ratio must 40 m³ be decreased to become 24 m³?

▼Solution

The required ratio = new value : old value
$$= 24 \text{ m}^3 : 40 \text{ m}^3$$
$$= 24 : 40 = 3 : 5$$

═ Exercise 11b ═

1. Increase 96 in the ratio 7 : 4; what is the result?

2. Decrease $288 in the ratio 2 : 9; what is the result?

3. Find the result of increasing or decreasing the quantities in the given ratios:

   (a) 40 kg, 5 : 8 (b) 56 m, 8 : 7
   (c) 35 hectares, 2.5 : 1
   (d) 2.5 cm², 2 : 5

4. (a) In what ratio must 35 be increased to become 49?
   (b) In what ratio must 72 kg be increased to become 96 kg?

5. (a) In what ratio must 105 be decreased to become 75?
   (b) In what ratio must 144 kg be decreased to become 108 kg?

6. The price of petrol drops from $1.20 per litre to 95 cents per litre. Find the ratio in which the price decreases.

7. Two sums of money are in the ratio 5 : 8. The smaller amount is $65. Find the larger amount.

8. A photograph measuring 5.5 cm by 9 cm is enlarged in the ratio 7 : 5. Find the dimensions of the enlarged photograph.

9. The cost of mutton has increased in the ratio 9 : 7. If the original price was $5.60 per kg, what is the new price?

10. Due to import duty, the price of a car increases in the ratio 11 : 8. What is the new price of a car which originally cost $25 600?

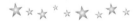

If it takes four minutes to boil one egg, how long will it take to boil three eggs?

Let us consider the following questions:

A : If one dozen eggs cost $1.80, what is the cost of 30 eggs?

B : If eight tins of a certain brand of tonic food beverage cost $26.40, what is the cost of 18 tins?

C : A car travels 570 km on 60 litres of petrol. If the car travels 190 km, what will the petrol consumption be in litres?

D : A boy works 5 hours and is paid $12.50. How much will he be paid if he works 12 hours?

To answer each of the above questions, we must first find

A : The cost of 1 egg = $\dfrac{1.80 \;\leftarrow\; \text{dollars}}{12 \;\leftarrow\; \text{eggs}}$ or $\dfrac{180 \;\leftarrow\; \text{cents}}{12 \;\leftarrow\; \text{eggs}}$

B : The cost of 1 tin = $\dfrac{26.40 \;\leftarrow\; \text{dollars}}{8 \;\leftarrow\; \text{tins}}$

C : The petrol consumption for 1 km = $\dfrac{60 \;\leftarrow\; \text{litres}}{570 \;\leftarrow\; \text{km}}$

D : The pay for 1 hour = $\dfrac{12.50 \;\leftarrow\; \text{dollars}}{5 \;\leftarrow\; \text{hours}}$

Each of above results is different from a ratio in that it involves two quantities of different kinds. Each of them is called a **rate**.

A : The rate = $\$\dfrac{1.80}{12}$ = $0.15 per egg

∴ the cost of 30 eggs = $0.15 × 30 = $4.50.

B : The rate = $\$\dfrac{26.40}{8}$ = $3.30 per tin

∴ the cost of 18 tins = $3.30 × 18 = $59.40.

Understand the problem by asking the questions:

1. *How far can a car travel on 1 litre of petrol?*
2. *How much petrol is needed to travel 1 km?*
3. *How many litres of petrol are required to travel 260 km?*

C : The rate = $\dfrac{60}{570} = \dfrac{2}{19}$ litre per km

∴ if the car travels 190 km, the petrol consumption = $\dfrac{2}{19} \times 190$

= 20 litres.

D : The rate = $\$\dfrac{12.50}{5}$ = $2.50 per hour

∴ he will be paid $2.50 × 12 = $30.00 for working 12 hours.

NB: We normally use the word "per" or the symbol "/" to denote a rate. Thus we have $2.50 per hour or $2.50/hour.

Example 5

How far can a car travel on 15 litres of petrol if it can travel 91 km on 7 litres of petrol? How much does the owner of the car spend on petrol, which costs $1.10 per litre, when he travels 260 km?

▼ **Solution**

Distance travelled on 1 litre of petrol = $\frac{91}{7}$ km = 13 km.

∴ distance travelled on 15 litres of petrol = (13 × 15) km = 195 km.

Consumption of petrol per km = $\frac{7}{91}$ litre = $\frac{1}{13}$ litre.

Consumption of petrol for 260 km = $\left(\frac{1}{13} \times 260\right)$ litres = 20 litres.

∴ the owner spends $1.10 × 20 = $22 on petrol when he travels 260 km.

══ Exercise 11c ══

1. Copy and complete the following:
   (a) If a typist types 900 words in 1 hour, her rate of typing is _____ words per minute.
   (b) If a man pays $600 rent for 3 months, the rental rate is _____ dollars per month.
   (c) If $14.06 is charged for 74 units of electricity, the rate is _____ cents per unit.
   (d) A machine is used to stamp bottle caps. If 150 bottle caps can be stamped in 30 seconds, the rate is _____ caps per second.

2. A man earns $250 in a five-day week. What is his pay for 3 days?

3. A car uses 40 litres of petrol to travel 340 km. How far can it travel if it has only 32 litres of petrol?

4. A machine stamps 720 bottle caps in 2 minutes. How many bottle caps can it stamp in 40 seconds?

5. A wire 22 cm long has a mass of 374 g. What is the mass of 13 cm of this wire?

6. A shopkeeper buys 72 articles for $82.80. How much will he have to pay if he buys 150 such articles?

7. 40 cm of a certain type of piping cost $2.00. What is the cost of 1 km of such piping?

8. The cost of a long-distance call lasting 4 minutes and 20 seconds was $23.40. At this rate, what was the cost of a call lasting 6 minutes 30 seconds?

9. 250 cm³ of a liquid weighs 125 g. Find the weight of 1 000 cm³ of the liquid.

10. 200 g of fertilizer is required for a land area of 8 m². At this rate,
    (a) how many grams of fertilizer are needed for a land area of 1 m²?
    (b) how many grams of fertilizer are required for a land area of 14 m²?
    (c) for what land area will 450 g of fertilizer be sufficient?

★11. A cook uses fifteen 2-kg bottles of cooking-oil over a 4-week period. If he decides to buy 5-kg tins of oil instead, how many tins of cooking oil will he use over a 10-week period if the rate of using it remains unchanged?

✳12. In a certain company, the amount of travelling expenses an employee may claim is calculated as follows:

If the distance travelled exceeds 20 km, claimable amount = 20 × rate + (number of km − 20) × $0.70.

Otherwise,

claimable amount = number of km × rate, where the rate in both instances is $0.55 per km if the engine capacity of the employee's car exceeds 1 000 cc, otherwise it is $0.50 per km.

Find the travelling expenses allowed in each case:

(a) **(i)** 18 km;
　　 (ii) 28 km travelled in a 1 298 cc car;

(b) **(i)** 16 km;
　　 (ii) 25 km travelled in a 998 cc car.

a.m. stands for "ante meridiem" (Latin word) meaning "before midday". p.m. stands for "post meridiem" meaning "after midday".

Time

To record the time of the day, we can either use the 12-hour clock or the 24-hour clock. In the 12-hour clock, morning (from midnight to just before noon) is denoted by a.m.; afternoon, evening and night are denoted by p.m. In the 24-hour clock, four digits are used to indicate time. The first two digits denote hours and the last two denote minutes.

12-hour clock

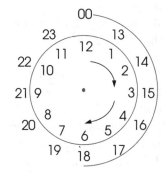

24-hour clock

The table below shows some examples.

Time	12-hour clock	24-hour clock
2 o'clock early morning	2.00 a.m.	02 00
5 to 11 in the morning	10.55 a.m.	10 55
Noon	12.00 p.m.	12 00
Half past 12 early afternoon	12.30 p.m.	12 30
Quarter to 3 in the afternoon	2.45 p.m.	14 45
5 past 8 in the evening	8.05 p.m.	20 05
One minute to midnight	11.59 p.m.	23 59
Midnight	12.00 a.m.	00 00
One minute past midnight	12.01 a.m.	00 01

Example 6

A journey starting at 08 40 takes $4\frac{3}{4}$ hours. Find the time the journey ends.

▼ **Solution**

A cashier of a bank is given one million one-cent coins to count. How long will she take if she can count five coins in one second?

	h	min
Starting time	08	40
Journey time	04	45
Arrival time	13	25

$\left(4\frac{3}{4}\text{ h}\right)$

$40 + 45 = 60 + 25 =$ ① h ㉕ min

$(8 + 4 + 1)$

∴ the journey ends at 13 25, or 1.25 p.m.

26 indicates that the car arrives in Kuala Lumpur the next day.

Example 7

A car leaves Singapore at 21 15 on Wednesday and arrives in Kuala Lumpur $5\frac{1}{2}$ hours later. At what time and day does the car arrive in Kuala Lumpur?

▼ **Solution**

	h	min
Starting time	21	15
Journey time	05	30
Arrival time	㉖	45

$\left(5\frac{1}{2}\text{ h}\right)$

→ ⑫ 45

-24

∴ the car arrives in Kuala Lumpur at 02 45, or 2.45 a.m., on Thursday.

Example 8

A train left Singapore at 07 35 and arrived in Seremban at 13 05. How long was the train journey?

▼ **Solution**

One hour is converted to 60 minutes.

	h	min
	12	65
Arrival time	~~13~~	~~05~~
Departure time	07	35
	5	30

∴ the train journey was 5 h 30 min long.

Example 9

A bus leaves Town A on Saturday night and is supposed to arrive at Town B at 08 17 on Sunday morning. If the estimated journey time is 10 h 43 min, at what time should the bus leave Town A?

24 h is added so that the arrival time is measured from 00 00 on Saturday.

Solution

	h	min	
Arrival time 08 17 (Sunday) =	$\overset{31}{\cancel{32}}$ +24	$\overset{77}{\cancel{17}}$	(Saturday)
Journey time	10	43	
Departure time	21	34	(Saturday)

∴   the bus should leave Town *A* at 21 34, or 9.34 p.m., on Saturday.

═ **Exercise 11d** ═

1. Convert the following times to 24-hour clock notation:

   (a) 8.00 a.m.   **(b)** 2 p.m.
   (c) 5.30 p.m.   **(d)** 9.42 p.m.
   (e) noon   **(f)** 12.45 a.m.
   (g) midnight   **(h)** 2.42 a.m.

2. Convert the following times to 12-hour clock notation:

   (a) 03 30   **(b)** 15 00
   (c) 23 12   **(d)** 19 15
   (e) 09 23   **(f)** 12 00
   (g) 00 05   **(h)** 24 00

3. Write down, using the 24-hour clock notation, the times shown:

   (a)   **(b)**

         a.m.   p.m.

   (c)

         a.m.

4. Copy and complete the following table:

	Departure time	Journey time	Arrival time
(a)	15 45	5 hours	
(b)	02 40	55 minutes	
(c)	08 45	$9\frac{3}{4}$ hours	
(d)	22 35	8 hours	
(e)	15 45		17 50
(f)	11 50		15 15
(g)	09 48		22 16
(h)	20 35 (Tue)		07 15 (Wed)
(i)		$1\frac{1}{4}$ hours	23 50
(j)		$17\frac{3}{4}$ hours	12 45 (Fri)

5. A train left a station at 8.35 a.m. and arrived at its destination at 3.12 p.m. How long did the journey take?

6. An overnight train left at 21 55 on a journey that took 9 h 18 min. Find the time at which it arrived at its destination.

7. A car arrived at a town at 15 06 after travelling for $4\frac{1}{4}$ hours. Find the time the car started its journey.

8. According to a timetable, a coach was due to leave a station at 22 55 and arrive at its destination at 06 05 the next day. How long would the journey take? If the train actually arrived 35 minutes early, at what time did it arrive?

∗9. Lessons in a certain school start at 7.45 a.m. and end at 3.45 p.m., with an hour's break at lunchtime and 20 minutes morning recess. If there are altogether 8 lessons of equal length, how long is each lesson?

∗10. Shown below is the schedule of the arrival and departure times of a long-distance express overnight coach.

Destination	Arrival	Departure
Singapore	—	21 30
Johor Baru	22 15	22 30
Seremban	02 25	02 30
Kuala Lumpur	03 50	04 20
Ipoh	07 50	08 00
Taiping	09 20	09 30
Butterworth	10 45	—

Find the time taken for the coach to travel from

(a) Singapore to Seremban;
(b) Johor Baru to Ipoh;
(c) Seremban to Taiping;
(d) Kuala Lumpur to Butterworth;
(e) Singapore to Butterworth.

Average Speed

Two cyclists, A and B, travel 90 km, in a race, in 5 hours and $4\frac{1}{2}$ hours respectively. Which cyclist travels faster?

Cyclist B travels faster since he takes less time to complete the race.

We can also find the **speed** at which each cyclist travels to find out who travels faster. As you can see, speed is a special kind of rate.

Cyclist A's speed $= \dfrac{90 \text{ km}}{5 \text{ h}} = 18 \text{ km/h}$

Cyclist B's speed $= \dfrac{90 \text{ km}}{4\frac{1}{2} \text{ h}} = 20 \text{ km/h}$

Cyclist B travels faster since he travels at a greater speed.

When calculating the speed of each cyclist, we assume that one travels at the same speed all the time. In reality, each cyclist will have difficulty cycling at the same speed all the time. For example, he may slow down when he is cycling up a slope or he may speed up when he is going down a slope. Thus, the speed calculated for each cyclist is not his exact speed at a particular instant. Instead, it is his **average speed**. For

If a cyclist is equipped with a speedometer, which gives his speed at a particular instant, the readings from the speedometer will change from time to time.

example, the average speed of cyclist A is 18 km/h. This means that on the average, he travels 18 km every hour. The average speed can be obtained by using the formula:

$$\text{Average speed} = \frac{\text{Total distance travelled}}{\text{Total time taken}}$$

NB: We can also express average speed in m/s.

The highest speed limit for cars on Singapore roads is 90 km/h. How many demerit points will a motorist be awarded if he is caught speeding on the expressway at

(a) 100 km/h;
(b) 120 km/h;
(c) 160 km/h?

Example *10*

A car travelled 510 km in 6 hours. Find the average speed of the car for the whole journey.

▼**Solution**

Distance travelled = 510 km
    Time taken = 6 hours

$$\text{Average speed} = \frac{\text{Distance travelled}}{\text{Time taken}} = \frac{510 \text{ km}}{6 \text{ h}} = 85 \text{ km/h}$$

Convert km to m and hour to seconds.

Example *11*

A cyclist is travelling at an average speed of 18 km/h.

(a) Express his average speed in m/s.
(b) Find the distance he travels in 3 hours.
(c) Find how far he travels in 25 seconds.

▼**Solution**

(a) 18 km = 18 × 1 000 m, 1 h = (60 × 60) s

   ∴ $18 \text{ km/h} = \frac{18 \text{ km}}{1 \text{h}} = \frac{(18 \times 1\,000) \text{ m}}{(60 \times 60) \text{ s}} = 5 \text{ m/s}$

(b) In 3 hours, the cyclist travels (18 × 3) km = 54 km

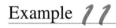

      Average speed in km/h   Time taken in hours

(c) In 25 seconds, he travels (5 × 25) m = 125 m

      Average speed in m/s   Time taken in seconds

In general,

$$\textbf{Distance travelled} = \textbf{Average speed} \times \textbf{Time taken}$$

A sports car leaves Singapore for Kuala Lumpur at the same time as a bus, which leaves Kuala Lumpur for Singapore. They travel along the same road, the sports car at 110 km/h and the bus at 55 km/h. Which vehicle is further away from Singapore when they meet?

Example 12

A train travels at an average speed of 15 m/s.

(a) Express its average speed in km/h.
(b) Find the time taken by the train to travel 750 m.
(c) If the train sets off from Station A at 8.00 a.m., find the arrival time of the train at Station B which is 36 km away.

▼ **Solution**

(a) $15 \text{ m} = \dfrac{15}{1\,000} \text{ km}$, $1 \text{ h} = 3\,600 \text{ s}$

In 1 second, the train travels $\dfrac{15}{1\,000}$ km.

In 1 hour, the train travels $\left(\dfrac{15}{1\,000} \times 3\,600 \right)$ km = 54 km.

∴ its average speed is 54 km/h.

(b) $15 \text{ m/s} = \dfrac{15 \text{ m}}{1 \text{ s}}$

In 1 second, the train travels 15 m.

The time taken to travel 1 m is $\dfrac{1}{15}$ s.

∴ the time taken by the train to travel 750 m $= \dfrac{1}{15} \times 750 \text{ s}$

$= \dfrac{750}{15} \text{ s}$  Distance travelled in m.
Average speed in m/s.

$= 50 \text{ s}$

(c) Similarly in 1 hour, the train travels 54 km.

The time taken to travel 1 km is $\dfrac{1}{54}$ h.

∴ the time taken by the train to travel 36 km $= \dfrac{1}{54} \times 36 \text{ h}$

$= \dfrac{36}{54} \text{ h}$ Distance travelled in km.
Average speed in km/h.

$= \dfrac{2}{3} \text{ h}$

$= \dfrac{2}{3} \times 60 \text{ min} = 40 \text{ min}$

∴ the arrival time of the train at Station B is 8.40 a.m.

In general,

$$\text{Time taken} = \dfrac{\text{Distance travelled}}{\text{Average speed}}$$

Exercise 11e

1. Copy and complete the following. The first one has been done for you.

	Distance travelled	Time taken	Average speed
(a)	180 km	$1\frac{1}{2}$ h	120 km/h
(b)	200 m	25 s	
(c)	400 m	1 min	
(d)		$5\frac{1}{2}$ h	80 km/h
(e)		$\frac{1}{3}$ min	25 m/s
(f)	100 m		20 m/s

2. Express the following in m/s:
   (a) 18 km/h   (b) 72 km/h
   (c) 90 km/h

3. Express the following in km/h:
   (a) 10 m/s   (b) 35 m/s
   (c) $\frac{1}{2}$ km/s

4. How long will a man take to run, once, round a circular track of radius 28 m at an average speed of 8 m/s? $\left(\text{Take } \pi = \frac{22}{7} \right)$

5. A cyclist begins on a 24-km journey at 09 23. When will he complete his journey if he travels at an average speed of 16 km/h?

6. A train leaves Town X at 12 57 and arrives at Town Y 45 minutes later.
   (a) At what time does the train arrive in Town Y?
   (b) What is the average speed of the train, in km/h, if the distance between the two towns is 84 km?

7. A car travels at an average speed of 24 km/h. Find, in metres, the distance travelled by the car in 12 seconds.

8. A car travelled on a B class road for 20 minutes at an average speed of 57 km/h. It then travelled a distance of 55 km in 30 minutes on an expressway. Find
   (a) the distance the car travelled on the B class road;
   (b) the average speed, in km/h, of the car when it travelled on the expressway.

9. A man cycles for two hours at an average speed of 16 km/h and then walks for 3 hours at an average speed of 6 km/h. Find his average speed for the whole journey.

10. A train travels 68 km at an average speed of 51 km/h. It then travels another 20 km at an average speed of 40 km/h before reaching its destination. Calculate the average speed for the whole journey.

*11. Two points, X and Y, are 120 m apart. M is the mid-point of X and Y. An object travels from X to M in 12 seconds and then from M to Y at an average speed of 15 m/s. Calculate
   (a) the average speed of the object from X to M;
   (b) the time taken to travel from M to Y;
   (c) the average speed for the whole journey from X to Y.

*12. Three points, L, M and N, lie on a straight line with $LN = 160$ m. An object travels from L to M at an average speed of 10 m/s in 6 seconds and then from M to N at an average speed of 25 m/s. Calculate
   (a) the distance from L to M;
   (b) the time taken to travel from M to N;
   (c) the average speed for the whole journey from L to N.

Direct Proportion

Have you ever borrowed books from the National Library? If you have, be thoughtful and return them before they are overdue. If you are late in returning books, as of September 1999, you are liable to a fine of 20 cents per day for each overdue book. The table below shows the possible fines for one overdue book.

No. of days (x)	1	2	3	4	5	6	7	8	9	10
Fine (y cents)	20	40	60	80	100	120	140	160	180	200

Clearly, the **longer** the book is overdue, the **greater** is the fine. When the number of days the book is overdue is doubled, is the fine also doubled? When the number of days the book is overdue is tripled, is the fine also tripled?

We notice that 4 days : 2 days = 80 cents : 40 cents

$$4 : 2 = 80 : 40 = 2 : 1$$

or $$\frac{4}{2} = \frac{80}{40} = \frac{2}{1}$$

and 6 days : 2 days = 120 cents : 60 cents

$$6 : 2 = 120 : 60 = 3 : 1$$

or $$\frac{6}{2} = \frac{120}{60} = \frac{3}{1}$$

We also notice that $\dfrac{x}{y} = \dfrac{1}{20} = \dfrac{2}{40} = \dfrac{3}{60} = \dfrac{4}{80} = \dfrac{5}{100} = \dfrac{6}{120} = \dfrac{7}{140} = \dfrac{8}{160} = \dfrac{9}{180} = \dfrac{10}{200}$.

In general, x_1 days : x_2 days = y_1 cents : y_2 cents, i.e.

$$x_1 : x_2 = y_1 : y_2 \quad \text{or} \quad \frac{x_1}{x_2} = \frac{y_1}{y_2} \quad \text{or} \quad \frac{x_1}{y_1} = \frac{x_2}{y_2}, \text{ where } x_1 \text{ and } x_2 \text{ are any two values of}$$

x while y_1 and y_2 are the corresponding values of y.

Thus, x and y are two quantities such that when one increases (or decreases), so does the other, and that the two quantities are always in the same ratio. We say that the two quantities x and y are **directly proportional**. In this case the fine is **directly proportional** to the number of days a book is overdue.

A **proportion** is a statement expressing the equivalence of two ratios. Hence, $\dfrac{x_1}{x_2} = \dfrac{y_1}{y_2}$, or $\dfrac{x_1}{y_1} = \dfrac{x_2}{y_2}$, is a statement of proportion, and x_1, x_2, y_1 and y_2 are said to be **proportional**.

Let $\dfrac{a}{b} = \dfrac{c}{d}$ be a statement of proportion. If we multiply both sides of the proportion by the common denominator bd, we have

$$\frac{a}{b} \times bd = \frac{c}{d} \times bd, \quad \text{i.e., } ad = bc.$$

Dividing both sides of $ad = bc$ by d, we obtain $a = \dfrac{bc}{d}$.

In the proportion

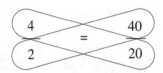

$$ad = 4 \times 20 = 80$$
$$bc = 2 \times 40 = 80$$

we have $ad = 4 \times 20 = 80$
and $\quad bc = 2 \times 40 = 80$
i.e., $\quad ad = bc$

This is a mathematical technique which is very useful in problem solving. It is sometimes called **cross-multiplication** and can be used to check whether a proportion is true.

For example, $\dfrac{75}{100} = \dfrac{3}{4}$ is true since $75 \times 4 = 3 \times 100 = 300$

but $\qquad \dfrac{6}{7} \neq \dfrac{18}{22}$ since $6 \times 22 = 132 \neq 18 \times 7 = 126$.

Example 13

Find x if 60 m : 100 m = 9 kg : x kg.

▼ Solution

$60 \text{ m} : 100 \text{ m} = 9 \text{ kg} : x \text{ kg}$

$$\frac{60}{100} = \frac{9}{x} \quad \text{i.e.,} \quad \frac{3}{5} = \frac{9}{x}$$
$$\therefore \quad 3x = 45 \quad \text{and} \quad x = 15$$

Example 14

Find the cost of 13 kg of biscuits if 6 kg of them cost $27.

▼ Solution

Strategy 1: Use increase in ratio

6 kg of biscuits cost $27.

$\therefore \quad$ 13 kg of biscuits cost $\$27 \times \dfrac{13}{6} = \$58.50$ (increase in the ratio 13 : 6)

Strategy 2: Use proportion

Let x be the cost of 13 kg of biscuits.

Then $\$x : \$27 = 13 \text{ kg} : 6 \text{ kg}$

i.e., $\qquad \dfrac{x}{27} = \dfrac{13}{6}$

$$x = \frac{13}{6} \times 27 = 58.50$$

$\therefore \quad$ 13 kg of biscuits cost $58.50.

Exercise 11f

1. Find x in each of the following cases:
   (a) $4 : 7 = x : 5$
   (b) $18 : 7 = 10 : x$
   (c) $9 : x = 24 : 88$
   (d) $x : 8 = 99 : 44$
   (e) x m $: 12$ m $= \$42 : \$63$
   (f) 1 km $: 32$ m $= 250$ g $: x$ g

2. Copy and complete the following:
   (a) If $\dfrac{18}{7} = \dfrac{10}{a}$, then $18a = $ _____
   (b) If $\dfrac{x}{y} = \dfrac{u}{v}$, then $xv = $ _____

3. Find the ratio of $x : y$ in each of the following cases:
   (a) $5x = 7y$
   (b) $3.2x = 1.2y$
   (c) $2\dfrac{1}{2}x = 4\dfrac{1}{2}y$
   (d) $1.2x = 2\dfrac{3}{4}y$

4. The lengths of two pieces of wire are in the ratio $4 : 7$. If the length of the longer piece is 3.5 m, what is the length of the shorter piece?

5. Find the cost of
   (a) 8 books when 6 books cost \$48, given that the price of each book is the same;
   (b) 10 kg of tea when 3 kg of tea cost \$18;
   (c) a kg of sugar when b kg of sugar cost c dollars.

6. $\dfrac{5}{9}$ of a piece of metal weighs 7 kg. What is the weight of $\dfrac{2}{7}$ of the metal?

7. In a bookstore, 60 books of the same kind occupy 1.5 m of shelf length. How much shelf length is required for 300 such books? If a shelf is 80 cm long, how many such books are needed to fill the shelf?

8. A pile of 108 identical books weighs 30 kg. Find
   (a) how many books weigh 20 kg and
   (b) the weight of 150 books.

 ## Inverse Proportion

The time taken by a car to travel a distance of 120 km at various speeds is displayed in the table below.

Speed (x km/h)	20	30	40	60	120
Time taken (y hours)	6	4	3	2	1

Clearly, the **greater** the speed of the car, the **shorter** the time taken to cover the distance, i.e., when the quantity x increases, the quantity y decreases, or when the quantity x decreases, the quantity y increases.

Notice also that the product of the two quantities x and y is always the same, i.e.

$$xy = 20 \times 6 = 30 \times 4 = 40 \times 3 = 60 \times 2 = 120 \times 1 = 120.$$

We say that the two quantities x and y are **inversely proportional**. In this case, the time taken is **inversely proportional** to the speed.

Reciprocals

Any two numbers whose product is 1 are called **reciprocals** of each other.

For example, 5 and $\frac{1}{5}$ are a pair of reciprocals. We say that $\frac{1}{5}$ is the reciprocal of 5 and vice versa. Other examples of pairs of reciprocals are $\frac{6}{7}$ and $\frac{7}{6}$, -3 and $-\frac{1}{3}$, $-\frac{3}{2}$ and $-\frac{2}{3}$.

The diagram below shows some numbers and their corresponding reciprocals.

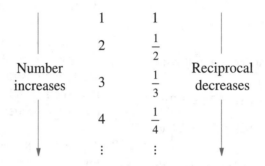

We see that the value of a number is inversely proportional to its reciprocal. Thus, in general, when a number gets bigger, its reciprocal becomes smaller. Conversely, the smaller the number, the bigger its reciprocal.

Example 15

Ten men can dig a trench in 4 hours. How long will 5 men take to dig the same trench? (Assume all the men are working at the same rate.)

▼Solution

Strategy 1: Use logical deduction

10 men take 4 hours

1 man will take (4×10) hours = 40 hours. Can you understand why?

5 men will take $(40 \div 5)$ hours = 8 hours.

Strategy 2: Use inverse proportion

Let x be the number of hours required.

$$\begin{array}{lcl} 10 \text{ men} & \longleftrightarrow & 4 \text{ hours} \\ 5 \text{ men} & \longleftrightarrow & x \text{ hours} \end{array}$$

Since product of two quantities, which are inversely proportional, is always the same,

$$5x = 10 \times 4$$
$$x = 8$$

Alternatively,

$$x \text{ hours} : 4 \text{ hours} = 10 \text{ men} : 5 \text{ men}$$

$$\frac{x}{4} = \frac{10}{5}$$

$$x = \frac{10}{5} \times 4 = 8$$

∴   5 men will take 8 hours to dig the trench.

Strategy 3: Use increase in ratio

10 men can dig the trench in 4 hours.

5 men can dig the trench in $\left(4 \times \dfrac{10}{5} \right)$ hours = 8 hours.

Example 16

A farmer has enough feed to last his 40 cattle 35 days. If he buys 10 more cattle, how long can the same feed last? Assume the cattle finish the feed at the same rate.

Solution

Strategy 1: Use inverse proportion

$$40 \text{ cattle} \longleftrightarrow 35 \text{ days}$$
$$(40 + 10) \text{ cattle} = 50 \text{ cattle} \longleftrightarrow x \text{ days}$$

Using the fact that the product of two quantities that are inversely proportional is always the same, we have

$$50x = 40 \times 35$$

$$x = \frac{40 \times 35}{50} = 28$$

Alternatively,

$$x \text{ days} : 35 \text{ days} = 40 \text{ cattle} : 50 \text{ cattle}$$

$$\frac{x}{35} = \frac{40}{50}$$

$$x = \frac{40}{50} \times 35 = 28$$

∴   the same feed can last 28 days.

Strategy 2: Use decrease in ratio

40 cattle have feed for 35 days.

50 cattle have feed for $\left(35 \times \dfrac{40}{50} \right)$ days = 28 days.

Exercise 11g

1. Which of the following are in inverse proportion?
   (a) The number of pencils you buy and their total cost.
   (b) The number of pipes filling a tank and the time taken to fill it.
   (c) The number of men doing a job and the time taken to finish it.
   (d) The number of cattle to be fed and the time taken to finish a certain amount of the feed.

2. Four pipes can fill a tank in 70 minutes. How long will it take to fill the tank if 7 pipes are used?

3. A school librarian has enough money to order 8 paperback books at $5.50 each. If the librarian decides instead to order books with hard covers at $8.80 each, how many books can the librarian buy?

4. Thirty-five workers build a house in 16 days. How many days will 28 workers working at the same rate take to build the same house?

5. An aircraft flying at an average speed of 770 km/h takes 15 hours to complete a journey. Find the time taken for the aircraft to complete the same journey if its average speed is 660 km/h.

6. A consignment of fodder lasts 1 260 cattle for 50 days. Given that the cattle consume the fodder at a constant rate, find
   (a) the number of cattle an equal consignment of fodder lasts for 75 days;
   (b) the number of days an equal consignment of fodder lasts 1 575 cattle.

★7. A contractor estimates that he would need 56 workers to complete a job in 21 days. If he is asked to complete the job in 14 days, find the additional number of workers he has to employ.

★8. At a scouts' camp, there is sufficient food to last 72 scouts for 6 days. If 18 scouts do not turn up for the camp, how much longer can the food last for the other scouts?

★9. It takes 12 men to make 12 tables in 9 hours. How long will it take 8 men to make 32 tables?

Proportional Parts, Scales and Mixtures

Study the examples below.

Example 17

Suppose a sum of money is divided among 3 people, John, Mary and Peter, in the ratio 2 : 3 : 7. This means that John's share: Mary's share: Peter's share = 2 : 3 : 7.
If the sum of money is $192, how much will each of them receive?

▼ **S o l u t i o n**

Strategy 1: Use proportion

Consider the sum of money divided into $(2 + 3 + 7) = 12$ equal parts.
John, Mary and Peter will get 2, 3 and 7 parts respectively.

John's share: $192 = 2 : 12$

$\therefore$ John's share = $\dfrac{2}{12} \times \$192 = \$32$

Similarly,

$$\text{Mary's share} = \frac{3}{12} \times \$192 = \$48$$

and $$\text{Peter's share} = \frac{7}{12} \times \$192 = \$112$$

Check: John's share + Mary's share + Peter's share
   = $(32 + 48 + 112) = \$192$

Strategy 2: Use an equation

Let John's share be $(2x)$.

∴   Mary's share = $(3x)$ and Peter's share = $(7x)$

$$\$(2x + 3x + 7x) = \$192$$
$$\text{i.e.,} \quad 12x = 192$$
$$x = 16$$

∴   John's share = $(2 \times 16) = \$32$
 Mary's share = $(3 \times 16) = \$48$
and   Peter's share = $(7 \times 16) = \$112$

Example 18

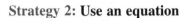

(a) Edward makes a model plane using a scale of 1 : 20. The model plane has an overall length of 1.2 m and its wingspan is 65 cm. Find the wingspan and the overall length of the actual plane in metres.
(b) On another occasion, he makes a model of another plane whose actual overall length of 35 m using a scale of 1 : 25. What is the overall length of the model plane in centimetres?

Solution

(a) Wingspan of the actual plane : wingspan of model plane = 20 : 1
 i.e.   wingspan of the actual plane : 65 cm = 20 cm : 1 cm

 ∴   wingspan of the actual plane = $\dfrac{20 \text{ cm}}{1 \text{ cm}} \times 65 \text{ cm} = 1\ 300 \text{ cm} = 13 \text{ m}.$

 The overall length of the model plane = 1.2 m = 120 cm

 Thus, the overall length of the actual plane = $\dfrac{20 \text{ cm}}{1 \text{ cm}} \times 120 \text{ cm} = 2\ 400 \text{ cm} = 24 \text{ m}$

(b) Length of the model : length of the actual plane = 1 : 25
 i.e.   length of the model : 35 m = 1 m : 25 m

 ∴   length of the model plane = $\dfrac{1 \text{ m}}{25 \text{ m}} \times 35 \text{ m} = 1.4 \text{ m} = 140 \text{ cm}.$

Example 19

Two chemicals, A and B, are combined in the ratio 5 : 11 by volume to form another solution X. A second solution Y is formed by combining chemicals A, B and C in the ratio 2 : 3 : 15 by volume. Calculate

(a) the volume of each chemical in 400 litres of solution X;
(b) the volumes of chemicals A and C in 400 litres of solution Y;
(c) the ratio of the three chemicals in a solution Z formed by mixing equal volumes of solutions X and Y;
(d) the volume of chemical C in 400 litres of solution Z.

▼Solution

(a) Volume of chemical A in 400 l of solution $X = \left(\dfrac{5}{16} \times 400 \right) l$

$$= 125 \ l$$

Volume of chemical B in 400 l of solution $X = (400 - 125) \ l$
$$= 275 \ l$$

(b) Volume of chemical A in 400 l of solution $Y = \left(\dfrac{2}{20} \times 400 \right) l$

$$= 40 \ l$$

Volume of chemical C in 400 l of solution $Y = \left(\dfrac{15}{20} \times 400 \right) l$

$$= 300 \ l$$

(c) Volume of chemical B in 400 l of solution $Y = (400 - 40 - 300)$
$$= 60 \ l$$

In 800 l of solution Z, the volumes of chemicals A, B and C are $(125 + 40) = 165 \ l$, $(275 + 60) = 335 \ l$ and 300 l respectively.

∴   the ratio of chemicals A, B and C in solution Z is 165 : 335 : 300, i.e., 33 : 67 : 60.

(d) $33 + 67 + 60 = 160$

∴   volume of chemical C in 400 l of solution $Z = \left(\dfrac{60}{160} \times 400 \right)$

$$= 150 \ l.$$

═ Exercise 11h ═

1. Divide $15 in the ratio 1 : 4 : 5; what is the result?

2. Divide 4 m in the ratio 1 : 3 : 4; what is the result?

3. Divide 110 g of salt in the ratio 5 : 8 : 9; what is the result?

4. Find the result of dividing 3 m 8 cm of ribbon in the ratio 2 : 3 : 6.

5. Three partners of a firm divide the profit of $6 720 among themselves in the ratio 2 : 3 : 7. What is the biggest share of the profit?

6. A man leaves $12 800 to his three children, *A*, *B* and *C*, in the ratio 4 : 5 : 7. How much does *B* receive?

7. A sum of money is divided among three persons, *X*, *Y* and *Z*, in the ratio 10 : 7 : 5. If *Y* gets $14 more than *Z*, how much will *X* get and what is the total sum of money?

8. Three families, *P*, *Q* and *R*, share 480 kg of rice. *Q* receives twice as much rice as *P*, and *R* receives half as much rice as *Q*. How much rice does each family get?

9. The model of an aircraft is in the scale 1 : 80.
    (a) If the wingspan of the model is 25 cm, what is the wingspan of the actual aircraft in metres?
    (b) If the real aircraft is 40 metres long, what is the length of the model in centimeters?

10. An architect's model of a block of flats is in the scale 1 : 50.
    (a) If the model is 0.8 metres wide, how wide is the actual block of flats?
    (b) If the block of flats is 30 metres tall, how tall is the model?

11. The scale of a map is given as 4 cm : 1 km.
    (a) Rewrite the ratio as simply as possible.
    (b) What is the length of a river, which is measured as 3 cm on the map?
    (c) The distance between two towns is 8 km. How far apart are the towns on the map?

12. Tea at $2.40 per kg is mixed with tea at $3.20 per kg in the ratio 1 : 3.
    (a) Calculate the weight of each type of tea in 40 kg of the mixture.
    (b) Calculate the price per kg of the mixture.

13. A certain solution is to be prepared by combining chemicals *X*, *Y* and *Z* in the ratio 18 : 3 : 2.
    (a) Calculate the volume of each chemical, *X*, *Y* and *Z*, in 69 litres of the solution.
    (b) How many litres of the solution can be prepared by using 36 litres of *X*?

∗14. A shopowner blends three types of coffee, *A*, *B* and *C*, in the ratio 3 : 5 : 7.
    (a) Calculate the weight of each type of coffee in 45 kg of the blended mixture.
    (b) Given type *A* coffee costs $7 per kg, type *B* coffee costs $10 per kg and type *C* coffee costs $13 per kg, calculate the cost per kg of the blended mixture.

∗15. Two types of coffee, *P* and *Q*, are blended in the ratio 3 : 13 by weight to form a standard blend *X*. A second standard blend, *Y*, is formed by blending type *P* coffee, type *Q* coffee and type *R* coffee in the ratio 1 : 7 : 12 by weight. Calculate
    (a) the weight of each type of coffee in 800 g of *X*;
    (b) the weights of type *P* coffee and type *R* coffee in 800 g of *Y*;
    (c) the ratio of the three types of coffee in a third standard blend *Z*, formed by mixing equal weights of *X* and *Y*;
    (d) the weight of type *P* coffee in 800 g of *Z*.

Strategies in Problem Solving

In this section, we shall look at some further examples of how some simple and effective strategies are used in problem solving.

Example 19

A farmer keeps some chickens and goats on his farm. One day, his son wants to know how many animals there are on the farm. The farmer wants his son to guess and tells him that there are altogether 50 heads and 140 legs of animals. How many goats and chickens are there?

Solution

The problem can be solved by either **making a systematic list, making a supposition, simplifying the problem** or **using equations**.

Strategy 1: Make a systematic list

Number of goats	Number of chickens	Number of heads			Number of legs		
		Goats	Chickens	Total	Goats	Chickens	Total
50	0	50	0	50	200	0	200
40	10	40	10	50	160	20	180
30	20	30	20	50	120	40	160
(20)	(30)	20	30	(50)	80	60	(140)

Thus, there are 20 goats and 30 chickens.

Strategy 2: Simplify the problem

Alternatively, imagine that all the goats stand on their hind legs. There were 50 heads counted. When the goats stand on their hind legs there would also be 50 pairs of legs on the ground. But 140 or 70 pairs of legs were counted. Therefore, the number of goat legs in the air must be 70 – 50 = 20 pairs.

Hence, there must be 20 goats.

∴   there were 50 – 20 = 30 chickens.

Strategy 3: Use an equation

Suppose x goats and $50 - x$ chickens were counted,

$$4x + 2(50 - x) = 140$$
$$4x + 100 - 2x = 140$$
$$2x = 40$$
$$x = 20$$
$$\therefore \quad 50 - x = 30$$

∴   20 goats and 30 chickens were counted.

Example 20

Two brothers, Peter and Paul, are vegetable sellers. One morning, they left home together at 5 o'clock for the market, each pushing a cart full of vegetables. Peter travelled at a constant speed of 100 m/min and Paul a constant speed of 60 m/min. After arriving at the market, Peter spent 5 minutes unloading the vegetables and immediately returned along the same route to help Paul. If Peter met Paul at 5 minutes to 6 o'clock, what is the distance between their house and the market?

▼**Solution**

Strategy: Use a diagram or a model

The diagram drawn below shows Peter's movement and Paul's movement between their house and the market.

Peter travelled $100 \times 50 = 5\,000$ m in 50 min.

NB: Peter spent 5 minutes unloading.

Paul travelled $60 \times 55 = 3\,300$ m in 55 min.

They travelled a total distance of $5\,000 + 3\,300 = 8\,300$ m.

From the diagram, the distance between their house and the market is half of the total distance travelled.

∴   the distance between their house and the market $= \dfrac{1}{2} \times 8\,300 = 4\,150$ m.

═══ Exercise 11i ═══

✳**1.** Five identical balls are marked with the numbers, 7, 3, 4, 2, 1 and are placed in a box. The balls are thoroughly mixed before three balls are drawn out all at one time from the box. A score is obtained by adding the numbers on the three balls drawn. Find how many different scores are possible and the possible scores.

✳**2.** A passenger train travelled at a speed of 72 km/h. A man on the passenger train observed a goods train travelling at a speed of 54 km/h in the opposite direction. If the goods train passed him in 8 seconds, find the length of the goods train. (*Hint:* model the problem and draw a diagram).

✳**3.** Steven left Town *A* and walked towards Town *B* at a speed of 100 m/min. At the same time, Jason and Melvin started from Town *B* and walked towards Town *A* at a speed of 80 m/min and 75 m/min respectively. If Steven met Melvin six minutes after passing Jason, find the distance between Town *A* and Town *B*.

✳**4.** A man can lift 200 kg, excluding the bar, of the dumbbell. There are weights in four sizes, 5 kg, 10 kg, 25 kg and 40 kg, which he can put on the bar. Assuming that he has unlimited weights in these four sizes and that the individual weights on both sides must be identical, find how many different combinations of weights he can put on the bar to make up the 200 kg.

Summary

1. A **ratio** is expressed as a fraction of the first quantity over the second. To find the ratio of two quantities, we must first express them in the same units. A ratio has no unit.

2. A **rate** expresses a relationship involving two quantities of different kinds.

3. Average speed of a moving object is given by the formula:

$$\text{Average speed} = \frac{\text{Distance travelled}}{\text{Time taken}}, \quad \text{Time taken} = \frac{\text{Distance travelled}}{\text{Average speed}}$$

   Also, Distance travelled = Average speed × Time taken.

4. A **proportion** is a statement that two ratios are equivalent.
   Two quantities are in **direct proportion** when one quantity is doubled, the other quantity is also doubled; when one quantity increases x times, the other quantity also increases x times.
   Two quantities are in **inverse proportion** when one quantity is doubled, the other is halved; when one quantity increases y times, the other quantity becomes $\frac{1}{y}$ of the original.

5. Any two numbers whose product is 1 are called reciprocals of each other. When a number gets bigger, its reciprocal becomes smaller. Conversely, the smaller the number, the bigger its reciprocal.

Review Questions 11

1. The bill for domestic power in a home is reduced from $120 to $90 per month. By what ratio has the bill decreased?

2. A poster measuring 150 cm by 180 cm is enlarged in the ratio 8 : 5. Find the length and breadth of the enlarged poster.

3. A manufacturing firm plans to increase its output in the ratio 2.25 : 1 next year. Its present output is 148 000 articles. How many articles does it hope to produce next year?

4. Goat's milk contains 27 g of protein, 30 g of fat and 36 g of carbohydrate. Find the ratio of protein to fat to carbohydrate in goat's milk.

5. Pupils in a class are told to choose one out of three sport options: tennis, basketball and badminton. Given that the pupils choose the options in the ratio 4 : 2 : 3 and that 20 choose tennis, find
   (a) the number of pupils in the class;
   (b) the number of pupils who choose badminton.

6. A student took 18 minutes to walk from home to school.
   (a) Given that he arrived in school at 07 05, find the time at which he left home.
   (b) Given also that he walked to school at an average speed of 4 km/h, calculate how far he had to walk.

7. A car took 2 hours and 15 minutes to travel 198 km. If it arrived at its destination at 12 06, find
   (a) the time it started on its journey;
   (b) the average speed of the car, giving your answer in kilometres per hour.

8. The cost of 1 kg of fish is $4.12.
   (a) Find the cost of $4\frac{1}{2}$ kg of fish.
   (b) How many kilograms of such fish can be bought for $20.60?

9. (a) Given that a typist can type 575 words in 25 minutes, how long will she take to type
       (i) 3 680 words?
       (ii) 8 855 words?
   (b) On another occasion, the typist started to type a report at 10 35 and finished it at 11 28.
       (i) How long did she take to type the report?
       (ii) Assuming she made no mistakes and typed non-stop at her usual speed, find the number of words in the report.

10. A rope is cut into three pieces in the ratio 1 : 3 : 5. Given that the length of the longest piece is 35 m, find
    (a) the length of the original rope;
    (b) the length of the shortest piece of rope.

11. A car travelled 100 km with half the distance at 40 km/h and the other half at 80 km/h. Find the average speed of the car for the whole journey.

12. (a) A photography competition offers $2 100 in prize money. Given that the prize money is divided among the first, second and third prize winners in the ratio 7 : 5 : 2, find the amount each prize winner gets.
    (b) It was decided later to introduce a fourth and fifth prize. The ratio of the first, second, third, fourth and fifth prize is then adjusted to 7 : 5 : 2 : 1 : 1. Given that the prize money is increased to $2 800, find how much each prize winner gets.

13. A model ship is $\frac{1}{2}$ metre long, and the actual ship is 30 metres long. What is the scale of model?

∗14. A lorry leaves a factory on a journey of 195 km at 08 45, travelling at an average speed of 52 km/h.
    (a) Find the time at which the lorry arrives at its destination.
    (b) On the return journey, the lorry leaves at 14 55 and arrives at the factory at 18 15. Calculate the time taken and the average speed of the lorry on the return journey.

∗15. A man parked his car in a carpark at 08 30 and retrieved it at 15 45 on the same day.
    (a) How long did he park his car in the carpark?
    (b) If the parking charges are $1.50 for the first hour and 80 cents for each subsequent half hour or part thereof, how much must he pay on parking his car there?

Problem Solving

1. Peter cycles to visit his grandmother and then returns home by the same route. He always cycles at 4 km/h when going uphill, 12 km/h when going downhill, and 6 km/h when on level ground. If his total cycling time is 2 hours and 20 minutes, what is the total distance he cycles in km?

2. Two candles of the same height are lit at the same time. Each candle burns at a constant rate and the first candle takes 5 hours while the second candle takes 4 hours to burn completely. Find the time, in hours, taken for the height of the first candle to be four times that of the second candle.

3. A container is filled with 56 litres of pineapple juice. 8 litres of pineapple juice are extracted and the container is refilled with mango juice. The content of the container is thoroughly mixed and 8 litres of the mixture are then extracted and the container is again refilled with mango juice. What is the ratio of mango juice to pineapple juice in the final mixture?

4. Twelve men take 6 hours to finish a piece of work. After the 12 men have worked for 1 hour, the contractor decides to call in 8 more men so that the work can be completed earlier. How many more hours would 20 men take to complete the remaining work?

5. Ahmad and Kumar together can paint a house in 12 days. Kumar and Chong Beng together can complete the same job in 15 days while Ahmad and Chong Beng together will take 20 days to paint the same house. How many days will it take Ahmad, Kumar and Chong Beng to complete the job together?

12

Arithmetical Problems

In this chapter, you will learn how to

▲ convert percentages into fractions;
▲ convert percentages into decimals;
▲ manipulate percentages and solve problems involving percentages;
▲ solve problems on personal and household finance and simple financial transactions.

Preliminary Problem

S ingaporeans consumed about 1 240 million eggs in 1999. Assuming that the population of Singapore was 3.85 million, how many eggs on average did each Singaporean consume in 1999?

Percentages, Fractions and Decimals

Percentages

We often see phrases like "Up to 75% off all items", "90% Housing Loan with Low Interest Rates" and "Fantastic Savings: 10–40% Genuine Discounts" in advertisements. 75%, 90%, 10% and 40% are examples of percentages.

Suppose there are 400 pupils in a school. During one afternoon, 120 pupils remain in school to participate in extra-curricular activities. We say that 120 out of 400 pupils participate in ECA that afternoon. The fraction of pupils who participate in ECA is equal to $\frac{120}{400}$, which can also be written as $\frac{30}{100}$. We say that 30 **per cent** (or percent) of the pupils participate in ECA. The expression "per cent" simply means **for every hundred**, or **out of every hundred**. Thus, a percentage is a fraction whose denominator is **100**. We use the symbol % to represent **per cent**.

So if a shop offers a customer 75% off an item which originally costs $600, then for every $100 of the original price, the customer will pay $75 less.

Similarly, if a bank provides a 90% housing loan to a customer who is buying a house, then the customer will get a loan of $90 for every $100 of the price of the house he is buying.

In another example, a mathematics examination paper is marked out of 50. If Meiling obtains 35 marks, Xiuyu 43 marks and Weiyun 32 marks, then we say that

Meiling gets $\frac{35}{50}$ of the marks or $\frac{70}{100}$, i.e., 70% of the marks.

Xiuyu gets $\frac{43}{50}$ of the marks or $\frac{86}{100}$, i.e., 86% of the marks.

Weiyun gets $\frac{32}{50}$ of the marks or $\frac{64}{100}$, i.e., 64% of the marks.

The word per cent originated from the Latin word "per centum" meaning "per hundred".

Changing Percentages to Decimals

We have seen that a percentage is simply a fraction with a denominator of 100. Thus, a percentage can be converted to a decimal by dividing the numerator of the fraction by 100.

Example *1*

Change each percentage to a fraction and then to a decimal:

(a) 25%   *(b) 65%*   *(c) 18%*   *(d) 4%*

▼ Solution

(a) $25\% = \frac{25}{100}$

$= 0.25$ (25 hundredths)

(b) $65\% = \dfrac{65}{100} = 0.65$ (65 hundredths)

(c) $18\% = \dfrac{18}{100} = 0.18$ (18 hundredths)

(d) $4\% = \dfrac{4}{100} = 0.04$ (4 hundredths)

> **To change a percentage to a decimal, express it as a fraction with a denominator of 100. Then convert it to a decimal.**

Example 2

Express each percentage as a decimal:
(a) 52%   *(b) 36%*   *(c) 125%*   *(d) 4.8%*
(e) 0.75%   *(f) 100%*

▼ **Solution**

(a) $52\% = \dfrac{52}{100} = 0.52$

(b) $36\% = \dfrac{36}{100} = 0.36$

(c) $125\% = \dfrac{125}{100} = 1.25$

(d) $4.8\% = \dfrac{4.8}{100} = 0.048$

(e) $0.75\% = \dfrac{0.75}{100} = 0.007\,5$

(f) $100\% = \dfrac{100}{100} = 1$

Example 3

Express each percentage as a decimal:

(a) $13\frac{1}{2}\%$ *(b) $8\frac{1}{4}\%$*   *(c) $134\frac{3}{4}\%$*   *(d) $\frac{2}{5}\%$*

▼ **Solution**

(a) $13\frac{1}{2}\% = 13.5\% = 0.135$ (First write the fraction as a decimal)

(b) $8\frac{1}{4}\% = 8.25\% = 0.082\,5$

(c) $134\frac{3}{4}\% = 134.75\% = 1.347\,5$

(d) $\frac{2}{5}\% = 0.4\% = 0.004$

 ## Changing Decimals to Percentages

We can also change a decimal to a percentage.

For example, $\quad 0.25 = \dfrac{25}{100}$ (25 hundredths)

$\qquad\qquad\qquad = 25\%$

To change a decimal to a percentage, write it as a fraction with denominator 100, then as a percentage.

Example 4

Express each decimal as a percentage:

(a) 0.24   (b) 0.72   (c) 0.09   (d) 0.136   (e) 1.12   (f) 3

Solution

(a) $0.24 = \dfrac{24}{100} = 24\%$

(b) $0.72 = \dfrac{72}{100} = 72\%$

(c) $0.09 = \dfrac{9}{100} = 9\%$

(d) $0.136 = \dfrac{13.6}{100} = 13.6\%$

(e) $1.12 = \dfrac{112}{100} = 112\%$

(f) $3 = \dfrac{300}{100} = 300\%$

Changing Fractions to Percentages

To change a fraction to a percentage, multiply it by 100%. Alternatively, change it to a decimal followed by expressing this decimal as a percentage.

Example 5

Change each fraction to a percentage:

(a) $\dfrac{7}{40}$ (b) $\dfrac{5}{8}$ (c) $1\dfrac{2}{3}$

Solution

For part (c), where the fraction is non-terminating, we may use the second method if we are not required to give the exact answer.

(a) $\dfrac{7}{40} = \dfrac{7}{40} \times 100\% = 17\dfrac{1}{2}\%$ or 17.5%

(b) $\dfrac{5}{8} = \dfrac{5}{8} \times 100\% = 62\dfrac{1}{2}$ or 62.5%

(c) $1\dfrac{2}{3} = \dfrac{5}{3} \times 100\% = 166\dfrac{2}{3}\%$

Alternatively,

(a) $\dfrac{7}{40} = 0.175 = 17.5\%$

(b) $\dfrac{5}{8} = 0.625 = 62.5\%$

(c) $1\dfrac{2}{3} = 1.667$ (correct to 3 decimal places)

  $= 166.7\%$

Changing Percentages to Fractions

To change a percentage to a fraction, reverse the process of converting a fraction to a percentage.

Example 6

Convert each percentage to a fraction:

(a) 15%   (b) 62.5%   (c) 215%

▼ **Solution**

(a) $15\% = \dfrac{15}{100}$ (Divide by 100%) or $15\% = 0.15$ (Change to decimal)

$= \dfrac{3}{20}$ $= \dfrac{15}{100} = \dfrac{3}{20}$

(b) $37.5\% = \dfrac{37.5}{100} = \dfrac{375}{1\,000} = \dfrac{3}{8}$ or $37.5\% = 0.375 = \dfrac{375}{1\,000} = \dfrac{3}{8}$

(c) $215\% = \dfrac{215}{100} = \dfrac{43}{20} = 2\dfrac{3}{20}$ or $215\% = 2.15 = 2\dfrac{15}{100} = 2\dfrac{3}{20}$

═ Exercise 12a ═

1. Express the following percentages as decimals:

(a) 6%   (b) 11%   (c) 22%
(d) 63%   (e) 179%   (f) 0.27%

(g) 28.7%   (h) 134.6%   (i) $3\dfrac{1}{2}\%$

(j) $5\dfrac{1}{4}\%$ (k) 0.074%   (l) 54.37%

(m) 0.0063%   (n) $1\dfrac{1}{8}\%$ (o) $\dfrac{7}{8}\%$

(p) $50\dfrac{3}{4}\%$

2. Write each decimal as a percentage:

(a) 0.17   (b) 0.575   (c) 0.83
(d) 2.36   (e) 0.09   (f) 0.025
(g) 0.008   (h) 2.564   (i) 0.000 5
(j) 1.2   (k) 4   (l) 6.25

3. Change each fraction to a percentage:

(a) $\dfrac{3}{4}$ (b) $\dfrac{9}{10}$ (c) $\dfrac{17}{20}$ (d) $\dfrac{6}{125}$

(e) $\dfrac{6}{5}$ (f) $\dfrac{12}{25}$ (g) $1\dfrac{6}{25}$ (h) $2\dfrac{2}{5}$

4. Express each fraction as a percentage, giving the answer to 1 decimal place:

(a) $\dfrac{2}{3}$ (b) $\dfrac{4}{7}$ (c) $\dfrac{2}{9}$ (d) $\dfrac{7}{12}$

(e) $1\dfrac{1}{3}$ (f) $\dfrac{5}{6}$ (g) $2\dfrac{3}{7}$ (h) $\dfrac{10}{11}$

5. Copy and complete the following table.

Percentage	Fraction	Decimal
	$\dfrac{3}{5}$	
Eleven per cent		
		0.175
		0.095
$78\dfrac{1}{2}\%$		

6. The forests of Singapore cover about $4\dfrac{1}{6}\%$ of the total land area. What fraction is this?

7. An electronic firm finds that $\frac{3}{64}$ of the resistors it makes are defective. What percentage is this?

8. Arrange the following in ascending order:

(a) 0.39, $\frac{12}{32}$, $4\frac{1}{2}\%$ (b) 0.222, 22%, $\frac{2}{9}$

(c) 64%, 0.6, $\frac{2}{3}$

Expressing One Quantity as a Percentage of Another

In a secondary school, 56 out of 70 teachers are female. What percentage of the teachers are female? What percentage of them are male?

We know that the fraction of female teachers in the school is $\frac{56}{70}$. Changing this fraction to percentage, we have $\frac{56}{70} \times 100\% = 80\%$. Hence 80% of the teachers in the school are female. The percentage of male teachers in the school = $100\% - 80\% = 20\%$.

In general, to express one quantity, a, as a percentage of another quantity, b, we

> 1. **write a as a fraction of b,**
>
> 2. **multiply the fraction $\frac{a}{b}$ by 100% to convert it to a percentage.**

Example 7

A pupil scored 108 out of 150 marks in Mathematics and 96 out of 160 marks in English. Find the percentage mark for each subject.

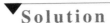
Solution

The pupil's percentage mark for Mathematics = $\frac{108}{150} \times 100\%$

$= 72\%$

The pupil's percentage mark for English = $\frac{96}{160} \times 100\%$

$= 60\%$

Ninety-nine boys and one girl are in a lecture theatre. How many boys must leave the theatre so that the percentage of boys becomes 98%?

Finding the Percentage of a Number

About 70% of the earth's surface is covered by water.

If you are told that 75% of the pupils in a class of 40 passed a Mathematics test, how many of them failed?

The number of pupils who passed the test = 75% of the 40 pupils

$$= \frac{75}{100} \times 40$$
$$= 30$$

∴ number of pupils who failed the test = 40 – 30 = 10

Alternatively, since 75% of the pupils passed the test, (100% – 75%) or 25% failed the test.

Number of pupils who failed the test = 25% × 40

$$= \frac{25}{100} \times 40 = 10$$

Example 8

Find   *(a)* 25% of $21.60,   *(b)* $37\frac{1}{2}\%$ of 1.60 m.

Solution

(a) 25% of $21.60 = $\frac{1}{4}$ × $21.60 $\left(25\% = \frac{1}{4}\right)$

$$= \$5.40$$

(b) $37\frac{1}{2}\%$ of 1.60 m = $\frac{75}{2}\%$ × 1.60 m

$$= \frac{1}{2} \times 75\% \times 160 \text{ cm} \quad \left(\frac{75}{2}\% = \frac{1}{2} \times 75\%; 1.60 \text{ m} = 160 \text{ cm}\right)$$

$$= \frac{1}{2} \times \frac{3}{4} \times 160 \text{ cm} \quad \left(75\% = \frac{3}{4}\right)$$

$$= 60 \text{ cm}$$

═══ Exercise 12b ═══

1. **(a)** Express 30 cents as a percentage of $1.
   (b) Express 45 m as a percentage of 1 km.
   (c) Express 1 kg as a percentage of 800 g.

2. Express the first quantity as a percentage of the second.

   (a) 45 min, 1 h   **(b)** 4 mths, 1 yr
   (c) 335 cm, 5 m   **(d)** 60°, 360°
   (e) 15 mm, 1 m   **(f)** 63¢, $2.10

3. **(a)** In a test, 30 of the 36 students obtained passing grades.
      (i) What fraction of the students passed?
     (ii) What percentage of the students passed?
   (b) In the same test, John scored 65 marks out of a possible total of 80 marks.
      (i) Write his score as a fraction.

   (ii) Write his score as a percentage.

4. A pupil saved $7.20 of his weekly pocket money of $24. What percentage did he save?

5. During the economic downturn, a company retrenched 24 out of its 400 employees. What percentage of employees was retrenched?

6. In a survey, 120 pupils were asked which learning site they would like to visit as part of the National Education learning journey.

   24 said National Heritage Board
   36 said Battle Box
   54 said Singapore Discovery Centre
   The rest said they would like to visit the People's Association.

Write these results as percentages.

7. Calculate the following:

  (a) $15\frac{1}{2}\%$ of $640

  (b) 6.5% of 5 000 people

  (c) 80% of 4.50 m

  (d) 125% of 50 cm

  (e) 30.6% of 300 l

  (f) 60.5% of 8 hrs

8. In a certain constituency, there are 8 500 voters and on election day, 15% of them failed to vote. Calculate the number of people who voted.

9. A company finds that $4\frac{1}{4}\%$ of the tyres made are defective. The company made 28 000 tyres. How many tyres were defective?

10. (a) Soyabeans on an average contain 39.5% protein. A bushel of soyabeans weighs 120 kg. How many kilograms of protein are contained in a bushel?

  (b) A 100-acre field yields 50 bushels per acre. How many kilograms of protein does the field yield?

11. In this question, take the Singapore population to be about 4 000 000.

  (a) Figure out, mentally, what 10% of the Singapore population is.

  (b) Use the answer in (a) to figure out the following percentages of the population:

    (i) 20%   **(ii)** 30%

    (iii) 40%   **(iv)** 50%

Percentage Change

The change in the value of an item can be expressed as a percentage increase or decrease in the original value. An **increase** of, say, 5% in the salary of a worker means that for every $100 in the **original** salary, there is an increase of $5, i.e., each $100 in the original salary becomes $105 in the **new** salary. Suppose the original salary for the worker is $1 600, how much will his new salary be after a 5% increase?

New salary : Original salary = 105 : 100

$$\frac{\text{New salary}}{\text{Original salary}} = \frac{105}{100}$$

$$\text{New salary} = \frac{105}{100} \times \text{Original salary}$$

$$= \frac{105}{100} \times \$1\ 600 = \$1\ 680$$

On the other hand, a **decrease** of, say, 5% in the salary means that for every $100 in the **original** salary, there is a decrease of $5, i.e., each $100 in the original salary becomes $95 in the **new** salary. In the above case,

New salary : Original salary = 95 : 100

$$\frac{\text{New salary}}{\text{Original salary}} = \frac{95}{100}$$

$$\text{New salary} = \frac{95}{100} \times \text{Original salary}$$

$$= \frac{95}{100} \times \$1\ 600 = \$1\ 520$$

1. Original salary increases in the ratio 105 : 100 and the new salary is 105% of the original salary.

2. Original salary decreases in the ratio 95 : 100 and the new salary is 95% of the original salary.

Example 9

The workers of an electronic company were given an increase amounting to 8% in their monthly salaries.

(a) If Peter earned $1 800 per month originally, find his monthly salary after the increment.
(b) If Paul's monthly salary after the increment is $1 728, find his original monthly salary.

▼**Solution**

(a) Peter's monthly salary after the increment is 100% + 8% = 108% of his original monthly salary.

His monthly salary after the increment = 108% of $1 800
$$= 1.08 \times \$1\ 800 = \$1\ 944$$

or
$$= \frac{108}{100} \times \$1\ 800 = \$1\ 944$$

Alternatively, the increment = 8% of $1 800 = $144

and thus Peter's new monthly salary = $1 800 + $144 = $1 944

(b) **Method 1: Use proportion**

Paul's salary after the increment : Paul's original salary = 108 : 100

Paul's original salary = $\frac{100}{108} \times \$1\ 728 = \$1\ 600$

Method 2: Use an equation

Let Paul's original salary be $x.

His monthly salary after the increment = 108% of $x = \$\frac{108}{100}x$.

$$\therefore \quad \frac{108}{100}x = 1\ 728$$

$$x = 1\ 728 \times \frac{100}{108} = 1\ 600.$$

$\therefore$ Paul's original salary is $1 600.

Example 10

After 6% of a bill has been deducted, $282 remains to be paid. How much was the original bill?

▼**Solution**

Strategy 1: Use proportion

Following a discount of 6%, 94% of the bill remains to be paid.

Original bill : $282 = 100 : 94

$\therefore$ original bill = $\frac{100}{94} \times \$282 = \$300$

Strategy 2: Use an equation

Let his original bill be x.

The deduction = $(x - 282)$

$\therefore$ 6% of $x = (x - 282)$

i.e., $\dfrac{6}{100}x = x - 282$

or $\dfrac{94}{100}x = 282$

$x = 282 \times \dfrac{100}{94} = 300$

$\therefore$ the original bill is $300.

Example 11

The cost of a television set is raised from $600 to $624. Find the percentage increase.

▼ Solution

The increase = $624 – $600 = $24

The percentage increase = $\dfrac{\text{Increase}}{\text{Original cost}} \times 100\%$

$= \dfrac{\$24}{\$600} \times 100\% = 4\%$

Example 12

The cost of a piece of furniture is calculated as follows:

Wood $300; Paint $200; Wages $200.

If the costs of the wood and paint are increased by 12% and 7% respectively, while the wages are decreased by 10%, find the percentage increase or decrease in the cost of the furniture.

▼ Solution

	Original cost ($)	Percentage change	New cost ($)
Wood	300	+12%	$\dfrac{112}{100} \times 300 = 336$
Paint	200	+7%	$\dfrac{107}{100} \times 200 = 214$
Wages	200	–10%	$\dfrac{90}{100} \times 200 = 180$
Furniture	700		730

The percentage increase in the cost of the furniture

$= \dfrac{\text{Increase}}{\text{Original cost}} \times 100\% = \dfrac{730 - 700}{700} \times 100\% = \dfrac{30}{700} \times 100\% = 4\dfrac{2}{7}\%$

Exercise 12c

1. Increase 28 by 125%; what is the result?

2. Decrease 216 by $37\frac{1}{2}$%; what is the result?

3. The result of a number, when increased by 15%, is 161. Find this number.

4. The result of a number, when decreased by 20%, is 192. Find this number.

5. A man spends $880 in a month. Out of this, 26% goes to his rent. How much is his rent?

6. A flat costs 36% more today than when it was built. If the original cost of the flat was $90 000, find its price today.

7. After spending 88% of his income, a man has $216 left. Find his income.

8. If 10% is deducted from a bill, $58.50 remains to be paid. How much is the bill?

9. A property company sold 20% more houses in 1999 than it did in 1998. If the company sold 426 houses in 1999, calculate how many houses it sold in 1998.

10. The height of a tree was 4.8 m. After one year, the height of the tree was increased by 12.5%. Find its new height.

11. A machinist is hired at $7.20 per hour.
    (a) On a particular day, he clocked in at 8.00 a.m. and clocked out at 3.45 p.m. Find his wage for that day.
    (b) At the end of a one-year probation period, his wage will increase by $27\frac{1}{2}$%. If the machinist successfully completes the apprenticeship,
       (i) what will his pay be per hour?
       (ii) what will his pay be per week, if he starts with a forty-hour week?

12. The production cost of a printer is as follows: overheads — $80; wages — $120; raw materials — $100.

    If the cost of overheads increases by 20%, wages by 15% and raw materials by 11%, find the percentage increase in the production cost of the printer.

13. A new car costs $120 000. After 1 year, its value decreases by 20%. For the second year, its value decreases a further 10%. What is the value of the car after 2 years?

14. James is 8% taller than John, and Wilson is 10% shorter than John. By what percentage is James taller than Wilson?

15. In 1998, a train carried 8% more passengers than in 1997. In 1999, it carried 8% more passengers than in 1998. What was the total percentage increase in the number of passengers from 1997 to 1999?

16. During 1998, a swimming lesson at a particular school lasted 45 minutes.
    (a) In 1999, the lesson time will be 50 minutes. Find the increase in the lesson time from 1998 to 1999 as a percentage of the lesson time in 1998.
    (b) The lesson time in 1999 will be 25% more than it was in 1997. Find how long the lesson lasted in 1997.
    (c) At present, James takes 240 seconds to swim 100 metres. In a year's time, he would have **improved** his swimming **time** by 25%. Calculate the time he will take to swim 100 metres in a year's time.
    (d) Robert, at present, also takes 240 seconds to swim 100 metres. In a year's time, he would have **increased** his swimming **speed** by 25%. Calculate the time he will take to swim 100 metres in a year's time.
    (e) Who will be the faster swimmer, James or Robert, in a year's time?

Profit and Loss

A manufacturer produces goods at a certain cost. If the goods are sold at a **higher** price than the cost price, then the manufacturer makes a **profit** or **gain**. But if, for some reason, the manufacturer sells the goods at a **lower** price than the cost price, he suffers a **loss** on the transaction. Thus,

> **Profit = Selling price – Cost price**
>
> **Loss   = Cost price – Selling price**

Percentage Profit and Percentage Loss

For comparison, we usually express the actual profit or loss as a percentage of the cost price. For example, a shopkeeper sold an article costing $50 for $60 and another article costing $100 for $110. We note that in each transaction, the shopkeeper made a profit of $10. It seems that both transactions are equally favourable. However,

the percentage profit for the first transaction is $\dfrac{\$10}{\$50} \times 100\% = 20\%$

and the percentage profit for the second transaction is $\dfrac{\$10}{\$100} \times 100\% = 10\%$.

Hence, the percentage profit gives a better comparison.

Example *13*

A bag costing $28 is sold for $35. Find the percentage profit.

▼**Solution**

Profit = Selling price – Cost price
= $35 – $28 = $7

∴   percentage profit = $\dfrac{7}{28} \times 100\% = 25\%$

Example *14*

A vase costing $60 is sold for $50. Find the percentage loss.

▼**Solution**

Loss = Cost price – Selling price
= $60 – $50 = $10

∴   percentage loss = $\dfrac{10}{60} \times 100\% = 16\dfrac{2}{3}\%$

Example 15

A bookseller gains 30% by selling a book for $65. Find the cost of the book.

▼**Solution**

Strategy 1: Use proportion

Selling price = Cost price + Profit

If cost price = 100%, then selling price = (100% + 30%) of the cost price

$\qquad\qquad\qquad\qquad\qquad\qquad$ = 130% of the cost price

Cost price : Selling price = 100 : 130

$$\text{Cost price} = \frac{100}{130} \times \text{Selling price}$$

$$= \frac{100}{130} \times \$65 = \$50$$

Strategy 2: Use an equation

Let the cost price be $x.

The profit = 30% of $x = $\frac{30}{100} \times \$x = \$\frac{3x}{10}$

Profit = Selling price − Cost price

$\frac{3x}{10} = 65 - x$

$3x = 650 - 10x$

$13x = 650$

$x = 50$

∴ the cost price of the book is $50.

Example 16

Desmond receives 400 kg of bananas, for which he pays $0.75 per kg. On average, 8% of the bananas will spoil. Find the selling price per kg to obtain a 75% profit on cost.

▼**Solution**

The cost of the bananas = $0.75 × 400 = $300.

The total selling price = 1.75 × $300 = $525 $\qquad$ (to obtain a 75% profit on cost)

He expects to sell (100 − 8)% = 92% of the bananas or 0.92 × 400 = 368 kg of the bananas

$$\text{Selling price per kg} = \frac{\text{Total selling price}}{\text{Number of kg of bananas expected to sell}} = \frac{\$525}{368}$$

$$\simeq \$1.427 \text{ or } \$1.43$$

Desmond must sell the bananas for $1.43 per kg to receive the profit he desires. He will receive additional profit if he sells more than 92% of the bananas.

 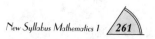

1. Find the gain or loss per cent in the following cases:

   (a) cost price = $40, gain = $5;
   (b) selling price = $30, gain = $2;
   (c) selling price = $60, loss = $20;
   (d) cost price = $16.25, selling price = $18.50.

2. A gold chain is sold for $635 at a gain of 27 per cent. Find the profit.

3. By selling a book for $16.50, a bookseller loses 12%. What is the cost price of the book?

4. Peter bought an antique chest for $600 and was forced to sell it for $500. Find the percentage loss.

5. If Susan sells her car at a loss of 6%, what is her selling price when she paid $18 400 for it?

6. To make a profit of $33\frac{1}{3}$%, a bicycle must be sold for $240. What is the cost price of the bicycle?

7. The profit on a certain refrigerator is 35% of the cost price. If the profit is $280, find

   (a) the cost price and
   (b) the selling price of the refrigerator.

8. The retail price of a television set is $840. If this is 140% of the wholesale price, find the wholesale price.

9. A man buys a dozen cameras for $1 800. He sells them at a profit of $36 each. Find his profit percentage.

10. A florist bought 360 roses at $10 per dozen. If he sold them at $1.10 each, what is his percentage profit?

∗11. Mr Lin buys an article and sells it to Mr Chen at a gain of 25%. Mr Chen sells the article to Mr Ang at a gain of 20%. How much money did Mr Lin pay for the article, if Mr Ang pays $360 for it?

∗12. A shopkeeper buys 300 identical articles at a total cost of $1 500. He fixes the selling price of each article at 20% above the cost price and sells 260 articles at this price. As for the remaining articles, he sells them at 50% of the selling price. Calculate the shopkeeper's total profit.

∗13. Simon ordered 200 boxes of Fuji apples from China. He paid $28 per box for the apples. There were 60 fruits in each box and he expected 15% of them to spoil. If he wants to make a profit of 80% on cost, what should be the selling price per fruit?

 ## Discount

Very often, retailers cannot sell defective merchandise, overstocked items, discontinued models and so on at the retail selling prices. To clear the merchandise in stock, the retailers usually sell the items at a lower price, called the sale price. The difference between the original selling price or the **marked price** and the cheaper price or the **sale price** is called the **discount**.

A discount
A reduction in the price of an article or commodity for payment in cash.

Discount = Marked price – Sale price

Discount is often expressed as a percentage of the original price.

Example 17

A watch priced at $160 is sold for $140. Find the percentage discount.

$\blacktriangledown$ **Solution**

Discount = Marked price − Selling price
    = $160 − $140 = $20

$\therefore$ percentage discount = $\dfrac{20}{160} \times 100\% = 12\dfrac{1}{2}\%$

Example 18

The charges for processing and printing a roll of film in a shop are as shown in the table.

Mr Lee sends 3 rolls of 36 prints and 6 rolls of 24 prints to a shop for processing and printing.

(a) How much does it cost him?
(b) How much will it cost him if a 15% discount is given?

Charges per roll	
24 prints	$9.00
36 prints	$12.00

$\blacktriangledown$ **Solution**

(a) $3 \times 12 + 6 \times 9 = 36 + 54 = 90$

$\therefore$ it costs him $90.

(b) Discounted price : original price = 85 : 100

$\therefore$ discounted price = $\dfrac{85}{100} \times \$90 = \$76.50$. It will cost him $76.50.

Alternatively, discount = 15% of the original price = 15% × $90 = $13.50
$\therefore$ it will cost him $90 − $13.50 = $76.50.

Example 19

A ladies' bag selling for $175 is marked down 20% for a special promotion. It is later marked down further by $17\dfrac{1}{2}\%$ of the sale price. Since it still has not sold, it is marked down further to a price 60% off the original selling price.

(a) What are the two sale prices of the bag?
(b) What is the final selling price of the bag?

$\blacktriangledown$ **Solution**

(a) The first sale price of the bag = (100 − 20)% of $175 = $\dfrac{80}{100} \times \$175 = \$140$.

The second sale price of the bag = $\left(100 - 17\dfrac{1}{2}\right)\%$ of $140 = $\dfrac{165}{2} \times \dfrac{1}{100} \times 140 = \$115.50$

(b) The final selling price of the bag = (100 − 60)% of $175 = $\dfrac{40}{100} \times \$175 = \$70$.

Commission

A **commission** is the payment an agent gets for selling or buying something on behalf of another person. It is usually given as a percentage of the cost price or the selling price.

Example 20

A flat was bought for $220 000 by an agent who received a commission of $1\frac{1}{2}\%$. How much commission did he receive?

▼ Solution

$$1\frac{1}{2}\% \text{ of } \$220\,000 = \frac{3}{2} \times \frac{1}{100} \times \$220\,000$$
$$= \$3\,300$$

∴ the agent received $3 300 as commission.

═══ Exercise 12e ═══

1. Find the percentage discount of the following, given the marked prices and the sale prices:

	Marked Price	Sale Price
(a)	$100	$88
(b)	$580	$464

2. A supermarket gives a 10% discount on the marked prices of all items during a sale. Find for the following marked prices

   (i) the amount of discount given and
   (ii) the sale price:
      (a) $45   (b) $110

3. Find the marked prices of the following, given the amount of discount:

   (a) A 7% discount which is $49.

   (b) A $33\frac{1}{3}\%$ discount which is $270.

4. Find the marked prices of the following, given the percentage discount and the sale prices:

   (a) 12% discount, $77
   (b) 25% discount, $123

5. At a sale, the price of a washing machine was reduced by 12% to $440. What was the original price of the washing machine?

6. A shopkeeper marks the price of an article at $80. Find the selling price of the article if

   (a) he gives a discount of 10%,
   (b) he gives two successive discounts of 5% each.

7. During a sale a shopkeeper reduced the prices of all his goods by 15%. Calculate the original selling price of a calculator, which was sold for $23.80 during the sale.

8. John bought an air-conditioner priced at $800, but was given a discount of $12\frac{1}{2}\%$. Calculate the price he paid.

9. A camcorder originally marked to sell for $2 000 was reduced 20% during a special promotion. The price was then reduced an additional 30% to clear the stock. What was the sale price for each reduction?

10. The cost of a colour film for 36 photographs is usually $3.60. Additionally, the cost of processing and printing the 36 photographs is usually $12.60.

    (a) Show that the **total** cost of each photograph is usually 45 cents.

(b) A shop keeps the price of the film at $3.60, and offers a reduction of 20% off the cost of processing and printing. Calculate the total cost of each photograph at this shop.

(c) Calculate the percentage reduction in the total cost, compared to the usual cost, of a photograph obtained from this shop.

11. A property agent charges a commission of 5% on the first $10 000 and $2\frac{1}{4}$% on the remainder of the selling price. Find the amount of commission he will receive if he sells a piece of property for $46 000.

12. Mr. Goh's monthly income consists of $500 plus a commission of 4% on all his sales.

Find his total sales for a particular month if his income was $1 220 that month.

13. A tour guide earns commission by bringing tourists to patronise a certain handicraft shop. Given that the commission he receives is 3% of the total sales, calculate his commission on a particular day when the 12 tourists he brought to the shop spent an average of $250 each.

14. Three salesmen went to 400 households to sell a certain brand of rice cookers costing $60 each. 15% of the households bought a rice cooker each from them. If the three salesmen sold the rice cookers in the ratio 3 : 4 : 5, find the commission each salesman received if the commission is 4% of the total sales.

Simple Interest

When you deposit money into a bank, you receive interest for allowing the bank to use your money. Similarly, when you borrow money from the bank, you must pay a certain interest for using its money. The interest in both cases is calculated as a percentage (called the **rate**) of the capital (called the **principal**) deposited or borrowed. Interest is usually calculated at a fixed yearly rate (called **rate per annum**).

Sometimes, interest rates are calculated on half-yearly or quarterly period, monthly or even daily basis. The amount of interest depends on the length of time the money is deposited or borrowed. If interest is always calculated on the original principal, it is called **simple interest**. When the interest is added to the principal, the sum is called the **amount**.

The principal is taken to be the same; i.e., $100 for each year.

Example 21

A man borrows $100 for 3 years at a rate of 6% per annum. What is the simple interest he has to pay?

▼
Solution

The principal is $100.

The interest on $100 for 1 year is $\frac{6}{100} \times \$100 = \$6$

∴ the interest on $100 for 3 years is $3 \times \$6 = \$18$.

From the above, we know that the interest payable (or earned) depends on

(i) the amount borrowed or lent, i.e., the principal,
(ii) the rate of interest charged, i.e., the rate %,
(iii) the period of the loan or deposit, i.e., the time.

For a sum of $P deposited in a bank at $R\%$ simple interest per annum

for T years, the simple interest (in $) is $\quad I = \dfrac{PRT}{100}$

Example *22*

Mary needed capital for her bakery. She borrowed $60 000 for 4 years at a simple interest rate of 8% per year.

(a) How much interest must be paid?
(b) How much money will Mary pay at the end of 4 years?

▼**Solution**

(a) $P = \$60\ 000$, $R = 8$ and $T = 4$

Simple interest $I = \dfrac{PRT}{100} = \dfrac{60\ 000 \times 8 \times 4}{100} = 19\ 200$

∴ $19 200 of interest must be paid.

(b) The amount of money Mary will pay at the end of 4 years = principal + interest
= 60 000 + 19 200 = $79 200.

Example *23*

To save money for a bookshop, Ronald invested $2 500 at 6% per annum simple interest. How long will it take for the amount to add up to $3 400?

▼**Solution**

Simple interest = $3 400 − $2 500 = $900

$I = \$900$, $R = 6$ and $P = \$2\ 500$

$$I = \dfrac{PRT}{100}$$

$$900 = \dfrac{2\ 500 \times 6 \times T}{100}$$

$$T = \dfrac{900 \times 100}{2\ 500 \times 6} = 6$$

∴   the time taken is 6 years.

Credit cards are widely used nowadays. Find out the rate of interest charged by credit card companies on card holders who do not pay up their bills in time. How much higher is it as compared to the rate of interest on savings account?

Example 24

Simon wanted to borrow some money to expand his fruit shop. He was told he could borrow a sum of money for 30 months at 12% simple interest per year and pay $1 440 in interest charges. How much money could he borrow?

▼ **Solution**

$$T = \frac{30}{12} = 2.5 \text{ year} \qquad I = \frac{PRT}{100}$$

$$1\,440 = \frac{P \times 12 \times 2.5}{100}$$

$$P = \frac{1\,440 \times 100}{12 \times 2.5} = \$4\,800$$

Simon could borrow $4 800.

Example 25

To buy a car, Raymond borrowed $20 000 for $3\frac{1}{2}$ years and paid $5 880 simple interest on the loan. What rate of interest did he pay?

▼ **Solution**

$$I = \frac{PRT}{100}$$

$$5\,880 = \frac{20\,000 \times R \times 3.5}{100}$$

$$R = \frac{5\,880 \times 100}{20\,000 \times 3.5} = 8.4$$

He paid 8.4% simple interest per year.

═ Exercise 12f ═

1. Copy and complete the following table:

	Principal	Interest rate	Time	Simple interest	Amount
(a)	$12 000	8%	7 years		
(b)	$500	11%		$220	
(c)		9%	4 years	$108	
(d)	$3 000		10 years	$1 200	
(e)			2 years	$360	$3 960
(f)	$1 800		18 months	$189	
(g)	$4 500		2 years		$5 040
(h)		5%		$90	$1 290

2. Kenneth's shoe repair shop borrowed $6 600 from a bank at 8% simple interest per annum. How much did he owe the bank at the end of 11 months?

3. A finance company charges $55 simple interest on a sum of money which is borrowed for five months. Given that the rate of interest is 12% per annum, find the sum of money.

4. A bank charges 2.25% per month simple interest on personal loans. If John borrows $6 400 for a period of 2 years 1 month, find the total interest he has to pay.

5. Mrs. Lee invests $800 at 6% per annum and $1 200 at 7% per annum. What is her total annual interest on these two investments?

6. How long would $1 250 have to be deposited at 6% per year simple interest to gain $750 simple interest?

7. Andrew lent Roger $4 800 for 7 months. At the end of this period Roger had to pay Andrew an interest of $119. What was the rate of simple interest per annum?

8. In a certain year, James puts $600 in a bank at the end of March and $400 in the same bank at the end of June. The bank offers 3% per annum simple interest rate. Find the total amount that James receives from the bank at the end of December in that year.

9. A bank increased the rate of interest, which it paid to depositors from 3.5% to 4% per annum. Find how much more interest Susan would receive if she deposited $6 400 in the bank for 6 months at the new interest rate.

10. Mrs. Jasmine invested $4 000 in a Building Society which paid simple interest at a rate of $7\frac{1}{4}\%$ per annum to its investors. After 2 years, the rate was increased to 7.6% per annum. Find the amount she had at the end of 7 years.

11. Mr. Chen deposits a certain sum of money in a bank. If the interest rate of the bank decreases from $3\frac{3}{4}\%$ per annum to $3\frac{1}{2}\%$ per annum, Mr. Chen's interest will decrease by $50 in a year. Find the sum of money he deposits.

 ## Compound Interest

The interest is not always calculated based on the original principal. Suppose John deposits $2 000 in his savings account in a bank for 2 years at 5% per annum and the interest due to him is calculated as follows:

First year: $P = \$2\,000, R = 5, T = 1, I = \dfrac{\$2\,000 \times 5}{100} = \$100.$

Second year: $P = \$2\,000 + \$100 = \$2\,100, R = 5, T = 1, I = \dfrac{\$2\,100 \times 5}{100} = \$105.$

The total interest for 2 years = **$100** + **$105** = **$205**.

In the above computation, the interest of **$100** due to him at the end of the first year is **compounded** with, i.e. added on, to the principal of $2 000. This amount $2 100 becomes the principal for the second year and is used to obtain the interest due to him at the end of the second year.

The total interest of **$205** is called the **compound interest** and the sum $2 000 is said to be deposited at compound interest **compounded** annually.

If the sum is deposited at 5% per annum simple interest for 2 years, calculate the simple interest. Which interest is larger, the simple interest or the compound interest?

Example 26

Find the compound interest on $600 for 3 years at $3\frac{1}{2}$% per annum, compounded annually.

▼**Solution**

First year, $P = \$600,$ $R = 3\frac{1}{2} = \frac{7}{2},$ $T = 1$ year

$$I = \$600 \times \frac{7}{2} \times \frac{1}{100} = \$21$$

By the end of the first year, the principal is $600 + $21 = $621.

Second year, $P = \$621,$ $R = \frac{7}{2},$ $T = 1$ year

$$I = \$621 \times \frac{7}{2} \times \frac{1}{100} = \$21.735$$

By the end of the second year, the principal is $621 + $21.735 = $642.735.

Third year, $P = \$642.375,$ $R = \frac{7}{2},$ $T = 1$ year

$$I = \$642.735 \times \frac{7}{2} \times \frac{1}{100} = \$22.495725.$$

By the end of the third year, the compound interest is

$21 + $21.735 + $22.495725 = $65.230725 = $65.23   (correct to the nearest cent.)

Example 27

Find the compound interest on $2 500 for 1 year at 4% per annum compounded half-yearly.

▼**Solution**

Since interest is calculated half-yearly, the rate of interest becomes 2% per half-year.

Principal for the first half-year = $2 500, interest at 2% = $2 500 × 0.02 = $50.

Principal for the second half-year = $2 550, interest at 2% = $2 550 × 0.02 = $51.

∴   total interest = $50 + $51 = $101.

Alternatively, *first half-year:* $P = \$2\,500, R = 4, T = \frac{1}{2}$ and $I = \$2\,500 \times \frac{4}{100} \times \frac{1}{2} = \$50$;

second half-year: $P = \$2\,550, R = 4, T = \frac{1}{2}$ and $I = \$2\,550 \times \frac{4}{100} \times \frac{1}{2} = \$51$;

∴   total interest = $50 + $51 = $101.

Exercise 12g

1. Find the compound interest on
   (a) $450 for 2 years at 10% per annum compounded yearly;
   (b) $700 for 3 years at 11% per annum compounded yearly;
   (c) $5 000 for 2 years at $11\frac{3}{4}$% per annum compounded yearly;
   (d) $1 200 for 3 years at 4% per annum compounded yearly;
   (e) $10 000 for 2 years at $7\frac{1}{2}$% per annum compounded annually.

2. Wilson invests $5 000 at $5\frac{1}{4}$% per annum compound interest compounded annually. Find the amount at the end of the third year.

3. Joan invests $800 at $12\frac{1}{2}$% per annum compound interest compounded half-yearly. What is the amount at the end of the first year?

4. Mr. Sim invests $9 000 at 2% per annum compound interest compounded daily. What is his amount at the end of the third day?

 ## Hire Purchase

The following is an advertisement for the sale of a bedroom set.

> **For Sale: $4 500**
> **$1 000 deposit**
> **Balance 7%, 2 years**

Hire Purchase is a method of buying goods in which payment of purchase price is spread over a specified period by payment of an initial deposit followed by regular instalments.

After a deposit of $1 000 is paid, you can take the bedroom set home. However, you are not the owner of the set. You are merely the hirer. The ownership of the set will be transferred to you only after you have paid off the balance of $3 500 plus the simple interest on $3 500 for 2 years at 7% per annum by making 24 equal monthly payments. This method of purchasing goods is called **hire purchase transactions**. Each monthly payment is known as an **instalment**.

In the above, interest $= \dfrac{\$3\ 500 \times 7 \times 2}{100} = \$490$

Total amount to be paid off = $3 500 + $490 = $3 990

∴ each monthly instalment $= \dfrac{\$3\ 990}{24} = \$166.25$

NB: The deposit of $1 000 is called the **down payment**. Sometimes, no down payment is required so the whole cost is paid by instalments only.

The simple interest rate 7% is also called the **flat rate**.

Example 28

A washing machine is priced at $450. It may be bought on the following hire purchase terms: a deposit of 15%, simple interest of $10\frac{2}{3}\%$ per year over 2 years; repayment to be paid monthly.

Find (a) the monthly instalment;
        (b) the total hire purchase price of the washing machine;
        (c) the percentage of money saved if a housewife buys the washing machine by paying $450 immediately.

Solution

The deposit = 15% of $450 = $\frac{15}{100} \times \$450 = $ **$67.50**

The amount remaining = $450 – $67.50 = $382.50

The interest on $382.50 for 2 years = $\$382.50 \times \frac{32}{3} \times \frac{1}{100} \times 2 = \$81.60$

Additional amount to pay in 24 monthly instalments = $382.50 + $81.60 = **$464.10**

(a) The monthly instalment = $464.10 ÷ 24 = $19.34 (correct to the nearest cent.)

(b) The total hire purchase price = the deposit + additional amount
                      = $67.50 + $464.10 = $531.60

(c) On hire purchase terms, the additional amount the housewife would have to pay
     = interest on $382.50 for 2 years = $81.60 (or $531.60 – $450)

     Percentage of money she could save on cash terms = $\frac{81.60}{450} \times 100\% = 18\frac{2}{15}\%$

= Exercise 12h =

1. For each of the following **(i)** find the additional amount you have to pay by hire purchase and **(ii)** express the additional amount obtained in (i) as a percentage of the cash price:

	Cash price	Hire purchase terms		
		Down payment	Monthly instalment of	Number of instalments
(a)	$360	$50	$40	10
(b)	$900	$150	$75	12
(c)	$25 000	$10 000	$500	36

2. Peter buys a window air-conditioner at $900. He pays 20% deposit and the outstanding balance plus interest in 48 months. Interest on the balance is charged at 10%. Find

(a) the cost of his monthly instalment;
(b) the amount he saves by paying cash.

3. On each of the following **(i)** find the hire purchase price of the goods and **(ii)** express the amount saved by paying cash as a percentage of the cash price:

Item	Cash Price	Deposit	Number of Instalments	Monthly Instalment
(a) VCD player	$200	10%	24	$9
(b) Printer	$450	15%	18	$25
(c) 3-seater sofa	$1 600	25%	30	$52

4. For each of the following, find **(i)** the monthly instalment and **(ii)** the difference in the hire purchase price and the cash price as a percentage of the cash price:

	Cash price	Hire purchase terms
(a)	$800	$100 deposit; balance 8%; 1 year
(b)	$8 000	$3 200 deposit; balance 10%; $2\frac{1}{2}$ years
(c)	$1 200	$200 deposit; balance 15%; $1\frac{1}{3}$ years

5. The cash price of a computer package deal was $3 200. Mary paid a 15% down payment and the outstanding balance plus interest over 24 months. Interest on the balance was charged at 9.5%.

   (a) Find the cost of the package deal if it is bought on hire purchase.
   (b) Find the difference between the hire purchase price and the cash price.
   (c) Express the difference obtained in (b) as a percentage of the cash price.

6. Answer the following questions by referring to the advertisement on the right.

   (a) Find the percentage discount for payment in cash compared to the original price, giving your answer correct to one decimal place.
   (b) What is the difference between the hire purchase price and the original price?
   (c) What is the rate of simple interest charged for hire purchase? (Give your answer correct to three significant figures.)

Multi-system CTV

~~was $2 198~~

Is **$1 798**

or

$55 monthly × 38

NO DEPOSIT

Money Exchange

Different countries use different forms of currency and their units of money are called by various names. The United Kingdom uses the sterling pound (£), the United States of America uses the American dollar (US$), Thailand uses the baht (B)), Malaysia uses the ringgit (M$), Indonesia uses the rupiah (R), the Philippines uses the peso (P) and Singapore uses the Singapore dollar (S$).

We can buy or sell foreign currencies at any bank or through a money changer.

The table below shows the exchange rates of the various currencies displayed by a major bank on July 1999.

	Currency	Buying	Selling
Singapore dollar to one unit of foreign currency	Australian dollar (A$)	1.1140	1.1300
	Canadian dollar (C$)	1.1350	1.1580
	New Zealand dollar (NZ$)	0.8820	0.9010
	Sterling pound (£)	2.6450	2.6730
	US dollar (US$)	1.6930	1.7040
Singapore dollar to 100 units of foreign currency	Chinese renminbi	19.10	19.60
	Deutschemark (DM)	88.10	89.10
	French franc (FR)	26.20	26.60
	Hongkong dollar (HK$)	21.70	22.00
	Indian rupee	3.750	4.150
	Indonesian rupiah (Rp)	0.02400	0.02700
	Japanese yen (¥)	1.3900	1.4200
	Philippines peso (P)	4.400	4.550
	Thai baht (B)	4.530	4.660

Table 12.1

The table shows that the bank will buy a currency at a lower rate than it will sell that currency. For example, we need to pay S$113 to buy A$100 from the bank but we will get only S$111.40 for selling A$100 to the bank. The difference is the profit the bank makes.

Example 29

Convert the following foreign currencies to Singapore dollars using Table 12.1. Give your answers correct to the nearest cent.
(a) US$185   *(b) 5 000 Thai baht*

Solution

(a) The bank will buy US dollars at US$1 = S$1.693.
   US$185 = 185 × S$1.693 = S$313.21   (correct to the nearest cent)

(b) The bank will buy Thai baht at 100 Thai baht = S$4.530.
   5 000 Thai baht = $\dfrac{5\ 000}{100}$ × S$4.530 = S$226.50.

Example 30

Convert   (a) S$250 to sterling pound;   (b) S$5 000 to Japanese yen.
Give your answers correct to the nearest unit of the foreign currency.

Solution

(a) The bank will sell sterling pounds at £1 = S$2.673   or   S$1 = £$\dfrac{1}{2.6730}$.
   S$250 = 250 × £$\dfrac{1}{2.6730}$ = £94   (correct to the nearest £)

(b) The bank will sell Japanese yen at ¥100 = S$1.4200   or   S$1 = ¥$\dfrac{100}{1.4200}$.
   S$5 000 = 5 000 × ¥$\dfrac{100}{1.4200}$ = ¥352 113   (correct to the nearest ¥)

1. Convert the following foreign currencies to Singapore dollars using Table 12.1. (Buying rate) Give your answers correct to the nearest cent where necessary.

   (a) US$450
   (b) £3 000
   (c) 8 000 Renminbi
   (d) 2 200 peso
   (e) C$720
   (f) 875 000 rupiah
   (g) 25 000 Thai baht
   (h) 980 French franc
   (i) ¥2 000 000
   (j) NZ$640
   (k) A$8 540
   (l) 4 200 rupee

2. Convert the following amounts in Singapore currency to the stated foreign currency using Table 12.1. (Selling rate) Give your answers correct to the nearest unit of the foreign currency.

   (a) S$7 500 to US$
   (b) S$875 to £
   (c) S$5 250 to NZ$
   (d) S$275 to Thai baht
   (e) S$5 000 to peso
   (f) S$225 to rupiah
   (g) S$420 to ¥
   (h) S$850 to French franc
   (i) S$370 to C$
   (j) S$1 250 to A$
   (k) S$2 200 to HK$
   (l) S$1 500 to Deutschemark

3. A money changer exchanged Thai baht (B) and US dollars (US$) at a rate of 7.70 B = US$1.

   (a) Calculate, in Thai baht, the amount received for US$150.
   (b) Calculate, in US$, the amount received for 1 617 B.

4. The exchange rate between the English pound (£) and the German mark (M) during a particular day was £1 to 3.10 M.

   (a) How many German marks would be equivalent to £320?
   (b) How many pounds would be equivalent to 868 M?

5. Roger put S$8 500 in a 1-year US$ fixed deposit account with a bank at 4% simple interest per annum when the exchange rate was at US$1 = S$1.70.

   (a) How much did he invest in US dollars?
   (b) At the end of one year he withdrew all his money when the exchange rate was at US$1 = S$1.65. Calculate the number of Singapore dollars he made from this investment.

Taxation

The government imposes various forms of taxes which include direct taxes and indirect taxes on its residents to finance public spending on national defence, education, etc. Direct taxes include income taxes, property taxes and profit taxes whereas indirect taxes include duties, motor vehicle taxes, goods and services taxes (GST), value-added taxes, etc.

Property Tax

A **property tax** is charged on the owner of land, houses, flats or buildings at a standard rate of 16%, as of 1998, on the **annual value** of the property.

Example 31

The annual value of a flat is $1 020. Find the half year tax payable at a rate of 16%.

Solution

Half year tax payable = $1 020 × 16% × $\frac{1}{2}$

$$= \$1\,020 \times 16 \times \frac{1}{100} \times \frac{1}{2} = \$81.60$$

Value-added Tax and GST

In some countries, when you buy an article, you have to pay a certain amount of tax known as the value-added tax in addition to the price of the article. The tax payable is usually given as a certain percentage of the selling price. In Singapore, a goods and services tax (GST) of 3% is imposed on goods bought and services rendered which came into effect on 1 April 1994.

Example 32

An article has a value-added tax of 15% imposed on it. If the marked price of the article is $64, calculate the total amount a man has to pay if he wants to buy it.

Solution

Value-added tax payable = 15% of $64 = $\frac{15}{100}$ × $64 = $9.60

∴   the total amount the man has to pay = $64 + $9.60 = $73.60.

Example 33

An ink jet printer is advertised as $618 inclusive of a 3% GST. What is the original price of the printer?

Solution

Original price : $618 = 100 : 103

∴   original price = $\frac{100}{103}$ × $618 = $600

Income Tax

Income tax is charged on all incomes derived from Singapore or received in Singapore from sources outside Singapore during the year started 1 January and ended 31 December. The income tax payable is calculated based on the chargeable income.

Chargeable income = Total income − Reliefs

The reliefs include personal relief, wife relief, child relief, life insurance premiums, contributions to the Central Provident Fund (CPF) and gifts to charitable organisations in the form of cash, etc. The amount of income tax payable is calculated according to the tax rates. Below is an extract of the tax rates from Explanatory Notes on how to prepare the returns sent to taxpayers in 1998 by the Inland Revenue Department:

	Chargeable Income ($)	Rate (%)	Gross Tax Payable ($)
On the first	7 500	2	150.00
On the next	12 500	5	625.00
On the first	20 000		775.00
On the next	15 000	8	1 200.00
On the first	35 000		1 975.00
On the next	15 000	12	1 800.00
On the first	50 000		3 775.00
On the next	25 000	16	4 000.00

Table 12.2

Example 34

Calculate the tax payable for a chargeable income of $8 450 according to the tax rates given in Table 12.2.

Chargeable income		Tax
On the first	$7 500	$150.00
On the next	$ 950 at 5%	$ 47.50
	$8 450	$197.50

∴   the tax payable = $197.50

Example 35

In 1998, Richard earned a gross annual income of $48 000. Calculate his income tax if he was entitled to the following reliefs: personal, $3 000; wife, $1 500; 3 children, $1 500 each; handicapped brother, $2 500; life insurance premiums and CPF contributions, $5 000; and gifts to charitable organizations, $200.

Total reliefs = $3 000 + $1 500 + 3 × $1 500 + $2 500 + $5 000 + $200 = $16 700

Chargeable income = $48 000 − $16 700 = $31 300

Chargeable income		Tax
On the first	$20 000	$ 775.00
On the next	$11 300 at 8%	$ 904.00
	$31 300	$1 679.00

∴   Richard's income tax was $1 679.00

═══ Exercise 12j ═══

1. The annual value of a property is $12 300. Find the property tax payable for a period of 8 months at the rate of 16%.

2. Calculate the total amount of money a man has to pay for an article marked at $85 with a 14% value-added tax imposed on it.

3. How much has a customer to pay for an article costing $240 with a 3% GST imposed on it?

4. An article is advertised for $169.95 inclusive of a 3% GST. Find the original price.

(For questions 5 and 6, refer to Table 12.2)

5. Find the income tax of a tax payer if his chargeable income is

   (a) $3 000,   (b) $6 000,
   (c) $12 000,   (d) $18 000.

6. For parts (a) and (b), use the following information:

Reliefs: personal, $3 000; wife, $1 500; children, $1 500 each; handicapped children, $2 500 each; parent, $2 500.

   (a) A married man with three children, one of whom is handicapped, earned $24 400 last year. Given that his wife is not working and that he contributed $3 660 towards CPF as well as paid $720 on his life insurance policy, find the income tax he has to pay.

  ✳(b) Mr Huang earned $18 000 in 1998. He has two children, a wife and a mother to support. He contributed $2 700 towards CPF and $120 to a charitable organisation. He also paid $640 for his life insurance premium. Calculate the amount of income tax Mr Huang has to pay.

Problems Involving the Use of Tables and Charts

A lot of information is often organized and put together in the form of tables and charts. The following in-class activity gives you some practice at using and interpreting tables and charts.

In-Class Activity

You can carry out these activities on your own.

MRT Travel Times and Fares

Table 12.3 shows travel times in minutes between some MRT stations and station-to-station fares in cents. Travel times include station stop but exclude transfer and waiting times. For example, you have to pay 60 cents to travel from City Hall to Somerset and the travelling time is 3 minutes.

1. Use Table 12.3 to find the fare payable and the travel time from
   (a) Tampines to Raffles Place;   (b) City Hall to Tiong Bahru;
   (c) Dhoby Ghaut to City Hall;   (d) Pasir Ris to Redhill.

Fares in Cents

Travel Times in Minutes   *Table 12.3 (as of 1999)*

Stations (diagonal labels): W5 Queenstown, W4 Redhill, W3 Tiong Bahru, W2 Outram Park, W1 Tanjong Pagar, C1 Raffles Place, C2 City Hall, E1 Bugis, E2 Lavender, E3 Kallang, E4 Aljunied, E5 Paya Lebar, E6 Eunos, E7 Kembangan, E8 Bedok, E9 Tanah Merah, E10 Simei, E11 Tampines, E12 Pasir Ris, M1 Marina Bay, N1 Dhoby Ghaut, N2 Somerset, N3 Orchard, N4 Newton

2. A man left his home at 08 45 and arrived at Simei station 8 minutes later. Three minutes later, he boarded an MRT train and alighted at Orchard station. After half an hour, he boarded another MRT train with his friends at Orchard station to visit someone in Tiong Bahru. Two and one-quarter hours later, he boarded a train at Tiong Bahru station to return home. Using Table 12.3, calculate

(a) the man and his friends' arrival time at Tiong Bahru station;
(b) the man's arrival time at Simei station on his return journey;
(c) the man's total MRT train fare.

Postal Charges

The table below shows the local mail postage rates for letters, postcards, small packets and printed papers as well as their respective surface mail rates to different places of the world in July 1999:

Service	Weight Step Not Over	Singapore	Malaysia and Brunei Darussalam		Other foreign countries
Letters	20 g	22¢	20 g	35¢	40¢
	50 g	30¢	50 g	50¢	70¢
	100 g	50¢	100 g	80¢	$1.00
	250 g	80¢	every		
	500 g	$1.50	additional	70¢	90¢
			100 g		
Postcards		22¢	30¢		30¢
Small packets & Printed papers	20 g	22¢	20 g	30¢	40¢
	50 g	30¢	50 g	40¢	60¢
	100 g	40¢	100 g	70¢	90¢
	200 g	50¢	every		
	300 g	60¢	additional	60¢	80¢
	400 g	70¢	100 g		
	500 g	80¢			

Table 12.4

For example, it will cost

(i)   35¢ to send a letter weighing 20 g to Malaysia;
(ii) 90¢ + 80¢ or $1.70 to send a packet weighing 200 g to the United Kingdom;
(iii) 70¢ + 7 × 60¢ or $4.90 to send some magazines weighing 790 g to Brunei.

3. Use Table 12.4 to find the cost for mailing the following articles:
   (a) 2 postcards to Malaysia, 1 postcard to Brunei and 4 postcards to Hong Kong.
   (b) 8 magazines to the same address in Thailand, each weighing 120 g.
   (c) a shirt weighing 110 g and a pair of trousers weighing 660 g to Indonesia.
   (d) a packet of curry powder weighing 990 g to New Zealand.
   (e) a letter with photographs enclosed weighing 220 g to USA.
   (f) 6 letters each weighing 49 g: 2 to Tokyo, 3 to Kuala Lumpur and 1 to Manila.
   (g) 4 letters to a Singapore address each weighing 18 g and 3 letters to a Singapore address each weighing 150 g.

ABC Photocopying Services

Table 12.5 provides the operators of the photocopying services a quick reference to the charges (in cents) of photocopying work. For example, the charge for 37 copies of the photocopying work is 185 cents or $1.85.

1	10	11	77	21	105	31	155	41	205		
2	20	12	84	22	110	32	160	42	210		101 to 150 copies 3 cents each.
3	30	13	91	23	115	33	165	43	215		
4	40	14	98	24	120	34	170	44	220	51 to 100 copies $3\frac{1}{2}$ cents each	More than 150 copies 3 cents each plus 10% off the first 100 copies.
5	50	15	105	25	125	35	175	45	225		
6	60	16	112	26	130	36	180	46	230		
7	70	17	119	27	135	37	185	47	235		For more than 100 copies 3% GST is chargeable on the amount payable.
8	80	18	126	28	140	38	190	48	240		
9	90	19	133	29	145	39	195	49	245		
10	100	20	140	30	150	40	200	50	250		

Table 12.5

4. (a) From the above table, what is the charge per copy if the number of copies of the photocopying work is
   (i) from 11 to 20 inclusive,   (ii) from 21 to 50 inclusive?
   (b) Use the table to find the cost of the following photocopying work:
   (i) 7 copies;   (ii) 19 copies;   (iii) 42 copies;
   (iv) 68 copies;   (v) 124 copies;   (vi) 220 copies.
   (c) (i) Do you notice that the charge for 10 copies is enough to pay for 14 copies when the number of copies of photocopying work exceed 10?
       (ii) Similarly, the charge for 50 copies is enough to pay up to how many copies of photocopying work when the number of copies exceed 50?

Example 36

A housewife bought a piece of curtain material. She used $\frac{1}{3}$ of the material and 2 m more to make her first curtain. For her second curtain, she used up $\frac{1}{2}$ of the remaining material less 4 m. She used 8 m for her third curtain and had 5 m of the material left. Find the length of the curtain material she bought.

▼ **Solution**

Strategy 1: Use a diagram and work backwards

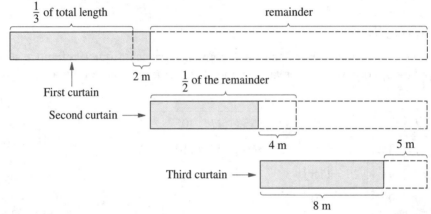

From the diagram (starting from the bottom):

(1) She had 8 + 5 = 13 m of the material remaining after making the second curtain.

(2) $\frac{1}{2}$ of the remaining = 13 − 4 = 9 m

∴ after making her first curtain, she had 2 × 9 = 18 m of the material left.

(3) $\frac{2}{3}$ of the total length of the material = 18 + 2 = 20 m.

∴ the length of curtain material the housewife bought = $20 \times \frac{3}{2} = 30$ m.

Strategy 2: Use an equation

Let x be the total length of the curtain material.

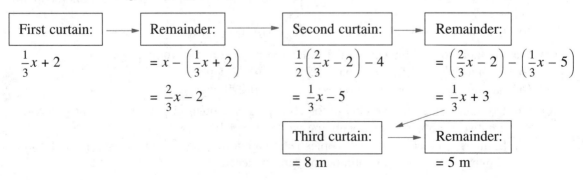

Hence, the remainder from the second curtain = length of third curtain + remainder of 5 m.

$$\therefore \quad \frac{1}{3}x + 3 = 8 + 5, \quad \frac{1}{3}x = 10 \quad \text{and} \quad x = 30 \text{ m}$$

Example 37

Su Mei, Li Li and Alvin each receives some sweets. Su Mei gives part of her sweets to Li Li and Alvin so that their respective number of sweets is doubled; Li Li gives part of her sweets to Alvin and Su Mei so that their respective number of sweets is doubled and Alvin also gives part of his sweets to Su Mei and Li Li so that their respective number of sweets is doubled. If all three of them eventually end up with 240 sweets, how many sweets did each of them receive originally?

▼ **Solution**

Sometimes, a combination of several heuristics is used to solve a problem. Example 37 makes use of three heuristics.

Strategy: Use tabulation, before-and-after comparison and work backwards

	Su Mei (S)	Li Li (L)	Alvin (A)
Original number of sweets	390	210	120
S ⟨ L / A	60	420	240
L ⟨ A / S	120	120	480
A ⟨ S / L	240	240	240

Note: A  indicates that Alvin gives part of his sweets to Su Mei and Li Li.

We can fill the table working from the bottom of the table.

(1) After Alvin has given part of his sweets to Su Mei and Li Li, each of them has 240 sweets (last line of the table).

(2) Before receiving sweets from Alvin,

Su Mei and Li Li each has $\frac{1}{2} \times 240 = 120$ sweets

Before giving sweets to Su Mei and Li Li,

Alvin has 240 + 120 + 120 = 480 sweets (second line from the bottom).

(3) Before receiving sweets from Li Li,

Su Mei has $\frac{1}{2} \times 120 = 60$ sweets and Alvin has $\frac{1}{2} \times 480 = 240$ sweets.

Before giving sweets to Su Mei and Alvin,

Li Li has $120 + 60 + 240 = 420$ sweets (third line from the bottom).

(4) Before receiving sweets from Su Mei,

Li Li has $\frac{1}{2} \times 420 = 210$ sweets and Alvin has $\frac{1}{2} \times 240 = 120$ sweets

Before giving sweets to Li Li and Alvin,

Su Mei has $60 + 210 + 120 = 390$ sweets.

Thus originally, Su Mei's number of sweets = 390, Li Li's number of sweets = 210, and Alvin's number of sweets = 120.

═══ Exercise 12k ═══

1. Wei Lin was trying a number trick on Edmond. She told him to choose a number, multiply it by 4, subtract 7 from the product, then add 11 and double the result. Edmond's final answer was 64. What number did he start with?

2. Mrs Yong bought some apples. She used 1 more than half of them for a pudding. She then used 1 more than half of the remainder for a pie. She gave 1 more than half of those that were left to her children and had 1 remaining. If she paid $4.40 for the apples, find the cost of 1 apple.

3. Forty eight marbles are divided into 3 groups. Then, some marbles are removed from the first group and put in the second group so that the number of marbles in the second group is doubled. Some marbles are removed from the second group and put in the third group so that the number of marbles in the third group is doubled and some marbles are removed from the third group and put in the first group so that the number of marbles in the first group is doubled. As a result, there are equal number of marbles in each group. Find the number of marbles in each group originally.

4. On a bus, 99 40-cent tickets and 80-cent tickets costing a total of $56 were issued. Find the difference between the number of 40-cent tickets and the number of 80-cent tickets issued.

5. In an examination consisting of 15 questions, 8 marks are awarded for a correct answer and 4 marks are deducted for a wrong answer. How many correct answers must one get to score 72 marks in this examination?

6. A durian seller sells half of his durians plus half a durian to his first customer. He then sells half of the remainder plus half a durian to his second customer, and half of the remainder plus half a durian to his third customer. He repeats the same process for the next customer and so on. After he has served the seventh customer, he finds that he has sold all his durians. How many durians had he originally?

1. A percentage is a fraction whose denominator is 100 and we use % to represent percent. A percentage can be converted to a fraction by dividing it by 100.

2. Profit = Selling price – Cost price, Loss = Cost price – Selling price

3. Discount = Original Selling price – Sale price

4. If the simple interest on $P for T years at R% per annum is I, then $I = \dfrac{PRT}{100}$.

5. Chargeable income = Total income – Reliefs

R e v i e w   Q u e s t i o n s   1 2

1. A school is given a 15% discount for buying textbooks in bulk. How much does the school have to pay for 110 books costing $10 each before the discount?

2. The profit made on a certain camera is 30% of the cost price. If the profit is $270, find
   (a) the cost price and
   (b) the selling price of the camera.

3. Yiwei receives $28 per week in pocket money. If she decides to save 20% of it, find how much she will
   (a) save and
   (b) spend in a year.

4. Calculate the simple interest on $5 640 invested for 7 months at 6% per annum.

5. Arrange 1.74, $1\dfrac{2}{3}$, 1.56, 173% and $1\dfrac{3}{4}$ in descending order.

6. Given that $0.7 : \dfrac{7}{8} = 7\% : x$, find x.

7. Given that a is 30% of b, find the value of $\dfrac{a}{4b}$, expressing your answer as a fraction in its lowest terms.

8. A bank offers two schemes of investment. Scheme A pays tax-free interest of 4%. Scheme B pays interest of 6% on which a tax of 20% has to be paid. A man has $5 000 to invest. Calculate his earnings under the two different schemes for 1 year.

9. A bank exchanges British currency for Singapore currency at the rate of S$2.30 to £1.
   (a) Calculate the amount of Singapore dollars that can be exchanged for £120.
   (b) Calculate, in £, the amount exchanged for S$1 600 by a customer who also had to pay an extra 3% commission for this transaction.

10. A fruit seller has 120 oranges. Given that he has 20% more apples than oranges and 40% less oranges than pears, find the number of apples and the number of pears the fruit seller has.

11. A shopkeeper sold two articles for $48 each. He made a 25% profit on one article and a loss of 20% on the other. What was his net gain or loss on the sale of the two articles?

12. Mr Chen and Miss Wang decided to buy a new car costing $60 000.

(a) Mr Chen paid for his new car in cash and was given a discount. Given that he paid $57 000 for his new car, calculate the percentage discount he received.

(b) Miss Wang agreed to pay 60% of the price of the car as a deposit and the balance at $3\frac{1}{2}\%$ simple interest per annum over a period of 3 years. Calculate the amount of each monthly instalment.

13. (a) After a company had paid $42\frac{1}{2}\%$ of the profit it had made as tax, $41 400 000 remained. Calculate the amount of the profit.

(b) Given that 26.9% of the profit remained after tax was set aside for further investment, calculate this amount set aside, correct to the nearest $100 000.

(c) If $26 496 000 was paid to share-holders, find what percentage this was of the $41 400 000 available.

∗14. (a) A retailer bought a compact disc from a manufacturer for $20. In addition to that, he paid a 15% value-added tax. If he sold the disc to a customer for $26, calculate the cash profit he made.

(b) The manufacturer later increased the price of the compact disc by 20%. At the same time, the value-added tax was increased to 25%.

(i) If the retailer made the same cash profit as before, calculate the price a customer had to pay for a disc.

(ii) Find the cash profit the retailer made on each disc if he sold each one at a price which was 30% more than the cost price.

Problem Solving

1. John accepted a reduction of 15% in his salary when his company was not doing well. Now his company's financial position has improved and his boss wants to restore his original salary. By what percentage must this reduced salary be increased?

2. The radius of a cylinder is increased by 15% and its height is decreased by 20%. Find the percentage change in the volume of the cylinder.

3. A man bought some articles at a discount of 25% of the list price. He set the marked price of each article such that after giving a discount of 20% of the marked price he still made a profit of $33\frac{1}{3}\%$ of the selling price. What percentage of the list price was his marked price?

4. Mr Sim instructed his assistant to place an order for 5 pairs of leather shoes and a number of pairs of canvas shoes. A pair of leather shoes costs two and a half times as much as a pair of canvas shoes. His assistant made a mistake in the order and the number of pairs of the two types of shoes had been inter-changed. This increased the bill by $33\frac{1}{3}\%$. Find the ratio of the number of pairs of canvas shoes to the number of pairs of leather shoes in the order that Mr Sim instructed his assistant to place.

5. Kelvin read 60 pages of a book on the first day. This was 20% more than the number of pages he read on the second day. Given that he read $\frac{1}{6}$ of the book on the second day, find the number of pages in the book he had read for both days.

Revision Exercise III No. 1

1. A shopkeeper bought a radio from a wholesaler for $25. In addition, he paid a value-added tax of 15% on the cost price. He then sold the radio for $31.50. Calculate the cash profit made by the shopkeeper.

2. A man walks at a rate of 1.25 m/s. Find the time he takes to walk 3.75 km.

3. Find the simple interest you will obtain if you deposit $600 in a bank for 9 months at $4\frac{1}{2}$% per annum.

4. Find the ratio of the weight of a Japanese car weighing 4 200 kg to that of a German car weighing 7 200 kg.

5. What is the difference in average wages between employing 18 men at a wage of $380 each and 33 women at a wage of $208 each?

6. A sum of money is distributed among 3 boys, A, B and C, in the ratio 2 : 4 : 14. If B gets $1.20 more than A, how much money does C get?

7. The figure shows a semicircle of radius 7 cm being enclosed in a rectangle of sides 14 cm by 12 cm. Calculate the area of the shaded region. $\left(\text{Take } \pi = \frac{22}{7}\right)$

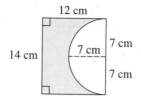

12 cm

14 cm

7 cm

7 cm

7 cm

8. It was projected that Singapore will need 1.2 million cubic metres of water daily at the turn of the 20th century. The Singapore Power (SP) planned to invest $900 million to build a desalination plant capable of producing 30 million gallons of water per day. If 1 gallon is equivalent to 4.5 litres,

   (a) how many m³ of water can the desalination plant produce per day?

   (b) how many desalination plants, correct to the nearest whole number, must be built if there are no other sources of water supply?

9. It took two and half years and 2.85 million m³ of earth to fill the disused Sin Seng quarry in Rifle Range Road. If each truck can carry 6.25 m³ of earth per trip, how many trips are needed to fill the quarry? If the cost of transport and material for each truck load is $45, how much would it cost for the transport and material?

10. The height of water inside a rectangular cuboid of length 8 cm and width 6 cm is $2\frac{1}{2}$ cm. This water is poured into an empty cylindrical tank of diameter 14 cm. Find the height of water in the cylinder. $\left(\text{Take } \pi = \frac{22}{7}\right)$

Revision Exercise III No. 2

1. A man earned an annual income of $24 500 in 1998. He was allowed a deduction of $1 500 relief for each of his three children and a personal relief of $3 000. If he was charged a tax rate of 4% on the first $5 000 and 6% on his remaining income, calculate the amount of tax he had to pay.

2. A bookseller bought 4 dozen books at $15.50 each. At what price was each book sold if his total profit was $240?

3. How many books costing $8.40 each can be bought with $200? How much money will then be left?

4. A man bought a car for $33 000. He made a first payment of $12 000 and borrowed the rest from a bank at 10% per annum simple interest. At the end of the first year, he repaid a certain sum to the bank after which he still owed the bank $9 000. Calculate the sum he repaid.

5. A car uses $27\frac{1}{2}$ litres of petrol for a journey of 220 km. How much petrol will it need to cover a distance of 680 km?

6. The volume of a rectangular box is 96 cm³ and its height is 4 cm. What is the area of its base? If the length of the base is 8 cm, find the width.

7. Find the total surface area and volume of a solid cylindrical block of diameter 28 cm and height 12 cm. $\left(\text{Take } \pi = \dfrac{22}{7} \right)$

8. Find the area of the shaded part in the figure below. If the figure represents the cross-section of a solid whose height is 7.5 cm, find the volume.

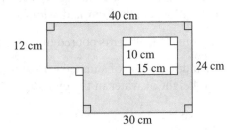

9. A pipe discharges 48 litres of water per minute into a rectangular tank of length 3.2 m and width 2.5 m. After 30 minutes, find the height of the water in the tank.

10. Carol deposits $800 in a bank that offers interest of 3% per annum. If the money and its interest are not withdrawn but allowed to compound annually, how much will she have at the end of 3 years? (Give your answer correct to the nearest cent.)

Revision Exercise III No. 3

1. (a) A shopkeeper sells an article for $250, thus making a profit of 25%. Find the cost price of the article.
(b) A new car cost $64 000. After one year its value depreciated by 20%. Find its value at the end of the first year.
(c) A man saves 20% of his income. What is his income if he spends $1 360 a month?

2. Two men, A and B, can paint a house in 8 days. A alone can paint it in 12 days. How long will B take to paint the house by himself?

3. Calculate the simple interest on $250 invested for 4 years at 8% per annum.

4. 784 marbles are shared among x, y and z in the ratio 3 : 5 : 8. How many marbles does each get?

5. Convert £53.35 to Malaysian ringgit if the exchange rate is M$5.95 to £1, giving your answer correct to the nearest ten cents.

6. Find the value of the following:
(a) 75% of $12;
(b) 3% of 40 kg;
(c) $8\dfrac{1}{2}$% of 200 m³;
(d) 45% of 500 km.

7. (a) A rectangular tank $1\dfrac{1}{2}$ m long and 88 cm wide contains water to a depth of 65 cm. The water is transferred to an empty rectangular tank 2 m long and 1 m wide. Find the depth of the water in centimetres.
(b) Find the total surface area and volume of a solid cylinder of diameter 14.6 cm and height 16.8 cm. If the density of the solid is 3.8 g/cm³, find its weight.
$\left(\text{Take } \pi = \dfrac{22}{7} \right)$

8. The figure shows a rectangle with a semi-circle on one of its sides. Calculate the perimeter and the area of the figure.
$\left(\text{Take } \pi = \dfrac{22}{7} \right)$

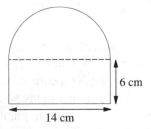

9. Find the volume of a solid of uniform cross-section with an area of 6.5 cm² and height, 24 cm. (Take π = 3.142)

10. (a) The perimeter of a rectangle is 24 cm and its length is twice its breadth. Find the area of the rectangle.

(b) A swimming pool is 50 m long and 20 m wide and its depth varies uniformly from 1 m to 3.5 m. Find the volume of the pool in cubic metres.

Revision Exercise III No. 4

1. A man buys 5 kg of beef at $12.50 per kg. In addition, for every kilogram of beef purchased, he has to pay a consumption tax of 6% on the selling price. Calculate the total amount of money that he has to pay.

2. The cash price of a television set is $940. However, it will cost more if it is bought by hire-purchase where a down payment of $160 and 24 equal monthly payments of $40 each have to be made. Find

(a) the extra cost involved if a man decides to buy it by hire-purchase;

(b) the difference between the hire-purchase price and the cash price as a percentage of the cash price.

3. There are 31 sweets to be shared among 3 boys, *A*, *B* and *C*. *A* has 2 sweets more than *B* and *B* receives 1 more than *C*. How many sweets does each receive?

4. The driver of a car 3 m long took 5 seconds to drive through a tunnel 44 m long. Find the average speed of the car in km per hour.

5. A man bought 400 dozen pencils at $0.80 a dozen. He sold half of them at $1.05 a dozen and the rest at $0.75 a dozen. Find his profit.

6. Mr Rajoo puts $4 500 in an insurance trust that offers 5.5% interest. If he does not make any withdrawals and the money and interest in the trust is allowed to compound annually, how much will he have at the end of 3 years? Give your answer correct to the nearest cent.

7. Find the area of the figures below.

(a)

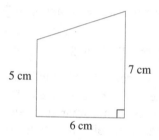

(b)

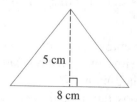

8. The height of water in a cylinder of radius 12 cm is 28 cm. This water is transferred into a rectangular cuboid of length 24 cm, width 18 cm and height 40 cm. Find the height of water level in the rectangular cuboid. $\left(\text{Take } \pi = \dfrac{22}{7} \right)$

9. Find the area of the cross-section of the metal plate shown in the figure. If its thickness is 1.5 cm, find the volume.

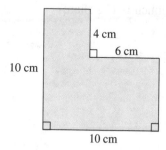

10. A rectangular tank measured internally is 2.5 m long, 1.5 m wide and 0.8 m high. How many litres of water are needed to fill the tank? The water in the tank is transferred into small cylindrical tanks each of diameter 70 cm and height 40 cm. Find the number of complete cylindrical tanks that can be filled. $\left(\text{Take } \pi = \dfrac{22}{7} \right)$

Revision Exercise III No. 5

1. **(a)** Given that $p = \dfrac{1}{4}$ and $q = \dfrac{2}{7}$, express $\dfrac{p}{q}$ as a percentage.

   (b) A school has 750 pupils and 32% of them wear spectacles. How many pupils do not wear spectacles?

   (c) If a man sells an article for $15, he would make a loss of 25%. How much must he sell it in order to make a profit of 5%?

2. **(a)** The average speed of a car is 108 km/h. How many metres can the car travel in 3 minutes?

   (b) At a book fair, a book was reduced in price from $7.50 to $6.00. If the first price gives a 50% profit, find the percentage profit of the book sold at the reduced price.

3. A shopkeeper buys a flower vase for $60 and prices it at $85. Find the cash price a customer has to pay if the shopkeeper gives him a 5% discount when he pays cash. Find also the percentage profit made by the shopkeeper.

4. A, B and C share a sum of money in the ratio $3 : 4 : 9$. If B has $2.80 more than A, how much is C's share?

5. **(a)** If I sold my car for $8 400, I would lose 25%. How much did I pay for my car?

   (b) A man bought a house for $327 500 and sold it at a gain of 12%. Find the gain.

6. The volume of a rectangular block is 720 cm³. Find its height if the area of the base is 60 cm².

7. Find the total surface area of a cube of side 6 cm.

8. If the area of a parallelogram is 32.8 cm² and the height between the two parallel sides is 16.4 cm, calculate the length of the base.

9. Mrs Li has 2 m of cake frill. She uses it for trimming a square cake of side 20 cm and the circumference of a round cake of diameter 28 cm. How much of the cake trimming is left over? $\left(\text{Take } \pi = \dfrac{22}{7} \right)$

10. 2.8 litres of paint of density 1.8 g/cm³ is mixed with 2.2 litres of turpentine of density 0.9 g/cm³. Find the mass and density of the mixture.

13

Basic Geometrical Concepts and Properties

In this chapter, you will learn how to

▲ identify various plane polygons and some simple solid figures;
▲ calculate unknown angles involving adjacent angles on a straight line, vertically opposite angles, angles at a point, alternate angles, corresponding angles and interior angles between parallel lines;
▲ draw parallel and perpendicular lines;
▲ construct angle bisectors and perpendicular bisectors.

Preliminary Problem

Many sports involve the effective use of angles. This billiard player needs to have a good judgement of angles when hitting the balls to score points.

Points

The basic geometric figure is a **point**. All other geometric figures are made up of a collection of points. The smallest dot you can mark on your paper with a sharp pencil will give you an idea of what is meant by a geometric point. A point is only an idea in our mind; it is not a physical object and we regard it as having a position but not size or shape. We use a dot or sometimes a cross to mark the position of a point. We normally use capital letters to name points. Thus we speak of point *A*, point *B*, point *C*, etc.

The word "geometry" is derived from the Greek words "ge" (earth) and "metrein" (to measure). Euclid's masterpiece, "The Elements", survived as the basic textbook for over 2 000 years. The geometry that we are to study in this book is sometimes referred to as Euclidean geometry.

$A^{\bullet}$ $_{\bullet}B$ $C^{\bullet}$

Lines

A **line** is the path described by a moving point. A straight **line segment** is formed when we use a ruler to join two points, say, *A* and *B*.

$A \bullet\!\!-\!\!-\!\!-\!\!-\!\!-\!\!-\!\!-\!\!-\!\!-\!\!-\!\!-\!\!-\!\!-\!\!-\!\!-\!\!\bullet B$

We call the line segment *AB* or *BA*. *A* and *B* are called the end-points. If we extend the line segment *AB* in each of the two directions indefinitely, we get a **line**. This is represented by the following diagram.

A B

The diagrams on the right show parts of lines with only one end-point and extending in only one direction. We call them **rays**.

Thus we have ray *XY*, ray *HK* and ray *PQ*.

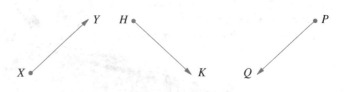

A line is either straight or curved. The diagram shows a curved line. A curved line is also called a **curve**.

a curved line

In this book, when we speak of a line, it refers to a straight line whereas a curve refers to a curved line. Also, we shall simply use *AB* to denote **line *AB*, line segment *AB*, ray *AB*** and the **length of *AB***.

Planes

A **plane** is a flat surface in which any two points are joined by a straight line lying entirely on the surface. The floor of a classroom is an example of a **horizontal plane** and the wall of a classroom is an example of a **vertical plane**.

Solids

A **solid** is a three-dimensional shape or object. The box shown in Fig. 13.1 has six flat surfaces of equal size and each surface is part of a plane. We call this solid figure a **cube**. The box shown in Fig. 13.2 has six flat surfaces of three different sizes. We call this solid figure a **cuboid**.

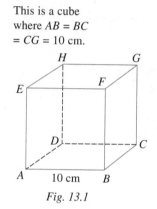

This is a cube where $AB = BC$ = CG = 10 cm.

Fig. 13.1

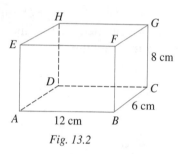

This is a cuboid where $AB = 12$ cm, $BC = 6$ cm and $CG = 8$ cm.

Fig. 13.2

Fig. 13.3 shows a **pyramid** which has five flat surfaces. Each surface is part of a plane. Fig. 13.4 shows a prism with five flat surfaces. Each surface forms part of a plane. Fig. 13.5 is an example of a prism with seven flat surfaces.

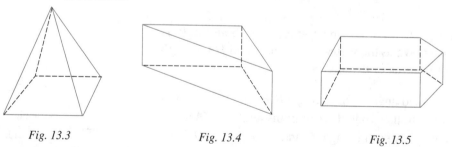

Fig. 13.3   Fig. 13.4   Fig. 13.5

Can you show a net of each of the above solids?

Curved Surfaces

A surface which is not flat does not form part of a plane. Such a surface is called a **curved surface**. For example, the surface of a basketball is a curved surface. The basketball is an example of a **sphere** (Fig. 13.6).

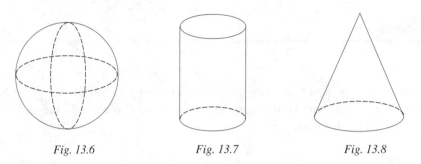

Fig. 13.6	*Fig. 13.7*	*Fig. 13.8*

Fig. 13.7 shows a solid figure which has two flat surfaces and a curved surface. It is called a cylindrical solid figure, or a **cylinder**.

A **cone** has only one flat surface and a curved surface (Fig. 13.8).

Intersecting Lines

Fig. 13.9 shows two lines, *AB* and *PQ*, on the same plane having a common point *X*. We say that the two lines **intersect** at *X*. Point *X* is called the **point of intersection**.

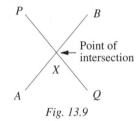

Fig. 13.9

Angles

When two rays *OA* and *OB* meet at a point *O*, an **angle** is formed. *O* is known as the vertex of the angle and *OA* and *OB* are the sides or arms of the angles.

The angle is called angle *AOB* or angle *BOA* and is written as *AÔB* or *BÔA*. Another way of writing this angle is $\angle AOB$ or $\angle BOA$. We may also call it angle *O* and write *Ô* or $\angle O$ when it is clear which angle we are referring to.

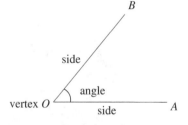

The Protractor and Angle Measure

The standard unit for measuring angles is one degree (written as 1°). It is defined as $\frac{1}{360}$ of a complete revolution. By definition, one complete rotation about a point has an angle of 360°.

How many different angles are there in the figure?

Fig. 13.10 shows a protractor which is used to measure angles. To measure an angle, place the protractor so that its centre A is at the vertex of the angle and its base AB along one side of the angle. Note under which graduation mark the other side passes. Thus, in Fig. 13.11(a), the angle x is 60°. Fig. 13.11(b) shows another way of measuring the angle.

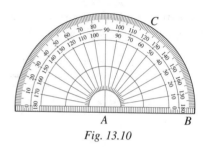

Fig. 13.10

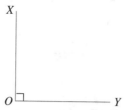

(a)

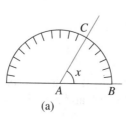

(b)

Fig. 13.11

Notice that the graduation marks on the protractor are marked with two sets of numbers, one greater than 90° and the other less than 90°. Hence, when using the protractor, use your common sense to choose the correct set of numbers. For example, if one arm of the angle to be measured lies along AB, the set of numbers to be used is the one in which the numbers increase as you read the graduations from AB towards AC.

Different Kinds of Angles

An **acute angle** is less than 90°.

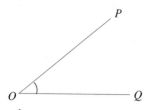

$P\hat{O}Q$ is an acute angle.

An **obtuse angle** is larger than 90° but less than 180°.

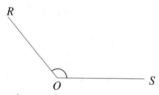

$R\hat{O}S$ is an obtuse angle.

A **right angle** is equal to 90°.

$X\hat{O}Y$ is a right angle.

A **straight angle** is equal to 180°.

180°

A ————————————— B
            O

$A\hat{O}B$ is a straight angle.

Can you name the angles formed by each of the following objects found in everyday life?

Look around your surroundings to see other examples of angles formed by everyday objects and instruments.

A **reflex angle** is larger than 180° but less than 360°. Both $A\hat{O}B$ and $C\hat{O}D$ are reflex angles.

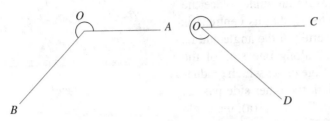

Complementary Angles

Two angles are called **complementary angles** if their **sum** is **90°**. The angles 28° and 62° are said to be complementary and so are the angles 40° and 50°, 30° and 60°, etc.

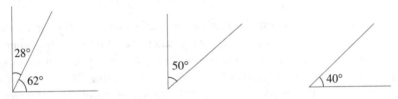

Supplementary Angles

Two angles are called **supplementary angles** if their **sum** is **180°**. The angles 45° and 135° are supplementary angles and so are 53° and 127°, 105° and 75°, etc.

Adjacent Angles on a Line

In Fig. 13.12, $X\hat{O}Z$ and $Y\hat{O}Z$ are called **adjacent angles** because

(a) they have a common vertex O,
(b) they have a common side OZ and
(c) they lie on opposite sides of the common arm.

The sum of adjacent angles on a line is equal to 180°.
(Abbreviation for reference: **adj. ∠s on a line.**)

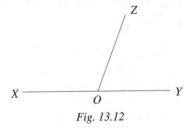

Fig. 13.12

To Construct an Angle Using a Protractor

Using the same method construct angles of sizes 35°, 83°, 110° and 165°.

Suppose you have a line *XY* and wish to construct angle *YXZ* of 64°. Place a protractor such that its centre is at *X* and its base is along *XY* as shown in Fig. 13.13(a). Make the 64° graduation with your sharp pencil and label it *Z*. Join *Z* to *X* and we have $X\hat{Y}Z = 64°$ (Fig. 13.13(b)).

Method: Use a protractor

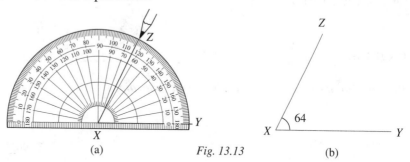

(a)   Fig. 13.13   (b)

Example 1

Find the values of a, b and c in the following diagrams:

(a)   (b)   (c)

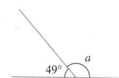 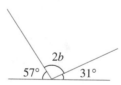 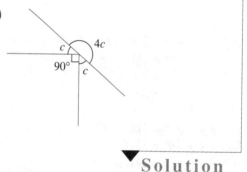

▼ **Solution**

(a) $49° + a = 180°$ (adj. ∠s on a line)
   ∴ $a = 180° - 49° = 131°$

(b) $57° + 2b + 31° = 180°$ (adj. ∠s on a line)
        $2b = 180° - 57° - 31° = 92°$
   ∴ $b = 46°$

(c) $90° + c + c + 4c = 360°$ (angles at a point)
         $6c = 270°$
   ∴ $c = 45°$

Vertically Opposite Angles

Vertically opposite angles are formed when two straight lines intersect each other. The angles *BOC* and *AOD* in Fig. 13.14 are said to be vertically opposite. The angles *AOC* and *BOD* are also vertically opposite each other. We shall prove that vertically opposite angles are equal.

With the notation in Fig. 13.14,

$$a + b = 180° \quad \text{(adj. } \angle \text{s on a line)}$$
$$b + c = 180° \quad \text{(adj. } \angle \text{s on a line)}$$
$$a + b = b + c$$
$$a = c$$

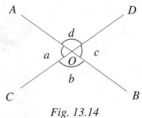

Fig. 13.14

Similarly, we can also show that $b = d$. Hence, **vertically opposite angles are equal**. (Abbreviation for reference: **vert. opp. $\angle$s.**)

Example 2

Find the values of x, y and z in the given diagram.

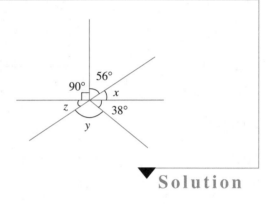

▼ **Solution**

$$90° + 56° + x = 180° \text{ (adj. } \angle \text{s on a line)}$$
$$\therefore \quad x = 180° - 90° - 56° = 34°$$
$$z = x = 34° \text{ (vert. opp. } \angle \text{s)}$$
$$\therefore \quad z = 34°$$

$$z + y + 38° = 180° \text{ (adj. } \angle \text{s on a line)}$$
$$34° + y + 38° = 180°$$
$$\therefore \quad y = 180° - 38° - 34°$$
$$= 108°$$

═══ Exercise 13a ═══

1. Give two examples of each of the following simple solids:

    (a) cube   (b) cuboid   (c) prism
    (d) cylinder   (e) pyramid   (f) cone
    (g) sphere

2. What shape is each of the following solids? Make a sketch of each:

    (a) a tennis ball   (b) a can of milk
    (c) a compact disc   (d) a tent
    (e) a heap of sand
    (f) the end of a sharpened pencil

3. Measure the angles marked in the following diagrams to the nearest degree:

    (a)   (b)

    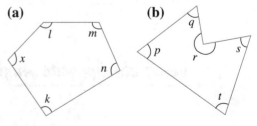

4. Name and measure each of the marked angles:

(a)

(b)

(c)

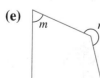

(d)

(e)

(f)

5. Find the measure of the complementary angle of each of the following angles:

(a) 18°   (b) 46°   (c) 53°
(d) 64°   (e) 7°

6. Find the measure of the supplementary angle of each of the following angles:

(a) 36°   (b) 12°   (c) 102°
(d) 171°   (e) 88°

7. Use a protractor to draw the following angles:

(a) 20°   (b) 157°   (c) 197°
(d) 242°   (e) 320°   (f) 285°

8. Refer to the figure on the right in which XOY is a straight line, and answer the following questions:

(a) Find a, given that $b = 45°$ and $c = 86°$.

(b) Find a, given that $b = 2a$ and $c = 3a$.

(c) Find b, given that $a + c = b$.

(d) Find c, given that $a = b = c$.

9. Using the figure on the right, find y in each of the following cases:

(a) If $a = 2y°$ and $c = (y + 30)°$.

(b) If $a = (3y + 40)°$ and $c = (y + 60°)$.

(c) If $a = (10y - 20)°$ and $c = (6y + 16)°$.

(d) If $a = y°$ and $b = 2y°$.

(e) If $b = (y + 30)°$ and $d = (4y + 16)°$.

10. In the diagram given,

(a) write an equation involving a and d;

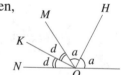

(b) find the value of $H\hat{O}K$;

(c) if $d = 25°$, find a.

11. In the diagram below, $A\hat{O}B = p°$. If $B\hat{O}C$ is two times $A\hat{O}B$, $C\hat{O}D$ is four times $A\hat{O}B$ and $D\hat{O}A$ is five times $A\hat{O}B$, find the values of all the four angles.

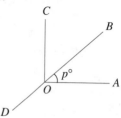

12. Calculate the unknown(s) in each of the following:

(a)

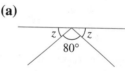

(b)

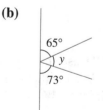

(c)

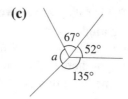

(d)

(e)

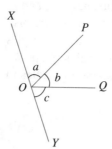

(f)

(g)

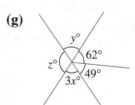

(h)

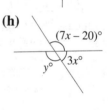

(i)

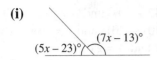
$(5x - 23)°$ $(7x - 13)°$

(j)

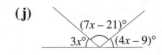
$(7x - 21)°$
$3x°$ $(4x - 9)°$

Parallel Lines

Parallel lines are lines which extend in the same direction and remain the same distance apart. We can take parallel lines as two points moving in the same direction. In geometry, a pair of parallel lines is represented by either a pair of single or double arrows (Fig. 13.15).

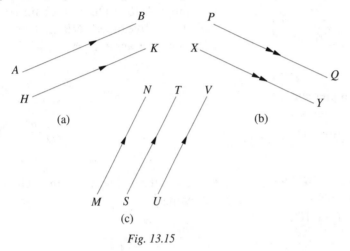

(a)

(b)

(c)

Fig. 13.15

We use the symbol "//" to represent "is parallel to". Thus, in Fig. 13.15(a), $AB//HK$ means that AB is parallel to HK and in Fig. 13.15(b), $XY//PQ$. In Fig. 13.15(c), $MN//ST$ and $ST//UV$. This also implies that $MN//UV$.

In Fig. 13.16, the line PQ is called a **transversal**. The angles k_1 and k_2 are called **corresponding angles (corr. ∠s)**. Similarly, l_1 and l_2 are also called corresponding angles. Use your protractor to measure the angles k_1, k_2, l_1 and l_2. What do you notice about the size of angles k_1 and k_2, and l_1 and l_2? Can you name two other pairs of corresponding angles in Fig. 13.16?

Fig. 13.16

Fig. 13.17 shows two parallel lines AB and CD cut by a transversal PQ. The angles a_1 and a_2 are called **alternate angles (alt. ∠s)**. Similarly, b_1 and b_2 are also called alternate angles. Use a protractor to measure the angles a_1, a_2, b_1 and b_2. What do you notice about the size of angles a_1 and a_2, and b_1 and b_2?

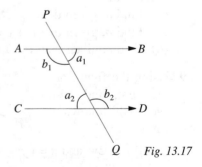

Fig. 13.17

Fig. 13.18 shows two parallel lines *AB* and *XY* cut by a transversal *PQ*. The angles *a* and *b* are called **interior angles**. The angles *x* and *y* are also interior angles. Use your protractor to measure the angles *a*, *b*, *x* and *y*. Find the value of $(a + b)$ and of $(x + y)$. Are the interior angles supplementary?

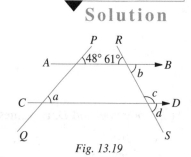

Fig. 13.18

We can conclude from the above discussion that when two parallel lines are cut by a transversal,

> 1. **the corresponding angles are equal;**
> 2. **the alternate angles are equal;**
> 3. **the interior angles are supplementary.**

The converse statements for the above are also true. That is, when two straight lines are cut by a transversal, and

> 1. **if the corresponding angles are equal, then the two lines are parallel;**
> 2. **if the alternate angles are equal, then the two lines are parallel;**
> 3. **if the interior angles are supplementary, then the two lines are parallel.**

Which of the following pairs of lines are parallel?

(a)

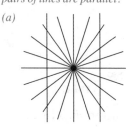

(b)

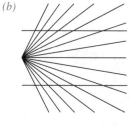

(c)

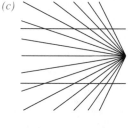

Example 3

Calculate the unknowns in Fig. 13.19.

Solution

$$a = 48° \qquad \text{(corr. } \angle\text{s, } AB//CD\text{)}$$
$$b = 61° \qquad \text{(vert. opp. } \angle\text{s)}$$
$$d = b = 61° \qquad \text{(corr. } \angle\text{s, } AB//CD\text{)}$$
$$b + c = 180° \qquad \text{(interior } \angle\text{s)}$$
$$c = 180° - 61° = 119°$$

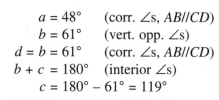

Fig. 13.19

Example 4

Find the unknowns in Fig. 13.20.

Solution

$$i + 30° = 69° \quad \text{(corr. } \angle\text{s, } OA//BC\text{)}$$
$$i = 69° - 30° = 39°$$
$$j = i \qquad \text{(corr. } \angle\text{s, } OA//BC\text{)}$$
$$j = 39°$$

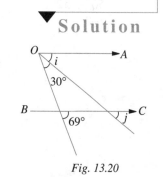

Fig. 13.20

Example 5

Find the values of f, g and h in Fig. 13.21.

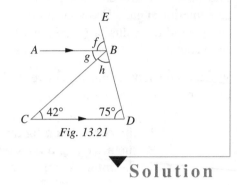

Fig. 13.21

Solution

$$g = 42° \quad \text{(alt. ∠s, } AB//CD)$$
$$f = 75° \quad \text{(corr. ∠s, } AB//CD)$$
$$f + g + h = 180° \quad \text{(adj. ∠s on a line)}$$
$$h = 180° - 42° - 75°$$
$$= 63°$$

Example 6

Find the value of x in Fig. 13.22.

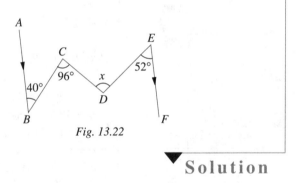

Fig. 13.22

Solution

At the points C and D, two lines both parallel to AB and EF are drawn as shown in Fig. 13.23.

$$y_1 = 40° \quad \text{(alt. ∠s, } AB//PQ)$$
$$\therefore \quad y_2 = 96° - 40°$$
$$= 56°$$
$$y_2 = y_3 = 56° \quad \text{(alt. ∠s, } PQ//RS)$$
$$y_4 = 52° \quad \text{(alt. ∠s, } RS//EF)$$
$$\therefore \quad x = y_3 + y_4$$
$$= 56° + 52°$$
$$= 108°$$

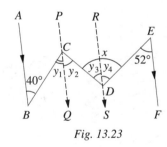

Fig. 13.23

Exercise 13b

1. From the diagram below, list
   (a) three pairs of corresponding angles;
   (b) three pairs of alternate angles.

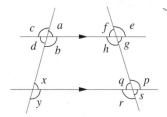

2. Refer to the diagram in Question 1. If $a = 73°$ and $e = 106°$, find the values of p, q, r, s, x and y.

3. Calculate the unknown(s) in the following diagrams:

(a) (b)

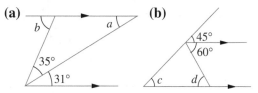

(c) (d)

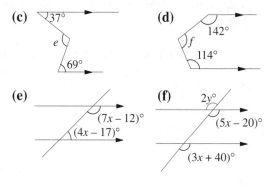

(e) (f)

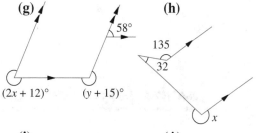

(g) (h)

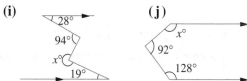

(i) (j)

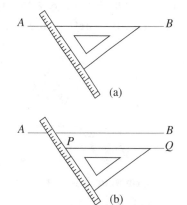

Drawing Parallel Lines Using a Set-square and a Ruler

Given: A straight line AB.

To construct: A line parallel to AB.

Construction steps:

(1) Place the set square on the line AB and place the ruler as shown in Fig. 13.24(a).

(2) By moving the set square along the length of the ruler, we can draw lines parallel to AB.

For example, by moving the set square down against the ruler, we can draw a line PQ parallel to AB (see Fig. 13.24(b)).

Fig. 13.24

Perpendicular Lines

Two lines which are at right angles to each other are said to be **perpendicular** to each other. We use the symbol "$AB \perp PQ$" to denote "AB is perpendicular to PQ".

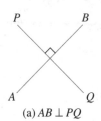
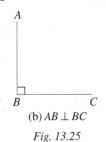
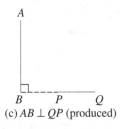

(a) $AB \perp PQ$ (b) $AB \perp BC$ (c) $AB \perp QP$ (produced)

Fig. 13.25

Geometers Sketch Pad (GSP) is a powerful tool to do geometrical constructions. Find out how you can draw (a) perpendicular lines, (b) parallel lines, (c) circles, (d) angle bisectors and (e) perpendicular bisectors using GSP.

Drawing Perpendicular Lines Using a Set-square and a Ruler

(a) **Given:** A point K on a line AB.

To construct: A line through K perpendicular to AB.

(i)
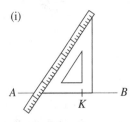

(ii)
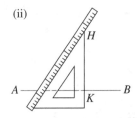

Fig. 13.26

Construction steps:

(1) Place the set-square on the line AB and place the ruler as shown in Fig. 13.26(i).

(2) Slide the set square along the length of the ruler until the other edge of the set square passes through K. Draw HK as shown in Fig. 13.26(ii). We write $AB \perp HK$.

(b) **Given:** A point K which is not on the line AB.

To construct: A line through K perpendicular to AB.

(i)
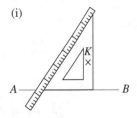

(ii)
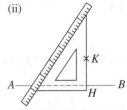

(iii)
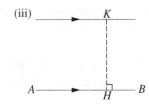

Fig. 13.27

Construction steps:

(1) Place one edge of the set square on AB as shown in Fig. 13.27(i).

(2) Slide the set square along the length of the ruler until the other edge passes through *K*. Draw *HK* as shown in Fig. 13.27(ii). We write $HK \perp AB$.

Note: The length of *KH* gives the distance of the point *K* to the line *AB*. In addition, if we draw a line passing through *K* and parallel to *AB*, *KH* also gives the distance between the two parallel lines.

Use of Compasses

A pair of **compasses** is a mathematical instrument often used for drawing circles, marking off lengths and measuring the length of a line segment.

drawing a circle   measuring a line segment

The following explains how to use a compass.

To mark off a length equal to *AB* on the line *PQ*, i.e., *HK*:

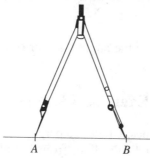
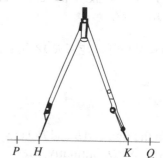

Construction steps:

(1) Adjust the arms of the compasses until they touch *AB*.
(2) Mark a point *H* on another line, *PQ*.
(3) With *H* as centre and radius *AB*, draw an arc to cut *PQ* at *K*. Hence, *AB = HK*.

In-Class Activity

You can create designs with your pair of compasses. Some of these designs are shown below. Try to create other designs of your own.

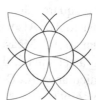

Perpendicular Bisector and Angle Bisector

Given: A straight line *PQ*.

To construct: A perpendicular bisector of a given line segment.

Construction steps:

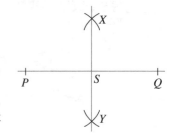

(1) Taking *P* and *Q* as centres and a radius greater than half of *PQ*, draw arcs above and below *PQ* such that the arcs cut each other at *X* and *Y*.

(2) Join *XY* to cut *PQ* at *S*. *XY* is called the **perpendicular bisector** of *PQ*. If you measure *PS* and *SQ*, you will find that *PS = SQ*. Thus, *S* is called the **midpoint** of *PQ*.

Given: An angle *PQR*.

To construct: The angle bisector of a given angle.

Construction steps:

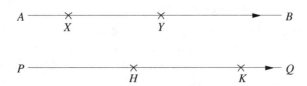

(1) Taking *Q* as centre and a fixed radius, cut *QP* at *X* and *QR* at *Y*.

(2) Taking *X* and *Y* as centres and the same radius, draw arcs to cut each other at *Z*.

(3) Join *QZ*.

You will find $P\hat{Q}Z = R\hat{Q}Z$ and hence *QZ* is the angle bisector of $P\hat{Q}R$.

⚍ Exercise 13c ⚍

1. In the figure, *AB* and *PQ* are parallel lines. Draw two perpendicular lines from points *X* and *Y*, on *AB*, to *PQ*. Similarly, draw two perpendicular lines from *H* and *K* to *AB*.

A ——✕——————————✕————————————▶ B
       X   Y

P ————————————✕————————✕——▶ Q
                H   K

Measure the lengths of these perpendicular lines. What do you notice about their lengths?

2. Draw the following triangle *ABC* with the given dimensions accurately and measure the angles marked *a* and *b*.

Using a set square, draw a line from *C* touching *AB* and perpendicular to *AB*. Also, draw a line from *B* touching *AC* and perpendicular to *AC*. Measure the length of these perpendicular lines. Using a set square, draw the line through *A* touching *BC* and perpendicular to *BC*. Do these three perpendicular lines meet at the same point?

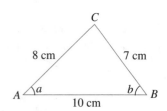

3. Draw the triangle *ABC* with the given dimensions accurately. Measure *AC* and *BC*.

   Using a pair of compasses, construct the angle bisectors of $B\hat{A}C$, $A\hat{B}C$ and $A\hat{C}B$. Do the angle bisectors meet at the same point?

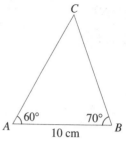

4. Draw a line *PQ* of length 8 cm. Construct the perpendicular bisector of *PQ*.

5. Draw an angle *ABC* of 78°. Construct the bisector of $A\hat{B}C$.

6. Draw the diagram shown accurately. Measure *HK*.

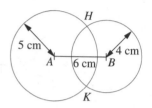

Summary

1. The **sum of all the angles at a point** is 360°.

2. The **sum of adjacent angles** on a straight line is 180°.

3. Fig. 13.28 shows two parallel lines, *AB* and *CD*, with a transversal *PQ*.
   - **(a)** *x* and *y* are **vertically opposite angles** and are equal in size.
   - **(b)** *x* and *q* are **corresponding angles** and are equal in size.
   - **(c)** *e* and *b* are **alternate angles** and are equal in size.
   - **(d)** *e* and *y* are **interior angles**. Their sum is equal to 180°.

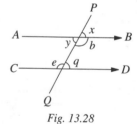

Fig. 13.28

Review Questions 13

1. Find the value of the unknown(s) in each of the following:

   (a)

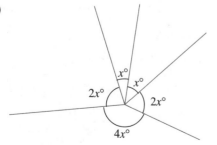

   (b)

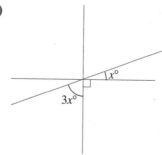

(c)

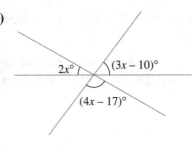

$y°$
$28°$ $70°$
$(3x - 5)°$

(d)

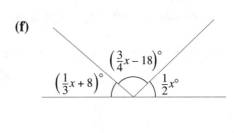

$2x°$ $(3x - 10)°$
$(4x - 17)°$

(e)

$4x°$ $84°$
$32°$
$2y°$

(f)

$\left(\frac{3}{4}x - 18\right)°$
$\left(\frac{1}{3}x + 8\right)°$ $\frac{1}{2}x°$

(g)

$(x + 15)°$
$(0.5x + 14)°$ $(0.2x + 15)°$

(h)

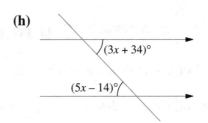

$(3x + 34)°$
$(5x - 14)°$

(i)

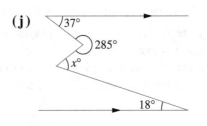

$(5x - 15)°$
$(75 - x)°$

(j)

$37°$
$285°$
$x°$
$18°$

(k)

$y°$
$x°$ $316°$
$58°$

(l)

$122°$
$123°$ $x°$

(m)

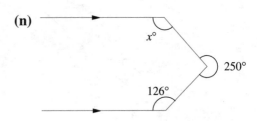

$122°$
$88°$
$x°$

(n)

$x°$
$250°$
$126°$

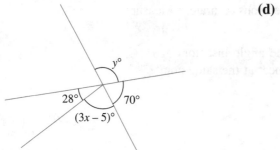
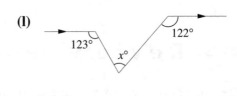

1. Draw the triangle PQR accurately. Measure $P\hat{Q}R$ and $R\hat{P}Q$. Using a pair of compasses, construct the angle bisectors of $P\hat{Q}R$ and $R\hat{P}Q$. Let the two lines meet at X. Measure the length of PX and RX. What is the distance of X from PQ? With X as centre, construct a circle to touch PQ, PR and QR.

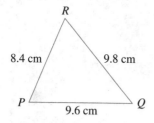

2. Construct triangle ABC such that $AB = 12$ cm, $BC = 11$ cm and $AC = 9.6$ cm. Construct the perpendicular bisectors of AB and BC. Let the two bisectors meet at K. With K as centre, construct a circle to pass through A, B and C. Find out the name of this circle from your library.

3. Draw the given quadrilateral $ABCD$ accurately. Construct a line parallel to AB and passing through D. Produce this line to cut BC at X. Measure DX and BX.

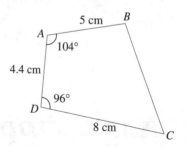

4. In the figure, $B\hat{A}C = a°$, $A\hat{C}D = b°$, $C\hat{D}F = c°$ and $D\hat{F}E = d°$. Form an equation connecting a, b, c and d.

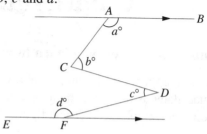

5. In the figure, AB is parallel to XY, $A\hat{B}P = a°$, $B\hat{P}Q = b°$, $P\hat{Q}Y = x°$ and $X\hat{Y}Q = c°$. Express x in terms of a, b and c.

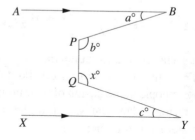

14

Angle Properties of Triangles and Quadrilaterals

In this chapter, you will learn how to

▲ calculate the unknown angles involving triangles and quadrilaterals using the angle properties of these figures;

▲ construct simple geometrical figures from given information.

Preliminary Problem

Triangles and quadrilaterals are common designs well-liked by people in the design of their houses and exteriors. Can you see triangles and quadrilaterals in this picture?

Polygons

A plane figure with three or more straight edges as its sides is called a **polygon**. Each polygon is named after the number of sides it contains. The following names are given to some common polygons.

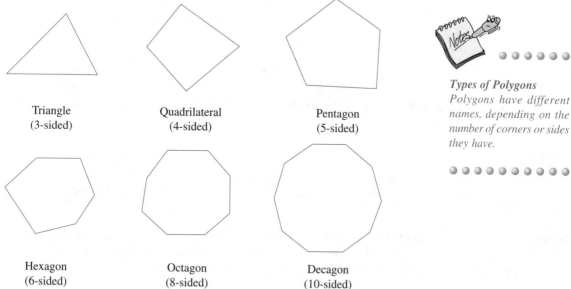

Triangle
(3-sided)

Quadrilateral
(4-sided)

Pentagon
(5-sided)

Hexagon
(6-sided)

Octagon
(8-sided)

Decagon
(10-sided)

Types of Polygons
Polygons have different names, depending on the number of corners or sides they have.

In general, a polygon with n sides is called an n-gon. Thus a polygon with 12 sides is called a 12-gon and a polygon with 25 sides is called a 25-gon. A **regular polygon** is one in which all its sides and all its angles are equal. The following figures are some examples of regular polygons.

In this chapter, you will learn about properties of triangles and quadrilaterals.

Triangles

A plane figure formed by having three straight edges as its sides is called a **triangle**

Fig. 14.1 shows a triangle *ABC,* which can be denoted by $\triangle ABC$, formed by the three sides *AB*, *BC* and *CA*. The points *A*, *B* and *C* are called the vertices (singular: vertex) of the triangle. $\angle ABC$, $\angle BAC$ and $\angle BCA$ are called the interior angles of the triangle, or simply the angles of $\triangle ABC$.

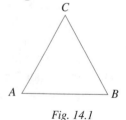

Fig. 14.1

Triangles can be classified according to:

(a) The number of equal sides

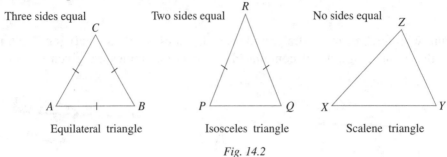

Three sides equal   Two sides equal   No sides equal

Equilateral triangle   Isosceles triangle   Scalene triangle

Fig. 14.2

(b) The types of angles

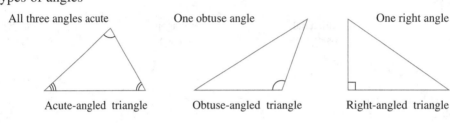

All three angles acute   One obtuse angle   One right angle

Acute-angled triangle   Obtuse-angled triangle   Right-angled triangle

Fig. 14.3

Notes: (1) All the three angles in an equilateral triangle are equal in size. Each angle is 60°.
(2) The two base angles of an isosceles triangle are equal, i.e., $\angle RPQ = \angle RQP$.
(3) All the three angles in a scalene triangle are different in size.

Construction of Triangles

To construct a triangle accurately, we use a pair of compasses, a ruler and a protractor. However, not all three instruments are often used at the same time.

Example 1

Construct $\triangle ABC$ in which $AB = 10$ cm, $BC = 6$ cm and $AC = 8$ cm. Measure $\angle ABC$, $\angle BCA$ and $\angle BAC$. What is the sum of the three angles? What type of triangle is this?

▼ **Solution**

Construction steps:

(1) Draw a line segment AB of length 10 cm.
(2) With A as centre, draw an arc of radius 8 cm with a pair of compasses.
(3) With B as centre, draw an arc of radius 6 cm to cut the first arc at C.
(4) Join AC and BC. $\triangle ABC$ is the required triangle.

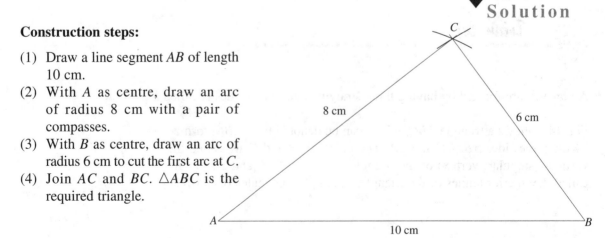

By measurement with a protractor, $\angle ABC \approx 53°$, $\angle BAC \approx 37°$ and $\angle ACB \approx 90°$. The sum of the three angles $\approx 53° + 37° + 90° = 180°$. $\triangle ABC$ is a right-angled triangle since $\angle ACB = 90°$. It can also be called a scalene triangle since all the angles are different.

Are the sides of the triangle straight?

Example 2

Construct $\triangle PQR$ in which $PQ = 9$ cm, $\angle PQR = 38°$ and $\angle QPR = 67°$. Measure the angle PRQ and the length of the sides PR and RQ. What is the sum of the three interior angles of the triangle. What type of triangle is this? What is the length of the side facing the smallest angle? And what is the length of the side facing the largest angle?

▼ Solution

Construction steps:

(1) Draw a line segment PQ 9 cm long.
(2) Using a protractor at points P and Q, draw an angle of 67° and one of 38° respectively.
(3) Produce the other arms of angles P and Q to meet at R. $\triangle PQR$ is the required triangle.

By measurement, $\angle PRQ = 75°$, $PR = 5.6$ cm and $QR = 8.5$ cm. The sum of the three interior angles = $38° + 67° + 75° = 180°$. $\triangle PQR$ is an acute-angled triangle. It can also be

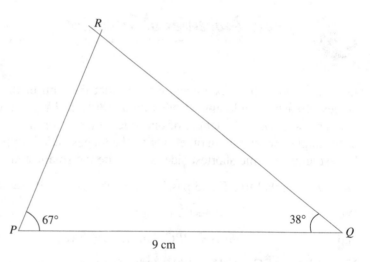

called a scalene triangle. The length of the side facing the smallest angle is 5.6 cm and that of the side facing the largest angle is 9 cm.

○ ○ ○ ○ ○ ○

The result of using a protractor to find the measure of an angle is not likely to be accurate.

○ ○ ○ ○ ○ ○ ○ ○ ○ ○

Example 3

Construct $\triangle XYZ$ in which $XY = 7.6$ cm, $\angle XYZ = 130°$ and $YZ = 4.8$ cm. Measure the length of XZ and the angles ZXY and YZX. What is the sum of the three interior angles of $\triangle XYZ$? What type of triangle is this? What is the size of the angle facing the shortest side?

▼ Solution

Construction steps:

(1) Draw a line segment XY of length 7.6 cm.
(2) Use a protractor to construct an angle of 130° at Y.

(3) Use a pair of compasses, set to a radius of 4.8 cm, to draw an arc to cut the produced arm of angle Y at Z. $\triangle XYZ$ is the required triangle.

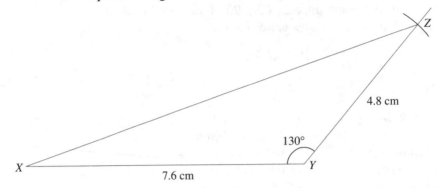

By measurement, $XZ = 11.3$ cm, $Y\hat{Z}X = 31°$ and $Y\hat{X}Z = 19°$. The sum of the three interior angles = $130° + 31° + 19° = 180°$, $\triangle XYZ$ is an obtuse-angled triangle. It is also an example of a scalene triangle. The size of the angle facing the shortest side is $19°$.

Angle Properties of Triangles

Use the Geometers' Sketch Pad to verify that the sum of the interior angles of a triangle is equal to 180°.

From the above three examples, we find that the sum of the interior angles of each triangle always adds up to $180°$, or 2 right angles. Do you also notice that the length of one side varies according to the size of the angle opposite it? In other words, the longest side is opposite the largest angle and the shortest side is opposite the smallest angle.

Draw PQ parallel to AC and passing through B.

We have $\qquad B\hat{A}C = P\hat{B}A$ (alt. $\angle$s, $PQ//AC$)

and $\qquad\qquad B\hat{C}A = Q\hat{B}C$ (alt. $\angle$s, $PQ//AC$)

Now, $P\hat{B}A + A\hat{B}C + Q\hat{B}C = 180°$ (adj. $\angle$s on a str. line)

$\therefore \quad B\hat{A}C + A\hat{B}C + B\hat{C}A = 180°$

(**Abbreviation:** $\angle$ sum of $\triangle$)

Exterior and Interior Opposite Angles

Fig. 14.4 shows $\triangle ABC$ with BA produced to P, BC produced to Q and CB produced to R. p, q and r are called the exterior angles of $\triangle ABC$. In particular, a and b are referred to as the interior opposite angles with reference to q. Similarly, a and c are the interior opposite angles with reference to r, etc.

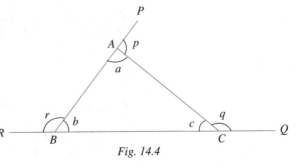

Fig. 14.4

Using a protractor, measure the angles a, b, c, p, q and r. Find the values of $(a + b)$, $(b + c)$ and $(a + c)$. What do you notice about these values? What can you say about the sum of the interior opposite angles?

Use Geometers' Sketch Pad to explore the relationship between the sum of the interior opposite angles and their corresponding exterior angles.

We can establish the fact that the sum of the interior opposite angles of a triangle is equal to its exterior angle by the following proof.

Refer to triangle ABC with notations as given in Fig. 14.5

We have $a + b + c = 180°$ ($\angle$ sum of $\triangle$)

and $\qquad q + c = 180°$ (adj. $\angle$s on a str. line)

$\qquad \therefore \quad a + b = q$

(**Abbreviation:** ext. $\angle$ = sum of int. opp. $\angle$s)

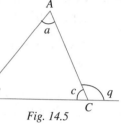

Fig. 14.5

Example 4

Find the unknown angles marked in each of the following diagrams:

(a)

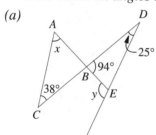

(b)

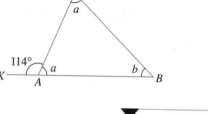

Solution

(a) $\qquad A\hat{B}C = 94°$ $\qquad$ (vert. opp. $\angle$s)

$x + 94° + 38° = 180°$ $\qquad$ ($\angle$ sum of $\triangle$)

$\qquad \therefore \quad x = 180° - 94° - 38° = 48°$

$\qquad \qquad y = 94° + 25°$ $\quad$ (ext. $\angle$ = sum of int. opp. $\angle$s)

$\qquad \therefore \quad y = 119°$

(b) $114° + a = 180°$ $\qquad$ (adj. $\angle$s on a str. line)

$\qquad \therefore \quad a = 180° - 114° = 66°$

$\qquad 114° = 66° + b$ $\quad$ (ext. $\angle$ = sum of int. opp. $\angle$s)

$\qquad \therefore \quad b = 114° - 66°$

$\qquad \qquad = 48°$

═══ Exercise 14a ═══

1. Sketch, in each case, a triangle ABC with the size of $\hat{A}$ and $\hat{B}$ given below. In each case find $\hat{C}$ and classify each triangle (i) by its sides (ii) by its angles:

(a) $\hat{A} = 20°$, $\hat{B} = 60°$ $\qquad$ (b) $\hat{A} = 70°$, $\hat{B} = 40°$ $\qquad$ (c) $\hat{A} = 60°$, $\hat{B} = 60°$

(d) $\hat{A} = 42°$, $\hat{B} = 48°$ $\qquad$ (e) $\hat{A} = 65°$, $\hat{B} = 50°$ $\qquad$ (f) $\hat{A} = 25°$, $\hat{B} = 112°$

2. The following are base angles of isosceles triangles. In each case, find the third angle of the isosceles triangle:

(a) $42°$ $\qquad \qquad$ (b) $82°$ $\qquad \qquad$ (c) $18°$ $\qquad \qquad$ (d) $64°$

3. Construct a triangle *ABC* such that *AB* = 85 mm, *BC* = 110 mm and *AC* = 95 mm. Name and measure the size of the smallest angle of the triangle.

4. Construct an equilateral triangle with sides 9.5 cm each.

5. Construct a right-angled triangle such that the two shorter sides are each equal to 6 cm. Measure the length of the longest side and the size of the smallest angle.

6. Construct a triangle *ABC* such that $\hat{A}$ = 75°, *AB* = 6 cm and *AC* = 7 cm. Measure *BC* and $\hat{B}$. What type of triangle is this?

7. Construct a triangle *PQR* such that *PQ* = 8 cm, $\hat{P}$ = 48° and $\hat{Q}$ = 56°. Measure *PR*, *QR* and $\hat{R}$. What type of triangle is this?

8. Construct a triangle *LMN* such that $\hat{L}$ = 90°, *LM* = 5 cm and *MN* = 9 cm. Measure *LN*, $\hat{M}$ and $\hat{N}$. What is the name of this triangle?

9. Calculate the values of the unknown in each of the following diagrams:

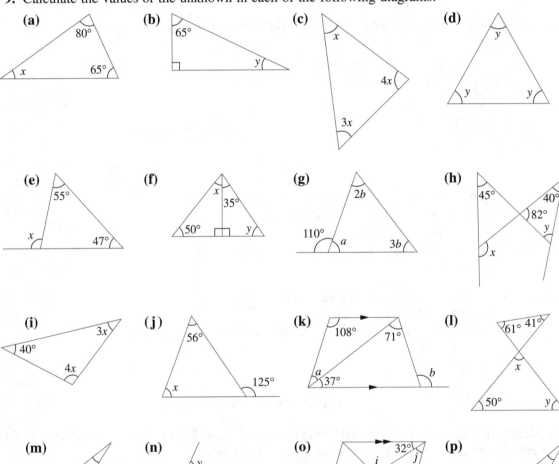

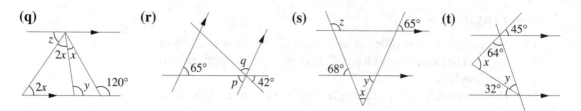

(q)

z
$2x$ x
$2x$ y $120°$

(r)

$65°$
q
p $42°$

(s)

z $65°$
$68°$
y
x

(t)

$45°$
$64°$
x
y
$32°$

$*$**10.** The angles of a triangle are $(x-35)°$, $(x-25)°$ and $\left(\dfrac{1}{2}x - 10\right)°$. Form an equation in x and hence find x.

$*$**11.** If the sizes of the angles of a triangle are $3x°$, $5x°$ and $4x°$, find the smallest angle of the triangle.

$*$**12.** In the triangle ABC, $\hat{A} = 50°$, $\hat{C} = 26°$ and AB is produced to D. Find $A\hat{B}C$ and $C\hat{B}D$.

Quadrilaterals

A quadrilateral is a plane figure with four sides and four angles. Fig. 14.6 shows a quadrilateral $ABCD$. It is named by taking the vertices in order either in a clockwise or anticlockwise direction. Thus, $ABCD$, $BCDA$, $DCBA$ and $CBAD$ are correct ways of naming the quadrilateral but $ABDC$, $ACBD$ and $CDBA$ are not. The line segments AC and BD that join the opposite vertices are called **diagonals**. The sum of the four angles of a quadrilateral equals $360°$.

The following are some quadrilaterals and their properties:

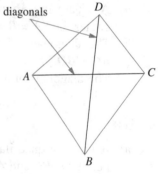

diagonals

Fig. 14.6

1. Trapezium

A trapezium is a quadrilateral with exactly one pair of opposite sides parallel, i.e., $AB//DC$.

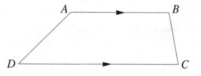

2. Parallelogram

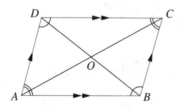

Use the open tool Geometers' Sketch Pad to explore the many properties of quadrilaterals.

(a) A parallelogram is a quadrilateral with two pairs of opposite sides parallel, i.e. $AB//DC$ and $AD//BC$.

(b) The opposite sides of a parallelogram are equal in length, i.e., $AB = DC$ and $AD = BC$.

(c) The diagonals of a parallelogram bisect each other, i.e., $AO = OC$ and $BO = OD$.

(d) The opposite angles of a parallelogram are equal, i.e., $\hat{A} = \hat{C}$ and $\hat{B} = \hat{D}$. Furthermore $\hat{A} + \hat{D} = 180°$ and $\hat{B} + \hat{C} = 180°$.

3. Rectangle

(a) A rectangle is a parallelogram where all its angles are right angles. The properties of a parallelogram are also applicable to a rectangle.

(b) The diagonals of a rectangle are equal in length, i.e., $AC = BD$.

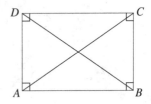

4. Rhombus

(a) A rhombus is a parallelogram with all its sides equal in length, i.e., $AB = BC = CD = AD$.

(b) The diagonals of a rhombus bisect each other at right angles, i.e., $A\hat{O}B = C\hat{O}D = B\hat{O}C = A\hat{O}D = 90°$ and $AO = OC$, $DO = OB$.

(c) The diagonals of a rhombus bisect the angles, i.e., $D\hat{A}O = B\hat{A}O$, $A\hat{B}O = C\hat{B}O$, $B\hat{C}O = D\hat{C}O$ and $A\hat{D}O = C\hat{D}O$.

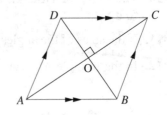

5. Square

(a) A square is a rhombus where all its angles are right angles, i.e., $\hat{A} = \hat{B} = \hat{C} = \hat{D} = 90°$.

(b) The diagonals of a square are equal in length, i.e., $AC = BD$.

The diagonals of a square bisect each other at right angles.

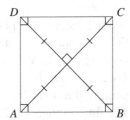

6. Kite

(a) A kite is a quadrilateral with 2 pairs of equal adjacent sides, i.e., $AB = BC$ and $AD = DC$.

(b) The longer diagonal bisects the other diagonal at right angles, i.e., $AO = OC$ and $A\hat{O}B = B\hat{O}C = A\hat{O}D = C\hat{O}D = 90°$.

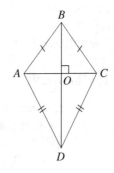

Example 5

ABCD is a rectangle in which $A\hat{K}D = 85°$ and $A\hat{D}K = 45°$. Calculate (a) $B\hat{A}K$; (b) $B\hat{K}A$.

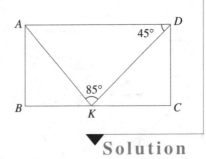

How many squares are there in the given figure?

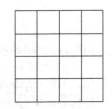

▼ **Solution**

(a) $K\hat{A}D + 85° + 45° = 180°$ ($\angle$ sum of $\triangle$)

$\qquad K\hat{A}D = 180° - 85° - 45° = 50°$

$\qquad B\hat{A}K + 50° = 90°$ ($B\hat{A}D$ is a right angle)

$\qquad \therefore \quad B\hat{A}K = 90° - 50° = 40°$

(b) $B\hat{K}A + 40° + 90° = 180°$ ($\angle$ sum of $\triangle$, $A\hat{B}K = 90°$)

$\qquad \therefore \quad B\hat{K}A = 180° - 40° - 90° = 50°$

═ **Exercise 14b** ═

1. For each of the rectangles given, calculate the unknown angles marked x and y:

(a)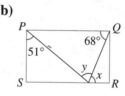

(b)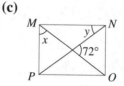

(c)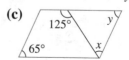

(d)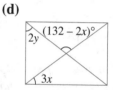

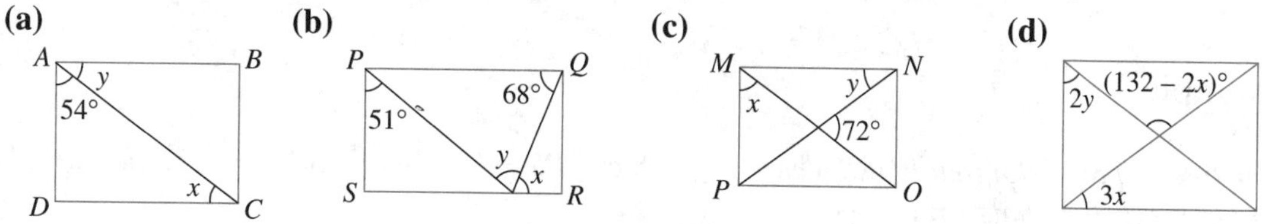

2. For each of the parallelograms given, calculate the values of x and y:

(a)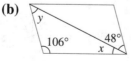

(b)

(c) 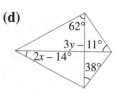

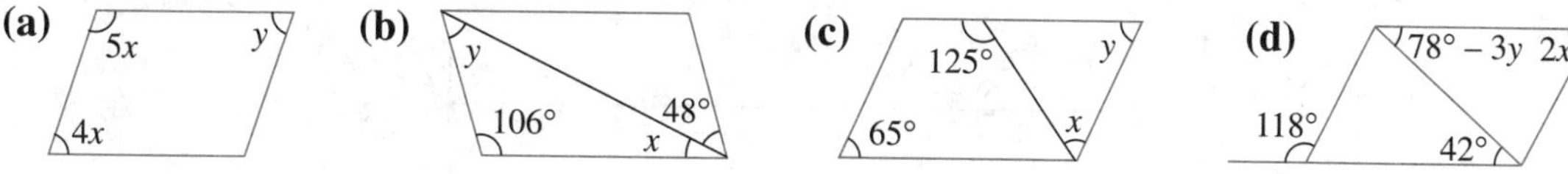

3. For each of the kites given, calculate the values of x and y:

(a)

(b)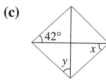

(c)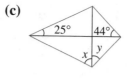

(d)

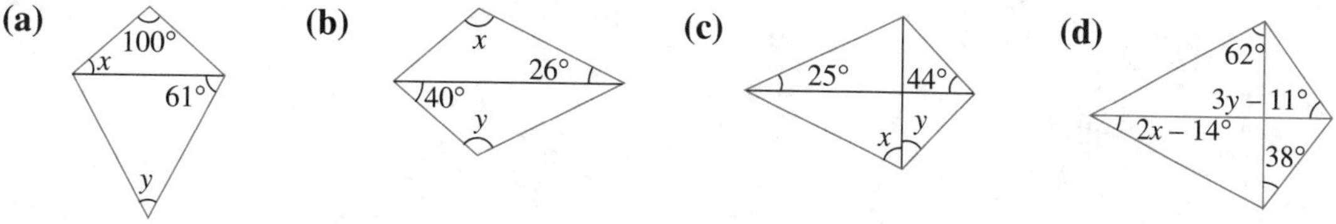

4. For each of the rhombuses given, calculate the unknown angles marked x and y:

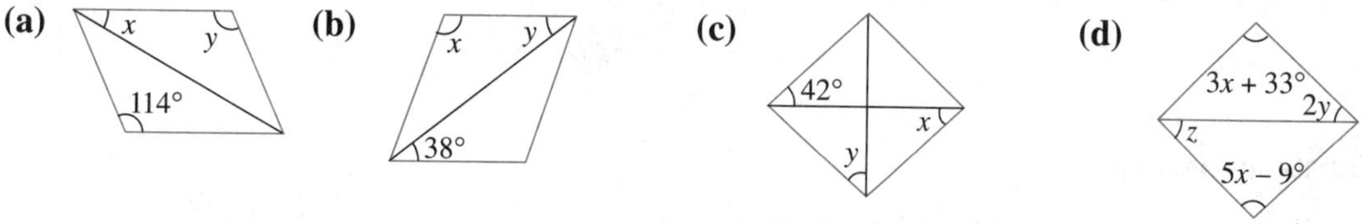

5. For each of the figures given, calculate the unknown angles marked x and y:

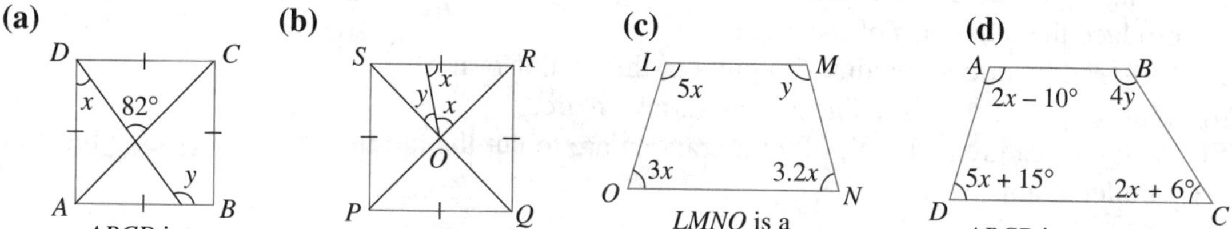

(a)
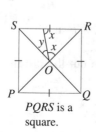
$ABCD$ is a square.

(b)
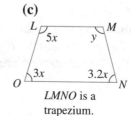
$PQRS$ is a square.

(c)
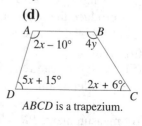
$LMNO$ is a trapezium.

(d)
$ABCD$ is a trapezium.

6. In a rectangle $ABCD$, X is the mid-point of AB and $C\hat{X}D = 118°$, calculate
    (a) $A\hat{D}X$ **(b)** $X\hat{C}D$

7. In a parallelogram $PQRS$, $Q\hat{P}R = 42°$ and $Q\hat{R}S = 70°$, calculate
    (a) $P\hat{Q}R$ **(b)** $P\hat{R}Q$

8. In a rhombus $PQRS$, $P\hat{Q}R = 108°$, calculate
    (a) $Q\hat{R}S$ **(b)** $Q\hat{P}R$ **(c)** $Q\hat{S}R$

9. In a kite $ABCD$, $AB = BC$, $AD = CD$, $A\hat{D}C = 64°$ and $B\hat{A}C = 42°$, calculate
    (a) $A\hat{C}D$ **(b)** $A\hat{B}C$

10. In a trapezium $PQRS$, PQ is parallel to SR, $PQ = PS$, $P\hat{S}R = 62°$ and $Q\hat{R}S = 52°$, calculate
    (a) $P\hat{Q}S$ **(b)** $S\hat{Q}R$

Construction of Quadrilaterals

The following examples illustrate the steps for the construction of quadrilaterals.

Example 6

Construct a parallelogram PQRS where PQ = 8 cm, PS = 5.6 cm and SP̂Q = 65°. Measure the length of the diagonals PR and QS.

▼ Solution

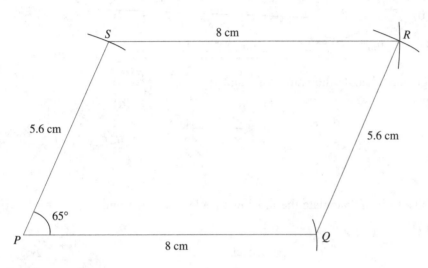

Construction steps:

(1) Draw a line segment *PQ* of length 8 cm.
(2) Using a protractor, construct an angle of 65° at *P*, so that *PQ* is one side of the angle, and produce the other arm of the angle.
(3) With *P* as centre and radius 5.6 cm, cut the arm of *P* at *S*.
(4) With *Q* as centre and radius 5.6 cm, draw an arc.
(5) With *S* as centre and radius 8 cm, draw an arc to cut the arc in (4) at *R*. *PQRS* is the required parallelogram.

By measurement, *PR* = 11.5 cm and *QS* = 7.6 cm.

Example 7

Construct a quadrilateral PQRS where PQ = 4.5 cm, QR = 5.6 cm. RS = 6.1 cm, PS = 4.3 cm and diagonal PR = 6.9 cm. Measure Q̂, R̂ and Ŝ.

▼ Solution

Construction steps:

(1) Draw a line segment *PR* of length 6.9 cm.
(2) With *P* and *R* as centres and radii 4.5 cm and 5.6 cm respectively, draw two arcs to cut at *Q*.
(3) With *P* and *R* as centres and radii 4.3 cm and 6.1 cm respectively, draw two arcs to cut at *S*.
(4) Join *PQ, QR, RS* and *PS*. *PQRS* is the required quadrilateral.

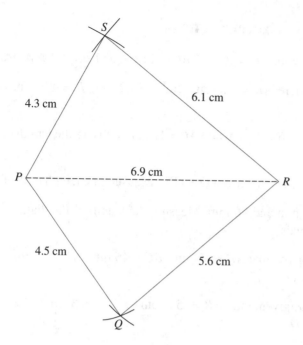

4.3 cm

6.1 cm

P ← - - - - - - - 6.9 cm - - - - - - - → R

4.5 cm

5.6 cm

Q

Draw a rectangle of any size. Use your ruler to locate the midpoints of the sides carefully. Join these midpoints to form a new quadrilateral. What is the name of the quadrilateral you have obtained? Repeat the above by drawing

(a) a trapezium;
(b) a parallelogram;
(c) a kite;
(d) a rhombus;
(e) a quadrilateral of 4 unequal lengths.

What conclusion can you draw?

By measurement, $\hat{Q} = 86°$, $\hat{R} = 78°$ and $\hat{S} = 81°$.

Example 8

Construct a quadrilateral PQRS where PQ = 6.5 cm, QR = 4.8 cm, RS = 8.5 cm, $\hat{Q} = 75°$ and $\hat{R} = 98°$. Measure the length of PS and the angles P and S.

▼ **Solution**

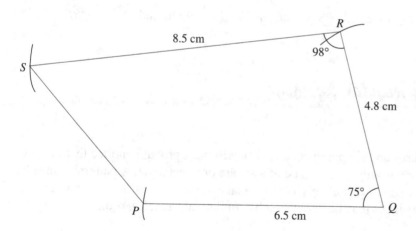

R

8.5 cm

98°

S

4.8 cm

75°

P

6.5 cm

Q

Construction steps:

(1) Draw a line segment PQ of length 6.5 cm.
(2) Using a protractor, construct $\hat{Q} = 75°$ and produce the arm of Q.
(3) With Q as centre and radius 4.8 cm, draw an arc to cut the produced arm of $\hat{Q}$ at R.
(4) Using a protractor, construct $\hat{R} = 98°$ and produce the arm of $\hat{R}$.
(5) With R as centre and radius 8.5 cm, draw an arc to cut the produced arm of $\hat{R}$ at S.
(6) Join PS and PQRS is the required quadrilateral.

By measurement, PS = 4.8 cm, $\hat{P} = 131°$ and $\hat{S} = 56°$.

Exercise 14c

1. Construct a parallelogram $ABCD$ with $AB = 10$ cm, $BC = 12$ cm and $\hat{B} = 80°$. Measure BD.

2. Construct a trapezium $ABCD$ where $AB = 5.6$ cm, $BC = 11.2$ cm, $\hat{B} = 80°$ and $\hat{C} = 70°$. Measure AC.

3. Construct a rhombus $ABCD$ where $AB = 7.5$ cm and $AC = 12$ cm. Measure the length of the other diagonal.

4. Construct a rhombus $PQRS$ where $PQ = 6$ cm and $\hat{Q} = 115°$. Measure the length of the diagonals.

5. Construct a rectangle of sides 84 mm and 96 mm. Measure the length of the diagonals and the acute angle made by these diagonals.

6. Construct a quadrilateral $ABCD$ given that $AB = 65$ mm, $BC = 46$ mm, $AD = 58$ mm, $\hat{A} = 105°$ and $\hat{B} = 120°$. Measure AC and BD.

7. Construct a quadrilateral $ABCD$ given that $AB = 5.3$ cm, $BC = 6.3$ cm. $CD = 6.7$ cm. $\hat{B} = 75°$ and $\hat{C} = 60°$. Measure AD.

8. Construct a quadrilateral $PQRS$ where $PQ = 5.6$ cm, $\hat{Q} = 80°$, $\hat{R} = 95°$, $QR = 6.2$ cm and $RS = 9.2$ cm. Measure PS.

9. Construct a quadrilateral $ABCD$ where $BC = 60$ mm, $CD = 90$ mm, $AD = 60$ mm, $AB = 45$ mm and $BD = 90$ mm. Measure $A\hat{D}C$.

10. Construct a quadrilateral $PQRS$ given that $PQ = PR = PS = 90$ mm, $RS = 75$ mm and $QR = 120$ mm. Measure $Q\hat{P}S$.

11. Construct a quadrilateral $PQRS$ where $PS = 6$ cm, $RS = QR = 9$ cm and $P\hat{S}R = Q\hat{R}S = 110°$. Measure PQ.

Tessellation of Regular Polygons

If you look at the floors of houses and shopping centres, you will most probably notice that many of them are tiled. The tiles used are usually in the shape of a square or a rectangle. A pattern formed by fitting together regular figures which completely cover a plane surface is called **tessellation**. The following diagrams show how planes may be tessellated by equilateral triangles, squares and regular hexagons.

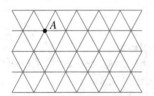

A tessellation formed
by equilateral
triangles.

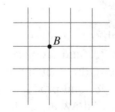

A tessellation
formed by
squares.

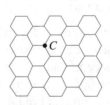

A tessellation formed
by regular hexagons.

What other tessellations are made up of combinations of other regular polygons? Can you design one on your own? What is the sum of the corner angles at each of the points *A*, *B* and *C*?

However, not all regular polygons tessellate. *For example*, regular pentagons do not tessellate. When they are put together as shown in Fig. 14.7, they leave a gap in between.

Fig. 14.7

Sometimes a tessellation may be make up of two or more regular polygons. Fig. 14.8 shows a tessellation formed by squares and regular octagons.

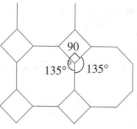

Fig. 14.8

Tessellation formed by squares and regular octagons.

The honeycomb illustrates tessellation found in nature.

We can also tessellate irregular polygons.

Tessellation formed by parallelograms

Tessellation formed by isosceles trapeziums (Two sides equal)

In-Class Activity

1. Which of the following figures will tessellate?

(a)

Isosceles triangle

(b)

Scalene triangle

(c)

Scalene trapezium (No sides equal)

(d)

Kite

(e)

Circle

(f)

Quadrilateral

2.

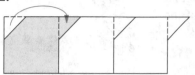 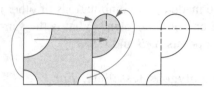

The Dutch artist, Maurits Escher, produced many tessellations of fishes, birds, reptiles and human beings. find out more on the works produced by Escher in your library.

We can design figures of different shapes which tessellate. In each of the diagrams above, we start with a simple design. Then, we remove a piece from a corner and add it onto the opposite side and we will have a new figure which tessellates. Create a few new tessellating patterns on your own in this way.

Summary

1. A **scalene triangle** is a triangle with no two sides being equal.
   An **isosceles triangle** is a triangle with two sides equal in length. The base angles of an isosceles triangle are equal in size.
   An **equilateral triangle** is a triangle with all three sides equal in length. The sizes of the three angles are also equal.

2. An **acute-angled triangle** is one where all the three angles are acute, i.e., less than 90°.
   An **obtuse-angled triangle** is a triangle with one of its angles obtuse, i.e., more than 90°.
   A **right-angled triangle** is a triangle with one of its angles equal to 90°.

3. The **sum of the angles of a triangle** is 180°.
   The **exterior angle** of a triangle is equal to the **sum of the interior opposite angles**.

4. A quadrilateral is a 4-sided plane figure. The sum of the angles of a quadrilateral is equal to 360°.

Review Questions 14

∗1. For each of the following figures, calculate the values of the unknowns:

(a)

(b)

(c)

(d)

(e)

(f)

(g)

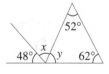

(h)

(i)

(j)

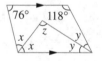

(k)

(l)

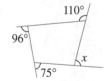

Exploration

1. Find the sum of the marked angles in each of the following diagrams:

   (a)

   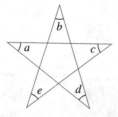

   (b)

   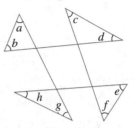

2. Construct a trapezium $PQRS$ where $PQ = 8.4$ cm, $QR = 4.8$ cm, $RS = 4.8$ cm and $\hat{Q} = 70°$. Measure PS, $\hat{R}$, $\hat{S}$ and $\hat{P}$.

3. $ABCD$ is a square and $\triangle DPC$ is an equilateral triangle. Find $A\hat{P}B$.

   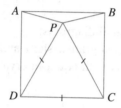

Statistics

In this chapter, you will learn how to

▲ collect, classify and tabulate data;
▲ read and interpret tables and statistical diagrams;
▲ construct bar graphs, pie charts, pictograms, stem and leaf
  diagram, line graphs and histograms with equal intervals.

Preliminary Problem

The government collects numerical information about all aspects of life, including education. Each year, the government has increased the level of spending on education in order to create a first-rate education system. Students including those in the picture benefit from the all-round Singaporean eduation system.

Introduction to Numerical Data

We live in a world of figures. Consider the following statements:

(1) The enrolment of students in a particular school is 1 000.
(2) There are altogether 152 secondary schools in Singapore.
(3) The literacy rate among local residents aged 15 years and above was about 95% in 1999.
(4) Deaths resulting from smoking was about 56 000 in a city in 1998.
(5) Eight out of 10 film stars use a certain brand of perfume.

We can continue to give figures like those shown above. Have you ever wondered how such figures are collected, summarised and finally presented so that a reader can easily understand them? Numerical data can be obtained in many ways. The data collected can be summarised and presented by means of tables and charts, or graphs.

Collection and Organisation of Data

We collect and analyse data to answer questions as well as solve problems.

Consider the following example:

Suppose Mr Wang of ABC Boys' School wants to know the type of sports his 40 students enjoy.

1. To **collect** the information, he gives each student a survey form containing the names of sports. Each student is to select only one favourite sport.

2. When the counting is done, he **organises** the results (information or data collected) in the form of a table as shown below.

Favourite sport	Basketball	Badminton	Hockey	Soccer	Table-tennis	**Total**
Number of students	10	7	5	12	6	40

3. He **presents** the information found in the table using a **diagram**.

4. He **interprets** the information and draws the following conclusions:

   (a) The most popular sport among his students is soccer.
   (b) More than half of the class prefer either soccer or basketball.
   (c) Hockey is the least popular sport.

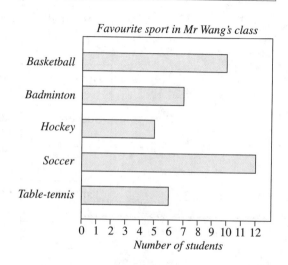

Favourite sport in Mr Wang's class

Number of students

Are the following statements true?

1. Students who smoke perform worse academically than non-smokers. Thus, smoking will make one stupid.

2. It is more dangerous to drive today than it was in 1950 because statistics have shown that there are more road accidents today than there were in 1950.

3. Of all car accidents, 20% are caused by people who drink alcohol and drive, whereas 80% are caused by those who are sober. Therefore, there is no cause for alarm when people drink alcohol and drive.

4. Singaporeans eat 1.2 hamburgers on the average per year.

The example in the previous page shows a very simple way of collecting and organising data. In practice, data can be collected in many ways, depending on the amount of data available and the purpose of the survey.

Collection of Data Using a Questionnaire

Suppose the principal of ABC Boys' School has to plan the Sports Budget. To make a better decision, he wants to know the relative popularity of the sports played in the school. He asks Mr Wang to conduct a survey by giving each student a copy of the questionnaire shown below:

QUESTIONNAIRE

on

Relative popularity of Sports played at ABC Boys' School

Which is your favourite sport?

Check the box next to the sport you like best.

Choose only ONE sport. Badminton ☐   Soccer ☐

Basketball ☐   Table-tennis ☐

Hockey ☐

Mr Wang records the results of the survey in a table as shown below.

Favourite sport	Tally	No. of students
Badminton	୦	136
Basketball	୦	180
Hockey	୦	84
Soccer	୦	212
Table-tennis	୦	108
Total		720

He does this in an organised manner by using the method of **tallying**. A tally is put in the corresponding space in the table, matching the checked box in the questionnaire. Tallies are grouped in fives (*////*) with the fifth tally crossing the first four for counting convenience.

From the table in the previous page, can you tell the relative popularity of the various types of sports in the school? You might have difficulty understanding and interpreting the information displayed in the table. You will probably be able to make better comparisons of the data if you present the information in a diagram as shown in the following sections.

Pictograms

Mr Wang can draw different diagrams to display the results of the survey, so as to give a clearer picture of the relative popularity of the various sports. One such diagram is a **pictogram**, shown in Fig. 15.1 below.

*A **pictogram** uses pictures to represent statistics.*

Popularity of sports played at ABC Boys' School

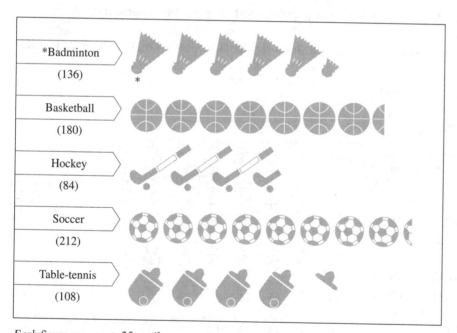

Each figure represents 25 pupils.

Fig. 15.1

Each figure in the pictogram above represents 25 pupils and a fraction of a figure means a corresponding fraction of 25. It should be noted that this is not a very accurate method of showing the **exact** number of pupils. It merely gives us a quick comparison of the relative popularity of the sports played in the school.

Bar Graphs

Mr Wang may also represent the information in a bar graph as shown in Fig. 15.2.

The vertical axis at the side shows the number of students in accordance to the different categories of their favourite sports, with these categories being labelled along the horizontal axis. A bar is constructed representing each category, with the length of the bar proportional to the number of students in that category. The bars should be of the same width. Note that there is a space between each category on the horizontal axis to distinguish clearly between the categories.

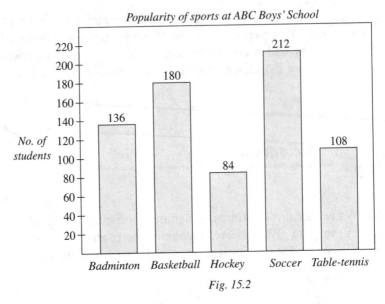

Popularity of sports at ABC Boys' School

Fig. 15.2

One can see at a glance that soccer is the most popular sport as it has the longest bar.

Can you tell which are the second, third and fourth most popular sports? Which is the least popular sport?

Example 1

The table below shows the profits, after taxation, of a company from 1995 to 2000.

(a) What was the profit in
   (i) 1998?
   (ii) 2000?

(b) In which year was the profit smallest? By how much had the profit decreased that year from the previous year?

Year	Profit
1995	💰 💰 💰 💰 💰 💰
1996	💰 💰 💰 💰 💰 💰
1997	💰 💰 💰 💰 💰
1998	💰 💰 💰 💰 💰 💰
1999	💰 💰 💰 💰 💰
2000	💰 💰 💰 💰 💰 💰 💰

Each 💰 represents 1 million dollars.

▼ **Solution**

(a) The profit in 1998 was about $5\frac{1}{2}$ million dollars and in 2000 it was 7 million dollars.

(b) In 1997 the profit was the smallest and it had decreased from 1996 by about $1\frac{1}{2}$ million dollars.

Example 2

A company owns five electrical shops. The bar graph at the side shows the number of television sets sold in the five shops in November and December in a certain year.

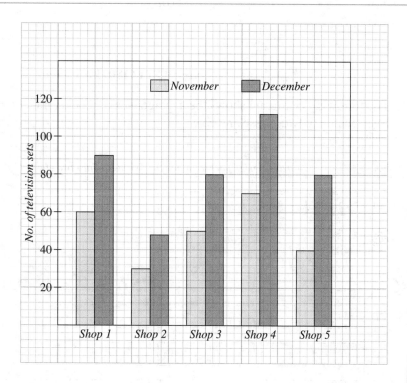

Study the graph above and answer the following questions:

(a) Find the total number of television sets sold in the five shops in
  (i)   November;
  (ii) December.

(b) Express the total number of television sets sold in December as a percentage of the total number of television sets sold in November and December.

(c) (i)   Which shop enjoyed the greatest increase in the sales of television sets?
  (ii) Express the increase as a percentage of the number of television sets sold in November.

Solution

(a) (i)   The total number of television sets sold in the five shops in November
      = 60 + 30 + 50 + 70 + 40
      = 250

  (ii) The total number of television sets sold in the five shops in December
      = 90 + 48 + 80 + 112 + 80
      = 410

(b) Percentage of the total number of television sets sold in December

   $= \dfrac{410}{250 + 410} \times 100\%$

   = 62% (correct to the nearest whole number)

(c) (i) Shop 4 enjoyed the greatest increase in sales.

(ii) Percentage increase in sales = $\dfrac{112 - 70}{70} \times 100\%$

$= 60\%$

═ Exercise 15a ═

1. The following pictogram shows the average weekly pocket money that students from each of the five secondary two classes receive.

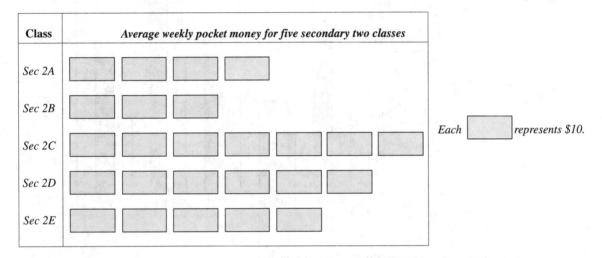

(a) What is the ratio of Sec 2D's average weekly pocket money to Sec 2B's average weekly pocket money?

(b) Express Sec 2A's average weekly pocket money as a percentage of Sec 2D's average weekly pocket money.

2. The bar graph illustrates the results of a survey carried out in the shops of a certain housing estate.

Calculate

(a) the total number of workers;

(b) the percentage of shops hiring 3 or more workers.

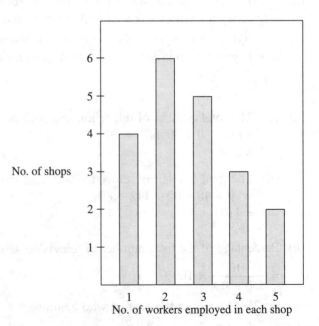

3. The graph below shows the number of candidates who sat for an examination and the number who were successful.

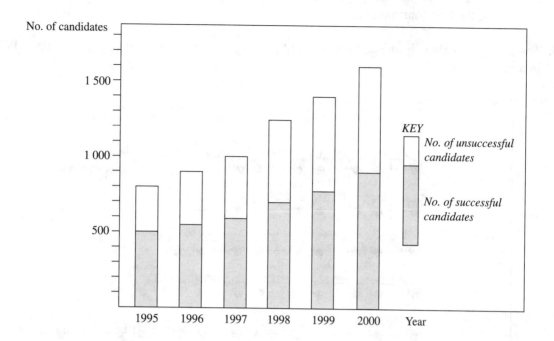

(a) How many candidates sat for the examination in 1997?

(b) How many passed in 2000?

(c) What fraction of the number who took the examination in 1999 passed?

4. The graph below shows the product sales of ABC Company in the first four months of 2000.

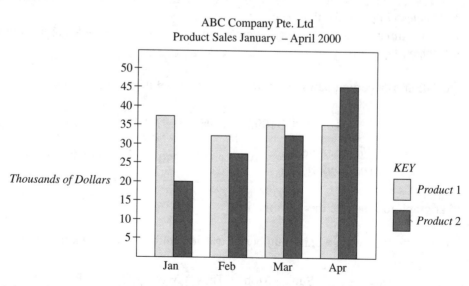

(a) Which product has almost the same amount of sales over the four-month period?

(b) Which month showed the greatest increase in the sales of product 2?

(c) How much were the sales of product 1 in January?

(d) How much were the sales of product 2 in April?

(e) What were the total sales of product 1?

(f) What were the total sales of product 2?

(g) What fraction of the total product sales of the company did the sales of product 1 make up during the first four months?

5. The pictogram below illustrates the number of private cars registered each year from 1995 to 1999 in a certain city.

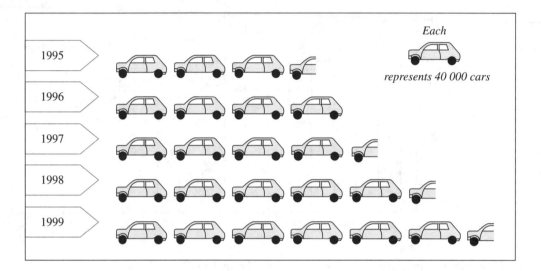

(a) In which year was the greatest number of vehicles registered? Estimate the number of vehicles registered in that year.

(b) Estimate the number of cars registered in each of the other years.

(c) If, in 1997, the registration fee for each car was $500, estimate the total amount the Registry of Vehicles collected for that year.

(d) Give an estimate of the percentage increase in the number of vehicles registered from 1998 to 1999.

6. The circulation of a certain newspaper from 1995 to 1999 is given as follows:

Year	1995	1996	1997	1998	1999
No. of copies (in thousands)	250	275	290	315	280

Use a bar graph to illustrate this information.

7. In a certain city, the average daily number of traffic accidents in a week is given as follows:

Day	Sun	Mon	Tues	Wed	Thur	Fri	Sat
No. of accidents	70	40	30	35	50	55	80

Illustrate this information with a bar graph.

8. The table below shows the number of students who play squash, tennis and badminton. Illustrate the data using a pictogram.

Sport	Squash	Tennis	Badminton
No. of students	40	60	50

(a) Find the ratio of the number of squash players to the number of badminton players.

(b) Calculate the percentage of pupils who play badminton.

Collection of Data Through Observation

In-Class Activity

(a) Carry out a traffic survey by watching and noting the types of vehicles which pass by your school during a 15-minute period.

(b) Copy and complete the survey sheet below.

Name : _____		Date : _____
Location		Time : From _____
of survey : _____		To _____

Types of vehicles	Tally	No. of vehicles
Bus		
Taxi		
Private car		
Motorcycle		
Lorry		
Pick-up or Van		
Total		

Note: You may change the list of vehicles to suit your situation. Students in the class should work in small groups and choose different times and locations to conduct the survey.

(c) Display the information you collected in the form of a pictogram or a bar chart. Remember to give a short title for your diagram.

(d) With the help of your diagram, interpret the information and draw some conclusions.

Pie Charts

If the principal of ABC Boys' School wants to know what fraction of the school chose a particular sport, then the diagram in Fig. 15.3, a **pie chart**, would be useful to him. The pie chart displays clearly the fraction of the school choosing a particular type of sport.

A **pie chart** represents *relative quantities by areas of sectors of a circle.*

Fig. 15.3 is constructed by dividing a circle into different sectors. Each sector corresponds to the percentage of a category of students who like a particular sport. The angle of each sector is proportional to the number the sector represents.

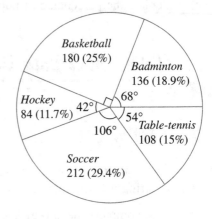

Fig. 15.3

The angle of each sector can be found easily, e.g. if 212 out of 720 students prefer soccer, then the angle of the sector for soccer is $\frac{212}{720}$ of $360° = \frac{212}{720} \times 360° = 106°$.

The table below shows the percentage of each category of students and the angle of the sector for each category.

These days, we usually use software programmes on the computer to help us construct bar graphs, pie charts, etc.

Favourite Sport	No. of students	Percentage	Angle of sector
Badminton	136	$\frac{136}{720} \times 100\% = 18.9\%$	$\frac{136}{720} \times 360° = 68°$
Basketball	180	$\frac{180}{720} \times 100\% = 25\%$	$\frac{180}{720} \times 360° = 90°$
Hockey	84	$\frac{84}{720} \times 100\% = 11.7\%$	$\frac{84}{720} \times 360° = 42°$
Soccer	212	$\frac{212}{720} \times 100\% = 29.4\%$	$\frac{212}{720} \times 360° = 106°$
Table-tennis	108	$\frac{108}{720} \times 100\% = 15\%$	$\frac{108}{720} \times 360° = 54°$

Although pie charts are particularly useful where the proportions of a whole are more important than the actual numerical values, they have some disadvantages. For instance, it is difficult to interpret a pie chart representing data which involves too many categories. In constructing pie charts, long calculations are often needed and actual measurements of angles using protractors are necessary to produce an accurate diagram.

Example 3

The bar graph illustrates the results of a survey conducted to find the number of people in each car in a random survey of 120 cars at a traffic junction.

Calculate

(a) the angle in a pie chart of the sector which represents cars with 2 people;
(b) the total number of people in these 120 cars;
(c) the percentage of cars with 4 or more people.

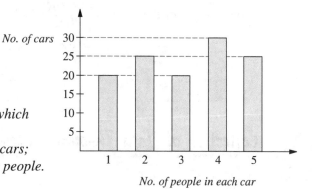

Solution

(a) No. of cars with 2 people = 25

∴ the angle of the sector in a pie chart representing this is $\dfrac{25}{120} \times 360° = 75°$

(b) Total no. of people in these 120 cars = $(1 \times 20) + (2 \times 25) + (3 \times 20) + (4 \times 30) + (5 \times 25)$
$= 375$

(c) No. of cars with 4 or more people = 30 + 25 = 55

∴ the percentage of cars with 4 or more people = $\dfrac{55}{120} \times 100\% = 45.8\%$

Example 4

The pie chart shows the nutritional composition of a fast-food product.

(a) Calculate the value of x.
(b) What is the percentage of fat in the fast-food product?
(c) Given that one such fast-food product contains 120 grams of carbohydrates, calculate the total weight of the fast-food product.

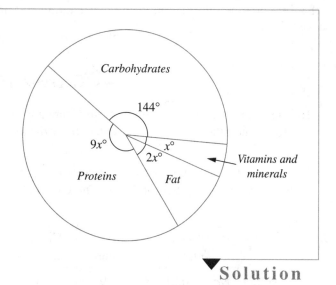

Solution

(a) $144° + 9x° + 2x° + x° = 360°$
$12x = 216$
∴ $x = 18$

(b) The angle representing fat in the product = $2 \times 18°$

$$= 36°$$

∴ the percentage of fat in the fast-food product = $\dfrac{36°}{360°} \times 100\%$

$$= 10\%$$

(c) The angle representing carbohydrates is 144° and this constitutes 120 g.

∴ the total weight of the product = $\left(\dfrac{360}{144} \times 120\right)$ g

$$= 300 \text{ g}$$

Collection of Data Through Interviews

In-Class Activity

(a) Conduct interviews with students in your class to find out their daily means of transport to school.

(b) Decide on the number of students you want to interview.

(c) Think of where and when to interview the students, e.g. in the canteen during recess time, or in the morning before students go to their classes for lessons. Do not forget to thank the students you have interviewed for their participation.

(d) Design a form for recording the results.

(e) Use a diagram, preferably a pie chart, to display your data.

(f) Interpret the information from your diagram and draw your conclusions.

═══ Exercise 15b ═══

1. The main products of a manufacturing company are corn oil (50%), margarine (30%), peanut oil (15%) and others (5%). Display the above data using a pie chart.

2. 72 students of a certain school were asked to indicate a place of interest in Singapore they would like to visit during their holidays. The table below shows the results.

Place of interest	Bird Park	Chinese Gardens	Science Centre	Sentosa Island	Zoo
No. of students	9	5	19	24	15

Use a bar graph to illustrate the results.

3. 100 people took part in a survey on their favourite fruit. The results were tabulated as follows:

Local Fruit	Banana	Durian	Mangosteen	Papaya	Rambutan
No. of people	30	25	10	15	20

(a) Illustrate the results using a
    (i) bar graph;   (ii) pie chart.

(b) Which diagram shows more clearly that one quarter of the people like durian most?

(c) Which diagram shows more clearly that banana is more popular than durian?

4. The pie chart below shows the health care expenditure for the year 1998:

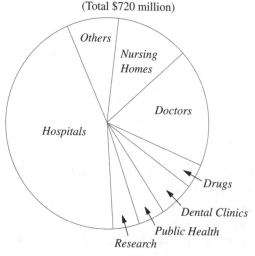

Health Care 1998 — Where the money goes
(Total $720 million)

(a) Measure the angle of each sector using a protractor and calculate the amount of money allocated to each category.

(b) Express the expenditure of each category as a percentage of the total expenditure on Health Care.

5. The pie chart shows the number of pupils and teachers in a certain school.

(a) Calculate the value of x.

(b) If there are 45 teachers in the school, how many
    (i) boys are there in the school?
    (ii) girls are there in the school?

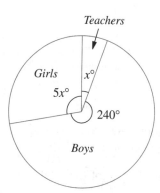

6. The bar graph shows the number of cars of different colours sold in one year in a certain city.

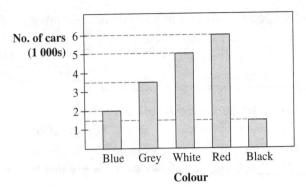

(a) Which colour is the most popular?

(b) Illustrate the information using a clearly labelled pie chart.

*7. Pupils in a class were asked to indicate which one of the four ice-cream flavours – vanilla, chocolate, yam or mango – they preferred. The following pie chart shows the results.

(a) If one-quarter of the class preferred yam flavour, state the angle in the yam sector.

(b) Calculate the angle in the vanilla sector.

(c) If 5 students indicated a preference for mango flavour, calculate the number of students in the class.

(d) Calculate the percentage of students in the class who preferred vanilla flavour.

*8. The daily output of two products, X and Y, in a factory are 6 tonnes and 14 tonnes respectively. If the output is represented by a pie chart, calculate the angle of the sector representing the output of product Y.

*9. A factory produces three products, A, B and C, in the ratio of $1 : x : 5$. When the output is illustrated by a pie chart, the angle of the sector representing the output of C is $120°$. Find x.

*10. The pie chart shows the sales of a publishing company.

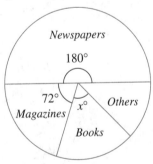

(a) What percentage of the total sales does each of the following make up?

(i) newspapers (ii) magazines

(b) Given that books make up $17\frac{1}{2}\%$ of the total sales, find x.

Line Graphs

The table below shows the government recurrent expenditure on university education in thousand dollars.

Year	87/88	88/89	89/90	90/91	91/92	92/93
Expenditure ('000)	293 443	259 014	288 571	351 476	841 154	412 524

Year	93/94	94/95	95/96	96/97	97/98
Expenditure ('000)	431 554	502 999	520 289	546 120	669 004

By plotting the points corresponding to the data and then joining the points by line segments, we obtain the line graph as shown in Fig. 15.4.

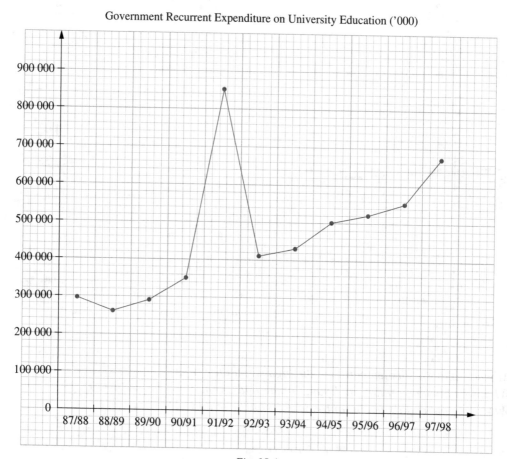

Fig. 15.4

A line graph is a suitable graph to construct when we wish to show a rising or a falling trend in a set of data over a period of time. The graph in Fig. 15.4 shows that the government recurrent expenditure on university education reached its lowest point in the 88/89 fiscal year, after which it increased gradually for the next two years. The expenditure hit the highest point in the fiscal year 91/92 following a big jump from the previous year. The expenditure then took a dip in the year 92/93 after which it rose gradually for the next five years.

NB: Although adjacent points are joined by a line segment, the intermediate values, other than the values recorded, have no meaning.

Example 5

The following graph shows the temperatures of a child who developed fever. His temperature was taken every two hours starting from 2 p.m.

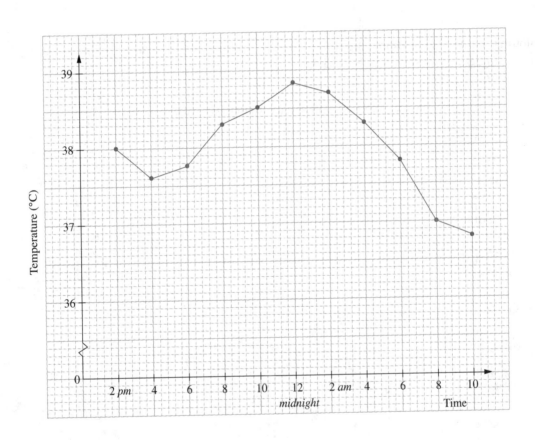

(a) At what time was his temperature the highest on the graph?
(b) What was his temperature at 4 p.m., 9 p.m. and 3 a.m.?
(c) When was the child's temperature 37°C, 37.4°C and 38°C?

Solution

(a) His temperature was the highest at 12 midnight.

(b) His temperature at 4 p.m. was 37.6°C. His temperatures at 9 p.m. and 3 a.m. can be estimated using intermediate values because it is reasonable to assume that the temperature changes gradually within a relatively short period of 2 hours.

From the graph,
his temperature at 9 p.m. was about 38.4°C;
his temperature at 3 a.m. was about 38.5°C.

(c) The child had a temperature of 37°C at 8 a.m., 37.4°C at 7 a.m., 38°C at 2 p.m., at about 6.50 p.m. and at about 5.10 a.m.

══ Exercise 15c ══

1. The line graph below shows the monthly tin output of a tin mine from July to December in 1999. Study the graph and estimate
   (a) the largest monthly output;
   (b) the smallest monthly output;
   (c) the total output for the six months.

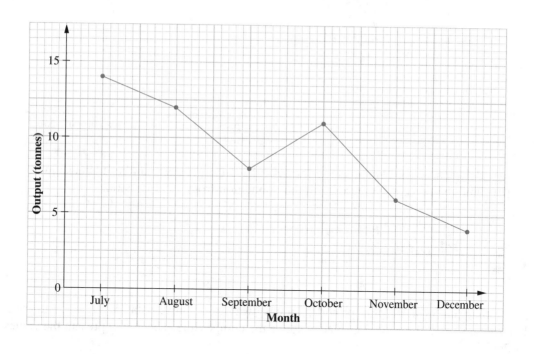

2. The temperature of a patient, taken every 3 hours, was recorded as shown in the table below:

Time	3 p.m.	6 p.m.	9 p.m.	12 midnight	3 a.m.	6 a.m.	9 a.m.
Temperature (°C)	39	39	39.5	37.5	39	38	37

(a) Display the data using a line graph.
(b) From the graph, estimate the patient's temperatures at 5 p.m. and at 1 a.m.

3. The line graph below shows the population of a town from 1990 to 2000.

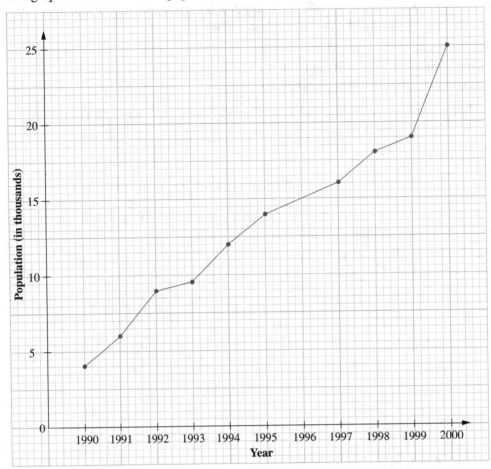

(a) Between which two years did the town have the greatest number increase in population?

(b) Find the percentage increase in the population from 1997 to 2000.

 # Dot Diagram

A dot diagram, or a dot plot, provides an easy way to organise data. A dot diagram consists of a horizontal number line and dots placed above the number line. The dots represent the values in a set of data.

Consider the marks scored by thirty students in a test.

48	20	27	26	24	39	40	30	37	37
29	44	37	38	25	44	25	30	28	37
38	24	30	36	39	37	25	38	37	36

Rearrange the marks in numerical order from the smallest to the biggest.

20, 24, 24, 25, 25, 25, 26, 27, 28, 29, 30, 30, 30, 36, 36, 37, 37, 37, 37, 37, 37, 38, 38, 38, 39, 39, 40, 44, 44, 48

Now create the dot diagram as shown below.

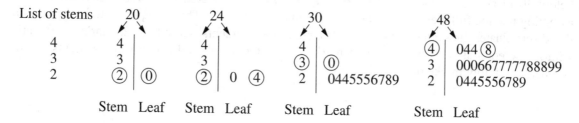

The diagram shows all the marks scored by the thirty students. It shows that the lowest score is 20, and that the highest score is 48. Most students score more than 35 marks. The most common score is 37.

 ## Stem and Leaf Diagram

The stem and leaf diagram is closely related to the dot diagram. In the stem and leaf diagram, however, numerical digits are used to present the data, instead of using number lines and dots. In constructing the stem and leaf diagram, two parts, a stem and a leaf, are extracted from each value.

Consider the set of same marks scored by the thirty students mentioned above. The first step in constructing the stem and leaf diagram is to arrange the marks in numerical order, the same way as that when constructing the dot diagram. Next, separate the numbers into their stem and leaf parts. For example, the first number is 20. We split it into its stem digit '2' and its leaf digit '0', and the leaf digit is written to the right of the corresponding stem as shown below. The same process is then repeated for each of the remaining numbers.

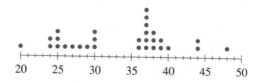

List of stems

	20		24		30		48	
4	4		4		4		④	044 ⑧
3	3		3		③	⓪	3	000667777788899
2	②	⓪	②	0 ④	2	0445556789	2	0445556789
	Stem	Leaf	Stem	Leaf	Stem	Leaf	Stem	Leaf

Alternatively, we may arrange the numbers as shown below first.

40 44 44 48
30 30 30 36 36 36 37 37 37 37 37 37 38 38 38 39
20 24 24 25 25 25 26 27 28 29

Next, split each number in the first column into its stem and leaf parts.

S	L
4	0 44 44 48
3	0 30 30 36 36 36 37 37 37 37 37 37 38 38 38 39
2	0 24 24 25 25 25 26 27 28 29

This is followed by removing the stem digit of each of the other numbers.

```
S | L
4 | 0  4  4  8
3 | 0  0  0  6  6  6  7  7  7  7  7  7  8  8  8  9
2 | 0  4  4  5  5  5  6  7  8  9
```

The final step is to simply bring the leaf digits closer together.

```
S | L
4 | 0448
3 | 0006667777778889
2 | 0445556789
```

To get a better picture of the distribution of the marks, we may choose to display a stem twice, i.e. one stem for the leaves 0 – 4 and the other for the leaves 5 – 9, as shown below.

```
4 | 8
4 | 044
3 | 667777778889
3 | 000
2 | 5556789
2 | 0444
```

From this stem and leaf diagram, the quick impression we have of the test is that most students score below 40 marks. No student scores below 20 marks and one student scores a high mark of 48, assuming that the full mark is 50. The most common score is 37. The test appears to be an easy one that discriminates the students quite well. The bulk of the students' score from 25 marks to 39 marks, with a few good students scoring high marks of 44 and above, and a few weak students scoring comparatively low marks of 24 and below.

═══ Exercise 15d ═══

1. The following data represent the travel times, in minutes, from home to office of 30 company executives:

68	37	18	48	25	12	64	35	40	43
34	28	54	57	43	31	38	43	50	39
44	41	26	17	19	12	35	53	60	48

   (a) Represent this data set in a dot diagram.
   (b) Represent this data set in a stem and leaf diagram.
   (c) What is the most common travel time?
   (d) What is the percentage of executives who take less than half an hour to reach the office?

2. The following are the weight, in kg, of 40 boxes.

80   83   84
86   86   86   87   88   88   89   89
90   90   90   90   90   90   90   91   91   92   92   93   93   93   94
95   96   96   97   97   99
100 101 102 104 104
106 108 108

(a) Represent this data set in a dot diagram.
(b) Copy and complete the stem and leaf diagram below.

$$
\begin{array}{c|ccc}
8 & 0 \\
8 & 6 & 6 \\
9 & 0 & 0 & 0 \\
9 & 5 & 6 \\
10 & 0 & 1 \\
10 & 6 \\
\end{array}
$$

(c) Write down the most common mass.
(d) 50% of the boxes have a mass of below a kg each. Find the value of a.

3. The following data represents the attention span, in minutes, of 30 preschool-age children.

5.4   2.0   6.3   5.5   3.0   5.4   3.6   5.4   3.3   4.6
7.3   4.4   6.6   5.4   5.2   7.0   3.8   5.8   5.7   4.5
5.7   4.9   6.5   2.7   6.1   7.2   2.2   6.7   4.1   5.6

(a) Draw a dot diagram to represent the data.
(b) Copy and complete the stem and leaf diagram below.

$$
\begin{array}{c|ccc}
7 & 0 \\
6 & 1 & 3 \\
5 & 2 & 4 & 4 \\
4 & 4 & 5 \\
3 & 0 & 3 \\
2 & 0 \\
\end{array}
$$

NB: The leaf unit = 0.1

(c) What is the most common attention span?
(d) What is the percentage of children with attention spans falling below 6 minutes?

4. The following diagram represents the scores of the students in two different schools for a common examination. In each school, 29 students took the examination.

ABC School		XYZ School
Leaves	Stem	Leaves
4 0	5	2 6 8 9
9 9 6	6	2 5 8 8 9 9
9 8 5 3 2 0	7	4 6 7 8 8 9
9 9 7 7 6 6 4 2	8	0 3 4 4 6 7 7
9 8 8 7 6 6 3 2 0	9	0 2 7 8
	10	0 0

(a) Which school had the "high scorer"?

(b) Which school had the "low scorer"?

(c) Which school did better in the examination?

(d) Combining the scores of the two schools, draw a dot diagram and also a stem and leaf diagram representing all 56 values.

Frequency Tables

Consider the marks scored by 40 students in a Science test marked out of a total of 10.

8	6	4	3	5	5	2	9	2	7
9	3	3	7	7	5	8	3	7	3
4	8	7	8	2	4	6	2	4	1
7	7	6	2	6	4	4	6	10	6

The teacher would like to know the overall performance of the students after the test to get a feedback on the students' progress. He may be interested in:

(a) the average score

(b) the middle score

(c) the most common score

(d) the highest score

(e) the lowest score

(f) the range of scores

(g) whether the test was too difficult or too easy.

He can find what he wants from the list of marks. But he will have some difficulty in doing so because the marks are not arranged in some convenient order. Hence, as discussed earlier, a set of unsummarised data, which we call raw data, has to be simplified and then arranged in an orderly fashion first, so that we will be able to understand and use them later.

We notice from the list of marks that some marks appear more than once. We arrange the marks according to the number of times each mark appears on the list.

Mark	Tally	Frequency
0		0
1	/	1
2	⫽⫽⫽	5
3	⫽⫽⫽	5
4	⫽⫽⫽ /	6
5	///	3
6	⫽⫽⫽ /	6
7	⫽⫽⫽ //	7
8	////	4
9	//	2
10	/	1
Total frequency		40

The marks are arranged in order of magnitude. We go through the list of marks and keep a tally as shown in the table above. The number of times each mark appears is called its **frequency**. The table which gives the frequency of each score is called a **frequency table**.

Histograms

A diagram can be constructed to illustrate the information given in the frequency table. Such a diagram is called a **histogram**. The histogram is easier to understand than the frequency table.

Fig. 15.5 below shows the histogram representing the frequency of the marks obtained in the Science test taken by 40 students.

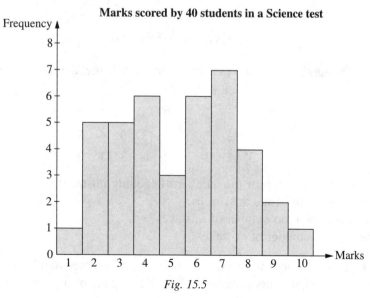

Fig. 15.5

A histogram is actually a vertical bar graph with no space in between the bars. However, the areas of the bars or the rectangles, and not the heights, are proportional to the numbers they represent. In our example, the bases of the rectangles are equal. So the height of each rectangle will be proportional to the frequency.

In-Class Activity

Using the histogram in Fig. 15.5, try answering questions like:

(1) What was the most common score?
(2) What was the middle score, that is, the score with half of the pupils scoring less than it?
(3) What was the highest score?
(4) What was the lowest score?
(5) What was the range, that is, the difference between the highest and the lowest scores?

Collection of Data by Measuring

This method of collecting data is useful in controlling the quality of products from a production line. For example, in a factory producing electrical light bulbs, the quality control process may involve measuring the lifespan of a certain number of bulbs selected at random from the production line. The results of the actual calculations involving this number of bulbs are then analysed to determine whether the electrical light bulbs produced overall are up to the acceptable standard.

In-Class Activity

(a) Measure the lengths, correct to the nearest cm, of the shoes worn by each of your classmates.
(b) Record the results and arrange them in the form of a frequency table.
(c) Display your information using a histogram.
(d) Comment on your results.

═ Exercise 15e ═

1. In a spelling test, the number of mistakes incurred by each of the 30 pupils in a primary one class is given below:

   3 4 6 0 2 2 4 3 5 3
   4 2 2 3 1 5 3 0 4 5
   4 3 4 0 3 2 6 3 1 0

   (a) Construct a frequency table for the number of spelling mistakes.
   (b) Draw a histogram to illustrate the results.
   (c) What is the most common number of mistakes?
   (d) What is the highest number of mistakes?

2. The teachers of a certain school were asked to indicate the average number of hours they spend on marking students' assignments each day. The following set of data was obtained.

$$
\begin{array}{ccccccccc}
6 & 4 & 3 & 1 & 2 & 2 & 3 & 1 & 4 \\
1 & 2 & 5 & 3 & 4 & 5 & 2 & 2 & 3 \\
3 & 1 & 2 & 2 & 3 & 1 & 4 & 2 &
\end{array}
$$

(a) Construct a frequency table and draw a histogram illustrating the results.
(b) How many teachers responded to the survey?
(c) What is the longest number of hours spent?
(d) What is the most common number of hours spent?

∗**3.** 100 crates of oranges imported from Country *A* were inspected and the number of rotten oranges recorded is shown below:

Rotten oranges	0	1	2	3	4	5	6	7	8	9
No. of crates	4	9	12	28	22	15	5	2	2	1

Another 100 crates of oranges imported from Country *B* were also inspected and the number of rotten oranges recorded was:

Rotten oranges	0	1	2	3	4	5	6	7	8
No. of crates	51	30	8	4	1	2	2	1	1

(a) Draw a histogram to represent each frequency table.
(b) What is the largest number of rotten oranges for each exporter?
(c) Find the total number of rotten oranges for each exporter.

Summary

1. (a) Numerical data can be obtained in many ways.
   (b) The data collected can be summarised in a systematic way by tabulation.
   (c) The tabulated data is usually presented in a graphical form.
   (d) Some common statistical graphs are **pictograms, bar graphs, pie charts** and **line graphs**.

2. Dot diagrams as well as stem and leaf diagrams provide an easy way of organising data.
   In a dot diagram, values are presented by dots above a horizontal number line.
   In a stem and leaf diagram, a value is split into two parts, namely a stem and a leaf.

3. (a) A set of data, or raw data, can be arranged in an orderly way in the form of a **frequency table**.
   (b) A frequency table can be represented graphically by a **histogram**.
   (c) A **histogram** is a vertical bar graph with no space in **between** the bars.
   (d) The **area** of each bar is proportional to the frequency it represents.

Review Questions 15

1. The bar graph below illustrates the monthly expenditure of a family.

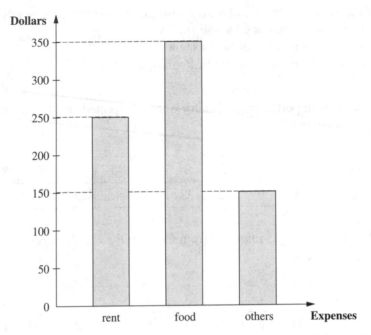

Draw a pie chart to represent this information, marking out the size of the angle in each sector clearly.

2. For the period of 1998–1999, the gross income of a company was $63 million. The profit of the company before tax was $8 million after the costs of running the company were deducted from the gross income.

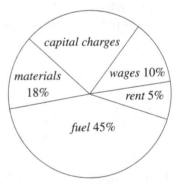

(a) Find the running costs for the period of 1998–1999.

(b) The running costs are represented in the following pie chart:

- **(i)** What percentage of the running costs belonged to capital charges?
- **(ii)** What is the measurement of the angle used to represent the materials in the pie chart?
- **(iii)** Find the actual amount of money spent on fuel.

3. The table shows the number of goals scored by each team in a soccer tournament.

(a) How many teams scored more than two goals?

(b) Draw a histogram to represent the data.

No. of goals	0	1	2	3	4	5
No. of teams	15	19	8	7	1	0

∗4. During a one-month period, the number of sick leave days of 100 workers in a factory was recorded as shown in the table below:

No. of sick leave days	0	1	2	3	4
No. of workers	45	32	14	6	3

(a) Represent the data using a histogram.

(b) What is the most common number of days of sick leave?

✳5. The following data represent the scores of 30 students in a quiz:

$$
\begin{array}{cccccccccc}
110 & 84 & 107 & 83 & 83 & 112 & 87 & 80 & 117 & 91 \\
104 & 113 & 110 & 124 & 118 & 79 & 116 & 116 & 94 & 113 \\
93 & 94 & 110 & 95 & 93 & 104 & 76 & 115 & 91 & 90
\end{array}
$$

(a) Draw a dot diagram to represent the data.

(b) Represent the data in a stem and leaf diagram.

(c) What is the most common score?

(d) There is an exceptionally high score. Identify this score.

6. The following data represent the weights, in grams, of 50 pencil sharpeners:

$$
\begin{array}{cccccccccc}
7.2 & 7.7 & 9.0 & 5.2 & 7.7 & 7.0 & 7.2 & 7.4 & 9.5 & 7.2 \\
8.4 & 6.9 & 7.4 & 7.2 & 8.5 & 7.1 & 8.0 & 10.5 & 7.6 & 10.2 \\
8.6 & 9.3 & 9.1 & 7.5 & 7.2 & 9.8 & 11.9 & 8.3 & 9.4 & 7.9 \\
6.8 & 9.2 & 8.6 & 8.6 & 8.4 & 7.2 & 7.4 & 8.5 & 7.7 & 7.0 \\
7.0 & 7.3 & 7.6 & 6.9 & 9.2 & 10.4 & 7.3 & 9.4 & 9.1 & 8.1
\end{array}
$$

(a) Draw a **(i)** dot diagram to represent the data;
       (ii) stem and leaf diagram to represent the data.

(b) Find the most common weight.

(c) Calculate the percentage of sharpeners having weights greater than 9.0 grams?

Exploration

1. The following table shows the amounts, in dollars, spent on food, rent, clothing, fuel and other items by two families in a week.

	Food	Rent	Clothing	Fuel	Others	**Total**
Family A	160	56	48	32	24	320
Family B	180	x	63	45	42	y

(a) Draw a pie chart of radius 4 cm to represent the amounts spent by Family A.

(b) In the pie chart for Family B, the angle of the sector representing the amount spent on rent is the same as that for Family A. Calculate the values of x and y.

Revision Exercise IV No. 1

1. The Political and Economic Risk Consultancy (PERC) ranked the following countries according to the level of corruption in the country based on a scale of 0 to 10: zero being the 'cleanest' and most transparent and 10 being the most corrupt. The following table show the results of the survey of some Asian countries in 1999. Represent the figures in the form of a bar chart.

Country	Corruption Score
China	9.00
India	9.17
Japan	4.25
Malaysia	7.50
Indonesia	9.91
Singapore	1.55
South Korea	8.20
Thailand	7.57
Vietnam	8.50
the Philippines	6.71

2. A triangle has sides 6 cm, 8 cm and 9 cm. Find the length of the shortest altitude of the triangle by means of an accurate drawing.

3. Draw a triangle with sides 12 cm, 8 cm and 10.5 cm. Bisect any two of the angles and let the bisectors meet at X. Construct the perpendicular from X to the longest side of the triangle. Measure this perpendicular.

4. A bus is supposed to start at 12 25 and to reach its destination at 13 50. It starts 3 minutes late and arrives 10 minutes late. How long did it take to reach its destination?

5. In the given diagram, find the values of x, y and z.

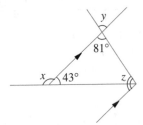

6. (a) A square piece of metal with side 14 cm costs $4.90. How much will a similar piece of metal in the shape of a rectangle with sides 20 cm by 12 cm cost? (Assume that the cost of the metal is proportional to the area.)

   (b) A trader buys a typewriter for $120 and sells it for $138. Find the profit percent.

7. (a) How long will it take a principal sum of $2 400 to amount to $2 880 at a simple interest rate of 6% per annum?

   (b) The driver of a train averaging 32 km/h takes 3 hours for a journey. What is the length of the journey? How long would the driver of an express train averaging 48 km/h take for the same journey?

8. In the figure, $d = 90°$, show that

   (a) $a - c = 90°$,　　(b) $a + b = 180°$.

   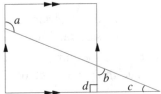

9. (a) Draw $\triangle PQR$ such that $PQ = 90$ mm, $QR = 100$ mm and $RP = 67.5$ mm. A point T lies on PQ such that $QT = 30$ mm. Draw a line through T parallel to QR to cut RP at S. Measure the length of RS.

   (b) Construct $\triangle ABC$ such that $BC = 7.5$ cm, $AC = 6$ cm and $A\hat{C}B = 60°$. Also construct the angle bisector of $A\hat{B}C$. Measure the length of AB.

10. Each student in a group of 240 was asked to choose his/her favourite subject from Mathematics, English and Geography. The result is represented on the pie chart given on the right.

    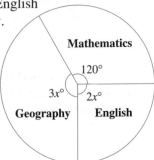

Calculate
(a) the value of *x*;
(b) the number of pupils who chose English;
(c) the fraction of pupils who chose Geography.

Revision Exercise IV No. 2

1. Draw $\triangle ABC$ with sides each of length 10.8 cm. Mark a point *P* on *AB* such that *PA* = 2.4 cm. On *BC*, mark a point *Q* such that *QC* = 8.6 cm. Measure *PQ*.

2. Construct a rhombus of side 6 cm and one of its diagonals 8 cm. Measure the length of the other diagonal.

3. In $\triangle ABC$, $A\hat{B}C = 64°$, *AB* = *AC* and *BC* is produced to *D*.
Calculate

(a) $B\hat{A}C$;   **(b)** $A\hat{C}D$.

4. In the given figure *AX* = *XC*, $A\hat{X}C = 130°$ and $A\hat{B}C = 56°$. Calculate the value of
(a) $C\hat{A}X$;   **(b)** $B\hat{A}X$.

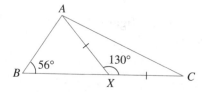

5. Two trains 245 m and 315 m long are travelling towards each other at 90 km/h and 54 km/h respectively on parallel lines. How long do the trains take to pass one another from the time they meet each other?

$\left(\textbf{Note:}\ 1\ \text{km/h} = \dfrac{5}{18}\ \text{m/s}\right)$

6. Construct a parallelogram with diagonals 7.5 cm and 10.2 cm, and with the shorter sides 3.6 cm long. Measure the length of the longer sides.

7. (a) If *x*% of 300 is equal to 15% of 220, find *x*.

(b) Express 5.4 km as a percentage of 6.4 km
  (i) exactly;
  (ii) in decimal form correct to 3 significant figures.

8. Find the angles marked *p*, *q*, *r* and *s* in the figure.

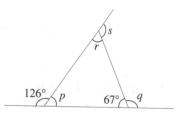

9. Construct $\triangle ABC$ where *AB* = 8 cm, *BC* = 7 cm and *CA* = 10 cm. Construct a point *X* inside the triangle such that it is lying on the bisector of $A\hat{B}C$ and is 3 cm from *AC*.

10. In a school, the pupils are divided into three groups, *A*, *B* and *C*. $\dfrac{1}{3}$ of the pupils are in group *A*, $\dfrac{5}{12}$ in group *B* and the rest in group *C*. If there are 150 pupils in group *C*, find

(a) the total number of pupils in the school;
(b) the ratio of the number of pupils in group *A* to the number of pupils in group *B*.

Revision Exercise IV No. 3

1. Construct a parallelogram with one of its diagonals 100 mm and two of its sides 48 mm and 109 mm. Measure the length of the other diagonal.

2. Construct a trapezium *PQRS* in which *PQ* is parallel to *SR*, $P\hat{S}R = 90°$, *QP* = 3.6 cm, *PS* = 7.2 cm and *SR* = 12.6 cm. Measure *QR* and $P\hat{Q}R$.

3. Find the angles marked *p*, *q* and *r* in the following figures.
(a)

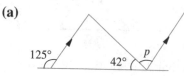

(b)

(c)

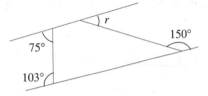

4. **(a)** The capacity of a tank is 60 000 litres. It is being filled at a rate of 1 250 litres per hour. How long will it take to fill $\frac{5}{8}$ of the tank?

   (b) A clock gains 12 min 15 s in one week. How many days will it take to gain 3 h 30 min?

5. Construct a quadrilateral $ABCD$ where $AB = CD = 8$ cm, $BC = 6$ cm, $A\hat{B}C = 90°$ and $B\hat{C}D = 130°$. Measure the length of AD.

6. If $1 560 amounts to $1 833 after 2 years and 4 months, find the rate of simple interest.

7. **(a)** If 80% of a number is 400, find the number.

   (b) What percentage of $55.00 is $13.20?

   (c) A bag was sold for $23.80 at a loss of $12\frac{1}{2}\%$. Find the cost price of the bag.

8. Find the unknown angles x, y and z in the figure below.

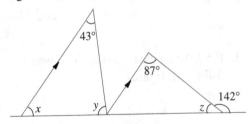

9. Given that $7x = 2y$, find the ratio $x : y$.

10. The pie chart below shows the number of people taking part in the big walk organised by the Singapore Sports Council. If 1 656 girls took part in the walk, find

   (a) x;

   (b) the percentage of participants who are men;

   (c) the number of participants who are boys.

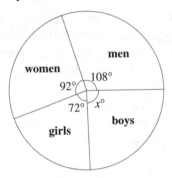

Revision Exercise IV No. 4

1. A Malaysian tourist exchanges M$480 for Singapore dollars at a rate of M$100 = S$45.50. Find the amount of Singapore dollars he can get.

2. Find, in the figure, the angles marked x and y.

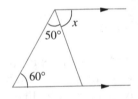
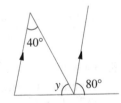

3. 12 men takes 5 days to build a road 200 m long. How many days will 20 men take to build a road 400 m long?

4. A bookseller bought 50 books for $225 and sold them for $5.40 each. Find his percentage profit.

5. Construct a parallelogram with sides 7.5 cm and 9 cm and with one of its interior angles as 62°. Measure its diagonals.

6. In the figure, $ABCD$ is a straight line, $BE = BC$, $A\hat{D}E = 35°$ and $A\hat{B}E = 140°$. Show that $CE = CD$.

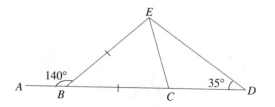

7. Construct $\triangle PQR$ such that $PQ = 10$ cm, $QR = 9$ cm and $RP = 8$ cm. A point S on PR is 2 cm from R. Draw a line through S parallel to RQ to cut PQ at T. Measure PT.

8. In an isosceles triangle the base angle is $12°$ greater than the vertical angle. Find the size of the vertical angle.

9. Each pupil in a class of 40 was asked to state the length of time he/she spends on private tuition in a week. The results are shown in the following table.

(t hours) Length of time spent	No. of pupils
$t = 0$	8
$0 < t \leqslant 2$	4
$2 < t \leqslant 4$	12
$4 < t \leqslant 6$	10
$6 < t \leqslant 8$	6

Illustrate the above information by using a pie chart. What is the angle representing pupils who have 2 to 4 hours of private tuition per week?

10. To ensure the long term availability of fresh water for its citizens, the Singapore Government decided to build a desalination plant scheduled for completion in the year 2004. Due to the Asian economic crisis in 1998, the cost of building the plant has dropped from an initial projected cost of S$1.2 billion to about $912 million. Find the percentage savings for building the plant.

Revision Exercise IV No. 5

1. In the figure, $AQ = BQ$ and PQ is parallel to BC. If $Q\hat{B}C = 28°$ and $Q\hat{C}B = 52°$, find $A\hat{P}Q$.

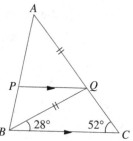

2. Construct a parallelogram $ABCD$ in which $AB = 7.5$ cm, $BC = 6$ cm and $A\hat{B}C = 50°$. Draw the perpendiculars from C to AB and AD. Measure the length of these perpendiculars.

3. From a square wooden disc of side 10 cm, a circular disc of radius 5 cm is cut out. What percentage of wood remains? (Take $\pi = 3.14$)

4. (a) If $5\frac{1}{2}\%$ of $2M$ is 110, find M.
 (b) A man bought a pen for $12.50. He sold it to a customer at 24% profit. Find the selling price.
 (c) A man bought an HDB flat for $150 000 and sold it later for $162 000. Find his percentage gain.

5. Find the angles marked x and y in the figure.

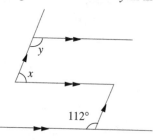

6. In the figure, BCD is a straight line and $\triangle ABC$ is an equilateral triangle. Given that $A\hat{D}C = 35°$ and $D\hat{A}C = x°$, find x.

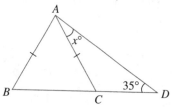

7. A man uses a ruler to measure a rectangle 45 cm by 36 cm. His result is 44.6 cm by 35.8 cm. Find his error per cent in the value he obtains for the perimeter.

8. Find x, y and z in the given figure.

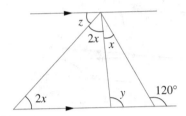

9. (a) *ABC* is a triangle in which $B = C = 70°$. *AC* is produced to P and the bisector of *BCP* cuts *AB* produced at Q. Find *AQC*.
   (b) Construct a rhombus of side 7 cm and one of the diagonals 11 cm. Measure the other diagonal. Measure also one of the acute angles.

10. The histogram displays the results of a survey on the number of children, the residents of a newly completed condominium have.

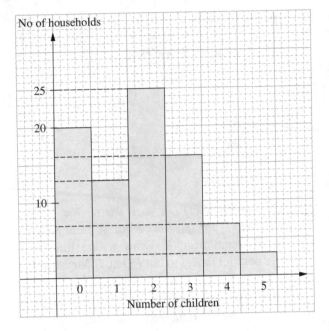

Find
(a) the number of households;
(b) the total number of children in the survey;
(c) the percentage of households having exactly 2 children.

Part I (50 marks)   **Time: 1 h**

*Answer **all** the questions. Calculators are **not** to be used in this section.*

1. Simplify (a) $4 - 1\frac{1}{2} \times 1\frac{3}{4}$, [2]

   (b) $3\frac{3}{8} \div \frac{3}{4} + \frac{5}{16}$. [2]

2. A ball-point pen weighs 12.4 g. Find the total mass of 2 560 such ball-point pens, giving your answer in kilograms. [3]

3. The perimeter of a rectangle is 28 cm and its width is 6 cm. Find its area. [3]

4. Evaluate each of the following, giving your answer correct to 2 decimal places:
   (a) $9.264\ 6 \div 0.6$ [2]
   (b) 3.156×27.2 [2]

5. A, B and C share $345 in the ratio 1 : 5 : 17. How much does each receive? [4]

6. A customer paid $117 for a watch after a 35% discount. What was the original price of the watch? [3]

7. A school librarian bought 56 books, some at $3.50 each and others at $4.50 each. If the total cost of these books was $240, how many books that cost $3.50 each were bought? [4]

8. Solve the following equations:
   (a) $4 = \frac{1}{5}(2x - 3)$ [2]
   (b) $3x - 4 = 7 - 4(x - 5)$ [2]

9. Simplify each of the following:
   (a) $12x - 2[2x - 3(x - 5)]$ [2]
   (b) $\frac{x-2}{5} - \frac{2x-3}{4} + \frac{5-x}{10}$ [3]

10. In the figure, ABC is a right-angled triangle with $A\hat{B}C = 90°$, $A\hat{C}B = 32°$ and $D\hat{A}B = D\hat{A}C$.
    Calculate
    (a) $D\hat{A}B$, (b) $A\hat{D}C$. [4]

11. Consider the number pattern below:
$$1 = 1$$
$$1 + 2 + 1 = 4$$
$$1 + 2 + 3 + 2 + 1 = 9$$
$$1 + 2 + 3 + 4 + 3 + 2 + 1 = 16$$
$$\vdots \quad \vdots$$

(a) Write down the 5th line of the sequence. [1]
(b) Find the value of
$1 + 2 + 3 + \ldots + 8 + 9 + 8 + 7 + \ldots + 3 + 2 + 1$. [1]
(c) If $1 + 2 + 3 + \ldots + (x - 1) + x + (x - 1) + \ldots + 3 + 2 + 1 = 169$, find the value of x. [1]

12. (a) A solid copper cylinder, 8 cm long and 4 cm in diameter, is melted and recast into a length of wire 2 mm in diameter. How long is the wire? [3]
    (b) Mr Lee puts $5 000 in a bank that pays a compound interest of 4% per year. If he leaves the principal and the interest in the bank for another year, how much will he have at the end of the second year? [2]

13. Construct a triangle ABC with AB = 7.8 cm. $A\hat{B}C = 55°$ and BC = 6.8 cm. Measure the length of AC. [4]

Part II (50 marks)   **Time: 1 h 15 min**

*Answer **all** the questions. Calculators may be used in this section.*

Section A (22 marks)

1. A lawn roller is 80 cm wide with a diameter of 42 cm. Find the area it covers in 40 revolutions. Give your answer in square metres and take π to be $\frac{22}{7}$. [4]

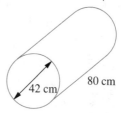

42 cm   80 cm

2. An open cylindrical tank with diameter 28 cm contains water to a depth of 30 cm. Find the volume of the water inside the tank, giving your answer in litres. Find also the total surface area of the tank that is in contact with the water. [6]

3. A rectangular field has sides $5x$ metres by $4x$ metres. Calculate the value of x in each of the following cases:

   (a) The perimeter of the field is 450 metres. [3]

   (b) The area of the field is 2 000 square metres. [3]

4. In the figure, HAK is parallel to BDE, $A\hat{D}E = 110°$, $A\hat{B}C = B\hat{A}C = 2x$, $C\hat{A}D = x$, $A\hat{C}D = y$ and $B\hat{A}H = z$. Calculate the values of x, y and z. [6]

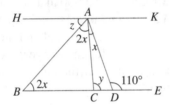

5. An open rectangular box 24 cm long, 18 cm wide and 10 cm deep internally is made of wood 2 cm thick.

   (a) What volume of wood is used to make the box? [4]

   (b) What is its capacity in litres? [3]

Section B (28 marks)

6. (a) Find the mass, in kg, of a cylindrical metal bar 3 m long and 7 cm in diameter if the density of the metal is 4.2 g/cm³.

$$\left(\text{Take } \pi = \frac{22}{7}\right) \quad [4]$$

   (b) Evaluate each of the following, giving your answer correct to 4 significant figures:

     (i) $\sqrt{432.9} \div 7.6$ [2]

     (ii) $\dfrac{5}{\sqrt[3]{965}} + \dfrac{3.2^2}{1.85^5}$ [2]

7. (a) Calculate the values of x and y in the diagram. [4]

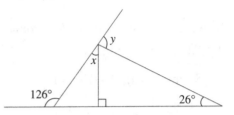

   (b) The amount of pocket money Alvin received is just enough for him to buy 10 plates of chicken rice or 15 plates of fried noodles. If he wishes to buy equal number of plates of chicken rice and fried noodles, how many of each type can he buy with the money? [3]

8. (a) Four people contributed sums of money to the Community Chest of Singapore in the ratio 2 : 3 : 5 : 8. If the largest amount contributed is \$24, calculate the total amount contributed by the four people. [3]

   (b) A tourist exchanged M\$900 for Singapore dollars (S\$) at M\$2.25 to S\$1. He spent S\$245 in Singapore and exchanged the remainder for Malaysian ringgit at the same rate. How many Malaysian ringgit did the tourist receive? Give your answer correct to the nearest ringgit. [3]

End-of-Year Examination Specimen Paper 2

Part 1 (50 marks)   Time: 1 h

*Answer **all** the questions. Calculators are **not** to be used in this section.*

1. Simplify   **(a)** $7\frac{1}{2} - 3\frac{3}{4} \div \frac{3}{8}$, [2]

           (b) $4\frac{2}{3} \times 3\frac{3}{8} - 9\frac{7}{8}$. [2]

2. (a) Express 0.035 as a fraction in its lowest terms. [1]

   (b) Express $1\frac{9}{40}$ as a decimal. [1]

(c) Express 2.004 56 correct to two decimal places. [1]

(d) Express 0.025 47 correct to two significant figures. [1]

3. **(a)** Find the LCM of 25, 80 and 120. [2]
   (b) Simplify $3(5x - 7) - 2(3x - 5y) + 2(3y - 7x) - (x - 2y)$. [2]

4. Solve the equation $x - \dfrac{x - 1}{4} = \dfrac{x + 2}{5}$. [3]

5. The area of a trapezium is 1 500 cm². Find the height between the parallel sides if their lengths are 14 cm and 36 cm. [3]

6. How many litres of water are required to fill a rectangular storage tank 12 m long, 6 m wide and 2 m deep? [3]
   (1 litre = 1 000 cm³)

7. A solid concrete cylinder of diameter 70 cm is 120 cm high. What is its volume in cubic metres? [3]

8. At a sale, a sofa set selling at a discount of 25% fetches $3 570. Find the original price of the sofa set. [3]

9. A trader buys x pencils at $\$y$ each and sells them at 3 for $\$z$. Find an expression for his total profit. [3]

10. A bicycle wheel has a diameter of 70 cm. Find
    (a) the circumference of the wheel; [2]
    (b) the distance the bicycle travels after the wheel has made 400 revolutions.
    $\left(\text{Take } \pi = 3\dfrac{1}{7}\right)$ [2]

11. A Singaporean obtained US$2 500 at a rate of S$1.70 to US$1. He spent US$1 850 and exchanged the remaining US dollars for Singapore dollars at a rate of S$1.68 to US$1. How many equivalent Singapore dollars had he used up? [4]

12. Construct a parallelogram $ABCD$ in which $AB = 9$ cm, $AD = 6$ cm and $B\hat{C}D = 55°$. On the same diagram, construct a perpendicular from D to AB and measure its length. [4]

13. Consider the following number pattern:
$$2 \times 2 = 1 \times 3 + 1$$
$$3 \times 3 = 2 \times 4 + 1$$
$$4 \times 4 = 3 \times 5 + 1$$
$$5 \times 5 = 4 \times 6 + 1$$
$$\vdots \qquad \vdots$$
$$n \times n = 13 \times 15 + 1$$

(a) Write down the 10th line in the pattern. [1]

(b) Find the value of n. [1]

(c) Use the above pattern to calculate the value of 199^2. [2]

14. The students of a Secondary 1 class were asked to name their favourite subject. The bar graph illustrates the result. Find

(a) the total number of students in the class; [1]

(b) the fraction of students who like Maths; [1]

(c) the fraction of students who like either History or Geography. [1]

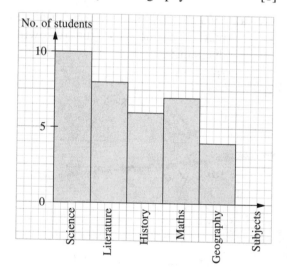

Part II (50 marks)   **Time: 1 h 15 min**

*Answer **all** the questions. Calculators may be used in this section.*

Section A (22 marks)

1. The density of a piece of metal is 5.8 g/cm³. Find the mass of a piece of the metal with a volume of 25 cm³. [3]

2. A father is four times as old as his son. Five years ago, the sum of their ages was 70. Find their present ages. [4]

3. (a) The figure shows a pattern made up of straight lines, semicircles and arcs of quadrants of circles. Calculate the total area of the shaded regions. [6]

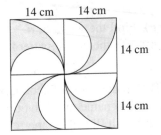

14 cm   14 cm

14 cm

14 cm

(b) A motorcycle wheel has a diameter of 42 cm. Find the number of complete revolutions it makes in moving a distance of 1.25 km. [3]

4. (a) Find the size of the unknown angles marked x and y on the following diagrams:

(i)

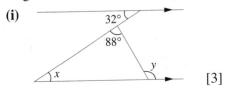

32°

88°

y

x [3]

(ii)

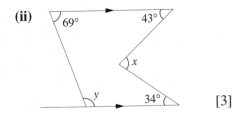

69°   43°

x

y 34°   [3]

Section B (28 marks)

5. (a) A man left $\frac{1}{8}$ of his money to a school, $\frac{1}{4}$ to charity and the remainder to his family. If the family received $15 000, how much money did the man have originally? [3]

(b) A sum of money is distributed among three people, A, B and C, in the ratio $5 : 7 : 13$. If B has $5 200 more than A, how much does C receive? [4]

6. (a) A man travelled 200 km at 60 km/h and then at 48 km/h for the next 160 km of his journey. Find his average speed for the whole journey. [4]

(b) A man earns a taxable income of $24 000 a year and pays $900 in taxes. What percentage of his income is taxed? [3]

7. (a) Evaluate each of the following, giving your answer correct to 4 significant figures:

(i) $84^2 \div 3.56^3$ **(ii)** $\dfrac{\sqrt{84.6}}{\sqrt[3]{0.014}} \times 0.6^3$ [4]

(b) Find the principal amount that will earn a simple interest of $1 638 in 3 years 3 months at 6% per annum. [3]

8. A rectangular pond 10 m by 8 m is surrounded by a concrete path 20 cm wide and 25 cm thick. Calculate the volume of concrete used in making the path, giving your answer in m^3. If the density of the concrete is 2.8 g/cm³, calculate the weight of the concrete. [7]

End-of-Year Examination Specimen Paper 3

Part I (50 marks)   **Time: 1 h**

*Answer **all** the questions. Calculators are **not** to be used in this section.*

1. Simplify

(a) $1\frac{1}{4} - \frac{1}{8} \times \left(2\frac{1}{3} + 1\frac{2}{9} \right)$; [2]

(b) $4\frac{2}{3} + 3\frac{1}{4} \div \left(3\frac{2}{5} + 3\frac{1}{10} \right)$. [2]

2. Simplify the following:

(a) $4a \times 5 + 3a$ [1]
(b) $18y - 5y \times 3$ [1]
(c) $2(a + b + c) - 4(2a - b - 3c)$ [2]

3. Solve the following equations:

   (a) $10 - 3y = 21 - 5y$ [2]

   (b) $11x + 10 - 6x = 23 + 4x - 9$ [2]

   (c) $\dfrac{4x - 2}{3} + \dfrac{2x + 17}{6} = \dfrac{7x - 3}{2}$ [3]

4. $ABCD$ is a parallelogram in which $A\hat{D}C = 108°$. Given that KB is perpendicular to BC and $K\hat{C}D = 23°$, find the values of x, y and z.   [4]

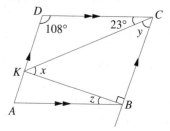

5. In the figure, ABC is a semicircle and ACD is a triangle. Find the area of the whole figure with the dimensions given.   [4]

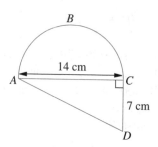

6. $\$2x$ is shared among 3 persons, A, B and C, in the ratio $3 : 2 : 5$. If B gets $\$45$, find the value of x.   [3]

7. The cost of material, labour and administration for an advertising campaign is in the ratio $8 : 5 : 2$. If the total cost of the campaign is $\$3\,525$, find the cost of labour.   [3]

8. A school field measures 120 m by 60 m. A plan of the field is drawn to a scale of $1 : 500$. Find the area of the field on the plan in cm².   [4]

9. The cost of a bottle of milk is NZ$0.65 in New Zealand. Find the cost of 20 bottles of milk in Singapore dollars.   [3]
   (Take NZ$1 = S$0.92)

10. A shopkeeper buys $143 worth of pens at $6.50 each. If he sells them at $7.80 each, find his profit percentage.   [4]

11. How long will it take to earn a simple interest of $337.50 from a principal sum of $2 500 at 6% per annum?   [3]

12. A driver covers 180 km in 2 h 30 min. If he is driving at a constant speed, find the distance he covers in 5 minutes.   [3]

13. Construct $\triangle PQR$ where $PQ = 6.4$ cm, $QR = 9.6$ cm and $PR = 8$ cm. Find, by measurement, the distance from P to the midpoint of QR.   [4]

Part II (50 marks)   Time: 1 h 15 min

*Answer **all** the questions. Calculators may be used in this section.*

Section A (22 marks)

1. When 8 is added to $\dfrac{4}{5}$ of a number x, the result is equal to x. Find x.   [3]

2. Find the volume of water that falls onto a flat roof 12.4 m long and 8.2 m wide during a day when 12 mm of rain is recorded. This water is later transferred into cylindrical containers each of radius 28 cm and height 60 cm. How many containers can be completely filled?   [6]

3. (a) The sum of three consecutive odd numbers is 63. Find the numbers.   [3]

   (b) A woman is 7 times as old as her daughter. If in 5 years' time she is 4 times as old as her daughter, what are their present ages?   [3]

4. (a) A housewife buys 11 m of cloth at $8.20 per metre. How much change will be given to her if she pays with 2 fifty-dollar notes?   [3]

   (b) Find the cost of painting the outer surface of a closed rectangular tank 3.6 m long, 2.5 m wide and 2 m deep with paint at 75 cents per square metre.   [4]

Section B (28 marks)

5. (a) A man cycles at v km/h. Find the distance he travels in t hours. How long will it take him to travel s km? [4]

(b) A car uses 1 litre of petrol to travel 9 km. If 1 litre of petrol costs $1.14, find the cost needed for the car to travel a distance of 135 km. [3]

6. (a) Find the angles marked x, y and z on the figure. [4]

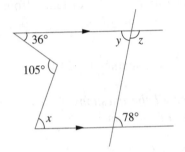

(b) Construct a parallelogram of sides 6.9 cm and 11.1 cm, and whose longer diagonal is 14.4 cm. Measure the length of the other diagonal. [4]

7. The inner dimensions of an open wooden rectangular box are 10 cm by 8 cm for the base and 5 cm for the height. If the thickness of the wood is 1 cm, calculate the volume of the material used in making the box. Find the weight of the box if the density of the wood is 0.7 g/cm³. [6]

8. (a) The pie chart below shows the sales of a shop dealing with telecommunications in a week.

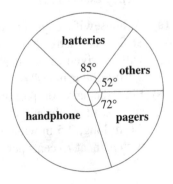

(i) What percentage of the sales were from pagers? [1]

(ii) If the total sales of the week amounted to $72 000, calculate the amount of sales for handphones. [3]

(b) 12 men can renovate a house in 15 days if they work 7 hours a day. If 14 men were asked to renovate a similar house in 10 days, how many hours a day must the men work? [3]

End-of-Year Examination Specimen Paper 4

Part I (50 marks)   **Time: 1 h**

*Answer **all** the questions. Calculators are **not** to be used in this section.*

1. Evaluate

(a) $(2 + 5)^2 - (17 - 15)^4 \div 2\frac{2}{3}$, [2]

(b) $1 - 0.04 + \frac{1}{4}$. [2]

2. (a) Express 0.086 479 as a decimal
(i) correct to 2 decimal places; [1]
(ii) correct to 2 significant figures. [1]

(b) Express 99 225 in prime factors and hence, find the value of $\sqrt{99\ 225}$. [2]

3. Solve the following equations:

(a) $5(3 - x) = 7(2x - 5)$ [2]

(b) $\frac{x}{3} - \frac{2x - 5}{5} = \frac{3}{15}$ [3]

4. Two towns, A and B, are 180 km apart. Motorist P sets off from A for B at 12 20 and travels at a speed of 50 km/h. Motorist Q sets off from A for B at 12 45 at a speed of 60 km/h. Who will arrive at B first and at what time? [3]

5. Copy and complete the following:

(a) 3 657 m = _____ km [1]
(b) 2.5 m² = _____ cm² [1]
(c) 1.864 l = _____ cm³ [1]
(d) 0.84 g = _____ kg [1]

6. A sum of money is divided among A, B and C in the ratio $15 : 8 : 7$. If B has \$4.50 more than C, find the original sum of money. [3]

7. A shopkeeper bought 650 eggs for \$70, 62 eggs were broken and the shopkeeper sold the rest at \$2 for 14 eggs. What was his gain or loss per cent? [3]

8. The histogram shows the number of absentees of a class during the first six months in a school in Singapore.

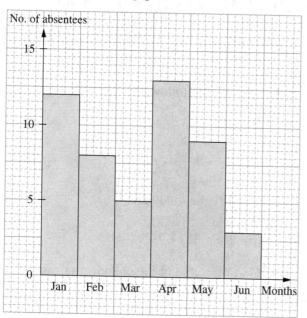

(a) Find the total number of absentees. [1]

(b) Suggest a simple reason why there were fewer absentees in the months of March and June. [2]

9. (a) If $2 : x = 5 : 9$, find x. [2]

(b) If $p = \dfrac{3}{4}$ and $q = 1\dfrac{5}{7}$, express $\dfrac{p}{q}$ as a percentage. [2]

10. Find two consecutive odd numbers such that the greater number added to 3 times the smaller number makes a total of 86. [4]

11. Simplify
(a) $2(5x - y) - 3(6x - 5y) + (x - 7y)$; [2]

(b) $\dfrac{x + 2}{3} - \dfrac{x - 5}{5} + \dfrac{2 - x}{4}$. [3]

12. In the diagram, AC is parallel to PQ, $CD = CB$, $B\hat{A}C = 44°$ and $C\hat{B}Q = 68°$. Calculate
(a) $A\hat{B}C$, (b) $A\hat{C}D$. [4]

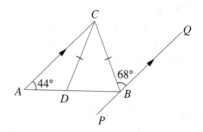

13. A motorist travels x km in t hours. If he travels at the same speed, how far will he travel in
(a) 3 hours; [1]
(b) y hours? [2]

Part II (50 marks)   **Time: 1 h 15 min**

*Answer **all** the questions. Calculators may be used in this section.*

Section A (22 marks)

1. Arrange the following numbers in descending order:
$$\frac{22}{7}, \ 3.142, \ \frac{47}{15}, \ 3\frac{3}{20}$$ [2]

2. Calculate the simple interest on \$7 800 for $3\dfrac{1}{2}$ years at 6% per annum. [3]

3. Construct a rhombus of side 8 cm with one of its interior angles measuring 70°. Measure the length of the diagonals. [4]

4. Find the value of x in each of the following diagrams:
(a)

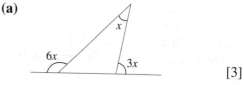

[3]

(b)

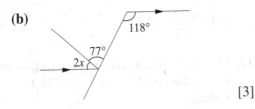

[3]

5. Construct the following in a single diagram.
   (a) $\triangle ABC$ in which $AB = 8$ cm, $A\hat{B}C = 65°$ and $B\hat{A}C = 42°$. [2]
   (b) The perpendicular from C to AB. [2]
   (c) The point E such that CE is parallel to AB and $C\hat{B}E = 58°$. [3]

Section B (28 marks)

6. A worker was paid $2.25 an hour and if he worked overtime, he was paid $3.50 an hour. If the worker received $127 for 52 hours of work, how many hours of overtime work did he do? [5]

7. A rectangular flower bed has a perimeter of 96 m. Given that its length is twice its breadth, calculate its length and its area. [4]

   The flower bed is surrounded by a concrete path of width 40 cm and height 15 cm. Calculate the volume of concrete used for the path, giving your answer in m³. [4]

8. A cylindrical water container of diameter 28 cm and height 35 cm is $\frac{7}{10}$ full of water.

   How many complete glasses of water, each of volume 186 cm³, can be filled? What is the volume of water left over then? [7]

   $\left(\text{Take } \pi = \frac{22}{7} \right)$

9. A rectangular hole measuring 2 cm by 3 cm is cut out from a solid cylinder of radius 12 cm and height 14 cm as shown in the diagram.
   (a) Find the volume of the remaining solid. [5]
   (b) If the density of the material used to make the solid is 1.5 g/cm³, find the weight of the remaining solid. [3]

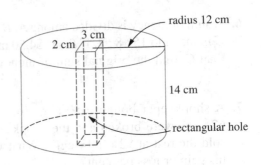

radius 12 cm
3 cm
2 cm
14 cm
rectangular hole

End-of-Year Examination Specimen Paper 5

Part I (50 marks)   **Time: 1 h**

*Answer **all** the questions. Calculators are **not** to be used in this section.*

1. Simplify the following:
   (a) $2\frac{3}{4} \div 1\frac{2}{3} - 1\frac{1}{3}$ [2]
   (b) $3\frac{2}{3} + 1\frac{1}{2} \times \frac{3}{4}$ [2]

2. Simplify the following:
   (a) $2(3x - 5) - 3(5x - 3)$ [2]
   (b) $2(a + 3b) + 7(2b - a)$ [2]

3. Find the value of the unknown in each of the following diagrams:
   (a)   (b)

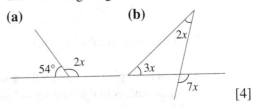

[4]

4. Estimate each of the following, giving your answer correct to 1 significant figure:
   (a) $\sqrt{905}$ (b) $\dfrac{586}{291}$
   (c) $8.01^2 - 0.48$ (d) $\sqrt[3]{8\,024}$ [4]

5. If $3(x - 1) - 5(x - 3) = 3$, find the value of $7x - 5$. [3]

6. Express (a) c cents in dollars, [1]
   (b) m millimetres in metres, [1]
   (c) k kilograms in grams. [1]

7. A tourist from England wishes to exchange sterling pounds for Singapore dollars. How many complete sterling pounds does he need to exchange for S\$1 800 if the exchange rate is £1 to S\$2.72? [3]

8. The results of a survey of the mode of transport used by the students of a school is illustrated by the pie chart. If the number of students travelling by car is 160, how many students travel by MRT? [3]

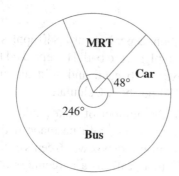

9. (a) The perimeter of a square is 36 cm. Find its area. [2]
   (b) The area of a triangle ABC is 36 cm² and $AB = 18$ cm. Find the perpendicular height from C to AB. [2]

10. A farmer uses $\frac{1}{3}$ of his land for rubber, $\frac{3}{8}$ for palm oil, $\frac{1}{6}$ for durians and the remaining 23 hectares for cocoa. Find the total area of the land. [3]

11. Meiling's mother is 8 times as old as Meiling. In 10 years' time, Meiling's mother will be only 3 times as old as Meiling. Find their present ages. [4]

12. The road distance between two towns, A and B, is 550 km. A car leaves A for B at an average speed of 72 km/h and a lorry leaves B for A, travelling along the same road as the car, at an average speed of 38 km/h at the same time. How long will it take before the two vehicles meet? [4]

13. Construct a parallelogram with sides 54 mm and 108 mm, and one of its angles, 64°. Measure the lengths of the two diagonals. [4]

14. The diagram shows a trapezium $ABCD$ with AB parallel to DC. Given that $AB = 6$ cm, $DC = 12$ cm and the height between the parallel sides equals 9 cm, calculate the area of $ABCD$. [3]

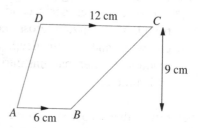

Part II (50 marks)   Time: 1 h 15 min

*Answer **all** the questions. Calculators may be used in this section.*

Section A (22 marks)

1. A man cycles at v km/h.
   (a) Find the distance he travels in 5 hours. [1]
   (b) Find the time needed to travel s km. [2]

2. A cylinder P has radius r cm and height $2h$ cm. A second cylinder Q has radius $3r$ cm and height h cm. Find the ratio of $\dfrac{\text{volume of } P}{\text{volume of } Q}$. [4]

3. (a) A motorist takes $5\frac{3}{4}$ hours to travel from P to Q at V km/h. If he increases his speed by 5 km/h, the time taken will be reduced by half an hour. Find V. [5]
   (b) The sum of 3 consecutive even numbers is 108. Find the numbers. [3]

4. Construct, in a single diagram,
   (a) $\triangle ABC$ where $AB = 9$ cm, $BC = 8$ cm and $AC = 7$ cm; [2]
   (b) a point D such that CD is parallel to AB and $CD = 5$ cm; [2]
   (c) the perpendicular from C to AB. [3]

Section B (28 marks)

5. **(a)** Solve the equation

$$\frac{2}{3}(4x - 1) - \frac{5}{6}(2x + 1) = \frac{1}{2}.$$ [3]

(b) If water is running into a tank at the rate of 3 metres per second along a trough of rectangular cross-section 18 cm wide and 15 cm deep, find the amount of water that runs into the tank in 1 minute. [4]

6. **(a)** Given that 12.5% of A is 42, find A.
   (b) Calculate the time needed for $4\,800 to earn a simple interest of $420 at 7% per annum. [3]

7. A cylindrical piece of cake of radius 14 cm and thickness 8 cm stands on a horizontal table. $\frac{1}{4}$ of the cake is removed by cutting vertically downwards through the radii OA and OB as shown in the diagram.

Find **(a)** the volume of the remaining cake. [3]

(b) the total surface area of the remaining cake. [5]

$$\left(\text{Take } \pi = \frac{22}{7} \right)$$

8. A shopkeeper bought 1 840 apples for $350. 52 apples were bad. He repacked the rest in boxes of 6 each and sold all of them at $1.80 per box. Calculate

(a) the number of boxes sold; [3]

(b) the total profit he made if the cost of an empty box was 6 cents each. Express this profit as a percentage of the total cost of apples and boxes, giving your answer correct to 1 decimal place. [4]

Answers

Exercise 1a *(Pg 5)*

1. (a) $a > 80\,000$
   (b) $b > 90$ $c > 80$
   (c) $83 \leqslant d \leqslant 95$
2. (a) 1, 2, 3, 4, 5, 6, 7
   (b) 26, 28, 30, 32, 34
   (c) 41, 43, 45, 47, 49, 51
   (d) 64, 65, 66, 67, 68, 69
   (e) 24, 27, 30, 33, 36, 39
   (f) 86, 88, 90, 92, 94, 96, 98
   (g) 55, 57, 59, 61, 63
   (h) 74, 76, 78, 80, 82, 84, 86, 88, 90

Exercise 1b *(Pg 6)*

1. (a) 1 735   (b) 15 455
2. (a) 58 257   (b) 2 368
3. (a)   249   (b)   284
        + 586   − 196
        ‾‾‾‾‾   ‾‾‾‾‾
          835   88
   (c)   663
            792
          + 587
          ‾‾‾‾‾
          2 042
4. (a) $x = 2, y = 2, z = 3$
   (b) $x = 6, y = 8, z = 7$
   (c) $x = 1, y = 7, z = 3$
   (d) $x = 2, y = 6, z = 9$
5. (a) 10 234, 98 765, 88 531
   (b) (i) 97 531, 86 420
       (ii) 10 468, 23 579
   (c) 97 531, 86 420

Exercise 1c *(Pg 8)*

1. (a) 15   (b) 854   (c) 18
   (d) 23
2. (a) 29   (b) 44   (c) 56
   (d) 68   (e) 152   (f) 266
   (g) 150 (h) 300   (i) 120
   (j) 130
3. (a) 143 (b) 128   (c) 280
   (d) 200 (e) 200   (f) 1 150

Exercise 1d *(Pg 10)*

1. (a) 6 194   (b) 85 920
   (c) 273 097

2. (a) 124   (b) 716   (c) 4 938
3. (a) 32   (b) 342   (c) 629

Exercise 1e *(Pg 12)*

1. (a) $\times, \times$ (b) +, + (c) +, +
   (d) $\times, \times$ (e) $\times, \times$ (f) +, +
2. (a) 7   (b) 4, 5   (c) 12
   (d) 6   (e) 13   (f) 6, 9

Exercise 1f *(Pg 13)*

1. (a) 242 424   (b) 242 424
2. 1 450 548
3. (a) 450   (b) 620
   (c) 590   (d) 770
   (e) 1 500   (f) 6 100
   (g) 12 910   (h) 81 600
   (i) 199 900   (j) 650 500
   (k) 44 400   (l) 222 200
   (m) 1 111 000 (n) 8 100
   (o) 7 200   (p) 7 700
   (q) 7 992   (r) 9 995

Exercise 1g *(Pg 15)*

1. (a) $=$ (b) $>$ (c) $<$
   (d) $>$ (e) $>$ (f) $=$
   (g) $<$ (h) $>$ (i) $<$
   (j) $<$
2. (a) $12 - (7 - 2) = 7$
   (b) $3 \times (5 + 7) = 36$
   (c) $3 \times (5 + 2 \times 4) = 39$
   (d) $3 \times (5 + 2) \times 4 = 84$
   (e) $(3 \times 5 + 2) \times 4 = 68$
   (f) $4 \times (6 - 3) \times 5 = 60$
3. (a) 72   (b) 112   (c) 1
   (d) 62   (e) 40   (f) 5
   (g) 440 (h) 45   (i) 15
   (j) 8   (k) 282   (l) 492
   (m) 209
4. 4, 12, $6
5. 8, 72, 4, 20, $98
6. 8
7. 5

Exercise 1h *(Pg 18)*

1. (a) (i) 590   (ii) 600
   (b) (i) 6 840 (ii) 6 800
       (iii) 7 000
2. (a) (i) 2 200 (ii) 2 000

   (b) (i)   10 080
       (ii) 10 100
       (iii) 10 000
       (iv) 10 000
3. (a) 82 650   (b) 82 600
   (c) 83 000   (d) 80 000
4. (a) (i)   55 730
       (ii) 55 700
       (iii) 56 000
   (b) (i)   380 010
       (ii) 38 000
       (iii) 38 000
   (c) (i)   9 969 970
       (ii) 9 970 000
       (iii) 9 970 000
   (d) (i)   76 636 790
       (ii) 76 636 800
       (iii) 76 637 000
5. (a) $14\,500 \leqslant a < 15\,500$ or
       $14\,500 \leqslant a \leqslant 15\,499$
   (b) $245\,000 \leqslant b < 255\,000$ or
       $245\,000 \leqslant b \leqslant 254\,999$

Exercise 1i *(Pg 20)*

1. (a) 8 400, 8 652
   (b) 50, 52
   (c) 80 000, 82 110
   (d) 13, 13
   (e) 3 400 000, 3 413 160
2. (a) (ii)   (b) (i)   (c) (ii)
   (d) (i)   (e) (i)
3. (a) 52 796 190
   (b) 26 011 001
   (c) 64 512 270
   (d) 1 091
   (e) 475 742 484
   (f) 25
   (g) 55 013
   (h) 13 805
   (i) 35 074 576
   (j) 6 991 771
   (k) 8 022 509
   (l) 30 838
   (m) 5 899
   (n) 53 935 970
   (o) 3 430 818
   (p) 138 479 550
   (q) 91 214 514

Review Questions 1 *(Pg 22)*

1. **(c)** 355   **(d)** 3 000
   (e) 1 600   **(f)** 8 684
   (g) 1 107   **(h)** 12 242
2. **(a)** 1 510   **(b)** 1 350
   (c) 720   **(d)** 7 700
   (e) 28   **(f)** 40 000
   (g) 998   **(h)** 2 024
   (i) 38 021
3. **(a)** 80   **(b)** 1 660
   (c) 37   **(d)** 1
   (e) 27   **(f)** 30
   (g) 0   **(h)** 1 150
   (i) 130   **(j)** 0
   (k) 19   **(l)** 220
4. **(a)** 97 000   **(b)** 3 648 000
   (c) 4 000 000   **(d)** 190
   (e) 70   **(f)** 200
   (g) 68   **(h)** 230
   (i) 200   **(j)** 20 000

Exercise 2a *(Pg 27)*

1. **(a)** 1, 2, 4, 8, 16
   (b) 1, 2, 4, 7, 14, 28
   (c) 1, 2, 3, 4, 6, 8, 12, 16, 24, 32, 48, 96
   (d) 1, 2, 4, 5, 10, 20, 25, 50, 100
   (e) 1, 2, 3, 4, 5, 6, 8, 10, 12, 15, 20, 24, 30, 40, 60, 120
   (f) 1, 2, 3, 5, 6, 7, 10, 14, 15, 21, 30, 35, 42, 70, 105, 210
2. **(a)** 4, 8, 12, 16, 20, 24
   (b) 7, 14, 21, 28, 35, 42
   (c) 9, 18, 27, 36, 45, 54
   (d) 12, 24, 36, 48, 60, 72
   (e) 17, 34, 51, 68, 85, 102
   (f) 21, 42, 63, 84, 105, 126
3. 54, 126, 196
4. 1, 2, 3, 4, 8, 9, 12, 16, 48, 144
5. 24, 32, 56, 72, 64, 40, 96, 120
6. 4, 14, 28, 32, 56
7. **(a)** 1, 2, 3, 4, 5, 6, 8, 10, 12, 15, 16, 20, 24, 30, 32, 40, 48, 60, 80, 96, 120, 160, 240, 480
   (b) 1, 2, 3, 4, 5, 6, 8, 10, 12, 15, 20, 24, 25, 30, 40, 50, 60, 75, 100, 120, 150, 200, 300, 600
   (c) 1, 2, 3, 4, 5, 6, 8, 10, 12, 15, 16, 20, 24, 30, 32, 40, 48,

60, 64, 80, 96, 120, 160, 192, 240, 320, 480, 960
   (d) 1, 2, 3, 4, 6, 8, 9, 12, 18, 24, 26, 36, 39, 52, 78, 104, 117, 156, 234, 312, 468, 936
   (e) 1, 2, 3, 4, 5, 6, 8, 9, 10, 12, 15, 18, 20, 24, 30, 36, 45, 54, 60, 72, 90, 108, 120, 135, 180, 216, 270, 360, 540, 1 080
   (f) 1, 2, 3, 4, 5, 6, 8, 10, 12, 15, 16, 20, 24, 25, 30, 40, 48, 50, 60, 75, 80, 100, 120, 150, 200, 240, 300, 400, 600, 1 200
8. **(a)** 2 bags of 24 gums, 3 bags of 16 gums, 4 bags of 12 gums, 6 bags of 8 gums, 8 bags of 6 gums, 12 bags of 4 gums, 16 bags of 3 gums, 24 bags of 2 gums
   (b) 3 bags of 15 gums, 5 bags of 9 gums, 9 bags of 5 gums, 15 bags of 3 gums
   (c) 3 bags each contains 16 orange-flavoured gums and 15 lime-flavoured gums
9. Prime numbers: (a), (c), (f); Composite numbers: (b), (d), (e)
10. 31, 37, 41, 43, 47
11. **(b)** Prime numbers: (i), (ii), (iv), (v)
12. 2, 3; Yes
13. **(a)** Yes **(b)** Yes **(c)** No
14. 13, 31 and 17, 71

Exercise 2b *(Pg 29)*

1. **(a)** 2, 5   **(b)** 2, 4
   (c) 2, 4, 5   **(d)** 2, 4
   (e) 5   **(f)** none
   (g) 2, 4, 5   **(h)** 5
   (i) 2, 4   **(j)** 2, 4
   (k) 2, 4   **(l)** 2, 5
2. **(a)** 3, 9 **(b)** 3, 9 **(c)** 3, 9
   (d) 3, 9 **(e)** 11 **(f)** 3, 11
   (g) 3, 11 **(h)** 3, 11 **(i)** 3, 11
3. **(a)** 6, 12 **(b)** 10 **(c)** 6, 12
   (d) 15 **(e)** 6, 10, 12, 15
   (f) 6, 10, 15
4. Unit digit 0, sum of digits divisible by 3. 660, 540 divisible by 30
5. No, Yes, Yes, No

6. Yes, Yes
7. No

Exercise 2c *(Pg 31)*

1. **(a)** 7^2 **(b)** $2^2 \times 5^2$
   (c) 3×7^3 **(d)** $5^2 \times 11^3$
   (e) $2^3 \times 13^2 \times 31$
   (f) $5^3 \times 19^2 \times 23 \times 29^2$
2. **(a)** $2^2 \times 7$ **(b)** $2^4 \times 3$
   (c) 2×3^3 **(d)** $2^3 \times 11$
   (e) $2^2 \times 3^3$ **(f)** $2^4 \times 3^2$
   (g) $2^6 \times 3$ **(h)** 2^8
3. **(a)** $2 \times 2 \times 2$
   (b) $2 \times 2 \times 3 \times 3$
   (c) $2 \times 3 \times 5$
   (d) $2 \times 2 \times 2 \times 3 \times 3$
4. **(a)** 2^4 **(b)** $2^3 \times 5$
   (c) $3^2 \times 5$ **(d)** $2^3 \times 7$
   (e) $2^2 \times 3 \times 5$ **(f)** $2^2 \times 3 \times 7$
   (g) $2 \times 3 \times 19$ **(h)** $2^3 \times 3 \times 5$
5. **(a)** $2^2 \times 5^2$ **(b)** 5^3
   (c) 3×7^2 **(d)** $2^3 \times 3^3$
   (e) $3^2 \times 5^2$ **(f)** $2^3 \times 3^2 \times 5$
   (g) $3^4 \times 7$ **(h)** $2^3 \times 3^4$

Exercise 2d *(Pg 33)*

1. **(a)** 3   **(b)** 2, 4
   (c) 3   **(d)** 7
   (e) 3, 9   **(f)** 3, 5, 15
   (g) 2, 3, 4, 6, 12
   (h) 3, 5, 15
2. **(a)** 6 **(b)** 6 **(c)** 14
   (d) 15 **(e)** 8 **(f)** 16
   (g) 5 **(h)** 7 **(i)** 8
   (j) 12 **(k)** 28 **(l)** 9
   (m) 3 **(n)** 18 **(o)** 33
   (p) 4
3. **(a)** 9 **(b)** 21 **(c)** 16
   (d) 12 **(e)** 16 **(f)** 15
   (g) 12 **(h)** 180 **(i)** 350
4. **(a)** 30 cm **(b)** 12
5. **(a)** 14 cm **(b)** 37

Exercise 2e *(Pg 36)*

1. **(a)** 21   **(b)** 65
   (c) 18   **(d)** 30
   (e) 21   **(f)** 24
   (g) 36   **(h)** 75
   (i) 72   **(j)** 150
   (k) 1 755   **(l)** 162
   (m) 300   **(n)** 1 080
   (o) 144   **(p)** 1 575
   (q) 250   **(r)** 400
   (s) 4 410

2. (a) 90   **(b)** 48
  (c) 72   **(d)** 126
  (e) 5 236   **(f)** 61 425
  (g) 72   **(h)** 72
3. (a) 1 417 500   **(b)** 16 200
  (c) 138 600
4. (a) 6, 126   **(b)** 7, 84
  (c) 13, 78   **(d)** 70, 420
  (e) 15, 450   **(f)** 112, 672
5. 8.01 p.m.
6. 5 p.m.

Exercise 2f *(Pg 38)*

1. 1, 4, 9, 16, 25, 36, 49, 64, 81, 100, 121, 144
2. 16, 25, 49, 81, 100, 1, 144, 169, 225, 400
3. 121, 144, 169, 196, 225, 256, 289, 324, 361, 400
4. (a) 8   **(b)** 12   **(c)** 17
  (d) 60
5. (a) 6   **(b)** 9   **(c)** 12
  (d) 14   **(e)** 16   **(f)** 18
  (g) 21   **(h)** 22
6. (a) 34   **(b)** 36   **(c)** 42
  (d) 99   **(e)** 105   **(f)** 186
7. 27, 64, 343, 512, 729, 1 000
8. (a) 11   **(b)** 19   **(c)** 13
  (d) 12   **(e)** 180
9. (a) $3^3 \times 5^3$; 15 **(b)** 2^{12}, 16
  (c) $2^9 \times 3^3$; 24 **(d)** $2^6 \times 7^3$; 28
  (e) $2^6 \times 3^6$; 36 **(f)** $3^6 \times 5^3$; 45
  (g) 2^{18}; 64   **(h)** $2^9 \times 3^6$; 72
10. 3 136 cm²
11. 48 cm
12. 1331 cm³
13. 14 cm

Exercise 2g *(Pg 42)*

1. (a) 1 600   **(b)** 3 600
  (c) 12 100   **(d)** 27 000
  (e) 64 000   **(f)** 1 000 000
  (g) 40 000   **(h)** 27 000 000
2. (a) 6   **(b)** 3   **(c)** 8
  (d) 5   **(e)** 9   **(f)** 12
  (g) 10   **(h)** 30
3. (a) 676   **(b)** 1 369
  (c) 6 084   **(d)** 9 801
  (e) 15 129   **(f)** 2 197
  (g) 24 389   **(h)** 39 304
  (i) 300 763   **(j)** 1 295 029
  (k) 31   **(l)** 47
  (m) 59   **(n)** 106

(o) 263   **(p)** 16
(q) 41   **(r)** 68
(s) 91   **(t)** 124
(u) 1 650   **(v)** 18 717
(w) 15 704   **(x)** 426
(y) 103

Review Questions 2 *(Pg 43)*

1. (a) F   **(b)** F   **(c)** T
  (d) F   **(e)** F   **(f)** F
  (g) T   **(h)** F
2. (a) 18   **(b)** 6   **(c)** 13
  (d) 5
3. (a) 60   **(b)** 144   **(c)** 630
  (d) 2 640
4. (a) 6   **(b)** 4   **(c)** 8
5. (a) 45   **(b)** 120
  (c) 7 689   **(d)** 8 165
  (e) 1 183
7. 30 m
8. 8 cm
9. (4, 120), (12, 40), (20, 24), (8, 60)
10. (8, 0), (4, 4), (0, 8), (9, 8)
11. 532 (19 × 7 × 2 × 2)

Exercise 3a *(Pg 47)*

1. (a) 14, 17, 20 **(b)** 40, 50, 60
  (c) 80, 87, 94 **(d)** 48, 40, 32
  (e) 46, 73, 82 **(f)** 55, 43, 39
2. (a) multiply the preceding term by 3; 81, 243, 729
  (b) multiply the preceding term by 2; 96, 192, 384
  (c) divide the preceding term by 2; 100, 50, 25
  (d) multiply the preceding term by 3; 324, 972, 2 916
3. (a) add 5 to preceding term; 34, 39
  (b) add 11 to preceding term; 72, 83
  (c) subtract 6 from preceding term; 49, 43
  (d) subtract 9 from preceding term; 63, 54
  (e) multiply preceding term by 2; 240, 480
  (f) divide preceding term by 3; 27, 9
4. (a) 15, 21, 28 **(b)** 37, 42, 47
  (c) 33, 32, 27 **(d)** 10, 8, 9
  (e) 29, 58, 61 **(f)** 21, 34, 55

Exercise 3b *(Pg 50)*

1. (a) $1 + 3 + 5 + 7 + 9 + 11 =$
  $36 = 6^2 = (5 + 1)^2$
  $1 + 3 + 5 + 7 + 9 + 11 + 13$
  $= 49 = 7^2 = (6 + 1)^2$
  (b) $1 + 3 + 5 + 7 + 9 + 11 + 13$
  $+ 15 + 17 + 19 + 21 + 23 =$
  $144 = 12^2 = (11 + 1)^2$
  (c) $a = 25$, $c = 13$, $d = 12$
2. (a) $2 + 6^2 = 38$ **(b)** 8
3. (a) $10^2 - 9^2 = 19 = 10 + 9$
  (b) 1 195
  (c) $m = 41$, $n = 40$
4. (a) $\dfrac{11 \times 12}{2} + (11 - 1)^2 = 166$
  (b) $p = 10$, $q = 136$
5. (a) 9, 12   **(b)** $t = 3n$
  (c) (i) 150   **(ii)** 29
6. (a) 16, 25
  (b) $T = (N + 1)^2$
  (c) (i) 100   **(ii)** 10

Exercise 3c *(Pg 57)*

1. (a) $3 + 1 = 4$, $4 + 1 = 5$,
  $5 + 1 = 6$, $6 + 1 = 7$
  (b) 50   **(c)** 100
2. (a) (i) $\dfrac{8 - 2}{2} = 3$, $\dfrac{10 - 2}{2} = 4$,
  $\dfrac{12 - 2}{2} = 5$, $\dfrac{14 - 2}{2} = 6$
  (ii) $2(3) + 2 = 8$,
  $2(4) + 2 = 10$,
  $2(5) + 2 = 12$,
  $2(6) + 2 = 14$
  (b) (i) 9   **(ii)** 14
  (c) (i) 46   **(ii)** 74
3. (a) $\dfrac{4 \times (4 - 1)}{2} = 6$,
  $\dfrac{5 \times (5 - 1)}{2} = 10$,
  $\dfrac{6 \times (6 - 1)}{2} = 15$,
  $\dfrac{7 \times (7 - 1)}{2} = 21$
  (b) 190
4. 120   **5.** 39 min
6. 5 games, 26 games
7. 15 minutes
8.

5 Cows	5 Cows	5 Cows

9.

Review Questions 3 *(Pg 60)*

1. (a) 25, 31, 37 (b) 42, 57, 75
   (c) 16, 26, 42 (d) 85, 81, 77
   (e) 21, 25, 29 (f) 27, 38, 51
2. (a) 9   (b) 6   (c) 16
   (d) 42   (e) 28   (f) 26
   (g) 95
3. (a) $1\,111\,111\,111 - 22\,222 =$
       $33\,333^2$
   (b) $x = 1\,111\,111\,111\,111\,111$
       $y = 22\,222\,222$
4. (a) (i) $1 + 2 + 3 + 4 + 5 + 6 +$
          $7 = 28 = \dfrac{7 \times (7 + 1)}{2}$
       (ii) $k = 9$
   (b) (i) $1^3 + 2^3 + 3^3 + 4^3 + 5^3 +$
          $6^3 = 1 + 8 + 27 + 64 +$
          $125 + 216 = 441 = 21^2$
       (ii) $x = 8^3, y = 512,$
            $z = 1\,296$
5. (a) 108
   (b) 630, 2 460

Exercise 4a *(Pg 64)*

1. (a) $\dfrac{1}{6}$ (b) $\dfrac{2}{9}$ (c) $\dfrac{5}{8}$
   (d) $\dfrac{6}{13}$ (e) $\dfrac{5}{12}$ (f) $\dfrac{11}{100}$
2. (a) one-ninth
   (b) two-sevenths
   (c) five-twentieths
   (d) thirty five-hundredths
3. (a) $\dfrac{5}{7}$ (b) $\dfrac{4}{9}$

Exercise 4b *(Pg 66)*

1. (a) 12 (b) 10 (c) 52
   (d) 3   (e) 135 (f) 187
2. $\dfrac{1}{4} = \dfrac{4}{16} = \dfrac{16}{64}$
4. (a) 12, 18, 30
   (b) 6, 32, 28
5. (a) $\dfrac{1}{2}$ (b) $\dfrac{8}{11}$ (c) $\dfrac{6}{13}$
   (d) $\dfrac{5}{6}$ (e) $\dfrac{5}{8}$ (f) $\dfrac{7}{13}$
6. (a), (b), (c)
7. (a) $\dfrac{7}{10}$ (b) $\dfrac{2}{3}$ (c) $\dfrac{6}{13}$
   (d) $\dfrac{1}{2}$ (e) $\dfrac{2}{3}$ (f) $\dfrac{7}{25}$
   (g) $\dfrac{3}{7}$ (h) $\dfrac{5}{11}$

Exercise 4c *(Pg 69)*

1. (a) (i)   (b) (ii)   (c) (i)
   (d) (iii) (e) (i)   (f) (iii)
   (g) (ii)   (h) (iii)
2. (a) $\dfrac{7}{3}$ (b) $\dfrac{14}{11}$
   (c) $\dfrac{68}{9}$ (d) $\dfrac{23}{5}$
   (e) $\dfrac{23}{4}$ (f) $\dfrac{23}{6}$
   (g) $\dfrac{31}{13}$ (h) $\dfrac{156}{11}$
3. (a) $3\dfrac{1}{7}$ (b) 3
   (c) $5\dfrac{5}{6}$ (d) $4\dfrac{2}{3}$
   (e) $16\dfrac{4}{5}$ (f) $15\dfrac{1}{2}$
   (g) $10\dfrac{1}{10}$ (h) $11\dfrac{2}{13}$
4. (a) $\dfrac{4}{10}$ (b) $\dfrac{1}{16}$
   (c) $\dfrac{1}{3}$ (d) $\dfrac{5}{9}$
5. (a) $\dfrac{6}{7}$ (b) $\dfrac{1}{2}$
   (c) $\dfrac{7}{8}$ (d) $\dfrac{2}{3}$
6. Peter
7. Susan
8. (a) $\dfrac{5}{8}, \dfrac{3}{4}, \dfrac{11}{12}$
   (b) $\dfrac{4}{9}, \dfrac{2}{3}, \dfrac{5}{6}$
   (c) $\dfrac{1}{3}, \dfrac{1}{2}, \dfrac{4}{7}$
   (d) $\dfrac{7}{11}, \dfrac{2}{3}, \dfrac{5}{6}$
9. (a) $\dfrac{5}{6}, \dfrac{3}{4}, \dfrac{7}{12}, \dfrac{5}{9}$
   (b) $\dfrac{11}{12}, \dfrac{4}{5}, \dfrac{3}{4}, \dfrac{7}{10}$
   (c) $\dfrac{2}{3}, \dfrac{5}{8}, \dfrac{1}{2}, \dfrac{5}{12}$
   (d) $\dfrac{5}{6}, \dfrac{7}{9}, \dfrac{13}{18}, \dfrac{2}{3}$

Exercise 4d *(Pg 73)*

1. (a) $\dfrac{3}{4}$ (b) $1\dfrac{1}{20}$
   (c) $1\dfrac{1}{2}$ (d) $1\dfrac{9}{14}$

2. (a) $\dfrac{1}{6}$ (b) $\dfrac{1}{4}$
   (c) $\dfrac{1}{6}$ (d) $\dfrac{2}{7}$
3. (a) $\dfrac{11}{14}$ (b) $1\dfrac{3}{70}$
   (c) $\dfrac{1}{10}$ (d) $\dfrac{11}{60}$
4. (a) $3\dfrac{4}{5}$ (b) $5\dfrac{13}{18}$
   (c) $5\dfrac{43}{56}$ (d) $9\dfrac{27}{200}$
   (e) $3\dfrac{29}{200}$ (f) $3\dfrac{3}{8}$
   (g) $3\dfrac{9}{10}$ (h) $2\dfrac{5}{12}$
   (i) $4\dfrac{1}{15}$ (j) $3\dfrac{5}{24}$
5. (a) $1\dfrac{1}{14}$ (b) $1\dfrac{7}{8}$
   (c) $4\dfrac{13}{28}$ (d) $5\dfrac{1}{60}$
   (e) $5\dfrac{11}{15}$ (f) $4\dfrac{3}{8}$
   (g) $\dfrac{29}{45}$ (h) $3\dfrac{5}{9}$
6. $4\dfrac{4}{15}$ km
7. $4\dfrac{3}{4}$ litres
8. (a) $2\dfrac{1}{3}$ hours or 2 hours and
       20 minutes
   (b) first classroom
   (c) $\dfrac{1}{6}$ hour or 10 minutes
9. (a) $4\dfrac{3}{4}$ cups
   (b) 2 cups
10. $4\dfrac{1}{2}$ hours

Exercise 4e *(Pg 78)*

1. (a) 16   (b) $6\dfrac{2}{3}$
   (c) $\dfrac{10}{21}$ (d) 1
   (e) 15   (f) $\dfrac{3}{8}$
   (g) 9   (h) $2\dfrac{34}{273}$
2. (a) 6   (b) $2\dfrac{1}{12}$

(c) $1\dfrac{7}{128}$ **(d)** $5\dfrac{1}{3}$

(e) $\dfrac{1}{4}$

3. (a) 4 pupils **(b)** 9 oranges
(c) 32 km **(d)** 15 hours
(e) 8 kg

4. (a) $\dfrac{9}{14}$ **(b)** $10\dfrac{1}{2}$ kg

(c) $3\dfrac{3}{4}$ kg

(d) (i) $5\dfrac{5}{8}$ kg

(ii) $1\dfrac{1}{8}$ kg

5. (a) $4\dfrac{2}{3}$ hours or 4 hours and

40 minutes

(b) (i) $9\dfrac{4}{5}$ hours or 9 hours

and 48 minutes

(ii) $1\dfrac{19}{30}$ hours or 1 hour

and 38 minutes

Exercise 4f *(Pg 80)*

1. (a) $\dfrac{7}{36}$ **(b)** $\dfrac{1}{6}$

(c) $3\dfrac{3}{4}$ **(d)** $1\dfrac{7}{10}$

(e) $6\dfrac{1}{6}$ **(f)** $1\dfrac{4}{5}$

2. (a) $\dfrac{13}{90}$ **(b)** $\dfrac{2}{9}$

(c) 10 **(d)** $1\dfrac{13}{36}$

(e) 0 **(f)** $18\dfrac{1}{24}$

Exercise 4g *(Pg 82)*

1. 216 hectres
2. $39
3. (a) 24 boys **(b)** 12 girls
4. 25
5. 85
6. 35

Exercise 4h *(Pg 85)*

1. (a) 0.43 **(b)** 0.057
(c) 0.000 8 **(d)** 1.35
(e) 8.25 **(f)** 2.3
(g) 15.096 **(h)** 7.000 5

(i) 85.12 **(j)** 2.62
(k) 19.024 **(l)** 101.000 11

2. (a) $\dfrac{3}{4}$ **(b)** $\dfrac{9}{25}$

(c) $\dfrac{1}{40}$ **(d)** $\dfrac{3}{500}$

(e) $\dfrac{21}{200}$ **(f)** $3\dfrac{3}{4}$

(g) $\dfrac{1}{80}$ **(h)** $15\dfrac{1}{4}$

(i) $84\dfrac{5}{8}$

3. (a) 1.625 **(b)** 0.837 5
(c) 2.687 5 **(d)** 0.875
(e) 0.593 75 **(f)** 1.468 75

Exercise 4i *(Pg 86)*

1. (a) $0.\dot{6}$ **(b)** $0.\dot{4}\dot{5}$
(c) $0.8\dot{7}$ **(d)** $0.2\dot{2}\dot{7}$
(e) $0.\dot{5}7142\dot{8}$
(f) $0.486\,\dot{1}$

2. (a) $0.\dot{4}$, R
(b) $2.\dot{3}$, R
(c) $0.6\dot{7}$, R
(d) $0.5\dot{9}$, R
(e) 0.776, N.R.
(f) $0.295\,\dot{4}$, R

Exercise 4j *(Pg 88)*

2. 1.04, 1.10, 1.115, 1.145, 1.18
3. (a) 2.1, 2.4, 2.7
(b) 3.03, 3.12, 3.16
(c) 0.02, 0.035, 0.065, 0.08
(d) 1.22, 1.25, 1.28, 1.31, 1.345, 1.38
4. (a) < **(b)** > **(c)** <
(d) > **(e)** >, > **(f)** <, <
5. (a) 0.8, 0.4, 0.3

(b) $1\dfrac{3}{4}$, 1.54, $\dfrac{5}{4}$

(c) 1.9, 1.88, 1.13

(d) $0.6\dot{5}$, $0.6\dot{5}$, $\dfrac{13}{20}$, $0.60\dot{5}$

(e) $3.1\dot{4}$, $\dfrac{22}{7}$, $3.\dot{1}\dot{4}$, 3.14

(f) 2.201, 2.102, $2.0\dot{2}$, 2.012

Exercise 4k *(Pg 89)*

1. (a) 1.358 **(b)** 336.728
(c) 916.462 **(d)** 267.203

2. (a) 597.45 **(b)** 271.91
(c) 0.061
3. (a) 18.97 **(b)** 297.102
(c) 127.18 **(d)** 32.365
4. (a) 2.47 **(b)** 13.28
(c) 4.849 **(d)** 9.634
(e) 8 **(f)** 306.826
5. (a) 88.578 **(b)** 215.23
(c) 11.219

Exercise 4l *(Pg 92)*

1. (a) 0.3 **(b)** 2.523
(c) 0.024 6 **(d)** 6.57
(e) 0.007 2 **(f)** 0.745 6
2. (a) 0.028 5 **(b)** 591.25
(c) 25.248 **(d)** 1 599.36
(e) 76.8 **(f)** 1.538 1
(g) 0.090 62 **(h)** 0.014
3. (a) 7.36 **(b)** 1 851.7
(c) 1 502.9 **(d)** 17 900
(e) 6.6 **(f)** 124
4. (a) 75.38 **(b)** 0.002 9
(c) 6.24 **(d)** 0.000 066
(e) 4 **(f)** 0.086 5
5. (a) 10.6 **(b)** 5.7
(c) 0.11 **(d)** 8 000
(e) 11.1 **(f)** 30.588
6. (a) 4 **(b)** 9
(c) 12.8 **(d)** 0.099
(e) 1 152 **(f)** 0.078 125

Exercise 4m *(Pg 93)*

1. 60
2. 40 cents
3. $12.05
4. $29.33; $20.67
5. packs of 5.

Exercise 4n *(Pg 96)*

1. (a) (i) 5 **(ii)** 5.42
(b) (i) 16 **(ii)** 15.82
(c) (i) 8 **(ii)** 7.86
(d) (i) 131 **(ii)** 130.83
2. (a) 712.893 **(b)** 0.003
(c) 0.827 **(d)** 7.024
3. 0.286
4. (a) 0.44 **(b)** 0.64
(c) 0.64 **(d)** 0.73

Exercise 4o *(Pg 97)*

1. (a) 467.622   (b) 35.8
   (c) 154.92   (d) 26.156
   (e) 15.846   (f) 51.791

2. (a) $\dfrac{19}{20}$, 0.95

   (b) $1\dfrac{5}{6}$, 1.83

   (c) $4\dfrac{1}{6}$, 4.17

   (d) $53\dfrac{19}{27}$, 53.70

   (e) $3\dfrac{1}{3}$, 3.33

   (f) $8\dfrac{63}{64}$, 8.98

3. (a) 70, 67.71
   (b) 1 000, 1 012.82
   (c) 3 101, 3 131.36
   (d) 290, 291.08
   (e) 20, 19.79

Review Questions 4 *(Pg 99)*

1. (a) $\dfrac{7}{10}$, $\dfrac{3}{4}$, $\dfrac{4}{5}$

   (b) $\dfrac{7}{12}$, $\dfrac{5}{8}$, $\dfrac{2}{3}$

   (c) $\dfrac{4}{7}$, $\dfrac{7}{12}$, $\dfrac{25}{42}$, $\dfrac{9}{14}$

2. (a) $\dfrac{5}{8}$, $\dfrac{7}{12}$, $\dfrac{5}{9}$, $\dfrac{13}{24}$

   (b) $\dfrac{2}{7}$, $\dfrac{4}{15}$, $\dfrac{5}{21}$, $\dfrac{6}{35}$

   (c) $\dfrac{6}{11}$, $\dfrac{13}{25}$, $\dfrac{7}{15}$, $\dfrac{9}{20}$, $\dfrac{2}{5}$

3. Xinyu

4. (a) $3\dfrac{3}{4}$ (b) $2\dfrac{10}{21}$

   (c) $\dfrac{13}{24}$ (d) $1\dfrac{3}{10}$

   (e) $4\dfrac{1}{9}$ (f) $3\dfrac{29}{72}$

5. (a) 3   (b) $1\dfrac{1}{2}$

   (c) $6\dfrac{2}{9}$ (d) $\dfrac{3}{10}$

   (e) $\dfrac{1}{2}$ (f) $\dfrac{3}{5}$

   (g) $5\dfrac{31}{42}$ (h) $22\dfrac{1}{2}$

6. (a) 31   (b) 9.26
   (c) 0.156 52   (d) 0.12
   (e) 120   (f) 413

7. (a) $\dfrac{9}{16}$ (b) 3.12

   (c) $\dfrac{2\,000}{16\,947}$ (d) 1 051.48

   (e) $\dfrac{361}{432}$

8. 25, yes.

Revision Exercise I No 1 *(Pg 101)*

1. (a) 34   (b) 160
   (c) 800   (d) 4 224
2. (a) 900   (b) 30   (c) 2
3. 3, 180

4. (a) 3   (b) $\dfrac{1}{2}$ (c) $\dfrac{3}{4}$

5. (a) 21, 25   (b) $\dfrac{5}{6}$, $\dfrac{6}{7}$

   (c) 5×7, 6×8
6. (a) 7.91   (b) 61.56
   (c) 29.63   (d) 10.89
7. (a) 3   (b) 2

   (c) $\dfrac{3}{40}$ (d) 2

8. (a) 2 900   (b) 0.67

   (c) $\dfrac{17}{40}$ (d) 2.84

9. (a) $89   (b) $11
10. (a) 5, 85
    (b) 3, 5, 7; 51, 85, 119

Revision Exercise I No 2 *(Pg 101)*

1. (a) 69, 61, 52 (b) 8, 7, 10
   (c) 0, 12, 24
2. (a) 5.476   (b) 4
3. (a) 180   (b) 52
4. (a) (i) 504   (ii) 280
     (iii) 3 465
   (b) (i) 8   (ii) 6
5. (a) 20   (b) 57   (c) 10

6. (a) 0.3 125   (b) $\dfrac{9}{40}$

   (c) (i) 9.91   (ii) 9.9
7. 500 g pack, 10¢ per kg
8. (a) 0.98   (b) 12.23
   (c) 2.04   (d) 2
9. (a) $6^2 - 2 \times 6 = 24$
   (b) 9

10. (a) $4\dfrac{1}{10}$ (b) $3\dfrac{5}{8}$

   (c) $\dfrac{1}{3}$

Revision Exercise I No 3 *(Pg 102)*

1. 10.5
2. (a) 907   (b) 22.7 022
   (c) 50

3. (a) $\dfrac{14}{25}$ (b) 0.29

4. (a) $\dfrac{13}{20}$ (b) $\dfrac{3}{13}$

   (c) $\dfrac{3}{4}$ (d) $\dfrac{57}{68}$

5. $x = 4$, $y = 1$, $z = 2$
6. (a) (i) 3×2^4 (ii) $2^2 \times 3^4$
   (b) (i) 7   (ii) 3
   (c) (i) 504   (ii) 210
7. (a) 3, 6   (b) 77, 88
   (c) 65, 78
8. 17, 19, 23, 29, 31, 37, 41, 43
9. $100

10. (a) $\dfrac{3}{4}$, $\dfrac{5}{6}$, $\dfrac{8}{9}$, $\dfrac{11}{12}$

    (b) $\dfrac{2}{5}$, $\dfrac{3}{8}$, $\dfrac{1}{3}$, $\dfrac{1}{4}$

Revision Exercise I No 4 *(Pg 103)*

1. (a) 3   (b) 47.7
   (c) 17.1   (d) −1.725

2. (a) $\dfrac{77}{96}$ (b) $\dfrac{11}{48}$

3. (a) No   (b) No   (c) No
   (d) Yes   (e) No   (f) No
4. (a) (i) 0.175   (ii) 0.4 125
     (iii) 0.36   (iv) 1.3 125

   (b) (i) $\dfrac{33}{500}$ (ii) $\dfrac{23}{40}$

     (iii) $\dfrac{7}{8}$ (iv) $\dfrac{7}{16}$

5. 5 h 36 min
6. 9
7. $48.09; $1.91
8. (a) 96, 4   (b) 840, 4
9. (a) 125, 216
   (b) 1 024, 4 096
   (c) 16, 22

10. (a) $\dfrac{1}{2}$ (b) $\dfrac{2}{9}$

Revision Exercise I No 5 *(Pg 103)*

1. (a) $\dfrac{5}{8}$ (b) $1\dfrac{6}{7}$

   (c) $5\dfrac{29}{48}$ (d) $\dfrac{17}{24}$

2. 720 m
3. (a) 104   (b) 11

4. (a) 80 **(b)** $1\frac{1}{4}$

(c) $1\frac{1}{3}$ **(d)** $1\frac{2}{5}$

5. (a) 8.03 **(b)** 1.67

(c) 36.04

6. (a) 2, 4, 6, 8, 10, 12, 14

(b) 1, 3, 5, 7, 9, 11

(c) 2, 3, 5, 7, 11, 13, 17, 19, 23

(d) 1, 2, 4, 8, 16, 32

7. (a) 16, 192 **(b)** 3, 756

(c) 12, 360 **(d)** 4, 1 344

8. $15 580

9. (a) $\frac{3}{56}$ **(b)** $\frac{2}{5}$

(c) $0.57\dot{1}\dot{4}$, $\frac{4}{7}$, $0.571\dot{4}$, $0.5\dot{7}1\dot{4}$

10. (a) 26, 37, 50

(b) 0.005, 0.000 6, 0.000 07

(c) 2, 0, –2

(d) 23, 37, 60

(e) $\frac{1}{16}$, $\frac{1}{32}$, $\frac{1}{64}$

Exercise 5a *(Pg 107)*

1. (a) negative

(b) (i) +20 **(ii)** +90

(iii) –9

2. (a) 30 m above sea-level

(b) –35

(c) rotating 30° anti-clockwise

(d) speed of 45 km/h of a car moving towards west

3. (a) –1 **(b)** +2 **(c)** –4

4. (a) < **(b)** > **(c)** <

(d) < **(e)** > **(f)** <

5. (a) –5° < 12°

(b) $200 > –$120

(c) –40 m < –25 m

6. (a) –90, –60, –6, –2, 0

(b) –1 500, –1, 1, 2

8. (a) > **(b)** < **(c)** >

(d) > **(e)** < **(f)** >

Exercise 5b *(Pg 109)*

1. (a) –5 **(b)** –5

(c) –7 **(d)** –6

(e) 8 **(f)** –9

2. (a) –11 **(b)** –16

(c) –14 **(d)** 20

(e) –21 **(f)** –20

(g) –30

Exercise 5c *(Pg 111)*

1. (a) 3 **(b)** –1

(c) –1 **(d)** –4

(e) 4 **(f)** –1

2. (a) 8 **(b)** 8

(c) 7 **(d)** 11

(e) –15 **(f)** –26

(g) –41 **(h)** –15

(i) –99

3. (a) –9 **(b)** –14

(c) 25 **(d)** 13

(e) –35 **(f)** 56

(g) 26 **(h)** –153

4. 9°C

5. (a) $ (6 000 – 2 000 – 5 500)

(b) $1 500 loss

Exercise 5d *(Pg 113)*

1. (a) –5 **(b)** –4

(c) –4 **(d)** –6

(e) 4 **(f)** 0

(g) 6 **(h)** –4

2. (a) 5 **(b)** –7

(c) –11 **(d)** –17

(e) 15 **(f)** 14

(g) 1 **(h)** 11

(i) –65 **(j)** 70

(k) –270 **(l)** –38

3. (a) 0 **(b)** –1

(c) –4 **(d)** 8

(e) 1 **(f)** 8

(g) 17 **(h)** –13

(i) –50

4. (a) –24 **(b)** –41

(c) –21 **(d)** –368

(e) –7 **(f)** 96

(g) –29 **(h)** –152

(i) –50

Exercise 5e *(Pg 115)*

(a) –21 **(b)** 6 **(c)** –32

(d) 0 **(e)** 280 **(f)** 0

(g) –2 **(h)** 61 **(i)** –6

(j) –55 **(k)** 0 **(l)** 8

(m) 0 **(n)** –16 **(o)** 192

(p) 0 **(q)** 0 **(r)** 28

Exercise 5f *(Pg 116)*

1. (a) ×, × **(b)** +, +

(c) +, + **(d)** ×, ×

2. (a) –28, 60 **(b)** 12, –120

(c) –14, –50 **(d)** 8, 9, 11

(e) 10, –20 **(f)** –15, –9, 90

3. (a) 13 **(b)** –80

(c) 4 **(d)** 125

(e) 40 **(f)** –18

(g) 28 **(h)** 0

(i) –4 **(j)** –9

(k) –17

Exercise 5g *(Pg 119)*

1. (a) $\frac{3}{4}$ **(b)** –1

(c) $-1\frac{1}{10}$ **(d)** $-3\frac{9}{10}$

(e) $-\frac{11}{12}$ **(f)** $-\frac{13}{20}$

(g) $\frac{3}{20}$ **(h)** $-7\frac{13}{28}$

(i) $\frac{7}{12}$ **(j)** $2\frac{7}{16}$

2. (a) $4\frac{1}{2}$ **(b)** $-\frac{2}{15}$

(c) $1\frac{11}{16}$ **(d)** $-\frac{1}{18}$

(e) 6 **(f)** $\frac{3}{13}$

(g) $\frac{112}{115}$

Exercise 5h *(Pg 121)*

1. (a) R **(b)** R **(c)** R

(d) I **(e)** I **(f)** R

(g) R **(h)** I **(i)** R

(j) R **(k)** R **(l)** R

(m) I **(n)** R **(o)** I

2. (a) T **(b)** F **(c)** T

(d) T **(e)** T **(f)** F

3. (a) 6 095 **(b)** 367 770

(c) –423 **(d)** –33 973

(e) $-\frac{65}{903}$ **(f)** $-3\frac{122}{539}$

(g) $2\frac{159}{184}$ **(h)** $-\frac{2\,821}{34\,542}$

(i) $\frac{598}{1\,225}$

4. (a) 11.36 **(b)** 4.33

(c) –2.47 **(d)** 2.37

(e) 0.50 **(f)** 23.60

(g) 19 940.66

(h) 113 269.73

(i) –0.07

(j) 0.79

1. (a) 67 (b) −28
   (c) −22 (d) −100
   (e) −36 (f) 390
   (g) 1 130 (h) −279
2. (a) −120 (b) −12
   (c) 56 (d) 3
   (e) 10 (f) −24
   (g) 6 (h) 54
   (i) 87
3. (a) 28 (b) −88 (c) −26
   (d) −4 (e) 3 (f) −102
4. (a) $-\dfrac{19}{30}$ (b) $-3\dfrac{5}{12}$ (c) $-\dfrac{4}{9}$

   (d) $-3\dfrac{5}{24}$ (e) $1\dfrac{5}{18}$ (f) 35

5. $-\dfrac{11}{13}$

6. (a) $1.428,\ 1.\dot{4}2\dot{8},\ 1\dfrac{3}{7},\ 1.428$

   (b) $-3.\dot{6},\ -3\dfrac{7}{11},\ -3.\dot{6}\dot{3},\ -3.63$

   (c) $-1\dfrac{4}{9},\ -1.43\dot{5},\ -1.\dot{4}3\dot{5},$

   $-1.43\ddot{5}$

Exercise 6a *(Pg 127)*

1. 4 kg   2. No.   3. B
4. (a) (iii) (b) (iii) (c) (ii)
   (d) (i) (e) (i)
5. (a) (iii) (b) (iii) (c) (ii)
   (d) (iii) (e) (iv)

Exercise 6b *(Pg 132)*

1. (a) 460 g (b) 700 g
   (c) 3 cm (d) 123.5 cm
   (e) 18 (f) 30 m
   (g) 12.4 cm
   (h) 4 300 pupils
   (i) 850 km (j) 22.6 mm
2. (a) 3 (b) 3 (c) 5
   (d) 3 (e) 2 (f) 2
   (g) 4 (h) 4
   (i) 1, 2, 3, 4, 5, 6 or 7
   (j) 3 (k) 2 (l) 2
3. (a) 3.1 (b) 1.484
   (c) 0.003 (d) 20
   (e) 3.1 (f) 0.57
   (g) 0.056 8 (h) 217.01
   (i) 3.60 (j) 15.70
   (k) 0.003 6 (l) 6.0
   (m) 0.035 (n) 18.0

   (o) 8.4 (p) 120.41
   (q) 4.83 (r) 12
   (s) 0.050 (t) 0.080
   (u) 0.010 1 (v) 0.103
4. (a) 4
   (b) 400 000 000
5. 0.05
6. (a) 0.010 5 (b) 0.442
   (c) 31.2 (d) 11.1
7. 28, 0
8. 0.211, 3
9. 0.008 3, 2
10. 117.96, 5

Review Questions 6 *(Pg 133)*

1. (a) (iii) (b) (ii)
   (c) (ii) (d) (ii)
2. (a) (i) (b) (ii)
   (c) (ii) (d) (i)
3. (a) 0.086 (b) 0.085 7
   (c) 5.10 (d) 730 000
   (e) 0.06 (f) 0.06
   (g) 0.006 14 (h) 0.004
4. 20
5. (a) 50 (b) 2 000

Exercise 7a *(Pg 137)*

1. (a) $\square \times 7 = 91$
   (b) $(\square - 5) \times 4 = 28$
   (c) $\square \times 5 + 4 = 19$
   (d) $(\square - 2) \times 3 = 12$
   (e) $(\square + 15) \times \triangle = 84$
   (f) $2\square = \$32$
   (g) $\square + 2\triangle = \$8.40$
   (h) $2\square + 5\triangle = 47$
   (i) $5\square + 3\triangle = \$98$
   (j) $320\square + 450\triangle = \$128$
   (k) $2 \times \dfrac{3}{4}\square + 4\square = 6$ days
   (l) $\square + 2\triangle \leqslant \$3\ 000$
   (m) $3\square + 2\triangle = 2\dfrac{2}{3}$ h

Exercise 7b *(Pg 141)*

1. (a) $-5x^3 + 7x^2 + 3x + 4$
   (b) $7x^4 + 7x^3 - 5x^2 - 4x$
   (c) $5x^3 + 4x^2 - 7x + 4$
   (d) $5x^5 - 6x^3 + 7x^2 + 7$
2. (a) $4 + 7x - 3x^2 + 4x^3$
   (b) $-4x - 9x^2 + 8x^3 + 4x^5$
   (c) $-4a + 2a^2 + 3a^5 - 4a^6$
   (d) $-3b - 4b^2 + 4b^3 + 7b^5$

3. (a) $2x + 14$ (b) $5a - 14$
   (c) $8k$ (d) $\dfrac{x}{3y}$
   (e) $2x + 6y$ (f) $\dfrac{y}{2} - 5x$
4. (a) $2x + y$ (b) $7k$
   (c) $2t - 15$ (d) $3u - 4$
   (e) $\dfrac{v}{2} + 8$ (f) $\$\left(\dfrac{h}{2} + 2k\right)$
   (g) $\$(1.82x + 2.22y)$
5. (a) −36 (b) 24
   (c) 2 (d) −6
   (e) −55 (f) 164
6. (a) $\$1.10x$ (b) $\dfrac{3x}{3 + k}$
   (c) $5(h + 3)$ (d) $\dfrac{1}{4}(m - 4)$
   (e) kn eggs (f) xz km
7. (a) $3(x + 1)$ (b) $5(x - 6)$
   (c) $4x + 8$ (d) $\dfrac{x - 14}{3}$
8. (a) $-1\dfrac{5}{6}$ (b) $-3\dfrac{1}{4}$
   (c) $-1\dfrac{1}{2}$ (d) $-\dfrac{1}{5}$
   (e) $-\dfrac{5}{6}$ (f) $-\dfrac{16}{21}$
   (g) $-\dfrac{8}{11}$ (h) $-\dfrac{7}{36}$

Exercise 7c *(Pg 143)*

1. (a) $14x$ (b) 0
   (c) $a - 6b$ (d) $2c - d$
   (e) $7x + 6y$ (f) $4pq$
   (g) $2ef$ (h) $13de - bc$
   (i) $2p^2$ (j) $4a^2$
   (k) $-q^3$ (l) $t^3 + t$
2. (a) $60n$ (b) $-12a$
   (c) $8k$ (d) $5a$
   (e) $\dfrac{3}{2}m$ (f) $-4b$
   (g) $-8n$ (h) $2a$
   (i) $3u$ (j) $-\dfrac{c}{11}$
   (k) $9v$ (l) $\dfrac{3}{a}$
   (m) $-\dfrac{3}{d}$ (n) $20m$
3. (a) $-14k^2$ (b) $32b^2$
   (c) $-9x^2$ (d) $\dfrac{2}{3}y^2$
   (e) $15ab$ (f) $-14mn$
   (g) $12uv$ (h) $\dfrac{6b}{a}$

(i) $\dfrac{4m}{3n}$ **(j)** $-70a^2b$

(k) d^2e **(l)** $\dfrac{10x^3}{3y}$

(m) $\dfrac{5c}{d}$ **(n)** $6d^3e^2f$

(o) $5c^3d^2$

Exercise 7d *(Pg 145)*

1. (a) $5a + 7b$ **(b)** $15v - 2u$
 (c) $3b - 5a$ **(d)** $4x - 8y$
 (e) $11m - 8n$ **(f)** $7k - 18h$
 (g) $5ax - 32bx + 27cx$
 (h) $13x - 4y$ **(i)** $27b - 9a$
 (j) $9p - 14q$
 (k) $7a - 9b + 10c$
 (l) $-6b - 4k$ **(m)** $9y - 5x - 6$
 (n) $6q - 5p + 20$

2. (a) $2x - 3$ **(b)** $4p - 2$
 (c) $a - b + c + d$
 (d) $28 - 4x$ **(e)** $a - 2$
 (f) $4p - 2q$ **(g)** $-6a - 16$
 (h) $25c + 5d$ **(i)** $17x - 2y$
 (j) $a - 2b$
 (k) $9w - 11r - 6t$
 (l) $3y - 6x$ **(m)** $-24x - 28y$
 (n) $200y$ **(o)** $12 - 13a$
 (p) $10b - 7a$ **(q)** $4a - 4b$
 (r) $-9x - 10y$

3. (a) $\dfrac{17x - 20}{35}$ **(b)** $\dfrac{28x + 26}{15}$

 (c) $\dfrac{23x - 3}{10}$ **(d)** $\dfrac{10x - 25}{28}$

 (e) $\dfrac{18 - 17x}{20}$ **(f)** $\dfrac{23x - 6}{20}$

Exercise 7e *(Pg 147)*

1. (a) $4x^2 - x + 8$
 (b) $x^3 + 9x^2 - 3x - 8$
 (c) $2a^2 + 4a + 13$
 (d) $2a + c$
 (e) $6p - 2q + 3r$
 (f) $x + 2y - 4z$
 (g) $x^3 + 5x^2 + 4x + 15$
 (h) $3p + 5q + 3r - 5s$
 (i) $2xz$
 (j) $2x^4 + 3x^3 - 4x^2 - 10x + 5$
 (k) $4x^4 + 8x^2 + 3x - 14$
 (l) $10x^2y + 10xy + xy^2$

2. (a) $x^2 + 4x - 2$
 (b) $-x^2 + x - 5$
 (c) $2a + 5b - 10c$

(d) $p - 6q - 3r + s$
(e) $x^3 - 6x^2 - 7x + 10$
(f) $-a^3 - 3a^2 + 2a - 2$
(g) $2a + 2b - 9c - 4d$
(h) $5a^5 + 7a^4 - 9a^3 + 3a + 8$
(i) $5a^5 + a^4 - 3a^3 - 2a^2 - 16$
(j) $2a^6 - 5a^5 - 10a^4 + 11a^3 - 12a^2 + 3a - 8$

3. (a) $5a^2 - 2a$ **(b)** $-3a + 3b$
 (c) $-8a + 26b - 62ab$
 (d) $13a - 8b - 2c$
 (e) $3a + 6b - 10c$
 (f) $-37a + 12b - 37c$
 (g) $7a - 7b - 12c$
 (h) $-12a - 53b + 54c$
 (i) $61a - 68b + 7c$
 (j) $18a + 60b - 52c$

Review Questions 7 *(Pg 148)*

1. (a) 27 **(b)** 8 **(c)** -34
 (d) -18 **(e)** 3 **(f)** 81

2. $-\dfrac{1}{2}$

3. 6

4. (a) $60f - 68e$ **(b)** $2m - 9$
 (c) $4 - k$ **(d)** $7 - 7x$
 (e) 17 **(f)** $-10x - 2$
 (g) $6x + 4$
 (h) $a - b + c - d - e$
 (i) $126 - 45a$ **(j)** $3x + 7y$
 (k) $13a - 18$ **(l)** $30y - 18x$
 (m) $\dfrac{34a - 5b - 21c}{30}$

 (n) $\dfrac{26a + 2b}{3a}$

 (o) $\dfrac{10x - 3y + 19}{15}$

 (p) $\dfrac{3x + 35y - 2z - 120}{42}$

5. $10p^2 + 7pq + 4q^2$

6. $-x^2 - x - 15$

7. $9a^2 - 10ab + b^2$

Exercise 8a *(Pg 152)*

1. (a) 2 **(b)** 47 **(c)** 4
 (d) 8 **(e)** 8 **(f)** 15
 (g) 12 **(h)** 12 **(i)** 9
 (j) 2 **(k)** 10 **(l)** 5

2. (a) 2 or -2
 (b) 3 or -3
 (c) not possible
 (d) 25 **(e)** 27 **(f)** -8
 (g) 60 **(h)** 24

Exercise 8b *(Pg 154)*

1. (a) 5 **(b)** 6 **(c)** 0
 (d) -5 **(e)** -3 **(f)** 0

 (g) 7 **(h)** -11 **(i)** $\dfrac{1}{3}$

2. (a) 2 **(b)** 3 **(c)** -2
 (d) -3 **(e)** 1 **(f)** 7

 (g) $1\dfrac{1}{2}$ **(h)** 7

3. (a) identity   **(b)** identity

 (c) -1 **(d)** $-16\dfrac{1}{2}$

 (e) identity   **(f)** $4\dfrac{1}{6}$

 (g) identity

Exercise 8c *(Pg 156)*

1. (a) 10 **(b)** $7\dfrac{1}{2}$

 (c) -21 **(d)** $1\dfrac{19}{21}$

 (e) $2\dfrac{2}{5}$ **(f)** 12

 (g) 36 **(h)** -60

 (i) $-2\dfrac{1}{2}$ **(j)** 15

 (k) $25\dfrac{5}{7}$ **(l)** 13

 (m) $2\dfrac{2}{3}$ **(n)** $\dfrac{-1}{3}$

 (o) $-4\dfrac{3}{4}$ **(p)** $-1\dfrac{1}{3}$

 (q) -2 **(r)** 22

2. (a) -10 **(b)** 2
 (c) 0.15 **(d)** 4
 (e) -0.64 **(f)** 1.21
 (g) 34 **(h)** 2.10
 (i) 2.92 **(j)** 0.907

Exercise 8d *(Pg 157)*

1. 86 **2.** 86 **3.** $1\,386$
4. 22 **5.** 5 **6.** 32

7. $1\dfrac{5}{6}$ **8.** $2\dfrac{1}{2}$ **9.** 15

10. 3 **11.** $4\dfrac{1}{8}$ **12.** 2

13. -123 **14.** -30 **15.** $6\dfrac{1}{3}$

16. $5\dfrac{3}{10}$

Exercise 8e *(Pg 158)*

(a) $S = a + b + c$ **(b)** $P = xy$
(c) $D = a - e$ or $e - a$
(d) $A = \frac{1}{2}\pi r^2$ **(e)** $C = \frac{3m}{25}$
(f) $A = \frac{1}{4}(m + n + p + q)$ years old
(g) $x = 180 - 2y$
(h) $T = 60a + b$
(i) $T = dp + cq$
(j) **(i)** $r = p + q$
(ii) $\frac{xy(p + q)}{py + qx}$ kmh^{-1}

Exercise 8f *(Pg 160)*

1. 5 000 g; 1 000x g
2. \$24; \$4p; \$$pq$ **3.** $\frac{1}{4}m$ kg
4. $2b$ km
5. 60 m minute
6. $\frac{y}{7}$ weeks **7.** $20x$
8. $\frac{1}{2}b$ **9.** $\frac{21}{v}$ hours
10. \$$(a + b)$
11. $6b$ years; $(7b + 2y)$ years
12. $(2x + 4)$ years
13. $n - 1, n, n + 1$
14. $(5u + 3v)$ km

Exercise 8g *(Pg 161)*

1. **(a)** $x + 7 = 18$
(b) $(x - 2) \times 3 = 24$
(c) $(x - 5) \times 7 = 63$
(d) $(24 - x) \div 5 = 4$
(e) $x + (x + 1) + (x + 2) = 63$
(f) $x + (x + 3) = 43$
(g) $6x = 2x + 16$
(h) $2[x + (x + 5)] = 32$
(i) $2(x + 2x) = 54$
2. \$70
3. 15
4. $3x + x + 2x = 4\ 800$
5. $3x + 2(2x) = 450$

Exercise 8h *(Pg 163)*

1. 11, 12, 13, 14 **2.** 14
3. 4 **4.** 16, 64
5. 19, 15 and 13 **6.** \$20, \$10
7. 8 700 kg **8.** 27
9. 9, 36 **10.** \$3.50
11. \$32, \$128, \$96
12. \$152 **13.** 12

Review Questions 8 *(Pg 164)*

1. **(a)** $2\frac{9}{11}$ **(b)** $-4\frac{1}{4}$ **(c)** 30
(d) $\frac{1}{4}$ **(e)** -6 **(f)** 4
(g) $\frac{17}{19}$ **(h)** $6\frac{3}{5}$
2. **(a)** identity **(b)** $-1\frac{3}{5}$
(c) -29 **(d)** identity
(e) identity **(f)** $2\frac{35}{37}$
3. 45
4. 120 kg, 240 kg, 120 kg
5. 120 **6.** 16 hours
7. 9 **8.** 24 days
9. 8 **10.** $3\frac{3}{5}$ km
11. 8, 40 **12.** 21, 24
13. 36 km/h **14.** 25, 13
15. 25 cents

Revision Exercise II No 1 *(Pg 167)*

1. $404x$
2. $20y - 8x$
3. **(a)** $3a$ **(b)** $28c^2$
(c) $5ab$ **(d)** $10a + c$
(e) $14a^2$ **(f)** 0
(g) $2xy$ **(h)** 0
(i) $20a$ **(j)** $8x$
4. **(a)** 6 **(b)** $5\frac{2}{11}$
(c) $12\frac{3}{7}$ **(d)** 11
5. **(a)** 138 **(b)** 10
6. 24 yrs
7. **(a)** -39 **(b)** -156
(c) 830
8. **(a)** $-7\frac{9}{20}$ **(b)** $1\frac{29}{72}$
9. **(a)** $>$ **(b)** $<$
(c) $>$ **(d)** $=$
10. **(a)** -450 **(b)** 26
(c) 16 **(d)** 12

Revision Exercise II No 2 *(Pg 167)*

1. $2b - 60a$
2. **(a)** -1 **(b)** 3
(c) 14 **(d)** -18
3. **(a)** $\frac{1}{6}$ **(b)** $-\frac{4}{7}$
4. 42 **5.** 9 mths
6. **(a)** 0 **(b)** -72
(c) 1 **(d)** -75
7. **(a)** $2\frac{1}{22}$ **(b)** $6\frac{1}{6}$ **(c)** $-5\frac{7}{8}$
8. **(a)** 40 **(b)** 20 **(c)** 4
9. $\frac{5x}{18t}$
10. **(a)** 49.735 **(b)** 14.442
(c) 111.595

Revision Exercise II No 3 *(Pg 168)*

1. $3r - 2q - s$
2. **(a)** 20 **(b)** -15
(c) 32 **(d)** 36
3. **(a)** 9 **(b)** 0.15
(c) 15 **(d)** $3\frac{14}{15}$
4. 135
5. 45 yrs
6. **(a)** -7 **(b)** -44 **(c)** 98
7. **(a)** 490.63 **(b)** 27.07
(c) 0.27
8. **(a)** $>$ **(b)** $<$ **(c)** $<$
(d) $>$ **(e)** $>$ **(f)** $<$
9. **(a)** 13.875 6 **(b)** 583.5
10. **(a)** $\frac{11}{13}$ **(b)** $-5\frac{1}{18}$

Revision Exercise II No 4 *(Pg 168)*

1. **(a)** 5.34 **(b)** 0.090
(c) 5 000 **(d)** 12 100
2. **(a)** $2x^2 - x - 2 - 6y^2$
(b) $6z - 2y$
3. $-\frac{1}{30}x - 1\frac{1}{6}y$
4. 6
5. **(a)** $1\frac{2}{3}$ **(b)** 8 **(c)** 14
(d) 4 **(e)** 2 **(f)** 5
6. $7\frac{1}{5}xy$ km
7. **(a)** 2 000 000 **(b)** 900 000
(c) 5 000 **(d)** 4 000
8. **(a)** 0.003 **(b)** 2 000
(c) 10 **(d)** 3
9. **(a)** 10 **(b)** -18
(c) $1\frac{3}{7}$ **(d)** $-\frac{4}{13}$
10. **(a)** 7 yrs **(b)** 56 yrs

Revision Exercise II No 5 *(Pg 169)*

1. **(a)** 5 **(b)** 6
(c) -1 **(d)** 12
2. $\frac{4x + 6}{3}$

3. 5

4. (a) 6   **(b)** $2\frac{2}{3}$ **(c)** 11

   (d) 5   **(e)** 8   **(f)** $-1\frac{1}{4}$

5. (a) 12 mn **(b)** 3xy

   (c) 28a **(d)** 8.5a

6. (a) 6.2   **(b)** 2.595

   (c) 10

7. (a) 4   **(b)** $-\frac{1}{4}$

   (c) 27   **(d)** $-\frac{3}{10}$

8. (a) 13   **(b)** $-$ 280

   (c) $-1\frac{11}{20}$ **(d)** $\frac{1}{4}$

9. (a) 25 yrs   **(b)** 18 yrs

10. (a) 8.840   **(b)** 212.3

   (c) 2 094   **(d)** 1.895

Mid-Year Examination Specimen Paper 1 *(Pg 170)*

Part I

1. (a) False   **(b)** True

   (c) False   **(d)** True

2. (a) 12   **(b)** 1 950

3. (a) $4\frac{5}{18}$ **(b)** $\frac{2}{9}$

4. (a) 24   **(b)** -4

   (c) -20 **(d)** 0

5. (a) $\frac{7}{8}$ **(b)** 1.387 5

6. (a) (i) 32.75 **(ii)** 32.7

   (b) 87.5

7. $2^4 \times 17^2$, 68

8. (a) $-7x^4 - 8x^2 + 10x + 3$

   (b) $2x^3 + 2x^2 + 8x + 10$

9. $\frac{1}{2}$

10. 251

11. -6

12. $(20x + 12y)$¢

13. $13\frac{1}{5}$

14. (a) 1.9, 2.5   **(b)** 94, 143

Part II

1. (a) $10 - 5x$ **(b)** 8

2. 64 kg

3. (a) $\frac{1}{8 \times 9} = \frac{1}{8} - \frac{1}{9}$

   (b) $\frac{1}{2\,550}$ **(c)** 18, 19

4. (a) $6\frac{1}{5}$ **(b)** $-\frac{3}{11}$

5. (a) $3\frac{24}{25}$ **(b)** 2 780

   (c) 1.474   **(d)** -6.514

6. (a) 30

   (b) (i) 0.150 8

     (ii) 0.002 32

7. (a) $6k - h + 18m$

   (b) $\frac{4x + 27y}{15}$

8. (a) $6\frac{3}{5}$ **(b)** 7.2

   (c) $-14 + 11x - 8x^2 + 2x^3$

Mid-Year Examination Specimen Paper 2 *(Pg 171)*

Part I

1. (a) 2 772   **(b)** 243

2. (a) $22\frac{1}{2}$ **(b)** 22.702 2

3. (a) 6a **(b)** $-y$

4. (a) $-2\frac{1}{3}$ **(b)** 3.2

5. 9 yrs

6. $11.25

7. (a) $\frac{15}{16}$ **(b)** $2\frac{13}{21}$

8. (a) $0.2\dot{1}$ **(b)** 0.212 1

9. (a) 60   **(b)** 6 000

10. 155y sec

11. (a) 69, 133   **(b)** $\frac{23}{29}$, $\frac{33}{40}$

12. (a) 38°C   **(b)** -3°C

13. $\frac{-38x - 31}{15}$

14. (a) -16 **(b)** 126

Part II

1. (a) 22   **(b)** 43

   (c) 1 086

2. (a) 33.98   **(b)** 4.829

3. (a) 5   **(b)** 10

4. (a) 14, 21   **(b)** $\frac{14a - 19}{20}$

5. $11

6. (a) $\frac{-45}{368}$ **(b)** 26, 10 cm

7. (a) $(-2, 6), (-1, 5), (1, 3)$

   (b) $(-2, -1), (1, 2)$

   (c) $(-1, 5, 6), (1, 3, 6),$

     $(1, 4, 5), (2, 3, 5)$

8. (a) $10x^2 - 5x - 2$

   (b) $6x^3 + 2x^2 - 2x + 1$

9. (a) $1 + 3 + 5 + \ldots + 17 + 19$

     $= 100 = 10^2$

   (b) 225   **(c)** 13

Mid-Year Examination Specimen Paper 3 *(Pg 173)*

Part I

1. 294

2. 15, 1 800

3. $2^6 \times 7^2$, 56

4. $2\frac{1}{2}$

5. (a) <   **(b)** <

   (c) >   **(d)** <

6. 7

7. 0.000 35

8. 336, 11 048

9. (a) $3\frac{1}{2}$ **(b)** $3\frac{3}{16}$

10. (a) 30, 38   **(b)** $7\frac{2}{3}$, 10

11. (a) 0.625   **(b)** $\frac{43}{50}$

   (c) 0.002 6   **(d)** 2.4

12. (a) $12x - 7y$ **(b)** $7z - 11x$

13. (a) 8   **(b)** 21

14. $23.50

Part II

1. (a) 3.629   **(b)** 65.99

2. (a) 85   **(b)** -3

3. 9 yrs, 36 yrs

4. (a) $(12a + 7b)$¢

   (b) (i) $5 < 7 < 10$

     (ii) $c < a < b$ or $b < a < c$

5. (a) 29, 37   **(b)** 50, 65

6. (a) $\frac{5}{24}$

   (b) $-4x^5 + 4x^4 + x^2 + 13x - 7$

7. (a) 0.016 26   **(b)** 37 560

8. (a) $x - 6$, 42   **(b)** 875 124

9. (a) $\frac{46}{3x}$ **(b)** $16\frac{2}{5}$

Mid-Year Examination Specimen Paper 4 *(Pg 174)*

Part I

1. $0.1\dot{7}$, 0.177, $0.1\dot{7}$, 0.178

2. 540, 45

3. $2^3 \times 3^6$, 18

4. 30

5. (a) $1\frac{2}{3}$ **(b)** $\frac{1}{4}$

6. $2\frac{3}{5}$

7. $\frac{4x + 7}{15}$

8. (a) 28   **(b)** 8

9. $4x^3 - 4x + 13$

10. $-\dfrac{1}{2}$

11. 15 yrs, 45 yrs

12. (a) $70x$ km   **(b)** $\dfrac{50x}{11}$

    (c) $1\,000k$

13. $28xy - 15x^2 - 4x - 26y$

14. $\dfrac{56}{135}$ **15.** $\dfrac{xy}{15}$

Part II

1. 1.17   **2.** 3

3. $11\dfrac{1}{6}$

4. $\dfrac{169}{273}, \dfrac{34}{51}, \dfrac{88}{121}, \dfrac{76}{95}$

5. $5\dfrac{2}{45}$ **6.** \$360

7. (a) (i) 66 000

     (ii) 168.7

   (b) $\dfrac{3x - y}{14}$

8. (a) (i) $10^2 - 9^2 = 19$

     (ii) 197

     (iii) $x = 79, y = 78$

   (b) $4x^2y^3 - 1 - 3x$

9. (a) $-24\dfrac{1}{2}$

   (b) (i) 441   **(ii)** 105

10. (a) 96, 145   **(b)** 81

Mid-Year Examination Specimen Paper 5 (Pg 176)

Part I

1. (a) 143   **(b)** $208\dfrac{3}{4}$

2. (a) $2\dfrac{1}{60}$ **(b)** $\dfrac{5}{6}$

3. 5, 3 780

4. (a) 2   **(b)** -1

   (c) $\dfrac{1}{4}$ **(d)** 7

5. (a) $a - 4b$ **(b)** $-5m - 4n$

6. -75

7. (a) $1\dfrac{3}{35}$ **(b)** $\dfrac{8}{15}$

8. $1\dfrac{2}{3}$ **9.** $2^8 \times 3^2$, 48

10. $\dfrac{8}{11}, \dfrac{5}{7}, \dfrac{2}{3}, \dfrac{4}{9}$

11. $2x^3 - 8x^2 + 8x - 5$

12. (a) 56 133   **(b)** 518

---

13. (a) $k = 5$ **(b)** 9

   (c) 1 200

14. (a) 5, 6, 7, 8   **(b)** -9

Part II

1. (a) 0.058 92   **(b)** -4.500

2. 3.5   **3.** \$502   **4.** $\dfrac{6}{17}$

5. (a) $5\dfrac{7}{24}$

   (b) $2x^3 - 12x^2 - 16x + 12$

6. (a) 49   **(b)** 49

7. (a) 1   **(b)** 32, 34

8. (a) 80¢   **(b)** \$565

   (c) $-6°C$

9. (a) 18   **(b)** 25 yrs

Exercise 9a (Pg 181)

1. (a) 27 cm   **(b)** 32 cm

   (c) 28 cm

2. (a) 41 cm   **(b)** 60 cm

   (c) 42 cm

3. 6

4. 1.65 km

5. 17 m

6. $(200a + 2b)$ cm

Exercise 9b (Pg 184)

1. (a) 0.000 85   **(b)** 0.025

   (c) 63 000   **(d)** 4 060

   (e) 4 440   **(f)** 31 000

   (g) 0.000 053 7

   (h) 280 000   **(i)** 0.053 2

   (j) 6.945   **(k)** 0.034

   (l) 0.046 2

2. (a) 20 m, 24 m²

   (b) 6 m, 28 m

   (c) 4 m, 12.4 m

   (d) 7 m, 31.5 m²

   (e) 23 mm, 598 mm²

3. 972   **4.** 2 460 cm²

5. 272 m²   **6.** 810 cm²

7. \$2 152.50   **8.** 275 m²

9. 81 cm²   **10.** 55.2 cm²

11. 5.65 ha

12. 18 cm, 180 cm²

Exercise 9c (Pg 190)

1. (a) 35 cm²   **(b)** 39 cm²

   (c) $13\dfrac{1}{2}$ cm²

2. 17 cm

3. (a) 102 cm²   **(b)** $17\dfrac{1}{2}$ cm²

   (c) 21 cm

---

4. (a) 84   **(b)** 7   **(c)** 5.5

5. 157.5 cm²

6. (a) 54   **(b)** 10   **(c)** 13

7. \$14 080

8. (a) 8   **(b)** 23

   (c) 12   **(d)** 21

9. (a) 60 cm²   **(b)** 762 cm²

   (c) 76 cm²   **(d)** 168 cm²

   (e) 659 cm²   **(f)** 63 cm²

   (g) 810 m²   **(h)** 1 040 m²

Exercise 9d (Pg 195)

1. (a) 20 m, $62\dfrac{6}{7}$ m, $314\dfrac{2}{7}$ m²

   (b) 28 mm, 56 mm, 2 464 mm²

   (c) 14 m, 28 m, 88 cm

   (d) 1.8 m, $11\dfrac{11}{35}$ m, $10\dfrac{32}{175}$ m²

2. (a) 220 mm, 3 850 mm²

   (b) 88 cm, 616 cm²

   (c) 110 cm, $962\dfrac{1}{2}$ cm²

   (d) $14\dfrac{2}{3}$ cm, $17\dfrac{1}{9}$ cm²

3. (a) 21.98 cm, 38.47 cm²

   (b) 86.66 m, 597.98 m²

   (c) 2.32 cm, 0.43 cm²

   (d) 32.97 cm, 86.55 cm²

4. (a) 72 cm, 308 cm²

   (b) 56 cm, 217 cm²

   (c) 96 cm, $661\dfrac{1}{2}$ cm²

   (d) 22.4 cm, 35 cm²

   (e) $28\dfrac{4}{7}$ cm, $50\dfrac{3}{7}$ cm²

   (f) 396 cm, 10 234 cm²

5. 20 cm

6. 3 684 cm²

7. 11.73 cm/min

8. $35\dfrac{1}{5}$ m/s

9. 301

10. 45.4 cm

Review Questions 9 (Pg 197)

1. 42 cm²   **2.** 18 cm²

3. 128 cm²   **4.** 13 cm, 117 cm²

5. 864

6. 12 cm; 8 cm, 4 cm

7. 14

8. 44 m

9. 88 cm, 154 cm²

Exercise 10a *(Pg 204)*

1. (a) 480 cm³, 376 cm²
   (b) 420 cm³, 358 cm²
   (c) 115 200 mm³, 27 360 mm²
   (d) $7\frac{1}{2}$ cm³, $41\frac{1}{2}$ cm²
   (e) $\frac{21}{64}$ cm³, $3\frac{43}{160}$ cm²
   (f) 4.095 cm³, 19.26 cm²
2. (a) 2 160 mm³, 1 284 mm²
   (b) 8 cm, 158 cm²
   (c) 2.5 cm, 89.5 cm²
   (d) 8 m, 432 m²
   (e) $3\frac{1}{4}$ cm, $102\frac{5}{8}$ cm²
   (f) 5 cm, 540 cm³
3. (a) 69 300 *l*   (b) 33 345 *l*
   (c) 6.84 *l*   (d) 35.568 *l*
4. 96 cm²
5. 702
6. 16 cm, 1 420 cm²
7. 2.9 m
8. 31.35 cm
9. (a) 456 000
   (b) $25.08 million, $836
10. 6 703.2 m³

Exercise 10b *(Pg 207)*

1. $3\frac{1}{8}$ g/cm³   2. 2.41 g/cm³
3. 1.3 g/cm³   4. 72.8 g
5. 125 cm³   6. 250 cm³
7. (a) 672 cm³   (b) 1881.6 g
8. (a) 1 232 cm³   (b) 7.63 g/cm³

Exercise 10c *(Pg 210)*

1. (a) 18 450 cm³
   (b) 600 cm³
   (c) 1 404 cm³
   (d) 369 840 cm³
   (e) 16 644 cm³
   (f) 960 cm³
   (g) 1 332 cm³
   (h) 770 cm³
   (i) 4 725 cm³
2. (a) 6 cm², 42 cm³
   (b) 14 cm, 693 cm³
   (c) 32 cm, 240 cm²
   (d) 400 cm, 95.94 cm²
3. 102 480 m³
4. 153 cm³, 250 cm²
5. 5 625 m³, 1 937.5 m²
6. 4 500 cm³, 1 650 cm²

7. $31\frac{1}{4}$ cm
8. 3.66 m²
9. (a) 180 cm³   (b) 264 cm²
10. 1 728 *l*, 0.872 m³
11. 49 500 cm³
12. 25 cm
13. 138.6 *l*

Exercise 10d *(Pg 216)*

1. (a) 1 848 cm³, 836 cm²
   (b) 4.526 m³, 17.35 m²
   (c) 44 550 mm³, 7 354.3 mm²
2. (a) 8 cm   (b) 28 cm
3. (a) 42 cm   (b) 21 cm
4. 400
5. 7.425 *l*
6. 1 056 cm³
7. 19 250 cm²
8. 20.1 m²
9. 11 550 m³, 154
10. 123.75 *l*, 206
11. (a) 4 400 cm³ (b) 37.84 kg
12. (a) 3 080 cm³
    (b) 0.844 g/cm³
13. 0.9856 cm³, 5.32 g, 10 348.8 m³, 55 881 tonnes

Review Questions 10 *(Pg 218)*

1. (a) 108 cm³, 168 cm²
   (b) 88 cm³, 152 cm²
   (c) 1 217.86 cm³, 1 233.57 cm²
2. (a) rectangular cuboid
   (b) cylinder
   (c) rectangular cuboid
   (d) triangular pyramid
   (e) triangular prism
   (f) square pyramid
3. 2.8 m
4. 3 000   5. 64
6. 1 800   7. 1 350 *l*
8. 104.16 kg   9. 172.8 kg
10. 1 690 kg   11. 0.81 m³
12. 105 cm   13. 1.216 kg
14. 1 h 55 min 30 sec
15. 291 000 m³, 366 660 kg
16. (a) 495 652 trips;
    (b) 543 truck loads

Exercise 11a *(Pg 223)*

1. (a) 6   (b) 3
   (c) 12   (d) 7
2. (a) 3 : 5   (b) 11 : 2

(c) 4 : 5   (d) 1 : 50
(e) 3 : 4   (f) 4 : 5 : 3
(g) 8 : 4 : 1   (h) 3 : 5 : 7
(i) 21 : 6 : 5   (j) 2 : 3 : 5

3. (a) (i) 5:16   (ii) $\frac{5}{16}$
   (b) (i) 7 : 12   (ii) $\frac{7}{12}$
   (c) (i) 5 : 2   (ii) $\frac{5}{2}$
   (d) (i) 2 : 3   (ii) $\frac{2}{3}$
   (e) (i) 5 : 12   (ii) $\frac{5}{12}$
   (f) (i) 7 : 120   (ii) $\frac{7}{120}$

4. 1 : 4
5. 4 : 21
6. (a) 8 : 3   (b) 5 : 8
7. 13 : 12 : 7
8. 2 : 3 : 6 : 7
9. (a) 4 : 9   (b) 2 : 3
10. 3 : 7 : 24 : 5

Exercise 11b *(Pg 225)*

1. 168
2. 64
3. (a) 25 kg   (b) 64 m
   (c) 87.5 ha   (d) 1 cm²
4. (a) 7 : 5   (b) 4 : 3
5. (a) 5 : 7   (b) 3 : 4
6. 19 : 24
7. $104
8. 7.7 cm by 12.6 cm
9. $7.20
10. $35 200

Exercise 11c *(Pg 227)*

1. (a) 15   (b) 200
   (c) 19   (d) 5
2. $150   3. 272 km
4. 240   5. 221 g
6. $172.50   7. $5 000
8. $35.10   9. 500 g
10. (a) 25 g   (b) 350 g
    (c) 18 m²
11. 15
12. (a) (i) $9.90 (ii) $16.60
    (b) (i) $8.00 (ii) $13.50

Exercise 11d *(Pg 230)*

1. (a) 08 00   (b) 14 00
   (c) 17 30   (d) 21 42

(e) 12 00   **(f)** 00 45
(g) 00 00   **(h)** 02 42
2. (a) 3.30 am   **(b)** 3 pm
(c) 11.12 pm   **(d)** 7.15 pm
(e) 9.23 am   **(f)** 12 pm
(g) 12.05 am   **(h)** 12.00 am
3. (a) 02 30 **(b)** 17 55 **(c)** 06 45
4. (a) 20 45 **(b)** 03 35 **(c)** 18 30
   (d) 06 35 the next day
   (e) 2 h 5 min
   (f) 3 h 25 min
   (g) 12 h 28 min
   (h) 10 h 40 min
   (i) 22 35
   (j) 19 00 (Thurs)
5. 6 h 37 min
6. 07 13 the next day
7. 10 51
8. 7 h 10 min, 05 30
9. 50 min
10. (a) 4 h 55 min
    (b) 7 h 20 min
    (c) 6 h 50 min
    (d) 6 h 25 min
    (e) 13 h 15 min

Exercise 11e *(Pg 234)*

1. (b) 8 m/s   **(c)** $6\frac{2}{3}$ m/s
   (d) 440 km   **(e)** 500 m
   (f) 5 s
2. (a) 5 m/s   **(b)** 20 m/s
   (c) 25 m/s
3. (a) 36 km/h   **(b)** 126 km/h
   (c) 1 800 km/h
4. 22 s
5. 10 53
6. (a) 13 42   **(b)** 112 km/h
7. 80 m
8. (a) 19 km   **(b)** 110 km/h
9. 10 km/h
10. 48 km/h
11. (a) 5 m/s   **(b)** 4 s
    (c) 7.5 m/s
12. (a) 60 m   **(b)** 4 s
    (c) 16 m/s

Exercise 11f *(Pg 237)*

1. (a) $2\frac{6}{7}$ **(b)** $3\frac{8}{9}$ **(c)** 33
   (d) 18   **(e)** 8   **(f)** 8

---

2. (a) 70   **(b)** *uy*
3. (a) 7 : 5   **(b)** 3 : 8
   (c) 9 : 5   **(d)** 55 : 24
4. 2
5. (a) $64 **(b)** $60 **(c)** $\dfrac{ac}{b}$
6. $3\frac{3}{5}$ kg
7. 7.5 m; 32 books
8. (a) 72 books   **(b)** $41\frac{2}{3}$ kg

Exercise 11g *(Pg 240)*

1. (b), (c), (d)
2. 40 min   **3.**   5 books
4. 20 days   **5.** $17\frac{1}{2}$ h
6. (a) 840 cattle **(b)** 40 days
7. 28   **8.** 2 days
9. 36 hours

Exercise 11h *(Pg 242)*

1. $1.50, $6, $7.50
2. 50 cm, 150 cm, 200 cm
3. 25 g, 40 g, 45 g
4. 56 cm, 84 cm, 168 cm
5. $3 920
6. $4 000
7. $70, $154
8. 120 kg, 240 kg, 120 kg
9. (a) 20 m   **(b)** 50 cm
10. (a) 40 m   **(b)** 60 cm
11. (a) 1 cm : 250 m
    (b) 750 m   **(c)** 32 cm
12. (a) 10 kg, 30 kg **(b)** $3
13. (a) 54 *l*, 9 *l*, 6 *l*   **(b)** 46 *l*
14. (a) 9 kg, 15 kg, 21 kg
    (b) $10.80
15. (a) 150 g, 650 g
    (b) 40 g, 480 g
    (c) 19 : 93 : 48
    (d) 95 g

Exercise 11i *(Pg 245)*

1. 9; 6, 7, 8, 9, 10, 11, 12, 13, 14
2. 280 m
3. 37 800 m
4. 37

Review Questions 11 *(Pg 246)*

1. 3 : 4
2. 240 cm by 288 cm
3. 333 000
4. 9 : 10 : 12

---

5. (a) 45   **(b)** 15
6. (a) 06 47   **(b)** 1.2 km
7. (a) 09 51   **(b)** 88 km/h
8. (a) $18.54   **(b)** 5 kg
9. (a) (i) 2 h 40 min
      (ii) 6 h 25 min
   (b) (i) 53 min
      (ii) 1 219 words
10. (a) 63 m   **(b)** 7 m
11. $53\frac{1}{3}$ km/h
12. (a) $1 050, $750, $300
    (b) $1 225, $875, $350, $175,
       $175
13. 1 : 60
14. (a) 12 30
    (b) 3 h 20 min; 58.5 km/h
15. (a) 7 h 15 min
    (b) $11.90

Exercise 12a *(Pg 253)*

1. (a) 0.06   **(b)** 0.11
   (c) 0.22   **(d)** 0.63
   (e) 1.79   **(f)** 0.002 7
   (g) 0.287   **(h)** 1.346
   (i) 0.035   **(j)** 0.052 5
   (k) 0.000 74   **(l)** 0.543 7
   (m) 0.000 063 **(n)** 0.011 25
   (o) 0.008 75   **(p)** 0.507 5
2. (a) 17%   **(b)** 57.5%
   (c) 83%   **(d)** 236%
   (e) 9%   **(f)** 2.5%
   (g) 0.8%   **(h)** 256.4%
   (i) 0.05%   **(j)** 120%
   (k) 400%   **(l)** 625%
3. (a) 75%   **(b)** 90%
   (c) 85%   **(d)** $4\frac{4}{5}$%
   (e) 120%   **(f)** 48%
   (g) 124%   **(h)** 240%
4. (a) 66.6%   **(b)** 57.1%
   (c) 22.2%   **(d)** 58.3%
   (e) 133.3%   **(f)** 83.3%
   (g) 242.9%   **(h)** 90.9%
5. 60%, 0.6; $\dfrac{11}{100}$, 0.11; 17.5%,
   $\dfrac{7}{40}$; 9.5%, $\dfrac{19}{200}$; $\dfrac{157}{200}$, 0.785
6. $\dfrac{1}{24}$
7. $4\frac{11}{16}$%
8. (a) $4\frac{1}{2}$%, $\dfrac{12}{32}$, 0.39

(b) 22%, 0.222, $\dfrac{2}{9}$

(c) 0.6, 64%, $\dfrac{2}{3}$

Exercise 12b *(Pg 255)*

1. **(a)** 30% **(b)** 4.5% **(c)** 125%

2. **(a)** 75%   **(b)** $33\dfrac{1}{3}$%

   (c) 67%   **(d)** $16\dfrac{2}{3}$%

   (e) 1.5%   **(f)** 30%

3. **(a) (i)** $\dfrac{5}{6}$ **(ii)** $83\dfrac{1}{3}$%

   (b) (i) $\dfrac{13}{16}$ **(ii)** $81\dfrac{1}{4}$%

4. 30%
5. 6%
6. 20%, 30%, 45%, 5%
7. **(a)** $99.20   **(b)** 325
   (c) 3.60 m   **(d)** 62.5 cm
   (e) 91.8 litres **(f)** 4.84 hours
8. 7 225 people
9. 1 190 tires
10. **(a)** 47.4 kg   **(b)** 237 000 kg
11. **(a)** 400 000
    (b) (i) 800 000
        (ii) 1 200 000
        (iii) 1 600 000
        (iv) 2 000 000

Exercise 12c *(Pg 259)*

1. 63   2. 135
3. 140   4. 240
5. $228.80   6. $122 400
7. $1 800   8. $65
9. 355 houses   10. 5.4 m
11. **(a)** $55.80
    (b) (i) $9.18 **(ii)** $367.20
12. 15%   13. $86 400
14. 20%   15. 16.64%

16. **(a)** $11\dfrac{1}{9}$%   **(b)** 40 minutes

    (c) 180 seconds
    (d) 192 seconds
    (e) James

Exercise 12d *(Pg 262)*

1. **(a)** 12.5%   **(b)** 7.14%
   (c) 25%   **(d)** 13.8%
2. $135   3. $18.75
4. 16.7%   5. $17 296
6. $180

7. **(a)** $800   **(b)** $1 080
8. $600   9. 24%
10. 32%   11. $240
12. $180   13. 99¢

Exercise 12e *(Pg 264)*

1. **(a)** 12%   **(b)** 20%
2. **(a) (i)** $4.50 **(ii)** $40.50
   (b) (i) $11   **(ii)** $99
3. **(a)** $700   **(b)** $810
4. **(a)** $87.50   **(b)** $164
5. $500
6. **(a)** $72   **(b)** $72.20
7. $28
8. $700
9. $1 600, $1 120

10. **(a)** 38cents   **(b)** $15\dfrac{5}{9}$%

11. $1 310   12. $18 000
13. $90
14. $36, $48, $60

Exercise 12f *(Pg 267)*

1. **(a)** $6 720, $18 720
   (b) 4 yrs, $720
   (c) $300, $408
   (d) 4%, $4 200
   (e) $3 600, 5%
   (f) 7%, $1 989
   (g) 6%, 540

   (h) $1 200, $1\dfrac{1}{2}$ yrs

2. $7 084   3. $1 100
4. $360   5. $132

6. 10 years   7. $4\dfrac{1}{4}$%

8. $1 019.5   9. $16
10. $6 100   11. $20 000

Exercise 12g *(Pg 270)*

1. **(a)** $94.50   **(b)** $257.34
   (c) $1 244.03 **(d)** $149.84
   (e) $1 556.25
2. $5 829.57   3. $103.13
4. $9 001.46

Exercise 12h *(Pg 271)*

1. **(a) (i)** $90   **(ii)** 25%

   (b) (i) $150   **(ii)** $16\dfrac{2}{3}$%

   (c) (i) $3 000
       (ii) 12%

2. **(a)** $21   **(b)** $288
3. **(a) (i)** $236   **(ii)** 18%
   (b) (i) $517.50 **(ii)** 15%
   (c) (i) $1 960 **(ii)** 22.5%
4. **(a) (i)** $63   **(ii)** 7%
   (b) (i) $200   **(ii)** 15%

   (c) (i) $75   **(ii)** $16\dfrac{2}{3}$%

5. **(a)** $3 716.80 **(b)** $516.80
   (c) 16.15%
6. **(a)** 18.2%   **(b)** $108
   (c) 5.13%

Exercise 12i *(Pg 274)*

1. **(a)** S$761.85   **(b)** S$7 935
   (c) S$1 528   **(d)** S$96.80
   (e) S$817.20   **(f)** S$210
   (g) S$1 132.5 **(h)** S$256.76
   (i) S$27 800   **(j)** S$564.48
   (k) S$9 573.56 **(l)** S$157.50
2. **(a)** US$4 401   **(b)** £327
   (c) NZ$5 827
   (d) 5 901 Thai baht
   (e) 109 890 peso
   (f) 833 333 rupiah
   (g) ¥29 577
   (h) 3 195 French franc
   (i) C$320
   (j) A$1 106
   (k) HK$10 000
   (l) 1 684 Deutschemark
3. **(a)** 1 155 Thai baht
   (b) US$210
4. **(a)** 992 M   **(b)** £280
5. **(a)** US$5 000 **(b)** S$330

Exercise 12j *(Pg 277)*

1. $1 312   2. $96.90
3. $247.20   4. $165
5. **(a)** $60   **(b)** $120
   (c) $375   **(d)** $675
6. **(a)** $276   **(b)** $90.80

Exercise 12k *(Pg 282)*

1. 7   2. 20 cents
3. 22, 14, 12   4. 17
5. 11   6. 127

Review Questions 12 *(Pg 283)*

1. $935
2. **(a)** $900   **(b)** $1 170
3. **(a)** $291.20   **(b)** $1 164.80

4. $197.40

5. $1\frac{3}{4}$, 1.74, 173%, $1\frac{2}{3}$, 1.56

6. $\frac{7}{80}$

7. $\frac{3}{40}$

8. $200, $240

9. (a) S$276   (b) £674.78

10. 144, 168

11. loss $2.40

12. (a) 5%   (b) $736.67

13. (a) $72 000 000
   (b) $11 137 000
   (c) 64%

14. (a) $3
   (b) (i) $33   (ii) $9.00

Revision Exercise III No 1 *(Pg 285)*

1. $2.75   **2.** 50 min

3. $20.25   **4.** 7 : 12

5. $24   **6.** $8.40

7. 91 cm²

8. (a) 135 000 m³   (b) 9

9. 456 000 trips, $20 520 000

10. $\frac{60}{77}$ cm

Revision Exercise III No 2 *(Pg 285)*

1. $920   **2.** $20.50

3. 23, $6.80   **4.** $14 100

5. 85 l

6. 24 cm², 3 cm

7. 2 288 cm², 7 392 cm³

8. 690 cm², 5 175 cm³

9. 18 cm

10. $874.18

Revision Exercise III No 3 *(Pg 286)*

1. (a) $200   (b) $51 200
   (c) $1 700

2. 24 days

3. $80

4. 147, 245, 392

5. M$317.43

6. (a) $9   (b) 1.2 kg
   (c) 17 m³   (d) 225 km

7. (a) 42.9 cm
   (b) 1 106 cm², 2 814 cm³,
       10.69 kg

8. 48 cm, 161 cm²

9. 156 cm³

10. (a) 32 cm²   (b) 2 250 m³

Revision Exercise III No 4 *(Pg 287)*

1. $66.25

2. (a) $180   (b) 19.15%

3. $A = 12, B = 10, C = 9$

4. 33.84 km/h

5. $40

6. $5 284.09

7. (a) 36 cm²   (b) 20 cm²

8. $29\frac{1}{3}$ cm

9. 76 cm³, 114 cm³

10. 3 000 l, 19

Revision Exercise III No 5 *(Pg 288)*

1. (a) 87.5%   (b) 510
   (c) $21

2. (a) 5 400 m   (b) 20%

3. $80.75, 34.58%

4. $25.20

5. (a) $11 200   (b) $39 300

6. 12 cm

7. 216 cm²

8. 2 cm

9. 32 cm

10. 7.02 kg, 1.404 g/cm³

Exercise 13a *(Pg 296)*

2. (a) spherical   (b) cylindrical
   (c) cylindrical   (d) prism
   (e) conical   (f) conical

3. (a) $x = 100°, k = 94°, l = 135°,$
      $m = 115°, n = 96°$
   (b) $p = 70°, q = 65°, r = 270°,$
      $s = 62°, t = 73°$

4. (a) $a = 62°, b = c = 118°$
   (b) $d = 74°, e = 97°, f = 107°$
   (c) $g = 245°, h = 50°$
   (d) $k = 180°, t = 132°, l = 28°$
   (e) $l = 90°, m = 68°, n = 225°$
   (f) $p = 248°, q = 99°, r = 90°,$
      $s = 55°$

5. (a) 72° (b) 44° (c) 37°
   (d) 26° (e) 83°

6. (a) 144° (b) 168° (c) 78°
   (d) 9°   (e) 92°

8. (a) 49° (b) 30°
   (c) 90° (d) 60°

9. (a) 30 (b) 10   (c) 9
   (d) 60 (e) $4\frac{2}{3}$

10. (a) $a + d = 90°$ (b) 90°
   (c) 65°

11. 30°, 60°, 120°, 150°

12. (a) 50°
   (b) 42°
   (c) 106°
   (d) 30°
   (e) $p = 35°, q = 145°$
   (f) 47°
   (g) $x = 23, y = 69, z = 111$
   (h) $x = 20, y = 120$
   (i) $x = 18$
   (j) $x = 15$

Exercise 13b *(Pg 301)*

1. (a) $b = y, h = r, e = p$
   (b) $x = d, q = g, p = h$

2. $p = 106°, q = 74°, r = 106°,$
   $s = 74°, x = 73°, y = 107°$

3. (a) $a = 31°, b = 66°$
   (b) $c = 45°, d = 60°$
   (c) $e = 106°$
   (d) $f = 104°$
   (e) $x = 19$
   (f) $x = 30, y = 65$
   (g) $x = 145, y = 223$
   (h) $x = 257$
   (i) $x = 275$
   (j) $x = 140$

Exercise 13c *(Pg 304)*

2. $a = 44°, b = 53°$; 5.6 cm, 7.0 cm,
   Yes

3. 12.3 cm, 11.3 cm, Yes

6. 6.6 cm

Review Questions 13 *(Pg 305)*

1. (a) $x = 36$
   (b) $x = 22.5$
   (c) $x = 29, y = 110$
   (d) $x = 23$
   (e) $x = 16, y = 48$
   (f) $x = 120$
   (g) $x = 80$
   (h) $x = 24$
   (i) $x = 30$
   (j) $x = 56$
   (k) $x = 44, y = 58$
   (l) $x = 65$
   (m) 150
   (n) 124

Exercise 14a *(Pg 313)*

1. (a) 100°
      (i) scalene △
      (ii) obtuse-angled △

(b) 70°
  (i) isosceles △
  (ii) acute-angled △
(c) 60°
  (i) equilateral △
  (ii) acute-angled △
(d) 90°
  (i) scalene △
  (ii) right-angled △
(e) 65°
  (i) isosceles △
  (ii) acute-angled △
(f) 43°
  (i) scalene △
  (ii) obtused-angled △

2. (a) 96°   (b) 16°
   (c) 144°   (d) 52°
3. $A\hat{C}B = 48°$
5. 8.5 cm, 45°
6. $BC = 8.0$ cm, $\hat{B} = 58°$; acute-angled triangle
7. $PR = 6.8$ cm, $QR = 6.1$ cm, $\hat{R} = 76°$; acute-angled triangle
8. $LN = 7.5$ cm, $\hat{M} = 56°$, $\hat{N} = 34°$; right-angled triangle
9. (a) 35° (b) 25° (c) 22.5°
   (d) 60° (e) 102°
   (f) $x = 40°$, $y = 55°$
   (g) $a = 70°$, $b = 22°$
   (h) $x = 127°$, $y = 58°$
   (i) 20° (j) 69°
   (k) $a = 35°$, $b = 108°$
   (l) $x = 78°$, $y = 52°$
   (m) $x = 35°$, $y = 125°$
   (n) $x = 25°$, $y = 97°$
   (o) $i = 101°$, $j = 42°$
   (p) 138°
   (q) $x = 24°$, $y = 96°$, $z = 48°$
   (r) $p = 65°$, $q = 73°$
   (s) $x = 47°$, $y = 65°$, $z = 112°$
   (t) $x = 77°$, $y = 39°$
10. 100
11. 45°
12. $A\hat{B}C = 104°$, $C\hat{B}D = 76°$

Exercise 14b *(Pg 317)*

1. (a) $x = 36°$, $y = 36°$
   (b) $x = 68°$, $y = 73°$
   (c) $x = 54°$, $y = 36°$
   (d) $x = 12°$, $y = 27°$
2. (a) $x = 20°$, $y = 80°$
   (b) $x = 26°$, $y = 48°$

(c) $x = 60°$, $y = 65°$
   (d) $x = 31°$, $y = 12°$
3. (a) $x = 40°$, $y = 58°$
   (b) $x = 114°$, $y = 114°$
   (c) $x = 65°$, $y = 46°$
   (d) $x = 21°$, $y = 21°$
4. (a) $x = 33°$, $y = 114°$
   (b) $x = 104°$, $y = 38°$
   (c) $x = 42°$, $y = 48°$
   (d) $x = 21°$, $y = 21°$, $z = 42°$
5. (a) $x = 37°$, $y = 127°$
   (b) $x = 67.5°$, $y = 22.5°$
   (c) $x = 22.5°$, $y = 108°$
   (d) $x = 25°$, $y = 31°$
6. (a) 59°   (b) 31°
7. (a) 110°   (b) 28°
8. (a) 72°   (b) 36°
   (c) 54°
9. (a) 58°   (b) 96°
10. (a) 31°   (b) 97°

Exercise 14c *(Pg 320)*

1. 16.9 cm   2. 11.6 cm
3. 9 cm
4. 6.4 cm, 10.1 cm
5. 128 mm, 82°
6. 97 mm, 98 mm
7. 1.7 cm   8. 7.0 cm
9. 65°   10. 133°
11. 14.4 cm

Review Questions 14 *(Pg 322)*

1. (a) $x = 40°$, $y = 70°$
   (b) $x = 39°$, $y = 63°$
   (c) $x = 66°$, $y = 66°$
   (d) 35°
   (e) $x = 244°$, $y = 26°$
   (f) $x = 39°$, $y = 63°$
   (g) $x = 56$, $y = 31°$
   (h) $x = 40°$, $y = 32°$
   (i) $x = 122°$, $y = 58°$, $z = 64°$
   (j) $x = 52°$, $y = 31°$, $z = 97°$
   (k) 20°
   (l) $x = 79°$

Exercise 15a *(Pg 330)*

1. (a) 2 : 1   (b) 66.7%
2. (a) 53   (b) 50%
3. (a) 1 000   (b) 900
   (c) $\dfrac{4}{7}$

4. (a) Product 1 (b) April
   (c) $37 500   (d) $45 000
   (e) $140 000 (f) $125 000
   (g) $\dfrac{28}{53}$
5. (a) 1999 – 260 000
   (b) 1995 – 140 000
       1996 – 160 000
       1997 – 180 000
       1998 – 220 000
   (c) $90 million
   (d) 18.2%
8. (a) 4 : 5   (b) $33\dfrac{1}{3}$%

Exercise 15b *(Pg 336)*

3. (c) A pie chart
   (d) A bar chart
4. Hospital   (a) $324 m
                    (b) 45%
   Research   (a) $25 m
                    (b) 3.5%
   Public Health   (a) $25 m
                    (b) 3.5%
   Dental Clinics   (a) $36 m
                    (b) 5%
   Drugs   (a) $40 m
                    (b) 5.6%
   Doctors   (a) $130 m
                    (b) 18.1%
   Nursing Homes   (a) $80 m
                    (b) 11.1%
   Others   (a) $60 m
                    (b) 8.3%
5. (a) 20
   (b) (i) 540   (ii) 225
6. (a) Red
7. (a) 90°   (b) 100°
   (c) 36   (d) 27.8%
8. 252°
9. 9
10. (a) (i) 50% (ii) 20%
    (b) 63

Exercise 15c *(Pg 341)*

1. (a) 14 tonnes
   (b) 4 tonnes
   (c) 55 tonnes
2. (b) 39°, 38°
3. (a) 1999 and 2000
   (b) $56\dfrac{1}{4}$%

Exercise 15d *(Pg 344)*

1. (c) 43 minutes
   (b) $26\frac{2}{3}\%$
2. (c) 90 kg   (d) 92 kg
3. (c) 5.4 minutes
   (d) $73\frac{1}{3}\%$
4. (a) XYZ school
   (b) ABC school
   (c) ABC school

Exercise 15e *(Pg 348)*

1. (c) 3   (d) 6
2. (b) 26   (c) 6   (d) 2
3. (b) Country A: 9; Country B: 8
   (c) Country A: 349;
        Country B: 99

Review Questions 15 *(Pg 350)*

2. (a) $55 million
   (b) (i) 22%   (ii) 64.8
       (iii) 24\frac{3}{4}$ million
3. (a) 8
4. (b) 0
5. (c) 110   (d) 124
6. (b) 7.2 grams   (c) 26%

Revision Exercise IV No 1 *(Pg 352)*

1. 50   2. 5.2 cm
3. 2.7 cm   4. 1 h 32 min
5. $x = 137°, y = 81°, z = 99°$
6. (a) $6   (b) 15%
7. (a) 3 years, 4 mths
   (b) 96 km, 2 h
9. (a) 22.5 m   (b) 6.9 m
10. (a) 48   (b) 64   (c) $\frac{2}{5}$

Revision Exercise IV No 2 *(Pg 353)*

1. 7.5 cm
2. 8.9 cm
3. (a) 52°   (b) 116°
4. (a) 25°   (b) 74°
5. 14 sec   6. 8.2 cm
7. (a) 11
   (b) (i) 84.375%
       (ii) 84.4%
8. $p = 54°, q = 113°, r = 59°,$
   $s = 121°$
10. (a) 600   (b) 4 : 5

Revision Exercise IV No 3 *(Pg 353)*

1. 136 mm
2. 11.5 cm, 141°
3. (a) $p = 83°$ (b) $q = 104°$
   (c) $r = 32°$
4. (a) 30 h   (b) 120 days
5. 11.3 cm
6. 7.5%
7. (a) 500   (b) 24%
   (c) $27.20
8. $x = 55°, y = 82°, z = 38°$
9. 2 : 7
10. (a) 88   (b) 30%
    (c) 2 024

Revision Exercise IV No 4 *(Pg 354)*

1. S$218.40
2. $x = 70°, y = 60°$
3. 6 days   4. 20%
5. 8.6 cm, 14.2 cm
7. 7.5 cm   8. 52°
9. 108°   10. 24%

Revision Exercise IV No 5 *(Pg 355)*

1. 78°
2. 4.6 cm, 5.7 cm
3. 21.5%
4. (a) 1 000   (b) $15.50
   (c) 8%
5. $x = 68°, y = 112°$
6. 25   7. 0.74%
8. $x = 24°, y = 96°, z = 48°$
9. (a) 15°   (b) 8.7 cm, 76°
10. (a) 84   (b) 154
    (c) 29.8%

End-of-Year Examination Specimen Paper 1 *(Pg 357)*

Part I

1. (a) $1\frac{3}{8}$ (b) $4\frac{13}{16}$
2. 31.744 kg   3. 48 cm²
4. (a) 15.44   (b) 85.84
5. $15, $75, $255
6. $180   7. 12
8. (a) $11\frac{1}{2}$ (b) $4\frac{3}{7}$
9. (a) $14x - 30$ (b) $\frac{17 - 8x}{20}$
10. (a) 29°   (b) 119°
11. (a) $1 + 2 + 3 + 4 + 5 + 4 + 3 +$
        $2 + 1 = 25$
    (b) 81   (c) 13

12. (a) 32 m   (b) $5 408
13. 6.8 cm

Part II

1. 42.24 m²
2. 18.48 l, 3 256 cm²
3. (a) 25   (b) 10
4. $x = 22°, y = 88°, z = 44°$
5. (a) 3 072 cm³ (b) 4.32 l
6. (a) 48.51 kg
   (b) (i) 2.738 (ii) 0.978 5
7. (a) $x = 36°, y = 80°$
   (b) 6 of each
8. (a) $54   (b) M$348

End-of-Year Examination Specimen Paper 2 *(Pg 358)*

Part I

1. (a) $-2\frac{1}{2}$ (b) $5\frac{7}{8}$
2. (a) $\frac{7}{200}$ (b) 1.225
   (c) 2.00   (d) 0.025
3. (a) 1 200
   (b) $18y - 6x - 21$
4. $\frac{3}{11}$
5. 60 cm
6. 144 000 l
7. 0.462 m³
8. $4 760
9. $\left($\frac{1}{3}$xz - xy\right)$
10. (a) 220 cm   (b) 880 m
11. S$3 158
12. 4.9 cm
13. (a) $11 × 11 = 10 × 12 + 1$
    (b) 14   (c) 39 601
14. (a) 35   (b) $\frac{1}{5}$ (c) $\frac{2}{7}$

Part II

1. 145 g
2. 64 yrs, 16 yrs
3. (a) 308 cm²   (b) 947
4. (a) (i) $x = 32°, y = 120°$
       (ii) $x = 77°, y = 111°$
   (b) 20
5. (a) $24 000   (b) $33 800
6. (a) 54 km/h   (b) 3.75%
7. (a) (i) 156.4 (ii) 8.243
   (b) $8 400
8. 1.84 m³, 5 152 kg